Trademark Acknowledgements

Wrox has endeavored to provide trademark information about all the companies and products mentioned in this book by the appropriate use of capitals. However, Wrox cannot guarantee the accuracy of this information.

Credits

Authors
Patrick Cauldwell
Rajesh Chawla
Vivek Chopra
Gary Damschen
Chris Dix
Tony Hong
Francis Norton
Uche Ogbuji
Glenn Olander
Mark A. Richman
Kristy Saunders
Zoran Zaev

Technical Architect
Peter Morgan

Technical Editors
Richard Deeson
P. Dennis Jackson
Sarah Larder
M. K. L. Lau
Simon Mackie
Chris Mills

Category Manager
Dave Galloway

Project Administrator
Beckie Stones

Author Agent
Trish Weir

Indexer
Fiona Murray

Proof Reader
Fiver Locker

Technical Reviewers
Dietrich Ayala
Dave Beauchemin
Martin Beaulieu
Michael Corning
Chris Crane
David I. Crowley
Steve Danielson
Mario Jeckle
Paul Kulchenko
Jim MacIntosh
Joel D. Munter
Gary L. Peskin
Jonathan Pinnock
Phil Powers-DeGeorge
Eric Rajkovic
Gareth Reakes
J. Andrew Schafer
David Schultz
Andrew Stopford
Dominic Tramontana
Adwait Ullal
Dmitry E. Voytenko
Paul Warren
Warren Wiltsie

Production Manager
Simon Hardware

Production Co-ordinator
Pip Wonson

Additional Layout
Paul Grove

Illustrations
Paul Grove
Pip Wonson

Cover
Dawn Chellingworth

About the Authors

Patrick Cauldwell

After completing a Bachelor's degree in the unlikely field of East Asian Studies, Patrick Cauldwell fell into the software industry. Since then he has worked on localizing software into 17 languages, helped design large e-commerce web sites like 800.com and gear.com, and spoken nation-wide about how to build large scalable sites. Patrick is currently embarking on a new project with Serveron Corp., which makes monitoring devices and software for the power industry.

Patrick Cauldwell contributed Chapter 4

Rajesh Chawla

Rajesh has been working with computers since his father bought him a Commodore 64 to play with many years ago. Since then, he has worked with a variety of technologies including C++, C, XML, Oracle, Unix, NT, Apache, and IIS, to name but a few. He currently works on middleware technologies for Sybase.

Rajesh lives near Denver, Colorado, with his wife Terri and is wrapped around the fingers of their three daughters, Katherine, Stephanie, and Angela.

I would like to take a moment to thank Phil Powers-DeGeorge, Jon Pinnock, Chris Crane, Dominic Tramontana, Warren Wiltsie, and Martin Beaulieu. Also thanks go to Phillip Jackson and Peter Morgan for pointing me in the right direction. Furthermore, thanks are due to Martin Lau and Chris Mills for bringing a polish to my work in progress, to Trish Weir for getting me involved in the first place, and to Beckie Stones for the gentle reminders.

Finally, I want to thank my wife, Terri, for her time, encouragement, and patience, without which my work on this project would never have become a reality.

Rajesh Chawla contributed Chapter 5

Vivek Chopra

Vivek Chopra has seven years of experience in software design and development, the last two years of which have been in Web Services, using the HP Web Services Platform, e-Speak, and various XML technologies. He works for Insight Solution Inc. at Cupertino, California, as a senior software engineer. His previous areas of experience and interest include compilers, middleware, clustering, and GNU/Linux. Besides work, he enjoys burning food on his barbecue and tries to avoid roller-blading for reasons that he does not wish to go into.

Vivek holds a Bachelor's degree in Electronics and a Master's in Computer Science, both from Pune University, India. He can be reached at vivek@soaprpc.com.

Vivek Chopra contributed Chapters 6 and 7

Gary Damschen

Gary Damschen is a Lead Programmer Analyst for Kelly Services, Inc. His love affair with computers began in High School when he wrote his first program on a TTY terminal and saved it on paper tape. Although he spent many years in a successful career in radiation safety, computers always found their way into what he was doing. Finally, he succumbed to the siren call and became an IT professional after teaching himself HTML and starting a web consulting business. He now develops online training delivery systems and courses. Gary now resides in California with his wife, daughter, cat, dog, and four computers.

Special thanks again to my wife Marilyn and daughter Charlotte for their help and support, even when I was still writing during our vacation. You guys are the greatest – I love you both.

Gary Damschen contributed Chapter 2

Chris Dix

Chris Dix has been developing software for fun since he was 10 years old, and for a living for the past 8 years. Chris specializes in Visual C++ development for Windows platforms. He has written articles for several magazines, and he contributes material on SOAP to vbxml.com. Now that he has been published in a book, Chris only needs to become mayor of a small town to complete his list of career goals. Chris is lead developer for NavTraK, Inc., a leader in automatic vehicle location systems located in Salisbury, Maryland, where he develops Web Services and Palm applications. He can be reached at cdix@navtrak.net.

I would like to thank my wife Jennifer, who doubles as my best friend. Without her love and support, this would not have been possible. For my sons, Alexander and Calvin, thank you for being more wonderful than I could have ever imagined; and to my parents, thanks for spending money you didn't have to get me a Commodore 64; it was worth the investment.

Chris Dix contributed Chapters 3 and 8

Tony Hong

Tony Hong founded and operates XMethods, an online listing of web services, and started the SOAPBuilders group on Yahoo. Before starting XMethods, he was building EAI and B2B integration systems for Ventro Corp, an early B2B marketplace operator. Tony lives in San Jose, CA with his wife Lisa and their three children Lauren, Andrew, and Anna. He can be reached at thong@xmethods.net.

Thanks to Paul Kulchenko, David Crowley, Dietrich Ayala, and the wonderful folks at Wrox for all of their help and support!

To Lisa, Lauren, Andrew, and Anna – thank you for your understanding, patience and love. I am truly blessed.

Tony Hong contributed Chapter 9

Francis Norton

Francis Norton works at iE (http://www.ie.com/) as a senior consultant where he has a special interest in the application of XML technologies to the many challenges of cross-platform retail finance applications. His interests include running, cooking, travel, and rather too much reading.

I'd like to thank my colleagues and employers at iE for giving me the space and opportunities to pursue my technical interests, especially those who've helped with questions, ideas, and reviews.

I'd also like to thank the Wrox team and technical reviewers for their patience and professionalism.

Francis Norton contributed Chapter 15

Uche Ogbuji

Uche Ogbuji is a computer engineer, and co-founder and CEO of Fourthought, Inc., a software vendor and consultancy specializing in open, standards-based XML solutions, especially as applicable to problems of knowledge management. He has worked with XML for several years, co-developing 4Suite, a pioneering library of open-source tools for XML development and object database management in Python. He also co-develops 4Suite Server, an XML data server using 4Suite to provide a flexible XML processing platform. Mr. Ogbuji also writes articles on XML for ITWorld and IBM developerWorks, where he is XML and Web Services columnist. He has also spoken extensively at conferences including: XML 2001, Web Services One, Software Development, Web Developer World, International Python Conference, and XML DevCon.

Mr. Ogbuji is a Nigerian immigrant with a B.S. in Computer Engineering from Milwaukee School of Engineering. He currently resides in Boulder, Colorado where he enjoys playing amateur softball in the summer and snowboarding in the winter. His main interest is literature, and poetry in particular.

Uche Ogbuji contributed Chapter 12

Glenn Olander

Glenn Olander is a musician living in Southern California. He also spends time as a software consultant, specializing in the design and implementation of client/server applications using Java, XML, SOAP, servlets, and Web Services. For contact information, see http://www.greenoak.com/consulting/.

Glenn Olander contributed Chapter 10

Mark A. Richman

Mark Richman has over 10 years experience as an independent consultant and software developer. He specializes in large-scale distributed web applications. Mark has demonstrated his technical expertise through engagements with both Fortune 500 corporations and small start-up firms. He frequently mentors software developers in object-oriented concepts and techniques. Mark has a personal interest in emerging technologies and platforms such as J2EE, XML, and Web Services. As a consultant, Mark provides technical leadership throughout the life cycle of a project including direction on systems architecture, code reuse, and development processes. Key responsibilities include guiding the architecture, user interface, and technology integration of projects; interfacing with client's technology and management teams; and gathering information on enterprise-wide trends. Mark holds a Bachelor of Science degree in Computer Science. He is also an avid Linux enthusiast, and enjoys playing and writing music. Mark and his wife, Tracey, currently reside in South Florida. He can be reached at http://www.markrichman.com/.

Mark A. Richman contributed Chapter 14

Kristy Saunders

Kristy Saunders has over 10 years professional experience, first programming on a number of OS/2 commercial products, and since 1995, developing Windows-based products and applications in C++, MFC, COM, and Microsoft web technologies.

She currently works as a developer/consultant/researcher/writer for SoftSource Consulting (http://www.sftsrc.com/), a Portland, Oregon-based organization that focuses on helping companies apply Web technologies and the Microsoft Windows platform in their development practices. She has spent most of the past year focusing on how to leverage the power of .NET and C# to build secure and scalable systems.

When she is not sitting in front of a computer she is chasing around her monkey of an 18-month old daughter.

She wishes to thank her husband Greg for his support, and her father, Wayne Smith, who gave her an Atari 800 and a couple of compilers for her 11th birthday.

Kristy Saunders contributed Chapter 11

Zoran Zaev

Zoran is a senior web solutions architect with Hitachi Innovative Solutions, Corp. in the Washington DC, area. He has worked in technology since the time when 1 MHz CPUs and 48Kb was considered "significant power", in the now distant 1980s. In mid 1990s, Zoran became involved in web application development. Since then, he has worked helping large and small clients alike to leverage the power of web applications. His more recent emphasis has been web applications and web services with XML, SOAP, and other related technologies. When he's not programming, you'll find him traveling, and exploring new learning opportunities. Zoran can be reached at zoran.zaev@hitachisolutions.net or zzaev@yahoo.com.

As always, I would like to thank my wife, Angela, for her constant support and restless encouragement. Thinking back, I am thankful to my grandpa Pavle, who years ago had fostered my curiosity and interest in science and math. I have to thank God for making impossible things possible (especially when deadlines seem impossible to meet!) and ensuring that our imagination and vision always takes us to better places that are not yet known. Finally, thanks to Peter, Beckie, and Trish from Wrox for their always-timely assistance.

Zoran Zaev contributed Chapters 1 and 13

Table of Contents

Introduction   1

Who Is This Book For?   2

What You Need To Use This Book   2

How Is This Book Structured?   2

Conventions   6

Customer Support   6

How to Download the Sample Code for the Book   7
Errata   7
E-mail Support   7
p2p.wrox.com   8

Chapter 1: Evolution Of Web Services   11

Web Services are the Future!   12

A Brief History of Distributed Computing   12

The Age of Local Networks   12
    CORBA/IIOP   13
    DCOM   13
    RMI   14
    Synchronous vs. Asynchronous Communication   14
The Age of the Internet and the Web   14
    Challenges with Existing Protocols   14
    Early Attempts at Connecting Web Applications   15
    Initial SOAP-type Implementations Using XML-RPC   17
    Web Services versus EAI   18

Enter Web Services   18

Architecture of Web Services   19

Invocation   20
    SOAP   20
    SOAP 1.2   23
    SOAP Bindings   24
    SOAP Extensions   25
    Description   31
    Discovery   32
    Web Services Framework Architecture   33

Table of Contents

Vendor Tools and Frameworks for Web Services   **34**

  HP and e-Speak   35
    e-Speak Engine   35
    Service Specification Framework (SFS)   37
    E-Services Village (ESV)   37
    HP Web Services Platform   38
  IBM's Dynamic e-Business   39
    Products   40
    Future Trends   42
  Microsoft's .NET Platform and Framework   42
    .NET Framework   43
  Sun Microsystems and Sun ONE   45
    JAXP (Java API for XML Parsing)   46
    JAXB (Java API for XML Binding)   46
    JAX-RPC (Java API for XML-based RPC)   46
    JAXM (Java API for XML Messaging)   46
    JAXR (Java API for XML Registries)   48
  Web Services and Other XML Initiatives   48
    ebXML   48
    RosettaNet   49
    Common Business Library (xCBL)   49
    BizTalk Framework   50
    Commerce XML (cXML)   50
    XML Repositories   51
    An Example Set of Web Services: HailStorm   51

The Service-Oriented Internet   **53**

  The Process Flow and Pattern Description   54
    RosettaNet   54
    XLANG and WSFL   54
  Web Agents   55
  The Semantic Web   56

Summary   **57**

Chapter 2: Internet Transport Protocols: An HTTP and SMTP Primer **59**

The Need for Protocols   **59**

The Internet Protocol Stack   **60**

  The OSI Reference Model   61
  The TCP/IP Model   62
  How SMTP and HTTP Fit Into The Internet Protocol Stack   62

Overview of SMTP   **63**

  Current Capabilities and Anticipated Enhancements   63
  Required Parameters and Common Commands   64
  A Simple SMTP Transaction Example   65
  Relay Agents   67
  Limitations   67
    MIME Overview   68

Overview of HTTP   **70**

    Current Capabilities and Anticipated Enhancements   70

    Required Parameters   71

    A Simple HTTP Transaction Example   71

        Client Connection and Request   72

        Server Response to Client   72

    HTTP Connection Types   74

    Extending HTTP Headers   74

Summary   **75**

Chapter 3: SOAP Basics   **77**

SOAP Fundamentals   **78**

    SOAP and Web Services   78

    The SOAP Message Exchange Model   78

        XML Documents As Messages   79

        Senders and Receivers   79

        Message Chains   79

    Endpoint Behavior   80

    Modular Design   80

SOAP Messages   **81**

    Envelope   83

        Envelope Namespace   84

        encodingStyle attribute   84

    Body   84

    Header   85

        actor attribute   85

        mustUnderstand attribute   86

    Fault   86

        faultcode element   87

        faultstring element   88

        faultactor element   88

        detail element   88

    Endpoint Behavior Revisited   89

    Body-Conscious   89

Data   **89**

    Encoding Style   90

    What About XML Schemas?   90

    SOAP Encoding   90

        Simple Data Types   90

        Compound Data Types   93

    Custom Encoding   96

    Multi-reference Values   96

    What's Simple About It?   98

Transports   **98**

    Separation of Message and Transport   98

    HTTP   99

        SOAPAction Header   100

        Status Codes   100

Table of Contents

SOAP and RPC	**102**
SOAP RPC Convention	102
The Call	102
The Return	103
RPC and HTTP	104
Beyond RPC - Working with XML Documents	106
Summary	**107**

Chapter 4: WSDL: the Web Services Definition Language   **109**

A Brief History of WSDL	**110**
Why WSDL?	**110**
WSDL Syntax	**111**
Putting it all Together	112
Namespaces	114
Elements of a Definition	115
documentation	115
types	115
Messages	117
Port Types	119
Bindings	120
Ports and Services	121
Transmission Primitives	**122**
One-way Operation	122
Request/Response Operation	123
Solicit/Response Operation	124
Notification Operation	125
Naming of Messages in an Operation	125
Protocol Bindings	**125**
SOAP	126
soap:binding	126
soap:operation	126
soap:body	127
soap:fault	130
soap:header and soap:headerfault	130
SMTP Example	130
HTTP GET/POST Binding	131
MIME Binding	133
mime:multipartRelated	134
mime:content	135
mime:mimeXml	135
WSDL Examples	**135**
Multiple Bindings	136
Microsoft SOAP Toolkit	139
IBM Web Services Toolkit	144
Summary	**147**

Chapter 5: SOAP Bindings   149

Detours into Background Information   150
DNS   150
MIME   152
URIs, URNs and URLs, Oh, My!   153

HTTP   154
HTTP Example   156
Passing SOAP using HTTP   158
Using the Microsoft SOAP Toolkit   159
    Server   159
    Client   161
Using the Echo Server   162

SMTP   163
SMTP Protocol   164
Example Overview   165
Example Setup   165
    Apache Web Server   166
    Apache SOAP, Tomcat and Xerces   167
Example Code   169

FTP   175
How Does it Work?   176
SOAP Example   177

Summary   179

Chapter 6: Universal Description, Discovery and Integration   181
Rationale for UDDI   182
UDDI Concepts   183
UDDI Deployment Scenarios   186
    Test Bed Deployment   187
Data Stored in the Registry   187

UDDI Specifications   187
UDDI Information Model   188
    Business Information   188
    Business Service Information   190
    Binding Information   191
    Specification Pointers and Technical Information   193
    Publisher Assertions   195
UDDI Programming Model   198
UDDI API   199
    Inquiry API   199
    Publishing API   203
    UDDI Errors   210
    Query patterns   211
    API Design principles   214
Specifications for UDDI Operators   214
    Managing Directory Information   215
    Security   215
    Data Management Requirements   215
    Custody Transfer   215
    UUID Generation Algorithm   216
    Operator Web User Interface   216
UDDI and WSDL   216
    Structure of WSDL Service Description   216
    Authoring the UDDI Service Descriptions   218

Table of Contents

Other Technologies   **219**
   ebXML   220
   JAXR   221
   DSML   221

Summary   **223**

References   **223**

Chapter 7: UDDI Implementations   227

Setup   **228**
   Software Downloads   228
   Setup Instructions   228
      Tomcat and Apache SOAP Setup   228
      Environment settings   231

Introduction to UDDI4J   **232**
   UDDI4J API   233
      Constructing a UDDIProxy object   233
      Getting an authentication token   234
      Methods to publish to the UDDI registry   234
      Methods for deleting from UDDI registry: 235
      Getting all Business Entities and tModels published by us   236
      Inquiry methods   236
   Programmatically Browsing the UDDI Registry   238
   Browsing the UDDI Registry Using GUI tools   245
   An Airline Web Service   249
      Creating an Account With the UDDI Registry   251
      Developing and Deploying the Web Service   252
      Programmatically Publishing the tModel   255
      Publishing the tModel Using GUI Tools   262
      Programmatically Publishing the Business Entity   262
      Publishing the Business Entity Using GUI Tools   271
      Finding and Invoking Methods on the Web Service   271
   Programmatically Deleting a Business Entity   280
      Deleting a Business Entity Using GUI Tools   284

Microsoft UDDI SDK   **285**

HP Web Services Platform   **286**
   HP UDDI Browser   287
   UDDI Client SDK   288
   UDDI Private Registry   291

UDDI::Lite   **291**

Other Implementations   **292**

Summary   **293**

References   **293**

Chapter 8: Microsoft SOAP Toolkit 2.0   295

SOAP for "Legacy" Windows   295
Did I Miss 1.0?   296
Downloading the Toolkit   296
The MSTK2 Model   296
WSDL Revisited   298
Introducing WSML   298
About the Samples   299

Cruising at 10,000 Feet – the High Level API   299
Building The SysInfo Object   300
Generating WSDL and WSML   303
   Listeners   309
The SoapServer Object   310
   The Init() Method   311
   The SoapInvoke() Method   312
The SoapClient Object   312
   The mssoapinit() Method   314
   SoapClient Extras   315
Debugging with the Toolkit   316
   The Fault Element   316
   Tracing Messages   317

Drilling Down – The Low Level API   318
Déjà vu – SystemInfoService the Hard Way   319
   At The Server   319
   Low Level Clients   323

Documents – The SMO Framework   326
   Code Generation   326
   SMO Objects At Work   330
   Why SMO?   330

Beyond the Basics   330
Working with Connectors   331
   Connectors and SoapClient   331
   Custom Connectors   332
Working with Complex Types   336
   Arrays   336
   Custom Types   338
Over-extended   341

Summary   341

Table of Contents

Chapter 9: Other SOAP Implementations   343

Before We Get Started   344
The Echo Service Example   344
Examining SOAP Wiredumps with tcpTrace   347

SOAP::Lite for Perl   349
Installing SOAP::Lite   349
    Prerequisites   350
    Preparing the Makefile   350
    Builiding, Testing, and Installing the Package   351
Implementing the Echo Services with SOAP::Lite   352
    Implementing the echoString Server and Client   352
    Implementing the echoIntegerArray Server and Client   357
    Implementing the echoStruct Server and Client   361
More SOAP::Lite Basics   365
    Fault Handlers for SOAP::Lite Clients   365
    Client Configuration via WSDL Binding   366
    Service Dispatching   367
    Character Set Encoding   367

EasySoap++   368
Installing EasySoap++   368
    Prerequisites   368
    Obtaining and Installing Expat   368
    Obtaining and Installing EasySoap++   370
Building the Echo Service and Clients   372
    echoString   372
    echoIntegerArray   379
    echoStruct   383
More EasySoap++ Basics   389
    Parameter Serialization   389
    XML Schema Version and Character Set Encoding   392

SOAPx4   392
Installing SOAPx4   393
    Prerequisites   393
    Download and Installing the SOAPx4 Package   393
Building the Echo Service and Clients   394
    echoString   394
    echoIntegerArray   398
    echoStruct   402
More SOAPx4 Basics   406
    Valid Data Types in Parameter Serialization   406
    XML Schema Version and Character Set Encoding   406
    Client Configuration via WSDL Binding   406

Summary   408

Chapter 10: Java Web Service Implementations — 411

Introduction — 411
Installation — 413

Simple First Demo — 417
The Server — 417
The Client — 420

Passing Objects — 422
Implementing Campsite Objects — 423
  Using the Tunneler — 428

Wrapping Strategies — 430

Proxy Generation With WSTK — 436

UDDI — 445
Setting Up Another Web Service — 453

End Game — 458
Writing a Serializer — 458
Using an Alternative Servlet Container — 462

Epilog — 463

Summary — 464

Chapter11: .NET Web Services — 467

Getting Started with Web Services for .NET — 468

Acquiring the Visual Studio .NET Beta 2 — 469

Acquiring the .NET Framework SDK Beta 2 — 469

Downloading the .NET Framework Redistributable — 470

A .NET Primer — 470
The Common Language Runtime — 470
  Common Type System — 471
  Assemblies — 471
.NET Framework Class Library — 472
C# — 472
ASP.NET — 474

An ASP.NET Web Service — 475
An Area Code Update Service — 475
  The Problem — 475
  The AreaCodeService Class — 475
AreaCodeService ASP.NET Web Service — 478
  .asmx Files — 479
  The System.Web.Services namespace — 479
  The WebService Directive — 479
  The WebMethod Attribute — 480
  The AreaCodeService.asmx — 481
Testing AreaCodeService — 481
Retrieving the WSDL — 484
ASP.NET Protocol Support — 484
  HTTP GET and HTTP POST — 485
  SOAP — 486
Creating a Web Service from a WSDL Description — 486

Table of Contents

ASP.NET Web Services with Visual Studio .NET   **488**

Using Visual Studio .NET's ASP.NET Web Service Template   488
Using Codebehind   492
Template-generated Files   494
     Dynamic Discovery and .VSDISCO Files   494
     AssemblyInfo.cs, Global.asax, Global.asax.cs, and Web.config   494
The WebService Class   495
More About WebMethod and WebService Attributes   496
     Using Attributes to Document our Web Service   496
     Changing the Default Namespace   498
     Renaming a Web Service or a Web Service Method   499
     Other WebMethod Attribute properties   502

Building Web Service Proxies   **502**

An Introduction to Web Service Discovery and DISCO   502
Our Client Test Application   504
Creating a Proxy with Visual Studio.NET   504
Creating an Asynchronous Proxy   513
Using the Web Services Description Language Utility to Generate a Proxy   516

Building a Web Service with .NET Remoting   **517**

ATL Server   518

Summary   **519**

Chapter 12: Developing Web Services With Python   **521**

Standard Python Library Modules of Interest to Web Services Developers   **522**

Web Architecture Modules   523
     BaseHTTPServer, SimpleHTTPServer and CGIHTTPServer   523
     urllib and urllib2   523
     httplib   524
Internet Data Format Modules   524
     xml.parsers.expat   524
     xml.dom   524
     xml.sax   524
     mimetools and MimeWriter   524
     uu, base64, md5, and sha   525

Third–party Python Modules and Tools of Interest to Web Services Developers   **525**

SOAP.py   525
SOAPy   526
soaplib.py   526
Orchard   526
Lye   526
PyXML   527
4Suite   527
4Suite Server   527

Installing the Required Software   **528**

Python   528
PyXML   528
4Suite   529

Python and SOAP   **529**

SOAP From First Principles   529
   Basic Python SOAP Server   529
   Basic Python SOAP client   533
   SOAP.py as SOAP client   535
   SOAPy as a SOAP client, Using WSDL   537

Python and WSDL   **539**

Processing WSDL With wsdl4py   539
   Reading in and Querying Existing WSDL Documents   539
   Creating and Manipulating WSDL   541
   Processing WSDL Using RDF   542

Web Services Implementation in 4Suite Server   **548**

WSDL Description of the Software Version Web Service   548
The SOAP Handler Code   550
Setting up the SOAP Handler   551
Testing the SOAP Implementation With SOAP.py   553
Testing the SOAP Implementation with the Basic Python Library   554

Summary   **555**

Further Resources   **556**

Chapter 13: Web Services Security   **559**

Security and XML Web Services   **560**

Security as an Afterthought   560
Security as a Process   561
Key Security Concerns   562
   Authentication   562
   Authorization   562
   Auditing and Logging   562
   Integrity and Encryption   563
   Privacy and Encryption   565
   Availability (Load Balancing, Failover, Backup)   565
   Nonrepudiation and Digital Signatures   566

Approaches to Web Services Security   **567**

Transport Level Security   568
HTTP   569
   Basic Authentication   570
   Forms-based Authentication   575
   Adding SSL to Basic Authentication   579
   Client Certificates   594
   Other Authentication Options   596
SMTP   597
   S/MIME   597

Application Level Security   **598**

Credentials in SOAP Messages   599
Kerberos and Ticket-Based Authentication   600
   Kerberos   600
XML Security Related Specifications   602
   XML Signature   603
   XML Encryption   603
   Digital Signatures Extensions to SOAP   604
   Privacy Via P3P   606
   Digital Rights Management   609

Summary   **610**

Table of Contents

Chapter 14: Case Study: A Java Filesystem Web Service — **613**

The Filesystem Web Service — **613**
Why Do We Need Security for Web Services? — 614

Apache SOAP and the Pluggable Provider — **615**

Setting Up The Server — **615**

Setting Up The Database — **618**

Writing a Pluggable Provider — **622**

Writing the Filesystem Web Service — **626**

Using SOAP Attachments — **627**

Deploying Web Services Using Pluggable Providers — **632**

Writing the Filesystem Proxy Class — **636**

Writing the Filesystem Client Class — **639**

Packaging the .jar File — **640**

Trying It Out — **641**

Summary — **641**

Chapter 15: Case Study: Wrox Online Auction Domain — **643**

Requirements — **644**
Selling an Item — 644
Sell Item — 646
Buying an Item — 646
Buy Item — 648
Transaction Analysis — 648
Specification — 650

Implementing the WOAD Web Services — **656**
Setting up the Projects — 656
Creating the Server Project — 656
Creating the Client Project — 657
Implementing the Ping Operation — 657
Implementing Ping on the Server — 658
Implementing Ping on the Client — 661
Implementing Business Transactions — 662
On the Server Project — 662
On the Client Project — 662
register() — 663
login() — 664
makeOffer() — 666
Integrating Web Services With Your Application — 667
State Management and Security — 667
Publishing the Service — 668

What Have we Achieved?   **673**
Case 1 – Retail Web Service Clients   673
Case 2 – Web Service Developers   674

Summary   **675**

Appendix A: Simple Object Access Protocol (SOAP) 1.1   **677**

Abstract   **678**

Status   **678**

Table of Contents   **678**

1. Introduction   **679**
1.1 Design Goals   680
1.2 Notational Conventions   680
1.3 Examples of SOAP Messages   680

2. The SOAP Message Exchange Model   **681**

3. Relation to XML   **682**

4. SOAP Envelope   **683**
4.1.1 SOAP encodingStyle Attribute   684
4.1.2 Envelope Versioning Model   684
4.2 SOAP Header   684
4.2.1 Use of Header Attributes   685
4.2.2 SOAP actor Attribute   685
4.2.3 SOAP mustUnderstand Attribute   686
4.3 SOAP Body   686
4.3.1 Relationship between SOAP Header and Body   686
4.4 SOAP Fault   687
4.4.1 SOAP Fault Codes   688

5. SOAP Encoding   **688**
5.1 Rules for Encoding Types in XML   689
5.2 Simple Types   692
5.2.1 Strings   693
5.2.2 Enumerations   693
5.2.3 Array of Bytes   694
5.3 Polymorphic Accessor   694
5.4 Compound types   695
5.4.1 Compound Values, Structs and References to Values   695
5.4.2 Arrays   697
5.5 Default Values   703
5.6 SOAP root Attribute   703

6. Using SOAP in HTTP   **703**
6.1 SOAP HTTP Request   703
6.1.1 The SOAPAction HTTP Header Field   703
6.2 SOAP HTTP Response   704
6.3 The HTTP Extension Framework   704
6.4 SOAP HTTP Examples   704

Table of Contents

7. Using SOAP for RPC   **705**
   7.1 RPC and SOAP Body   706
   7.2 RPC and SOAP Header   706

8. Security Considerations   **706**

9. References   **707**

A. SOAP Envelope Examples   **707**
   A.1 Sample Encoding of Call Requests   707
   A.2 Sample Encoding of Response   708

Appendix B: Web Services Description Language WSDL) 1.1   **713**

   Abstract   714
   Status   714
   Table of Contents   714

1. Introduction   **715**
   1.1 WSDL Document Example   716
   1.2 Notational Conventions   718

2. Service Definition   **719**
   2.1 WSDL Document Structure   719
   2.2 Types   724
   2.3 Messages   725
   2.4 Port Types   727
   2.5 Bindings   730
   2.6 Ports   731
   2.7 Services   731

3. SOAP Binding   **732**
   3.1 SOAP Examples   732
   3.2 How the SOAP Binding Extends WSDL   736
   3.3 soap:binding   736
   3.4 soap:operation   737
   3.5 soap:body   737
   3.6 soap:fault   739
   3.7 soap:header and soap:headerfault   739
   3.8 soap:address   740

4. HTTP GET & POST Binding   **740**
   4.1 HTTP GET/POST Examples   740
   4.2 How the HTTP GET/POST Binding Extends WSDL   742
   4.3 http:address   742
   4.4 http:binding   743
   4.5 http:operation   743
   4.6 http:urlEncoded   743
   4.7 http:urlReplacement   743

5. MIME Binding   **744**
   5.11 MIME Binding example   744
   5.2 How the MIME Binding extends WSDL   746
   5.3 mime:content   746
   5.4 mime:multipartRelated   747
   5.5 soap:body   747
   5.6 mime:mimeXml   747

6. References   **747**

A 1. Notes on URIs   748

    A 1.1 XML namespaces & schema locations   748

    A 1.2 Relative URIs   748

    A 1.3 Generating URIs   748

A 2. Wire format for WSDL examples   748

    A 2.1. Example 1   748

A 3. Location of Extensibility Elements   749

A 4. Schemas   750

    A 4.1 WSDL Schema   750

    A 4.2 SOAP Binding Schema   755

    A 4.3 HTTP Binding Schema   756

    A 4.4 MIME Binding Schema   757

Appendix C:UDDI 2.0 Data Types   **759**

Data Structure Notation   **760**

The businessEntity Structure   **761**

Structure Specification   761

Substructure Breakdown   761

    discoveryURLs   762

    name   763

    contacts   763

    businessServices   766

    identifierBag   766

    categoryBag   766

The businessService Structure   **766**

Structure Specification   767

Substructure Breakdown   767

    bindingTemplates   768

The bindingTemplate Structure   **769**

Structure Specification   769

Substructure Breakdown   769

    accessPoint   771

    hostingRedirector   771

    tModelInstanceDetails   772

The tModel structure   **774**

Two Main Uses   774

    Defining the Technical Fingerprint   774

    Defining an Abstract Namespace Reference   775

Structure Specification   775

Substructure Breakdown   775

The publisherAssertion Structure   **776**

Structure Specification   777

Substructure Breakdown   777

Index   **779**

Introduction

If you believe all the hype written about Web Services over the past 18 months or so, you'd probably think they were going to solve world debt problems, eliminate hunger, and bring back Elvis! Yet most of us in the computing world have seen enough radical proclamations such as these to know that the reality is never quite so sweet. In this book, we're going to give you a pragmatic, programmer's view of Web Services, focusing on what can be done with the tools and technology **today**.

The premise of Web Services technologies (such as SOAP and WSDL) forms the natural next step in the evolution of distributed computing. "Evolution" is the key word here. These technologies are still at a nascent stage, and their development will continue apace over the coming months. Huge investment is being poured into this area by all of the major software companies. Perhaps you're thinking it's all a load of bandwagon jumping? Maybe so in some cases, but when a company such as Microsoft turns its whole focus towards service-oriented software, and Sun, HP, and IBM (to name just three) are enthusiastic backers, then you really ought to be sitting up and taking notice.

One of the most compelling reasons to go down the route of Web Services development is their high level of interoperability. As you are probably aware, the invocation of a Web Service is a platform- and language-independent operation. So, for example, a Perl client can invoke a Java Web Service. That's great news for you as a developer, but it has given us a few headaches in developing this book. Since all major programming languages and platforms are provided for in the Web Services framework, how can we satisfy such a widespread audience? To do so in a single book would be impossible. Instead, our approach has been to start with a detailed study of SOAP, WSDL, and UDDI, which are the technologies forming the cornerstone to the Web Services framework. The book then provides some in-depth coverage of some of the tools and software that cater for the more popular development languages and platforms. We complete the book with some case studies showing how Web Services can be implemented, and appendices of the SOAP, WSDL, and UDDI specifications.

Please bear in mind that we are providing a snapshot of a rapidly changing landscape. Most of the book has been written with SOAP 1.1 as its focus, since this is widely supported and implemented. During the writing of this book, the W3C XML Protocol Working Group (the group developing the successor to SOAP 1.1) delivered its first Working Draft of SOAP 1.2. In the book we provide an overview of the design goals of SOAP 1.2 and the future is it leading us towards. However, given that at time of writing there are no implementations supporting this Working Draft, and the fact that the specification will change on its course to becoming a fully-fledged Recommendation, we do not cover it in any detail. Any references to "SOAP" within the book refer to SOAP 1.1, unless specified otherwise.

Who Is This Book For?

This book is for developers who want to get to grips with programming Web Services. An intermediate level of XML knowledge is assumed, and experience of distributed application development is helpful, but not essential. In addition, you will benefit from experience with at least one programming language – we have catered for web services implemented using Microsoft's .NET platform (Beta 2), Java, C++, Perl, VB6, Python, and PHP.

What You Need To Use This Book

The different chapters of the book require you to download several programs and accessories, depending on which client language you're dealing with at the time. It would be unhelpful to mention all of these downloads at this point, as they are detailed in their respective chapters.

The code included in this book can be downloaded from http://www.wrox.com/. More details are given in the *Customer Support* section.

How Is This Book Structured?

To give you the best possible understanding of the technologies involved in generating web services, we have arranged the book into three main sections, along with appendices:

❑ **Introduction to Web Services**: This gives you an in-depth introduction to Web Services, its core protocols, and to Web Service implementations.

❑ **Web Services Languages**: Here we go in-depth into the technologies that make up Web Services, such as SOAP, WSDL, and UDDI.

❑ **Web Services Implementations**: We look at how these technologies have been implemented in languages such as C++, Perl, PHP, Java, .NET, and Python. In this section we also look at Web Services security.

❑ **Appendices**: We have included the SOAP 1.1 W3C Note, the WSDL 1.1 W3C Note, and material from the UDDI version 2.0 Data Structure Reference as handy references

Introduction to Web Services

1. Evolution of Web Services

Chapter 1 covers the history of distributed computing, general Web Services architecture, and a brief look at the core protocols that make it up – SOAP 1.1 and 1.2, as well as WSDL and UDDI. Also, Web Services implementations are looked at, such as ebXML, xCBL and RosettaNet, and Hailstorm. We finish the chapter by looking at the future – the semantic web.

2. Internet Transport Protocols (Primer)

Chapter 2 is a primer on SMTP and HTTP, the important protocols that allow reliable data transfer across the World Wide Web. The simplicity, robustness, and extensibility of these protocols are looked at, and the aim is to give the reader a well-grounded understanding of their capabilities.

Web Services Languages

3. SOAP Basics

In Chapter 3 we take a look at SOAP and its core role in the Web Services Framework. We look at how SOAP can be used as a messaging protocol for Web Services and why it is usually the protocol of choice. We also examine the syntax of SOAP messages, SOAP binding to HTTP, and the SOAP Encoding rules for representing data types. At the end of the chapter we look at Remote Procedure Calls (RPCs) and where the future of SOAP may lie.

4. WSDL

In Chapter 4 we look at how WSDL provides a much-needed part of the Web Services picture. If Web Services are to proliferate, then there needs to be a common way to describe them, and WSDL does this. We look at the history and syntax of WSDL, as well as its bindings to the existing standards it builds on, such as XSD, SOAP, and MIME. We look at how WSDL fills the gap between SOAP and UDDI by providing the ability to programmatically bind to Web Services, and also at creating WSDL with IBM's WSTK, and Microsoft's SOAP Toolkit WSDL.

5. SOAP Bindings

Chapter 5 looks at transporting SOAP with a variety of protocols, including HTTP (using Microsoft's SOAP Toolkit), SMTP (using Apache SOAP), and FTP. Each of these protocols is reviewed, and the reasons for using them examined. There are code samples and examples of SOAP implemented on each of these transports.

6. UDDI

In Chapter 6 we take a detailed look at the rationale and concepts behind the UDDI 2.0 specification, its syntax, data structures, and API. We examine global and intranet deployment scenarios for UDDI registries, and their importance. We look at the areas of overlap between ebXML and the UDDI specification, ebXML features being added to UDDI, and how UDDI seems to have more momentum than ebXML at the moment. We show how UDDI does not concern itself with Web Services themselves, and that it is just a simple specification for business registries, that defines a standard XML API for publishing and finding information. We finish the chapter by looking at different technologies such as ebXML, DSML, and JAXR.

7. UDDI Implementations

In Chapter 7 we see an end-to-end example of a Web Service. Using Tomcat, Apache SOAP, Xerces, Java, and IBM's UDDI4J we develop the service, publish information about it, find it, and invoke methods on it (both using tools and programmatically). In addition we briefly cover a few other UDDI implementations such as Microsoft's UDDI SDK, and UDDI::Lite.

Web Services Implementations

8. Microsoft SOAP Toolkit 2.0

Chapter 8 is a detailed examination the Microsoft SOAP Toolkit 2.0, and how we can use it to work with Web Services using Visual Studio 6.0. We look at how it is a powerful tool, with an important role in Web Services development. We also look at the three APIs of the toolkit: the high level API that relies on WSDL and WSML; the more flexible, and powerful, low level API; and the SMO Framework tool that is useful when working with documents as message payloads. The chapter also looks at how to control SoapConnectors, and how to build a simple SoapConnector implementation in Visual Basic. The chapter goes on to explain that although Microsoft's SOAP Toolkit 2.0 is not the only COM based implementation, it is the most distributed, and a "legacy" windows developer's greatest web Service asset.

9. Other SOAP Implementations

In Chapter 9 we examine three different SOAP implementations based on C++ (Easy SOAP), Perl (SOAP::Lite), and PHP (SOAPx4) and set up SOAP Echo services for each. We demonstrate SOAP RPC messaging using parameter encoding, and look at the similar patterns in the workings of all three toolkits. We also see how any language on any platform, scripted or compiled, can be a participant in a SOAP encoded message exchange if its internal structures can be mapped into SOAP-encoded parameters.

10. Java Web Service

In Chapter 10 we show you how to implement a Java-based server-client web service application through Apache and Tomcat, using SOAP to access and transmit objects. We also show how to monitor the passing of these SOAP objects through the serialization/deserialization process using a tunneler, and how to add a proxy class to the application to deal with the SOAP complexities, making the Java code easier to implement. Finally we see how to use the IBM WSTK to automatically generate the proxy class, and how to register the web service and add additional services to our application through the use of an UDDI site, thus enabling the client to discover the presence and location of Web Services.

11. .Net Web Services

Chapter 11 starts with a .NET primer. We then go on to see how the .NET framework class library gives us classes and attributes containing all the Web Service plumbing. We look at the new .asmx file and how we can deploy our application logic under ASP.NET by merely adding a few attributes and a new page directive. We look at how the ASP.NET platform gives us save state, authentication, authorization, and caching abilities, and how it also includes a built in mechanism for testing Web Services using the HTTP GET or POST protocols. We also see how building Web Services is a simple task with VS.NET, and how with Web Service project templates we can create and deploy simple "Hello World" Web Services in a matter of seconds. Also in the chapter we look at Microsoft's C# programming language, .NET Remoting, building Web Services proxies, and VS.NET.

12. Python Web Services

In Chapter 12 you will see that there are many tools and techniques for Web Services programming in Python. We discuss a selection of modules that come with Python, as well as third-party Python tools and modules that are available for Web Services development and deployment. We look at sending and receiving SOAP messages using facilities in the core Python library as well as SOAP.py, and SOAPy. We also show how to manage and process WSDL documents using wsdl4py, and how to implement Web Services using 4Suite Server.

13. Web Services Security

In Chapter 13 we investigate some of the most important security concepts related to building secure applications utilizing Web Services. We look at authentication, authorization, auditing, logging, integrity, privacy, encryption, availability, non-repudiation, digital signatures, and S/MIME. We will examine how to implement security at the transport layer (that is: HTTP and SMTP) with basic authentication, certificates, and SSL, and also look at security in the application level. Towards the end of the chapter we discuss ticket-based security such as Kerberos, and finally look at the future of XML security standards, including XML Signature, XML Encryption, and P3P. Throughout the chapter we also show how to modify a Web Service and its clients (written in Visual Basic, Java, and Perl) to support Basic Authentication and SSL.

14. Filesystem Case Study

Chapter 14 gives a tour of the features and facilities offered by the Apache SOAP Toolkit. The aim of the chapter is to give the reader a solid starting point from which to explore the areas of Web Service development that are of particular interest to them. The chapter goes through setting up a database (MySQL) and a server (Tomcat), writing a pluggable provider (using Apache SOAP) and a filesystem Web Service, and using SOAP attachments.

15. Wrox Auction Case Study

The goal of Chapter 15 is to demonstrate a set of skills and techniques that will enable you to design and implement a Web Services interface to an existing application. In the chapter we work through a C# case study using SOAP, WSDL, and UDDI to design, build, and publish the Web Services layer of an online auction application. We look at the business activities of our auction application, such as: selling, searching, and bidding, and how each of these areas involves providing Web Services to support client transactions with fundamentally synchronous or asynchronous server responses.

Appendices

Appendix A

Simple Object Access Protocol (SOAP) 1.1 W3C Note 08 May 2000

Appendix B

Web Services Description Language (WSDL) 1.1 W3C Note 15 March 2001

Appendix C

Material from the UDDI version 2.0 Data Structure Reference UDDI Open Draft Specification 08 June 2001

This gives a detailed list of all UDDI Structures and Substructures, a description of their fields, and the lengths and data types of these fields.

Conventions

To help you get the most from the text and keep track of what's happening, we've used a number of conventions throughout the book.

For instance:

> **These boxes hold important, not-to-be forgotten information, which is directly relevant to the surrounding text.**

> *While this style is used for asides to the current discussion.*

As for styles in the text:

- ❑ When we introduce them, we **highlight** important words
- ❑ We show keyboard strokes like this: *Ctrl-A*
- ❑ We show filenames, and code within the text like so: `sample.cs`
- ❑ Text on user interfaces is shown as: File | Save
- ❑ URLs are shown in a similar font, as so: http://www.wrox.com/
- ❑ Namespace URIs, however, are shown like this: `http://www.w3.org/2001/XMLSchema`
- ❑ When referring to chapter sections or titles, we italicize them, as so: *Introduction*

We present code in two different ways. Code that is new or important is shown as so:

```
In our code examples, the code foreground style shows
new, important, and pertinent code
```

Code that is an aside, or has been seen before is shown as so:

```
Code background shows code that's less important in the present context,
or that has been seen before.
```

In addition, when something is to be typed at a command line interface (for example, a DOS/Command prompt), then we use the following style to show what is typed:

```
> set WSTK_HOME=c:\wstk-2.3
```

Customer Support

We always value hearing from our readers, and we want to know what you think about this book: what you liked, what you didn't like, and what you think we can do better next time. You can send us your comments, either by returning the reply card in the back of the book, or by e-mail to feedback@wrox.com. Please be sure to mention the book title in your message.

How to Download the Sample Code for the Book

When you visit the Wrox site, http://www.wrox.com/, simply locate the title through our Search facility or by using one of the title lists. Click on Download in the Code column, or on Download Code on the book's detail page.

The files that are available for download from our site have been archived using WinZip. When you have saved the attachments to a folder on your hard-drive, you need to extract the files using a de-compression program such as WinZip or PKUnzip. When you extract the files, the code is usually extracted into chapter folders. When you start the extraction process, ensure your software (WinZip, PKUnzip, etc.) is set to use folder names.

Errata

We've made every effort to make sure that there are no errors in the text or in the code. However, no one is perfect and mistakes do occur. If you find an error in one of our books, like a spelling mistake or a faulty piece of code, we would be very grateful for feedback. By sending in errata you may save another reader hours of frustration, and of course, you will be helping us provide even higher quality information. Simply e-mail the information to support@wrox.com, your information will be checked and if correct, posted to the errata page for that title, or used in subsequent editions of the book.

To find errata on the web site, go to http://www.wrox.com/, and simply locate the title through our Advanced Search or title list. Click on the Book Errata link, which is below the cover graphic on the book's detail page.

E-mail Support

If you wish to directly query a problem in the book with an expert who knows the book in detail then e-mail support@wrox.com, with the title of the book and the last four numbers of the ISBN in the subject field of the e-mail. A typical e-mail should include the following things:

❑   The **title of the book**, **last four digits of the ISBN**, and **page number** of the problem in the Subject field.

❑   Your **name, contact information**, and the **problem** in the body of the message.

We *won't* send you junk mail. We need the details to save your time and ours. When you send an e-mail message, it will go through the following chain of support:

❑   Customer Support – Your message is delivered to our customer support staff, who are the first people to read it. They have files on most frequently asked questions and will answer anything general about the book or the web site immediately.

❑   Editorial – Deeper queries are forwarded to the technical editor responsible for that book. They have experience with the programming language or particular product, and are able to answer detailed technical questions on the subject.

❑   The Authors – Finally, in the unlikely event that the editor cannot answer your problem, he or she will forward the request to the author. We do try to protect the author from any distractions to their writing; however, we are quite happy to forward specific requests to them. All Wrox authors help with the support on their books. They will e-mail the customer and the editor with their response, and again all readers should benefit.

The Wrox Support process can only offer support to issues that are directly pertinent to the content of our published title. Support for questions that fall outside the scope of normal book support, is provided via the community lists of our http://p2p.wrox.com/ forum.

p2p.wrox.com

For author and peer discussion join the P2P mailing lists. Our unique system provides **programmer to programmer**™ contact on mailing lists, forums, and newsgroups, all in addition to our one-to-one e-mail support system. If you post a query to P2P, you can be confident that it is being examined by the many Wrox authors and other industry experts who are present on our mailing lists. At p2p.wrox.com you will find a number of different lists that will help you, not only while you read this book, but also as you develop your own applications. Particularly appropriate to this book are the various Web Services and XML lists.

To subscribe to a mailing list just follow these steps:

1. Go to http://p2p.wrox.com/.

2. Choose the appropriate category from the left menu bar.

3. Click on the mailing list you wish to join.

4. Follow the instructions to subscribe and fill in your e-mail address and password.

5. Reply to the confirmation e-mail you receive.

6. Use the subscription manager to join more lists and set your e-mail preferences.

Why this System Offers the Best Support

You can choose to join the mailing lists or you can receive them as weekly digests. If you don't have the time, or facility, to receive the mailing list, then you can search our online archives. Junk and spam mails are deleted, and your own e-mail address is protected by the unique Lyris system. Queries about joining or leaving lists, and any other general queries about lists, should be sent to listsupport@p2p.wrox.com.

1

Evolution Of Web Services

In this chapter we will introduce the core concepts of XML Web Services – services-oriented computing that brings a new paradigm to the process of creating highly distributed applications. XML Web Services are modular applications that are self-describing, and can be published, located, and invoked from anywhere on the Web (or within any local network based on open Internet standards). XML Web Services are powered by XML (Extensible Markup Language), which is at the core of most of the technologies presented in this book. We will look at the technologies, standards, and specifications that form the main building blocks used in creating XML Web Services. More specifically, in this chapter:

- ❑ We will start with a brief history of distributed computing. Then, we will consider the strengths and weaknesses of some of the main pre- XML Web Services distributed computing technologies.

- ❑ Next, we will turn towards reviewing the architecture of XML Web Services by showing how the different technologies fit together. This chapter will provide an overview of the building blocks for XML Web Services. The later chapters in this book will provide full details and examples using the various building block technologies.

- ❑ Finally, we will venture into some of the new and upcoming efforts that are being undertaken around the topic of XML Web Services. These efforts promise to bring the Web to its new level of functionality and usefulness.

Web Services are the Future!

The power of the Web Services model of developing distributed applications is quite exciting. A company, for example, can offer an online electronic payment service and expose it to its partners, who can connect to it and use it regardless of the platform that they are using. Car-rental companies can link their online reservation systems with airlines and hotels, so that travelers can book a car and a flight, and make a hotel room reservation at the same time. As shipping, fulfilment, and electronic payment companies start to expose their systems via Web Services, you will be able to easily plug these into the e-Commerce site that you may be building. These are early examples that cover only a few of the possibilities – many more will surely follow. So, before we take a look at the Web Services architecture that makes these exciting capabilities possible, let's take a quick look back into the history of distributed computing in order to see how it developed through the years and eventually lead to the onset of Web Services.

A Brief History of Distributed Computing

Once upon a time there were computers called mainframes. All serious computing applications ran on them at that time. Later, terminals were added in order to connect to these mainframes, and people could work on these machines by typing in commands in plain text. Some years passed and a new type of a machine arrived, called the personal computer or PC. People quickly started to love the idea of having their own personal computer and being able to run their own applications on it.

At this time (back in the 1980's), particularly in the personal computer world, developers did not care much about communications protocols. Making applications talk to each other on the same machine was a challenge enough. By the early 1990's a few object frameworks became popular, such as **COM** (**Component Object Model**) introduced by Microsoft and **CORBA** (**Common Object Request Broker Architecture**) introduced as a cross-vendor initiative by the **OMG** (**Object Management Group**). In general, COM and CORBA are models or architectures for writing and encapsulating binary code, that is, components, that programmers can easily and in a standard way call from any application that supports COM or CORBA. COM and CORBA are not easily interoperable however, so COM can only call COM and the same applies to CORBA components (we will describe these architectures and protocols in further detail in the next section). So, this was the distant era when mostly **stand-alone computing machines** ruled the Earth.

Keep in mind that in this discussion of distributed computing, we are emphasizing the perspective of application-to-application communication that works in a standard way on top of an operating system. Lower level machine-to-machine communication offered by various networking technologies was already available in the 1990s and even earlier.

The Age of Local Networks

Once local networks became more widespread in the 1990's, particularly among personal computers, connecting one machine to another became a much higher priority than ever before. Vendors and organizations that already had their own object model frameworks extended them to support the ability to communicate across networks. The OMG established **IIOP** (**Internet Inter–ORB Protocol**) as the CORBA standard wire protocol. Microsoft came up with **DCOM** (**Distributed COM**) as its wire protocol, which can cross machine boundaries. Another strong contender, created at a later date than IIOP or DCOM, and which the Java community uses is Sun Microsystems' **RMI** (**Remote Method Invocation**) protocol.

Utilizing one of these protocols, an application that supports them can call components that reside on other computers across the network. Typically, this call would be in the form of **RPC** or **Remote Procedure Call**, where a remote procedure is being called. The remote procedure would then send a reply back to the calling application. Keep in mind that these protocols are not interoperable, at least not without a significant effort. So, in general, clients using DCOM will call only servers that support DCOM, and the same applies to IIOP and CORBA. There have been some efforts in the industry for interoperability, but they have not been widely successful (or widely used).

Our review of these distributed applications protocols in the next few sections will be brief, mainly mentioning what they are, and some of their key characteristics. For a more in-depth review of these protocols, you can go to the URLs provided for more information.

CORBA/IIOP

As we said above, OMG introduced IIOP as the CORBA standard wire protocol for TCP/ IP. IIOP is the TCP/ IP specialization of the **GIOP** (**General Inter-ORB protocol**), which specifies the basic wire protocol. Extending the object model, so it can be used as an application-to-application communication protocol between computers and across the network created a rich programming environment. CORBA/ IIOP has a connection oriented and stateful programming model and as such is not as scalable as stateless architectures.

A **Stateful Programming Model**, usually refers to a situation where a server has to hold state information, such as caller addresses for example, for a duration longer than a single request and reply. This usually means that we have a connection-oriented programming model, where we establish a connection between the client and the server first and then perform multiple request/response type interactions within that connection. Connection-oriented and stateful programming models involve some additional overhead that the server would not have to implement if the communication had a stateless architecture. In a stateless architecture, the server does not require connections any longer than a single request/response communication. In addition, in stateless architectures the server does not have to keep track of any session related information for the client, and this lowers the overhead on the server. Lowering the overhead is especially important when serving many clients in a large distributed network scenario.

> *To learn more about CORBA and IIOP, visit the OMG web site at http://www.omg.org/ or the CORBA dedicated site at http://www.corba.org/.*

DCOM

Microsoft developed DCOM (Distributed COM) as its wire protocol, which can cross machine boundaries. DCOM is one of the most complex distributed computing protocols. It also has a connection-related overhead conceptually similar to CORBA/IIOP, therefore scalability is not one of its main strengths (for more information see the paragraph on stateful vs. stateless model discussion within the previous section). DCOM performs some other tasks such as garbage collection and it has a very solid security implementation that adds to its functionality, but at the expense of increased complexity.

> *Find out more about DCOM at the Microsoft COM technologies web site http://www.microsoft.com/com/ or go directly to its DCOM section at http://www.microsoft.com/com/tech/dcom.asp*

RMI

Another contender in the distributed computing arena is Sun Microsystems' RMI (Remote Method Invocation) protocol. RMI was built with performance in mind, although only one of its three sub-protocols is connectionless oriented (for discussion on connectionless vs. connection-oriented communication, please see the *CORBA* section). RMI implements garbage collection (by extending the Java Virtual Machine or JVM built-in garbage collection capabilities over the network) and is quite security conscious. One of the main disadvantages of RMI however, is that it is tightly bound to a single language platform namely Java.

There is much more about Java's RMI on the Sun Microsystems web site located at http://java.sun.com/products/jdk/rmi/index.html

Synchronous vs. Asynchronous Communication

It's important to mention that protocols such as DCOM and RMI are inherently request/response oriented, that is, they are made to work synchronously and thus do not support a one-way exchange of messages. This is where some different vendor-specific technologies should be mentioned. On the Java side, we have **Java Message Service** (**JMS**) and on the Microsoft side we have **Microsoft Message Queuing** (**MSMQ**).

JMS supports both message queuing (best suited for guaranteed delivery of messages), as well as the publish-and-subscribe model (better for implementing less-critical data exchanges). MSMQ has comprehensive functionality with support for reliable message delivery, full security, transaction support, and more.

Both of these asynchronous messaging technologies are feature rich, complex, and tightly bound to the particular vendor standards, the Windows operating system in the case of Microsoft and the Java language platform in the case of Sun Microsystems.

You can read more about JMS on the Sun Microsystems web site located at http://java.sun.com/products/jms/index.html. *For more information on MSMQ, visit Microsoft's web site at* http://microsoft.com/msmq/default.htm.

The Age of the Internet and the Web

Connecting applications using any of the described protocols works quite well, especially when those same applications reside on the same local network. However, with the emergence of the Internet and particularly the Web, the network became very large, very distributed, and extremely decentralized. No single person or company had the power to make the decision of which operating system or programming/language environment would run on the various computers that are connected on the Internet. This means that the same rules that apply within a local area network do not work very well for the Internet and the Web. So, what are the challenges in using some of the existing distributed application protocols over the Internet and the Web?

Challenges with Existing Protocols

In order to implement a rich application-to-application communication across machines, we would typically use CORBA/IIOP, DCOM, or RMI (or some of the asynchronous communication technologies, if we wanted to implement a one-way method of communication). As rich environments for implementing application-to-application communications, these protocols tend to get quite complex. Configuration and installation are usually accompanied by errors and it is very difficult to set things up where they work properly "right out of the box". Once we add security and transaction management, the installation and configuration becomes even more difficult.

Another major obstacle is communication over the Internet. The distributed communication technologies described earlier have a **symmetrical** requirement, meaning that both ends of the communication link would typically need to have implemented the same distributed object model. With the Internet we **cannot** guarantee that both ends of the communication link will have implemented the same distributed object model. Assuring this on the Internet is difficult and often simply impossible.

Furthermore, the above-mentioned protocols rely on **single vendor solutions** in order to gain the maximum advantage of the protocol. There has been some implementation of these communications protocols (DCOM, CORBA/IIOP, or RMI) on operating systems and language platforms, other than the primary one, but this has been limited and not very successful. For example, the primary language platform for the CORBA/IIOP protocols has been the Java programming language, and the primary operating system environment for DCOM has been the Windows operating system. Use of these protocols with other language platforms/environments has not been very significant.

An even more limiting issue is the difficulty of getting these protocols to work over firewalls or proxy servers; in other words, they are **firewall-unfriendly**. They are firewall-unfriendly because their architecture typically forces them to listen to port numbers that may not be easily or widely known. The challenge with proxy servers is that clients using these protocols typically require having a direct connection to the server (versus an indirect connection via a proxy server). Of course, there are some workarounds, such as RDS (Remote Data Services) for DCOM, but these types of workarounds tend to be slower, more challenging to configure properly, and are typically not implemented in various operating systems or language platforms. In general, firewall administrators are very reluctant to open many ports, except some widely used ones, such as the ports for HTTP (Hypertext Transfer Protocol) and SMTP (Simple Mail Transfer Protocol).

Although CORBA/IIOP, DCOM, and RMI are respectable protocols, the industry has not yet shifted entirely to one in particular. The lack of universal industry **acceptance** is marked by all sides pointing out the other's shortcomings. Each side finally realized that the strategy of attempting to persuade the customers and users that "our protocol is better than theirs" did not work. The solution to being able to have an application-to-application communication from any machine to any other, regardless of the operating system, language environment, or distributed object model includes the use of existing Internet standards. Even though none of these protocols is a good candidate for a universal communication protocol, it does not mean that we do not need them anymore. They will continue to be used in the building of individual Web Services for some time to come.

Once people started creating applications that were accessible via the Web, that is, web applications, the need for connecting these web applications became quite important. So, how did web applications achieve interoperability before the move towards Web Services?

Early Attempts at Connecting Web Applications

Applications and web pages started as islands of information, with **links** that allowed users to move from one place to another. When using links, however, the user had to leave everything that was on the first page in order to move to the second. Therefore, links provided a very crude way of connecting web applications (more precisely, it was not a matter of connecting applications directly, but simply redirecting users from one web application to another).

Probably the most common interoperability between web sites and web applications has been via the use of **frames**. Frames can be HTML (Hypertext Markup Language) frames where the content from one web site is displayed in a separate HTML frame alongside the content of another. However, the frames approach works with other client-side environments in addition to HTML, such as Java applets, Java applications, Windows applications, ActiveX controls, etc. All of these can open windows for various web applications and frame the content within those windows side by side.

The frames technique brought the impression that users can work with different web applications at the same time. The limitation of the frames approach, similar to the links approach, is that it does not really connect the applications, but just the front end user interface (UI). Furthermore, regardless of how well this approach is implemented, it is still quite difficult to get many web applications to look and behave like one seamless application, in terms of their graphical appearance, layout, form style, and other user experience elements. For instance, we may have tried to frame other web sites in our site, so that users don't completely leave our site (maybe for maps or stock quotes information). However, it is very likely that users would be able to easily tell that the framed web site is not part of our web site. Now, imagine that the web site we are framing in our site provides a **Web Service** for the information that we need (again, maybe this is for the purpose of dynamically obtaining map or stock quote information). In this case, we would be able to fully integrate their service within our application and follow our own graphical, layout, and style choices.

Another approach to connecting web applications was to have the web server act as a client to another web application, and then "**screen scrape**" the page for relevant content. The application would need to process the returned HTML, extract relevant information and then present its version of the content. This approach was often difficult to do appropriately and it was susceptible to errors due to visual changes in the web application serving the information. For example, this is how third party developers today have built applications that let you sell on the online auction site, eBay. They take data from eBay's site and then they post data back to it. When the web site changes, their software would tend to break, so eBay frequently received calls from third party developers saying that their software had broken because eBay had changed something as little as a category. Today eBay is looking into leveraging Web Services.

When using this approach, the only way to send information to a web site was to **post information** as if it had been submitted from an HTML form. Posting information is done via HTTP POST or GET, which are the two methods of submitting information when using HTTP (the most common transport protocol that the World Wide Web uses). If the posting of information is not done in co-operation with the web site, it is prone to similar problems as screen scraping, as most changes in the form receiving code will break the client application. Sometimes, posting information was known as the early generation of Web Services, before the time of XML. However, this method lacked structure, such as the structure of XML. In addition, it was difficult to create a more sophisticated RPC type of communication between the servers. Note that Web Services that utilize HTTP as their transport protocol will still use HTTP POST or GET for submitting information.

A number of first generation portal applications and "**digital dashboard**" type applications used the methods of links, frames, "screen scraping", and posting information to assemble different applications under one place and with a single interface. "digital dashboard" is an application type that collects and presents information from various sources in separate windows or sections – all organized in one screen. The analogy is to the dashboard that you have in your car that provides you with an overall view of the status of your car by pulling information from various car subsystems, such as the gas tank, speed, engine temperature, and so on. Those of you who've worked with "digital dashboard" type applications know that the interoperability was not always at the level where users and developers wanted it to be.

At the surface, it may seem that the challenge of these early approaches in connecting web applications has to do with not having full control of the target application. For example, you may not know when the server application gets updated, and when it does your application will break. There may be some valid legal issues involved, as well, such as that some web applications may not allow their content to be framed. Even though these are all valid points, there are still some very important technical challenges involved with these integration approaches. The above techniques of integrating web applications allow primarily user interface (UI) integration, with little control over visual style – something that is surely very important to your marketing department or customer's marketing department. Furthermore, trying to integrate at the application level, for example using the posting approach is quite difficult, due to the lack of standardized structure (something that was addressed with the use of XML).

Some companies and developers have chosen to integrate and try to semi-implement Web Services without the use of a standard XML based protocol, but rather using custom defined **XML messages over HTTP**. With this approach comes a challenge similar to that with the posting approach. It lacks the structure in creating more sophisticated RPC type message exchanges between computers in a standard way. There are simply too many different ways to structure XML in connecting applications and sending messages without the use of a standard XML based protocol – just like there are too many ways to structure plain text or ASCII (American Standard Code for Information Interchange) text, without the fine structural rules imposed by XML.

Web Services address the need for interoperability between web applications by specifying a standard XML based protocol. With Web Services as a new application development possibility, we need to think of web sites as functions (in other words, Web Services). One web application calls another, as a regular application would call another, by invoking a function and getting a result back. Or, if communicating in an asynchronous mode, a web application would send a message to another web application, without the need to receive an immediate response. Having this type of programmatic interface, a company can focus on its core competencies within its web application and add the other needed capabilities from others. At the same time, the end–user can experience a full–fledged application even though a single vendor provides only part of the overall functionality.

An XML based protocol that uses established Internet transport protocols would enable web applications to offer rich Web Services, and it would overcome the challenges of these early methods of connecting web applications. So, let's look at one of the first attempts for an XML-based communication protocol.

Initial SOAP-type Implementations Using XML-RPC

When XML arrived in the later part of the 1990s, suddenly developers had a way to express a rich structure of information and messages in a uniform and self-describing way. This matured into using XML in formatting the messages exchanged between systems. This approach would allow us to exchange well-formatted messages between systems in a self-documented/self-describing and extensible way, regardless of what operating system or language environment those systems may have.

One of the better-known early implementations of XML-based communication protocols is **XML–RPC** (XML Remote Procedure Call). XML-RPC allows us to call procedures on remote machines without having to worry about the specifics of their operating system or language environment. These machines can be anywhere on the Internet or within our Intranet, as long as they are connected via HTTP. XML-RPC is a very simple protocol that is easy to handle (it's simply XML, no binary specification to worry about), and it is very easy to use. There are implementations of XML-RPC for most language environments and operating systems freely available. However, despite these strengths of XML-RPC and despite it being a notable pioneer in this space, most vendors did not fully embrace it, but rather chose to embrace its successor, **SOAP** (**Simple Object Access Protocol** – more about this below).

XML-RPC has two important shortcomings: it is quite verbose in the way it represents data, and it lacks good data typing. XML–RPC has challenges when encoding structures of data and other more complex data types such as arrays. At the time when XML–RPC was created, the work on XML data types via the XML Schemas specification was not even close to being ready. The experience from XML-RPC was used in the design of SOAP.

For more information on XML–RPC you can visit http://www.xmlrpc.com/

Before embracing the details of Web Services and their architecture, let's look at **EAI** (**Enterprise Application Integration**) and how it relates to the area of Web Services.

Web Services versus EAI

When thinking about the subject of connecting applications and enabling them to talk to each other, the concept of Enterprise Application Integration (EAI) often comes to mind. In enterprises, applications were often created with various technologies to address various needs. Some of these applications were created by specific vendors and were actual commercial products; some were custom applications. These applications were great in addressing the particular need for which they were created, such as human resources needs, sales force management, financials management, etc. However, these applications were not able to connect to each other and exchange information easily. The area of EAI emerged as a solution to offer ways of connecting these various enterprise applications.

So, how are Web Services different from EAI? These two areas are sometimes understood to be one and the same. However, EAI tends to be more specific to a particular business process, such as connecting a specific human resources application to a specific financials application. In addition, EAI is typically designed as a much more tightly bound implementation of connected systems. Web Services, on the other hand, are typically thought of as loosely bound collections of services that are much easier to plug in and out, discover, and bind to dynamically. EAI is less flexible and more expensive to implement than Web Services using open Internet standards and technologies.

So, Web Services are, overall, a better solution for a larger, less specific scale. Let's concentrate on this area from now on.

Enter Web Services

Web Services are **modular applications** that are self-describing and that can be published, located, and invoked from anywhere on the Web or within any local network based on open Internet standards. They combine the best aspects of component-based programming and web programming, and come packaged in the form of modules that can be reused without worrying about how the service is implemented, or even what language, operating system, or component model was used to create it. This is also known as "black box reuse", meaning that we don't have to know what is "in the box" and how it works in order to use its functionality. Web Services are accessible via ubiquitous Internet protocols such as HTTP or SMTP, and they are of course based on XML. The consumers of the XML Web Service can be implemented in any language, component model, and hosted on any operating system.

At a high level, it is interesting to note that building applications with Web Services would allow us to move from building tightly coupled or bound applications into building applications that are built with **loosely bound** components. In general, we can think of tightly bound components or applications as ones that have to be bound at design time, and loosely bound components as ones that can often be bound or even discovered and then bound at run-time. Loosely bound components and applications tend to be more scalable, manageable, extensible, and less susceptible to errors from modifications than tightly bound implementations.

However, loosely bound components have some disadvantages on the side of the application programmer such as more error conditions to handle. In addition, the tools and infrastructure needed for the implementation of loosely bound components are often more difficult to design and create. Finally, implementing loosely bound applications in the past has been a challenge due to the lack of necessary standards. The area of Web Services is set to bring us closer to creating more applications that we can bind and discover dynamically, thus experiencing the benefits that this improved application architecture brings.

Web Services are modular, self-describing applications that can be published, located, and invoked from just about anywhere on the Web or a local network. The provider and the consumer of the XML Web service do not have to worry about the operating system, language environment, or component model used to create or access the XML Web service, as they are based on ubiquitous and open Internet standards, such as XML, HTTP, and SMTP.

The concept of Web Services started to take a fuller shape with the introduction of **SOAP (Simple Object Access Protocol)** as the messaging protocol between computers. SOAP is a simple wire protocol that is based on XML. It was designed to connect computers regardless of their operating system, programming language, or object model utilized (or even lack of object model altogether). Even though, from its name it may appear that it mandates the use of particular objects, that is not the case, because SOAP specifies the message format that accesses and invokes the objects, rather than the particular objects themselves.

The W3C (World Wide Web Consortium, see http://www.w3c.org/) acknowledged the submission of SOAP in May of 2000. Ariba Inc., CommerceOne Inc., Compaq Computer Corp, DevelopMentor Inc., Hewlett–Packard Co., IBM Corp., IONA Technologies PLC, Lotus Development Corp., Microsoft Corp., SAP AG, and Userland Software Inc. jointly submitted the specification to the W3C. Having such a group of diverse companies support the submission of SOAP was a good sign towards industry acceptance and implementation of an open standards-based interoperability protocol. Currently, SOAP is being further developed under the XML Protocol Working Group at W3C, which is to develop the next version of SOAP, **SOAP 1.2** (for more on SOAP 1.2, see the section on SOAP later in this chapter).

XML and SOAP are the base technologies of Web Services architectures.

We have mentioned that Web Services are based on XML and other open Internet standards, such as HTTP and SMTP. We briefly touched upon SOAP as the standard messaging protocol for Web Services. What else is there to discuss about Web Services?

When talking about Web Services, we typically think of certain architecture with some standard building blocks that can plug into that architecture in a specific way. Now let's take a look at that architecture.

Architecture of Web Services

The main building blocks of Web Services are three-fold and they go along the concepts of discovery, description, and invocation – see the diagram over for how they fit together. Each one of these building blocks consists of number of layers. Later in this chapter, we will expand on the details of the various building blocks vertically. Let's first get familiar with these building blocks as entities.

In order for a consumer application (the application consuming the service or asking for the service) to use an XML Web Service, they would first have to find or **discover** it. Next, a consumer would need to learn more about what the XML Web service does or more about its **description**. Another way to think of the description building block is to think of it as the representation of the meaning of the XML Web Service, or alternatively as the meta data, that is, descriptive data about the XML Web service. Finally, the consumer would need to be able to call the XML Web service by providing it the necessary input elements and receiving any output that is appropriate (that is, **invoke** it). This block contains the SOAP Protocol with its various extensions. The Message building block sits on top of the **Transport** layer, which consists of transport protocols – typically open Internet standards based protocols such as HTTP and SMTP.

Message/ Wire (Invocation)	Description (Meaning)	Discovery
Transport		

From an Web Services provider or developer perspective, it is easier to look at the Web Services architecture starting from the Invocation block, and then going up to the Description and Discovery section. This is how we will continue our discussion.

Invocation

The Invocation block of Web Services focuses on the message or wire level of the architecture. Here, SOAP is the key component to the architecture. SOAP is an extensible message format protocol and it can bind on top of various Internet standard protocols for transport, such as HTTP and SMTP. We'll look at the core SOAP protocol first, and then we will review some of its extensions.

SOAP

SOAP is an XML based communication protocol for exchanging information between computers regardless of their operating system, programming environment, or object model framework. In the specification, SOAP is defined as a lightweight protocol for exchange of structured and typed information between peers (that being computers) in a decentralized and distributed environment. A "decentralized and distributed environment" usually refers to networks such as the Internet, but it does not have to be limited to this. For example, SOAP can easily be used for communication between computers on your own LAN (Local Area Network). SOAP does not define a programming model or implementation-specific semantics (such as an API or Application Programming Interface). It defines a simple mechanism for exchanging messages, by simply providing a model for modular packaging and a way of encoding data within messages that is based on XML Schemas.

SOAP specifies the message format of the communication that occurs between computers. An easy way to think of SOAP is to make analogy to regular postal mail. Similar to how postal mail has to follow certain specifications for most letters that are mailed, SOAP addresses similar needs for the computer-to-computer communications. The postal mail system specifies an envelope for standard letters, and SOAP specifies an envelope for the data payload, for instance.

It is important to highlight that SOAP does not define the transport protocol that is used for sending the message. In the same postal mail example, an envelope itself typically does not specify whether a letter is sent via plane or via ground transportation, however some of the stamps or other stickers on it would. The SOAP specification does describe how HTTP can be used to carry SOAP messages. However, it also states that SOAP is not limited to HTTP in any way and that it can be used with a variety of other protocols.

> **SOAP is a simple and extensible computer-to-computer communication protocol that leverages existing Internet standards: XML for message formatting, HTTP and other Internet protocols for message transport.**

By supporting SOAP, web sites and applications in general can offer Web Services that are accessible programmatically to other computers, without the need for human interaction or intermediation. In this way, one application can assemble solutions from any combination of software components, applications, processes, or devices. For example, an ASP (Application Service Provider) can use SOAP to build a generic solution for customer authentication, payment, tax calculation, shipping, and more, and then sell or give away this service.

Those thinking that we already have too many protocols to worry about may be wondering if we really need yet another one? SOAP came to light as a protocol that tries not to invent anything new, but to use existing technologies such as XML, HTTP, SMTP, and other common Internet protocols. XML is used to define the format of the message, envelope, and RPC mechanism, and HTTP, SMTP, or other Internet protocols define the transport mechanisms for the message. Therefore, we do need a protocol to allow for "componentization" of the Web and making these "components" universally accessible. No established standard communication protocol today is completely platform, language, and component model independent (aside from HTTP, SMTP, etc, that are different from SOAP, which is a messaging protocol). So, how does SOAP compare with the distributed communications technologies, CORBA/IIOP, DCOM, and RMI that were described earlier in this chapter?

SOAP vs. Other Distributed Protocols

As its name suggests, SOAP is a **simple** protocol – with a few lines of code, an XML parser, and an HTTP server, we can quickly have a SOAP object request broker. Commercial Object Request Brokers or ORBs are system services that assist in object invocation, often managing the object lifetime, performing object pooling for enhanced performance, and more. SOAP, being a very simple protocol addresses the complexity issue that impeded the universal adoption of a number of the distributed protocols we had described earlier

SOAP goes a step further – it is **extensible** via the use of XML. No single protocol can guarantee that it will be applicable to all situations and all times, and SOAP addresses this via a standard way of extensibility. SOAP also establishes a framework of sending messages or conducting RPC type communications, but it does not limit us to the use of a single transport protocol. In essence, this makes SOAP extensible in the selection of these protocols.

SOAP works with the existing Internet infrastructure. No special configurations have to be done to routers, firewalls, or proxy servers to get SOAP to work. By using HTTP or other common Internet transport protocols, SOAP becomes very **easy to deploy**, with no firewall modifications. It's worth mentioning that ease of deployment with no firewall modifications could be seen as a drawback as well, making it more difficult to filter unwanted or malicious traffic at the firewall level (at least until firewall and Web Services security standards catch up with the new Web Services technologies).

The various vendors and organizations that have supported the implementation of SOAP, from IBM and Microsoft, to the open source community and organizations such as OASIS (Organization for the Advancement of Structured Information Standards) and RosettaNet (we'll discuss these organizations later in this chapter), should address the issue of **vendor acceptability.** Finally, being recognized by the W3C as a Working Draft at the time of writing this book, and a Recommendation or standard (sometime later in 2001 or early 2002) should ensure that no single vendor has full control over SOAP, and that it becomes as common as some of the other Internet standards (such as HTML, XML, HTTP, and SMTP).

Keep in mind that most standards work on XML related technologies (this includes SOAP) traditionally has been coordinated at the W3C (World Wide Web Consortium), and most Internet transport protocol level standards work, such as HTTP and SMTP, has been traditionally done at the IETF (Internet Engineering Task Force). You can find W3C at http://www.w3.org/ and the IETF at http://www.ietf.org/.

One point to remember is that SOAP does not fully replace the existing protocols such as DCOM, CORBA/IIOP, or RMI. SOAP purposefully leaves several features from traditional messaging and distributed object systems out of its specification. For example, object-type functionality such as: activation, object-by-reference, distributed garbage collection, and batching of messages, are purposely left to the infrastructure where the SOAP client and server are implemented. SOAP has no object model, but it binds applications implemented in various object models and languages.

SOAP Messages

SOAP messages are fundamentally one-way transmissions from a sender to a receiver. Often messages are combined to implement request/response communications. All SOAP messages are XML documents with their own schema; they include proper namespaces on all elements and attributes. Namespaces uniquely define elements or attributes within XML, and SOAP defines two namespaces, **SOAP envelope** and **SOAP serialization** or **encoding**. Some of the rules that SOAP Specifies are stricter than XML itself, for example SOAP messages cannot contain DTDs (Document Type Definitions) or PIs (Processing Instructions). This should be no surprise, as one of the goals of SOAP was to remain a simple protocol.

> *For a comprehensive overview of XML and the various XML related technologies, please see Professional XML 2nd Edition, by Mark Birbeck et al, also by Wrox Press (ISBN: 1-861005-05-09).*

As an XML document, SOAP message consists of three sections: SOAP envelope, SOAP header, and SOAP body (see the following diagram). The body contains the payload of the message, the header provides identifying information about the payload, and the envelope wraps the payload.

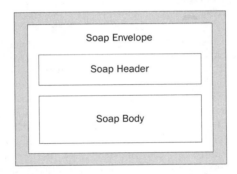

> *In this chapter we are providing only a very brief overview of SOAP. For a detailed overview of this technology please see Chapter 3, SOAP Basics.*

Simple SOAP Example

The following snippet of code comes from the SOAP specification and it illustrates a simple example of a SOAP message used to call a procedure that requires a single parameter.

```
<SOAP-ENV:Envelope
    xmlns:SOAP-ENV="http://schemas.xmlsoap.org/soap/envelope/"
    SOAP-ENV:encodingStyle="http://schemas.xmlsoap.org/soap/encoding/">
    <SOAP-ENV:Body>
        <m:GetLastTradePrice xmlns:m="Some-URI">
            <symbol>DIS</symbol>
        </m:GetLastTradePrice>
    </SOAP-ENV:Body>
</SOAP-ENV:Envelope>
```

We can see that within the `Body` of this SOAP message (the `SOAP-ENV:Body` element), a procedure is being called by the name of `GetLastTradePrice()`, and a parameter (inside the `symbol` element) is being passed to it with a value of `DIS`. Note that the `Envelope` and `Body` have the namespace of `http://schemas.xmlsoap.org/soap/envelope/` and that the encoding has a namespace of `http://schemas.xmlsoap.org/soap/encoding/`. The method itself (`m:GetLastTradePrice`) references a user-defined schema, because it is prefixed with a namespace qualifier (`m`).

> *For more details on SOAP, its main sections, and much more complete details along with examples, please refer to Chapter 3 in this book. There is also the SOAP 1.2 Working Draft at* http://www.w3.org/TR/soap12/.

SOAP 1.2

Individuals from various organizations and companies are working under the umbrella of the W3C organization, within its XML Protocol Workgroup, with the intent of updating SOAP. The XML Protocol Workgroup is comparing the various XML based protocols that are out today before determining the final draft for SOAP 1.2. The XML Protocol Workgroup is planning to work with other groups and standards bodies in an attempt to coordinate the finalization of SOAP 1.2. Some of these standards groups are the sponsors of ebXML (the Electronic Business XML standard), which we will discuss in further detail later in this chapter (you can find ebXML at http://www.ebXML.org/).

It appears, by looking at the current stage of affairs of the XML Protocol Working group that, in all likelihood, SOAP 1.2 will be in essence the next version release of SOAP 1.1. Over the time of writing, the XML Protocol Working Group released the Working Note (that is, draft) on the next version of SOAP 1.2, which you may also hear called XML Protocol (as this was an early working title). The SOAP 1.1 functionality will cover the core of SOAP 1.2, and more capabilities will be available in terms of expandability and layered modularity of the entire framework. Some of the current ideas for the overall framework of the upcoming SOAP 1.2 Protocol are described in the following diagram. Note that in this diagram, we are expanding the details of the messaging and transport building blocks described earlier in this chapter, in order to get a more complete view of the architecture of these Web Services building blocks, and the layers within them.

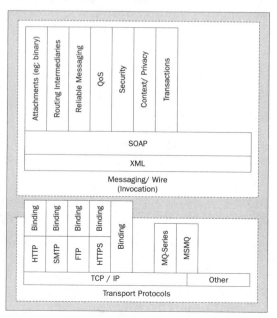

The **core section** of the message building block will be SOAP 1.2, the next updated version of SOAP. This core section is based on XML as the universal base for the syntax of messages. The core SOAP 1.2 Protocol specifies the **envelope** and also, the **extensibility** of the protocol. SOAP 1.2 will be extensible in its ability to bind to just about any transport protocol (bottom of the diagram). In addition, SOAP 1.2 would be extensible in its ability to allow additional functionality to be plugged in and layered in a modular fashion (top level of the diagram). The extensibility should be controlled, to ensure easier and consistent interoperability throughout time.

At the bottom end, very similar to current SOAP functionality, the SOAP 1.2 would be able to bind to various transports, HTTP, SMTP, etc. Then, the transport protocols such as HTTP and SMTP would be layered on top of the TCP (Transmission Control Protocol) or other networking protocols. To some, this may bring about the idea of the OSI (Open Systems Interconnection) model of layering the networking protocols from physical to application layer. It almost looks as if SOAP 1.2 will expand the OSI model further and in more detail, particularly within the application layer of the OSI model (or you could also think of SOAP 1.2 as building on top of the application layer of the OSI model).

> *Once again, for more details on SOAP 1.1, its main sections, and comprehensive coverage of the details, please refer to Chapter 3 in this book. Additionally, you can follow some of the workings of the XML Protocol group at http://www.w3.org/2000/xp/*

Optional **extension modules** "sit" on top of SOAP 1.2. These will not be specified by the protocol itself, although it will allow them to "plug-in" in a standard way. These modules or extensions will include ones for security, routing, and other similar needs that computer-to-computer communications require, and that some have criticized SOAP for not providing.

We will discuss the elements in this diagram in subsequent sections. First, let's make a few general points about SOAP bindings.

SOAP Bindings

We had described earlier that SOAP does not tie itself to any particular transport protocol; in fact, SOAP documents can be carried by almost any transport protocol. The SOAP specification describes how SOAP can be used in combination with HTTP and the HTTP Extension Framework, but it provides this as an example only.

> *The HTTP Extension Framework is an extension to HTTP and can be used optionally, over HTTP. In order to use the HTTP Extension Framework both the client and the server have to support it. Please see Chapter 5 for more information on SOAP binding to transport protocols, such as HTTP, as well as binding to the HTTP Extension Framework.*

In addition, SOAP messages defined in XML can be exchanged using enterprise-messaging technologies such as MSMQ or Queued Components by Microsoft, or JMS (Java Message Service) for the Java community. These messaging technologies can provide all of their features, such as built in security and transaction support, to the SOAP messages being submitted in their payloads. While the benefits of using some of the enterprise-messaging technologies are widely known, the drawbacks lie with the difficulties in communication across platforms and across the Internet as we described earlier.

Now we will look at some of the potential extensions to the core functionality of SOAP.

SOAP Extensions

The SOAP extensions are additional modules of functionality that can be "plugged-in" to the protocol. This approach allows developers to use only the modules and functionality that they need, without the complexity of having to understand or implement all modules. For example, if we need to implement a simple system that doesn't require any of the additional modules, all that we would have to know is SOAP (and XML, of course) and we could connect the two systems. However, if we are looking at building sophisticated interconnectivity between two large systems, where the requirements demand much more than the functionality of the core SOAP specification, then we have the option of "plugging-in" these additional modules. This extensibility of SOAP provides the best of both worlds: easy and simple to implement for small systems and powerful enough with high-end features for large and more demanding systems.

At the time of writing, the SOAP extensions are largely in the process of development. However, from the work of the XML Protocol Workgroup at the W3C and the work in the Web Services area in the developers' community in general, there are indications that the message or wire building block of the Web Services architecture will develop in the direction indicated in the following diagram:

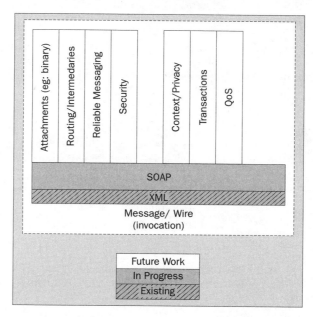

In general, the extensions to SOAP would be implemented as additional header entries within the SOAP message. To allow an understanding of what this means, let's briefly discuss the SOAP `Header` element.

The `Header` element is an optional element, but when present, it has to be the first immediate child of the `Envelope` element and it has to come before the `Body` element. The `Header` element may contain attributes and elements within, and they have to be identified by namespace. The following is an example usage of the `Header` element within the same simple example of a SOAP message that we saw earlier in the chapter.

```
<SOAP-ENV:Envelope
    xmlns:SOAP-ENV="http://schemas.xmlsoap.org/soap/envelope/"
    SOAP-ENV:encodingStyle="http://schemas.xmlsoap.org/soap/encoding/">
<SOAP-ENV:Header>
```

```
    <t:Transaction xmlns:t="some-URI" SOAP-ENV:mustUnderstand="1">
      5
    </t:Transaction>
  </SOAP-ENV:Header>
    <SOAP-ENV:Body>
      <m:GetLastTradePrice xmlns:m="Some-URI">
          <symbol>DIS</symbol>
      </m:GetLastTradePrice>
    </SOAP-ENV:Body>
  </SOAP-ENV:Envelope>
```

The SOAP `Header` element provides a mechanism for extending a message in a decentralized fashion without prior knowledge between the communicating parties. Note that in our example, the optional `Header` element contains entries for tracking transactions. The `Transaction` element used is uniquely identified with a namespace. It also has an attribute that specifies if the extension must be understood or not. This attribute is a standard attribute that is defined with the current SOAP specification. It can have the values of `"1"` or `"0"` (default). A value of `"1"` indicates that the recipient of the message must understand all of the attributes provided in the header, and if not, it is required to return an error message and not process the message.

Some of the functionality of the extensions to the SOAP Protocol is implemented by other organizations, such as with the ebXML standard. For example, the ebXML functionality that parallels the functionality of some of the SOAP extensions was not done in the form of SOAP extensions, but rather, was implemented as part of the overall ebXML framework.

Keep in mind that the intent of the XML Protocol Working Group would be to specify how the core protocol can be extensible, but not to specify all of these extensions. Various extensions may come up throughout time, and vendors or customers may decide to implement their own extensions, if needed. Some of the most desired and widely discussed extensions to SOAP fall in the following areas:

❑ Attachments

❑ Routing/Intermediaries

❑ Reliable Messaging

❑ Security

❑ Quality of Service

❑ Context/Privacy

❑ Transactions Support

These are all described in more detail below.

Attachments

This extension will describe the need for a standard way of attaching or including non-XML or binary files. The SOAP "Messages with Attachments" Specification is likely to be used as the base for this functionality. A few of the vendors that offer Web Services or SOAP toolkits have already implemented or have pledged to implement this extension to SOAP.

Within this specification, content is often encoded with an encoding mechanism called MIME (Multipurpose Internet Mail Extensions). This is the standard used to send e-mail attachments. MIME is a multipart mechanism for encapsulation of compound documents and it can be used to bundle both SOAP messages and other related documents, such as binary document attachments. Binary content is Base64 encoded, and is then included within the SOAP message or attached to a SOAP message. If we think about the possibility of being able to submit SOAP messages with attached fax documents, legal documents, medical images, engineering drawings, or any other type of images, we can see the great potential of the attachments extension to SOAP.

In general, three key ways of handling non-XML or binary content can be applied. First, binary content can be encoded (such as with Base64 encoding) and then included within the XML based SOAP message. In a second option, a binary file can be encoded and then attached with the SOAP message via MIME. Finally, there can be a method of attaching binary content without the need of it to be encoded (this may prove helpful, as encoding binary content may prove to be expensive in terms of usage of resources). The last method works by providing a link reference to the binary or non-XML content, conceptually similar to how a HTML page provides a link reference to an image that is stored as a separate file on the server (using the img tag for example).

> *The Specification that describes how to bind SOAP 1.1 to MIME in greater detail is called: "SOAP Messages with Attachments" and can be found at http://www.w3.org/TR/SOAP-attachments/. The latest version of the "SOAP Messages with Attachments" document can be found at http://www.w3.org/TR/.*

Routing/Intermediaries

Extensions for routing/intermediaries are related to the process of routing SOAP messages through intermediaries. Here we are talking about different routing and intermediaries than the routers found on the Internet that forward and route various Internet traffic, such as TCP/IP (Transmission Control Protocol/Internet Protocol) traffic. The SOAP routers will operate at the message level. For example, if we think about being able to aggregate various Web Services and offer them as part of our application, then our servers would route the execution of the particular XML Web Service request to the company providing the service. The response would also be sent to our servers, which we would have to route further to the service requester. The current SOAP specification allows for routing, however these extensions are not precisely determined at this point. The need to correlate the proper request with the proper response message is very important when intermediaries are involved.

Extensions for routing/intermediaries will have an impact on the ways that XML Web Service **scalability** is addressed (scalability refers the way well the software can adapt to increased demand for service). Scalability is a very important aspect of many web applications, and therefore of Web Services as well. In Web Services, scalability is typically addressed by making them available on multiple servers (similar to how web farms for web sites work, with multiple and less expensive web servers serving the content of a single web site that otherwise would have required one large and expensive computer). A single server can be enlarged to a certain degree, but that approach has the limitation of reaching a point where the cost outpaces the benefits. Intermediary servers are often required to spread the load across multiple web servers, as well.

Using more intermediary servers would be one of the appropriate ways to address the scalability of Web Services. – There are several ways in which they can achieve this. They can take the function of caching servers because caching is a technique very common for scaling distributed systems. Caching stores frequently requested data locally, and then serves requests using the local data, therefore saving more expensive requests or trips across the network. Another way of improving scalability is the store-and-forward approach, where multiple messages with the same destination are stored up and can be sent down a single network connection, reducing the overhead of initiating multiple network connections. This is similar to "batching" used by the SMTP protocol. The efficiency of intermediaries is accomplished by: avoiding the data transfers, avoiding round trips, and moving data closer to the "edge" of the network, that is, closer to the end user's location.

Web Services must have a clear way of addressing the routing and intermediaries extensions in order for us to address scalability appropriately.

Reliable Messaging

Reliable messaging extensions relate to the capability of being able to guarantee delivery in some fashion. For example, when a message does not reach the destination, how many times should the sending party retry before giving up and reporting an error? Another question would be what happens if two of the same message were sent, due to traffic congestions or slow connections? The receiving party should be able to determine that it had received a duplicate message and it should not process both of the messages.

One obvious example of the importance of reliable messaging is that when a system debits an account, we would want to make sure this is done only once, regardless of whether the system had to resubmit the message a few times, or send the message only once. Reliable messaging relates in some aspects to transactions, which we'll talk about in a subsequent section. However, reliable messaging is more than concerns about typical short-running transactions and ensuring that our debit and credit either both happen or don't happen at all. Reliable messaging has to deal with the issue of ensuring that a message requesting a transaction or multiple transactions is processed only once. For example, when a request is sent to an XML Web Service with our purchase for two books, we want to make sure not only that our account is only properly debited for the two books, but also that our order is placed only once, despite the fact that, due to traffic congestion, the system had to retransmit the order three times and the XML Web Service received all three of those requests at different times throughout the day. All order requests are the same and only one of them should be processed. As you can see, reliable messaging and ensuring guaranteed delivery is another important aspect of Web Services.

Security

Security is a very important extension of the SOAP Protocol. When talking to customers about implementing solutions that leverage Web Services, security seems to be one of the most important questions that they bring up to the discussion. With security for Web Services, we are talking about message level security at this point. Transport level security is already available and that may be sufficient for a number of implementations of Web Services. Transport level security options depend on the transport protocol used. For example, the safe way to use HTTP would be to apply SSL (Secured Sockets Layers), which will turn HTTP into HTTPS (HTTP Secure). However, especially when intermediaries are involved in transferring the message from one end-point in the communication to another, message level security is needed, which would provide end-to-end security, rather than the hop-to-hop security provided by the transport stack security methods.

Some of the security needs of SOAP may be addressed with a few of the specifications that are under development at the W3C at the time of writing. The **XML Signature** specification will help to answer the question: who sent the message and was the message altered on-route to us. It is important to understand that the mechanism to apply a digital signature provided by XML Signatures is going to be independent of specific signature technology and is separate from any protocols or techniques used to verify signatures, mange keys, and determine authorization.

For more on the workings of XML Signatures you go visit W3C at
http://www.w3.org/Signature/

The **XML Encryption** specification will provide a standard way of encrypting the content of a message by the sending party, and a standard way of decrypting the message by the destination party, therefore making the message unreadable by any other parties during transport. Optionally, digital signatures should provide the capability to encrypt and sign the entire message or only parts of it. As with XML Signatures, XML Encryption is a mechanism for applying encryption, is independent of specific encryption technology, and is separate from any protocols or techniques used to manage keys. An example is the case where the communication between the order service and the credit card service is encrypted to prevent anybody from being able to read the sensitive content while in transport.

For more information on the XML Encryption specification, you can go to
http://www.w3.org/Encryption/2001/

Security is a complex discipline and involves other issues such as authentication, privacy (discussed below in the *Context/Privacy* section), and authorization (which is typically the responsibility of the end point, and would likely not be part of the SOAP Security Extensions).

We will examine the various issues of security as they relate to Web Services in much further detail in Chapter 13. We can also take a look at the latest SOAP Security Extensions. See the Digital Signatures Specification at http://www.w3.org/TR/SOAP–dsig/ or go to http://www.w3.org/TR/ and then look for the latest SOAP and Digital Signatures document.

Quality of Service (QoS)

Quality of Service (QoS) is determined by the satisfaction of the user about the overall service performance. It is a subjective concept, and as such requires business agreements to determine the finer details. These business agreements are known as **Service Level Agreements (SLAs)**. SLAs are contracts between the service provider (such as an ISP or Internet Service Provider or an ASP or Application Service Provider) and the end user of that service. SLAs cover a number of QoS issues and relevant performance and quality metrics, such as: it commits the service provider to a particular level of service, support options, penalties if promised level of service is not provided, guaranteed level of system performance, maximum allowed service downtime before penalties are applied, minimum network bandwidth, the software and hardware provided for a particular fee, and other details.

The QoS extension for SOAP is related to the reliable messaging XML Web Service extension described earlier (in the *Reliable Messaging* section). It would address questions such as guarantees about service uptime, and actions to be taken if the service is down or fails. Web Services, at the time of writing this book, do not provide standard mechanisms of specifying SLAs and the QoS issues covered in them. Implementing QoS on network traffic that is based on the current version of TCP/IP or more specifically IPv4 (the protocol used as the base for most Internet protocols such as HTTP and SMTP), has proved to be challenging. Various companies have been creative in finding ways to address this challenge to some degree via QoS enabled devices such as routers and network based management software as well as some newer methods of QoS appliances typically installed between the LAN and the WAN, but many analysts agree that the situation will not improve dramatically until the newer version of TCP/IP (or more specifically, IPv6) is widely adopted. Implementing Web Services QoS will likely be strongly impacted by the available QoS offerings for TCP/IP, as Web Services traffic will in most cases occur over transport protocols that are based on TCP/IP (such as HTTP and SMTP).

Despite some of the challenges of addressing QoS on today's Internet, the situation is not as hopeless as it may appear at first sight. For example, there are ongoing discussions about addressing these needs in the Web Services community and the various companies involved at the standards processes at the W3C, as well as coming up with a standard way of providing many of the QoS attributes within the Web Services Description. A number of the QoS approaches used by ISPs and ASPs today for web sites would likely apply to Web Services as well, so stay tuned for more news this area in the near future.

Context/Privacy

Context support is often related to the topic of **Intelligent Web Services**. By knowing the context or the situation and the environment that exists at the time of the execution of the XML Web Service, intelligent decisions can be made automatically on behalf of the user or owner of the service. For example, with wireless devices it would be helpful to know the GPS coordinates of where the device is located, the current time, language preferences, and other caller-related information. This information is useful for providing appropriate choices.

Context sensitivity is one part of the intelligent XML Web service topic. The other part is being able to share the context with other services. Overall, information about the context of the Web Service will significantly lessen the classical problem that computer applications have – presenting many non-relevant choices to the user.

Another use of context information is as a reference to a user profile, providing the service with certain information about the user, such as preferences. This use of context information ties into the need of privacy and being able to appropriately handle this information (that is, being able to protect the privacy of the user).

> *The Platform for Privacy and Preferences (P3P) Recommendation found at the W3C is promising to work on addressing these issues, and may at least partially address the need for context of Web Services as well. There is more information about P3P at http://www.w3.org/P3P/.*

Currently there are no standards for this need, and just about every site that provides a personalized experience maintains identity and history information in a proprietary format. A standard framework for privacy and a standard for keeping and exchanging context information would greatly help in creating "Intelligent" Web Services.

Transactions Support

Transactions permit a group of operations or actions to either all succeed or all fail as a single unit. If the group of operations is to fail, then the particular operations that have executed already should be rolled back or their actions should be undone.

In general, we have short transactions, such as the ones found in typical databases and transaction management systems. However, with Web Services, transactions that span transaction infrastructures, models, and domains of control can often be long-running. These transactions can take minutes and sometimes perhaps hours or more to complete. Handling long-running transactions is quite different than handling short-running transactions. Both long-running and short transactions are to be addressed as extensions to SOAP.

Now that we have covered a few of the most likely SOAP extensions, we'll discuss the description stack of Web Services.

Description

The description of an XML Web Service, that is, the description of the messages it can accept and generate (in essence, part of the XML Web Service contract) is currently done primarily by WSDL (Web Services Description Language), which has other XML technologies as its base, such as XML Schemas, and XML namespaces.

The architecture of the Description stack for Web Services is provided in the following diagram:

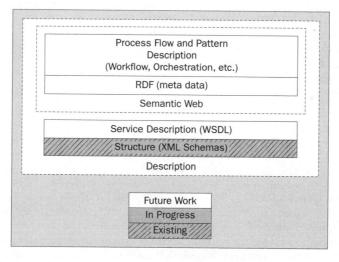

We can see that the description stack starts with the description of the structure, utilizing **XML Schemas**. XML Schemas provide a way of specifying data types, starting from simple ones such as `integer` and `string`, to more complex data types such as arrays, and arbitrary user-defined constructs.

> *For more information on XML Schemas, see Professional XML Schemas, by Jon Duckett et al (ISBN: 1-861005-47-4), also by Wrox Press. In addition, see the W3C section dedicated to XML Schemas at http://www.w3.org/XML/Schema/.*

The next level of the description stack is the description of the service, done typically with the usage of WSDL. WSDL is an XML format for describing network services. It does this by considering network services as a set of endpoints operating on messages containing either document-oriented or procedure-oriented information. The operations and procedures are described firstly in an abstract manner, and then they are bound to a specific network protocol (or transport protocol) and message format. WSDL is extensible to allow describing network services regardless of their network and messaging protocols. The current specification only describes bindings to SOAP, HTTP GET/POST, and MIME. It does not include a complete framework for describing the composition and orchestration of network services, which is part of the higher-level layers of the description stack.

WSDL was brought together to represent the current thinking of defining Web Services by Ariba, IBM, and Microsoft. In March 2001, WSDL received the status of a Note with the W3C, meaning that it is not a full specification as of yet, but is being considered by the W3C and the vendors that are members of W3C. When it comes to defining the services provided with SOAP, the most current implementations use WSDL.

> *For more information on WSDL see chapter 4, and refer to the WSDL specification in Appendix B, or at http://www.w3.org/TR/wsdl/.*

The "Semantic Web" layers are still at an early stage of evolution. The goal of these layers is to describe, in a way that is understandable to software, the various characteristics of a Web Service. This includes characteristics such as reliability and capabilities, as well as the sequencing of messages and a description of who sends what message and at what time. The exact set of describable characteristics is still being developed. RDF (Resource Description Framework) is considered by various experts in the field as the foundation for this effort because of its ability to be used for defining ontology or providing meaning to terms. In addition, process flow and pattern description techniques can be used to describe the processes within an enterprise or an application. Some of the process description languages could evolve to satisfy this area – these process flow technologies would enable a developer writing code to connect their application to an XML Web Service, use the process flow description file, and determine the sequence of messages at the XML Web Service site.

Discovery

Once we know how to invoke an XML Web Service and we can describe it, we need a way to allow others to find out about it. Analogous to search engines, the **UDDI** (**Universal Description, Discovery, and Integration**) Specification describes how a provider can advertise the existence of their XML Web service in a **directory**. A consumer of an XML Web Service can search the UDDI registry to find out about the Web Services that they need, by category – UDDI 1.0 allows businesses to describe themselves in one or more standard taxonomies, such as NAICS (North American Industry Classification System) and UNSPSC (Universal Standard Products and Services Classification). Taxonomies are similar to vocabularies, where a term is assigned a meaning; however these terms can be categorized in hierarchical structures. With UDDI 2.0 new taxonomies should be allowed for describing businesses.

> *We talk more about UDDI in Chapters 6 and 7. Also, we suggest visiting http://www.uddi.org/ for the latest work on the UDDI specification.*

So, once we find out which XML Web Service we need, the next step is to be able to **inspect** the details of it, such as its service description, and process flow orchestration contract.

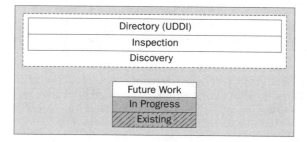

We have just become familiar with the three main building blocks of Web Services: the message (or wire), the description, and the discovery. These building blocks are related, and are meant to work together within one **Web Services Framework**. In the next section, we will look at the Web Services Framework as a whole, and its layered and modular architecture, how it comes together, and we will learn more about the status of the various technologies.

Web Services Framework Architecture

We started with a very simple diagram of the architecture of Web Services. Then, we worked through the three main building blocks. Now, when we expand the main building blocks of the Web Services Framework architecture, we get the following diagram:

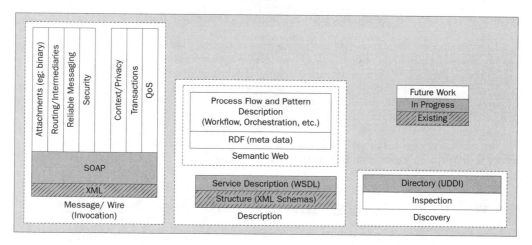

In this diagram, we can see that the building blocks already in existence are XML and XML Schemas. The components that are in the process of being developed are SOAP, UDDI, and WSDL. SOAP is the foundation for the Web Services Framework. The framework will allow decentralized services to be defined, deployed, manipulated, and evolved in an automated fashion without a centralized control. This framework is the basis for services-oriented applications and eventually a services-oriented Internet. The framework would allow for scalable, layered architecture that can meet the demands of both simple and very complex implementations.

The Web Services Framework does not overly restrict the technologies that may be used to implement Web Services, and certainly does not limit developers to a particular vendor's products. This means that we can implement the Web Services Framework (and not necessarily all of it at once) with various technologies, such as Java on the Linux operating system, or Visual Basic and Visual C++ on the Windows operating systems. The sections of this book that discuss the various Web Services implementations offered by different vendors at this time will go into further detail on this topic.

According to some of the authors of the Web Services Platform at the W3C, a common framework helps to ensure that implementations are less complex, with lesser probability of having different companies creating overlap in frameworks, and with greater probability of achieving interoperability.

Another very important point about having a common framework is that development and adoption of individual components of the framework can happen in parallel and asynchronously, allowing implementations to be created without first having to study all of the components of the framework. In addition, new components and modules can be added at a later time, a critical feature, which allows the system to evolve without changing the entire system. The components are developed in an incremental, layered manner, from the bottom up. This allows each component to be fully functional on its own. Also, each component would serve as a foundation for the implementation of the components in the layers above it.

The Web Services Framework allows for subsets of components to be used to provide specific levels of service that particular scenarios require. For example, if a company wants to develop a simple application-to-application communication for their Intranet, they can use SOAP without the need to concern themselves with most of the other components of the Web Services platform. This is a key in reducing the complexity of an implementation and making it appropriate for users from all needs and situations, from the smallest companies to some of largest international enterprises. Building monolithic standards that address entire usage-domains leads to creation of different standards. By creating a collection of building-block standards that can be combined into domain standards as required, we simplify implementation, interoperability, and compliance verification. In return, this makes the development of Web Services standards and infrastructure more practical and cost effective.

We described that the Web Services Framework does not specify the implementation of the various modules specified. In other words, the Web Services Framework allows for it to be implemented in any programming language, using any operating system, database, or middleware technology. This interoperability is based on standard data formats and protocols, not APIs (Application Programming Interfaces). This allows software vendors the flexibility and autonomy to implement the Web Services Framework in the way that they best know how.

Next, we will briefly cover the various implementation initiatives that the vendors are taking, that is: the various Web Services toolkits and frameworks that they provide.

Vendor Tools and Frameworks for Web Services

Although SOAP and some of the other related Web Services building blocks have only been around for a relatively short time, there are already a number of implementations on the market. Most key vendors have their own implementation of SOAP within their preferred programming language or environment. These implementations are typically in the form of **toolkits**.

In the Java community, the Apache SOAP (originally donated by IBM and its alphaWorks division to the care of the Apache organization), and the IBM Web Services Toolkit are the key implementations. Microsoft has the SOAP Toolkit 2.0, however in the long term Microsoft's implementation of Web Services will be within its .NET framework.

Other large vendors offer Web Services toolkits and frameworks, such as Sun Microsystems offering its Web Services Development Pack, and HP with its Core Services Framework. There are a number of other vendors that provide various Web Services toolkits and SOAP implementations for various language platforms and operating systems (such as toolkits for PERL, Python, C++, PHP, etc.).

There is more about Web Services implementations for Java, Microsoft, and other Web Services implementations later in the book.

While the Web Services tools are generally focused on providing the core capability for developing and deploying Web Services, some of the vendors provide wider and more encompassing offerings. These are the so-called **frameworks** or sometimes also referred as platforms. Besides the core Web Services toolkits, the frameworks include architectural specifications and guidelines and additional tools and utilities for deploying Web Services. Let's take a look at some of the better-known frameworks and platforms offered by some of the larger vendors.

HP and e-Speak

Hewlett Packard has been a pioneer in the area of Web Services, even before the term became popular. Their first product offering was **e-Speak**, which is an open platform for developing and deploying e-Services. An e-Service corresponds closely to a Web Service, as we now know it. An e-service is a service that is available via the Internet and performs a given task or transaction. It can be dynamically discovered, invoked and composed with other e-services. e-Speak started in HP as a research project back in 1995, and in 1998 a software project was initiated to develop it into a product. The first e-Speak product launch was in May 1999.

Since then however, HP has moved towards the XML based standards for Web Services like SOAP and UDDI which seem to have greater industry acceptance, and their new product – the **HP Web Services Platform** is built around these standards. HP is increasingly playing a larger role in these Web Service standards, and will also be an operator node for the UDDI Business Registry by sometime towards the end of 2001.

e-Speak has been developed in Java, and clients need to use its Java API (called J-ESI – Java e-Speak Service Interface) for building e-services and clients. In addition it also has XML-based mechanisms to interact with e-Speak services.

e-Speak has a very strong security model, which is based on the SPKI (Simple Public Key Infrastructure) standard – something that is still not available in today's web service offerings. However, for whatever reasons, it did not get the mind share that newer technologies proposed by Microsoft, IBM and others did. More details on SPKI can be found at http://www.ietf.org/html.charters/spki-charter.html.

e-Speak defines three technical components: the **e-Speak Engine** (also called the **e-Speak Core**), the **Service Framework Specification** (SFS) and the **E-Services Village**. The e-Speak engine consists of the engine itself and a Java API for interacting with it. SFS defines a protocol for exchanging XML documents between services. The e-Service Village is a hosted directory for web services.

e-Speak Engine

The e-Speak engine has API for building services and clients to interact with the services. A service would need to conform to a **contract** and be published in a **vocabulary**. A contract is an interface that a service implements and a vocabulary is set of attributes that associated with a service.

Lets take a simple example to illustrate these concepts. In order to implement an e-Service for a printer, we would first define its interface or contract. This would define methods that all printers would need to support- like `print()` or `isPaperFinished()` etc.

Next, the vocabulary for the printer service would contain the meta data about the service. This would be in the form of name-value pairs specifying the attributes of the printer, such as *manufacturer name, model, colour, DPI,* etc.

Typically, standards bodies define the contracts and vocabularies for a market segment, and service developers write their services based on these specifications. Once the service had been written, it is deployed and advertised in an advertising service. The advertising service itself is an e-Speak service.

Users or clients of the service can search for a service based on either the contract or attributes of the vocabulary. The following piece of client code, adapted from an example in the e-Speak Programmers guide gives a flavour of what's involved in finding and using a printer service.

First, make a connection to the e-Speak engine. The parameter `connectionProperties` contains properties for the connection, like the username, password, hostname, and the port number e-Speak is running on etc.

```
/* Connect to the e-Speak engine */
ESConnection coreConnection = new ESConnection (connectionProperties);
```

The engine to which the client connects doesn't need to be the same as the engine that the service provider had registered with, so long that they are in the same **community**. A community consists of a number of e-Speak engines connected together.

Next, we locate the service name. For this, we need to construct a service finder (`ESServiceFinder`) object, setting it with the name of the interface that we are interested in finding.

```
String intfName = PrinterServiceIntf.class.getName ();

/* Set the interface that the service implements */
ESServiceFinder printFinder = new ESServiceFinder (coreConnection, intfName);
```

Then we set the search attributes. In the example below, we are interested in printer service that can print in colour and has a DPI speed of 1400.

```
/* Set the search attributes- these attributes are searched in the vocabulary */
ESQuery printQuery = new ESQuery ("Color == 'yes'");
printQuery.addConstraint ("DPI == 1400");
```

Now we do a find call to locate a printer that matches our search criteria. The find call returns a service stub object on success.

```
/* Find all printer services that conform to our requirements */
PrintServiceIntf printer = (PrintServiceIntf) printFinder.find (printQuery);
```

We can then invoke the service methods on the stub object. In this case, we send it a document to print.

```
printer.print (someDocument);
```

The diagram below shows this use case.

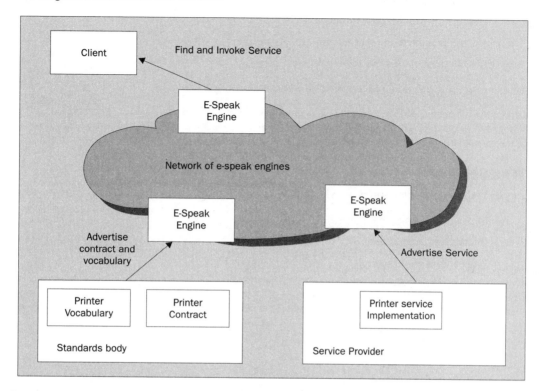

In order to enable and use security, no additional code needs to be written on the service or client side. The e-Speak engine has a configuration file where security can be enabled or disabled. It also comes with tools to generate and manage certificates for users. This allows for a very fine-grained security model – it is possible to specify access restrictions for users at the service method level.

In e-Speak, all access to the service is **mediated** through the e-Speak engine. This allows for accounting for service usage.

Service Specification Framework (SFS)

The e-Speak SFS defines standards that allow interaction between e-Services. SFS supports asynchronous messaging using an XML document exchange model. Using this, it builds support for higher-level business abstractions, negotiations, dynamic binding. Thus entities in a business relationship could use SFS for B2B interactions such as discover each other, negotiate using user-defined criteria and reach agreement on product, pricing and delivery terms.

E-Services Village (ESV)

The e-Services Village is a directory of e-Services. It organizes e-services into business categories, and allows for searching for the services via a variety of mechanisms – web browser, PDAs, XML messages over HTTP in addition to programmatic access via the e-Speak engine. The typical use case for the ESV would be

❑ The service provider implements and deploys his e-Service on his own local e-Speak engine

❑ The service provider (or someone on his behalf) advertises the service at the ESV.

❑ A client discovers the service either programmatically or through a web browser.

❑ The client then uses the service.

The e-Services village can be accessed at http://www.hpespeak.com/

Most of the e-Speak platform code base has been turned over to public domain. The e-Speakweb site (http://www.e-Speak.net/) has downloads of the source code, documentation as well as binary releases. HP's e-Speak site is at http://www.e-Speak.hp.com/.

HP Web Services Platform

The HP Web Services Platform is an XML platform consisting of the following components:

❑ Messaging Component

❑ Interaction Component

❑ Processing Component

❑ Security Component

❑ Transaction Component

The diagram below shows these components and their place in this XML stack.

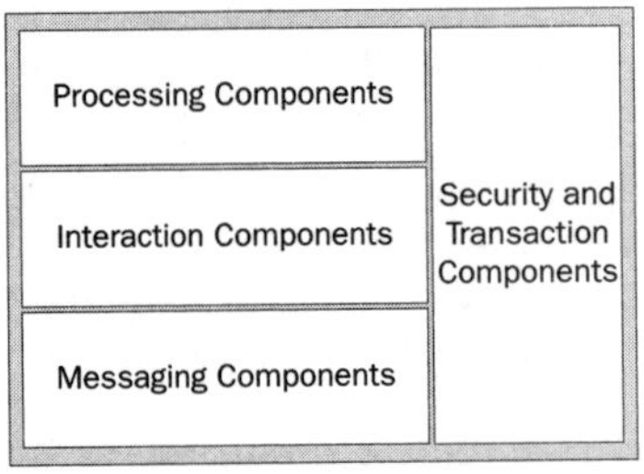

Messaging Components

The messaging component consists of listeners and in boxes for incoming messages. A listener is a generic socket-based component, and there are listeners for standard transport protocols like HTTP, HTTPS, SMTP and FTP. They can be configured to run in a load-balancing broker for scalability.

Interaction Components

The interaction component facilitates dispatching an incoming request to an application component. This layer will have support for both simple dispatches to application (for example SOAP RPC requests) as well as multi-node message conversations (for example ebXML business scenarios).

This component also has an interaction controller supporting **conversations** between business partners. The conversation is described using the WSCL (Web Service Conversation Language) protocol. This protocol specification is proposed by HP to standardize conversation description. It describes business level conversation and specifies the XML documents exchanged and their sequence.

Further details on WSCL can be found at http://www.e-Speak.hp.com/specifications/wscl.shtm/.

Processing Components

The processing component supports three levels of application processing models:

- ❑ A high-end solution using a business process engine/workflow system in the HP Process Manager
- ❑ A scripting solution built around Cocoon 2/XSP. This would be useful for developing the middle tier business logic
- ❑ A low-level J2EE solution in which the business logic is developed in a Java Bean/EJB. It can then be exposed as a Message-Driven Bean (MDB) and the request dispatched through JMS

Security Components

This component focuses on security aspects, and has implementations of the emerging security standards:

- ❑ XML Digital Signature
- ❑ XKMS (XML Key Management Specification)
- ❑ XML encryption

Transaction Components

This component provides support for transaction, and well as Quality of Service (QoS) issues.

More details about the HP Web Services Platform can be found at http://www.hp.com/go/webservices/. Currently the complete Web Services Platform is not available for download. The components available at the time of writing this chapter include:

- ❑ HP SOAP
- ❑ HP UDDI implementation, including a UDDI private registry, UDDI browser and client SDK
- ❑ Parts of the security component, including XML Digital Signature implementation
- ❑ Cocoon2 with SOAP logicsheets

IBM's Dynamic e-Business

IBM's web services product offerings are collected under the concept of a "dynamic e-business". This concept refers to the use of Internet technologies to make a business more flexible and able to adapt to change. The dynamic e-business concept recognizes that the costs of building business processes and infrastructure are often dominated not by their initial creation, but rather by their evolution to meet new needs not anticipated when originally designed. This evolution can be dictated by changing needs of customers or business partners, and generally entails integrating a system into a new environment or reorganizing components of business logic into novel combinations.

Traditionally, achieving this kind of flexibility via component-wise system design has meant use of a sophisticated framework to provide the necessary component management that permits inexpensive reorganization of the components. The problem is that systems like this, for example CORBA, tend to impose a relatively high amount of structure on the components themselves, with the result that one kind of inflexibility (monolithic system design) has been replaced with another (tight coupling to the framework). One of the predictable results of this is that interoperation of components built with frameworks from different vendors can be difficult to achieve.

The dynamic e-business approach uses a looser coupling, based on Internet standards, such as XML, SOAP, WSDL, and UDDI, to achieve the desired flexible system design without the overbearing influence of a complex framework. A system built with these standards can be designed as a set of components, i.e. Web Services, which can be modified and rearranged to reflect changing business strategies, and can use standard interfaces which can interact with other systems with minimum integration costs.

Products

IBM's goal is to serve as a purveyor of tools, which can be used to build such a system. The key first step however, is the widespread adoption of the standards upon which Web Services will be built. To this end, IBM has been active in the standards community. IBM donated their SOAP toolkit to Apache and has been active in the standardization efforts for WSDL and UDDI. Indeed, IBM's web services infrastructure is characterized by a greater degree of openness than competing offerings, according to IBM's sources. Compared to Microsoft, which has a vested in interest in building their XML Web Service models on their own proprietary operating system (that is: the Windows operating system), IBM has embraced a support for multiple operating systems via their use of Java as their primary programming language of implementing Web Services. Microsoft's side of the story is that they have embraced a multi-language environment (via .NET) and thus they show openness in their language selection – something that vendors that standardize on Java do not. We'll cover the .NET Framework later in this chapter, and also in chapter 11.

IBM's web service products are based on the following model:

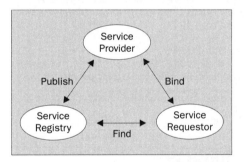

In this model, the Service Provider implements the business logic to be delivered and it advertises its existence by publishing information with the Service Registry.

The Service Requestor would like to employ the services of the Service Provider, so it consults the Service Registry to find an appropriate provider for the service it desires.

Equipped with the information from the Service Registry, the Service Requestor can find the Service Provider and learn about its interface. That information is sufficient for the Service Requestor to contact, or Bind, the Service Provider and thus make use of the services it provides.

This model is an excellent representation of a Web Service, and exploits that feature of Web Services which is most valuable: the components are only loosely coupled, thus simplifying the inevitable adaptation of the system to meet new requirements, which is so common in today's business world.

Using IBM's tools, the developer of such a system would employ standardized technologies. For example, the communication between the parties in this model would typically be via SOAP messages, which are formatted according to the XML protocol, and transmitted over HTTP. The Service Provider would employ the WSDL standard (in XML format) to describe the service. The Find and Publish operations would occur by using the UDDI standard, which uses SOAP messages, to communicate with the Service Registry.

IBM provides tools to build the system according to this model. Rather than being found in a single product, IBM's strategy is to include these tools in a range of products, including DB2 (database management), Lotus Notes (groupware), Tivoli (network management), and, most notably, WebSphere (internet infrastructure). For example, DB2 includes a variety of tools for converting database contents back and forth between XML, and the Domino server within Lotus can export services as web services.

WebSphere, however, is the most important IBM product connected to web services. WebSphere itself is a broad collection of tools, all of which are related by virtue of the fact that they can be considered, however distantly, to be of use in creating a web-based application. Among its components are a web server, directory server, web page authoring tools, security services, session management, and a wide range of tools for building an e-commerce site. The most important component of WebSphere with regard to web services is the WebSphere Application Server. This application server includes tools such as a J2EE framework for developing and deploying Enterprise Java Beans, JDBC drivers for connecting to databases, a servlet container, a Java development kit, transaction services, and a set of tools especially targeted for development of an application based on the web services model described above.

These web service-specific tools include Java libraries for producing and parsing XML, for transmitting SOAP messages, for creating WSDL files, and for communicating with a Service Registry via UDDI.

The SOAP toolkit that IBM includes in the WebSphere Application Server is the same as the one freely available from Apache. However, as is the case with the JDK that is shipped with WebSphere, the version is carefully selected to ensure compatibility with the remainder of WebSphere. For that reason, it is best to use the JDK and SOAP that come with WebSphere when using any of the other WebSphere tools.

WebSphere includes a tool called `wsdlgen` that can be used to produce WSDL files to describe a service. The information in a WSDL file includes operational descriptions of the functions a service is capable of performing, the protocols which can be used to communicate with it, and the endpoints on the Internet where it can be contacted. A WSDL file is human-readable but, being XML, it is just barely so. The `wsdlgen` tool is therefore useful since it acts as a "wizard" that facilitates WSDL file creation.

Also included with WebSphere is the uddi4j Java library for communicating with a UDDI Service Registry. UDDI is a standard system for publishing and locating services, somewhat like a phone directory. Also like a phone directory, UDDI is divided into white pages, which contain information about how to contact an organization, yellow pages that categorize services, and green pages that contain information on how to do business with Service Providers. While it is possible to use a private UDDI registry, there is a single, global, UDDI registry that may be used by contacting any of the UDDI "operator sites". The operator sites are themselves web services, and use SOAP (and therefore XML), for communication. However, UDDI is a sophisticated protocol, and IBM has implemented uddi4j, which may be used to simplify the task of writing an application, which communicates with an operator site to Publish, and Find services. Although it is not required for UDDI, WSDL makes a natural complement to UDDI by acting as the protocol with which a service may be described and uddi4j includes tools that assist in the use of WSDL to describe the service to be registered.

Future Trends

One thing shared by a number of the technologies in the WebSphere Application Server is that they originated as tools in IBM's Alphaworks program. Alphaworks is a program in which early versions of technologies and tools are delivered to interested developers. The idea is that IBM can put early, or "alpha" versions, of the tools into the hands of developers before actually committing to supporting them as products. Developers can thus get early looks at new technologies and tools and benefit from their usage, while IBM can get feedback from developers in order to refine the tools before putting them into products. For example, uddi4j, wsdlgen, and even the Apache SOAP toolkit were originally (and still are) available as downloads from the Alphaworks site as components of the Web Services Toolkit.

WebSphere, like almost all application servers, is undergoing product definition by accretion, meaning that it is an ever-growing collection of generally cooperating tools, some of which were created without the idea that they would become a component within an application server. However, it is possible to detect a direction of growth in WebSphere and that direction is upward, away from low-level, fundamental tools such as XML which bear little resemblance to solutions to real-world business problems, and towards higher-level, more abstract tools, such as UDDI, where it is fairly easy to see how they could be employed by an end-user.

A new example of a higher-level tool at Alphaworks is **WSFL**, Web Services Flow Language. WSFL is an attempt to put a tool in the hands of domain experts that can be used to produce a Web Services-based application. In other words, the tools available for building Web Services so far are fairly complex and require a fair bit of computer science background. It would be better to have tools that are within the reach of business experts, who generally don't have that computer science background, so that they can directly express what the application should do. This division of labour is similar to Java Server Pages where a computer science expert builds tag libraries and a domain expert can write the .jsp files to build an application from those tags.

WSFL is an XML grammar that is used to describe a business process. The building blocks of the business process are Web Services. The WSFL model describes how to combine the Web Services, or "activities", into a process that accomplishes something useful to the business. Usually this requires two complementary views of the process, the "flow model" which describes the sequence of activities, which must occur in an assembly line-like manner, and the "global model" which describes the nature of the interactions, or messages, that link the activities.

A key feature of WSFL is recursive composition, meaning that once a process has been defined with WSFL, it can be used as a single activity within a larger model, and meaning that you can build a process once and reuse it multiple times within other models.

While WSFL is described with XML, it is convenient to think of business models in graphical terms with pictures. It is therefore very likely that tools will become available which permit a user to draw pictures of a business model and have the corresponding WSFL automatically generated.

Microsoft's .NET Platform and Framework

Microsoft's strategy in developing and deploying Web Services, especially in the longer run, is the .NET Framework. The .NET initiative was announced in July of 2000. It is centered at the .NET platform, which consists of a few building blocks, with the .NET Framework being at the core. Let's quickly take a look at the .NET platform and its building blocks and then we'll focus back to its core: the .NET Framework.

Visual Studio .NET		
.NET Enterprise Servers	.NET Framework	.NET Building Block Services
Operating System on Servers, Desktops, and Devices		

The **operating systems** layer consists of Microsoft's operating systems for servers such as Windows 2000 Server, operating systems for desktop computers such as Windows XP, Windows 2000 Professional, or Windows ME, and operating systems for devices, such as Windows CE.

In the next layer, we have the **.NET Enterprise Servers** such as the BizTalk 2000 Server (EAI or Enterprise Application Integration and B2B server), Commerce Server 2000 (e-Commerce solutions server), SQL Server 2000 (database server), Exchange Server 2000 (email and collaboration server), Application Server 2000 (management for high availability web sites and server farms), Content Management Server 2001 (web content management), Host Integration Server 2000 (connecting to legacy systems), Internet Security and Acceleration Server 2000 (firewall and proxy server), Mobile Information Server 2001 (gateway for connecting to mobile devices), SharePoint Portal Server 2001 (document management, enterprise search, and portal engine). For more information on the .NET Servers, please visit: http://www.microsoft.com/Servers/.

The **.NET Building Block Services** are collections of Web Services that Microsoft plans to release. These can be used as building blocks by developers in the applications they create, therefore avoiding having to spend lots of time on number of "pluming" type aspects of their applications, such as authentication for example. One of these services is available in its early edition and that is the Passport service. It allows a single login across web sites. Microsoft has announced the services called "HailStorm" that would be centred on user experiences (we'll cover HailStorm in further detail, later in this chapter).

The top layer of the .NET platform is the **Visual Studio .NET**. This is an application development tool intended for rapid development of Web Services and other applications (it's the next version of the Visual Studio 6 IDE or Integrated Development Environment).

.NET Framework

The final part of the .NET platform is the .NET Framework (in the centre of our earlier diagram). The .NET Framework is the new development platform offered by Microsoft and it contains a new programmatic interface to Windows services and APIs, integrating technologies such as COM+ component services, the ASP (Active Server Pages) web development framework, reliability, security, simple deployment, and the Web Services protocols such as SOAP, WSDL, and UDDI. The architecture of the .NET Framework is shown in the diagram below:

Web Services	Web Forms	Windows Forms
Data and XML classes		
Base Classes		
Common Language Runtime (CLR)		

Going from bottom and then up, first with start with the **Common Language Runtime (CLR).** The CLR runs on the top of the operating system. The CLR is the heart of the .NET Framework. It is the runtime infrastructure that abstracts the operating system implementations. In particular, the CLR handles tasks such as activating objects, garbage collection, memory handling, code execution, security checks on objects, etc.

You can think of the CLR as similar to the Java Virtual Machine (JVM), if you are familiar with Java. The difference with the JVM is that the CLR supports all languages that can be represented in the **Common Intermediate Language (CIL)** or the Microsoft's intermediate language to which code is initially compiled (this multilanguage capability is possible due to the common data types, including even base data types such as Long or Boolean). The JVM however supports only one language, and that is Java. On the other hand, the CLR runs only on Windows operating systems, at least at the time of writing this chapter (although there have been some indications that other companies create version of the CLR for Linux). The JVM is available for most operating system platforms. In short you can compare the CLR and JVM in the following fashion: the CLR has single operating system but multiple language support, while the JVM has multiple operating system but single language support.

The CIL was submitted by Microsoft to the **ECMA** or the European Computer Manufacturers Association (http://www.ecma.ch/), a standards organizations that manages C# (C sharp) – the new language that Microsoft has introduced with its .NET platform. ECMA also manages ECMAScript, a scripting language that is found in major web browsers such as Internet Explorer (known as JScript in this browser) and Netscape Navigator (called JavaScript in Netscape Navigator). Other languages that will run on .NET, besides C#, will be Visual Basic (VB), C++ (if using managed code), and JScript. Some of the third party languages that will run on .NET are COBOL, Pascal, Eiffel, PERL, Python, Smalltalk, and more. For more on support for various languages in .NET please see http://msdn.microsoft.com/net/languages/default.asp and http://msdn.microsoft.com/net/thirdparty/default.asp#lang.

The next level up in our diagram is the layer of **base classes**. These are similar to sets of classes in ATL (Active Template Library) and MFC (Microsoft Foundation Classes) or some of the Java base classes. It includes input/output functionality, string manipulation, security management, thread management, network communications, handling collections, and more.

The data and XML classes extend the base classes by providing a set of **classes for handling data and XML manipulation**. For example, this includes management of data that is stored in databases via ADO.NET and SQL. The XML data related support is about access and manipulation of XML data, XML searches by incorporating XPath, and XML transformations with XSLT.

The top layer of building blocks for the .NET Framework consists of Web Services, Web Forms, and Windows Forms. The **Web Services** are the program interfaces and they provide classes for creating, deploying and utilizing Web Services via the support for standard protocols, such as SOAP, WSDL, and UDDI.

Web Forms and Windows Forms provide user interface capability. **Web Forms** provide classes for handling the design and development of web forms (HTML based that run within a web browser). **Windows Forms** provides classes for building native-Windows Graphical User Interface (GUI) applications.

For more information on the .NET Framework and examples on building Web Services using .NET, please see Chapter 11.

Sun Microsystems and Sun ONE

Sun's offering for Web Services include its **Sun ONE** (Open Network Environment), a platform built around the Sun-Netscape Alliance iPlanet server suite, and the new XML API for Web Services called the JAX Pack.

The Sun ONE platform has the following components:

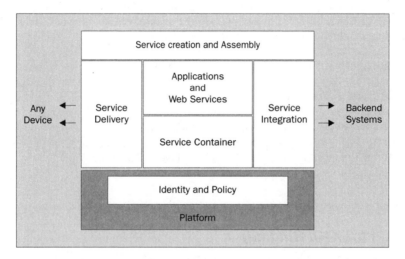

The **Service Creation and Assembly layer** contains tools that help in the development of services and applications. It includes the Forte Developer tools from Sun.

The **Service Delivery layer** includes technologies that locate, connect, aggregate, present, communicate, personalize, notify, and deliver content. The iPlanet Portal Server is meant for this layer.

The **Applications and Web Services layer** is designed to transform traditional business productivity applications into collaborative Web Services. The iPlanet Commerce products (iPlanet BuyerXpert, BillerXpert, SellerXpert, MarketMaker) address this layer.

The **Service Container layer** includes products that help deploy the services and make them available to the end-user. This layer includes the iPlanet Application and Web Servers.

The **Service Integration layer** helps connect existing systems and applications. The products that comprise this layer include the iPlanet Integration Server and iPlanet ECXpert. The Integration server enables access to data and logic stored in applications such as SAP, or even custom or "home-grown" applications.

The **Identity and Policy layer** deals with user management profiles, users, context, roles, and security. The iPlanet User Management products - iPlanet Directory Server, Meta-Directory, Directory Access Router, Administrator, Proxy Server and the iPlanet Certificate Management System- address this layer.

The **Platform layer** is the recommended operating system platform for these services. Sun recommends the Sun operating system platform and Sun Cluster 3.0, though the tools and products mentioned in the above layers should work on most UNIX operating system platforms and the Windows operating system.

The components in this stack are based upon standard XML technologies like SOAP, SOAP with Attachments, WSDL, UDDI etc. and on Java API. Sun has also defined a set of Java API for XML – both document-oriented API like JAXP, JAXB as well as procedure-oriented ones like JAXM, JAXR and JAX-RPC. They are discussed below.

More details on Sun ONE can be found at http://www.sun.com/sunone/.

In addition, Sun and some other companies are involved in defining a set of standard Java API for XML. These will be a part of JDK 1.4, and will also be available as an optional package called JAX Pack (http://java.sun.com/xml/jaxpack.html) for older JDKs.

JAX Pack includes the following packages: JAXP and JAXB.

JAXP (Java API for XML Parsing)

JAXP provides a uniform API for processing XML documents using various parsers. It supports the SAX (Simple API for XML) and DOM (Document Object Model) parser standards. JAXP does not provide any XML parsing capabilities, instead it allows for any parser implementation compliant with these standards to be plugged in, using a 'pluggability layer'. This layer also allows a XSL (XML Stylesheet Language) processor to be plugged in.

You can find more about JAXP at http://java.sun.com/xml/xml_jaxp.html.

JAXB (Java API for XML Binding)

JAXB provides a fast and convenient way of mapping an XML file to java object and vice versa. JAXB uses a DTD (Document Type Definition) to generate code to parse XML documents conforming to that DTD.

JAXB does not have tree management capabilities like JAXP. You should choose the API that best suits the application. For instance you should uses JAXP's SAX API if you just need to grab a piece of data from a large XML document, and want a fast and efficient way of doing it. You should use the DOM API if you don't have a large document, and you need to do complex manipulations with it, such as removing or adding data from it. Finally, you should use JAXB when you need to have a java object representation of the XML data, and wish to avoid the large memory footprint that a DOM tree has.

You can find more details on JAXB at http://java.sun.com/xml/jaxb/index.html.

JAX-RPC (Java API for XML-based RPC)

JAX-RPC provides support for XML-based RPC. It is targeted towards Web Service applications, and clients can make calls to Web Services using JAX-RPC. It internally makes use of SOAP for the call request and response, though this detail is shielded from user programs.

More details on JAX-RPC can be found at http://java.sun.com/xml/xml_jaxrpc.html.

JAXM (Java API for XML Messaging)

The JAXM API provides a standard way of sending XML messages over the Internet. It supports SOAP 1.1 and SOAP With Attachment Specifications and can be extended to work with ebXML and BizTalk.

JAXM has the following features over and above JAX-RPC:

- ❑ Asynchronous messaging
- ❑ Routing of messages to more than one recipient
- ❑ Reliable messaging

JAXM uses a message provider for the actual task of transporting and routing the message. The following shows sample usage of the JAXM API for sending a SOAP message.

First, we need to create a message. This involves getting a connection to the messaging provider. In the code below, we first JNDI (Java Naming and Directory Interface) to locate the appropriate `ConnectionFactory` object. This is under the assumption that it was first registered with the naming service under the name "SomeProviderName".

```
Context context = getInitialContext ();
ConnectionFactory connectionFactory =
            (ConnectionFactory) context.lookup ("SomeProviderName");
```

We then use the `getConnection()` method to obtain a connection to the messaging provider.

```
Connection connection = connectionFactory.getConnection ();
```

We then construct a message using `MessageFactory`. The `getMessageFactory()` method can take a (optional) profile argument, and this can specify additional header information. This is useful when building messages for ebXML or BizTalk protocols.

```
MessageFactory messageFactory = connection.getMessageFactory();
Message message = messageFactory.createMessage ();
```

In the code below, we build a SOAP message- we first extract the `SOAPEnvelope` out from the message, and then add a XML document to its body.

```
SOAPPart soapPart = message.getSOAPPart ();
SOAPEnvelope soapEnvelope = soapPart.getSOAPEnvelope ();
```

The document referred to below is some XML document that we need to send across. This could be read from a file or generated by an application.

```
// Document document;
DOMSource domSource = new DOMSource (document);
SoapEnvelope.setContent (domSource);
```

We then set the end point URL for the message recipient.

```
Endpoint endpoint = new Endpoint ("http://endpointURL");
```

Finally, we can send the message across to the endpoint.

```
connection.send (message, endpoint);
```

If the application is running standalone (and not in a J2EE container), we need to use the `call()` method to send the message. Unlike the `send()` method, this method blocks until it receives a reply.

```
Message reply = connection.call (message, endpoint);
```

More details on JAXM can be found at http://java.sun.com/xml/jaxm/index.html.

JAXR (Java API for XML Registries)

JAXR provides a uniform API for accessing XML based business registries. JAXR was originally intended to provide an API for accessing ebXML business registries, but is now targeted for heterogeneous XML registries: ebXML, UDDI or any other. This is done by using "pluggable providers" for different registry types: for instance one for ebXML, one for UDDI and so on.

It also provides two flavours of API: a Business API that is influenced by the UDDI API and has fewer capabilities, and a Generic API with more capabilities and targeted to the ebXML Registry specifications.

JAXR uses JAXM internally for messaging between the client and the business registry.

More details on JAXR can be found at http://java.sun.com/xml/xml_jaxr.html.

Web Services and Other XML Initiatives

In this section, we will describe various XML initiatives, most of which started before some of the Web Services specifications were brought to life. Some of these initiatives are working to find ways to incorporate the various Web Services specifications such as SOAP, WSDL, and UDDI within their own frameworks. Some are utilizing the Web Services specifications and are building on top of them.

ebXML

The ebXML (Electronic Business XML) is a B2B XML framework. This initiative is managed by UN/CEFACT (a United Nations body that has done work on EDI or Electronic Data Interchange standards, such as the UN/EDIFACT) and OASIS (a consortium that operates the XML.org registry for industry XML schemas and vocabularies). ebXML is a complete B2B framework that enables business collaboration through the sharing of web-based business services. The framework supports choreographed sequences of business service exchanges. It defines specifications for Message Service, Core Components, Business Process Methodology, Registry and Repository, Transport/Routing and Packaging, Collaboration Protocol Profile, and Agreements.

For more on ebXML please see Chapter 6 or visit http://www.ebxml.org/.

The ebXML framework will incorporate the SOAP and SOAP Messaging with Attachment specifications into its upcoming releases. Building the messaging infrastructure of ebXML on top of SOAP will give SOAP another further sign of industry-wide acceptance.

RosettaNet

The RosettaNet is a consortium organization with member companies coming from three vertical industries (industries that deal with the same products, but in different stages of their evolution): Information Technology, Electronic Components, and Semiconductor Manufacturing. The consortium provides standards for these companies for implementing industry-wide and open e-business processes such as catalogs, invoices, and purchase orders. It does this by defining the RosettaNet XML standard DTD and XDR (XML Data Reduced) schemas. The XML Data Reduced format is a proprietary precursor to XML Schema.

The framework that RosettaNet provides has a layered approach and starts from the bottom with Messaging Services, then on to Registry and Repository, Business Dictionary Structure and Business Processes, Supply Dictionary and Business Processes, and finally Universal Specification Schema and Architecture. RosettaNet has been following the activities of the Web Services framework and ebXML, and it has recently announced support for the Messaging Services component of the ebXML architecture. The Messaging Services component of ebXML incorporates SOAP and SOAP with Attachments as we described when talking about ebXML in the previous section. Therefore, RosettaNet will support SOAP as well. An interesting note is that it was announced that the BizTalk Server 2000 EAI and B2B product by Microsoft would provide a bridge that should help interoperability between BizTalk and RosettaNet.

RosettaNet can be found at http://www.rosettanet.org/.

Common Business Library (xCBL)

The Common Business Library (xCBL) is a set of XML building blocks and a document framework. The "x" in xCBL was added to indicate its relationship to XML. The xCBL documents are available in various XML repositories (such as XML.org), and both the xCBL documents and the component library are available free of charge. We can either use the existing documents found in the repositories or create our own XML documents for e-commerce.

xCBL was created by Commerce One, which has indicated that it is interested in distributing xCBL under the supervision of XML repositories such as XML.org and BizTalk.org. xCBL is not a single standard, but a collection of common business elements. It has been developed and modeled after EDI semantics such as X12 and EDIFACT, in order to preserve and extend the EDI investments of the trading partners. RosettaNet was also analyzed before the creation of xCBL, although xCBL is more horizontally oriented (meaning across various vertical industries) than the fully vertical approach of RosettaNet (which as we had described earlier focuses on three vertical industries).

xCBL is a single vocabulary that allows for data typing and validation between documents exchanged in e-commerce transactions. xCBL is made available as a set of SOX (Schema Language for Object-Oriented XML, created by Commerce One) schemas, as a single XML DTD, and as a set of XDR schemas. SOX is the primary language for validating and processing xCBL documents at the moment, but xCBL intends to support the W3C XSD (Schema Definition Language) specification in the future. Also, xCBL intends to be compliant to ebXML in its future versions, which means it will likely be compliant with SOAP, as well.

There is more about xCBL at http://www.xcbl.org/.

BizTalk Framework

The BizTalk Framework is an XML framework created by Microsoft for application integration and electronic commerce. It addresses interoperability in a platform and technology neutral manner, providing specifications for the design and development of XML-based messaging solutions, for communications between applications and organizations. It includes an XML Schema with a set of XML elements and attributes used in messages sent between applications. Also, the BizTalk Framework defines rules for formatting, transmitting, receiving, and processing standard XML messages. It does not specify particualr business processes however, as some of the other initiatives described in this section do.

The BizTalk Framework in its latest edition has support for SOAP messages, and supports other Internet standard protocols such as HTTP, and MIME. There are indications that the BizTalk Framework will adopt the various Web Services technologies, as they become standards. SOAP, along with its extensions, would address many of the aspects that the BizTalk Framework does, such as security, reliable delivery, and handling of attachments.

> *To learn more about the BizTalk Framework go to:*
> *http://www.microsoft.com/biztalk/techinfo/framwork20.asp*

Commerce XML (cXML)

Commerce XML (cXML) is an open Internet-based standard for e-commerce or B2B protocol. cXML was created to reduce on-line business trading costs by facilitating the exchange of content and transactions over the Internet and between procurement applications, e-commerce hubs, and suppliers. It is a set of XML DTDs that were developed in concert with more than 40 leading companies. Schemas are not supported at the time of writing this book, although there are indications for this support in the future.

cXML supports various supplier content and catalog models, including buyer-managed, supplier-managed, content management services, electronic marketplaces, and web-based sourcing organizations. Additionally, cXML defines request/response business processes for the exchange of transaction information. These business processes include purchase orders, change orders, acknowledgments, status updates, ship notifications, and payment transactions, to name a few. In particular, the current standard includes documents for setup (company details and transaction profiles), catalogue content, application integration (including the widely-used PunchOut feature), and also *original, change,* and *delete* purchase orders (and responses to all of these requests), as well as new order confirmation and ship notice documents.

In comparison to RosettaNet and xCBL, cXML is unique as a protocol for B2B interactions over the Internet; it does not attempt to translate the EDI business process and documents into the syntax of XML. This approach allows it to avoid the problems of EDI, such as point-to-point mappings that would make it rather unsuitable for the Internet. Comparing it to RosettaNet in particular, cXML is much more of a horizontal initiative, focusing mostly on the wire protocol. Therefore, cXML has overlaps with SOAP, and will probably adopt it as its transport protocol layer over time. However, at the time of writing this book, there have been no indications of a SOAP version of cXML.

> *Find out more about cXML at http://www.cxml.org/.*

XML Repositories

XML repositories can be thought as libraries of various XML resources, such as XML Schemas or DTDs. The general public or members (usually membership is free with registration) can use the resources provided by XML repositories. We will briefly cover some of the more-well-known XML repositories in order to become familiar with the nature of these types of initiatives.

BizTalk.org

The BizTalk.org site is a library of XDR schemas (XML Data Reduced Schemas, a proprietary precursor to XML Schema), W3C approved XML Schemas (XSD), and vocabulary definitions created and submitted by various companies. The library of schemas is intended for connecting to partners, suppliers, and customers, both within an enterprise and over the Internet. The schemas that are submitted are verified and then placed on the site where others can access and use them. The site helps with versioning of the schemas by notifying users when new versions are posted, etc.

> Go to *http://www.BizTalk.org/* for more information on the BizTalk library and repository.

XML.org

The XML.org is described as an XML Industry Portal. It is hosted by OASIS (Organization for the Advancement of Structured Information Standards) and funded by various organizations. In addition to news and educational information, XML.org provides its registry and repository of vocabularies, schemas, namespaces, and DTDs. As well as having a registry of schemas, XML.org has a catalog of organizations known to be producing industry-specific or cross-industry XML specifications.

> Go to *http://www.xml.org/* for more information on the services provided.

An Example Set of Web Services: HailStorm

When Web Services are put to work, we can create new opportunities that did not previously exist. The following is one of the examples of just such a use of Web Services that we will see fully implemented in the future. We are sure to see more offerings of publicly available Web Services made available by a number of other companies. We chose to use HailStorm as an example of a Web Services set due to its high publicity, making it likely that you will have heard about it.

HailStorm is the codename for a set of Web Services with user-centric architecture, to be implemented and made available by Microsoft. HailStorm will allow applications and services to cooperate to their user's benefit, as well as allowing users, groups, and organizations to share information and collaborate. The information in the HailStorm-enabled services (for instance, a personal calendar that is HailStorm enabled) will be accessed through any PC, smart phone, PDA, or any other smart Web-connected device. HailStorm services will be accessed through SOAP and XML, thus any network-connected device will be able to access its services, regardless of operating system, language environment, or object model framework.

> **HailStorm is a collection of Web Services. In particular, it is a set of user-centric Web Services that would be made available on the Internet, and it could be used as building blocks by incorporating them into any solution or application with access to the Internet.**

With HailStorm, the emphasis is on the user and the user's control of their data. From a **privacy** perspective, the model used by HailStorm is known as "affirmative consent" or "opt-in" model. This means that the user has to provide explicit approval for using certain data, how much of the data can be used, and for how. The set of services provided by HailStorm will help manage and protect the information and the interactions of the user across all the applications, devices, and services. HailStorm is based on Microsoft Passport for its basic handling of user credentials. Microsoft Passport offers single sign-in for users on web sites that support it (meaning being able to log in to multiple applications or web sites by entering one set of credentials, that is, usernames and passwords, once). The security model that HailStorm will use is Kerberos-based authentication (*for more on Kerberos-based authentication, please see Chapter 13*). Overall, privacy appears to be one of the main goals of the platform, and rightly so.

HailStorm will be based on a **subscription business model**, not based on advertisers' revenue. Following the dot-com meltdown, this seems to be a reasonable approach. Microsoft seems to see two opportunities for developers of applications, first in creating applications, devices, or services that use HailStorm services, and second in exposing their own HailStorm-compatible services. Developers ought to see benefits due to having to spend less time creating the plumbing for their systems and instead using some of the services already offered by HailStorm.

The **Core HailStorm Services** will manage elements such as calendar, location, and profile information. Any solution that uses HailStorm could take advantage of these elements, saving the user time otherwise taken up by re-entering this information, and saving the developer time in creating applications to handle these needs.

For example, take a company that utilizes Web Services such as HailStorm. In order to notify the user of an application or web site of the availability of a part that has been placed on backorder, this company would only have to submit a SOAP message to the HailStorm `myNotifications` service. They can do this using SOAP and XML regardless of what application, platform, or language environment is being used. Furthermore, the company would not have to worry about building a system that authenticates the user, tracks their presence, routes notifications, handles receiving of the notification message, manages various methods that a user can use to be notified (e-mail, pager, instant messaging, etc). Instead of spending valuable time on building the plumbing of the application or web site, the company can focus on delivering the services that they provide.

At the time of writing, HailStorm was reported to be on schedule for availability as a public beta by the end of 2001, with a full release in production sometime in 2002. Microsoft created the core functionality of HailStorm, and extensions of additional services are to be created via the Microsoft Open Process with the involvement of the developer community. Microsoft seems to be working hard in getting support from developers for HailStorm Web Services. Furthermore, Microsoft pledges that all of its products will support HailStorm, such as Microsoft Office, Microsoft games, MSN, bCentral small business portal, as well as devices such as the Microsoft XBox video game console, Pocket PC, Microsoft's smart phone software platform, and operating systems such as Windows XP and Windows CE.

For more information on Microsoft's HailStorm, please visit http://www.microsoft.com/net/hailstorm.asp.

The entire description of HailStorm may sound amazing in that it connects to lots of applications, devices, and users. However, keep in mind that HailStorm only addresses some end user needs, such as calendar, location, notification, and profile information. There are so many other services that could be offered in a number of other domains and areas for universal use online in the form of Web Services by any application, any device, and any user. The opportunities are immense and it is very likely that we will see other companies follow suit and offer various competitive XML Web services online. So, once we have many services available for universal use online, by any application, device, or user, these very exciting opportunities would just start to make themselves more obvious. The development of the services-oriented Internet, is where we will pick up the discussion in the following section.

The Service-Oriented Internet

XML is deceptively simple, but it is changing the way we build software. HTML is deceptively simple as well, but it proved that it could change the way we present and share information with each other. XML with its accompanying technologies (for example: SOAP, WSDL, and UDDI) that form the Web Services Framework are revolutionizing how applications talk to other applications. Web Services can allow universal access, from any computer or any device, regardless of the proprietary technology base. In essence, we have a universal language – the language of Web Services. Web sites that were about presenting information to users can now become Web applications that can communicate with each other. As a matter of fact, any application can communicate to any other application, as long as it implements the necessary Web Services. Moreover, as more people and businesses connect together, the value to the consumer increases dramatically.

> **Web Services can allow universal access, from any computer or any device to any other, regardless of the proprietary technology that is the base of the particular device.**

In the previous section, we described examples of a set of user-centric Web Services and some of the new possibilities that they can create, but we only covered a few types. If we image having any kind of Web Service available, from some of the more user-centric ones (such as user profile and preferences), to various commercial Web Services (such as shipping service, tax calculating services, collaboration-related services, etc), the possibilities and opportunities that would be created are enormous. Soon enough, the Internet could turn into a large services oriented network, where we could find just about any service that we, or our application, may need.

> **The services-oriented Internet would have just about any XML Web Service available, from consumer related ones to commercial services; in a similar fashion to how the current Internet has just about all types of content on it.**

We will start our discussion of the services-oriented Internet by returning to the description building block of the Web Services Framework, and its process flow and pattern description layer.

The Process Flow and Pattern Description

Once Web Services are commonplace on the Internet, there will likely be a market for composing new services by **aggregating** existing services. Doing this though would require technologies that would be able to describe workflows within a newly created application and potentially even between companies. Some of the technologies that can be used as the base in this space of process flow and pattern description are XLANG and WSFL (XML process flow languages, see the next section for more details).

So, why would we need a process flow or workflow XML-based language? Typical enterprise workflow systems today support the definition, execution, and monitoring of long running processes that coordinate the activities of multiple business applications. However, they do not separate internal implementation from external protocol description. This behavior is fine when dealing with systems that are based on the same technology. However, for systems spanning enterprise boundaries and systems that are made from different technologies, this would not work well. An XML based process flow and pattern description language would however, address this need.

Once we have a good hold on process flow and pattern description, we can specify better **agreements** that would define items such as:

❑   Which principals in each organization can invoke which services in other organizations

❑   What are the particular QoS parameters that are acceptable when using the service

We will not go much further into agreements in this chapter. Let's take a quick look at what initiatives are available in this area of XML based process flow.

RosettaNet

The RosettaNet Partner Interface Processes (PIPs) and the RosettaNet Implementation Framework (RNIF) are examples of business protocol specification. However, one of the limitations of PIPs is that they are essentially paper specifications and are meant to be used for human understanding and enforcement. This is not adequate for a process flow standard that needs to be understood by computers. In addition, it would not scale sufficiently, as the business protocols would have to be automated.

XLANG and WSFL

XLANG is an early implementation provided by Microsoft for the automation of business processes based on Web Services. This specification provides details about the message exchange behavior among participating Web Services. XLANG in itself is just a specification on the use of XML in this field of business process automation. An engine would have to be created to use XLANG to actually track the state of process instances and help enforce protocol correctness in message flows. This engine could be implemented in any programming language or environment.

The XLANG Specification has been used in BizTalk Server 2000, an Enterprise Application Integration (EAI) and B2B server provided by Microsoft. In BizTalk Server 2000, business processes are diagrammed using a Visio-like interface (Visio is a diagramming product owned by Microsoft). Then, these diagrams are automatically converted into XLANG files that are used by the system to run any business processes that were created and specified within the XLANG file.

For more information on BizTalk Server 2000, see Professional BizTalk Server 2000 by Stephen Mohr and Scott Woodgate (ISBN: 1-861003-29-3), also by Wrox Press. For the latest XLANG Specification, please visit: http://www.gotdotnet.com/team/xml_wsspecs/xlang-c/default.htm

Similar to the XLANG workflow language, IBM has created an XML-based workflow language called **WSFL (Web Services Flow Language)**. It has a similar purpose to XLANG. Both XLANG and WSFL are among the first XML based workflow languages and future standards in this area are likely to draw from the experience of these languages.

> *You can find more about the WSFL at:*
> *http://www-4.ibm.com/software/solutions/webservices/pdf/WSFL.pdf*

In order to further understand why we need languages like XLANG and WSFL, let's take a look at Web Agents.

Web Agents

Some Web Services could be implemented as autonomous agents (Web agents). An autonomous agent is software that can run for a long time and can take actions on its own without having to wait to be called upon for each task individually. An example of an agent would be software that can crawl a web site and index it, and that can usually be scheduled. A service that is an autonomous agent can support stateful and long-running interactions, with a beginning, a defined protocol for operation invocation, and an end. XML-based agent markup languages could be important for the services-oriented Internet.

> *There is more about the DARPA Agent Markup Language (DAML) at http://www.daml.org/.*

Now that we understand what agents are all about, let's go back and take another look at what WSDL does within the Web Services architecture. The unit of action offered by a service described in WSDL is an operation, which can be an asynchronous message or request/response pair of messages. WSDL does not tell us more about the operation, such as what the operation being executed actually is. The operation could be a **stateless service**, or it could be an operation on a **stateful object**. However, the operation could be over a service that is a **stateful autonomous agent**. For instance, a supply chain service may start with the submission of a purchase order, with an acknowledgement sent back, and then proceed with further messages about the shipping and invoicing. The input and output operations happen in exactly predefined order or sequence. An XML language such as XLANG or WSFL would define that operation sequence.

In distributed environments there would be no central authority that would manage the entire business process of all participating parties. The coordination is achieved by the different process-capable services acting as autonomous agents, with message exchanges expressed as WSDL operations. XLANG and WSFL help to formally specify business processes as stateful long-running interactions. Business processes, besides showing the public behavior of each participant (and they always involve more than one participant, otherwise it would not be a process), would also have to show how the behaviors work together to produce the overall process, via message exchanges. Note that the details of the private implementations of the participant are not a concern of the business process protocol, and aren't specified at this level.

The Semantic Web

In this chapter we have discussed Web Services as a means for computers to talk to other computers. Then, we added to the mix the possibilities of meaningful description of content and services (think of the description stack that we described earlier in this chapter) via WSDL, RDF, and some of the process flow protocols. When all of these technologies are placed together, some people such as Tim Berners-Lee (creator of the Web) speculate that the Web will slowly evolve into its new form – a **Semantic Web**, with content that is meaningful to computers. In this brief section, we will cover some of the main ideas about the Semantic Web. First we will look at RDF, which is one of the key components needed by the Semantic Web.

The **Resource Description Framework** (**RDF**) provides a technique for describing resources on the Web. These resources can be just about anything that has a unique address, and the properties that can be described can be any information about those resources. RDF is a framework for specifying meta data, the data about resources such as web pages for example. The RDF specification describes the model of describing meta data, as well as the XML syntax of describing the meta data. In Chapter 12 we illustrate how to process WSDL using RDF.

> *You can learn more about RDF in Professional XML 2nd Edition by Mark Birbeck et al (ISBN: 1-861005-05-9), also by Wrox Press. Additionally, the RDF Specifications can be viewed at* http://www.w3c.org/TR/REC-rdf-syntax/ *and* http://www.w3c.org/TR/rdf-schema/.

The Semantic Web, as its names implies, would be the current Web, only evolved with increasing presence of structure – one that can be understood by computers. The essential property of the World Wide Web is its universality, where anything can link to anything else. The Web has been very decentralized and has been able to increase its size and scope to unimaginable proportions. The Semantic Web would be no different than the current Web, in terms of universality and decentralization. However, the Semantic Web would have content and services that contain description understandable to computers, based on XML, RDF, Web Services and some of the other XML based technologies.

> *"The Semantic Web is an extension of the current web in which information is given well-defined meaning, better enabling computers and people to work in cooperation." -- Tim Berners-Lee, James Hendler, Ora Lassila*
>
> *You can learn more about the Semantic Web activities taken by the W3C at* http://www.w3c.org/2001/sw/.

Summary

In this chapter we became familiar with the core concepts and technologies that create Web Services. More specifically, we were able to cover the following:

- ❑ The history of distributed computing and some of the most important distributed computing technologies and frameworks

- ❑ The three main building blocks that form Web Services: invocation, description, and discovery

- ❑ The most important technologies, standards, and specifications that represent the building blocks of the Web Services Framework. Some of most notable ones are SOAP, with its envelope specification and extensibility capability (all part of the Message/Wire/Invocation building block), the WSDL for Web Services description, and UDDI as part of the discovery building block

- ❑ Some other XML related initiatives and how they relate to Web Services

- ❑ A brief overview of some new technologies that promise to bring the services oriented Web to an even higher level of the "Semantic" Web

The beginning of the charter for the XML Protocol Workgroup at W3C states:

"Today, the principal use of the World Wide Web is for interactive access to documents and applications. In almost all cases, such access is by human users, typically working through Web browsers, audio players, or other interactive front-end systems. The Web can grow significantly in power and scope if it is extended to support communication between applications, from one program to another."

The Web Services computing model promises to bring universal application-to-application connectivity, leading to better cross-business integration, improved efficiency, cost-savings in applications development via faster application development, and closer customer and vendor relationships. Various types of devices, from personal computers and different servers to many types of smart devices will collaborate seamlessly. This is bound to bring a range of new opportunities in business and technology. Just as HTML and HTTP enabled people to connect to each other and browse any kind of information on the Web, the utilization of XML and the Web Services technologies will bring the Internet to its new level. The services-based Internet will be a place where machine-to-machine communication is commonplace, as well as services-based application development. In the services-based Internet, new opportunities for an even richer and more meaningful collaboration between people and businesses will abound.

2

Internet Transport Protocols: An HTTP and SMTP Primer

In this chapter, we look at the Internet transport protocols, HTTP and SMTP. We will look at their history, their syntax, and some basic examples of their use. This chapter provides a fairly high-level overview of these technologies, which will come in handy when we get onto Web Services, in which these protocols play a very important part. Chapter 5 recaps some of this information in the context of SOAP messaging, and shows the parts these protocols play in Web Services, with some in-depth examples.

The Need for Protocols

Rudimentary networking and electronic messaging have been available since the 1920s in the form of telex communication services. These required dedicated communication lines, telex terminals, and trained operators. Telex was (and is, since it is still in operation) an expensive messaging solution that typically was used only by medium to large companies that could justify the cost. Telex uses a basic "handshaking" method to identify other machines on the network, allowing machines anywhere in the world to connect with each other. However, telex suffers from the fact that inter-machine communication requires dedicated hardware that cannot be used for any other purpose. Under this model, the Internet would require machines all using the same hardware platform and operating system!

In the mid-1960s and early 1970s, the United States Department of Defense recognized the need for a robust wide-area communication system that would allow a diverse mixture of hardware platforms running different operating systems to communicate reliably, even during a nuclear war. Their research produced the Internet's immediate forerunner, the ARPANET. As the ARPANET developed, it became clear that a heterogeneous computer network required agreed formats for everything from hardware interconnection to message content. These formats (or protocols) formed the basis for the TCP/IP protocols used on the Internet and World Wide Web today. Although the development histories of these protocols are beyond the scope of this book, there are many web sites that cover them. For example, M.A. Padlipsky's paper *A Perspective on the ARPANET Reference Model* offers a look at the design framework of ARPANET, and is available at:

http://www.cis.ohio-state.edu/cgi-bin/rfc/rfc0871.html

According to legend, in 1971 Ray Tomlinson, then an engineer for Bolt, Beranek, and Newman, sent the first message that could be considered a modern e-mail. After a modest start (Ray thinks QWERTYUIOP was the first message sent between machines whose sole physical connection was the ARPANET/Internet), messaging services became a major driving force for the development of what was to become the Internet and World Wide Web. The second driving force was the development of a graphical **user agent (UA)** for accessing linked data over a network in the 1990s, using HTTP. Both of these services required a stable underlying data transport system, leading to the development of the **Internet Protocol Stack**.

The Internet Protocol Stack

The **Internet Protocol Stack** is a hierarchical arrangement (or architecture) of predefined standards (protocols) that allows machine-to-machine communication over the Internet. Protocols define all aspects of the intercommunication process from hardware, electrical, and physical standards (low-level protocols) to message syntax, data sequencing, and character sets (high-level protocols). By dividing the protocols into functional groups, libraries of related services can be developed and updated without revising the entire protocol stack. There are two architecture models commonly used to describe the Internet Protocol Stack: the four-level **Transmission Control Protocol/Internet Protocol (TCP/IP)** Protocol Suite, and the seven-level **Open Systems Interconnect (OSI)** architecture. The models are functionally equivalent, even though they group the protocols into different modules. The following diagram shows how the TCP/IP architecture maps to the OSI architecture:

OSI Reference Model	TCP/IP Model
7. Application	Process/ Application
6. Presentation	
5. Session	
4. Transport	Transport
3. Network	Internet
2. Data Link	Network Access
1. Physical	

Each level of the Internet Protocol Stack builds on the services provided by the layer below it. Inter-communication requirements are handled at the lowest possible level within the stack, so a communication session may not require the use all of the stack's layers to pass data from one machine to another. Note that there is no standard TCP/IP model, and some sources include an additional Physical Layer at the bottom of the TCP/IP stack. Here, however, we include the physical connection standards as part of the Network Access Layer. While an in-depth look at the stack layers and the methods for determining which layers will be used in a given data transfer are beyond the scope of this book, let's take some time out to look briefly at each model.

The OSI Reference Model

The **OSI Reference** model was developed by the **International Organization for Standardization (ISO)** in 1983. It contains seven layers that are arranged according to the typical progression of events that happen during communications sessions. The following table lists the layers and their primary functions:

OSI Layer	Function
7. Application Layer	Provides an interface between user applications and network services. For example, a web client (such as a browser) may generate a request to retrieve a web page from a server. It will send this request to the appropriate Application Layer protocol(s) and launch a communications session to retrieve the desired files.
6. Presentation Layer	Manages data encoding, including translation between incompatible formats such as the American Standard Code for Information Interchange (ASCII) and the Extended Binary Coded Decimal Interchange Code (EBCDIC). Encryption and decryption services are also usually located here.
5. Session Layer	Manages data flow between two computers, including whether the flow is uni- or bi-directional.
4. Transport Layer	Ensures end-to-end integrity of transmitted data, including data received from sources outside the local LAN segment. Can detect packets discarded by routers and automatically generate retransmit requests. Unlike the Data Link Layer, the Transport Layer can also re-sequence packets received out of order. This must be done before sending them up to the Session Layer.
3. Network Layer	Establishes the route that data will travel between the sending and receiving computers. It contains no error detection/correction methods, and so depends on the Data Link Layer for the reliability of its data. Its use is optional on most Local Area Networks (LANs), but is required if the two computers are on different network segments separated by a router.
2. Data Link Layer	Provides end-to-end validity of transmitted data. Detects damaged, unusable, and undelivered packets and ensures they are repaired or replaced by the originating layer prior to assembly into a data frame and transfer to the Physical Layer for transmission. Also buffers incoming data from the Physical Layer and assembles it into data frames for transfer to the Network Layer.

Table continued on following page

OSI Layer	Function
1. Physical Layer	Transmits the bit stream generated by the higher layers. It receives frames of data from the Data Link Layer and transmits their structure and content in a serial stream, one bit at a time. Also receives incoming data one bit at a time and passes them to the Data Link Layer for re-framing. It does not include the transmission media for sending the bit stream to another computer.

Outgoing data travels from higher layers to lower layers with each layer adding its own header to the data and header packet passed to it from above. In this way, an outbound data packet sent from the Application Layer will consist of the data packet itself and seven headers. In contrast, incoming data travels from bottom to top with each layer stripping its header from the packet as it travels up the stack. In this way, a data packet bound for the User Application will consist of only the data packet itself when it leaves the Application Layer, even though it included seven headers when it arrived at the bottom of the stack.

The TCP/IP Model

The **TCP/IP** model approaches network interconnectivity from a different perspective to the OSI Reference model. Focused more on the hierarchical arrangement of the functions necessary to provide intercommunication services than on a strict adherence to functional layers, the TCP/IP model provides a much greater degree of flexibility to developers than the OSI model. However, it does not explain the actual mechanics of computer communication as clearly. Therefore, although TCP/IP is the predominant Internet protocol, it is often "mapped" to the OSI model in an effort to show the approximate relationships between the mechanics of internetwork communication and the functional protocols that provide the intercommunication services.

When looking at XML Web Services, we are primarily interested in the Process/Application level at the top of the stack. There are many Process/Application Level services that are already defined as part of the general TCP/IP stack. Some examples that you may have heard of are: whois, finger, Telnet, and FTP. Extensions to the stack are being developed almost daily; XML Web Services are an example of this. To help us understand the underpinnings of the XML Web Services that are the subject of this book, let's take a closer look at how two of the most used services, the **Simple Mail Transfer Protocol (SMTP)** and the **Hypertext Transfer Protocol (HTTP)**, function.

How SMTP and HTTP Fit Into The Internet Protocol Stack

SMTP and **HTTP** are Process/Application level TCP/IP protocols that can provide data transfer services to a variety of clients, or user agents. SMTP was one of the early TCP/IP services and was implemented in 1982 to allow the transfer of electronic mail over the fledgling ARPANET. HTTP is a relatively new service that was added in the 1990s to control the delivery of hypertext data. Without it, the point-and-click interface to the World Wide Web that we now take for granted would not exist. As Process/Application level services, HTTP and SMTP rely on the underlying TCP/IP layers to provide the cross-platform/cross-OS communication foundation that makes the heterogeneous construction of the Internet and World Wide Web possible. The figure below illustrates this:

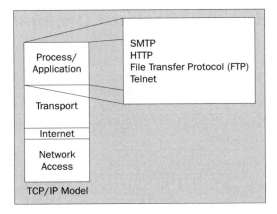

Note that SMTP and HTTP are just two of the many protocols in the Process/Application layer. A small sample of these protocols is shown in the diagram.

Overview of SMTP

Electronic mail is one of the major sources of data transferred across the Internet. From its beginnings as a way for multiple users of a single computer to leave text messages for each other, it has grown into a method for transferring almost any kind of data between users on Internet-capable machines across the planet. In this section we will explore the basic operation and structure of SMTP.

Current Capabilities and Anticipated Enhancements

Simple Mail Transfer Protocol (SMTP) is a Process/Application level protocol for providing messaging services over TCP/IP networks, usually through TCP port 25 (this port is assigned by the SMTP specifications in the RFC 2821 document, see below for more details). Designed during the much more trusting, low traffic, text-only, pre-World Wide Web era, the SMTP command set has been extended via a well-defined framework, the **Extended Simple Mail Transfer Protocol (ESMTP)** to allow greater control over the e-mail transaction process. It has also been supplemented with **Multipurpose Internet Mail Extensions (MIME)** so that non-textual data can be encapsulated in the SMTP message. This is accomplished by converting the non-textual data into ASCII text using an encoding method such as Base64, BinHex, or UUEncode. **S/MIME (Secure/Multipurpose Internet Mail Extensions)** is an addition to MIME that allows MIME to support encrypted messages. Originally based on the RSA's public key encryption methods, it has been expanded to include other encryption methods. We will see more of MIME in the section on SMTP limitations.

There are several **Internet Engineering Task Force (IETF) Requests For Comments (RFCs)** that define SMTP, ESMTP, MIME and S/MIME. A searchable RFC index is available at:

http://www.rfc-editor.org/rfcsearch.html

The major RFCs for SMTP are 2821 and 2822. Of particular interest is RFC 1869, which defines the ESMTP framework. At the time of writing, there are 98 RFCs defining MIME types. Some important SMTP-related MIME RFCs are 2045 – 2049, and 2442. S/MIME and its supporting encryption technologies are defined in RFCs 2311, 2312, 2630 – 2634, 2785, 2876, 2984, and 3058.

Required Parameters and Common Commands

One of the strengths of SMTP is its simple four-letter command set. There are ten SMTP commands specified in RFC 2821. This RFC is relatively new and is backwardly compatible with the earlier standards. The current commands are not case-sensitive, although some earlier systems did require upper-case command strings. The table below lists the commands in the order they appear in a typical SMTP transaction:

SMTP Command	Description
HELO	HELO (hello) identifies the SMTP client to the SMTP server. HELO is sent with the client's domain name or address literal. In ESMTP, this is changed to EHLO (extended hello) to identify the client as supporting ESMTP and request ESMTP support information from the server. The server information is sent in response to this command.
MAIL	MAIL starts the actual mail transaction from the client to the server. It usually includes the sender's e-mail address, preceded by the FROM: argument, but may be left empty (null).
RCPT	RCPT identifies the message's recipient and is repeated for multiple recipients. RCPT identifies the recipient using the TO: argument. Under ESMTP, RCPT may be extended as agreed between the client and host.
DATA	DATA identifies the start of the actual message content. Messages may contain any of the 128 ASCII codes. Messages are terminated by a single line that contains only a period (for example: <CRLF>.<CRLF> (where <CRLF> is a carriage return-line feed).
RSET	RSET (reset) aborts the current transaction. The host should dump any data buffered prior to replying to the RSET command.
VRFY	VRFY (verify) requests that the receiving host verifies that the recipient is a user or mailbox and not a mailing list.
EXPN	EXPN (expand) requests that the receiving host verifies that the recipient is a mailing list and returns the list's membership information to the sending host.
HELP	HELP is used by the client to request additional information from the host. It does not affect the message transaction and may be issued at any time.
NOOP	NOOP (no operation) signals that no action other than returning OK should be performed by the receiving host.
QUIT	QUIT requires that the recipient host send an OK reply, and then close the transmission channel.

The following commands are deprecated: SEND, SOML, SAML, and TURN. Although they may still be encountered, they are being phased out in favor of the current command set and will not be addressed here.

A Simple SMTP Transaction Example

E-mail users compose their messages on User Agents such as Outlook, Eudora, or an Internet-capable cell phone. The UA connects to, or acts as, a **Mail Transfer Agent (MTA)** to initiate an SMTP transaction with another MTA. SMTP transactions occur between MTAs in four steps:

1. The client (sender MTA) issues a HELO or EHLO command to the recipient MTA's TCP port 25. The recipient host responds by either accepting or denying the connection. If it accepts the connection, the transaction proceeds to step 2.

2. The client sends the MAIL command, including the sender's identification. The receiving host typically does not confirm the validity of the sender's information. Consequently, the sender's ID information can be easily faked (as you may have seen if you have ever looked at the header information for a spam, or unsolicited e-mail message). If the host accepts the sender's ID information, the transaction proceeds to step 3.

3. The client issues one or more RCPT commands to identify the intended recipients for the message. This may include forwarding information for multiple hosts or systems. The host is not required to process the forwarding request, so it is unwise to depend on recipients to forward SMTP data unless you know that the receiving host will process the request. Once the host signals that it accepts the RCPT data, the transaction proceeds to step 4.

4. The client issues the DATA command to indicate that the data transferred from this point on is message data. If the host accepts the transmission, it treats all data as message content until it receives the message end identifier which is a line containing only a period (<CRLF>.<CRLF>, where <CRLF> is a carriage return and line feed; line feeds without carriage returns are no longer recognized as message end identifiers). Note that the first <CRLF> in the set comes from the end of the preceding line.

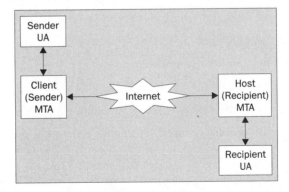

Below is an example of a simple SMTP transaction. After the client requests that the server open port 25, the following exchange occurs (client statements are in **bold** text):

```
220 X1 NT-ESMTP Server targetHost.com (Imail 5.03 2618-2)
HELO
250 hello targetHost.com
MAIL FROM:<sender@sendingMTA.com>
250 ok
RCPT TO:<recipient@targetMTA.com>
```

```
250 ok
DATA
354 ok, send it; end with <CRLF>.<CRLF>
This is the test message.<CRLF>
.<CRLF>
250 Message queued
QUIT
221 Goodbye
```

In this example, upon opening its TCP/IP port 25, the host identifies itself as an NT server supporting ESMTP that is ready to receive data (Status Code 220) by issuing the statement:

```
220 X1 NT-ESMTP Server targetHost.com (Imail 5.03 2618-2)
```

The transaction then continues until the sending MTA sends the QUIT command. After sending the 221 Goodbye statement, the receiving MTA disconnects and waits for the next connection on TCP port 25. The host lines start with a number. This number is the host's SMTP status code. Some common SMTP status codes are listed in the table below. A complete set of codes is available from ftp://ftp.isi.edu/in-notes/rfc2821.txt.

Status Code	Meaning
214	Help message
220	Service is ready
221	Closing connection
250	Requested action is okay
251	User not local, forwarding message to <path>
354	Start message input
421	Requested service not available
450	Requested action not taken, mailbox not available (may be busy)
451	Requested action aborted, local processing error
452	Requested action not taken, insufficient system storage
500	Syntax error, command unrecognized
501	Syntax error in parameters or arguments
502	Command not implemented
503	Bad command sequence
504	Command parameter not implemented
550	Requested action not taken, mailbox unavailable

Status Code	Meaning
551	User not local, please try `<otherMailBox@server2.com>`
552	Requested mail action aborted, exceeded storage allocation
553	Requested action not taken, mailbox name not allowed (possible incorrect mailbox syntax)
554	Transaction failed (if responding to connection-opening request, means no SMTP service here)

Relay Agents

Most e-mail is no longer sent directly from the sender's mail UA to the recipient's mail UA. Instead, the mail is typically queued for delivery in batches and transferred between MTAs by **relay agents**. Relay agents allow greater flexibility in routing and processing SMTP traffic than direct MTA-to-MTA transactions. By using a relay agent that understands proprietary data transfer protocols, companies and service providers can use more efficient and secure protocols than SMTP for internal mail transactions, while maintaining the ability to relay SMTP-based mail to external recipients. The following diagram illustrates a network that uses relay agents to improve the flexibility of the mail system:

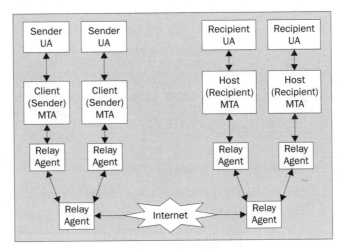

Limitations

SMTP's primary functional limitation is its inability to support any data format other than text. This limits the usefulness of basic SMTP, as it cannot be used to send binary data between users. The solution to this problem has been for the sender to encode the binary data as 7-bit ASCII text characters, then send a MIME type identifier with the encoded data to the recipient MTA for decoding and processing according to the passed MIME type. Since this method is also used for HTTP, let's look at it in more depth.

MIME Overview

Normally, SMTP uses the US-ASCII 7-bit character set that contains 128 (or 2^7) characters with assigned codes ranging in value from decimal 0 – 127. This does not allow the transmission of international characters with assigned values ranging from decimal 128 – 255 that are coded using the 256 (or 2^8) character 8-bit ASCII standard. It also precludes the transmission of 8-bit binary data. The MIME protocol was developed to allow the transmission of data values equivalent to decimal value 128 - 255 (the eighth bit) using the 7-bit US-ASCII character set. This is accomplished using an encoding method that must be available on both the sending and receiving devices.

To ensure that a message is usable on the recipient device, the sending device sends one or more of the five defined MIME header fields described here:

MIME Header Field	Description
MIME-Version	Identifies the MIME version used by the sender. This header is always required.
Content-Type	Identifies how to interpret the MIME object. Defaults to `text/plain; charset=us-ascii`.
Content-Transfer-Encoding	Identifies the encoding technique used to render the data in a mail-safe format.
Content-Description	Plain-text identification of the MIME object's content. Generally used when the encoded object is not human readable (for example, audio, video, or image data).
Content-ID	Globally unique identifier that specifies the MIME object's content.

After the version header, the most important MIME headers are probably the Content-Type and Content-Transfer-Encoding headers. There are seven standard Content-Types:

Content-Type	Description
text	The MIME object contains unformatted text
multipart	The MIME object contains multiple items with independent data types
message	The MIME object contains an encapsulated message or portion of a message (messages may be segmented to allow multiple transfers to recipients that limit mail content length)
image	The MIME object contains graphical data, usually in JPEG or GIF format
video	The MIME object contains image data for moving images, usually MPEG format
audio	The MIME object contains audio data
application	Catch-all category for MIME objects whose contents do not easily fit into other categories, typically PostScript or streaming data.

Additional `Content-Types` may be defined for private use by prefixing an `X-` to the private `Content-Type`'s name.

The `Content-Transfer-Encoding` header specifies the method that was used by the sender to encode the MIME object. This is required for encoded MIME objects to ensure that the recipient properly decodes them. The most common method for encoding non-textual data is probably **Base64** encoding. Although there are 128 characters in US-ASCII, only 73 of them are safe for mail transmission due to the requirements for cross-standard translation by some mail servers. Since the 73 safe characters do not fill the 128-character space defined by the 7-bit US-ASCII standard, 6-bit encoding is used, leaving only 64 (or 2^6) usable characters, hence the name Base64. Under this scheme, three 8-bit input bytes are translated into four 6-bit output bytes (that are padded to 7-bits to comply with the US-ASCII standard). Here's how it works:

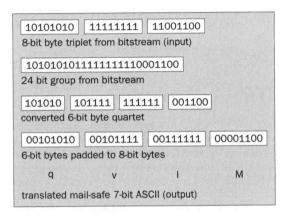

As you can see, this process substantially inflates the amount of data that must be transferred and can be fairly resource intensive for large data objects. Given the computing power of most modern clients, this is not too much of a concern on the client side. On the server side, however, resources can be rapidly depleted if a large number of clients are demanding data that must be encoded "on the fly", such as streaming live audio or video. For this reason there has been some research into extending or revising SMTP and HTTP to allow the direct transfer of binary data without encoding it to ASCII text first. To date, no standards have been proposed.

SMTP also suffers from substantial security problems that must be addressed outside of the protocol itself. There are two basic approaches to addressing this problem: extending SMTP (through the ESMTP framework) encrypting message contents before delivery to SMTP so that they are not passed across the Web as clearly readable text. These methods have met with varying degrees of success, and it is important to verify the security of any proposed encryption method before using it.

SMTP has fairly restrictive size limits for many of its objects. Several methods have been developed within the ESMTP framework for increasing the limits by using extensions or sending multiple lines. The following table summarizes SMTP's general object size limits and identifies objects that can be extended:

Object	Character Limit
User name	64
Domain name/number	255
MTA Path	256 including punctuation and element separators.
Command line	512 including command word and <CRLF>. May be increased through the use of extensions.
Reply line	512 including reply code and <CRLF>. More information may be conveyed by sending multiple lines in a single message
Text line	1000 including <CRLF>, but not the leading dot duplicated for transparency. May be increased through the use of extensions.
Recipients buffer	100 recipients maximum capacity

Overview of HTTP

Hypertext Transfer Protocol (HTTP) was implemented in the early 1990s. It was originally designed to transfer text-based data, and this limitation has remained through to the current revision, HTTP 1.1. As the World Wide Web has evolved, the need to transfer binary data such as images and applets has grown substantially. Current HTTP implementations address this by requiring the server to deliver the binary data as text via MIME, with the client decoding the textual data into binary data upon receipt. This is an inefficient system (recall the encoding process in the SMTP section), and research into the direct transfer of binary data over HTTP was carried out between 1997 and 1999 as part of the W3C **HTTP-NG (HTTP-Next Generation)** Draft. Interest in implementing the HTTP-NG proposals has not been sufficient for it to move forward and it is currently inactive. To study the HTTP-NG proposal further, see http://www.w3.org/Protocols/HTTP-NG/Activity.html. HTTP 1.1 is currently defined by RFC 2616. There are twenty other RFCs defining HTTP extensions listed in the searchable RFC index at http://www.rfc-editor.org/rfcsearch.html, which are available for further study.

Current Capabilities and Anticipated Enhancements

HTTP is a Process/Application Level protocol that controls the transmission of textual data (usually over TCP/IP port 80, but any available port can be used). Each content item in an HTTP document (for example, an HTML web page) is requested using a separate HTTP request, so if we have five rollover buttons on our page, a background image, and two foreground images, the page will require fourteen HTTP transactions (the page source code, plus 2 images x 5 rollovers, plus the background image, plus the two other images) to load completely. This results in a substantial data overhead since the standard HTTP connection is closed after each request and must therefore be re-opened for each item.

This can be alleviated somewhat by holding connections open for multiple transactions as allowed in HTTP 1.1 (but not HTTP 1.0). However, holding connections open places its own demands on the HTTP server. Although HTTP only allows the transfer of text, it can deliver other types of data by using MIME technology (originally introduced for SMTP) to encode non-textual data and send it, along with MIME type information for proper decoding, to the client for reconstruction and rendering in the client's UA. HTTP can be adapted to the needs of higher-level Web Services (such as the XML Web Services covered in this book) by adding additional information headers and other methods that we will look at in depth in later chapters.

Required Parameters

The HTTP protocol uses a request/response model, where a client UA makes a data request to a host server and waits for its response. If the response is not received within a predetermined period of time, the client assumes that the server does not exist (or is not available), and displays an appropriate error message. Since HTTP is a stateless protocol, the server and client do not maintain any information about connections. Therefore, methods such as writing client-side **cookies** (small packets of data for **ID** purposes) or sending identifier strings in the HTTP headers are required to track clients or resume dropped connections. HTTP's request/response model means that its command set (or method set) is even more basic than the SMTP command set. It is summarized in the table below:

Command	Description
GET	Requests the specified document. Data is passed to the server as text appended to the requested document's URL and is visible in the URL window in web browsers.
HEAD	Requests only the specified document's header.
POST	Requests that the server treats the specified document as a server-executable file and passes it the information included in the request (which is hidden from the URL window in web browsers). The actions performed on the data are determined by the server.
PUT	Requests that the server replaces the contents of the specified document with the data sent by the client.
DELETE	Requests that the specified page be deleted from the server.
OPTIONS	Requests that the server returns its capabilities/requirements to the client.
TRACE	Requests that the server returns information detailing how the message was received. Generally only used for testing.

A Simple HTTP Transaction Example

HTTP transactions are extremely simple, consisting of four steps:

1. The client connects to the server, usually using port 80, although any port can be used as long as the server is configured to respond to an HTTP request on that port (this is a common method for segregating sites on a development server; one site is delivered over port 80, another over port 81, and so on). If the connection is accepted, the process continues to step 2.

2. The client requests a document from the server, usually using the GET method, although HEAD or POST may also be used in typical transactions. The process then continues to step 3.

3. The client waits for the server's response. If the server responds within the UA's response window, the response is displayed by the UA, otherwise an error message is displayed and the transaction proceeds to step 4.

4. The server and/or client drops the connection.

In HTTP 1.1, the client can hold a connection open for more than one transaction, but this is generally limited to the contents of a single web page due to the toll that maintaining the open connection places on the server's resources. Additionally, servers will usually limit the time that they will hold a connection open. This allows the server to balance the performance gains from using a single TCP connect transaction to service several data requests against the resource drain imposed by holding the connection open for a given client. On a busy server, hundreds of connections (and potentially hundreds of fast clients) might be served in the time that a single connection is held open by a slow client. Let's look at our simple transaction in a little more depth.

Client Connection and Request

Client requests consist of three parts: the **request method**, the **request header**, and the **request data**. Only the request method is required. When included, the request header is used to identify additional information (such as the type of requesting UA, form data collected from a web page, or the contents of a cookie) that will be sent to the server. If the request method requires that data be sent from the client, it is included in the **response data**. The table below summarizes some common request headers:

Header Name	Description
Accept	Provides a list of MIME types that the client will accept
User-Agent	Provides details regarding the type of client software that is making the request, typically including at least the UA name, version, client operating system, and claimed compatibility
Authorization	Provides user authentication information such as user names, IDs, and passwords
Referer	Provides information about the server that sent the user to the current server

Let's look at a simple client request:

```
GET /default.htm HTTP/1.1
Accept: text/plain
Accept: text/html
Accept: image/jpeg
Accept: image/gif
User-Agent: Mozilla/4.0 (compatible; MSIE 5.5; Windows NT 5.0)
```

Here, the client asks for the server's default.htm page using HTTP 1.1. It tells the server it will accept plain text, HTML text, and GIF and JPEG images. It also identifies itself as Internet Explorer 5.5 running on Windows 2000. Note that the request ends with a single blank line.

Server Response to Client

HTTP server responses also consist of three parts: the status code, the response header, and the response data. An exhaustive list of status codes is beyond the scope of this chapter. However a concise summary of the code categories is provided in the table opposite:

Code Series	Status Category
100 - 1XX	Server Status or Informational Messages
200 - 2XX	Successful Connection
300 - 3XX	Redirection Notification
400 - 4XX	Client (Request) Errors
500 - 5XX	Server Errors

The status code may be followed by response header data that usually includes at least the server's identification and the transaction date. The Content-Type, Content-Length, Expiration date, and Last-Modified date may also be included if data was requested by the client. If the client has requested data (a web page, image, etc.), it is included after the response header. Let's look at a typical server response to our earlier client request:

```
HTTP/1.1 200 OK
Date: Friday, 22-Jun-2001 18:26:07 GMT
Server: IIS/5.0
MIME-Version: 1.0
Content-Type: text/html
Last-Modified: Wednesday, 06-Jun-2001 04:18:08 GMT
Content-Length: 1658

<html>
   <head>
      <title>Index Page</title>
   </head>
   <body>
      ...
   </body>
</html>
```

Here, the server acknowledges that the client's request has been successfully processed (status code 200) under HTTP 1.1 and identifies itself as a Windows 2000 server using MIME version 1.0. It reports the date and time of the request (note that Greenwich Mean Time or GMT is used so that there are no time zone adjustment problems between the client and server) and the date that the requested file was last modified. A blank line then follows the header and the actual file data is returned. If the file had not been found, the response would have looked something like this:

```
HTTP/1.1 404 NOT FOUND
Date: Friday, 22-Jun-2001 18:26:07 GMT
Server: IIS/5.0
```

This response is the source of the dreaded Error 404: page not found HTTP status code message displayed by many browsers to indicate that the server could not find the requested page. Note that even this short response ends in a single blank line.

HTTP Connection Types

In HTTP 0.9 and HTTP 1.0, each client data request required the negotiation of a new TCP connection to the server. Because the connection applies to only a single data request and the HTTP server does not keep track of any of the connection information, these are known as **transient connections**. Since the standard HTTP connection was closed after each request and a new TCP connection had to be negotiated for each data item on a web page, there was a substantial data overhead.

As the traffic on the Web grew and web pages became more complex, the amount of traffic generated by the TCP "open connection" requests began to have a detrimental effect on the speed of the Web. Several methods of addressing the slowdowns caused by all of the connection requests required under HTTP 1.0 resulted in the development of **persistent connections** that allow clients to make multiple data requests over a single TCP connection. With the implementation of HTTP 1.1, persistent connections became the default connection type for HTTP transactions. Under HTTP 1.1, a client can open a connection with the server and "pipeline" its data requests by sending multiple requests without waiting for acknowledgement from the server. Using persistent connections, all of the fourteen items on our previous example page can be retrieved using a single connection, saving the traffic that would be generated by establishing the thirteen additional transient connections that were previously required.

However, persistent connections do have some drawbacks. A major problem when providing services over persistent connections is that clients must be careful to close connections as soon as the data transfer is complete. This permits efficient use of server connection resources while optimizing data transfer to the server's clients. Consistent use of the Content-Length header field to inform the server of the content's length so that it can close the connection upon completion of the transfer(s) is also important to efficient server operation. When the Content-Length is specified for a document, the server can more effectively allocate resources, and so improve its performance.

Abandonment of a connection by the client without notifying the server of the closure can result in severely degraded performance of the server as it struggles to determine which connections are really active and which are dormant. To help minimize the effects of dropped connections, most servers implement a timeout policy that terminates a connection when it has been inactive for some predefined period of time. This timeout period is usually determined by the system administrator based on the server's purpose. It is also important that proxy servers (servers between the client and the host that relay client requests and host responses) pass the persistent connection request properly, along with any requests to close the connection. Otherwise, the proxy may end up "hung", with the host in an open connection, even though the client is no longer active and has gone on to another connection request, thinking that it has properly closed its earlier connection.

Extending HTTP Headers

Although there are forty-six predefined general HTTP headers in the defining RFC, it is sometimes necessary to add additional headers to accomplish certain tasks or provide enhanced services that were not included in the HTTP Specification. Fortunately, it is fairly simple to add custom HTTP headers, called **extension headers**, when needed. This allows the development of new services such as those outlined in this book without requiring revisions to the protocol. If the client or server does not understand the use or content of the extension header, it simply ignores it, much as an HTML client ignores HTML tags that it does not understand. More information regarding the exact use of extension headers is available in RFC 2616 at ftp://ftp.isi.edu/in-notes/rfc2616.txt. The following table lists some common HTTP headers and their uses:

HTTP Header	Description
Accept	Identifies media types that are acceptable to the sending user agent.
Accept-Charset	Identifies the character sets that are acceptable to the sending user agent. Frequently used on non-English sites to indicate the need for specific charactersets.
Authorization	Contains identification information (credentials) used by clients wanting to authenticate themselves to the server, usually after receiving notification that they are not authorized to access the requested data.
Cache-Control	Specifies caching requirements for all caching agents along the request/response chain. May not be implemented, even in HTTP 1.1 environments.
Content-Length	States the decimal number of octets containing the data that are about to be sent to the recipient (or that would be sent if HEAD is used to request the data instead of GET).
Content-Type	Identifies the media type of the data about to be sent to a recipient (or that would be sent if HEAD is used to request the data instead of GET).
Expires	Defines the date/time when the data will be considered "stale" and will be checked against the server if pulled from a cache or a proxy source.
Host	Contains the host and port number for the requested resource. If the port number is not present, the default number is assumed (80 for HTTP, 25 for SMTP).
If-Modified-Since	Makes a request conditional. If the requested resource has not been modified since the specified date/time, it is not returned by the server and the client must retrieve it from a cache or other source. This method is commonly used to reduce network traffic by sending unchanged data that is already present in the client code.
Referer	Contains information about the address of the user agent making the request.
User-Agent	Contains information about the user agent making the request. Commonly used on the server to dynamically customize content to avoid problems with specific user agents.

Summary

SMTP and HTTP are important protocols that allow us to reliably transfer many types of data between networked computers composed of a huge array of hardware and software combinations. Neither the most efficient nor the most elegant of possible or available protocols, their simplicity, robustness, and extensibility have nonetheless earned them positions as the protocols of choice for moving data across the World Wide Web. A well grounded understanding of their capabilities and workings will help ensure the smooth development of additional web services founded upon their capabilities, just as SMTP and HTTP build upon the capabilities of the TCP/IP layers below them.

3

SOAP Basics

With Web Services, we are on the verge of a new programming model. A set of standards has been developed that gives us programmatic access to the application logic of the web. This application logic is accessible to clients on every platform, and in every programming language. Using this model, we can build applications that integrate components using standard Internet protocols. As has already been touched upon in Chapter 1, at the core of the Web Services model is **SOAP** (**Simple Object Access Protocol**), the protocol that allows messages to be transmitted as XML documents and invokes the capabilities of Web Services. The SOAP standard is the key to Web Services.

This chapter delves into SOAP 1.1, and the concepts needed to start using SOAP in applications. We will cover the fundamentals of SOAP and its design, and then we will drill down into the details of SOAP messages, transports, and conventions.

> Note that this chapter, and the majority of the rest of the book will focus on SOAP version 1.1, because this is the newest final version, which has support available for it, so is currently the relevant version to learn about.
>
> This chapter will not cover SOAP 1.2, because at the time of writing, it is currently a Working Draft on the W3C, and therefore prone to significant change. SOAP 1.2 is briefly discussed in Chapter 1.
>
> To track the progress of SOAP 1.2, go to the W3C SOAP 1.2 Working Draft document at http://www.w3.org/TR/soap12/, and visit the XML Protocol working group main page at http://www.w3.org/2000/xp/.

SOAP Fundamentals

SOAP is a specification for using XML documents as messages. The SOAP Specification contains:

❑ A syntax for defining messages as XML documents, which we refer to as SOAP messages

❑ A model for exchanging SOAP messages

❑ A set of rules for representing data within SOAP messages, known as SOAP encoding (or **section 5 encoding** due to the section of the specification it appears in)

❑ A guideline for transporting SOAP messages over HTTP

❑ A convention for performing remote procedure calls (RPC) using SOAP messages

SOAP and Web Services

With all the buzz and acronyms surrounding the topic of Web Services, it can get a little confusing. The list of protocols and technologies related to Web Services grows everyday. Of all the Web Services acronyms, SOAP is probably the most important. It is rapidly becoming the standard protocol for accessing a Web Service, and accessing the service is key. For Web Services to work as a technology, there must be well-defined approaches for discovering a service (UDDI – Universal Description Discovery and Integration) and determining its capabilities (WSDL – Web Service Definition Language). For any individual Web Service to succeed, however, these technologies are optional: written documentation or even a conversation over coffee can define the location of a service and its methods. However, without a protocol to access the methods, the service is useless. SOAP is the best choice today for that protocol.

Although SOAP is a great choice for a Web Services messaging protocol, it is not the only choice. Web Services can simply operate on HTTP GET, or only expose functionality through XML-RPC. This does not make these components any less of a Web Service than a component that works with SOAP. Generally, however, SOAP is the messaging protocol of choice for Web Services. There is widespread acceptance of SOAP both by vendors and independent developers, and the tools and implementations that work with SOAP are improving all the time.

The first version of the SOAP Specification that was available to the public was released in 1999, and it was a result of collaboration between developers at Microsoft, DevelopMentor, and UserLand Software. The current version, SOAP 1.1, was released on May 8th 2000 as a Note by the W3C with additional contributions from IBM and Lotus. Since then more than twenty different implementations have been started covering a wide variety of languages and platforms.

> *For a complete list of SOAP implementations, go to http://www.soapware.org/directory/4/implementations. Here you will be able to find a SOAP implementation that fits your needs, or if there isn't one yet, you will find the resources to help you build it.*

The SOAP Message Exchange Model

The SOAP specification defines a model for exchanging messages. It relies on three basic concepts: messages are XML documents, they travel from a sender to a receiver, and receivers can be chained together. Working with just these three concepts, it is possible to build sophisticated systems that rely on SOAP.

XML Documents As Messages

The most fundamental concept of the SOAP model is the use of XML documents as messages. SOAP messages are XML. This provides several advantages over other messaging protocols. XML messages can be composed and read by a developer with a text editor, so it makes the debugging process much more simple than that of a complex binary protocol. As XML has achieved such widespread acceptance, there are tools to help us work with XML on most platforms.

We won't examine a SOAP message in detail until later in the chapter, but here is an example of one:

```
<soap:Envelope xmlns:soap="http://schemas.xmlsoap.org/soap/envelope/"
               soap:encodingStyle="http://schemas.xmlsoap.org/soap
                                   /encoding/">
   <soap:Body>
      <w:Greeting xmlns:w="http://www.wrox.com/helloworld/">
         <w:message>Hello world!</w:message>
      </w:Greeting>
   </soap:Body>
</soap:Envelope>
```

Senders and Receivers

When SOAP messages are exchanged, there are two parties involved: a sender, and a receiver. The message moves from the sender to the receiver. This operation is the basic building block of SOAP message exchanges, the smallest unit of work. The figure below illustrates this simple operation:

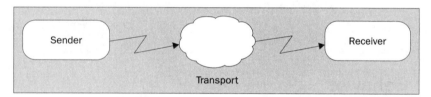

In many cases, however, this type of operation is not enough. A more common requirement would be for messages to be exchanged in request-response pairs. As we will see later in the chapter, this is the method SOAP uses with the HTTP transport and/or the RPC convention. Requiring that model, however, would make it difficult to design one-way message exchanges. By starting with the most basic operation, a one-way message exchange from sender to receiver, more complicated exchanges can be composed without preventing the simplest exchanges from occurring. This gives us the ability to construct message chains.

Message Chains

SOAP messages do not have to follow a traditional client-server model. Messages might be exchanged in this manner, as in the case of HTTP, or a chain of logical entities might process the messages. This concept of a logical entity that performs some processing of a SOAP message is referred to as an **endpoint**. Endpoints are receivers of SOAP messages. It is the responsibility of an endpoint to examine a message and remove the part that was addressed to that endpoint for processing.

It is worth mentioning here that despite the "O" in SOAP, there is nothing object-oriented about the SOAP model. Endpoints, as well as clients, can be written in any language, and there is no presumption of "objects" existing on either end of the wire.

As the model allows us to combine one-way messages into more complex operations, endpoints can function as both receiver and sender. This capability allows for a processing chain to be created, with messages being routed through the chain with some potential processing occurring at each step. Endpoints that function as both sender and receiver, passing messages that they receive on to another endpoint, are referred to as **intermediaries**. Intermediaries and the message chain concept allow developers the opportunity to construct sophisticated systems based on SOAP. The figures below show some examples of message patterns that can be achieved through chaining endpoints together:

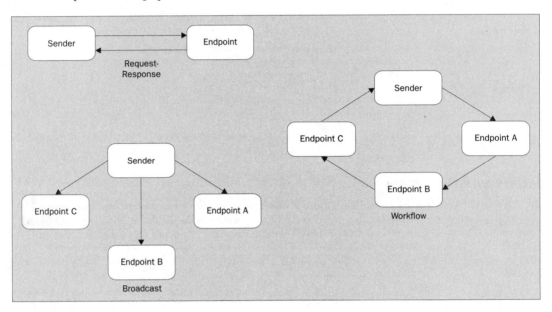

Endpoint Behavior

Thinking of SOAP in terms of endpoints helps to understand the flexibility of SOAP messaging. No matter what route a message takes, or how many endpoints may process it, all endpoints must handle messages in a certain way. Here are the three steps that an endpoint must take to conform to the specification:

- ❏ Examine the SOAP message to see if it contains any information addressed to this endpoint
- ❏ Determine which of the parts addressed to this endpoint are mandatory, if any. If the endpoint can handle those mandatory parts, process the message. If not, reject it
- ❏ If this endpoint is an intermediary, then remove all the parts identified in the first step before sending the message to the next endpoint

We will revisit these steps later in the chapter. By conforming to these three requirements, endpoints can be chained together to form complex systems.

Modular Design

SOAP is open and extensible. That means that all of the following scenarios are acceptable and allowed by the SOAP specification:

❑   A desktop application composes a SOAP message that requests stock quotes and sends it as the body of an HTTP POST. A web server receives the POST, processes the message, and returns a SOAP message in the HTTP response

❑   A server process composes a SOAP message that describes a system event and broadcasts the message over named pipes to other servers on the network

❑   A software developer with limited social skills decides to compose a SOAP message declaring his love for a co-worker and sends it as an e-mail attachment (this is likely to be a one-way message)

How is it that SOAP can support such different scenarios with the same model? The answer is in SOAP's modular design. Throughout the specification, there are placeholders left open for future extensibility of the protocol. SOAP is designed to be extensible in all of the following areas:

❑   **Message Syntax** – the SOAP message format does have an area set aside for extensions to be added (we will examine this area, the `Header` element, in the next section)

❑   **Data** – the SOAP payload can contain any type of data. SOAP provides one method for serializing data, but applications can define their own rules as well

❑   **Transport** – SOAP does not dictate how messages will be transported during the exchange. SOAP defines how messages should be exchanged over HTTP, but any communications protocol or method can be substituted for HTTP

❑   **Purpose** – SOAP does not define what you want to put into a message. Although this may sound like we are counting data twice, there is a difference between data and purpose, as we will see later in the chapter

Extensibility is important, but without some concrete implementations of these concepts, SOAP would be just a lot of interesting concepts. Luckily, the authors of SOAP provided a description of one implementation each of: data, transport, and purpose. For data, the Specification provides the SOAP encoding rules (section 5 encoding). For Transport, a transport binding for HTTP is defined. Finally, for purpose, the specification defines a convention for using SOAP messages for RPC.

We will cover each of these topics in more detail in this chapter. It is important to remember these four concepts, because the fact that they are separate from the protocol and therefore extensible is one of the biggest advantages of SOAP.

SOAP Messages

Now that we have covered SOAP at a high level, let's examine the most important detail of SOAP: the structure of a message. First and foremost, SOAP uses XML syntax for messages. The structure of a SOAP message is shown overleaf:

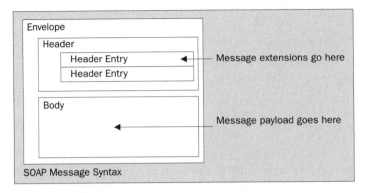

The diagram shows how a SOAP message can be broken down into components, and we will cover each of these in detail. A SOAP message contains a payload, the application-specific information. Here is an example of a SOAP message as an actual XML document:

```
<soap:Envelope xmlns:soap="http://schemas.xmlsoap.org/soap/envelope/"
               soap:encodingStyle="http://schemas.xmlsoap.org/soap/
                                   encoding/">
    <soap:Header>
        <h:from xmlns:h="http://www.wrox.com/Header">SoapGuy@wrox.com</h:from>
    </soap:Header>
    <soap:Body>
        <w:GetSecretIdentity xmlns:w="http://www.wrox.com/heroes/">
            <w:codename>XSLT-Man</w:codename>
        </w:GetSecretIdentity>
    </soap:Body>
</soap:Envelope>
```

Before we go into the contents of the SOAP message, let's take a quick glance at the XML of the message. As can be seen, SOAP messages rely heavily on XML Namespaces. All of the elements in this document are prefixed with a namespace, and there is a good reason why the SOAP specification uses namespaces so extensively. In order for a SOAP message to carry any arbitrary XML payload, all the elements of the message must be scoped in some fashion to avoid conflicts in the names of elements.

> *The Namespaces in XML Recommendation can be found at http://www.w3.org/TR/REC-xml-names/.*

The namespace prefix soap is used on most of the elements in the above message. In this example, the prefix is associated with the namespace URI http://schemas.xmlsoap.org/soap/envelope/, and it identifies the elements that are part of a standard SOAP message. Like all namespace prefixes, the choice of soap is irrelevant. The namespace prefix could have been something else entirely, as in this message:

```
<blah:Envelope xmlns:blah ="http://schemas.xmlsoap.org/soap/envelope/"
               blah:encodingStyle="http://schemas.xmlsoap.org/
                                   soap/encoding/">
    <blah:Header>
        <h:from xmlns:h="http://www.wrox.com/Header">SoapGuy@wrox.com</h:from>
    </blah:Header>
    <blah:Body>
        <w:GetSecretIdentity xmlns:w="http://www.wrox.com/heroes/">
```

```
            <w:codename>XSLT-Man</w:codename>
         </w:GetSecretIdentity>
      </blah:Body>
   </blah:Envelope>
```

The namespace prefix could also be eliminated completely if the namespace is the default namespace for the document. The default namespace is assigned using just the `xmlns` attribute, as shown here:

```
<Envelope xmlns="http://schemas.xmlsoap.org/soap/envelope/"
          encodingStyle="http://schemas.xmlsoap.org/soap/encoding/">
   <Header>
      <h:from xmlns:h="http://www.wrox.com/Header">SoapGuy@wrox.com</h:from>
   </Header>
   <Body>
      <w:GetSecretIdentity xmlns:w="http://www.wrox.com/heroes/">
         <w:codename>XSLT-Man</w:codename>
      </w:GetSecretIdentity>
   </Body>
</Envelope>
```

All three of these messages are acceptable and equivalent. For the sake of readability, it is better to use the `soap` namespace prefix for elements.

All of the elements in the message that are associated with the `soap` namespace are standard elements of a SOAP message, as are the attributes. Any other elements are either related to message extensions or the message payload. There are three standard SOAP elements that appear in this sample message: the `Envelope`, the `Body`, and the `Header`. There is also one other standard element that does not appear in this example message, the `Fault` element, which we will discuss later in this chapter.

Envelope

The `Envelope` element, as its name would suggest, serves as a container for the other elements of the SOAP message. As it is the top element, the `Envelope` is the message. The example below shows the same message we saw earlier, but this time, the `Envelope` element has been highlighted to stress its position in the message.

```
<soap:Envelope xmlns:soap="http://schemas.xmlsoap.org/soap/envelope/"
               soap:encodingStyle="http://schemas.xmlsoap.org/soap/
                                    encoding/">
   <soap:Header>
      <h:from xmlns:h="http://www.wrox.com/Header">SoapGuy@wrox.com</h:from>
   </soap:Header>
   <soap:Body>
      <w:GetSecretIdentity xmlns:w="http://www.wrox.com/heroes/">
         <w:codename>XSLT-Man</w:codename>
      </w:GetSecretIdentity>
   </soap:Body>
</soap:Envelope>
```

Envelope Namespace

SOAP messages indicate their version by the namespace of the Envelope element. The only version recognized by the 1.1 Note is the URI "http://schemas.xmlsoap.org/soap/envelope/". Messages that do not use this namespace are invalid, and endpoints that receive messages with another namespace must return a "fault". We will discuss Fault elements later in this section.

> *The use of the Envelope namespace to indicate message versions is a good example of how much the SOAP specification relies on XML Namespaces. Without XML Namespaces, it would be extremely difficult to define an open XML format for messages that did not result in name conflicts with the payload XML of the message.*

encodingStyle attribute

The specification defines an attribute called encodingStyle that can be used to describe how data will be represented in the message. Encoding is the method used to represent data. The encodingStyle attribute can appear on any element in the message, but in the case of SOAP encoding, it often appears on the Envelope element. We will discuss the encodingStyle attribute and encoding in general in more detail later in the chapter.

Body

The Body element of a SOAP message is the location for application-specific data. It contains the payload of the message, carrying the data that represents the purpose of the message. It could be a remote procedure call, a purchase order, a stylesheet, or any XML that needs to be exchanged using a message. The Body element is highlighted in the message below:

```
<soap:Envelope xmlns:soap="http://schemas.xmlsoap.org/soap/envelope/"
               soap:encodingStyle="http://schemas.xmlsoap.org/soap/
                                    encoding/">
    <soap:Header>
        <h:from xmlns:h="http://www.wrox.com/Header">SoapGuy@wrox.com</h:from>
    </soap:Header>
    <soap:Body>
        <w:GetSecretIdentity xmlns:w="http://www.wrox.com/heroes/">
            <w:codename>XSLT-Man</w:codename>
        </w:GetSecretIdentity>
    </soap:Body>
</soap:Envelope>
```

The Body element must appear as an immediate child of the Envelope element. If there is no Header element, then the Body element is the first child; if a Header element does appear in the message, then the Body element immediately follows it. The payload of the message is represented as child elements of Body, and is serialized according to the chosen convention and encoding. Most of this chapter deals with the contents of the Body and how to build payloads.

Header

The SOAP message structure of `Envelope` and `Body` elements is an open one that maps well to many messaging scenarios. The `Body` element encapsulates the payload for the message, but in some instances, the payload data is not enough. Perhaps a message is part of a set of messages that must be treated as a single logical transaction, or the message should be executed on a persistent object that resides at the server. Issues like transactions and object references are vital to the message, but are separate from the payload.

It is unrealistic to think that we can predict every type of extension that will be needed by a SOAP message. So, in a wise design choice, the authors created the `Header` element. The purpose of the `Header` element is to encapsulate extensions to the message format without having to couple them to the payload or to modify the fundamental structure of SOAP. This allows extensions like transactions, encryption, object references, billing, and countless others to be added over time without breaking the specification. The text below illustrates our original example message with an additional `Header` entry. The entire `Header` element is highlighted in the example below.

```
<soap:Envelope xmlns:soap="http://schemas.xmlsoap.org/soap/envelope/"
               soap:encodingStyle="http://schemas.xmlsoap.org/soap
                                    /encoding/">
    <soap:Header>
        <h:from xmlns:h="http://www.wrox.com/Header">SoapGuy@wrox.com</h:from>
        <h:report xmlns:h="http://www.wrox.com/Header">1</h:report>
    </soap:Header>
    <soap:Body>
        <w:GetSecretIdentity xmlns:w="http://www.wrox.com/heroes/">
            <w:codename>XSLT-Man</w:codename>
        </w:GetSecretIdentity>
    </soap:Body>
</soap:Envelope>
```

In this example, the header entry `h:from` could be used to send a report via e-mail to the address that is indicated. By agreeing upon a set of extensions, a sender and receiver can build additional capabilities into a message exchange without requiring additional features from SOAP.

> *As this chapter is being written, there is still little detail out about SOAP 1.2, the very likely successor to SOAP 1.1. However, what information is available suggests that the XMLP working group will be leveraging the extensibility of the `Header` element to build additional capabilities on top of SOAP 1.1. If SOAP 1.2 develops in this manner, it should help early adopters of SOAP significantly.*

Just like the `Body` element, the `Header` element must appear as an immediate child of the `Envelope` element. It is optional, but if it does appear, it must appear as the first child. The `Header` element contains one or more child elements known as entries. Header entries can be used to add any type of extension to a message, and by default, an endpoint will ignore the extension unless it can understand it. This allows the extensions to be developed over time without breaking existing endpoints. Some extensions have additional requirements, however, that are dealt with using the `mustUnderstand` and `actor` attributes.

actor attribute

As the SOAP model allows for endpoints to be chained together, it is necessary to identify what parts of a message are meant for what endpoint on the chain. In the case of the payload, it is not necessary to do this: the final endpoint on the chain is the target of the payload. However, in the case of `Header` elements, the issue of addressing becomes important.

The actor attribute can be used to address a Header element to a particular endpoint. The value of the actor attribute is a URI that identifies the endpoint the Header element entry is targeted for. SOAP attaches special significance to two values of the actor attribute to address issues of message chaining. If the value is "http://schemas.xmlsoap.org/soap/actor/next", then the entry is targeted for the first endpoint that finds it. Omitting the actor attribute indicates that the entry is intended for the final endpoint, the same endpoint that will process the payload.

The issue of the actor attribute becomes important when it comes to intermediaries and the Header element. There has been quite a bit of debate on the behavior of intermediaries towards Header elements. In the end, the consensus is that well-behaved intermediaries know whether or not they are the last endpoint in the chain, and if they are not, they should not modify Header elements that have no actor attribute. In addition, intermediaries must remove the Header elements they process.

mustUnderstand attribute

In the example of a Header element that represents a transaction, developers will not be able to accept the endpoint ignoring the extension. If a message is part of a transaction, it must be part of a transaction, and endpoints that cannot support transactions should not try to process a message. This is where the mustUnderstand attribute is useful.

The mustUnderstand attribute can be used anywhere in a SOAP message, but it commonly appears on a Header element. The value of the attribute is either a 1, indicating that the element is mandatory, or a 0, indicating that it is optional. The absence of the attribute is equivalent to the 0 value.

Let's take another look at the example message, this time with a mandatory Header element that is addressed to the final endpoint.

```
<soap:Envelope xmlns:soap="http://schemas.xmlsoap.org/soap/envelope/"
               soap:encodingStyle="http://schemas.xmlsoap.org/soap
                                   /encoding/">
    <soap:Header>
        <h:from xmlns:h="http://www.wrox.com/Header" soap:mustUnderstand="1">
            SoapGuy@wrox.com
        </h:from>
    </soap:Header>
    <soap:Body>
        <w:GetSecretIdentity xmlns:w="http://www.wrox.com/heroes/">
            <w:codename>XSLT-Man</w:codename>
        </w:GetSecretIdentity>
    </soap:Body>
</soap:Envelope>
```

Fault

Everything we have discussed about the SOAP message format so far covers how to build good clean messages that are successfully sent to and processed by the receiver every time. Of course, that is not a realistic view of how a real application will behave. Just as SOAP messages have a specified location and format for versioning, encoding style, payload, and extensions, they also have a location and format for errors. The element in a SOAP message that represents an error is the Fault element. You can think of the Fault element as exceptions for Web Services, a standard way to throw back a report on unexpected behavior to the originator of the message.

Faults are typically associated with a response message. Although the specification does not rule out
Fault elements in requests, do not expect existing server implementations to behave well in the face
of such requests!

If the Fault element appears, it must be in the payload of the SOAP message, which means that it must appear as a child element of the Body.

The example message below is a response that contains a Fault element.

```
<soap:Envelope xmlns:soap="http://schemas.xmlsoap.org/soap/envelope/"
               soap:encodingStyle="http://schemas.xmlsoap.org/soap/
                                    encoding/">
   <soap:Body>
      <soap:Fault>
         <faultcode>soap:MustUnderstand</faultcode>
         <faultstring>Mandatory Header error.</faultstring>
         <faultactor>http://www.wrox.com/heroes/endpoint.asp</faultactor>
         <detail>
            <w:source xmlns:w="http://www.wrox.com/">
               <module>endpoint.asp</module>
               <line>203</line>
            </w:source>
         </detail>
      </soap:Fault>
   </soap:Body>
</soap:Envelope>
```

faultcode element

The faultcode element contains a value that identifies the error condition to the application. This means this value is for machine use and is not intended for display to potential users. The faultcode element value must be a qualified name, as if it were an element in the message itself. In the above example, the faultcode element's value is soap:MustUnderstand, indicating that the MustUnderstand fault is a SOAP standard fault. This allows us to define our own values for the faultcode element and identify them by their namespace.

The following standard faultcode element values are defined in the SOAP 1.1 specification:

❑ **VersionMismatch** – this value indicates that the namespace of the SOAP Envelope element was not http://schemas.xmlsoap.org/soap/envelope/. Currently that value is the only acceptable version of a SOAP message, and it indicates that the message conforms to the 1.1 Note.

❑ **MustUnderstand** – this value is returned in a faultcode element when the endpoint encounters a mandatory Header element entry (one with a mustUnderstand attribute set to 1) that it does not recognize.

❑ **Client** – this value should be used in the faultcode element when a problem is found in the message that was received. This could be anything from a missing element to an incorrect namespace in the body, but this faultcode element value states that the message that was received was to blame for the error.

❑ **Server** – in contrast to the `Client` fault code, `Server` indicates that a problem occurred during processing that was not directly related to the content of the message. An example of this type of fault would be that the database used by the endpoint to return information is down.

The standard `faultcode` element values listed here represent classes of faults rather than a single error. They are extensible in that more specific codes that fit into these classes can be defined. This is done by appending a period to the code and adding an additional name to the code. For example, if the machine the endpoint is running on were to run out of memory, the endpoint could potentially return a `Server.OutOfMemory` fault code.

faultstring element

If the `faultcode` element contains the fault information that is meant for the machine, then the `faultstring` element value is what is meant for the user. The `faultstring` element contains a string value that briefly describes the fault that occurred in a way that would make sense if it were displayed to the user in an error dialog. That is not to suggest that it could not be technical in nature.

faultactor element

It is often just as important to know where the error occurred as it is to know what error occurred. This is especially true in systems that involve SOAP intermediaries. If a message must pass through a dozen endpoints before it can reach its final destination for payload processing, the developer needs to know at what point on the message routing chain an error occurred. The `faultactor` element is a placeholder for that type of information. The `faultactor` element contains a URI that identifies the endpoint where the fault originated.

The `faultactor` element is only mandatory for intermediaries. If a fault occurs at an intermediary, then that fault must have a `faultactor` element. If the fault occurs at the final destination, then the endpoint is not required to populate that value (although it may choose to do so, and it would probably be the nice thing to do for developers who are using our endpoints). This means that a fault with no `faultactor` element can be assumed to have originated from the final endpoint.

detail element

It is possible to provide descriptive error information with just the three elements above, but additional information would be helpful, if not necessary. For instance, we might want to include in the `Fault` element the module and source code line of the error while still debugging the application. In this case, the additional error information can be included as `detail` element entries, as seen in the example below.

The specification allows us to define any `detail` element entries we choose to, but it does define one case in which the endpoint returning the `Fault` element must return information in the detail entries: when an error occurs because the server could not process the message correctly. This is an important requirement, especially in the development of SOAP, because it helps to debug problems that arise from poorly formed messages. This example shows a SOAP message that might have resulted from such a message:

```
<soap:Envelope xmlns:soap="http://schemas.xmlsoap.org/soap/envelope/"
               soap:encodingStyle="http://schemas.xmlsoap.org/soap
                                    /encoding/">
   <soap:Body>
      <soap:Fault>
         <faultcode>soap:Client.MissingParameter</faultcode>
         <faultstring>A parameter was missing</faultstring>
```

```
            <faultactor>http://www.wrox.com/heroes/endpoint.asp</faultactor>
            <detail>
                <w:error xmlns:w="http://www.wrox.com/">
                    <code>178</code>
                    <desc>The codename parameter was missing.</desc>
                </w:error>
            </detail>
        </soap:Fault>
    </soap:Body>
</soap:Envelope>
```

Endpoint Behavior Revisited

Now that we know more about the structure of a SOAP message, let's consider what is really involved in the three steps of message processing:

❑   Examine the SOAP message to see if it contains any information addressed to this endpoint. Examine the header for entries addressed to this endpoint, either by position (next or last endpoint) or by URI. If this endpoint is the last, look for the body as well.

❑   Examine the header entries targeted at this endpoint. If any are marked with mustUnderstand="1" and are not recognized by the endpoint, a fault code of MustUnderstand must be returned.

❑   If this endpoint is an intermediary, then remove the processed header entries before sending the message to the next endpoint. This does not apply to the body, since only the last endpoint can process that.

These steps, and other requirements of SOAP, will be transparent to most developers. The various SOAP tools and implementations will take into account these requirements when generating endpoints. Part of the beauty of SOAP, however, is the minimal requirements for endpoints. If our application meets these three, it is a valid SOAP endpoint.

Body-Conscious

The elements that make up the SOAP message structure provide a framework for a message. Working with those elements, we know where to put our data, where to extend the message, and how to report errors, among other things. Using the Envelope, Header, Body, and Fault elements, we can assemble a SOAP message to accomplish what we need. Other than the Fault element, which appears inside the body, we have not discussed the actual payload of the message. The rest of the chapter deals with specific uses for the body, how we can represent data in the body, and what XML we can place in the body.

Data

In order to build SOAP messages from our language of choice, we need to know how to serialize data. We need to know the rules for representing an integer, string, or floating point number in a SOAP message so that we can exchange messages freely between languages and platforms. The serialization of data inside a SOAP message is referred to as **encoding**. As this section focuses on the payload of the message, the XML in the examples represents only a SOAP message payload and not a complete message.

89

Encoding Style

The ability to decide on a set of rules for representing data in a message is very important to the open nature of SOAP. It doesn't do much good of course to define a set of rules if we cannot tell what encoding rules were used to serialize a particular SOAP message. The encodingStyle attribute defined by the SOAP specification is used to identify the encoding rules used in a particular message.

The encodingStyle attribute is commonly located on the Envelope element. It is possible, however, to use the encodingStyle attribute on any element in a SOAP message. Although the SOAP specification defines a set of encoding rules that map well to programming constructs, **there is no default encoding**. This means that if the encodingStyle attribute does not appear in the message, the receiver cannot make any assumptions about how data will be represented within the message. By the same token, the zero length encodingStyle="", is equivalent to a missing encodingStyle attribute. In either case, no encodingStyle means that the implementation will have to try to figure out how to deserialize data without any help.

What About XML Schemas?

Those familiar with XML Schemas may be wondering what relationship exists between encoding and XML Schemas. Encoding can make use of XML Schemas. In the case of SOAP encoding, the URI used in the encodingStyle attribute points to a schema. As we will see in the next section, the SOAP encoding rules use XML Schemas heavily, relying on the XML Schema datatypes namespace and the type attribute. The key difference is that encoding does not mandate XML Schemas. Encoding rules are simply identified by a URI. The rules implied by that URI could be backed up by nothing more than a verbal agreement, or possibly some written documentation. This allows developers who do not necessarily need the capabilities of XML Schemas to forego their use and start sending messages with encoding rules based on an accepted URI.

Although we can have encoding without a corresponding schema, it's not recommended. Most XML parsers will soon be schema-aware (in fact, some like Xerces already are), and we can save ourselves a lot of trouble when parsing messages if we rely on the parser and schema to validate and convert data instead of doing it manually.

SOAP Encoding

The SOAP Specification defines a single set of encoding rules that are referred to as **SOAP encoding**. SOAP encoding is based on XML Schemas and as such it closely models many of the standard types and constructs that developers would be familiar with. The value of the encodingStyle attribute for SOAP encoding is http://schemas.xmlsoap.org/soap/encoding/, which points to the XML Schema that defines the encoding rules.

Simple Data Types

In SOAP encoding, simple types are always represented as single elements in the body. SOAP encoding exposes all the simple types that are built into the XML Schemas Specification. If we are using a simple type with SOAP encoding, then it must come from XML Schemas, or be derived from a type that does. The namespace associated with the XML Schemas data types is http://www.w3.org/1999/XMLSchema. This provides the common types that many programmers will expect, like: string, integer, float, date, and so on. If we assume the xsd prefix is associated with the XML Schemas URI, and the soapENC prefix is associated with the SOAP encoding URI, then both of these payload values work with strings. This refers to XML Schemas:

```
<codename xsi:type="xsd:string">Hulk</codename>
```

while this refers to SOAP encoding:

```
<codename xsi:type="soapENC:string">Hulk</codename>
```

For a XML Schemas tutorial, including a list of the types available in XML Schemas (and therefore, SOAP encoding), go to http://www.w3.org/TR/xmlschema-0/.

xsi:type attribute

SOAP tries to make it possible for a wide variety of languages to communicate, and not all languages are created equal. In many scripting languages, type is a loose concept. To help level the playing field, SOAP borrows from XML Schemas once again and uses the `xsi:type` attribute.

The `xsi:type` attribute is a way for elements in the payload to indicate their type. It is associated with XML Schemas, and the `xsi` prefix in this case is associated with the URI `http://www.w3.org/1999/XMLSchema-instance`. It can appear on any payload element.

Developers not familiar with namespaces and schemas in XML need to be aware that the `xsi` *prefix of the* `xsi:type` *is insignificant. The attribute could easily appear in the message as* `foo:type`*, provided that the foo prefix is associated with the namespace URI* `http://www.w3.org/1999/XMLSchema-instance`*. Likewise, the xsd prefix commonly used on the values of the* `type` *attribute is assumed here to be associated with* `http://www.w3.org/1999/XMLSchema`*. Be aware of this and other namespace issues as you work with SOAP messages.*

If the application knows what type is being sent and retrieved from some outside source (for example, a schema, a WSDL document, or other metadata), then the `xsi:type` attribute is not required. The fact remains that not all languages will be supporting WSDL in the near future, if ever, and so the good neighbor approach suggests that including `xsi:type` will help make our SOAP messages more interoperable with "type-challenged" languages like XSLT.

So what does this mean for the SOAP message as a whole? In order to use the `xsi:type` attribute and the `xsd` prefix for data types, we must define what these prefixes mean inside the message. Let's consider another example message with encoding in mind.

```
<soap:Envelope xmlns:soap="http://schemas.xmlsoap.org/soap/envelope/"
               soap:encodingStyle="http://schemas.xmlsoap.org/soap
                                   /encoding/">
    <soap:Body>
       <m:MixedMessage xmlns:m="http://www.wrox.com/mix/">
          <param1>OU812</param1>
          <param2>2001</param2>
          <param3>3.14159</param3>
       </m:MixedMessage>
    </soap:Body>
</soap:Envelope>
```

That message meets all the requirements of SOAP, but many implementations would not be able to process it because they would not be able to map the values in the payload to types in the target language. We don't want to require a language to use a union type like the variant in COM, or to try to map the type by trial and error. Therefore, we add a little information to our message to make it more readable:

```
<soap:Envelope xmlns:soap="http://schemas.xmlsoap.org/soap/envelope/"
               soap:encodingStyle="http://schemas.xmlsoap.org/soap
                                    /encoding/"
               xmlns:xsi="http://www.w3.org/1999/XMLSchema-instance"
               xmlns:xsd="http://www.w3.org/1999/XMLSchema">
    <soap:Body>
        <m:MixedMessage xmlns:m="http://www.wrox.com/mix/">
            <param1 xsi:type="xsd:string">OU812</param1>
            <param2 xsi:type="xsd:integer">2001</param2>
            <param3 xsi:type="xsd:double">3.14159</param3>
        </m:MixedMessage>
    </soap:Body>
</soap:Envelope>
```

Now all the data in the payload is identified by type, and it becomes much easier for a SOAP implementation to process.

Enumerations

SOAP encoding allows us to define enumerated types. It borrows once again from XML Schemas, which also has the concept of an enumeration. An enumeration is a named set of values, based on a basic type. For example, we could define an enumeration that represented geographical locations ("North, "South", etc). To define an enumeration, we must use XML Schemas.

Here is an example of an enumeration that defines a set of geographical regions.

```
<simpleType name="Region" base="xsd:string">
    <enumeration value="North"/>
    <enumeration value="South"/>
    <enumeration value="East"/>
    <enumeration value="West"/>
</simpleType>
```

If this enumeration appeared in a referenced schema, we could then use this type in a SOAP message just as we would any other type.

```
<soap:Envelope xmlns:soap="http://schemas.xmlsoap.org/soap/envelope/"
               soap:encodingStyle="http://schemas.xmlsoap.org/soap
                                    /encoding/"
               xmlns:xsi="http://www.w3.org/1999/XMLSchema-instance">
    <soap:Body>
        <m:GetSalesTotals xmlns:m="http://www.wrox.com/sales/">
            <m:reg xsi:type="m:Region">East</m:reg>
        </m:GetSalesTotals>
    </soap:Body>
</soap:Envelope>
```

Binary Data

As part of the simple types it supports, SOAP and XML Schemas provide a type for representing binary data. One approach for working with binary data is to use the `base64` type. We can represent binary data, such as an image file, as an array of bytes in the message. The `base64` type converts binary data to text using the base64-encoding algorithm of XML Schemas. There is no relationship between SOAP and base64-encoding; if we use it, our application (or implementation of SOAP for your platform) must be able to understand and work with base64-encoding.

Catch All

In addition to the simple types, many languages have a "universal" data type or placeholder, something that can represent a variety of types within that language. In COM, the `variant` serves this purpose, as does the `any` type in CORBA. SOAP accounts for this possibility with the **polymorphic accessor**. If we are serializing a value in the form of a polymorphic accessor, we must provide the `type` attribute.

The polymorphic accessor is more difficult to pronounce than to use! Let's assume we are passing in a value representing a person's age, and that type could vary depending on how the information was to be used. If the value of our data is a `float`, it would appear like this:

```
<age xsi:type="xsd:float">3.5</age>
```

If is a `string`, it would appear like this:

```
<age xsi:type="xsd:string">3 and a half years old</age>
```

Both examples are legal if the `age` element has been defined as being a polymorphic accessor, meaning that its data type will vary.

What About XML?

Those frequenting the SOAP discussion lists and newsgroups will notice the recurring question: "How do I send XML in a SOAP payload?" or something to that effect. This is a general problem related to XML, but there are a couple of approaches we can use to transmit XML inside SOAP. We can:

❏ Rely on our toolkit or XML parser to properly encode the XML when we pass it in as a string parameter. If our implementation is based on RPC and does not encode the XML we pass in as a string properly, that is a bug. Let the implementation's author know.

❏ Consider why we are passing XML. If we are using SOAP RPC to pass XML as a string parameter, check to see if the implementation supports passing arbitrary XML in the payload. A good implementation should. As we will discuss later, SOAP does not have to be RPC, and if we are passing XML in string parameters, our application probably doesn't need RPC.

Compound Data Types

Sometimes, simple types are not enough. Just like the programming languages it must support, SOAP encoding provides structures for representing compound types. SOAP encoding handles two compound types: structs (records), and arrays. Complex types are serialized as payload elements, just like simple types, but they have child elements. The child elements are the fields or elements of the type. SOAP had to invent its own rules for structs and arrays because, as of this writing, XML Schemas does not pay special attention to these compound types.

Structs

Let's start with a struct (or structure, or record, whichever you prefer). Structs are easy to represent as XML because they have unique named members. Consider this C++ struct definition of a super-hero:

```
struct SuperHero
{
    string sCodename;
    string sFirstName;
    string sLastName;
    int nAge;
};

SuperHero hero = { "Hulk", "Bruce", "Banner", 32 };
```

We've chosen a simple struct to illustrate the basics of compound types. If we serialize the variable "hero" into a SOAP message payload using SOAP encoding, it would look like this:

```
<hero xsi:type="x:SuperHero">
    <sCodeName xsi:type="xsd:string">Hulk</sCodeName>
    <sFirstName xsi:type="xsd:string">Bruce</sFirstName>
    <sLastName xsi:type="xsd:string">Banner</sLastName>
    <nAge xsi:type="xsd:integer">32</nAge>
</hero>
```

As can be seen in this example, the xsi:type attribute is used on compound data types as well as simple types. In this case, the type is x:SuperHero, and the x namespace would point to a schema that represents our SuperHero struct.

Arrays

Arrays are compound types as well, and they are represented in much the same way that structs are. As we might expect, the difference between arrays and structs is in how we refer to their members. Structs have data that is identifiable by name, and array members are identified by position. The names of array elements are insignificant, so they cannot be used to look up a value.

In SOAP encoding, arrays are considered a special type. This type is indicated by their xsi:type attribute, which is SOAP-ENC:Array. As with all SOAP encoding, the namespace associated with the Array type is http://schemas.xmlsoap.org/soap/encoding. Elements with this xsi:type are declared as SOAP encoding arrays. The type of the array members is declared using another attribute, SOAP-ENC:arrayType. This attribute indicates the type and size of the array. Arrays in SOAP encoding can be confusing, so let's take a look at a simple array of five integers to see how these attributes are used to define an array:

```
<numbers xsi:type="SOAP-ENC:Array" SOAP-ENC:arrayType="xsd:integer[5]">
    <item>10</item>
    <item>20</item>
    <item>30</item>
    <item>40</item>
    <item>50</item>
</numbers>
```

The `numbers` element is declared as a SOAP array, and the `arrayType` attribute states that it contains five elements of the `integer` type. This is accomplished by combining the values we used earlier in the `type` attribute (values from XML Schemas) and the square brackets `[]` with a size value. As can be seen, each of the array elements has the name `item`. This could have been any name as the member values are determined solely by the order of the elements.

Before we look at the more complex features of arrays, let's see another simple array. This array contains four names, each as a `string`. The differences occur in the `arrayType` attribute, and in the names of the members (which are irrelevant).

```
<names xsi:type="SOAP-ENC:Array" SOAP-ENC:arrayType="xsd:string[4]">
    <e>John Doe</e>
    <e>John Q. Public</e>
    <e>John Smith</e>
    <e>John Elway</e>
</names>
```

By setting the `arrayType` attribute on a SOAP array, we are able to define the type of members that will appear. The `arrayType` attribute is the only restriction on member types; SOAP arrays do not place restrictions on member types by default, so we can mix types inside of an array. We can accomplish this by using an `arrayType` attribute value of `SOAP-ENC:ur-type[]`. The `ur-type[]` is a universal data type for the SOAP encoding data types, so arrays that use this can have mixed members. The only catch to using `ur-type[]` is that like the polymorphic accessor for simple types, we must use the `xsi:type` attribute on the accessors to indicate each element's type. Below is an example of a SOAP array that contains a mixed set of types as members. Notice that each member uses the `xsi:type` attribute to specify its type.

```
<mix xsi:type="SOAP-ENC:Array" SOAP-ENC:arrayType="SOAP-ENC:ur-type[4]">
    <e xsi:type="xsd:string">John Elway</e>
    <e xsi:type="xsd:integer">7</e>
    <e xsi:type="xsd:string">Denver Broncos</e>
    <e xsi:type="xsd:date">1999</e>
</names>
```

Besides using mixed types, arrays have some other sophisticated features that we can take advantage of if our application needs them. Because arrays can be costly as parameters in remote procedure calls, SOAP defines two attributes that give us the flexibility to pass the portion of the array that we need to work with in our application. These attributes are the `offset` and `position` attributes.

The `SOAP-ENC:offset` attribute lets us specify where in the array we are beginning, so transmitting only part of the array. All elements before the offset are assumed to contain the default value, or NULL, depending on the application's behavior. The `offset` attribute appears on the array element, as shown below. In that case, the elements are the third and fourth of the array.

```
<names xsi:type="SOAP-ENC:Array" SOAP-ENC:arrayType="xsd:string[4]"
                SOAP-ENC:offset="[2]" >
    <e>John Smith</e>
    <e>John Elway</e>
</names>
```

The `SOAP-ENC:position` attribute specifies the position in the array of a particular member (like `offset`, the `position` attribute is zero based). As might be expected, that means that the position attribute must appear on the member itself rather than the array element. If the `position` attribute appears on one member, it must appear on all the members. This example shows how the `position` attribute can be used to pass a large array that is almost empty (this is referred to in the Specification as **sparse arrays**):

```
<names xsi:type="SOAP-ENC:Array" SOAP-ENC:arrayType="xsd:string[100]">
    <e SOAP-ENC:position="[11]">John Smith</e>
    <e SOAP-ENC:position="[45]">John Elway</e>
</names>
```

These two attributes (`offset` and `position`) are to some extent interchangeable in that the `offset` attribute implies position for all the elements that appear. That means that it is possible to describe an array in minimal fashion using either technique.

Custom Encoding

SOAP encoding is just one example of a set of encoding rules. This is a topic that deserves a level of detail beyond the slope of this chapter. Suffice it to say that we can define our own encoding, and there are many reasons that we might want to. SOAP encoding will probably handle most needs because the rules for data representation match up well with the customary programming types.

Multi-reference Values

Whether a value is represented as a simple or compound type, it is not uncommon for the same value to appear multiple times in a single payload. Because XML is a verbose representation of data, there is an opportunity to write more efficient XML documents by eliminating redundant data. SOAP follows the lead of XML Schemas by allowing values to be referenced multiple times inside a document. SOAP uses the `id` and `href` attributes to allow values to be referenced inside of a message. This allows for redundant data to be eliminated, and for the payload to more accurately reflect the language models it represents (if we are serializing a reference, why not serialize it as a reference?).

Let's look at an example of multi-reference values in use. In this example, we have a struct that represents an employee. The employee struct contains the employee's name, identification number, and address. The address is also represented as a struct.

```
<m:Employee>
    <idno>12345</idno>
    <fname>Billy</fname>
    <lname>Batson</lname>
    <address>
        <street>1000 Sharon Drive</street>
        <city>Charlotte</city>
        <state>North Carolina</state>
        <zip>28211</zip>
    </address>
</m:Employee>
```

When we introduce a second employee record, it turns out that these two employees live at the same address. There is redundant data in the address member if both these employees appear in the message payload.

```
<m:Employee>
    <idno>12345</idno>
    <fname>Billy</fname>
    <lname>Batson</lname>
    <address>
        <street>1000 Sharon Drive</street>
        <city>Charlotte</city>
        <state>North Carolina</state>
        <zip>28211</zip>
    </address>
</m:Employee>
<m:Employee>
    <idno>23456</idno>
    <fname>Wally</fname>
    <lname>West</lname>
    <address>
        <street>1000 Sharon Drive</street>
        <city>Charlotte</city>
        <state>North Carolina</state>
        <zip>28211</zip>
    </address>
</m:Employee>
```

By using the `id` and `href` attributes, we can make the address field of these two structs a multi-reference value. The example below shows what the resulting payload would look like:

```
<m:Employee>
    <idno>12345</idno>
    <fname>Billy</fname>
    <lname>Batson</lname>
    <address href="#address1"/>
</m:Employee>
<m:Employee>
    <idno>23456</idno>
    <fname>Wally</fname>
    <lname>West</lname>
    <address href="#address1"/>
</m:Employee>
<m:address id="address1">
    <street>1000 Sharon Drive</street>
    <city>Charlotte</city>
    <state>North Carolina</state>
    <zip>28211</zip>
</m:address>
```

If we are working with a SOAP message with only two structs in the payload, multi-reference values might seem like overkill. The real advantage to using multi-reference values becomes obvious when we are working with large amounts of data, such as an array of structs. Let's assume our redundant address in this example is a high-rise apartment building one block away from our company. If we were passing an array of 100 structs in a payload, perhaps 50 or more employees might all have the same address. The reduction in message size by using multi-reference values would be significant.

> *For many SOAP implementations, supporting multi-reference values has come late, and some still do not support this capability. On the other hand, implementations like Microsoft's .NET Framework took the approach of using multi-reference values to represent every element of an array, whether the values appear more than once or not. Interoperability tests between SOAP implementations have made great progress in identifying these types of issues.*

What's Simple About It?

At this point, many developers ask, "Whatever happened to 'Simple'?" It's fair to say that with advanced topics like multiref accessors and sparse arrays, the "Simple" part of SOAP seems like a distant memory, and it is tempting to use XML-RPC or even a home-grown solution. For SOAP to be able to function as a generic messaging protocol, it must be extensible, and this extensibility does not come without a price. This is an advantage of SOAP, not a handicap. SOAP is simple when the needs of the application allow it to be, and yet its open nature allows it to handle the complexities of more sophisticated systems. As yet, not all SOAP implementations handle the more advanced aspects of the specification. As SOAP implementations mature, complex topics like multirefs will be handled transparently for most users. Until then, be extra nice to those developers working on SOAP implementations.

> *For any developers out there who are working on an implementation of SOAP for their platform, we highly recommend checking out both the SOAPBuilders group at Yahoo (http://groups.yahoo.com/group/soapbuilders) and the DevelopMentor SOAP discussion list (http://discuss.develop.com). They are both great sources of information on interoperability, advanced topics, and what the specification really means, as the best of the SOAP community and many of the authors of SOAP frequent them.*

Now that we have covered the details of what goes into a SOAP message, let's turn our attention to how we move a message from point A to point B. This mechanism for moving messages is called the transport.

Transports

Once we have a SOAP message, we will probably want to send it to someone. After all, what good is a message if it never goes anywhere? The transport is the method by which a SOAP message is moved from sender to receiver. One example of a transport is HTTP, the Hypertext Transfer Protocol.

Separation of Message and Transport

One of the best design decisions made by the authors of SOAP was to separate the message definition from the message transport. It may sound ridiculous, but there is nothing in the specification that requires computers be involved in the transport of a SOAP message. Given that, here is a list of possible transports for SOAP messages (some more likely than others):

- ❏   HTTP
- ❏   SMTP
- ❏   MQSeries
- ❏   Raw sockets
- ❏   Files
- ❏   Named Pipes
- ❏   Carrier Pigeon

Granted, not many developers will be exercising stock options after developing SOAP-enabled carrier pigeons, but this helps to illustrate the modular nature of the specification. Most developers are going to focus on HTTP as the standard transport for their SOAP messages, and that is the transport that we will focus on in this chapter. As SOAP support continues to grow, there will be SOAP transport bindings defined and implemented for any number of protocols.

HTTP

When many developers think of SOAP, they think of XML over HTTP. HTTP is an excellent transport for SOAP because of its wide acceptance. HTTP is the ubiquitous protocol for the Web, a constant reminder that standards can actually work. Combining HTTP, the standard transport protocol for the Web, and SOAP, the leading candidate for the standard messaging format, gives us a powerful tool. HTTP makes such a great transport for SOAP that the authors made sure that the rules for using HTTP as a transport are part of the SOAP specification.

There are only a couple of basic rules for using HTTP as a SOAP transport. The mechanism for sending a SOAP message over HTTP is the standard HTTP POST method. An HTTP POST sends a block of data to a particular URI on the web server. In the case of SOAP messages, this block of data is the SOAP message itself. Because the SOAP message is XML, the Content-Type header of the HTTP POST must be text/xml. If there is a response to the message, it is returned in the HTTP response.

Let's take another look at the example SOAP message we used earlier, this time transporting the message over HTTP.

```
POST /endpoint.asp HTTP/1.1
Content-Type: text/xml
Content-Length: ###
SOAPAction: "urn:wroxheroes"
```

```
<soap:Envelope xmlns:soap="http://schemas.xmlsoap.org/soap/envelope/"
               soap:encodingStyle="http://schemas.xmlsoap.org/soap
                                   /encoding/">
    <soap:Header>
       <h:from xmlns:h="http://www.wrox.com/Header">
          SoapGuy@wrox.com
       </h:from>
    </soap:Header>
    <soap:Body>
       <w:GetSecretIdentity xmlns:w="http://www.wrox.com/heroes/">
          <codename>XSLT-Man</codename>
       </w:GetSecretIdentity>
    </soap:Body>
</soap:Envelope>
```

The first four lines of this example are related to the HTTP transport. The first line contains the HTTP method, POST, and the URI indicating the location of the endpoint. This example might represent a SOAP message request sent to the URL http://www.wrox.com/endpoint.asp. The first line also indicates that version 1.1 of HTTP is being used in this request.

The next three lines are the HTTP headers. The first two are standard HTTP. `Content-Type` indicates the MIME type of the POST content. All SOAP messages must use `text/xml`. `Content-Length` tells the size in bytes of the content. The last header, `SOAPAction`, is SOAP specific. We will examine that next, but before that, notice the remainder of the HTTP request. There is an additional carriage-return/line feed that separates headers from the body, and the body content itself is a SOAP message. The message itself does not change because it is being transported by HTTP, and other than the `SOAPAction` header, HTTP does not change just because it is sending a SOAP message.

SOAPAction Header

The SOAP specification does define a single additional HTTP header to be used when SOAP messages are transported over HTTP, and that header is the `SOAPAction` header. The `SOAPAction` header provides a hint to servers that a particular HTTP POST contains a SOAP message, and the value of the header is a URI that indicates the intent of the SOAP message. This allows firewalls and other servers to perform conditional processing based on the presence of the `SOAPAction` header.

Version 1.1 stated that the `SOAPAction` header must be present in HTTP transports, although it may be blank. Since then, that requirement has been removed. A blank `SOAPAction` on an HTTP POST means that the intent of the message can be inferred from the target of the POST, the URI. Although this may sound confusing, it is actually pretty straightforward. There are some messages whose purpose is obvious by where they are going (what URL they are posted to). If our methods are implemented at one URL, we may need to use the `SOAPAction` header to make the intent of an incoming message clearer. The need for `SOAPAction` largely depends on how the endpoint is implemented.

Status Codes

You will recall that HTTP returns status information in the form of status codes. These codes are integers, and they are sectioned into classes of 100. For example, anything in the range 200-299 indicates success. SOAP places a requirement on the HTTP transport when it is used to exchange SOAP messages. If the response message contains a fault, then the status code of the HTTP response must be 500, which indicates an Internal Server Error. We will see examples of both success and failure status codes later in the chapter.

Let's take a look at the response to our `GetSecretIdentity` call (below) to see the relationship between request and response, as well as message and fault.

```
HTTP/1.1 200 OK
Content-Type: text/xml
Content-Length: ###

<soap:Envelope xmlns:soap="http://schemas.xmlsoap.org/soap/envelope/"
                soap:encodingStyle="http://schemas.xmlsoap.org/soap
                                     /encoding/"
                xmlns:xsi="http://www.w3.org/1999/XMLSchema-instance"
                xmlns:xsd="http://www.w3.org/1999/XMLSchema">
    <soap:Body>
        <m:GetSecretIdentityResponse xmlns:m="http://www.wrox.com/heroes/">
            <return xsi:type="xsd:string">Michael Kay</return>
        </m:GetSecretIdentityResponse>
    </soap:Body>
</soap:Envelope>
```

The above response is successful, returning the identity of Wrox's resident XSLT super-hero. Notice the first line of the example response, which contains the status code 200. Now, let's call the `GetSecretIdentity` method again, but this time we will send a different request, one with problems:

```
POST /endpoint.asp HTTP/1.1
Content-Type: text/xml
Content-Length: ###
SOAPAction: "urn:wroxheroes"

<Envelope>
   <Body>
      <w:GetSecretIdentity xmlns:w="http://www.wrox.com/heroes/">
         <codename>XSLT-Man</codename>
      </w:GetSecretIdentity>
   </Body>
</Envelope>
```

In this case, the SOAP namespace is missing completely, so the endpoint must return a fault, which means it must use a status code of 500 on the response. The response message is shown below, and it contains a `VersionMismatch` fault as well as the appropriate status code:

```
HTTP/1.1 500 Internal Server Error
Content-Type: text/xml
Content-Length: ###

<soap:Envelope xmlns:soap="http://schemas.xmlsoap.org/soap/envelope/"
               soap:encodingStyle="http://schemas.xmlsoap.org/soap
                                   /encoding/"
               xmlns:xsi="http://www.w3.org/1999/XMLSchema-instance"
               xmlns:xsd="http://www.w3.org/1999/XMLSchema">
   <soap:Body>
      <soap:Fault>
         <faultcode>soap:VersionMismatch</faultcode>
            <faultstring>The SOAP namespace is incorrect.</faultstring>
         <faultactor>http://www.wrox.com/endpoint.asp</faultactor>
         <detail>
            <w:errorinfo xmlns:w="http://www,wrox.com/">
               <desc>The SOAP namespace was blank.</desc>
            </w:errorinfo>
         </detail>
      </soap:Fault>
   </soap:Body>
</soap:Envelope>
```

These examples show how to use HTTP as the transport binding for SOAP. It is not difficult to use HTTP, which is one of the reasons for its popularity. For more information on HTTP, including the status codes, consult Chapter 2.

If we think of transport as "how" the message is sent, then the purpose of the message is the "why". HTTP is SOAP's "how" of choice for the time being, and our next topic, RPC, is the "why".

SOAP and RPC

We have spent much of this chapter trying to show that SOAP does not necessarily have to be used for remote procedure calls. The truth is that RPC is what gets most developers excited about SOAP, and with good reason. The idea that the complexities of CORBA and DCOM can be forgotten with a little XML is an attractive concept. The SOAP specification clearly describes how remote procedure calls should be represented in SOAP messages.

Saying that SOAP replaces CORBA or DCOM is an oversimplification, however. SOAP is missing most of the features that developers expect from a robust distributed object protocol, such as garbage collection or object pooling. Despite the letter "O" in SOAP, as the Specification stands today, there are no "objects" in the DCOM or CORBA sense. The SOAP Specification makes it clear that this was not a design goal of the authors. On the other hand, it is clear that SOAP was designed with RPC in mind.

SOAP RPC Convention

We already discussed the open nature of the SOAP specification as it relates to message transport. SOAP defines a message syntax and exchange model, but it does not try to define the "how" of message exchange. The **convention** is the set of rules applied to a particular use of SOAP messages. The Specification defines rules for a single convention: remote procedure calls, or RPC. The RPC convention can be defined as a way of serializing remote procedure calls and responses as SOAP messages. At the end of this chapter we will discuss the implications of using some alternative conventions.

Like its partner HTTP, SOAP RPC uses a request-response model for message exchanges. Making a remote procedure call with SOAP just involves building a SOAP message. The request SOAP message that is sent to the endpoint represents the call, and the response SOAP message represents the results of that call. Let's take a look at the rules for building method calls and returns in SOAP messages.

The Call

Making a remote procedure call with SOAP just involves building a SOAP message. The message that is sent to the endpoint represents the call. The payload of that request message contains a struct that is the serialized method call. The child elements of that struct are the inbound parameters of the method. The end result is an XML representation of a call that looks the way we would expect.

When RPC calls are serialized in a SOAP message, the name of the element must match the name of the method, as do the parameters. Consider this method signature:

```
// Return the current stock price, given the company symbol
double GetStockQuote ( [in] string sSymbol );
```

If our method namespace is `http://www.wroxstox.com/`, then the serialized method call that requests the stock quote using symbol OU812 would look like this:

```
<q:GetStockQuote xmlns:q="http://www.wroxstox.com/">
    <q:sSymbol xsi:type="xsd:string">OU812</q:sSymbol>
</q:GetStockQuote>
```

The method name matches the element, as does the parameter. While the parameter names match the child elements, only inbound parameters appear in the serialized call. To illustrate this, let's look at three very similar methods signatures:

```
// Reverse the string, s, and return the new string.
string ReverseString ( [in] string s );

// Reverse the string, s, and return the new string.
void ReverseString ( [in] string s, [out] string sRev );

// Reverse the string, s, passed in by reference.
void ReverseString ( [in, out] string s );
```

All three methods would be represented by the same serialized call. If we called the `ReverseString()` method with the parameter s containing a value of ROHT, the call would be represented as shown (below):

```
<x:ReverseString xmlns:x="http://www.wrox.com/">
    <s xsi:type="xsd:string">ROHT</s>
</x:ReverseString>
```

Now we'll take a look at how the return from a remote procedure call is serialized, and also how the returns from the different forms of the `ReverseString()` method shown here, would look.

The Return

As we mentioned earlier, the RPC convention uses a request-response model. Just as the call is represented in the request SOAP message, the results of the call are returned in the response SOAP message. The payload in the response also contains a struct, and the child elements are the outbound parameters and/or the return value of the method.

The name of the method response struct can be anything, but it is a convention to append the word "Response" to the name of the method call struct. For example, `ReverseString` would result in `ReverseStringResponse`. Just as in the call, the names of parameter elements are significant and should match the parameters. If the method returns a value, the name is irrelevant, but it must be the first child of the method struct.

So how do we know the difference between a single out parameter and a return value? In one sense, there is no difference. Both are returning a single value as part of the method return. The real answer lies in the name of the parameter. If the name of the parameter matches a parameter of the method, then it is an out parameter. Return values cannot be identified by name, only position, but the name should not conflict with the parameters of the method.

Now that we know how a serialized return should look, let's continue to use our `ReverseString` example. As we saw before, all three method signatures for `ReverseString` result in the same serialized call. However, how do the serialized returns differ? The first version reverses the string and returns the result as the return value of the method:

```
<x:ReverseStringResponse xmlns:x="http://www.wrox.com/">
    <x:ret xsi:type="xsd:string">THOR</x:ret>
</x:ReverseString>
```

The second version has no return value, but instead uses an out parameter called sRev:

```
<x:ReverseStringResponse xmlns:x="http://www.wrox.com/">
    <x:sRev xsi:type="xsd:string">THOR</x:sRev>
</x:ReverseString>
```

The final version reverses the string after passing it by reference, so the parameter s is both an in and out parameter:

```
<x:ReverseStringResponse xmlns:x="http://www.wrox.com/">
    <x:s xsi:type="xsd:string">THOR</x:s>
</x:ReverseString>
```

As can be seen, the difference between values returned in parameters and the value of the method itself is all in the name. In the first case, the element was named ret, and in the second case, it was named s. We can access parameters by name or position as elements of the RPC struct, but the return value can only be accessed by position.

What if there are no out parameters or return values? In that case, we still have a response that represents a method return, but with no data:

```
<m:GetNothing xmlns:m="http://tempuri.org/"/>
```

Now that we know how to work with remote procedure calls, let's look at a more complete example that uses full messages and a transport.

RPC and HTTP

We have been looking at RPC in isolation, but in order to perform a remote procedure call, we need a way to move our message to the "remote" location. Here is where SOAP really shines: when we combine RPC and HTTP to make calls against Web Services.

Assume we need to call a remote procedure on a web server to validate a city and state combination and return a zip code. Our hypothetical Web Service will exist at www.livezipcodes.com (this is not a real endpoint, don't bother trying!). We do not know how the method is implemented; all we know is how to access it. The method can be invoked at the URL http://www.livezipcodes.com/call.asp, the method is associated with the namespace URI http://www.livezipcodes.com/methods/, and the SOAPAction for this method is urn:livezipcodes. The signature for the method is shown below:

```
string GetZipCode ( string city, string state );
```

In building the request message, we do not need any extensions, so the Header element can be left out. The payload will be a struct representing the method call. The method parameters are passed as child elements. Here is the HTTP request, including the request SOAP message, sent to www.livezipcodes.com.

```
POST /call.asp HTTP/1.1
Content-Type: text/xml
Content-Length: ###
SOAPAction: "urn:livezipcodes"
```

```
<soap:Envelope xmlns:soap="http://schemas.xmlsoap.org/soap/envelope/"
               soap:encodingStyle="http://schemas.xmlsoap.org/soap
                                   /encoding/"
               xmlns:xsi="http://www.w3.org/1999/XMLSchema-instance"
               xmlns:xsd="http://www.w3.org/1999/XMLSchema">
   <soap:Body>
      <m:GetZipCode xmlns:m="http://www.livezipcodes.com/methods/">
         <city xsi:type="xsd:string">Modest Town</city>
         <state xsi:type="xsd:string">Virginia</state>
      </m:GetZipCode>
   </soap:Body>
</soap:Envelope>
```

Since there is actually a place named Modest Town, Virginia, the response from the endpoint would look like this.

```
HTTP/1.1 200 OK
Content-Type: text/xml
Content-Length: ###

<soap:Envelope xmlns:soap="http://schemas.xmlsoap.org/soap/envelope/"
               soap:encodingStyle="http://schemas.xmlsoap.org/soap
                                   /encoding/"
               xmlns:xsi="http://www.w3.org/1999/XMLSchema-instance"
               xmlns:xsd="http://www.w3.org/1999/XMLSchema">
   <soap:Body>
      <m:GetZipCodeResponse xmlns:m="http://www.livezipcodes.com/methods/">
         <zip xsi:type="xsd:string">23412</zip>
      </m:GetZipCodeResponse>
   </soap:Body>
</soap:Envelope>
```

If we were to execute this same method, but the endpoint is unable to access its database of geographical information, the response would be more like this.

```
HTTP/1.1 500 Internal Server Error
Content-Type: text/xml
Content-Length: ###

<soap:Envelope xmlns:soap="http://schemas.xmlsoap.org/soap/envelope/"
               soap:encodingStyle="http://schemas.xmlsoap.org/soap
                                   /encoding/"
               xmlns:xsi="http://www.w3.org/1999/XMLSchema-instance"
               xmlns:xsd="http://www.w3.org/1999/XMLSchema">
   <soap:Body>
      <soap:Fault>
         <faultcode>soap:Server.DatabaseDown</faultcode>
         <faultstring>The database is unavailable.</faultstring>
         <faultactor>http://www.livezipcodes.com/call.asp</faultactor>
      </soap:Fault>
   </soap:Body>
</soap:Envelope>
```

Beyond RPC - Working with XML Documents

Although RPC has certainly received the most attention, SOAP messages can be used to transfer arbitrary XML documents. For a given document type, we can define a new convention that describes the purpose of the message transfer.

Here's something we don't see everyday: a SOAP message that has nothing to do with RPC.

```
<soap:Envelope xmlns:soap="http://schemas.xmlsoap.org/soap/envelope/"
               soap:encodingStyle="http://schemas.xmlsoap.org/soap
                                   /encoding/"
               xmlns:xsl="http://www.w3.org/1999/XSL/Transform">
    <soap:Body>
        <xsl:stylesheet version="1.0">
            <xsl:template match="/">
                <html>
                    <body>
                        <p><xsl:value-of select="Envelope"/></p>
                    </body>
                </html>
            </xsl:template>
        </xsl:stylesheet>
    </soap:Body>
</soap:Envelope>
```

This message contains a payload that is an XSLT stylesheet (one that happens to be written to manipulate a SOAP message). Consider the implications of having the SOAP Body element be an arbitrary XML document (in this case, an XSLT stylesheet) instead of RPC. In that sense, SOAP is a general-purpose mechanism for transporting an XML document. This is how SOAP is being applied in both Microsoft's BizTalk Server and in the ebXML protocol, but the potential uses do not stop there.

> *For more information on BizTalk, go to the BizTalk Home Page at*
> http://www.biztalk.org/home/default.asp. *Additional information about ebXML is provided in Chapter 1 of this book, and* http://www.ebxml.org/

For every potential application of XML, SOAP provides the mechanism for extending that use via messaging. This is an area of development that is still largely untapped because of the excitement surrounding RPC. **Web Services can be composed with SOAP but without RPC**. As more developers realize this, the excitement surrounding SOAP will continue to grow. Inserting an XSLT transform into a SOAP message gives us a mechanism to trigger an XML transformation on a remote machine, and that's a Web Service. A SOAP message that carries a Vector Markup Language (VML) document could be used to insert new graphical elements into a diagram that exists on another machine, and that's a Web Service too. The possibilities are endless!

Summary

In this chapter we have taken a look at SOAP and how it relates to Web Services. SOAP is a messaging protocol based on XML. The SOAP specification defines a modular architecture for messaging that allows any combinations of message routing, transports, and conventions to be used to build systems. SOAP can be used as a messaging protocol for Web Services, and it is the protocol of choice for most vendors because of its growing acceptance as a standard.

We examined the syntax of the SOAP message itself. SOAP messages have an `Envelope` element as the document element, which provides version information. The `Envelope` element contains a `Body` element that holds the payload of the message, and it may also contain a `Header` element. The `Header` element contains one or more entries that represent extensions to the message syntax. SOAP defines another standard element, `Fault`, which is used to carry error information inside the `Body` element.

SOAP messages contain data, and there are rules for how data types are represented in a message. SOAP defines one set of rules, called SOAP encoding, but new encoding rules can be defined. SOAP encoding relies on XML Schemas for most of its data types, and it adds structs and arrays as well.

Messages in SOAP can be transported by any mechanism, whether by socket or by hand. The specification defines a transport binding for HTTP, which does not stray far from the general mechanisms for XML transfer over HTTP. SOAP adds one twist, the `SOAPAction` header, to help servers route SOAP messages without needing to examine their contents.

The last area of SOAP we focused on is remote procedure calls, or RPC. SOAP messages can be used to perform remote procedure calls, and the Specification defines how calls and returns should be serialized in messages. RPC is just one convention for SOAP messages, and we saw how the future of SOAP might be in other XML document conventions.

4

WSDL: the Web Services Definition Language

While **SOAP** (**Simple Object Access Protocol**) provides a standard way of transporting messages for use by Web Services, it doesn't provide any way of describing what the format of those messages should be for a given Web Service. When the SOAP specification first arrived on the scene and developers started to implement real SOAP based Web Services, they quickly discovered that the only way for someone to know how to call a Web Service was to publish a sample SOAP document illustrating a call to the web service in question. The problem with this approach was that it didn't go far enough in describing how to call the Web Service. For example, if we think of an **RPC** (**Remote Procedure Call**)-style Web Service as a library we want to call, simply getting an example SOAP document would be the equivalent of someone giving you a C++ library and some example code, but no header file, or a Java server with no corresponding IDL. You would know how to make the function calls demonstrated in the example code, but not the formal definition of those functions, or how many other functions there might be that aren't called in the example.

When you compile a C++ program that calls a library, you need a header file, not only so that you, the developer, know how to write your code, but also so that the compiler knows that you did it correctly. The same problem became apparent when companies like IBM and Microsoft started developing toolkits for working with SOAP. On the receiving end (the server side), it's easy to write code to parse a specific SOAP message and turn that into a call to a binary function (such as a C++ function or a Java method). On the calling (client) side however, it turned out to be hard to programmatically "know" how to create a SOAP message representing the call, without a "header file" to describe the creation of the SOAP message.

WSDL (**Web Services Definition Language**) grew out of Microsoft and IBM's efforts to address this issue. WSDL seeks to define and describe Web Services, just as header files (or type libraries) define and describe traditional binary libraries.

A Brief History of WSDL

The first two major efforts at building toolkits to work with SOAP came from two of the flagship companies behind the development of the SOAP 1.1 spec: IBM and Microsoft. IBM developed the **IBM SOAP for Java** toolkit, and Microsoft released the **SOAP Toolkit for Visual Studio**. Both implementations sought to solve the "header file" problem (how to programmatically discover how to format a SOAP message to call a specific SOAP service).

IBM's solution was **NASSL**, the **Network Accessibility Service Specification Language**, which was released with the first version of the SOAP for Java toolkit. NASSL uses XML to describe interfaces for Web Services and how they are bound to specific web addresses (URLs). It also uses the W3C XML Schema Language (**XSD**) to describe the data types passed to and from Web Services.

At around the same time (Spring of 2000) Microsoft released **SCL**, the **Service Contract Language**, with its first release of the SOAP Toolkit for Visual Studio. SCL also uses XML to describe Web Services, but it used Microsoft's **XML Data-Reduced** (**XDR**) format for defining data types. Microsoft soon followed with an updated version called **SDL**, or the **Services Description Language**, which was released with the first public preview of Visual Studio.NET.

One major problem became rapidly apparent to the development community. The whole point of SOAP and Web Services is to allow cross platform communication, and the two major SOAP implementations were incompatible.

The solution to this problem became WSDL. IBM and Microsoft, working together with Ariba, developed the first version of WSDL, which brought together ideas from all of their current work on Web Services definition. The focus of WSDL is around open standards, so it uses XSD (now a fully fledged W3C Recommendation at http://www.w3.org/XML/Schema) to describe its types, and other standards such as SOAP and MIME to describe specific bindings. WSDL 1.1 was itself submitted to the W3C as a Note in March 2001. The latest version of the Specification can now be found at http://www.w3.org/TR/wsdl.

WSDL 1.1 is now supported by Microsoft's SOAP Toolkit 2.0 (http://msdn.microsoft.com/xml), IBM's Web Services Toolkit 2.3 (http://alphaworks.ibm.com/tech/webservicestoolkit), and the latest version (Beta 2) of Microsoft's .NET Framework (http://msdn.microsoft.com/net/).

Why WSDL?

To fulfill the Web Services vision of millions of independent pieces of components all available over the Internet and usable on any platform from any development language, Web Services need to be self-describing. Just as Java class files and COM objects are self-describing (through reflection and type libraries respectively) so too are Web Services, by using WSDL to describe their interfaces and bindings. If Web Services all publish their interfaces using WSDL, it should be possible for any Web Services client to call them programmatically without having to know anything about the implementation details of the individual Web Service, or what platform or OS the service is running on.

WSDL is built on top of open standards like XML, XSD, SOAP, and MIME in an effort to make platform, implementation, and device independence for Web Services a reality.

WSDL Syntax

WSDL provides a grammar for describing services as a set of endpoints that exchange messages. One of the central concepts behind these descriptions is the idea that there is a difference between the abstract definition of a message, and the concrete way in which those messages are mapped to a specific transport and/or data encoding protocol.

In practice, most developers will use a tool (two are discussed at the end of this chapter) to create their WSDL documents rather than coding them by hand. However, I think it makes sense to tackle the underlying syntax of WSDL before looking at the tools, since even if the tool does most of the work, in reality most developers know that you use code generation tools to give you a head start, and then tweak the results by hand. To do that kind of customization, it is important to understand the basic structure of WSDL.

A WSDL document is composed of definitions. These define a **service** as a set of one or more network endpoints, or **ports**. Each port is associated with a specific **binding**. It is the binding that defines how an abstract set of operations and messages are bound to a port according to a specific protocol. A binding maps a specific protocol to a **port-type**. A port-type is composed of one or more **operations**. Operations represent an abstract set of things the service can "do". Each operation is composed of a set of abstract **messages**. Messages represent the data being communicated during the operation. Each message contains one or more pieces of data, which are defined by **types**.

Each WSDL document is composed of the following elements, which will be discussed in a moment:

- ❑ Types
- ❑ Messages
- ❑ Operations
- ❑ Port types
- ❑ Bindings
- ❑ Ports
- ❑ Services

Each abstract definition of a type, message, or operation can be bound to more than one concrete port, so that the same message can be sent to different ports using different encoding.

WSDL is designed to be highly extensible, and in theory any protocol can be defined and used for binding messages. However, only three bindings to message formats/transports are defined as part of the WSDL 1.1 spec:

- ❑ SOAP 1.1
- ❑ HTTP GET/POST
- ❑ MIME

WSDL is also not bound to a specific schema language for defining types. Any way of describing types can be used, but the default is XSD. In the following sections, note will be made of how to extend WSDL to use other methods for mapping to a specific protocol.

111

Putting it all Together

Before describing each element of a WSDL document in detail, let's take a look at a complete definition. The following WSDL example defines a Web Service that has one **operation** called `GetCurrentTemperature`. `GetCurrentTemperature` takes a three-letter city code and returns the current temperature for that city. Since the service is composed of types, messages, etc, each building on the preceding definition, the document starts with types and builds up to a service at the end of the document. This makes it much easier to see the hierarchy of composition at work in WSDL. Each component part is defined and then built upon to arrive at the final service definition. This example uses SOAP 1.1 as its encoding style, and is bound to HTTP.

```
<?xml version="1.0"?>
```

First the top level `definitions` element:

```
<definitions name="CurrentTemp"
            targetNamespace="http://example.com/currenttemp.wsdl"
            xmlns:tns="http://example.com/currenttemp.wsdl"
            xmlns:xsd1="http://example.com/currenttemp.xsd"
            xmlns:soap="http://schemas.xmlsoap.org/wsdl/soap/"
            xmlns="http://schemas.xmlsoap.org/wsdl/">
```

The `documentation` element can be used for comments:

```
<documentation>
    the documentation element can have mixed <content/>.
</documentation>
```

Next, the individual data types that will make up the messages:

```
<types>
    <schema targetNamespace="http://example.com/currenttemp.xsd"
            xmlns="http://www.w3.org/2000/10/XMLSchema">
        <element name="CurrentTemperatureRequest">
            <complexType>
                <all>
                    <element name="cityCode" type="string"/>
                </all>
            </complexType>
        </element>
        <element name="CurrentTemperature">
            <complexType>
                <all>
                    <element name="temp" type="float"/>
                </all>
            </complexType>
        </element>
    </schema>
</types>
```

Now those types are associated with `message` elements:

```
<message name="GetCurrentTemperatureInput">
   <part name="body" element="xsd1:CurrentTemperatureRequest"/>
</message>
<message name="GetCurrentTemperatureOutput">
   <part name="body" element="xsd1:CurrentTemperature"/>
</message>
```

message elements are grouped into operation elements, and operations grouped to make a portType element:

```
<portType name="CurrentTemperaturePortType">
   <operation name="GetCurrentTemperature">
      <input message="tns:GetCurrentTemperatureInput"/>
      <output message="tns:GetCurrentTemperatureOutput"/>
   </operation>
</portType>
```

A binding element maps the operation elements in a portType element (referenced by the type attribute) to a specific protocol:

```
<binding name="CurrentTemperatureSoapBinding"
        type="tns:CurrentTemperaturePortType">
   <soap:binding style="document"
                 transport="http://schemas.xmlsoap.org/soap/http"/>
   <operation name="GetCurrentTemperature">
      <soap:operation soapAction="http://example.com/
                                  GetCurrentTemperature"/>
      <input>
         <soap:body use="literal"/>
      </input>
      <output>
         <soap:body use="literal"/>
      </output>
   </operation>
</binding>
```

Finally, the service is composed of port elements, which associate an address or endpoint with a specific binding:

```
<service name="CurrentTemperatureService">
   <documentation>My first service</documentation>
   <port name="CurrentTemperaturePort"
        binding="tns:CurrentTemperatureSoapBinding">
      <soap:address location="http://example.com/currenttemp"/>
   </port>
</service>
</definitions>
```

Note that in this example, all the definitions for the service being described are present in the same document. WSDL also supports an import element, which allows the parts of the document to be physically separated into different files. This is useful if any of the components are to be reused in other definitions. For example, if we define a set of types representing often-used data structures, we can put those type definitions in a separate file and include them in other service definitions using the import element. The following example is the same as the previous example document, but with the types element replaced with an import element:

```
<?xml version="1.0"?>
<definitions name="CurrentTemp"
             targetNamespace="http://example.com/currenttemp.wsdl"
             xmlns:tns="http://example.com/currenttemp.wsdl"
             xmlns:xsd1="http://example.com/currenttemp/schemas"
             xmlns:soap="http://schemas.xmlsoap.org/wsdl/soap/"
             xmlns="http://schemas.xmlsoap.org/wsdl/">
    <import namespace="http://example.com/currenttemp/schemas"
           location="http://example.com/currenttemp/currenttemp.xsd"/>
    <message name="GetCurrentTemperatureInput">
       <part name="body" element="xsd1:CurrentTemperatureRequest"/>
    </message>
    <message name="GetCurrentTemperatureOutput">
       <part name="body" element="xsd1:CurrentTemperature"/>
    </message>

       ... deleted for brevity...

    <service name="CurrentTemperatureService">
       <documentation>My first service</documentation>
       <port name="CurrentTemperaturePort"
             binding="tns:CurrentTemperatureSoapBinding">
          <soap:address location="http://example.com/currenttemp"/>
       </port>
    </service>
</definitions>
```

Namespaces

The following table illustrates the set of namespaces used in WSDL, and the prefixes used for them in all of the examples in this chapter. Other namespaces can be used for additional bindings, such as SMTP, but those are up to the author of the document, and aren't defined in the Specification.

Prefix	Namespace URI	Definition
wsdl	http://schemas.xmlsoap.org/wsdl/	WSDL namespace for WSDL framework.
soap	http://schemas.xmlsoap.org/wsdl/soap/	WSDL namespace for WSDL SOAP binding.
http	http://schemas.xmlsoap.org/wsdl/http/	WSDL namespace for WSDL HTTP GET & POST binding.
mime	http://schemas.xmlsoap.org/wsdl/mime/	WSDL namespace for WSDL MIME binding.
soapenc	http://schemas.xmlsoap.org/soap/encoding/	Encoding namespace as defined by SOAP 1.1.

soapenv	`http://schemas.xmlsoap.org/soap/envelope/`	Envelope namespace as defined by SOAP 1.1.
xsi	`http://www.w3.org/2001/XMLSchema-instance`	Instance namespace as defined by XSD.
xsd	`http://www.w3.org/2001/XMLSchema`	Schema namespace as defined by XSD.
tns	Whatever the current document namespace is	The "this namespace" (`tns`) prefix is used as a convention to refer to the current document.

Elements of a Definition

Now that we've seen how the whole WSDL document fits together, we'll look at what each element means and how it's used.

documentation

There is a specific element called `wsdl:documentation` that is meant to hold human readable documentation, and is allowed inside any other WSDL language element. The contents of the `documentation` element can be "mixed" (text and XML elements). The `documentation` element is meant to be used for comments inside a WSDL document, and should be used rather than the XML comment tag (`<!-- -->`), since application-specific parsers may, for example, want to use the `documentation` elements to generate human readable specs for WSDL documents.

types

The `types` element is used to describe the types or structures of the data to be contained in messages. In theory, any schema language can be used inside the `types` element to describe the format of a message, but according to the W3C Specification, "WSDL prefers the use of XSD as the canonical type system, and treats it as the intrinsic type system" which means that type definitions are assumed to use XSD unless specified otherwise. This is reasonable, since XML Schema is a full Recommendation now, and the industry seems to be converging on XSD as the best way to represent XML Schemas.

However, one important thing to take into account is that although XSD is used to describe the schema of a type, the actual wire representation of that type may not be XML. For example, the following example schema describes a type called `CurrentTemperatureRequest`, which has two child elements, `cityCode` (a string), and `tempFormat` (a string which can be either `celsius` or `fahrenheit`). The attributes of the `definitions` element have been omitted for brevity:

```
<definitions...>
    <types>
        <xsd:schema xmlns:xsd="http://www.w3.org/2000/10/XMLSchema"
                elementFormDefault="qualified">
            <xsd:element name="CurrentTemperatureRequest">
                <xsd:complexType>
                    <xsd:sequence>
```

```
                    <xsd:element name="cityCode" type="xsd:string"/>
                    <xsd:element name="tempFormat">
                        <xsd:simpleType>
                            <xsd:restriction base="xsd:string">
                                <xsd:enumeration value="celsius"/>
                                <xsd:enumeration value="fahrenheit"/>
                            </xsd:restriction>
                        </xsd:simpleType>
                    </xsd:element>
                </xsd:sequence>
            </xsd:complexType>
        </xsd:element>
    </xsd:schema>
  </types>
</definitions>
```

If the type defined in the example above were part of a message bound to SOAP encoding, the wire format could be:

```
<GetCurrentTemperatureRequest>
    <cityCode>PDX</cityCode>
    <tempFormat>celsius</tempFormat>
</GetCurrentTemperatureRequest>
```

However, if that same message were bound to HTTP GET/POST, the actual wire format would be something like:

```
POST /CurrentTemperature HTTP/1.1
Host: www.tempserver.com
Content-Type: application/x-www-form-urlencoded
Content-Length: ###

cityCode=PDX&tempFormat=celsius
```

The data structures described by the types element are **abstract** types. They are representations of the conceptual data format of a message, not the wire format. The wire or implementation format is determined by the protocol used for binding. Since the types are abstract, there are a few guidelines on how to use XSD schemas to represent them:

❏   Use elements, not attributes

❏   Don't represent any protocol specific types (soap:encodingStyle for example)

❏   Arrays should use the SOAP 1.1 array encoding format

❏   Use xsd:anyType if the type doesn't matter

If we follow these guidelines, it is relatively easy to map an XSD schema to non-XML wire formats. There are some other caveats regarding array type encoding, but these are outside the scope of this chapter. For full details, see the SOAP (http://www.w3.org/TR/SOAP/#_Toc478383522) and WSDL Specifications (http://www.w3.org/TR/wsdl#_types).

Messages

Once a set of types is defined, they can be composed into messages. Each message definition (and again, these are abstract messages, not concrete wire format messages) is composed of one or more logical parts. Each part is associated with a type as defined by the type system in use. In other words, a message element contains part elements, and each part refers to a type defined in the types element. Since WSDL uses XSD (see http://www.w3.org/TR/xmlschema-2/ for available types) as its native type system, the two default bindings for a part are:

❑   element – a single XSD element by name

❑   type – can be either an XSD simpleType or complexType by name

These bindings take the form of attributes on the part element.

```
<definitions...>
   <message name="nmtoken">
      <part name="nmtoken" element="qname" | type="qname"/>
   </message>
</definitions>
```

If we choose not to use XSD as our type system, we can create type system appropriate bindings to take the place of element or type, as long as they are in a namespace other than that of WSDL. For example, if the document used a proprietary type system called myTypes, the mapping between the part and the type might look like the following:

```
<definitions…>
   <message name="mymessage" xmlns:myType="http://my.proprietary.type.com">
      <part name="firstpart" myType:type="myfavoriteproprietarytype"/>
   </message>
<definition>
```

The name of the message element and of each of its parts is up to us, as long as it is unique within the scope of the document.

There are a couple of different ways to approach mapping message parts to types. Consider the following schema:

```
<xsd:schema xmlns:xsd = "http://www.w3.org/2000/10/XMLSchema">
   <xsd:element name = "ShippingAddress">
      <xsd:complexType>
         <xsd:element name = "StreetAddress" type = "xsd:string"/>
         <xsd:element name = "City" type = "xsd:string"/>
         <xsd:element name = "State" type = "xsd:string"/>
         <xsd:element name = "Zip" type = "xsd:string"/>
         <xsd:element name = "Country" type = "xsd:string"/>
      </xsd:complexType>
   </xsd:element>
   <xsd:element name = "BillingAddress">
      <xsd:complexType>
         <xsd:element name = "StreetAddress" type = "xsd:string"/>
         <xsd:element name = "City" type = "xsd:string"/>
         <xsd:element name = "State" type = "xsd:string"/>
         <xsd:element name = "Zip" type = "xsd:string"/>
```

117

```
            <xsd:element name = "Country" type = "xsd:string"/>
        </xsd:complexType>
    </xsd:element>
</xsd:schema>
```

`part` elements are meant to be a logical separation of data inside a single message. If we wanted to separate the notion of "Shipping Address" from "Billing Address" using `part` elements, we might end up with this:

```
<definitions...>
    <message name="SetCustomerAddress">
        <part name="ShippingAddress" element="ShippingAddress"/>
        <part name="BillingAddress" element="BillingAddress"/>
    </message>
</definitions>
```

However, at some point the structure of the message may become sufficiently complex so that it is easier to manage that complexity in XSD, rather than separating the message into parts. The same thing could be accomplished by defining the schema as:

```
<xsd:schema xmlns:xsd = "http://www.w3.org/2001/XMLSchema">
    <xsd:element name = "ShippingAddress">
        <xsd:complexType>
            <xsd:element name = "StreetAddress" type = "xsd:string"/>
            <xsd:element name = "City" type = "xsd:string"/>
            <xsd:element name = "State" type = "xsd:string"/>
            <xsd:element name = "Zip" type = "xsd:string"/>
            <xsd:element name = "Country" type = "xsd:string"/>
        </xsd:complexType>
    </xsd:element>
    <xsd:element name = "BillingAddress">
        <xsd:complexType>
            <xsd:element name = "StreetAddress" type = "xsd:string"/>
            <xsd:element name = "City" type = "xsd:string"/>
            <xsd:element name = "State" type = "xsd:string"/>
            <xsd:element name = "Zip" type = "xsd:string"/>
            <xsd:element name = "Country" type = "xsd:string"/>
        </xsd:complexType>
    </xsd:element>
    <xsd:complexType name="CustomerAddresses">
        <xsd:sequence>
            <xsd:element ref="ShippingAddress"/>
            <xsd:element ref="BillingAddress"/>
        </xsd:sequence>
    </xsd:complexType>
</xsd:schema>
```

Then the message definition becomes:

```
<definitions...>
    <message name="SetCustomerAddress">
        <part name="Addresses" type="CustomerAddresses"/>
    </message>
</definitions>
```

Both methods are equally valid. It is up to the developer to decide which makes more sense, or is easier for the end users of the service to understand. Once again, keep in mind that since these are abstract message definitions, the ultimate concrete format may or may not be the same as the abstract form. For some bindings, such as SOAP 1.1, the actual concrete format may be almost if not exactly the same as the abstract definitions, but that isn't always the case.

Port Types

A port type is a set of messages grouped into **operations**. Operations represent a single unit of work for the service being described. A port type can be composed of more than one operation. We'll look at what types of operations (called **transmission primitives**) are available a bit later in the *Transmission Primitives* section. For now, we'll look at the structure of the portType element:

```
<definitions...>
    <portType name="nmtoken">
        <operation name="nmtoken">
            <input name="nmtoken" message="qname"/>
            <output name="nmtoken" message="qname"/>
            <fault name="nmtoken" message="qname"/>
        </operation>
    </portType>
</definitions>
```

Each operation can be composed of input, output, and fault messages. Whether or not each one of these three appears depends on which transmission primitive we are using. Think of an operation as equivalent to a method. Methods have [in] (parameters), [out] (output parameters), and potentially errors (exceptions). Operations are laid out the same way, with input being the data passed in to the operation, output being the data passed back from the operation, and the optional fault being data passed out indicating an exception. Note that this fault is application-specific fault information (used for application-level errors) separate from any protocol specific fault information (for example: soap:fault), which are handled by the underlying SOAP implementation.

In our original example, there was a single operation GetCurrentTemperature, which had input and output elements, but no fault element. The following example shows how that operation is defined as part of a port type:

```
<definitions...>
    <message name="GetCurrentTemperatureInput">
        <part name="body" element="xsd1:CurrentTemperatureRequest"/>
    </message>
    <message name="GetCurrentTemperatureOutput">
        <part name="body" element="xsd1:CurrentTemperature"/>
    </message>
    <portType name="CurrentTemperaturePortType">
        <operation name="GetCurrentTemperature">
            <input message="tns:GetCurrentTemperatureInput"/>
            <output message="tns:GetCurrentTemperatureOutput"/>
        </operation>
    </portType>
</definitions>
```

A message of type `GetCurrentTemperatureInput` is sent to the operation, and a message of type `GetCurrentTemperatureOutput` is received back. The operation in this case is meant to be abstract and doesn't include any details about how to bind to a specific protocol. In practice, when bound to a specific protocol, the above operation could result in a single request/response pair (bound to HTTP, for example), or two altogether separate messages (bound to SMTP, for example). How the operation maps to a given protocol is defined by **bindings**.

The `operation` element can also have an optional attribute `parameterOrder`, which is used to specify the order of parameters in an RPC-style binding. It is not required, and if present simply provides added data for applications that are binding Web Services to RPC-style code. The `parameterOrder` attribute can help with mapping an operation to an actual function signature.

Bindings

A **binding** defines how a given operation is bound to a specific protocol. Each operation is mapped to a specific protocol using a protocol specific syntax. We'll look at the three bindings defined by the WSDL spec shortly in the *Protocol Bindings* section.

The syntax of a binding is similar to that of a port type, but each operation is mapped to a protocol specific operation. The following shows how a `binding` element contains operations, and where the protocol-specific information fits in:

```
<definitions...>
    <binding name="nmtoken" type="qname">
        <!--binding specific mapping info goes here-->

        <operation name="nmtoken">
            <!--operation specific mapping info goes here-->

            <input name="nmtoken">
                <!--input specific mapping info goes here-->

            </input>
            <output name="nmtoken">
                <!--output specific mapping info goes here-->

            </output>
            <fault name="nmtoken">
                <!--fault specific mapping info goes here-->

            </fault>
        </operation>
    </binding>
</definitions>
```

Since an operation can be bound to more than one protocol, and multiple WSDL ports can use each binding, each binding must specify only one protocol, and cannot specify an address.

The following illustrates a sample binding that maps the `GetCurrentTemperature` operation to the SOAP 1.1 protocol:

```
<definitions>
    <binding name="GetCurrentTemperatureSOAP"
            type="GetCurrentTemperaturePortType">
        <soap:binding style="rpc"
                    transport="http://schemas.xmlsoap.org/soap/http"/>
```

```
        <operation name="GetCurrentTemperature">
          <soap:operation soapAction="http://example.com
                                 /GetCurrentTemperature"/>
          <input name="GetCurrentTemperatureInput">
            <soap:body use="encoded"
                      namespace="http://example.com/currenttemp"
                      encodingStyle="http://schemas.xmlsoap.org
                                 /soap/encoding/"/>
          </input>
          <output name="GetCurrentTemperatureOutput">
            <soap:body use="encoded"
                      namespace="http://example.com/currenttemp"
                      encodingStyle="http://schemas.xmlsoap.org
                                 /soap/encoding/"/>
          </output>
        </operation>
      </binding>
</definitions>
```

In this example, the operation is using the RPC-style (style="rpc") encoding over HTTP (transport="http://schemas.xmlsoap.org/soap/http"), and encoding the message according to SOAP's encoding rules (use="encoded"). For more details see Chapter 3.

Ports and Services

A **port** associates a binding with a protocol-specific address. This represents the actual network endpoint(s) on which the service communicates. A **service** represents a collection of ports as a logical unit. The following shows the relationship of port to service:

```
<definitions...>
   <service name="nmtoken">
      <port name="nmtoken" binding="qname">
         <!--protocol specific address information goes here-->
      </port>
   </service>
</definitions>
```

Each port specifies a binding, which refers to a previously defined binding element, and refers to one and only one address. The way in which the address is specified is protocol-specific. An example of using the SOAP binding would be:

```
<definitions...>
   <service...>
      <port name="CurrentTemperaturePort"
            binding="GetCurrentTemperaturSOAP">
         <soap:address location="http://example.com/currenttemp"/>
      </port>
   </service>
</definitions>
```

A single service can contain multiple ports that all use the same `portType`, but have different bindings and/or addresses. In this case, these ports are alternatives, so that the user of the service can choose which protocol they want to use to communicate with the service (possibly programmatically by reading the namespaces in the bindings), or which address is closest. For example, a single service could contain three ports, all of which use the same port type (for example `GetCurrentTemperaturePortType`) but are bound to SOAP over HTTP, SOAP over SMTP, and HTTP GET/POST respectively. This would give the user of the `CurrentTemperature` service a choice of protocols over which to use the service. A PC-based desktop application might use SOAP over HTTP, while a WAP application designed to run on a cellular phone might use HTTP GET/POST, since an XML parser is typically not available in a WAP application. All three services are semantically equivalent in that they all take a city code and return the current temperature, but by employing different bindings, the service is more readily accessible on a wider range of platforms.

Transmission Primitives

WSDL defines four basic types of operations, called transmission primitives. These "styles" of operations represent the most common usage patterns for Web Services. Since each operation defined by WSDL can have an input and/or an output, the four transmission primitives represent possible combinations of inputs and outputs. The primitives are:

- One-way
- Request/Response
- Solicit/Response
- Notification

While all four kinds of operations are described by the WSDL 1.1 specification, it only includes bindings for One-way and Request/Response operations. The actual bindings for Solicit/Response and Notification operations are essentially left as an exercise for the reader of the spec. Presumably, subsequent versions of the WSDL specification may include formal bindings for these operations, but it is unclear as to how these primitives would map to SOAP or HTTP GET/POST at this time.

One-way Operation

A one-way operation is one in which the service endpoint receives a message, but does not send a response. An example of this might be an operation representing the submission of an order into a purchasing system. Once the order is sent, no immediate response is expected. In an RPC-style context, a one-way operation represents a subroutine, in which no return value is given.

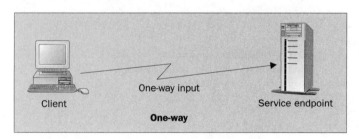

A one-way operation defines an input message, but no output message, and no fault. This means that there is no way to tell if an error has occurred on a one-way message, or to return data. An example of a one-way message might be as follows:

```
<definitions...>
    <portType name="SubmitOrderType">
        <operation name="SubmitOrder">
            <input message="SubmitOrderInput"/>
        </operation>
    </portType>
</definitions>
```

One possible way to deal with the issue of missing error data might be to establish two one way messages to take the place of a request/response pair.

Request/Response Operation

A request/response operation is one in which the endpoint receives a message and returns a message in response. An example of this is the GetCurrentTemperature operation, which receives a message containing a city code and responds with a message containing the current temperature. In an RPC-style context it is equivalent to a function call, which takes a list of parameters and returns a value. As the request/response operation is expected to return a value, and it can also return a fault if there is an error.

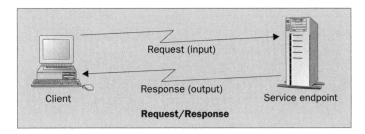

The request/response operation is defined as:

```
<definitions...>
    <portType...>
        <operation name="nmtoken">
            <input name="nmtoken" message="qname"/>
            <output name="nmtoken" message="qname"/>
            <fault name="nmtoken" message="qname"/>
        </operation>
    </portType>
</definitions>
```

To continue the sales order system example, a request/response pair might look like the following, in which the request is for an item description, and the description is the response:

```
<definitions...>
    <portType name="ItemDescriptionType">
        <operation name="GetItemDescription">
            <input message="ItemDescriptionRequest"/>
```

```
            <output message="ItemDescription"/>
        </operation>
    </portType>
</definitions>
```

Solicit/Response Operation

A Solicit/Response operation is one in which the service endpoint sends a message, and receives an answering response. This is the opposite of Request/Response, since the service is initiating the operation (soliciting the client), rather than responding to a request.

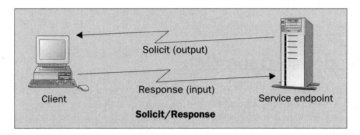

A Solicit/Response operation is defined as:

```
<definitions...>
    <portType...>
        <operation name="nmtoken">
            <output name="nmtoken" message="qname"/>
            <input name="nmtoken" message="qname"/>
            <fault name="nmtoken" message="qname"/>
        </operation>
    </portType>
</definitions>
```

Since none of the protocol bindings defined by WSDL 1.1 define a binding for the Solicit/Response operation, it is an abstract notion of a transport primitive. It would be up to a future binding to determine if this operation is bound to a single HTTP-style request/response, or two completely separate messages. An example might be a service that sends out order status, and receives back a receipt, as in the following example:

```
<definitions...>
    <portType name="OrderStatusType">
        <operation name="SendOrderStatus">
            <output message="OrderStatus"/>
            <input message="OrderStatusReceipt"/>
        </operation>
    </portType>
</definitions>
```

Notification Operation

A Notification Operation is one in which the endpoint sends a message and receives no response. An example would be a model in which events are reported, and where an endpoint periodically reports its status. No response is required in that case, since most likely the status data is logged and not acted upon immediately.

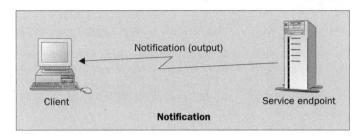

Notification

The format of a notification operation is:

```
<definitions...>
   <portType...>
      <operation name="nmtoken">
         <output name="nmtoken" message="qname"/>
      </operation>
   </portType>
</definitions>
```

The notification operation is also abstract, since no binding is currently defined for it.

Naming of Messages in an Operation

Each input and output message in an operation has a unique name, which identifies it within its port type. However, to avoid the necessity of having to name each message manually (GetCurrentTemperatureInput, GetCurrentTemperatureOutput, etc.), WSDL provides a scheme for assigning default names to these messages. For messages in a one-way or Notification operation, if no name is provided the name of the message is assumed to be the same as the name of the operation. If no name is given for the input and output messages of a Request/Response or Solicit/Response operation, the name is assumed to be the same as the name of the operation, with Request, Solicit, or Response appended as appropriate.

Protocol Bindings

Now that we've seen the basic syntax and construction of a WSDL document, let's take a closer look at the three protocols for which the WSDL 1.1 spec defines bindings:

- ❑ SOAP
- ❑ HTTP GET/POST
- ❑ MIME

SOAP

The SOAP 1.1 binding for WSDL provides ways of indicating that SOAP is the protocol to bind to, which SOAPAction header should be used, additional SOAP headers to include, and what address the message should be sent to (see Chapter 3, *SOAP Basics*, for more details on SOAP encoding). The Specification leaves open the possibility of additional binding elements being added as SOAP and SOAP bindings continue to evolve.

soap:binding

The soap:binding element is used inside the binding element to indicate that the binding is to SOAP, and which transport mechanism and document encoding style should be used:

```
<definitions...>
    <binding...>
        <soap:binding style="rpc | document" transport="uri"/>
        <operation...>
        </operation>
    </binding>
</definitions>
```

The required transport attribute indicates which transport protocol to use for SOAP binding. The only value defined in the Specification is http://schemas.xmlsoap.org/soap/http, which indicates that SOAP will be bound to HTTP. Other URIs can be used to indicate other transport bindings such as SMTP, FTP, etc.

The optional style attribute indicates what style of message the operation represents. A value of rpc indicates that the message uses the RPC style encoding, and the message is meant to represent a method call and a parameter list. A value of document indicates that the message is in document style, meaning that the message represents a single document. If no style is specified, a value of document is assumed.

soap:operation

The soap:operation element is used to indicate how an operation should be bound to the SOAP protocol. This includes specifying a SOAPAction header to use for the SOAP binding, and optionally specifying an encoding style:

```
<definitions...>
    <binding...>
        <operation...>
            <soap:operation soapAction="uri" style="rpc | document"/>
        </operation>
    </binding>
</definitions>
```

The soapAction attribute specifies the SOAPAction HTTP header to use for the SOAP message. If using the HTTP transport, soapAction is required. For other transports, it may not be used, and the soap:operation element can be omitted. The URI used for soapAction should exactly match the contents of the SOAPAction header. Do not use relative URIs, as they will not be converted into absolute addresses. The style attribute is the same as for soap:binding above. It can be used to override the default specified at the binding level.

soap:body

The `soap:body` element defines which parts of the message will be included in the SOAP Body, and how they will be included. This is one area where the binding gets fairly complex, as several elements combine to determine the final outcome.

```
<definitions...>
   <binding...>
      <operation...>
         <input...>
            <soap:body parts="nmtokens" use="encoded | literal"
                       namespace="uri" encodingStyle="uri"/>
         </input>
      </operation>
   </binding>
</definitions>
```

The `parts` attribute is optional, and indicates which parts should be included in the SOAP Body. Not all of the parts of the message need to be included in the body, but if the `parts` attribute is omitted, all the message parts are assumed to be included.

The attributes `use`, `namespace`, and `encodingStyle` combine with the operation `style` to determine how the parts are mapped to the SOAP Body. Each part can represent either an abstract message, in which case it's up to the `encodingStyle` to determine how the part is mapped to the actual SOAP Body, or it can be a concrete message, in which case the schema associated with the part is used as a rule set with which to create the message. If the `use` attribute has the value `literal`, then the parts represent a concrete format. If it has the value `encoded`, then the value of `encodingStyle` is used to determine how to map the abstract message to the SOAP body. Additionally, if the operation `style` is `rpc`, then the message parts are wrapped with an element with the same name as the operation, and each part corresponds to a parameter. If `style` equals `document`, then no additional wrapper is added, and the SOAP Body directly contains the parts. To help clarify this consider the following example WSDL document:

```
<definitions name="CurrentTemp"
             targetNamespace="http://example.com/currenttemp.wsdl"
             xmlns:tns="http://example.com/currenttemp.wsdl"
             xmlns:xsd1="http://example.com/currenttemp.xsd"
             xmlns:soap="http://schemas.xmlsoap.org/wsdl/soap/"
             xmlns="http://schemas.xmlsoap.org/wsdl/">
   <message name="GetCurrentTemperatureInput">
      <part name="cityCode" element="xsd:string"/>
   </message>
   <message name="GetCurrentTemperatureOutput">
      <part name="currentTemp" element="xsd:float"/>
   </message>
   <portType name="CurrentTemperaturePortType">
      <operation name="GetCurrentTemperature">
         <input message="tns:GetCurrentTemperatureInput"/>
         <output message="tns:GetCurrentTemperatureOutput"/>
      </operation>
   </portType>
   <binding name="CurrentTemperatureSoapBinding"
            type="tns:CurrentTemperaturePortType">
      <soap:binding style="document"
```

```
                            transport="http://schemas.xmlsoap.org/soap/http"/>
        <operation name="GetCurrentTemperature">
          <soap:operation soapAction="http://example.com
                                      /GetCurrentTemperature"/>
          <input>
             <soap:body use="literal"/>
          </input>
          <output>
             <soap:body use="literal"/>
          </output>
        </operation>
    </binding>
</definitions>
```

Since the operation `style` is `document`, and the `use` is `literal`, the resulting SOAP message for the input message for the operation `GetCurrentTemperature` (as defined above) would be:

```
POST /CurrentTemperature HTTP/1.1
Host: www.tempserver.com
Content-Type: text/xml; charset="utf-8"
Content-Length: ###
SOAPAction: " http://example.com/GetCurrentTemperature "

<soapenv:Envelope xmlns:soapenv="http://schemas.xmlsoap.org/soap/envelope/">
   <soapenv:Body>
      <cityCode>PDX</cityCode>
   </soapenv:Body>
</soapenv:Envelope>
```

However, if the document `style` is `rpc`:

```
    ...
    <binding name="CurrentTemperatureSoapBinding"
            type="tns:CurrentTemperaturePortType">
       <soap:binding style="rpc"
                     transport="http://schemas.xmlsoap.org/soap/http"/>
       <operation name="GetCurrentTemperature">
          <soap:operation soapAction="http://example.com
                                      /GetCurrentTemperature"/>
          <input>
             <soap:body use="literal"/>
          </input>
          <output>
             <soap:body use="literal"/>
          </output>
       </operation>
    </binding>
    ...
```

then the wrapper (`GetCurrentTemperature`) is added to the SOAP Body as shown below:

```
POST /CurrentTemperature HTTP/1.1
Host: www.tempserver.com
Content-Type: text/xml; charset="utf-8"
Content-Length: ###
SOAPAction: " http://example.com/GetCurrentTemperature "

<soapenv:Envelope xmlns:soapenv="http://schemas.xmlsoap.org/soap/envelope/">
   <soapenv:Body>
      <GetCurrentTemperature>
         <cityCode>PDX</cityCode>
      </GetCurrentTemperature>
   </soapenv:Body>
</soapenv:Envelope>
```

If we now change use to encoded, and set the encodingStyle to the SOAP 1.1 encoding, as below:

```
   ...
   <binding name="CurrentTemperatureSoapBinding"
            type="tns:CurrentTemperaturePortType">
      <soap:binding style="rpc"
                    transport="http://schemas.xmlsoap.org/soap/http"/>
      <operation name="GetCurrentTemperature">
         <soap:operation soapAction="http://example.com
                                     /GetCurrentTemperature"/>
         <input>
            <soap:body use="encoded"
                       encodingStyle="http://schemas.xmlsoap.org
                                      /soap/encoding/"
                       namespace="http://example.com/currenttemp"/>
         </input>
         <output>
            <soap:body use="encoded"
                       encodingStyle="http://schemas.xmlsoap.org
                                      /soap/encoding/"
                       namespace="http://example.com/currenttemp"/>
         </output>
      </operation>
   </binding>
   ...
```

we get the following SOAP request:

```
POST /CurrentTemperature HTTP/1.1
Host: www.tempserver.com
Content-Type: text/xml; charset="utf-8"
Content-Length: ###
SOAPAction: " http://example.com/GetCurrentTemperature "

<soapenv:Envelope xmlns:soapenv="http://schemas.xmlsoap.org/soap/envelope/">
   <soapenv:Body>
      <m:GetCurrentTemperature xmlns:m="http://example.com/currenttemp">
         <m:cityCode>PDX</m:cityCode>
      </m:GetCurrentTemperature>
   </soapenv:Body>
</soapenv:Envelope>
```

In this case, the SOAP encoding style didn't change the underlying schema much, but with a more complex data type the changes might be more noticeable.

soap:fault

The `soap:fault` element binds a message part to the SOAP Fault Details, which is used to convey error information.

```
<definitions...>
   <binding...>
      <operation...>
         <fault...>
            <soap:fault name="nmtoken" use="encoded | literal"
                        namespace="uri" encodingStyle="uri"/>
         </fault>
      </operation>
   </binding>
</definitions>
```

The `name` attribute maps the `soap:fault` element to the correspondingly named `wsdl:fault` element. The other attributes (use, namespace, and encodingStyle) are the same as for `soap:body`. The only difference is that fault messages may only have one part, so the `parts` attribute is omitted, and `style="document"` is assumed, since faults don't have parameters.

soap:header and soap:headerfault

The elements `soap:header` and `soap:headerfault` essentially correspond to `soap:body` and `soap:fault` respectively. There are some small differences in the way in which parts are associated with these header elements. See the WSDL spec for details (http://www.w3.org/TR/wsdl).

SMTP Example

The following example shows a SOAP binding of a one-way operation over SMTP. SMTP lends itself to one-way operations, since the transport protocol itself is essentially one-way and asynchronous. HTTP on the other hand is inherently two way (Request/Response) and synchronous. For one-way messaging, in which no response is required, and synchronicity isn't necessary, SMTP is a good choice. The example service below takes the name of a list and an email address (represented as separate message parts `email_address` and `name_of_list`), and subscribes the given email address to the named mailing list:

```
<definitions name="ListSubscription"
             targetNamespace="http://example.com/sublist.wsdl"
             xmlns:tns="http://example.com/sublist.wsdl"
             xmlns:xsd1="http://example.com/sublist.xsd"
             xmlns:soap="http://schemas.xmlsoap.org/wsdl/soap/"
             xmlns="http://schemas.xmlsoap.org/wsdl/">
```

Below we define a message with two parts representing the parameters:

```
<message name="SubscribeMailingList">
   <part name="email_address" element="xsd:string"/>
   <part name="name_of_list" element="xsd:string"/>
</message>
```

Then we create a `portType` with a single `input`, since this is a one-way operation:

```
<portType name="SubscribePortType">
  <operation name="SendSubscription">
    <input message="tns:SubscribeMailingList"/>
  </operation>
</portType>
```

Now we bind the port-type to SMTP, using both parts of the message as SOAP parameters:

```
<binding name="SubscribeListSoapBinding" type="tns:SubscribePortType">
  <soap:binding style="document" transport="http://example.com/smtp"/>
  <operation name="SendSubscription">
    <input>
      <soap:body use="literal" parts="email_address name_of_list"/>
    </input>
  </operation>
</binding>
```

Lastly, we bind to a specific e-mail address:

```
<service name="MailingListService">
  <port name="MailingListPort" binding="tns:SubscribeListSoapBinding">
    <soap:address location="mailto:subscribe@example.com"/>
  </port>
</service>
</definitions>
```

HTTP GET/POST Binding

The HTTP GET/POST binding defines three different ways of binding a message to a specific HTTP address:

❑   HTTP GET with URL encoding

❑   HTTP GET with URL replacement

❑   HTTP POST

These methods allow a service to be used by a standard HTTP browser, which makes the service accessible to a wide range of clients, from desktop web browsers, to WAP based cellular phones or PDAs. Any platform that supports HTTP can use the service if bound this way.

Take, for example, a service that adds two integers together and returns the result as text. The port-type is defined as:

```
<definitions...>
  <message name="AddInput">
    <part name="op1" element="xsd:int"/>
    <part name="op2" element="xsd:int"/>
  </message>
  <message name="AddOutput">
```

```
          <part name="result" element="xsd:string"/>
       </message>
       <portType name="AddPortType">
          <operation name="Add">
             <input message="AddInput"/>
             <output message="AddOutput"/>
          </operation>
       </portType>
    </definitions>
```

This port type can be bound in three ways. Firstly to HTTP POST as follows:

```
    ...
    <binding name="b3" type="AddPortType">
       <http:binding verb="POST"/>
       <operation name="Add">
          <http:operation location="o1"/>
          <input>
             <mime:content type="application/x-www-form-urlencoded"/>
          </input>
          <output>
             <mime:content type="text/html"/>
          </output>
       </operation>
    </binding>
    ...
```

This will result in a binding to an HTTP POST to the address http://example.com/o1, with the body of the POST being op1=1&op2=2 for example. The server portion of the address (http://example.com/) comes from the port element, as shown in the final code block below.

We can also bind the same message as an HTTP GET, and there are two different ways. With one method, the parts of the message are used as query string parameters on the GET request by using the http:urlEncoded element:

```
    ...
    <binding name="b2" type="AddPortType">
       <http:binding verb="GET"/>
       <operation name="Add">
          <http:operation location="o1"/>
          <input>
             <http:urlEncoded/>
          </input>
          <output>
             <mime:content type="text/html"/>
          </output>
       </operation>
    </binding>
    ...
```

This results in a mapping to a specific HTTP address with the parts of the message appearing as a query string parameter, http://example.com/o1?op1=2&op2=2 for example. Since location is o1 and the two parts of the AddInput message are op1 and op2, the page requested is http://example.com/o1, and the parameters are called op1 and op2.

The other method of binding to an HTTP GET uses replacement characters in the URL, which correspond to the names of message parts, with the `http:urlReplacement` element:

```
...
<binding name="b1" type="AddPortType">
    <http:binding verb="GET"/>
    <operation name="Add">
        <http:operation location="o1/(op1)/(op2)"/>
        <input>
            <http:urlReplacement/>
        </input>
        <output>
            <mime:content type="text/html"/>
        </output>
    </operation>
</binding>
...
```

This would result in a binding to a specific URL with no query string parameters, but with certain characters in the location replaced. The names of message parts in parentheses (in the above code) are replaced with the parameter values, resulting in a call to http://example.com/o1/1/2.

It is possible to use all three encodings (POST and GET with URL encoding, and GET with URL replacement) in the same service, which would give potential clients three different methods of using the service depending upon their preferences and/or abilities as shown below:

```
...
<service name="AddService">
    <port name="p1" binding="tns:b1">
        <http:address location="http://example.com"/>
    </port>
    <port name="p2" binding="tns:b2">
        <http:address location="http://example.com"/>
    </port>
    <port name="p3" binding="tns:b3">
        <http:address location="http://example.com"/>
    </port>
</service>
...
```

MIME Binding

WSDL also allows parts of a message to be bound to implementation data types using MIME types. Explicit bindings are defined for the types: `multipart/related` and `text/xml`. All other MIME types can also be represented using the `mime:content` element. It is also possible to use MIME types in conjunction with SOAP to bind to different parts of the same message.

MIME data bindings can be used inside either the `input` or `output` sections of a `binding` element.

```
...
<binding...>
    <operation...>
        <input>
            <!-- MIME elements here-->
        </input>
```

```
            <output>
                <!-- MIME elements here-->
            </output>
        </operation>
    </binding>
    ...
```

mime:multipartRelated

The `mime:multipartRelated` element can be used to bind different parts of a message to different MIME types. The following example shows SOAP used together with MIME bindings to describe a service that takes a city code as a string and returns a float representing the current temperature, and a document in HTML format describing the weekly forecast.

```
<definitions...>
```

First is the request, which needs a city code:

```
<message name="CurrentTempRequest">
    <part name="cityCode" element="xsd:string"/>
</message>
```

Then the response part, which is split into two parts, the current temperature (as a float), and the weekly forecast (as a string):

```
<message name="CurrentTempResponse">
    <part name="currentTemp" element="xsd:float"/>
    <part name="forecast" element="xsd:string"/>
</message>
<portType name="TempPort">
    <operation name="GetCurrentTemp">
        <input message="tns:CurrentTempRequest"/>
        <output message="tnd:CurrentTempResponse"/>
    </operation>
</portType>
```

The binding is declared as a SOAP message over HTTP:

```
<binding name="CurrentTempSOAP" type="tns:TempPort">
    <soap:binding style="document"
                  transport="http://schemas.xmlsoap.org/soap/http"/>
    <operation name="GetCurrentTemp">
        <input>
            <soap:body use="literal"/>
        </input>
        <output>
```

The value of `literal` (for the use attribute above) means the body of the soap request will be:
`<cityCode>XXX</cityCode>`.

The return value is encoded as a multipart-related mime document, with the first part for the current temperature, and the second part the weekly forecast. Because the first part is set to use="literal", that part of the return value will be a literal XML fragment (<currentTemp>YYY</currentTemp>). The second part is the weekly forecast encoded as HTML.

```
                <mime:multipartRelated>
                   <mime:part>
                      <soap:body parts="currentTemp" use="literal"/>
                   </mime:part>
                   <mime:part>
                      <mime:content part="forecast" type="text/html"/>
                   </mime:part>
                </mime:multipartRelated>
            </output>
        </operation>
    </binding>
</definitions>
```

mime:content

The mime:content element is used to represent an arbitrary MIME type. The part attribute relates the content to a message part, and the type attribute specifies the MIME type to use. Some common types are text/html, image/gif, and application/x-www-form-urlencoded (the type used by HTML forms).

```
<mime:content part="nmtoken" type="string"/>
```

mime:mimeXml

The mime:mimeXml element is used to bind to an implementation message format without the use of SOAP encoding or a SOAP envelope. The mime:mimeXml element specifies a single part (optional if the message has only one part) and will use the element or type defined by the part as the root XML element in the concrete message without any additional encoding.

```
<mime:mimeXML part="nmtoken"/>
```

WSDL Examples

The following examples are meant to be real world examples built both by hand and by using some currently available tools. They should give you a good idea of how WSDL can be used to describe Web Services for use on the Internet today.

It's a fact that most people will probably never write very much WSDL from scratch, but will instead rely on tools to generate WSDL for them. However, even if this is the case, it is important to know how to do it by hand, since most of the tools available right now are not production quality, and take different approaches to WSDL, so it's often necessary to tweak the results they produce. To do this, it is important to understand what the underlying structure of the WSDL should be. If nothing else, we will know how far we can trust the tools if we can verify the output produced ourselves.

Multiple Bindings

The first example is a complete description of the Current Temperature service. It was coded by hand in an XML editor, and shows how a simple set of messages can be bound to multiple transports and encodings. In the example, the same request for a temperature and forecast can be sent as a SOAP request (with a response of either straight XML or multipart encoded), or via HTTP using all three HTTP bindings (POST, GET with URL encoding, and GET with URL replacement).

This shows the real advantages of WSDL. Given a document such as the one following, a client could programmatically determine which binding to use to talk to this service, and the same service is therefore available to a wide range of clients.

```
<?xml version="1.0"?>
```

First we need to declare all the right namespaces:

```
<definitions name="CurrentTemp"
             targetNamespace="http://example.com/currenttemp.wsdl"
             xmlns:tns="http://example.com/currenttemp.wsdl"
             xmlns:xsd1="http://example.com/currenttemp.xsd"
             xmlns:soap="http://schemas.xmlsoap.org/wsdl/soap/"
             xmlns="http://schemas.xmlsoap.org/wsdl/"
             xmlns:mime="http://schemas.xmlsoap.org/wsdl/mime/"
             xmlns:http="http://schemas.xmlsoap.org/wsdl/http/">
```

Next, we define the type of the request, a string called `cityCode`. This example uses an XSD schema to define the request type:

```
<types>
   <schema targetNamespace="http://example.com/currenttemp.xsd"
           xmlns="http://www.w3.org/2000/10/XMLSchema">
      <element name="CurrentTemperatureRequest">
         <complexType>
            <all>
               <element name="cityCode" type="string"/>
            </all>
         </complexType>
      </element>
      <element name="temp" type="float"/>
      <element name="forecast" type="string"/>
   </schema>
</types>
```

Next, two messages are defined. First, the input message, which has one part (body) of type `CurrentTemperatureRequest`:

```
<message name="GetCurrentTemperatureInput">
   <part name="body" element="xsd1:CurrentTemperatureRequest"/>
</message>
```

Second, the output message, which has two parts (`Temperature` and `Forecast`) each with the appropriate element type referenced from the schema above.

```
<message name="GetCurrentTemperatureOutput">
   <part name="Temperature" element="xsd1:temp"/>
   <part name="Forecast" element="xsd1:forecast"/>
</message>
```

One port type is defined, which takes a `cityCode`, and returns a temperature and forecast:

```
<portType name="CurrentTemperaturePortType">
   <operation name="GetCurrentTemperature">
      <input message="tns:GetCurrentTemperatureInput"/>
      <output message="tns:GetCurrentTemperatureOutput"/>
   </operation>
</portType>
```

Next, five bindings are defined. The first uses SOAP encoding over HTTP. The input message uses literal encoding, which means that the SOAP body will contain a literal `cityCode` element, without being wrapped in the method name (`GetCurrentTemperatureInput`). The return value is also using literal encoding, which means that the SOAP body will contain two elements, `temp` and `forecast`:

```
<binding name="CurrentTemperatureSoapBinding"
       type="tns:CurrentTemperaturePortType">
   <documentation>a binding to SOAP over HTTP</documentation>
   <soap:binding style="document"
               transport="http://schemas.xmlsoap.org/soap/http"/>
   <operation name="GetCurrentTemperature">
      <soap:operation soapAction="http://example.com
                                 /GetCurrentTemperature"/>
      <input>
         <soap:body use="literal"/>
      </input>
      <output>
         <soap:body use="literal"/>
      </output>
   </operation>
</binding>
```

The second binding also uses SOAP, but with a different encoding of the return value. The input is the same literally encoded `cityCode` as above, but the return value is encoded as a MIME multipart-encoded document, with the temperature as an XML element (`temp`), and the forecast as an HTML document:

```
<binding name="CurrentTemperatureMIMEBinding"
       type="tns:CurrentTemperaturePortType">
   <documentation>
      a binding to SOAP over HTTP using MIME types
   </documentation>
   <soap:binding style="document"
               transport="http://schemas.xmlsoap.org/soap/http"/>
   <operation name="GetCurrentTemperature">
      <soap:operation soapAction="http://example.com
                                 /GetCurrentTemperature"/>
      <input>
         <soap:body use="literal"/>
      </input>
```

```
              <output>
                  <mime:multipartRelated>
                      <mime:part>
                          <soap:body parts="temp" use="literal"/>
                      </mime:part>
                      <mime:part>
                          <mime:content part="forecast" type="text/html"/>
                      </mime:part>
                  </mime:multipartRelated>
              </output>
          </operation>
      </binding>
```

The third binding uses an HTTP GET binding with URL replacement. Since the location is specified as `tempForecast/(cityCode)`, the part in parentheses must be replaced with the `cityCode` value. Therefore, the final URL for a `cityCode` of PDX would be http://example.com/tempForecast/PDX. The return value is a single HTML document, since this method is intended for use by HTML browsers:

```
      <binding name="CurrentTemperatureUrlReplacementBinding"
              type="tns:CurrentTemperaturePortType">
          <documentation>
              an HTTP GET binding using urlReplacement
          </documentation>
          <http:binding verb="GET"/>
          <operation name="GetCurrentTemperature">
              <http:operation location="tempForecast/(cityCode)"/>
              <input>
                  <http:urlReplacement/>
              </input>
              <output>
                  <mime:content type="text/html"/>
              </output>
          </operation>
      </binding>
```

The fourth binding is the same as the third, but with URL encoding. This means that the same request for PDX will result in a URL of `http://example.com/tempForecast?cityCode=PDX`, since each part of the message is encoded as query string parameter:

```
      <binding name="CurrentTemperatureUrlEncodingBinding"
              type="tns:CurrentTemperaturePortType">
          <documentation>an HTTP GET binding using urlEncoded</documentation>
          <http:binding verb="GET"/>
          <operation name="GetCurrentTemperature">
              <http:operation location="tempForecast"/>
              <input>
                  <http:urlEncoded/>
              </input>
              <output>
                  <mime:content type="text/html"/>
              </output>
          </operation>
      </binding>
```

The fifth, and last, binding is an HTPP POST, so the request will be encoded according to HTML form posting rules, in the body of the HTTP POST as `cityCode=PDX`:

```
<binding name="CurrentTemperaturePOSTBinding"
        type="tns:CurrentTemperaturePortType">
  <documentation>an HTTP POST binding</documentation>
  <http:binding verb="POST"/>
  <operation name="GetCurrentTemperature">
    <http:operation location="tempForecast"/>
    <input>
      <mime:content type="application/x-www-form-urlencoded"/>
    </input>
    <output>
      <mime:content type="text/html"/>
    </output>
  </operation>
</binding>
```

Finally, the service is defined, with each binding bound to a different port of the same service. Since they are all part of the same service, WSDL interprets them to be alternatives. An application can pick any of these protocols to get the same results:

```
<service name="CurrentTemperatureService">
  <port name="CurrentTemperaturePort"
        binding="tns:CurrentTemperatureSoapBinding">
    <soap:address location="http://example.com/currenttemp"/>
  </port>
  <port name="CurrentTemperatureMIMEPort"
        binding="tns:CurrentTemperatureMIMEBinding">
    <soap:address location="http://example.com/mime/currenttemp"/>
  </port>
  <port name="p3" binding="tns:CurrentTemperatureUrlReplacementBinding">
    <http:address location="http://example.com"/>
  </port>
  <port name="p4" binding="tns:CurrentTemperatureUrlEncodingBinding">
    <http:address location="http://example.com"/>
  </port>
  <port name="p5" binding="tns:CurrentTemperaturePOSTBinding">
    <http:address location="http://example.com"/>
  </port>
</service>
</definitions>
```

Microsoft SOAP Toolkit

Now let's take a brief look at Microsoft's SOAP implementation, and how it can be used to generate WSDL.

Microsoft's latest version of the SOAP Toolkit for Visual Studio (v2.0) uses WSDL to describe Web Services. The wizards provided by the SOAP toolkit not only make it easy to create a WSDL document describing a COM object, but also provide the necessary infrastructure to expose a COM object as a fully-fledged web service using HTTP and SOAP. The following example was created using the Microsoft SOAP Toolkit for Visual Studio v2.0 (available from http://msdn.microsoft.com/xml). It is based on a COM object created in Visual Basic, which looks like this in UML:

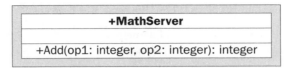

+MathServer
+Add(op1: integer, op2: integer): integer

This COM object supports just one method called `Add()`, which takes two integers (`op1` and `op2`) and returns an integer as the result. The SOAP Toolkit 2.0 provides a simple wizard-style tool called `wsdlgen.exe`, which can be used to create a WSDL document representing a specific COM object.

The initial screen of the wizard asks for a name for the service, and the location of the `.dll` containing the COM object(s) to expose. The name of the service will be used for the filenames of the generated files.

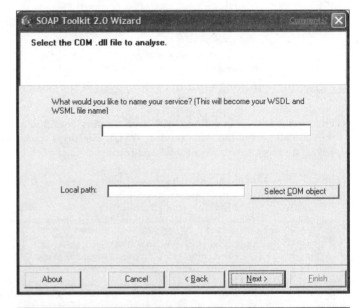

The next screen allows us to specify which methods of which objects/interfaces we want to expose as part of our web service. Here, only one of the three available methods, `Add()`, has been selected:

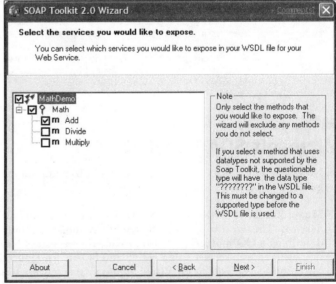

Next, we are asked for a URL for the new service. This will be used in the `port` element to describe the target URL for the service. We are also given the choice of listener, and the desired XSD namespace. There are two listeners, Active Server Pages, (ASP) and Internet Server Application Programming Interface (ISAPI). The ASP listener creates a new ASP with code to parse incoming SOAP requests and instantiate the target COM object. The ISAPI listener associates an ISAPI extension with the WSDL file on the server, and processes incoming requests within the extension's compiled code. The advantage to the ASP listener is that if we don't like the default behavior we can change the ASP code. The ISAPI extension has better performance, but we can't change the default behavior without recompiling the C++ code for the extension (which is provided). The last choice is which XSD namespace to use. 2001 is correct for the Final Recommendation, but some older tools may not support the use of that namespace.

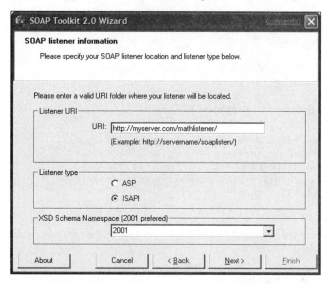

Finally, we're asked which character set the generated WSDL file should use (UTF-8 or UTF-16), and where the new files should be created:

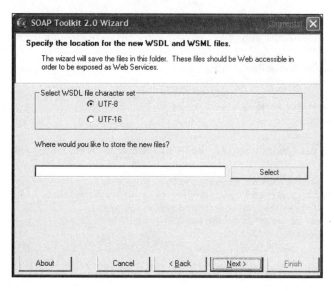

When the wizard is finished, the following WSDL is created:

```
<?xml version="1.0"?>
<!--
   Generated 07/17/01 by Microsoft SOAP Toolkit WSDL File Generator,
   Version 1.02.813.0
-->
<definitions name="MathServer"
             targetNamespace="http://tempuri.org/wsdl/"
             xmlns:wsdlns="http://tempuri.org/wsdl/"
             xmlns:typens="http://tempuri.org/type"
             xmlns:soap="http://schemas.xmlsoap.org/wsdl/soap/"
             xmlns:xsd="http://www.w3.org/2001/XMLSchema"
             xmlns:stk="http://schemas.microsoft.com
                         /soap-toolkit/wsdl-extension"
             xmlns="http://schemas.xmlsoap.org/wsdl/">
   <types>
```

First the schemas are defined in an external XSD file:

```
      <schema targetNamespace="http://tempuri.org/type"
              xmlns="http://www.w3.org/2001/XMLSchema"
              xmlns:SOAP-ENC="http://schemas.xmlsoap.org/soap/encoding/"
              xmlns:wsdl="http://schemas.xmlsoap.org/wsdl/"
              elementFormDefault="qualified"/>
   </types>
```

Next is the message element, named `MathServer.Add`, with the two parameters `op1` and `op2` defined as `shorts`:

```
   <message name="MathServer.Add">
      <part name="op1" type="xsd:short"/>
      <part name="op2" type="xsd:short"/>
   </message>
```

The response also contains `op1` and `op2`, indicating that they are in/out parameters.

```
   <message name="MathServer.AddResponse">
      <part name="Result" type="xsd:short"/>
      <part name="op1" type="xsd:short"/>
      <part name="op2" type="xsd:short"/>
   </message>
```

`parameterOrder` is used to indicate that the two parameters should be passed in the order op1, op2:

```
   <portType name="MathServerSoapPort">
      <operation name="Add" parameterOrder="op1 op2">
         <input message="wsdlns:MathServer.Add"/>
         <output message="wsdlns:MathServer.AddResponse"/>
      </operation>
   </portType>
```

The operations are bound using `use="encoded"`, so the message parts will be wrapped by a tag named after the operation inside the SOAP body element.

```
<binding name="MathServerSoapBinding"
        type="wsdlns:MathServerSoapPort">
   <stk:binding preferredEncoding="UTF-8"/>
   <soap:binding style="rpc"
                 transport="http://schemas.xmlsoap.org/soap/http"/>
   <operation name="Add">
      <soap:operation soapAction="http://tempuri.org/action
                                  /MathServer.Add"/>
      <input>
         <soap:body use="encoded"
                    namespace="http://tempuri.org/message/"
                    encodingStyle="http://schemas.xmlsoap.org
                                   /soap/encoding/"/>
      </input>
      <output>
         <soap:body use="encoded"
                    namespace="http://tempuri.org/message/"
                    encodingStyle="http://schemas.xmlsoap.org
                                   /soap/encoding/"/>
      </output>
   </operation>
</binding>
```

Lastly, the port is bound to a specific `.asp` file:

```
<service name="MathServer">
   <port name="MathServerSoapPort"
        binding="wsdlns:MathServerSoapBinding">
      <soap:address location="http://myservice.com/soap
                              /MathServer.WSDL"/>
   </port>
</service>
</definitions>
```

The SOAP toolkit also creates the code necessary to expose a COM object as a web service. That code uses the above WSDL document to configure itself. Another file is generated with a WSML extension. The WSML file is used by the SOAP toolkit infrastructure to map an incoming SOAP request to a specific COM object. Either an ASP or an ISAPI extension can be used to listen for SOAP requests, instantiate the object, and process the request. The server side code uses the WSML file to map to the right COM object, and the client side proxy that comes with the SOAP toolkit uses the WSDL file to make the right SOAP calls to the server. The SOAP toolkit provides a quick and easy way to expose our existing COM objects as Web Services, and uses WSDL to provide a platform independent description of those services.

For a much more in-depth look at the Microsoft SOAP Toolkit, see Chapter 8.

IBM Web Services Toolkit

The next example was created using IBM's Web Services Toolkit v2.3 (available from http://www.alphaworks.ibm.com). The Web Services Toolkit contains a utility (wsdlgen) that reads a Java class, EJB jar file, or a COM object and creates a WSDL document which describes the Web Service based on that class or EJB.

For the following example, we'll use a very simple Java class that looks like this:

```
public class MathServer {

public MathServer() {
    super();
}
public int Add(int op1, int op2) {
    return 0;

}
}
```

When we start the wizard using wsdlgen.bat, we get the following choice:

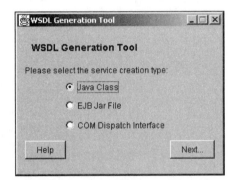

We can generate a service from an existing Java .class file, an EJB .jar file, or a COM .dll that supports IDispatch. If we choose Java Class, the next screen looks like this:

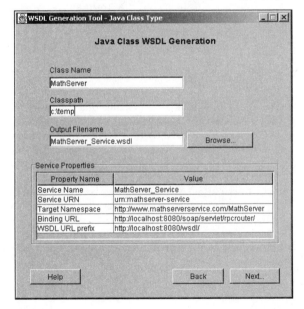

Once the **Class Name** and **Classpath** are entered, the wizard generates all the correct names and paths to the new service. By default, the Web Services Toolkit installs its own HTTP server on port 8080, so all the references use that port by default. Next, we specify which methods on the class we want to expose as part of the new web service.

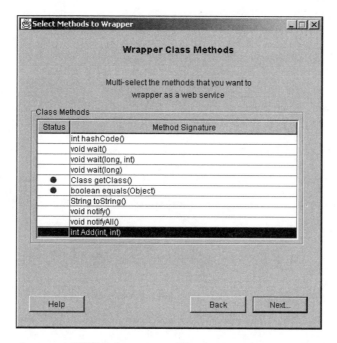

Running the tool results in two WSDL documents. The first, `MathServer_Service-interface.wsdl`, contains the definitions of types, messages, port-types, and bindings:

```
<?xml version="1.0" encoding="UTF-8"?>
<definitions name="MathServer_Service"
             targetNamespace="http://www.mathserverservice.com/MathServer-
                              interface"
             xmlns="http://schemas.xmlsoap.org/wsdl/"
             xmlns:soap="http://schemas.xmlsoap.org/wsdl/soap/"
             xmlns:tns="http://www.mathserverservice.com/MathServer"
             xmlns:xsd="http://www.w3.org/1999/XMLSchema">
```

The tool creates two messages called `InAddRequest`, and `OutAddResponse`. In this case the two parameters are defined as `xsd:int`, as is the return value in `OutAddResponse`:

```
<message name="InAddRequest">
   <part name="meth1_inType1" type="xsd:int"/>
   <part name="meth1_inType2" type="xsd:int"/>
</message>
<message name="OutAddResponse">
   <part name="meth1_outType" type="xsd:int"/>
</message>
```

The port-type is fairly straightforward. Notice that unlike with the Microsoft tool, `parameterOrder` is not used:

```
<portType name="MathServer_Service">
   <operation name="Add">
      <input message="InAddRequest"/>
      <output message="OutAddResponse"/>
   </operation>
</portType>
```

While Microsoft's tool used `document` style binding, the IBM tool uses `rpc` instead. Other than that, the bindings look pretty much the same, although IBM's tool uses a URN for the namespace rather than a URL, which potentially makes more sense.

```
<binding name="MathServer_ServiceBinding" type="MathServer_Service">
   <soap:binding style="rpc"
                 transport="http://schemas.xmlsoap.org /soap/http"/>
   <operation name="Add">
      <soap:operation soapAction="urn:mathserver-service"/>
      <input>
         <soap:body encodingStyle="http://schemas.xmlsoap.org
                                    /soap/encoding/"
                    namespace="urn:mathserver-service" use="encoded"/>
      </input>
      <output>
         <soap:body encodingStyle="http://schemas.xmlsoap.org
                                    /soap/encoding/"
                    namespace="urn:mathserver-service" use="encoded"/>
      </output>
   </operation>
</binding>
</definitions>
```

The second file, `MathServer_Service.wsdl`, contains the actual service definitions:

```
<?xml version="1.0" encoding="UTF-8"?>
<definitions name="MathServer_Service"
             targetNamespace="http://www.mathserverservice.com/MathServer"
             xmlns="http://schemas.xmlsoap.org/wsdl/"
             xmlns:soap="http://schemas.xmlsoap.org/wsdl/soap/"
             xmlns:tns="http://www.mathserverservice.com/MathServer"
             xmlns:xsd="http://www.w3.org/1999/XMLSchema">
```

The definitions we just saw are imported here from an absolute URL rather than a relative reference:

```
<import location="http://localhost:8080/wsdl
                  /MathServer_Service-interface.wsdl"
        namespace="http://www.mathserverservice.com
                   /MathServer-interface"/>
```

Finally, the service is defined with one port bound to the file `rpcrouter`, which is the Java servlet that the Web Services Toolkit uses, to map the incoming SOAP request to the correct Java class, and to instantiate that class to execute the right method:

```
      <service name="MathServer_Service">
         <documentation>
            IBM WSTK 2.0 generated service definition file
         </documentation>
         <port binding="MathServer_ServiceBinding"
               name="MathServer_ServicePort">
            <soap:address location="http://localhost:8080/soap/servlet
                                    /rpcrouter"/>
         </port>
      </service>
   </definitions>
```

The Web Services Toolkit also contains all the tools and infrastructure needed to expose a Java class as a Web Service using one of several web servers (see Chapter 10 for more in-depth practical applications of the Web Services Toolkit). Just as the Microsoft toolkit creates a WSML file to map the web service's requests to COM objects, the IBM toolkit's `wsdlgen` creates a file called `DeploymentDescriptor.xml`, which contains information about the Java class to be instantiated for the incoming request. That file is then installed in the correct directory (which differs depending on which web server we use) to make sure that the appropriate class handles incoming requests.

Summary

WSDL provides a much-needed part of the Web Services picture. If we are to see the proliferation of Web Services on the Internet, it will take the common definition language provided by WSDL to see that dream become reality. There must be a common way of describing Web Services, how they are bound to transport protocols, and the types that they use. As more and more XML standards are finalized, it becomes easier to build upon them to create new standards. WSDL builds heavily upon existing standards like XSD, SOAP, and MIME.

At least two of the major players in the push toward Web Services, IBM and Microsoft, have adopted WSDL and hopefully others will follow their lead in the near future. WSDL fills the gap between SOAP for message encoding, and UDDI for service discovery by providing the ability to programmatically bind to a web service. A WSDL document can be stored directly in the UDDI registry, which makes it even easier to use Web Services programmatically.

5

SOAP Bindings

Up to this point, you have read about SOAP (Simple Object Access Protocol). This chapter is all about passing SOAP messages from one point to another. SOAP can be transmitted in a variety of ways, including HTTP and SMTP (which we were introduced to in Chapter 2), and FTP. This is a good thing as there has been a debate raging as long as distributed systems have been built whether to use message passing or the request/response paradigm. Message passing applications are typically connectionless since they contain session-like information in each message. Request/response type applications are generally in lock step with each other, providing synchronous behavior, and in general are easier to use. The designers of SOAP realized that each method of transmission is appropriate under different circumstances. This is one of the reasons that SOAP does not specify the transport protocol, but can be bound to a variety of transportation mechanisms, some being request/response, some being message-based. Another reason for not specifying the underlying protocol for SOAP is that the designers wanted to leverage exiting protocols as much as possible. For example, since SOAP can be a payload for HTTP, benefits from the fact that nearly every operating system has a web server, and security is well defined, as well as caching schemes. On the other hand, let us assume that a proprietary system is using it's own protocol, but wishes to leverage the fact that SOAP is on a standards track which makes it easier to specify. This also is accomplished by not specifying the transport mechanism for SOAP.

This chapter examines a variety of ways to transmit SOAP, including HTTP and SMTP. The reason for choosing these two transports is that each illustrates a different paradigm for building distributed systems. HTTP provides an example of a protocol that is in widespread use that uses the request/response paradigm. SMTP, on the other hand, provides a widespread example of the message passing paradigm.

This chapter will provide two detours from SOAP. The first detour describes MIME and its use in HTTP and SMTP. The second detour provides a background into the difference between a URI, URL and a URN. The purpose for these detours is to provide a solid framework to describe HTTP, SMTP and finally how SOAP is bound to these two transport protocols.

At the end of this chapter, you will be able to:

❏ Explain why SOAP does not specify a transport mechanism (For those of you who just like reading bullets, you already missed this one. Go back and read the first paragraph;-)

❏ Understand what MIME is and why it is used in HTTP and SMTP.

❏ Differentiate between a URI, URL, and URN and understand their importance in HTTP and SOAP.

❏ Describe pros and cons for choosing HTTP (including the extension mechanism) as a SOAP transport mechanism.

❏ Describe pros and cons for choosing SMTP as a SOAP transport mechanism.

❏ Have code that provides a sample implementation of SOAP over HTTP.

❏ Have code that provides a sample implementation of SOAP over SMTP.

Since the SOAP protocol does not specify any transport mechanism, any transport may be used. Since this would take a very long time, this chapter will not describe all possible transports for SOAP.

Detours into Background Information

In this section we will take three brief detours to describe DNS, MIME, and URIs, URLs and URNs. This is background material only, and if you are already comfortable with these concepts, lick you finger and turn the page!

DNS

DNS is short for Domain Name System. The Domain Name Systems or DNS is a distributed database that allows TCP/IP applications to translate a symbolic name or hostname into an IP address. DNS is an essential tool for any application or protocol that uses TCP/IP. Since no single site maintains an entire directory of all mappings, this provides the distributed nature of DNS. Each site maintains its own DNS information and queries other DNS servers on the Internet for mappings that are not local. An interesting note is that if the DNS servers for a particular site are compromised, all TCP/IP access to that site is essentially halted. For this reason, it is imperative that you design your DNS servers to be resilient from outside hackers. DNS is a subject that can fill a book by itself, so we only provide a brief introduction here. For those of you with more interest check out RFC 1034 and RFC 1035 (http://andrew2.andrew.cmu.edu/rfc/rfc1034.html and http://rfc.fh-koeln.de/rfc/html/rfc1035. html, respectively).

So, given that DNS is a distributed database, how is it managed? DNS is organized into a namespace that is hierarchical. A non-profit agency known as ICANN or Internet Corporation for Assigned Name and Numbers is responsible for the top level of the tree for DNS. Originally, there were seven top-level domains. Recently, ICANN has approved an additional seven top-level domains bringing the total to 14 (seen below in the following table). In addition to these 14 top-level domains, ISO 3166 defines a 243 country domains (see http://stiwww.epfl.ch/utile/iso_3166.html for a list of these, and go to http://www.iso.ch to order a hardcopy of this standard, and the others maintained by ISO).

Top Level Domain	Description
Com	Commercial Organization
Edu	US Universities
Gov	US Government
Int	International
Mil	US Military
Net	Networks
Org	Non-commercial organizations
Aero	Air-transport industry
Biz	Business
Coop	Cooperatives
Info	Unrestricted
Museum	Museums
Name	Individuals
Pro	Accountants, lawyers, and physicians

The diagram below shows a small portion of the DNS namespace. The top circle represents a special node in the tree designated with a null label. Every other circle in the tree has a label. This label has a maximum length of 63 characters. The domain name of a circle in the namespace is obtained by concatenating the label of each circle as you work your way to the root of the tree. The separator between the labels is the "." symbol. So for example, the circle with the label sub2 has a domain name of sub2.sub1.com. If the domain name ends with a ".", the domain name is known as a fully qualified domain name or FQDN. If, however, the domain name does not end with a ".", how the domain name is completed is implementation specific.

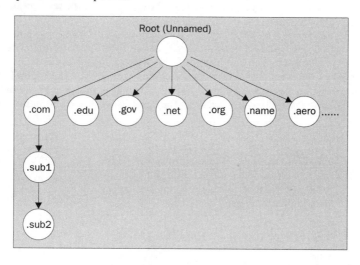

Now that we know how the namespace is organized, let us examine how DNS is managed in a distributed manner. Each subtree in the DNS namespace may be considered a zone if it is administered separately. For example, .sub1 may be administered in New York, NY, but .sub2 may be administered in Denver, CO. Once the zones are set up, the administrators are responsible for setting up one or more name servers for the zone under their control. An interesting point to note about name servers is that they may contain mappings for one or more zones. This provides the ability to have primary and secondary name servers. Generally, the only difference between a primary and secondary name server is that the administrator is responsible for the primary name server while the secondary name server is automatically populated at regular intervals from the primary name server. This population of the secondary name server is known as **zone transfer**.

The process of actually transforming a symbolic name or domain name into an IP address that can be used is conceptually simple. We start at the root and query the next lower layer of the tree until we find the appropriate label. This process continues until we have fully resolved the name to an IP address. In practice, this would take an unacceptable amount of time, so caching DNS entries is a vital part of any DNS implementation.

So, in a quick recap, DNS provides a mechanism for transforming a symbolic name or domain name into an IP address that can be used for TCP/IP connections. DNS is used heavily for a variety of widely deployed protocols on the Internet, including HTTP, FTP, and SMTP.

MIME

MIME stands for Multipurpose Internet Mail Extensions. The MIME standard specifies formatting of messages so that a variety of different data formats can be sent together. By creating a standard that identifies where specific pieces of data reside in a data stream, different readers can be attached to different parts of the same stream. For example, a single e-mail message may contain a video image, a sound image, and text. Using MIME to delineate the different pieces of the message, the e-mail reader can provide the user with a far better experience for reading e-mail by either automatically spawning the applications to read the appropriate streams or allowing the user the option of doing it himself. Another example is a web browser that receives a data stream from a web server over HTTP. The web browser must decide if the data is to be interpreted as HTML, Postscript, a video image, or an audio image. To make the decision the web browser reads the `Content-Type` header of the HTTP request and interprets it as a mime type. As you can see, even though MIME started out just for mail, it has a variety of uses beyond just e-mail.

The central body that manages MIME types is IANA, or the Internet Assignment Name Authority, formed in 1988 with Jon Postel as its head (see http://www.iana.org for more information). This agency provides a central authority to manage MIME types so that there is one definition for them. The format of a MIME type provides for five top level media types. They are: text, image, audio, video and application. The following table provides a brief description as well as examples of each type:

Mime Type	Description	Example
Text	Textual information. Assuming the subtype is plain, no special software is required to get the full meaning of the text, aside from support for the indicated character set.	`text/plain` `text/xml`

Mime Type	Description	Example

Image	Image data. Requires a display device (such as a graphical display, a graphics printer, or a FAX machine) to view the information.	`image/jpeg`
		`image/gif`
		`image/tiff`

Audio	Audio data. "Audio" requires an audio output device (such as a speaker or a telephone) to "display" the contents.	`audio/tone` `audio/basic`
Video	Video data. "Video" requires the capability to display moving images, typically including specialized hardware and software.	`video/mpeg` `video/quicktime`
Application	Other kind of data, typically either uninterpreted binary data or information to be processed by an application.	`application/postscript` `application/pdf`

In addition to these five top level media types, there are two composite types: **multipart** and **message**. Multipart indicates to the reader of the MIME message to expect multiple MIME parts in the same stream seperated by a boundary line. Message is used in mail to forward an e-mail message as an attachment.

Even though MIME was originally defined for e-mail messages, it has been widely used for the Internet in HTTP. The use of MIME types allow the web browser to automatically play a video clip or audio clip or to send XML to the parser properly. The way this is done in a web browser is that there is a mapping between MIME types and readers of that particular data. For example, if a MIME type of `video/mpeg` is detected, a video player may be invoked to process the incoming data stream. In the same manner, a web browser may be configured to send MIME data streams of the type `text/xml` to an XML parser.

For more information on MIME, go to http://www.faqs.org/rfcs/, and search for RFC numbers 2045 to 2049.

URIs, URNs and URLs, Oh, My!

A Uniform Resource Identifer (URI) provides a simple and extensible means for identifying a resource. In other words, it is a specification of how to name a resource. For a wealth of in-depth information on URIs, look at RFC 2396 (http://andrew2.andrew.cmu.edu/rfc/rfc2396.html), which formally defines a URI. You may specify a URI in two ways:

❑   location dependent – Specifies an exact resource and a path to get to it. For example:
    `http://www.wrox.com/`.

❑   location independent – Requires interpretation to find the exact resource.

For example, if you choose to specify a URI as location dependent, you have chosen to specify a URL (Uniform Resource Locator). The location independent version is called a URN or Uniform Resource Name. The interesting thing about URNs is that there is no specified way to resolve a URN to a specific address. With the widespread use of web browsers, URLs are understood by most people. URNs, however, are not used by web browsers, but by software in conjunction with a resolution mechanism that finds a URL given a URN.

An example of a URL that is familiar is the one used to specify a resource using HTTP. The syntax is as follows:

```
http:// <host> [":" <port>]  [<absolute path> [ "?" <query>]]
```

<host> may be the IP address of the server, or a symbolic name that can be translated to an IP address using DNS. The <port> field is optional, and if not specified, defaults to 80 because the HTTP protocol is registered to use this port by default with IANA. The <absolute path> field specifies the contents of the Request-URI field in the HTTP request. Finally, the optional <query> field represents a set of key-value pairs that are delimited using &. The only required portion of this syntax is the <host> field. Sample URL's include: http://www.wrox.com:80, http://www.trcs.com/family, or http://search.yahoo.com/bin/search?p=xml.

A URN has the following syntax:

```
urn: <NID> : <NSS>
```

<NID> represents the Namespace Identifier while <NSS> represents a Namespace Specific String. As stated earlier, translating a URN into a location specific identifier is implementation specific. An example of a URN is:

```
urn:ISBN:1861005091
```

The NID in this example is ISBN while the NSS may be the specific ISBN number for a book (in the actual example shown, it's the ISBN for this one).

HTTP

Hypertext Transfer Protocol, also known as HTTP defines how web servers and web browsers communicate, although more and more standalone programs are using HTTP for purposes other than just web browsing. HTTP is a stateless request/response oriented protocol. HTTP is defined in RFC 2068 (http://www.cis.ohio-state.edu/cgi-bin/rfc/rfc2068.html), and we will review the basics of HTTP here (some of which we have already met in Chapter 2) to get a good understanding of the protocol before describing how SOAP maps onto HTTP.

An interesting point about HTTP versus most other protocols is that all control information is in plain text. This makes it much easier to debug and to view the data that is being put on the wire. So, let us take a look at an example HTTP request. The example is a POST request in HTTP – one way of sending SOAP requests is to use HTTP POST requests.

```
POST /http_post_example HTTP/1.1
HOST: www.wrox.com
Content-Type: text/plain
Content-Length: 15

String to count
```

The first line of the HTTP request defines the action that is being requested. In addition to the action, the first line signifies the Request-URI and the HTTP version. There are a total of eight actions that are defined for use in HTTP. They are:

- ❑ **OPTIONS** – This method allows the client to determine the options and/or requirements associated with a resource or with the capabilities of a server, without initiating a resource retrieval

- ❑ **GET** – Retrieves whatever information is identified by the Request-URI

- ❑ **HEAD** – Identical to GET, except that the server does not return a message body in the response

- ❑ **POST** – Request an action on the server based on parameters passed in

- ❑ **PUT** – Request storage of the data at the Request-URI

- ❑ **DELETE** – Requests deletion of resource at the Request-URI

- ❑ **TRACE** – Used for debugging

- ❑ **CONNECT** – Open a connection

By far the most used of these methods are GET and POST. The GET method provides a way for a web browser to retrieve information from a web server and the POST method provides a way to send arbitrary data to the web server. The GET method is most commonly used for retrieving HTML pages for display, while the POST method is most commonly used for sending form information to the server for processing. A common use for the POST method is to process forms on web pages. It is also used as a tunnel for other protocols, such as the Internet Printing Protocol (IPP) and SOAP, to use HTTP. The second item in the first line, the Request-URI, specifies to the web server the URI to process. In this case, the Request-URI is /http_post_example. Finally, the third item on the first line is the HTTP version number. In this case, we are using HTTP version 1.1. The other two options for HTTP version numbers are 1.0 and 0.9.

HTTP has been in use since 1990, and at that time the version of HTTP was 0.9. Version 1.0 of HTTP added MIME-like improvements, and finally, version 1.1 added support for hierarchical proxies, caching, persistent connections, and virtual hosts.

The second line of the HTTP request specifies the host to contact. The host may be a specific IP address or a name that can be translated to an IP address using DNS. The third line specifies the format of the payload as a MIME type – in this case, the payload is identified as being in plain text format. The fourth line specifies the length of the payload. In this case we have 15 characters being sent in the payload. Finally, a blank line follows which signifies the end of the HTTP header information and the beginning of the HTTP payload information.

The headers discussed here are a small subset of what is possible in HTTP. We have restricted our discussion to these headers in HTTP since these are the ones that will be primarily used in passing SOAP.

Once these headers have been sent, it is expected that the HTTP server will respond with a HTTP response. A sample response to the above request is as follows:

```
200 OK
Content-Type: text/plain
Content-Length: 2

15
```

In the HTTP response the first line specifies the HTTP status. The options for the status are organized into five categories, with three digits representing the status information. The first digit represents the type of response, while the remaining two digits represent the actual status code being sent back. In this summary the characters "xx" represent the remaining two digits. They are:

- 1xx: Informational – Request received, continuing process

- 2xx: Success – The action was successfully received, understood, and accepted

- 3xx: Redirection – Further action must be taken in order to complete the request

- 4xx: Client Error – The request contains bad syntax or cannot be fulfilled

- 5xx: Server Error – The server failed to fulfill an apparently valid request

The return codes in the 3xx category are interesting as they indicate that the URI requested in the HTTP request has been moved. As an example, if a URI at http://www.wrox.com/http_post_example had been moved, the web server may return the following:

```
301 Moved Permanently
Location: http://www.wrox.com/new_http_post_example
Content-Length: 0
```

HTTP Example

To implement the HTTP request example we use a Java class to create and send a POST request. The class, PostExample, contains only one method, main(), which is invoked on executing the PostExample class. The PostExample class will open a connection to a URL, format a POST message, populate the content of the message with the characters "String To Count" and send the request. Once the request has been sent, the HTTP reply is read and the count of the string received.

A caveat to using this class is to make sure that you replace the URL used when destinationAddress is initialized from www.wrox.com to something that you know works. So, how do you decide which destinationAddress works? This Java class is designed to send a POST request with a string and expects back a number that is the length of the string. Conveniently enough, the following example shows an example (in C) of just how to create this. Other than that, this class has been tested on Windows 2000 using Visual J++ 6.0 and JDK 1.3. It should work with no problems using any standard JVM and compilation environment.

The PostExample class illustrates how to retrieve information from the reply of the POST method, but does not do anything useful with it. Feel free to insert your patented algorithm for saving the world here!

```java
// Make sure we have access to all the classes we need.

import java.net.*;
import java.io.*;

public class PostExample
{
public static void main (String[] args) throws MalformedURLException, IOException
    {
        URL destinationAddress;
        HttpURLConnection connection;
        DataOutputStream postStream;
```

```
            DataInputStream dataStream;
            int stringLength;

            // Set up the server address. Note this must contain the
            // URL of the CGI script that will process the request.
            // Note that the current address will not work! You must change the URL to
            // one that works!

            destinationAddress = new URL ("www.wrox.com");

            connection = (HttpURLConnection) destinationAddress.openConnection ();

            // We are doing a POST request.
            connection.setRequestMethod ("POST");

            // We must set the Content-Type of the data.
            connection.setRequestProperty ("Content-Type", "text/plain");

            // We will be doing input as well as output.
            connection.setDoInput (true);
            connection.setDoOutput (true);

            // Let's make sure we are connected.
            connection.connect ();

            // Write out the body of the Post request.
            postStream = new DataOutputStream (connection.getOutputStream ());
            postStream.writeChars ("String to Count");

            // Now that we are done, make sure that all buffering is
            // flushed and we clean up by closing the stream.
            postStream.flush ();
            postStream.close ();

            // Read an integer on the inputstream that represents the
            // number of characters sent.
            dataStream = new DataInputStream (connection.getInputStream ());
            stringLength = dataStream.readInt ();

            // Clean up, now that we have gotten all the data.
            dataStream.close();

            // We don't do anything useful with stringLength, but this is where
            // additional logic would be inserted to use the result of the POST
            // method.
    }
}
```

If on compiling and running this example you find you get the following exception: **java.net.MalformedURLException: no protocol: www.wrox.com;** you must change the URL from www.wrox.com to a valid one.

Another exception you may encounter is on the line where the dataStream variable is populated by creating a new DataInputStream. If this exception is like a java.io.FileNotFoundException exception, the URL you specified is not returning a reply to the POST request. The following C example provides a sample that will respond properly to the POST request.

This example is used in conjuction with the previous Java program creates a complete working sample – it is set up to be a CGI program. It reads the data from a standard input, which web servers map to the data stream from an input HTTP request. It is up to you to configure your web server to allow access to this executable. Once the data has been read in, the length of the string is calculated. Next, the HTTP response header is generated by writing to `stdout` using `printf` statements, and the CGI protocol will map this stream back to the browser or program that initiated the HTTP request.

```c
#include <stdio.h>
#include <io.h>

void main (void)
{
    int stringLength;
    char bufferRead[1024];

    stringLength = _read (0, bufferRead, sizeof (bufferRead));

    // Set up the return header information for the HTTP response.
    // We send back a status indicating everything worked.
    printf ("200 OK\r\n");

    // We set the content-type to be text/plain as we are returning
    // the length of the string as characters.
    printf ("Content-type: text/plain\r\n");

    // We specify the length of the data in the HTTP response.
    printf ("Content-Length: %d\r\n", stringLength);

    // Signal the end of the headers.
    printf ("\r\n");

    // Append the data to return that is the length of the
    // string passed in.
    printf ("%d", stringLength);
}
```

Passing SOAP using HTTP

HTTP is an excellent transport for SOAP when a request/response paradigm is required. HTTP provides an excellent equivalent to an RPC transport, such as DNC RPC or ONC RPC. This is because URIs identify the endpoint to connect to in HTTP. Another significant advantage to using HTTP is that it will work with firewalls. This feature of HTTP makes it far more suitable for use on the Internet than other protocols such as CORBA or DCOM.

HTTP would be a poor transport if a reply could not be provided in a reasonable amount of time. A reasonable amount of time here depends on the client requirements and network timeouts. A guideline for interactive time limits that is often used is described in the work of Card and Mackinlay – the assumption is that if the delay to an interactive user is 0.1 seconds, the user considers the response instantaneous. If the user perceives a delay of 1 second, there is no loss in the train of thought for the user. Finally, if the delay is over 10 seconds, the user is likely to lose interest and move on. In a web environment, the user losing interest is of vital importance, as keeping the user on a page is the key to generating revenue. Given this scenario, the use of HTTP to translate SOAP requests and responses into web pages may not be desirable if the percieved user response time is greater than 10 seconds.

In this scenario, a store and forward method of passing SOAP should be considered. This method of transmitting SOAP is discussed in more detail in the upcoming section on passing SOAP using SMTP. Other options in this area would include FTP, MSMQ, or a proprietary protocol for the transmission of SOAP.

Given our understanding of MIME, HTTP, URIs, URLs and URNs, let us examine how HTTP sends the SOAP packets. HTTP sends the SOAP packets in the POST method with the header tag of `Content-Type: text/xml`. This type of binding is important, as it works with existing infrastructure, that is, a proxy web server needs to do nothing special to be able to store a SOAP request or response encoded in this manner. However, it is a double edged sword – the SOAP packet will go through firewalls that have a port open for HTTP, the default being port 80. The advantage to this is that no additional configuration is required to begin using SOAP. The downside to this is that anyone can send a SOAP message to your computer. One alternative is to bind SOAP to HTTPS instead of HTTP. This automatically provides a level of security and there is no difference, from a SOAP packet point of view, whether the transport is HTTP or HTTPS.

In mapping SOAP onto HTTP, the request and response for HTTP stay largely the same, with some restrictions. As we have seen, one of these restrictions is that the content-type must be `text/xml`. This is done since the SOAP payload is represented entirely as XML, so the content-type of the request and response must reflect this. In addition, the HTTP request must have an additional header field named `SOAPAction`, which provides the URI that is to be executed. A major reason for having this additional header field is that it allows firewalls to understand the destination of the SOAP request without having to decipher the payload of the SOAP message. This provides two advantages for firewalls. The first is speed – a request can be filtered by only examining the headers. The second is that a variety of firewalls already allow the creation of rules to inspect HTTP headers.

In the HTTP response, the existing status codes defined for HTTP are used in the headers. For example, a 2xx code indicates that the SOAP request was understood and processed. The interesting thing to note, however, is that if a SOAP request fails for any reason, resulting in a Fault element, the HTTP status code must be set to 500. The status code of 500 indicates an "Internal Server Error".

An interesting scenario becomes possible with the use of the status codes in the 3xx series. These codes provide the ability to indicate that a URI has moved temporarily or permanently. In using these codes with SOAP, you can provide a mechanism to automatically upgrade the client to the latest implementation, simply by providing a redirection to the new URI.

Using the Microsoft SOAP Toolkit

In creating the following example of sending SOAP over HTTP, we have used the Microsoft SOAP Toolkit, version 2.0, which is freely available from Microsoft at http://msdn.microsoft.com/webservices. Installation of the toolkit on Windows 2000 using IIS 5.0 was reasonably straightforward, and it has also been shown to work using PWS. A setup wizard guides you through the steps, working seamlessly. We then created a new virtual directory in IIS to hold the examples. We named this virtual directory `Wrox`.

Server

The sample is an Echo server. The server has two methods. The first, `EchoString()`, returns the string that is passed in. The second method, `EchoReverseString()`, invokes the function `StrReverse` to reverse the string and then return it. The code for the server (`EchoSvcRpcVB.vbp` – written in VB 6.0) is shown overleaf:

```
Option Explicit

Public Function EchoString(ByVal S As String) As String
    EchoString = S
End Function

Public Function EchoReverseString(ByVal S As String) As String
    EchoReverseString = StrReverse(S)
End Function
```

Once the server code is created, we need to package it into a VB .dll using Visual Studio. Next, we run the WSDL Generator utility (supplied with the Microsoft SOAP toolkit) to generate the .wsdl and .wsml files. Click Next to get past the first screen. The next screen we come to requests that we enter the name to be used for our service (and our file names), and the location of the COM objects to analyse. We choose MyEcho for our service name, and navigate to our newly compiled EchoSvcVB.dll. Our screen now looks like this:

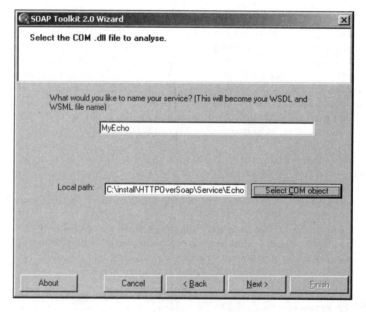

We then click Next (and we won't include any more screenshots, as the remainder of the screens are fairly easy to work out, and have already been seen in Chapter 4). The remaining screens are as follows:

❑ The next screen requires us to select which services to expose, and include in our WSDL file. We check both boxes, and click Next.

❑ Next, we are required to enter a valid URI for our listener to be located at – we entered the URL to our test directory (http://localhost/wrox). The other options (listener type and preferred XSD Schema Namespace to use) were kept as their defaults (ISAPI and 2001, respectively).

❑ The fourth screen requires us to enter our preferred character set to use for the WSDL file, and a path to the place where we want our files generated. We selected the default encoding – UTF-8 for the character set, and the physical location on our drive where the contents of our test directory are located for the path. We click the Next button to commence generating the files.

❑   The final screen is a confirmation that it has worked successfully (hopefully!). We click Finish to exit.

You should now have a WSDL file and a WSML file. The generated files define how the exposed web methods are to be called by SOAP and allow auto discovery by the client. This is a feature of the Microsoft SOAP toolkit and is not a part of the SOAP standard.

For a more in-depth look at the Microsoft SOAP toolkit, see Chapter 8.

Client

The client to test the SOAP server is also a simple VB application, though it has a few more lines, the ones of interest being shown below. The variable sc is dimensioned as a SoapClient. The SoapClient is created using a New call, and then initialized by calling mssoapinit (see sample below). The value of the variable cbWSDLURL.Text is the location of the .wsdl file that was generated for the server (it can be manually set – see below). Once this is done, the Web Services can be remotely invoked by calling the appropriate method, such as sc.EchoReverseString, and passing the appropriate argument, which in this case is a string. Finally, we do some error checking and wrap up. The entire source code can be found on the Wrox web site at http://www.wrox.com/.

```
Dim sc As SoapClient
...
...
Set sc = New SoapClient
sc.mssoapinit cbWSDLURL.Text
...
...
ResultString = sc.EchoReverseString(InputString)
...
...
If sc.faultcode <> "" Then
    MsgBox "Fault Recieved. " & vbCrLf & sc.faultstring & vbCrLf & _
    sc.detail, vbExclamation
    Exit Sub
End If
```

Now we can run the sample by clicking on our EchoCliRpcVB.exe. The front end looks like this:

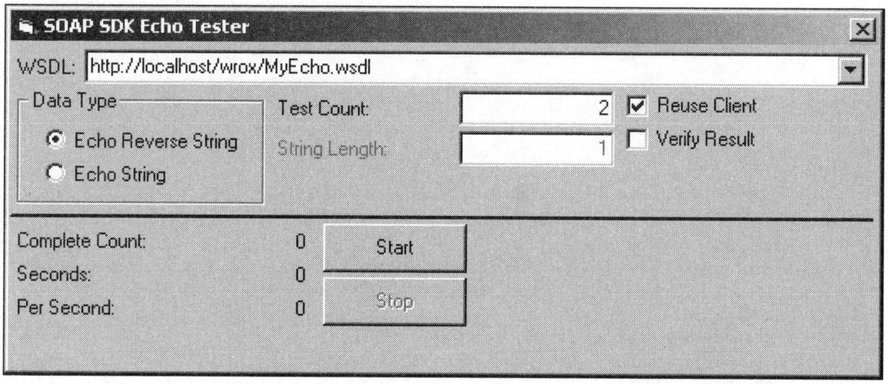

As you can see, we need to enter the URL to out WSDL file in the WSDL: box. We can test it by clicking the Start button. The three numbers at the bottom of the window should return some count values.

Using the Echo Server

The echo sample created the following HTTP request and response. The XML has been formatted by adding spaces and carriage returns so the `Content-Length` field is not accurate in the example. If however, you remove all the blanks and carriage returns, the count is accurate. You will notice that the HTTP request is a POST request with the URI set to `/Wrox/Service/MyEcho.WSDL`. The interesting thing about this particular SOAP implementation is that the `SOAPAction` is set to a URI that has the consistent prefix of `http://tempuri.org/action`. This is the default namespace generated by the WSDL Generator. As we also discussed, the Content-Type is set to `text/xml`, but in addition the charset has been specified as "UTF-8". While this is not required for SOAP, it is good practice to specify which charset you are using. Finally, you will note the body of the HTTP request is a valid SOAP packet including the `Envelope` and `Body` elements. In this case we have no need for a header, so it has been eliminated.

Request

```
POST /Wrox/Service/MyEcho.WSDL HTTP/1.1
Content-Type: text/xml; charset="UTF-8"
Host: Eiffel
SOAPAction: http://tempuri.org/action/EchoServer.EchoReverseString
Content-Length: 360

<?xml version="1.0" encoding="UTF-8" standalone="no"?>
<SOAP-ENV:Envelope
SOAP-ENV:encodingStyle="http://schemas.xmlsoap.org/soap/encoding/"
xmlns:SOAP-ENV="http://schemas.xmlsoap.org/soap/envelope/">
   <SOAP-ENV:Body>
     <SOAPSDK1:EchoReverseString xmlns:SOAPSDK1="http://tempuri.org/message/">
       <S>A</S>
     </SOAPSDK1:EchoReverseString>
   </SOAP-ENV:Body>
</SOAP-ENV:Envelope>
```

The HTTP response shows a successful SOAP request by virtue of the status code for the HTTP response being 200. Just as in the HTTP request, the Content-Type and Content-Length are also specified. In the response, the header field `Expires` indicates to the software that invoked the HTTP request that the response should not be cached.

Response

```
HTTP/1.1 200 OK
Server: Microsoft-IIS/5.0
Date: Thu, 14 Jun 2001 21:39:50 GMT
Content-Type: text/xml; charset="UTF-8"
Content-Length: 386
Expires:-1;

<?xml version="1.0" encoding="UTF-8" standalone="no"?>
<SOAP-ENV:Envelope
SOAP-ENV:encodingStyle= "http://schemas.xmlsoap.org/soap/encoding/"
    xmlns:SOAP-ENV="http://schemas.xmlsoap.org/soap/envelope/">
   <SOAP-ENV:Body>
     <SOAPSDK1:EchoReverseStringResponse
      xmlns:SOAPSDK1="http://tempuri.org/message/">
       <Result>A</Result>
     </SOAPSDK1:EchoReverseStringResponse>
   </SOAP-ENV:Body>
</SOAP-ENV:Envelope>
```

To recap, we saw that HTTP is a valuable transport for SOAP because of its widespread use, framing, content negotiation and endpoint addressing. We have examined the basics of HTTP and then saw how a simple SOAP server and client can be created using the Microsoft SOAP toolkit. Finally, we examined what is actually sent on the wire between the server and the client. Although we have not shown examples of all possible scenarios and error conditions, we have covered what is to be expected in case of success as well as failure.

SMTP

SMTP stands for Simple Mail Transfer Protocol. It is one of the key protocols that have enabled e-mail to become ubiquitous. To fully appreciate the usefulness of SMTP, a brief overview of how e-mail is delivered is in order. Let's say a user named Katherine is on a host named Eiffel. Katherine's e-mail address is Katherine@eiffel.trcs.com. She wishes to send a message to Stephanie, who is on a computer named Colorado. Stephanie's e-mail address is Stephanie@colorado.trcs.com. So, how does an e-mail message get from the host Eiffel to Colorado? We will follow one possible scenario.

First Katherine creates a message using her mail user agent or MUA. This may be Microsoft Outlook, Eudora, or any other mail client. She populates To and Subject fields, and then writes something into the body of the message. When Katherine is ready to send, she asks her MUA to send it. The MUA adds various header fields, such as Date and Message-Id. Also any resolution of destination addresses that can be done is done. From here, the MUA may open a SMTP connection directly or forward the mail message to a mail transfer agent or MTA. For each operating system there are a variety of MTA's. On Unix, you can nearly always count on sendmail being present. On NT and Windows 2000, Microsoft Exchange also serves this purpose. Regardless of the specific MTA, once the MUA passes the message to the MTA, it is completely the MTA's responsibility to deliver the message.

The MTA now opens an SMTP connection to the remote system. The IP address of the remote system is determined either through a local host lookup or a DNS lookup if a local host cannot be found. Once the connection is established, an SMTP dialogue takes place which will send the message in two parts, first the envelope and then the message itself. The envelope contains the destination address and the return address. In this case the destination address is Stephanie@colorado.trcs.com and the return address is Katherine@eiffel.trcs.com. At this point, the MTA on Eiffel may reject the message because there is no way to deliver it to Stephanie. If this occurs, an error message is generated and delivered to the return address – in other words, the source e-mail is "bounced back".

Let's suppose the MTA on Colorado accepted the message. The MTA would examine the recipient address and follow the same procedures. If the destination is on a remote machine, another SMTP communication takes place, otherwise, the mail is sent to a MDA or mail delivery agent. On Unix systems, programs in this category are /bin/mail or procmail. On Windows platforms, Microsoft Exchange can also fill this role. If the delivery of the mail succeeds, the message will wait in Stephanie's mailbox until she reads the mail using her MUA.

It is useful to point out that each MUA and MTA may have (and generally do have) queues, that is, each MTA or MUA may have a queue that stores messages until a later time where they can be delivered. This provides a great deal of tolerance for network failures.

As you can see from this scenario, a great deal occurs when sending an e-mail, however, the key point for our discussion is that SMTP is used nearly universally. For this reason, it provides two unique properties as a transport for SOAP. First, almost all firewalls hold open the SMTP port of 25. Second, since it is a store and forward protocol, it can deliver messages even when target machines are not online when the message is sent. This property is vital if you cannot guarantee reasonable connectivity with the destination host.

So, if you are looking for a way to send an asynchronous request using SOAP, SMTP can be a good option, especially if you are looking for a way to send an event notification through SOAP and do not expect a reply, and/or if you believe that the method you are invoking through SOAP may take a long time to complete.

On the other hand, if you are interested in having the request arrive in a timely fashion, SMTP will most likely not be the approach you should choose to send a SOAP request. The reason is that SMTP allows the receiver to be down at the time of delivery, and, depending on the individual server configuration, will retry delivery for up to three to five days. This potential for long timeouts would of course play havoc with a system that intended delivery in a matter of seconds or minutes.

Additionally, a SOAP request sent through SMTP may take up to a day to discover that the endpoint address or the e-mail recipient is invalid. Your application must be able to tolerate this type of delay or be in a position where this error can be ignored.

SMTP Protocol

So, now that we know how SMTP is used, what does the SMTP protocol look like? The SMTP protocol is a simple protocol that runs over port 25. There is no encryption available in SMTP, though you may encrypt the message. An SMTP conversation consists of a client connecting to a server. Once the connection has been established, the server may either accept, temporarily reject or permanently reject the connection. This is known as the server's greeting. If the connection is successfully established, the client will send a request which consists of a SMTP verb optionally followed by a parameter. The RFC 821 (http://www.faqs.org/rfcs/rfc821.html) defines in great length the SMTP verbs and their meanings, but it is required that all support the following verbs.

SMTP Verb	What it means
HELO	Open a channel
RSET	Abort current mail transaction
NOOP	Perform no action other than to receive an OK response from the server
MAIL	Indicates sender of mail
RCPT	Identifies recipient of mail
DATA	Indicates the data of the mail message is to follow
QUIT	Close the channel

The following may have been the SMTP conversation that took place as Katherine (on the Eiffel host) sent an email to Stephanie (on the Colorado host):

```
Eiffel:    MAIL FROM:<Katherine@eiffel.trcs.com>
Colorado: 250 OK

Eiffel:    RCPT TO:<Stephanie@colorado.trcs.com>
Colorado: 250 OK

Eiffel:    DATA
Colorado: 354 Start mail input; end with <CRLF>.<CRLF>
```

```
Eiffel:    Blah blah blah...
Eiffel:    ...etc. etc. etc.
Eiffel:    <CRLF>.<CRLF>
Colorado: 250 OK
```

Example Overview

So, how can a SOAP request be processed using SMTP? There must be something listening for an e-mail message that in turn does something with it. In our example, we will have a standalone process that is listening using SMTP and then takes any SOAP messages received and relays them using HTTP. After receiving the SOAP response over HTTP, the response is then relayed using SMTP to a POP3 mailbox. The POP3 mailbox is specified at the time of making the initial SMTP request. POP3 is the third version of the Post Office Protocol as specified in RFC 1725 (http://www.freesoft.org/CIE/RFC/1725/). POP3 represents a protocol that implements the necessary commands to allow the user of such machines to poll a larger computer at the intervals that the user sees as most convenient to get the mail messages stored at the server and transfer them to his personal computer (usually, but not always, deleting them from the server).

Example Setup

In creating an example of sending a SOAP request using SMTP, let's use the SOAP implementation in Apache running on Windows 2000 (an implementation that we will revisit to varying degrees in Chapters 7, 10 and 14). The units of software required are as follows (the version suggested are those used to test this code):

- ❏ JDK Version 1.3.1 from Sun. This software download is over 30 MB, but installs cleanly. (Download from http://java.sun.com/). You need the JDK to get the compiler that does not come with the Java runtime environment.

- ❏ JDK Documentation Version 1.3.3 from Sun. This software is over 20 MB, and comes as a .zip file. Download from http://java.sun.com/

- ❏ Apache version 1.3.17 for Windows. The core web server. Download from http://www.apache.org/

- ❏ Apache SOAP version 2.2. Download from http://xml.apache.org/soap/

- ❏ Apache Jakarta Tomcat version 3.2.2. Download from http://jakarta.apache.org/site/binindex.html

- ❏ Apache Xerces XML Parser version 1.4.0: http://xml.apache.org/xerces-j/index.html.

- ❏ Mod_jk.dll Download from: http://jakarta.apache.org/builds/jakarta-tomcat/release/v3.2.3/bin/win32/i386/

- ❏ Perl version 5.6.1, build 626. Download from http://www.activestate.com

- ❏ JavaMail version 1.2: http://java.sun.com/products/javamail/

- ❏ JavaBeans Activation Framework version 1.0.1: http://java.sun.com/products/javabeans/glasgow/jaf.html

- ❏ The SMTP and POP3 beans from IBM Alphaworks: go to http://www.alphaworks.ibm.com/alphabeans/ to download them.

Since the configuration of these items is not intuitively obvious, please follow these steps. First, let us install the JDK. The JDK comes packaged as an `.exe` file that spawns an installation wizard. The installation wizard should work fine and set up the JDK properly. If it doesn't automatically set the environment variable `JAVA_HOME`, set it to the directory where the JDK has been installed, for example, `c:\JDK1.3.1`. Also, add the directory `c:\JDK1.3.1\bin` to the `PATH` environment variable for convenience. The documentation can be installed anywhere you think appropriate. It is a good idea to unzip the documentation and install it into the directory `c:\JDK1.3.1`, for the main reason that to remove.

Apache Web Server

The next step is to install the Apache web server and get it running. This also is reasonably straightforward. After the installation wizard installed the base code, go to the `conf` subdirectory of the installation and modify the `httpd.conf` file for the following three parameters:

```
#
# ServerAdmin: Your address, where problems with the server should be
# e-mailed.  This address appears on some server-generated pages, such
# as error documents.
#
ServerAdmin rajesh@trcs.com
```

This is done so that error pages would have the correct e-mail address to send administration errors to. The next item modified is the `ServerName`.

```
#
# ServerName allows you to set a host name which is sent back to clients for
# your server if it's different than the one the program would get (for example,
use
# "www" instead of the host's real name).
#
# 127.0.0.1 is the TCP/IP local loop-back address, often named localhost. Your
# machine always knows itself by this address. If you use Apache strictly for
# local testing and development, you may use 127.0.0.1 as the server name.
#
ServerName 127.0.0.1
```

As the comments indicate, do not just invent a name for the `ServerName` – this name must be a valid TCP/IP address. If you are not sure what that is, please consult your system adminstrator. In our case, we are using the web server for testing purposes only, so we named the server 127.0.0.1, which is the default TCP/IP address for a localhost. The final item we modified was the port that Apache listens for HTTP request on. This was set to 8000 instead of 80 to prevent any conflicts with existing web servers as follows:

```
#
# Port: The port to which the standalone server listens.
#
Port 8000
```

To test that Apache is functioning properly, fire up Apache. This can be done from the command line by going to the directory where Apache is installed and keying in **apache**. This will run the Apache executable using the httpd.conf file for its configuration. On the command line you should see the following:

```
c:\Apache> apache
Apache/1.3.17 (Win32)
```

As a final test to make sure the web server is running properly, point your browser to
http://127.0.0.1:8000. You should see the default Apache page with the Apache logo. We will come
back to the `httpd.conf` file to modify it again once Tomcat is installed, but for now, we can be
satisfied that we have a running web server.

Apache SOAP, Tomcat and Xerces

The next step is to get SOAP running. To get SOAP running with Apache we need three components,
Tomcat (for servlets), the SOAP distribution for Apache, and Xerces (for the XML parser). These were
unpacked in their default directories.

Of course, you can unpack them anywhere you like, as long as you set the environment variables
accordingly. At this stage, we need to set two more – CLASSPATH and TOMCAT_HOME. In setting
CLASSPATH, add the full pathname to `xerces.jar` and `soap.jar`, so if you do set up the above
directory, add the following to CLASSPATH:

```
c:\xerces-1_4_0\xerces.jar
c:\soap-2.2\lib\soap.jar
```

and this line to the value of TOMCAT_HOME:

```
c:\Jakarta-tomcat-3.2.2
```

Now we have servlets installed into the system. To get SOAP processing we add the following Context
into the `server.xml` file for Tomcat. This file is found in the `conf` subdirectory of the Tomcat
installation. The following context associates the path "/soap" with the SOAP 2.2 distribution.

```
<Context path="/soap"
         docBase="c:\soap-2_2\webapps\soap"
         reloadable="true" >
</Context>
```

We now need to tell Apache about Tomcat. This allows Apache to redirect the servlet requests to Tomcat,
which in turn also allows all the SOAP requests to be handled. To create this communication, we again
modify the httpd.conf file for Apache. At the end of the httpd.conf file, add an include statement to the
`mod_jk.conf-auto` file in the Tomcat distribution. On my system, I added the following line:

```
include c:\jakarta-tomcat-3.2.2\conf\mod_jk.conf-auto
```

This line loads a module into Apache at runtime named `mod_jk.dll`. This .dll file should be copied
to the `modules` subdirectory of the Apache installation so that it can be found when Apache starts. Now
when we start Apache, the `mod_jk` module is loaded, and will communicate with Tomcat and Apache
SOAP as appropriate.

Note that when we start Apache we do not automatically start Tomcat. We must do this in another window. So after all this work of installing and configuring where are we? We now have Apache configured so that Java servlets can be run using Tomcat and SOAP request can be received and sent using the SOAP subsystem. However, you will find that there is one more thing to be done before you have full functionality – you need to add two .jar files – activation.jar from the JavaBeans Activation Framework, and mail.jar, from JavaMail, as you did the others, previously. Without these two items in your CLASSPATH, you will not be able to run the admin client (see later).

One more gotcha was found by reading the documentation for Apache SOAP. The xerces.jar file must be in the CLASSPATH before the tomcat .jar files. To remedy this, edit the tomcat.bat file (in the bin subdirectory of the tomcat installation directory) so that the line

```
set CP=%CP%;%CLASSPATH%
```

Is replaced with the following line:

```
set CP=%CLASSPATH%;%CP%
```

Note the reversal of %CLASSPATH% with %CP%. As stated before, this allows for the xerces.jar file to be found first in the CLASSPATH environment variable.

Once this is all done, we can now test to see that Apache SOAP is running properly. First, you need to go to the directory in which you will run the example code and make sure the classpaths are set properly, then type **tomcat run** to start Tomcat. Then, point the web browser to http://127.0.0.1:8080/soap – if it is working ok, we will see the Apache-SOAP welcome screen, which looks like this:

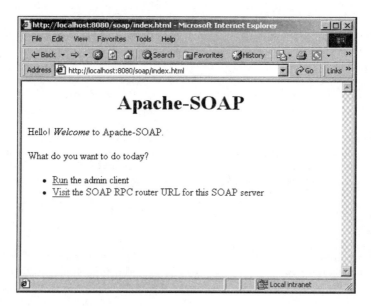

One final consideration concerns the two beans downloaded from IBM Alphaworks – SMTP and POP3. As you will discover in the next section, these are needed to use SOAP with these two protocols. Unzip the downloads into respective SMTP and POP3 folders on c:.

Example Code

The first thing to do is to create a mapping of SOAP calls from SMTP to HTTP. This is done to leverage the HTTP SOAP code already written. To do this, we create a bridge that maps the SMTP calls into SOAP requests that were sent using HTTP. This is done using a class supplied in Apache SOAP named SMTP2HTTPBridge. This class is located in the org.apache.soap.server package. To run the bridge we supply the following arguments:

Argument Name	Argument Description	Default Value in Script
Polldelay	Length of delay between polling the POP3 mailbox	30000 (30 seconds)
Pop3Host	Name of the POP3 host to retrieve e-mail from.	Your POP3 host
Pop3Login	Username to login as to the POP3 host	Your username
Pop3Password	Password provided in conjunction with the Pop3Login	Your password
RouterURL	SOAP Server URL	http://localhost:8000/soap/servlet/rpcrouter
SmtpHostName	SMTP server to send reply with.	Your SMTP host

Supplied in the sample code for this chapter is a batch file (smtpBridge.bat) that specifies these values and creates a command line. For the script to work properly you must supply the Pop3Host, Pop3Login, Pop3Password and SmtpHostName. If you have configured Apache SOAP following the instructions provided, the default RouterURL is correct. The batch file is shown below:

```
@echo off

REM
REM Launch Apache SOAP SMTP Bridge
REM

REM Set up XERCES Directory and Apache SOAP root directories.

set XERCES_DIR="c:\xerces-1_4_0"
set SOAP_DIR="c:\soap-2_2"
set SMTP_DIR="c:\smtp"
set POP3_DIR="c:\pop3"

REM Build the Class path.

Set
SOAPCP="%XERCES_DIR%\xerces.jar;%SOAP_DIR%\lib\soap.jar;%POP3_DIR%\lib\pop3.jar;%S
MTP_DIR%\lib\smtp.jar"

REM
REM     All values will be hard coded in the script for now.
REM


REM    Number of milli seconds delay between polls
```

```
set polldelay="30000"

REM    Name of the POP3 server
set pop3host="INSERT YOURS HERE"

REM    LoginId for the POP3 Account
set pop3login="INSERT YOURS HERE"

REM    Password for the POP3 Account
set pop3passwd="INSERT YOURS HERE"

REM    HTTP URL for the SOAP Router to bridge to
set routerURL="http://localhost:8080/soap/servlet/rpcrouter"

REM    smtp hostname of SMTP server
set smtphostname="INSERT YOURS HERE"

REM run the bridge!
echo Running the SOAP Bridge using classpath: %SOAPCP%

java -classpath %SOAPCP% org.apache.soap.server.SMTP2HTTPBridge %polldelay%
%pop3host% %pop3login% %pop3passwd% %routerURL% %smtphostname%
```

The SMTP_DIR should point to the base directory of the SMTP bean from IBM Alphaworks. The POP3_DIR should point to the base directory for the POP3 bean from IBM Alphaworks. In addition to setting the SMTP_DIR and POP3_DIR environment variables, the CLASSPATH environment variable must include the paths to the .jar files. It is important to have the complete pathnames to the .jar files.

Now assuming that you have set the variables properly, run the bridge from the ApacheSOAPSMTPExample directory using the following:

c:\install\ApacheSOAPSMTPExample> **smtpBridge.bat**

Of course, the setting for your CLASSPATH environment variable may be different based on the exact directory paths used, but in general this should be what you see:

All of the setup is now complete. We have set up a POP3 mailbox to receive e-mail, in which we will recognize the payload as a SOAP message. Once a SOAP message is recognized it will be re-routed over HTTP to a SOAP method. After receiving the SOAP response over HTTP, a SOAP payload is created and sent back over SMTP.

Now we can actually create some code to call a SOAP message using SMTP! We can create a web service that has similar functionality to that of the Microsoft SOAP Toolkit, but in the Apache SOAP environment. Once the service is created and deployed, we will create a client for the service that invokes it using HTTP. Finally, we will modify the client to invoke the service using SMTP and the SMTPBridge that we have already seen. This service will take an input of a string and return the count of the string as an int. The code for the service is shown below:

```
public class MyStringService
{
    public int countString (String inputString)
    {
        return (inputString.length());
    }
}
```

The next step is to compile the code and to deploy the service with Apache SOAP. To deploy the service, use go to http://127.0.0.1:8000/soap/admin and click the Deploy button on the left side of the screen. The following screen displayed is:

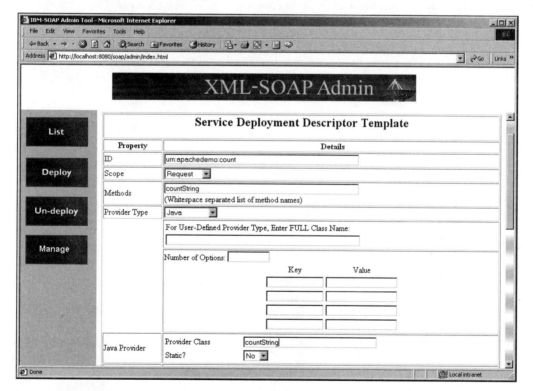

Here you provide information about the class you wish to deploy with Apache Soap. The fields I entered are as follows:

❑   ID – Specify a URN for the service. This can be just about anything you wish to call it, but if you stick to the URN naming schema, you will be in good shape – go for urn:apachedemo:count

- ❑ **Scope** – What should the scope of the service be? You should set yours to Request, which means the service should be instantiated every time the server receives a request, the other choices being Session and Application (indicate that the service should either be instantiated once per session, or once in the lifetime of the tomcat server, respectively).

- ❑ **Methods** – Enter countString here as this is the method to be invoked.

- ❑ **Provider Type** – Choose Java. The other options are Script and User Defined.

- ❑ **Java Provider** – Provide the class name and indicate that the method to be invoked, countString, is not static, but an instance method. So, if your code directory is c:\install, and you are invoking it fro the same place, you just need to enter countString here.

The other fields allow you to map functions in scripting languages (including JavaScript, JScript, Python and others) as well as user defined ones, where you can define your own mappings for arguments. Once you have entered all the items, click the Deploy button at the bottom of the form. You can then review your deployment's success by clicking the List button (you can select this service from a list of services, then bring up a list of the details we just entered into the deployment form).

Next, we will create a client that sends an SMTP message and waits for a reply. This example uses the transport that is provided by the Apache SOAP package. In the client, the values used for smtpServer, popServer, and popPassword have been removed, in the interest of not compromising the author's ISP! If you do use your existing e-mail account, you will not lose any e-mail from this exercise, but you will end up with a lot of extra mail messages in your mailbox. Just replace these values with ones of your own and you will be on your way!

The client code is as follows:

```java
import java.net.*;
import java.util.*;
import org.apache.soap.*;
import org.apache.soap.rpc.*;
import org.apache.soap.transport.*;

public class SMTPClient
{
    public static void main( String[] args ) throws Exception
    {
        URL url;
        Call call;
        Vector params;

        url = new URL ("mailto:smtpsoap@trcs.com");
        String urn = "urn:apachedemo:count";

        // Here we start settting up the SOAP call. We include the
        // URI to connect to as well as the method name.

        call = new Call();
        call.setTargetObjectURI (urn);
        call.setMethodName ("countString");
        call.setEncodingStyleURI (Constants.NS_URI_SOAP_ENC);

        // Since we are sending the SOAP message using SMTP, we
        // initialize the server parameters here. In the way we
```

```
        // have done it, not only do we need a SMTP server,
        // but a POP3 server as well! The POP3 mailbox in
        // our example serves to hold the response from the SOAP
        // request.

        String smtpServer = "INSERT YOURS HERE";
        String popServer = "INSERT YOURS HERE";
        String popLogin = "smtpresponse";
        String popPassword = "INSERT YOURS HERE";
        String fromAddress = popLogin + "@" + popServer;

        SOAPTransport smtpTransport =
        new org.apache.soap.transport.smtp.SOAPSMTPConnection
                        (fromAddress, "SOAP SMTP TEST", smtpServer,
                         30000, popServer, popLogin, popPassword);

        call.setSOAPTransport (smtpTransport);

        // Now we add the arguments to the SOAP message.

        params = new Vector();
        params.addElement (new Parameter ("inputString", String.class,
                        "StringToCount", null));

        call.setParams (params);

        try
        {
            System.out.println ("invoke service\n" + "  URL= " + url +
                            "\n  URN =" + urn);
            Response response = call.invoke (url, "");

            if (!response.generatedFault())
            {
                Parameter result = response.getReturnValue ();
                System.out.println ("Result= " + result.getValue ());
            }
            else
            {
                Fault f = response.getFault (); // an error occurred
                System.err.println ("Fault= " + f.getFaultCode () + ", " +
                f.getFaultString ());
            }
        }
        catch (SOAPException e) // call could not be sent properly
        {
            System.err.println ("SOAPException= " + e.getFaultCode () +
                            ", " + e.getMessage ());
        }
    }
}
```

Compile the SMTPClient class and now we have all the pieces to send an SMTP message over SOAP. Let us recap the pieces and see what we need to have running for this example to work. First we must have Apache running with the countString() method installed as a valid SOAP message. Next, we must have the SMTPBridge.bat file running as this translates the SOAP requests coming in on SMTP to a corresponding method over HTTP. Finally, we run the client in the class SMTPClient to invoke the method.

So what is actually sent over the wire using SMTP? The interesting thing to note here is that there is no correlation between SOAP and the SMTP headers. The SOAP request (seen below) is simply carried as the payload of the SMTP message. The one header that does get set is the content-type which is set as `text/xml`. This is the same setting as we saw in the HTTP request.

```
From smtpresponse@trcs.com   Sat Jun 16 13:39:46 2001
Return-Path: <smtpresponse@trcs.com>
Received: from [192.168.0.1] (starlite.rmii.com [166.93.12.26])
          by web04.bigbiz.com (8.8.7/8.8.7) with SMTP id NAA13433
          for <smtpsoap@trcs.com>; Sat, 16 Jun 2001 13:39:45 -0700
Date: Sat, 16 Jun 2001 13:39:45 -0700
From: smtpresponse@trcs.com
Message-Id: <200106162039.NAA13433@web04.bigbiz.com>
To: <smtpsoap@trcs.com>
MIME-Version: 1.0
Subject: SOAP SMTP TEST
Content-Type: text/xml
Content-Transfer-Encoding: 7bit
Content-Disposition: inline

<?xml version="1.0" encoding="UTF-8"?>
<SOAP-ENV:Envelope xmlns:SOAP-ENV=http://schemas.xmlsoap.org/soap/envelope/
                   xmlns:xsi=http://www.w3.org/1999/XMLSchema-instance
                   xmlns:xsd="http://www.w3.org/1999/XMLSchema">
   <SOAP-ENV:Body>
      <ns1:countString xmlns:ns1="urn:apachedemo:count"
          SOAP-ENV:encodingStyle="http://schemas.xmlsoap.org/soap/encoding/">
      <inputString xsi:type="xsd:string">StringToCount</inputString>
      </ns1:countString>
   </SOAP-ENV:Body>
</SOAP-ENV:Envelope>
```

The SOAP response in SMTP is very similar to the SOAP request in that the only header in SMTP that is modified is the content-type, to indicate that the payload is `text/xml`.

```
Return-Path: <smtpsoap@trcs.com>
Received: (from trcs@localhost)
          by web04.bigbiz.com (8.8.7/8.8.7) id NAA13165
          for postmaster@trcs.com; Sat, 16 Jun 2001 13:38:19 -0700
From: smtpsoap@trcs.com
Received: from [192.168.0.1] (starlite.rmii.com [166.93.12.26])
          by web04.bigbiz.com (8.8.7/8.8.7) with SMTP id NAA13158
          for <smtpresponse@trcs.com>; Sat, 16 Jun 2001 13:38:17 -0700
Date: Sat, 16 Jun 2001 13:38:17 -0700
Message-Id: <200106162038.NAA13158@web04.bigbiz.com>
To: <smtpresponse@trcs.com>
MIME-Version: 1.0
Subject: Re: SOAP SMTP TEST
Content-Type: text/xml; charset=utf-8
Content-Transfer-Encoding: 7bit
Content-Disposition: inline
X-UIDL: 960d55f79a912e0eabe6f56c00b06349
```

```
<?xml version="1.0" encoding="UTF-8"?>
<SOAP-ENV:Envelope xmlns:SOAP-ENV=http://schemas.xmlsoap.org/soap/envelope/
                   xmlns:xsi=http://www.w3.org/1999/XMLSchema-instance
                   xmlns:xsd="http://www.w3.org/1999/XMLSchema">
   <SOAP-ENV:Body>
      <ns1:countStringResponse xmlns:ns1="urn:apachedemo:count"
         SOAP-ENV:encodingStyle="http://schemas.xmlsoap.org/soap/encoding/">
         <return xsi:type="xsd:int">13</return>
      </ns1:countStringResponse>
   </SOAP-ENV:Body>
</SOAP-ENV:Envelope>
```

Now that we have two functional SOAP implementations, it is interesting to note the differences between them. The Apache SOAP package provides SOAP on a variety of platforms, allows SOAP transport over HTTP and SMTP, and allows the use of Java and scripting languages. The Microsoft SOAP implementation provides functionality on Microsoft platforms and allows the use of any language that can take advantage of COM. It does, however, only allow SOAP transport over HTTP, but it is interesting to note that the Microsoft SOAP toolkit makes the client invoking the SOAP method easier to write by using WSDL. The IBM web services toolkit that is based on Apache extends the SOAP implementation to include WSDL.

We have now examined SMTP and its advantages, and how to create a working client and server using SMTP as a transport. As a useful recap, the limitations of using SMTP as a transport include:

❑　No guaranteed delivery.

❑　No guaranteed time of delivery.

❑　No transaction support.

❑　No filtering support.

FTP

FTP stands for **File Transfer Protocol**. It provides a mechanism to transfer files using TCP/IP. This transport provides unique qualities that HTTP and SMTP cannot provide, which are as follows:

❑　You can use anonymous FTP as your transport protocol, if you want to, say, set up a SOAP method that could be invoked anonymously

❑　FTP allows file sharing between systems without needing to know about the remote systems

❑　FTP provides commands to perform content translation and directory navigation

Even to this day there are extensions being proposed to FTP. These can be found at http://www.ietf.org/html.charters/ftpext-charter.html. Although FTP came originally bundled with Unix systems, its popularity has grown, and now web browsers on a variety of operating systems support FTP.

How Does it Work?

FTP uses two socket connections. The first provides a control connection, made using port 21. Interestingly, this connection stays open for the entire time the FTP session is active. The second socket connection is the data connection, which is made on a negotiated port between the FTP client and server. The data connection is used for sending files to and from the server as well as sending listings of files or directories from the server to the client – this connection comes and goes during the session, as needed.

Though the FTP specification provides broad control over how to transfer files between client and server, in practice you will generally find there is only one option to toggle. This option specifies the file format as ASCII or binary (or image). The specification of ASCII requires the sender to convert the file to ASCII. This can require the sender to scan each byte of the file search for a <CR><LF> pair of characters. The other option is to send the file using the binary format. In this mode, no translation is done and the file is sent as a continuous stream of bits over the wire.

Although the specification for FTP provides for 33 commands, most are not used. The replies that are sent in response to these commands is a three digit number in ASCII. This number is followed by an optional messages. The following table summarizes some of the most commonly used commands and their functionality:

Common FTP command	Description
User	Username to login to the server
Pass	Password to login to the server
Cwd	Print the current working directory
Cdup	Change directory "up" one level
Quit	Terminate session
Type	Specify file type (ASCII or binary)
Retr	Retrieve a file
Stor	Store a file
Rest	Provides a marker to restart a file transmission
Abor	Abort the current FTP command
List	List contents of directory
Port	Client specifies port to use for data connection
Nlst	Send directory listing

Now, lets take a look at a sample FTP session to see how these commands are used:

```
C:\Documents and Settings\rajesh>ftp -d ftp.wrox.com
Connected to ftp.wrox.com.
220 WROXIIS1 Microsoft FTP Service (Version 5.0).
User (ftp.wrox.com:(none)): ftp
---> USER ftp
```

```
331 Anonymous access allowed, send identity (e-mail name) as password.
Password:
---> PASS rajesh@trcs.com
230 Anonymous user logged in.
ftp> ls
---> PORT 166,93,12,26,15,232
200 PORT command successful.
---> NLST
150 Opening ASCII mode data connection for file list.
beginning
ChinaShop
instant
masterclass
noscan
Preview
Private
professional
tools
226 Transfer complete.
ftp: 91 bytes received in 0.01Seconds 9.10Kbytes/sec.
ftp> quit
---> QUIT
221
```

In this session of FTP, we connected to the WROX FTP server at ftp://ftp.wrox.com/ using an anonymous login, ftp. In doing so, we used the -d option on the command line for ftp so that the client FTP commands that were sent to the server would be shown. As you will note, the commands used were USER, PASS, PORT, NLST, and QUIT. For each of these client commands, the server replied with a status code of three digits as well as a brief explanation that is human readable.

SOAP Example

The example that uses FTP as a transport for SOAP is built using Apache SOAP. Specifically, it mimics the SMTP example by creating an FTP transport class as well as an FTP bridge that maps FTP SOAP request to HTTP SOAP requests. The FTP bridge then takes the result of the HTTP SOAP request, packages it, and sends the result back to the client via FTP.

The SOAP method to be invoked is the same as in the SMTP example. The method counts the number of characters in a string. Ok, so it's not as imaginative as we'd like, but we're more interested in the transport here, right? In creating this example, we will create a Java class named FTP2HTTPBridge that takes in FTP requests and reroutes them over HTTP. Once the SOAP request is completed over HTTP, the response is then routed back through FTP to the requestor. In addition to the bridge, we will create an FTP transport that takes in a SOAP request, creates appropriately named files, and sends them to an FTP server monitored by the FTP2HTTPBridge. Finally, we will create a client to call the FTP transport.

The sample code provided is not production ready. To go to production ready, you should consider adding more robust error handling! In the code sample for the FTP client, the only difference between this and the SMTP client is in setting up the call using the SOAPFtpTransport class. Another change is specifying the FTP server, FTP login and FTP password as opposed to the SMTP and POP3 information for the SMTP client. The most interesting thing is that the handling of the SOAP message is unchanged. In fact, the handling of the SOAP message is the same whether the transport is HTTP, SMTP, or FTP, provided of course you use the same SOAP toolkit (whether it be the Microsoft SOAP toolkit, or the Apache SOAP toolkit, which we used). The main functional part of the FTP SOAP client is as follows (see http://www.wrox.com/ for the full code):

```
import java.net.*;
import java.util.*;
import org.apache.soap.*;
import org.apache.soap.rpc.*;
import org.apache.soap.transport.*;

public class FTPClient
{
    public static void main( String[] args ) throws Exception
    {
        URL url;
        Call call;
        Vector params;

        String urn = "urn:apachedemo:count";

        call = new Call();
        call.setTargetObjectURI (urn);
        call.setMethodName ("countString");
        call.setEncodingStyleURI (Constants.NS_URI_SOAP_ENC);

        url = new URL ("ftp://REPLACE WITH YOUR FTP SERVER");

        String ftpServer = "REPLACE WITH YOUR FTP SERVER";
        String ftpLogin = "REPLACE WITH YOUR FTP LOGIN";
        String ftpPassword = "REPLACE WITH YOUR FTP PASSWORD";

        SOAPTransport ftpTransport = new SOAPFTPConnection (ftpServer,
                                                            30000,
                                                            ftpLogin,
                                                            ftpPassword);
```

Let us recap the pieces and see what we need to have running for this example to work. First, we must have Apache running with the count method installed as a valid SOAP message. Next, we must have the FTPBridge.bat file running as this translates the SOAP requests coming in on FTP to a corresponding method over HTTP. Finally we run the client, in the class FTPClient to invoke the method.

Let us follow the flow of the code. First the FTPClient makes a SOAP request using the programming interface supplied as part of the Apache SOAP package. The Apache code creates the proper XML in response to the client request and passes the XML to the SOAPFTPConnection class for transport. The SOAPFTPConnection class creates a file and populates it with the XML information for the SOAP request. This file is sent to a known ftp site where the FTPBridge is polling for new files. Once the SOAPFtpConnection class sends the file to the directory that the FTPBridge is polling, the SOAPFTPConnection class then waits for a response in a file is retrieved using FTP. The FTPBridge takes the contents of the file, and assumes the contents are a SOAP request. The request is then forwarded to the Apache SOAP server over HTTP, and the results are obtained, then placed in a file, which is picked up by the polling SOAPFTPConnection class. The SOAPFTPConnection class finally reads the file, retrieves the result and returns the result to the FTP Client.

The SOAP request looks like this:

```
<?xml version="1.0" encoding="UTF-8"?>
<SOAP-ENV:Envelope xmlns:SOAP-ENV=http://schemas.xmlsoap.org/soap/envelope/
              xmlns:xsi="http://www.w3.org/1999/XMLSchema-instance"
              xmlns:xsd="http://www.w3.org/1999/XMLSchema">
    <SOAP-ENV:Body>
        <ns1:countString xmlns:ns1="urn:apachedemo:count"
```

```
                SOAP-ENV:encodingStyle="http://schemas.xmlsoap.org/soap/encoding/">
            <inputString xsi:type="xsd:string">StringToCount</inputString>
        </ns1:countString>
    </SOAP-ENV:Body>
</SOAP-ENV:Envelope>
```

The SOAP response is the same whether the transport is HTTP, SMTP or FTP.

```
<?xml version="1.0" encoding="UTF-8"?>
<SOAP-ENV:Envelope xmlns:SOAP-ENV="http://schemas.xmlsoap.org/soap/envelope/"
                   xmlns:xsi="http://www.w3.org/1999/XMLSchema-instance"
                   xmlns:xsd="http://www.w3.org/1999/XMLSchema">
    <SOAP-ENV:Body>
        <ns1:countStringResponse xmlns:ns1="urn:apachedemo:count"
            SOAP-ENV:encodingStyle="http://schemas.xmlsoap.org/soap/encoding/">
            <return xsi:type="xsd:int">13</return>
        </ns1:countStringResponse>
    </SOAP-ENV:Body>
</SOAP-ENV:Envelope>
```

The main difference in these three transports (HTTP, FTP, and SMPT) is the mechanism of delivering the data. It is vital to note that the SOAP payload is the same regardless of the transport.

Summary

In this chapter, we have examined how to transport SOAP using a variety of protocols. The protocols have included HTTP, SMTP, and FTP. For each of these protocols, we have reviewed the protocol itself, examined what reasons may exist to use the protocol as a transport for SOAP, and also why the protocol might not be suitable in your circumstances. Finally, we have implemented SOAP on each of these transports and provided code samples.

6

Universal Description, Discovery and Integration

In this chapter, we will be covering the UDDI specifications in some detail, it's data structures and API, and also some deployment related issues. The current version of the UDDI specification is 2.0 (released June 2001), though most implementations support version 1.0 only. We will also look at some other related technology areas, such as ebXML, DSML, and the JAXR (Java API for XML Registries) API. There are a number of implementations of UDDI 1.0 already on the market, and the next chapter deals with some of them, and specifically with IBM's UDDI4J.

To understand what **UDDI** or "**Universal Description, Discovery and Integration**" is, and where it fits in, we need to revisit the Web Services stack and its different components.

A Web Service is a self-contained application or component that has the following characteristics – it can be described in a service description language and this description can be published. Client programs can find these descriptions, bind to the service so described and finally invoke the services.

UDDI provides the registry piece in this stack. It enables the three basic functions of Web Services, popularly known as "publish, find, and bind".

- ❑ The **publish** function is concerned with how the provider of a Web Service registers itself and its services

- ❑ The **find** function deals with how a client application finds the description of a Web Service or a service provider

- ❑ Finally, **bind** deals with how a client application connects to and interacts with the Web Service after finding it

UDDI defines standards for web-based registries. Companies can register information in these registries about themselves, about the services they offer and technical information on how these services can be accessed. They can also search the registry for other companies or service providers (that is: search by service information in addition to company information). These registries can either be privately hosted ones, or the global UDDI Business Registry.

The figure below shows the Web Services stack and where UDDI figures in it.

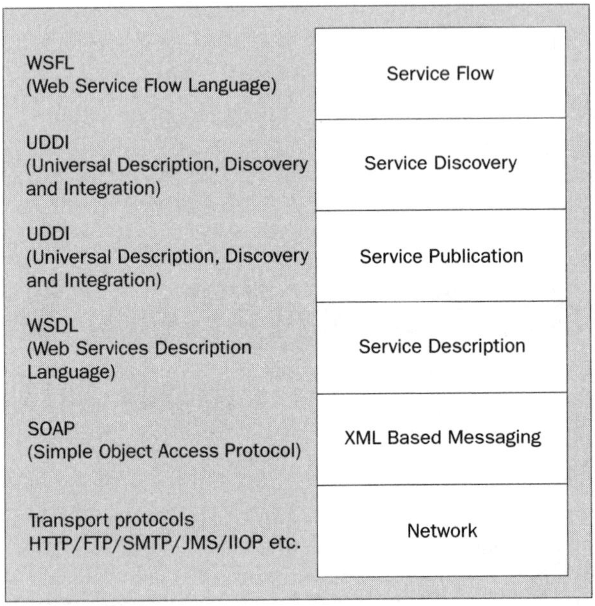

WSFL (Web Service Flow Language)	Service Flow
UDDI (Universal Description, Discovery and Integration)	Service Discovery
UDDI (Universal Description, Discovery and Integration)	Service Publication
WSDL (Web Services Description Language)	Service Description
SOAP (Simple Object Access Protocol)	XML Based Messaging
Transport protocols HTTP/FTP/SMTP/JMS/IIOP etc.	Network

Rationale for UDDI

Three companies – IBM, Microsoft, and Ariba started the UDDI initiative. Their aim was to define standards for enabling businesses to discover each other, interact and share information in a global registry.

UDDI is intended to be standards-based and cross platform. It builds upon existing Internet standards of XML, HTTP, and DNS (Domain Name System). Since then, a number of other companies have pledged to support this standard. The UDDI.org web site lists the supporting companies.

❑ UDDI was designed to solve problems in the business-to-business (B2B) interaction arena, provide a facility for a "smarter search" for Web Services, and allow for easier aggregation of services.

UDDI uses **SOAP** as its transport layer. SOAP, or **Simple Object Access Protocol** is a new standard for XML based messaging, including both synchronous (Remote Procedure Call-like) messaging as well as asynchronous messaging (see Chapter 3).

UDDI Concepts

Version 2 was released in June 2001, but most implementations still support the previous version. The UDDI Global Business Registry is already in operation, and was originally hosted by the three founding companies – IBM, Microsoft, and Ariba. Since then, Ariba has dropped out, and Hewlett Packard has signed up to be an UDDI operator. The companies that host the UDDI global registry are called the UDDI **operators**. These operators need to follow a defined process for managing directory information, replication, etc. This is more formally specified in UDDI version 2. For more information, check out the UDDI production operator sites listed at http://www.uddi.org/. Microsoft's UDDI site is at http://uddi.microsoft.com/, and IBM's is at https://www-3.ibm.com/services/uddi/protect/home.jsp. These sites provide a web interface to the registry for browsing, publishing, and un-publishing business information. The figure below shows the UDDI registry web interface at IBM. Other operator nodes (at present only Microsoft) would have a similar web interfaces too.

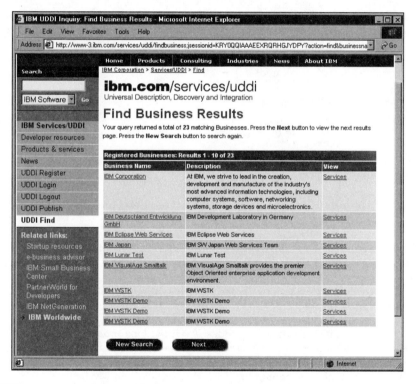

These UDDI operators are free, and businesses can publish their information and details about their services. A business does not need to register with each one separately – it can register at any one of the operator companies, also referred to as the **operator nodes**. The registry works on a "register once, published everywhere" principle, that is, any business registering with one of the registries has its information replicated in all the other registries within a specified time. This is the concept of the UDDI **service cloud** shown in the following diagram, which essentially is a replicated registry. A client searching for a business or a service can do so at any of the registry operators – they should get the same information. There may be a time delay in propagating information between operator nodes; hence if a service provider updates some information at the operator node where they are registered, it may be a little while before clients searching at other nodes in the registry are able to view it.

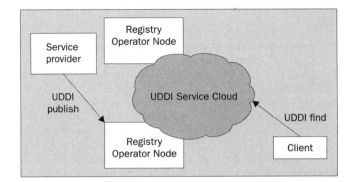

If a company needs to change any information that it has published, it would need to do that with the same operator that it originally registered with. This simplifies security in the UDDI protocol, as it prevents conflicting changes at different operator nodes. In some ways, the UDDI registry parallels the role that the Domain Name System (DNS) plays – it maintains a database of services and service providers similar to DNS maintaining information about domain names. However, unlike DNS, the information here is replicated on all nodes.

In brief, the way the UDDI Business Registry works is:

1. Standards bodies populate the UDDI registry with descriptions of various kinds of services

2. Businesses (service providers) populate the registry with descriptions of the services that they provide

3. The UDDI Business Registry assigns unique identifiers to each service and business registration

4. Online marketplaces, search engines, and business applications query the registry to discover services

5. Businesses will use this data to invoke methods on remote services and integrate with each other over the Web

A company's services can be classified using industry standard taxonomies like **NAICS, UNSPSC,** or **SIC** codes. These taxonomies are used to classify businesses, industries and product categories and define unique category codes for businesses and are pre-existing standards defined by the industry. In addition to these, geographic taxonomies like ISO 3166 or GeoWeb can be used.

❑ SIC, or the Standard Industrial Classification classifies establishments by their primary type of activity. This is a US classification mechanism, and dates back to the 1930's. It is now being replaced by NAICS.

❑ NAICS, or the North American Industrial Classification System, is a classification mechanism specific to US, Canada and Mexico. As the name suggests, it defines classification codes for industries. For example, mining companies have been assigned a NAICS classification code "21", non-oil and gas mining companies the value "212", and under that hierarchy, coal mining companies have the NAICS code "2121"..

❑ UNSPSC, or Universal Standard Products and Services Classification, is an open global coding system for classifying products and services. It is used extensively in electronic catalogs, procurement applications and accounting systems. It is a new system, and is supposed to supercede the Dun & Bradstreet Standard Product and Services Classification (SPSC) and the United Nations Development Program's UNCCS (United Nations Common Coding System). It uses a 10 digit hierarchical code for classification, consisting of the product segment, product family, class, commodity, and business type. For example, mining machinery and accessory companies have the UNSPSC code "20". Under this, quarrying machinery and equipment manufacturers have the code "2010", and still further down the hierarchy, cutting equipment manufacturers have the UNSPSC code "201015".

❑ Geographic taxonomies are a location-based classification for business organizations. UDDI supports the ISO 3166 standard. This defines standard numeric and 2/3 letter alphabetic codes for countries and regions. For example, businesses in California would have "US-CA" as their ISO 3166 geographic taxonomy code. However, Microsoft is pushing its own GeoWeb taxonomy – this allows for a more fine-grained classification, up to the level of cities.

UDDI 2.0 has added the functionality for supporting validated classification and identification taxonomies. Identification taxonomies include Dun & Bradstreet's Data Universal Numbering System and Thomas Register – these are discussed later in the chapter.

A business could be classified under multiple taxonomies. For example, i2 Technologies, which is a software company with offices in Dallas (Texas) and California, is classified as shown below.

GeoWeb classification codes for California, Dallas (Texas) and World:

```
<businessEntity>
   ...

   <categoryBag>
      <keyedReference tModelKey="uuid:297aaa47-2de3-4454-a04a-cf38e889d0c4"
                      keyName="California" keyValue="301364" />

      <keyedReference tModelKey="uuid:297aaa47-2de3-4454-a04a-cf38e889d0c4"
                      keyName="Dallas" keyValue="518350" />

      <keyedReference tModelKey="uuid:297aaa47-2de3-4454-a04a-cf38e889d0c4"
                      keyName="World" keyValue="100016" />
```

NAICS classification code for "Software Publisher":

```
      <keyedReference tModelKey="uuid:c0b9fe13-179f-413d-8a5b-5004db8e5bb2"
                      keyName="Software Publishers" keyValue="5112" />

   </categoryBag>
</businessEntity>
```

UDDI was not the first proposal to address business registries – proposals already exist, for example the ebXML Registry and Repository Specification, with significant areas of overlap. However, UDDI seems to be gaining a lot more momentum than others. It has the backing of major software vendors like BEA, HP, IBM, Intel and Microsoft, Sun, etc.

The term UDDI is often used to mean both the protocol, with its data structures and API, and the global UDDI Business Registry. This is however not the only way that a UDDI registry can be deployed – some alternative deployment scenarios are discussed below.

Given the sheer number of business entities and the services they provide, it is expected that the global UDDI Business Registry may easily have millions of entries. Another issue would be that of validation of content published by companies, and some kind of ratings for the organization information stored in the registry. For example, a customer searching for a supplier for specific materials would have no idea if the found businesses are whom they claim to be, or of their reliability. Given these considerations, business portals and online marketplaces will need to provide value added services on top of the UDDI Business Registry for end users.

UDDI Deployment Scenarios

❑　Global Business Registry

❑　B2B Marketplace Deployment

❑　Private Business Partners

❑　Portal Deployment

❑　Intranet Deployment

The first deployment scenario for a UDDI registry is the one described above consisting of a **global business registry**, the UDDI service cloud, and operator nodes with well defined replication protocols between them. An Operator's Council governs the UDDI operator nodes. This UDDI Operator Council is composed of all current UDDI Public Registry operators. The council will set policy for the UDDI Public Registry and will control future expansion in the body of operators. The list of operator nodes is available at the UDDI.org web site. As mentioned earlier, it currently includes IBM and Microsoft and HP has signed up to be the third operator.

This, however, is not the only way it can be deployed. A closed **business-to-business marketplace deployment** could run a local version of a UDDI registry with its data shielded from the global UDDI registry. This kind of marketplace can then provide value added services like service monitoring, ensure that participants in the UDDI registry have been vetted by a rigorous selection procedure, and also ensure that all entries pertain to the market segment of interest. In such a deployment, publish and find operations could be restricted to the legitimate businesses registered with the marketplace. Such a deployment might not be free like the global registry and may charge a fee, either from the service providers or from the users for providing such value added services.

A variant of the above is a **private business partner UDDI registry** catalog, in which the registry is hosted behind one partner's firewall and only trusted, or "vetted" partners can access the registry. Other names for such a deployment are Vetted Partners or Rolodex-like UDDI.

Yet another deployment of the registry could be in a web portal (hence called **Portal UDDI** deployment) that has the registry behind a firewall. External users of the portal would be allowed to do find operations on the registry, however publish would be restricted to services internal to the portal.

An **Intranet deployment** is another way to deploy the UDDI registry. This allows applications in different departments of the organization to publish and find services, and would be useful for large corporations. These kinds of deployments are called **Internal Enterprise Application Integration UDDI**, for they allow corporations to deploy and advertise Intranet Web Services.

All these deployment scenarios above (with the exception of the global UDDI registry) are examples of **private UDDI registries**. These closed registries offer some advantages over the global UDDI Business Registry. The global Business Registry does not restrict how the service is described, hence a company could describe its services by a variety of means – it could be a URL, pointing to a text description of the service, a description in WSDL, or whatever means the company desires to use. While this allows for flexibility, it severely restricts the ability of an application to do anything meaningful with the results of a find. Instead, if the description were modeled in a way that was well defined, for example using WSDL (this is recommended as best practice), an application could use dynamic find and bind operations on the service. The section on UDDI and WSDL later in the chapter discusses this in greater detail. Private UDDI deployments can thus restrict publishing to allow only WSDL-based `tModel`, or only screened and approved businesses and hence can provide a **target-rich** environment to users.

Some UDDI toolkits, like IBM's UDDI4J and Idoox's WASP UDDI, come with a UDDI server that can be used in private UDDI deployments. These, and other toolkits are covered in the next chapter.

Test Bed Deployment

Before a service is deployed in a production UDDI registry where it has a lot of visibility, it should be deployed in a **test bed registry**. The UDDI operator nodes at IBM and Microsoft host test versions of their global Business Registry nodes, and advise service providers to first publish to the test registry to iron out any errors. Similarly, private UDDI registries could have test bed deployments too.

Data Stored in the Registry

UDDI stores three kinds of data published by businesses in its registry – these are named in terms borrowed from phone books, as White pages, Yellow pages, and Green pages. These terms are representative of the type of data stored in the registry.

❑ **White pages** contain information like the name of the business, contact information, and human-readable descriptions of the company. It also has a list of alternative identifiers that a business may be known by.

❑ **Yellow pages** contain information that classifies the company. This information is based on standard industry classification mechanisms like NAICS, UNSPSC, or geographic index-based classifications and a company could have multiple entries for all the different services or products that it provides. More detail about these classification taxonomies is given later in the chapter.

❑ Finally, **Green pages** contain technical information about the services that a company provides. This is useful for partners who want to do e-commerce interactions with the company, and it contains information about business processes, service descriptions and binding information about the services.

In addition, the standards bodies and businesses also register information about their service types. These are called the **Service Type Registrations** (called `tModels` in UDDI), and they contain information that a programmer would need to know in order to use a particular service. These are discussed in greater detail later in the chapter.

UDDI Specifications

The UDDI 2.0 specifications defined the information model (that is: the UDDI data structures) and the API that the registry operator is expected to support. These specifications are available for free from the UDDI.org web site.

UDDI Information Model

The information model of the UDDI registry is defined in an XML Schema (uddiAPI2.xsd). This schema is published on the UDDI.org website – you can find it on http://www.uddi.org/specification.html. An XML Schema defines the structure of an XML document. The UDDI XML Schema defines five core types of information that a business organization would need to know in order to use a partner's Web Service. These types are business information, service information, binding information, specification pointers and technical information, and publisher assertions. Publisher assertions are new in UDDI 2.0.

Business Information

Business information is a top-level structure and contains information about the business entity itself. It is modeled by the UDDI data structure **businessEntity**, and also corresponds to the "white pages" maintained about a company.

The specification for a business entity is given below.

```
<element name = "businessEntity">
   <complexType>
      <sequence>
         <element ref = "discoveryURLs" minOccurs = "0"/>
         <element ref = "name" maxOccurs = "unbounded"/>
         <element ref = "description" minOccurs = "0"
                  maxOccurs = "unbounded"/>
         <element ref = "contacts" minOccurs = "0"/>
         <element ref = "businessServices" minOccurs = "0"/>
         <element ref = "identifierBag" minOccurs = "0"/>
         <element ref = "categoryBag" minOccurs = "0"/>
      </sequence>
      <attribute ref = "businessKey" use = "required"/>
      <attribute ref = "operator"/>
      <attribute ref = "authorizedName"/>
   </complexType>
</element>
```

The businessEntity element contains:

❑ businessKey attribute: A unique business key, which is an identifier for the business entity. This service key is assigned to the business entity by the UDDI operator node when it registers, using a well-defined algorithm – the DCE UUID (Universal Unique Identifier) algorithm is required by the UDDI specifications. These keys are guaranteed to be unique across all operator nodes. Further details of this algorithm can be obtained from the UUID Internet Draft document listed in the reference section at the end of the chapter.

❑ authorizedName attribute: The name of the individual that publishes the business entity.

❑ operator attribute: Name of the UDDI registry operator site where this entry is published.

❑ discoveryURLs element: URLs that point to alternative discovery mechanisms for the service.

❑ name element: Name of the organization.

❑ description element: A short business description.

188

- ❏ `contacts` element: Contact information for the organization.

- ❏ `businessServices` element: List of business services that this business entity provides (see below).

- ❏ `identifierBag` element: A list of name-value pairs that act as alternative identifiers for the company. For example, the US Tax code Id, the **D-U-N-S** (Dun & Bradstreet's Data Universal Numbering System) identifier, Thomas Register ID, etc. These allow clients to search a company using alternative identification names. The example below shows the IBM's business entity structure, and its D-U-N-S ID `00-136-8083` published in it. A company could have multiple entries in this field.

- ❏ `categoryBag` element: A list of name-value pairs that tag the business entity with specific classification information. This could be in the form of industry taxonomy classifiers (for example: UNSPSC) or geographic classifiers.

A prospective partner can now search the UDDI registry based on any one or more of these attributes and locate matching companies.

A sample business entity structure is shown below. As can be seen, it contains a `businessService` element, the details of which are discussed in the *Business Service Information* section below. The `operator` attribute specifies the UDDI operator node where this information was published. The `authorizedName` attribute in the `businessEntity` element contains the name of person who published this listing:

```
<businessEntity authorizedName="0100000MDJ"
                businessKey="D2033110-3AAF-11D5-80DC-002035229C64"
                operator="www.ibm.com/services/uddi">
  <discoveryURLs>
    <discoveryURL useType="businessEntity">
      http://www.ibm.com/services/uddi/uddiget?businessKey=D2033110-
      3AAF-11D5-80DC-002035229C64
    </discoveryURL>
  </discoveryURLs>
  <name>IBM Corporation</name>
  <description xml:lang="en">At IBM, we strive to lead in the
    creation, development and manufacture of the industry's most
    advanced information technologies, including computer systems,
    software, networking systems, storage devices and
    microelectronics.
  </description>
  <description xml:lang="en"></description>
  <description xml:lang="en">This service enables direct purchasing from
    IBM through the ShopIBM web site.</description>
  <description xml:lang="en">Register to ShopIBM</description>
    ...
    ...
  <contacts>
    <contact useType="US general">
      <personName>IBM Corporation</personName>
      <phone useType="">1 800 IBM 4YOU</phone>
      <email useType="">askibm@vnet.ibm.com</email>
      <address sortCode="" useType="">
        <addressLine>IBM</addressLine>
        <addressLine>New Orchard Road</addressLine>
        <addressLine>Armonk, NY 10504</addressLine>
```

```
            </address>
        </contact>
    </contacts>
    <businessServices>
        <businessService businessKey="D2033110-3AAF-11D5-80DC-002035229C64"
                        serviceKey="894B5100-3AAF-11D5-80DC-002035229C64">
            ...
        </businessService>
        ...
    </businessServices>

    <identifierBag>
        <keyedReference keyName="D-U-N-S" keyValue="00-136-8083"
                        tModelKey="UUID:8609C81E-EE1F-4D5A-B202-
                                    3EB13AD01823"/>
    </identifierBag>

    <categoryBag>
        ...
    </categoryBag>
</businessEntity>
```

Business Service Information

The business service models descriptive information about a family of services offered by a company. The top-level businessEntity element described earlier can contain one or more businessService elements for each of these service families. The businessService element, as the name suggests, contains the business service information. This information includes:

❑   serviceKey attribute: A unique service key that identifies this service. This service key is assigned by operator node when the service is registered.

❑   businessKey attribute: The business entity key – this is the key for the business entity that contains this service.

❑   name element: The name of this service family.

❑   description element: A text description of the service family.

❑   bindingTemplates element: The binding templates, giving the technical service description. More on binding templates is given below.

❑   categoryBag element: A list of name-value pairs that tag the business entity with specific taxonomy information. These, as discussed earlier, can be product, service, or geographic codes. The example below for a "Buy from IBM" service shows it classified under multiple classification codes – for example: for database software (UNSPSC code 43161501), etc.

The business service structure specification is given below:

```
<element name = "businessService">
    <complexType>
        <sequence>
            <element ref = "name" maxOccurs = "unbounded"/>
            <element ref = "description" minOccurs = "0"
                    maxOccurs = "unbounded"/>
            <element ref = "bindingTemplates"/>
```

```
                <element ref = "categoryBag" minOccurs = "0"/>
            </sequence>
            <attribute ref = "serviceKey" use = "required"/>
            <attribute ref = "businessKey"/>
        </complexType>
    </element>
```

The kind of information contained in the businessService element maps to the "yellow pages" information about a company. The example below shows a sample business service entry in the registry. As can be seen in the example, the binding templates are contained in the businessService element. The bindingTemplate element structure is discussed in greater detail a bit later. The example below shows the business service with businessKey and serviceKey attributes. In addition, the child elements of businessService, namely name (name of service), description, bindingTemplate and categoryBag (taxonomy classification information) can be seen. The description string in the example is in English (as can be seen by the xml:lang="en" attribute), though this could very well have been in any language:

```
<businessService businessKey="D2033110-3AAF-11D5-80DC-002035229C64"
                 serviceKey="894B5100-3AAF-11D5-80DC-002035229C64">
    <name>Buy from IBM</name>
    <description xml:lang="en">
        This service enables direct purchasing from IBM through the
        ShopIBM web site.
    </description>
    <bindingTemplates>
        ...
    </bindingTemplates>

    <categoryBag>
        <keyedReference keyName="UNSPSC: Database software"
                        keyValue="43161501"
                        tModelKey="UUID:DB77450D-9FA8-45D4-A7BC-
                                   04411D14E384"/>
        <keyedReference keyName="UNSPSC: Single optical drives"
                        keyValue="43172310"
                        tModelKey="UUID:DB77450D-9FA8-45D4-A7BC-
                                   04411D14E384"/>
        <keyedReference keyName="NAICS: Other Computer Related Services"
                        keyValue="541519"
                        tModelKey="UUID:C0B9FE13-179F-413D-8A5B-
                                   5004DB8E5BB2"/>
    </categoryBag>
</businessService>
```

There is also provision for the business service to be reused between business entities, and typically businesses that publish multiple business entities would like to do this. In this case the business service is managed by one business entity, and other entities have **projections,** or references to the business service.

Binding Information

Binding information contains technical information about a Web Service, also called the "green pages" data. This information helps clients to connect and then invoke the service. The complete list of attributes and elements contained in the bindingTemplate element structure (the structure that models binding information) is below:

❑ bindingKey attribute: A unique binding key identifying this binding template. This again is a unique ID assigned by the operator node.

❑ serviceKey attribute: The business service key – this is the key of the businessService element that contains this binding template.

❑ description element: A text description of the binding template.

❑ accessPoint element: The access point for the information. This contains the entry point for the service. Valid access point values can include the URL, email address or even a phone number. The access point has a urlType attribute, and valid values that it can contain include http, https, ftp, fax, phone and mailto.

❑ hostingRedirector element: This points to another binding template, and is used when the access point is not specified.

❑ tModelInstanceDetails element: A list of tModel info structures. A tModel acts as a fingerprint for the service – more information on tModels is given below.

The structure definition for a binding template is given below.

```
<element name = "bindingTemplate">
    <complexType>
        <sequence>
            <element ref = "description" minOccurs = "0"
                    maxOccurs = "unbounded"/>
            <choice>
                <element ref = "accessPoint" minOccurs = "0"/>
                <element ref = "hostingRedirector" minOccurs = "0"/>
            </choice>
            <element ref = "tModelInstanceDetails"/>
        </sequence>
        <attribute ref = "bindingKey" use = "required"/>
        <attribute ref = "serviceKey"/>
    </complexType>
</element>
```

Let's look at an example of a binding template. As can be seen, it contains references to tModels – the tModelKeys. The example below shows a binding template with the bindingKey (it's unique key) and serviceKey (key of the containing business service) attributes. We can also see the description element, the access point with a URLType of https, and the tModelInstanceDetails element containing the tModel key(s) that this binding templates conforms to:

```
<bindingTemplate bindingKey="6D8F8DF0-3AAF-11D5-80DC-002035229C64"
                serviceKey="894B5100-3AAF-11D5-80DC-002035229C64">
    <description xml:lang="en">Register to ShopIBM</description>
    <accessPoint URLType="https">
        https://commerce.www.ibm.com/cgi-bin/ncommerce
        /RegisterForm?Krypto=rux5N33YF4onmRRYrM2MK6JbZDJCQIqsYZ
        jyy6s330dHEcqYH6sVJako2B%2FwXQuQ
    </accessPoint>
    <tModelInstanceDetails>
        <tModelInstanceInfo tModelKey="UUID:68DE9E80-AD09-469D-8A37-
                                        088422BFBC36"/>
    </tModelInstanceDetails>
</bindingTemplate>
```

A service can have more than one binding template.

Specification Pointers and Technical Information

The binding information discussed above defines how to contact a Web Service. Access information is often not sufficient, as a programmer would need to know a lot more information about the Web Service. This could be information about the kinds of methods that the service exposes, the expected data format, and so on. A lot of this information is application-specific. This information is kept in a tModel (see details below), and has been kept deliberately vague. It has a key, a name, an optional description, and a URL that points to a location that has more description related to the service or taxonomy:

- ❑ tModelKey attribute: A unique tModel key identifying the tModel. These too are assigned by the operator node in a manner similar to the business, service, and binding keys.

- ❑ authorizedName attribute: The name of the individual that published this tModel information.

- ❑ operator attribute: Name of the UDDI registry operator site where this information is published.

- ❑ name element: Name of the tModel.

- ❑ description element: Description of the tModel.

- ❑ overviewDoc element: A reference to remote instructions or descriptions related to the tModel. For example, this could contain a URL pointing to the WSDL description of the Web Service

- ❑ identifierBag element: A list of name value pairs used to record identification numbers for this tModel.

- ❑ categoryBag element: A list of name value pairs used to record classification information for this tModel.

The structure definition for a tModel is given below:

```
<element name = "tModel">
   <complexType>
      <sequence>
         <element ref = "name"/>
         <element ref = "description" minOccurs = "0"
                  maxOccurs = "unbounded"/>
         <element ref = "overviewDoc" minOccurs = "0"/>
         <element ref = "identifierBag" minOccurs = "0"/>
         <element ref = "categoryBag" minOccurs = "0"/>
      </sequence>
      <attribute ref = "tModelKey" use = "required"/>
      <attribute ref = "operator"/>
      <attribute ref = "authorizedName"/>
   </complexType>
</element>
```

A tModel has two main uses; it defines a "technical fingerprint" for the service (when used in binding templates) and it defines an abstract namespace reference (when used in category and identifier bags).

- ❑ Used in a binding template, the tModel key refers to a technical service type. It defines the "technical fingerprint" for the service and thus helps a client program to determine if a Web Service implements a particular programming interface (and hence is compatible with the client program).

```
<bindingTemplate bindingKey="6D8F8DF0-3AAF-11D5-80DC-002035229C64"
                 serviceKey="894B5100-3AAF-11D5-80DC-002035229C64">
    <description xml:lang="en">Register to ShopIBM</description>
    <accessPoint URLType="https">https://someurl</accessPoint>
    <tModelInstanceDetails>
        <tModelInstanceInfo
           tModelKey="UUID:68DE9E80-AD09-469D-8A37-088422BFBC36"/>
    </tModelInstanceDetails>
</bindingTemplate>
```

❑ The tModel key in a category element defines the type of taxonomy. For example, different tModel keys would identify NAICS, UNSPSC, and other taxonomy types. The tModel key shown in the example below is the one for UNSPSC codes:

```
<categoryBag>
    <keyedReference keyName="UNSPSC: Database software" keyValue="43161501"
                    tModelKey="UUID:DB77450D-9FA8-45D4-A7BC-04411D14E384"/>
```

❑ In an identifier element, the tModel key is the type of the identifier – for instance the D-U-N-S number or Taxpayer ID number:

```
<identifierBag>
    <keyedReference keyName="D-U-N-S" keyValue="00-136-8083"
                    tModelKey="UUID:8609C81E-EE1F-4D5A-B202-3EB13AD01823"/>
```

❑ In a business relationship (publisher assertion structure), the tModel key is the type of the relationship. In the example below, it used to define the relationship to be that of a "holding company". Publisher assertions are new in UDDI 2.0, and are discussed later:

```
<publisherAssertions generic="2.0" operator="www.ibm.com/services/uddi/"
                     authorizedName="John J. Doe"
                     xmlns="urn:uddi-org:api_v2">
    <publisherAssertion>
        <fromKey>F5E65...</fromKey>
        <toKey>A237B...</toKey>
        <keyedReference tModelKey="uuid:807A2C6A-EE22-470D-ADC7-
                                   E0424A337C03"
                        keyName="Holding Company"
                        keyValue="parent-child"/>
        </keyedReference>
    </publisherAssertion>
</publisherAssertions>
```

❑ In an address structure, the tModel key specifies the organization structure of the address – for example addresses in USA would be formatted differently from those in other countries. Again, this use is new in version 2.0:

```
<address useType="office" tModelKey="uuid:A345...">
    <addressLine>180 Elm Court</addressLine>
    <addressLine>Sunnyvale, CA 94086</addressLine>
</address>
```

A sample `tModel` entry in the UDDI registry is shown below:

```
<tModel authorizedName="0100000M99"
        operator="www.ibm.com/services/uddi"
        tModelKey="UUID:68DE9E80-AD09-469D-8A37-088422BFBC36">
   <name>uddi-org:http</name>
   <description xml:lang="en">
      An http or web browser based web service
   </description>
   <description xml:lang="en">
      This tModel is used to describe a web service that is invoked
      through a web browser and/or the http protocol.
   </description>
   <overviewDoc>
      <description xml:lang="en">
         This tModel is used to describe a web service that is invoked
         through a web browser and/or the http protocol.
      </description>
      <overviewURL>http://www.uddi.org/specification.html</overviewURL>
   </overviewDoc>
   <categoryBag>
      <keyedReference keyName="tModelType" keyValue="transport"
                      tModelKey="UUID:C1ACF26D-9672-4404-9D70-
                                 39B756E62AB4"/>
   </categoryBag>
</tModel>
```

A set of **canonical** `tModels` has been defined that standardize commonly used classification mechanisms. These include `tModels` for NAICS, UNSPSC, and ISO 3166 categorization taxonomies, identification taxonomies like Dun & Bradstreet's D-U-N-S and Thomas Register supplier identification codes.

Not only that, canonical `tModels` have also been defined for use internally within the registry for its core services. For example, `tModels` have been defined for the UDDI Inquiry API etc.

Publisher Assertions

This is a new data structure that has been introduced in UDDI version 2.0 for modeling business relationships. These can be published by one or both business entities, however for an assertion to be visible, both business entities must publish the same information in the assertions. This prevents businesses from claiming a relationship unilaterally. However, if a publisher is responsible for both the business entities, then publishing just one assertion is enough.

The publisher assertion structure contains the following:

❑   The `fromKey` element or the first business entity the assertion is made for

❑   The `toKey` element or the second business entity the assertion is made for

❑   The `keyedReference` element. This designates the relationship type

The structure definition for the publisher assertion is shown below:

```
<element name = "publisherAssertion">
   <complexType>
      <sequence>
         <element ref = "fromKey"/>
```

```
            <element ref = "toKey"/>
            <element ref = "keyedReference"/>
        </sequence>
    </complexType>
</element>
```

A sample publisher assertion is given below. It models a relationship between a holding company and its subsidiary:

```
<publisherAssertions generic="2.0" operator="www.ibm.com/services/uddi/"
                     authorizedName="John J. Doe" xmlns="urn:uddi-
                                             org:api_v2">
    <publisherAssertion>
        <fromKey>F5E65...</fromKey>
        <toKey>A237B...</toKey>
        <keyedReference tModelKey="uuid:807A2C6A-EE22-470D-ADC7-
                                   E0424A337C03"
                        keyName="Holding Company"
                        keyValue="parent-child">
        </keyedReference>
    </publisherAssertion>
</publisherAssertions>
```

In the sample above, the `fromKey` and `toKey` elements contain the business keys of the two companies. The `tModelKey` attribute in the `keyedReference` element refers to the type of the relationship (for example business partners or holding company, or franchise etc.). UDDI has also defined a canonical `tModel` (see description of canonical `tModels` earlier) for such business relationship types. This allows for three kinds of relationships between business entities – parent-child, peer-peer, and identity (that is: both the entities are the same).

To summarize what we have discussed so far about UDDI data structures: a business publishes a **business entity** containing, among other things, one or more business services. A **business service** has descriptive information about a service that the business provides. A business service can have one or more bindings (**binding templates**). The binding template has information on how to access a service (it's entry point). It also has references to `tModels` (using `tModel` keys) that point to the specification or interface definitions for a service. The interface definitions are usually in the form of WSDL documents. Businesses can model relations between themselves using **publisher assertions**. The following diagram shows the relationship between these five UDDI data structures:

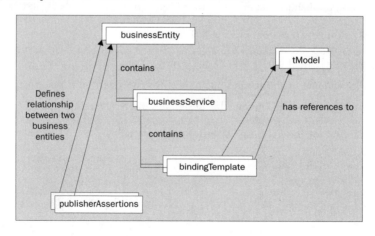

Let's look at a complete example of a registration – so far we have seen the individual data structure elements. The following XML document is the actual registration for IBM published in the UDDI registry. It has been edited for readability and considerably shortened – the original was longer than 700 lines! And no wonder, for it has information about all the services that IBM provides. In the example below, the business entity and the contained business service and binding template information have been highlighted. We can also see some additional structures – for example: the businessDetail element (contains list of business entities), the businessService element (contains list of business service structures) and the bindingTemplates element (list of binding templates). These are messages structures that are returned as response to the inquiry API calls.

```
<businessDetail generic="1.0" operator="www.ibm.com/services/uddi"
                truncated="false" xmlns="urn:uddi-org:api">
    <businessEntity authorizedName="0100000MDJ"
                businessKey="D2033110-3AAF-11D5-80DC-002035229C64"
                operator="www.ibm.com/services/uddi">
        <discoveryURLs>
            <discoveryURL useType="businessEntity">
                http://www.ibm.com/services/uddi
                /uddiget?businessKey=D2033110-3AAF-11D5-80DC-002035229C64
            </discoveryURL>
        </discoveryURLs>
        <name>IBM Corporation</name>
        <description xml:lang="en">
            At IBM, we strive to lead in the creation, development and
            manufacture of the industry's most advanced information
            technologies, including computer systems, software, networking
            systems, storage devices and microelectronics.
        </description>
        <contacts>
            <contact useType="US general">
                <personName>IBM Corporation</personName>
                <phone useType="">1 800 IBM 4YOU</phone>
                <email useType="">askibm@vnet.ibm.com</email>
                <address sortCode="" useType="">
                    <addressLine>IBM</addressLine>
                    <addressLine>New Orchard Road</addressLine>
                    <addressLine>Armonk, NY 10504</addressLine>
                </address>
            </contact>
        </contacts>
        <businessServices>
            <businessService businessKey="D2033110-3AAF-11D5-80DC-
                                    002035229C64"
                        serviceKey="894B5100-3AAF-11D5-80DC-
                                    002035229C64">
                <name>Buy from IBM</name>
                <description xml:lang="en">
                    This service enables direct purchasing from IBM through
                    the ShopIBM web site.
                </description>
                <bindingTemplates>
                    <bindingTemplate bindingKey="6D8F8DF0-3AAF-11D5-80DC-
                                    002035229C64"
                        serviceKey="894B5100-3AAF-11D5-80DC-
                                    002035229C64">
```

```
                    <description xml:lang="en">
                       Register to ShopIBM
                    </description>
                    <accessPoint URLType="https">
                       https://commerce.www.ibm.com/cgi-bin/ncommerce/
                       RegisterForm?Krypto=rux5N33YF4onmRRYrM2MK6
                       JbZDJCQIqsYZjyy6s330dHEcqYH6sVJako2B%2FwXQuQ
                    </accessPoint>
                    <tModelInstanceDetails>
                       <tModelInstanceInfo tModelKey="UUID:68DE9E80-AD09-
                                              469D-8A37-088422BFBC36"/>
                    </tModelInstanceDetails>
                 </bindingTemplate>
              </bindingTemplates>

              <categoryBag>
                 <keyedReference keyName="UNSPSC: Database software"
                                 keyValue="43161501"
                                 tModelKey="UUID:DB77450D-9FA8-45D4-
                                            A7BC-04411D14E384"/>
                 <keyedReference keyName="UNSPSC: Single optical drives"
                                 keyValue="43172310"
                                 tModelKey="UUID:DB77450D-9FA8-45D4-
                                            A7BC-04411D14E384"/>
                 <keyedReference keyName="NAICS: Other Computer Related
                                          Services"
                                 keyValue="541519"
                                 tModelKey="UUID:C0B9FE13-179F-
                                            413D-8A5B-5004DB8E5BB2"/>
              </categoryBag>
           </businessService>
        </businessServices>

        <identifierBag>
           <keyedReference keyName="D-U-N-S" keyValue="00-136-8083"
                           tModelKey="UUID:8609C81E-EE1F-4D5A-B202-
                                      3EB13AD01823"/>
        </identifierBag>
     </businessEntity>
  </businessDetail>
```

Further detailed information on these different data structures is available in the technical white paper and the Data Structure Reference available at the UDDI.org website (http://www.uddi.org/).

UDDI Programming Model

The UDDI 2.0 API Specification document defines the programming interface for the UDDI registry. This document can be found at the UDDI.org website.

UDDI API

The UDDI API is an interface that accepts XML messages wrapped in SOAP envelopes. A programmer typically would not be creating messages in this format – there are toolkits available that shield programmers from the task of manipulating XML documents. These toolkits (or the API they provide) internally talk to the UDDI registry using the XML message formats defined by the UDDI protocol. Programmers can build applications in Java, Visual Basic or any language of their choice to access UDDI registries and either publish their services, find services provided by other companies or un-publish their service listings. Currently, UDDI client side libraries/toolkits exist for Visual Basic, Java, and Perl. The UDDI registry understands SOAP messages, and can even be thought of as a SOAP-enabled Web Service itself. Even though most programmers would not be using these directly, an understanding of these API formats is useful, not only for implementers of UDDI tools, but also developers interested in what happens under the hood. Further details on the API can be obtained from the UDDI Programmer's API version 2.0 document at the UDDI.org website.

Inquiry API

The inquiry API that needs to be exposed by the UDDI registry is given below. These API calls are discussed below. UDDI 2.0 adds one new API call – `find_relatedBusinesses` – to this list. At the end of this section, we will look at some sample interactions with the UDDI registry.

find_binding

This is used to locate specific bindings within a registered business service. It takes as arguments the service key, which is a unique identifier for a business service, the technical fingerprints for the desired services (sent as a list in `tModelBag`) and some optional (signified by `[]`) search criteria. This call returns the binding template(s) that match the search criteria. The binding templates have information on invoking services. The syntax of this call as given in the UDDI v 2.0 Programmer API document is:

```
<find_binding serviceKey="uuid_key"
              [maxRows="nn"]
              generic="2.0"
              xmlns="urn:uddi-org:api_v2" >
  [<findQualifiers/>]
   <tModelBag/>
</find_binding>
```

Errors messages, if any, are passed back through a "Disposition Report" – more about this is explained later. There can be three cases in which this call can fail, and the error codes for these are:

❑   `E_invalidKeyPassed`: Invalid key for service or `tModel`

❑   `E_unsupported`: Invalid values were passed in the find qualifiers

The find qualifiers have the following syntax:

```
<findQualifiers>
   <findQualifier>fixedQualifierValue</findQualifier>
  [<findQualifier>fixedQualifierValue</findQualifier> ...]
</findQualifiers>
```

The values that can go in the find qualifier are one –`exactNameMatch`, `caseSentiveMatch`, `sortByNameAsc`, `sortByNameDesc`, `sortByDateAsc`, `sortByDateDesc`. These are self-descriptive in their meaning; and they modify the default search behavior of the inquiry methods. The UDDI API document defines precedence rules for them.

a. `exactNameMatch` and `caseSensitiveMatch` can be combined but are equal in precedence

b. `sortByNameAsc` and `sortByNameDesc` are mutually exclusive, but equal in precedence

c. `sortByDateAsc` and `sortByDateDesc` are mutually exclusive, but equal in precedence

UDDI 2.0 has defined four new find qualifiers in addition to these. They are:

a. `orLikeKeys`: When a category bag/identifier bag contains multiple entries, they should be logically OR'ed for the search and not AND'ed

b. `orAllKeys`: Logically OR all keys in the identifier and category bag, instead of ANDing them

c. `andAllKeys`: Logically AND all keys in the identifier and category bag
(As expected, the above three are mutually exclusive.)

d. `soundex`: Do a "sound-alike" search on the names

❑ `E_tooManyOptions`: Some of the arguments passed were mutually exclusive. Some find qualifiers are mutually exclusive – for example: `sortByNameAsc` (sort by name ascending) and `sortByNameDesc` (sort by name descending) are mutually exclusive.

find_business

This method helps locate one or more business entities that match search criteria. The search can be performed on the partial name of the business, the business identifiers, the category/classification identifiers or the technical fingerprints of the services. The operator node might truncate the search result if the number of businesses is too large – UDDI does not define what being too large means, and individual operator nodes define this for themselves. The syntax of the call is given below:

```
<find_business [maxRows="nn"] generic="2.0" xmlns="urn:uddi-org:api_v2" >
  [<findQualifiers/>]
  [<name/> [<name/>]... ]
  [<discoveryURLs/>]
  [<identifierBag/>]
  [<categoryBag/>]
  [<tModelBag/>]
</find_business>
```

In addition to the find qualifier described in `find_binding`, there are two specifically for `find_business` (new in UDDI 2.0):

❑ `CombineCategoryBags` – Combine the category bag entries in the business service with that of the business entity while performing a search

❑ `ServiceSubset` – Use the category bag entries of the business service only for the search

The possible errors for this call include:

❑ `E_nameTooLong`: The partial name value passed exceeds the maximum name length designated by the Operator Site

❑ `E_tooManyOptions`: More than 5 names arguments passed

❑ `E_unsupported`: One of the `findQualifier` values passed was invalid

find_service

The `find_service` method returns a list of business services that match the search conditions. The input parameters to this method are the unique business entity key, the partial name of the service, a list of category references for the service, and other search qualifiers.

```
<find_service businessKey="uuid_key" [maxRows="nn"] generic="2.0"
              xmlns="urn:uddi-org:api_v2" >
  [<findQualifiers/>]
  [<name/> [<name/>]... ]
  [<categoryBag/>]
  [<tModelBag/>]
</find_service>
```

The find qualifiers are the same as described in `find_binding`.

The errors that can occur in this call are:

❑ `E_invalidKeyPassed`: The `uuid_key` value passed did not match with any known `businessKey` key or `tModel` key values

❑ `E_nameTooLong`: The partial name value passed exceeds the maximum name length as specified in the UDDI Data structure reference

❑ `E_unsupported`: Can be one of multiple causes – the error text would have more details. Some possible causes are – invalid `findQualifier` values, blank name value

find_tModel

This method, as the name suggests, finds `tModels`. The input is a partial name of the `tModel` or a list of business identifiers or a list of category/classification identifiers in addition to other find qualifiers. The business identifiers are logically OR 'ed with each other while the category identifiers are AND 'ed in the search query.

```
<find_tModel [maxRows="nn"] generic="2.0" xmlns="urn:uddi-org:api_v2" >
  [<findQualifiers/>]
  [<name/>]
  [<identifierBag/>]
  [<categoryBag/>]
</find_tModel>
```

The find qualifiers are the same as described in `find_binding`.

In case of an error, the disposition report will contain of the following errors:

❑ `E_nameTooLong`: The partial name value passed exceeds the maximum name length designated by the Operator Site

❑ `E_unsupported`: One of the `findQualifier()` values passed was invalid

get_bindingDetail

This method returns the run-time binding template information (`bindingTemplate` structure) used for invoking methods against a business service. The binding templates specified by the `bindingKeys` are the input parameters to the call:

```
<get_bindingDetail generic="2.0" xmlns="urn:uddi-org:api_v2" >
   <bindingKey/>
   [<bindingKey/> ...]
</get_bindingDetail>
```

The error that can be returned by this call is:

- ❑ E_invalidKeyPassed: One of the uuid_key values passed did not match with any known bindingKey key values

get_businessDetail

The get_businessDetail method returns the complete businessEntity object for one or more business entities. The input parameter is a list of businessKeys that uniquely specify the business entity.

```
<get_businessDetail generic="2.0" xmlns="urn:uddi-org:api_v2" >
   <businessKey/>
   [<businessKey/> ...]
</get_businessDetail>
```

The error that can be returned by this call is:

- ❑ E_invalidKeyPassed: One of the uuid_key values passed did not match with any known businessKey key values

get_businessDetailExt

This method is identical to the get_businessDetail method, but returns extra attributes in case the source registry is not an operator node:

```
<get_businessDetailExt generic="2.0" xmlns="urn:uddi-org:api_v2" >
   <businessKey/>
   [<businessKey/> ...]
</get_businessDetailExt>
```

The errors that can be returned by this call are:

- ❑ E_invalidKeyPassed: One of the uuid_key values passed did not match with any known businessKey key values

- ❑ E_unsupported: The operator node does not implement the extended detail function

get_serviceDetail

The get_serviceDetail method returns the complete businessService object for one or more business services specified by their service keys:

```
<get_serviceDetail generic="2.0" xmlns="urn:uddi-org:api_v2" >
   <serviceKey/>
   [<serviceKey/> ...]
</get_serviceDetail>
```

The error that can be returned by this call is :

❑   E_invalidKeyPassed: One of the uuid_key values passed did not match with any known serviceKey key values

get_tModelDetail

This method returns the tModel details. One or more tModel keys can be passed as an argument:

```
<get_tModelDetail generic="2.0" xmlns="urn:uddi-org:api_v2" >
  <tModelKey/>
  [<tModelKey/> ...]
</get_tModelDetail>
```

The error that can be returned by this call is:

❑   E_invalidKeyPassed: One of the uuid_key values passed did not match with any known tModelKey key values

All the inquiry methods can have their results truncated by the operator site. If this is the case, the truncated attribute in the response is set to true. The methods can control the number of rows desired using the maxRows input parameter.

find_relatedBusinesses

This is used to locate information about business entity registrations that are related to the business entity. The business entity's unique key is passed as the input parameter. This functionality is used to manage registrations of business units and relate them based on organization hierarchies or business partner relationships. This call returns a list of related business entities. The syntax for this call is:

```
<find_relatedBusinesses generic="2.0" xmlns="urn:uddi-org:api_v2" >
  [<findQualifiers/>]
  <businessKey/>
  [<keyedReference/>]
</find_relatedBusinesses>
```

Possible errors from this call include:

❑   E_invalidKeyPassed: A uuid_key or tModel key value passed did not match with any known businessKey key or tModel key values.

❑   E_unsupported: The findQualifier values passed was invalid

This API call is new in UDDI version 2.0.

Publishing API

The Publishing API essentially allow programs to save and delete the five data types supported by UDDI and described earlier in the UDDI information model.

These calls are used by service providers and companies to publish and un-publish information about themselves in the UDDI registry. These API calls require authenticated access to the registry, unlike the Inquiry API. All these calls, except for `get_authToken`, require an authorization token to be passed as a parameter. The authentication token is an opaque data value – it is up to the operator node to implement a mechanism for generation of the authorization token, and these tokens are not portable across operator nodes. The publishing API provides two calls – `get_AuthToken` and `discard_authToken` – for getting an authorization token and invalidating it respectively. The `get_AuthToken` call takes the user ID and credentials and returns the token. The user ID and password for this call is set when the user sets up a publisher account at an operator node. The UDDI operators provide a web-based interface for setting up publisher account, and these often involve entering some contact information about the business. This token is then used in all subsequent publishing calls – these and other calls are discussed in greater length later.

The figure below shows the web interface for creating a publisher account at IBM's UDDI node:

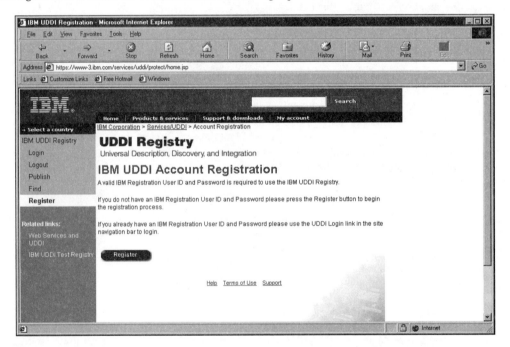

A UDDI implementation need not use this kind of login-based mechanism for authentication. It could very well use a certificate based authentication scheme that directly passes an authorization token (in this case the certificate value) with each publish API message. In such an implementation, the use of `get_authToken` and `discard_authToken` messages would not be required.

In addition to this, these calls are transported over HTTPS, thus securing their transmission over the network.

UDDI 2.0 introduces five new publishing API calls for publisher assertions – `add_publisherAssertions`, `delete_publisherAssertions`, `set_publisherAssertions`, `get_publisherAssertions`, and `get_AssertionStatusReport` calls. These are discussed below, along with calls that were introduced in UDDI 1.0.

delete_binding

Removes one or more binding templates from the registry. The binding templates to be deleted are specified by their unique binding keys. The calls syntax is given below, and as can be seen, it takes one or more binding keys as input:

```
<delete_binding generic="2.0" xmlns="urn:uddi-org:api_v2" >
   <authInfo/>
   <bindingKey/>
   [<bindingKey/> ...]
</delete_binding>
```

The errors that can occur in this call are:

- ❑ E_invalidKeyPassed: One of the uuid_key values passed did not match with any known bindingKey values. No partial results will be returned – if any bindingKey values passed are not valid, this error will be returned

- ❑ E_authTokenExpired: The authentication token value passed in the authInfo argument is no longer valid because the token has expired

- ❑ E_authTokenRequired: The authentication token value passed in the authInfo argument is either missing or is not valid

- ❑ E_userMismatch: One or more of the bindingKey values passed refers to data that is not controlled by the individual who is represented by the authentication token

- ❑ E_operatorMismatch: One or more of the bindingKey values passed refers to data that is not controlled by the operator site that received the request for processing

delete_business

Removes one or more businessEntity structures from the registry. The business entities to be deleted are specified by their unique business keys. The syntax of this call is shown below, and it takes one or more business keys along with the authorization information as its parameters:

```
<delete_business generic="2.0" xmlns="urn:uddi-org:api_v2" >
   <authInfo/>
   <businessKey/>
   [<businessKey/> ...]
</delete_business>
```

The errors that can occur in this call are the same as in delete_binding.

delete_service

Removes one or more businessService structures from the registry. The business services to be deleted are specified by their unique service keys:

```
<delete_service generic="2.0" xmlns="urn:uddi-org:api_v2" >
   <authInfo/>
   <serviceKey/>
   [<serviceKey/> ...]
</delete_service>
```

The errors that can occur in this call are the same as in delete_binding.

delete_tModel

Removes one or more tModel structures from the registry. The tModel to be deleted are specified by their unique tModel keys.

```
<delete_tModel generic="2.0" xmlns="urn:uddi-org:api_v2" >
    <authInfo/>
    <tModelKey/> [ <tModelKey/> ...]
</delete_tModel>
```

The errors that can occur in this call are the same as in delete_binding.

discard_authToken

This call informs the UDDI site that the authentication token may be discarded, and all subsequent calls using this token are to be rejected.

```
<discard_authToken generic="2.0" xmlns="urn:uddi-org:api_v2" >
    <authInfo/>
</discard_authToken>
```

Once a client has finished publishing to the UDDI registry, it should expire the token using this call. The error that can occur in this call is:

❑   E_authTokenRequired: The authentication token value passed in the authInfo argument is either missing or is not valid

get_authToken

This call is used to obtain an authentication token. The input parameters are username and credentials/password. The token obtained is used for all subsequent calls that require authentication. This token is valid until it either expires or is invalidated by a discard_authToken call.

```
<get_authToken generic="2.0" xmlns="urn:uddi-org:api_v2"
                userID="someLoginName"
                cred="someCredential"
</get_authToken>
```

The error that can occur in this call is:

❑   E_unknownUser: The operator site that received the request does not recognize the userID and/or credential argument values passed to be valid.

get_registeredInfo

The get_registeredInfo() call returns an abbreviated list of all business entity keys and tModel keys that are controlled by the individual whose credentials are passed as input to the call:

```
<get_registeredInfo generic="2.0" xmlns="urn:uddi-org:api_v2" >
    <authInfo/>
</get_registeredInfo>
```

The errors that can occur in this call are:

- ❏ E_authTokenExpired: The authentication token value passed in the authInfo argument is no longer valid because the token has expired

- ❏ E_authTokenRequired: The authentication token value passed in the authInfo argument is either missing or is not valid

save_binding

The save_binding call is used to save or update a complete bindingTemplate structure. One or more binding templates may be passed to the call, as shown in the syntax of the call below:

```
<save_binding generic="2.0" xmlns="urn:uddi-org:api_v2" >
   <authInfo/>
   <bindingTemplate/> [<bindingTemplate/>...]
</save_binding>
```

The errors that can occur in this call are:

- ❏ E_invalidKeyPassed: One of the uuid_key values passed did not match with any known bindingKey values. No partial results will be returned – if any bindingKey values passed are not valid, this error will be returned

- ❏ E_authTokenExpired: The authentication token value passed in the authInfo argument is no longer valid because the token has expired

- ❏ E_authTokenRequired: The authentication token value passed in the authInfo argument is either missing or is not valid

- ❏ E_userMismatch: One or more of the bindingKey values passed refers to data that is not controlled by the individual who is represented by the authentication token

- ❏ E_accountLimitExceeded: User account limits have been exceeded

save_business

This method is used to save or update a business entity structure. One or more business entity structures may be passed to this call, and it updates these in the registry. Since the business entity contains the business services, which in turn contain the binding templates, this call is very broad in its effect!

```
<save_business generic="2.0" xmlns="urn:uddi-org:api_v2" >
   <authInfo/>
   <businessEntity/> [<businessEntity/>...]
</save_business>
```

The errors that can occur in this call include the ones for save_binding, and the following errors:

- ❏ E_invalidValue: The given keyValue did not correspond to a category within the taxonomy identified by a tModelKey value within one of the categoryBag elements provided

- ❏ E_valueNotAllowed: Restrictions have been placed by the taxonomy provider on the types of information that should be included at that location within a specific taxonomy. The validation routine chosen by the operator site has rejected this businessEntity for at least one specified category

save_service

This method is used to save or update a business service structure. It takes an input one or more business service structures, and updates the registry with it. This can be seen in the syntax for the call below:

```
<save_service generic="2.0" xmlns="urn:uddi-org:api_v2" >
   <authInfo/>
   <businessService/> [<businessService/>...]
</save_service>
```

The errors that can occur in this call are the same as in save_business.

save_tModel

The save_tModel method is used to add or update tModel structures. As can be seen from the syntax below, it takes one or mode tModel structures as input.

```
<save_tModel generic="2.0" xmlns="urn:uddi-org:api_v2" >
   <authInfo/>
   <tModel/> [<tModel/>...]
</save_tModel>
```

The errors that can occur in this call are the same as in save_business.

add_publisherAssertions

Adds a relationship to the existing set of assertions about relationship. The syntax of this call is:

```
<add_publisherAssertions generic="2.0" xmlns="urn:uddi-org:api_v2" >
   <authInfo/>
   <publisherAssertion>
      <fromKey/>
      <toKey/>
      <keyedReference/>
   </publisherAssertion>
[<publisherAssertion/> ...]
</add_publisherAssertions>
```

As can be seen, the publisher assertions consist of a "from" key, a "to" key and a keyed reference. This is explained in more detail in the section on the new data structures.

The following errors are relevant for this call:

❑ E_invalidKeyPassed: One of the uuid_key values passed did not match with any known businessKey or tModelKey values

❑ E_authTokenExpired: The authentication token value passed in the authInfo argument is no longer valid because the token has expired

❑ E_authTokenRequired: The authentication token value passed in the authInfo argument is either missing or is not valid

❑ E_userMismatch: Neither of the businessKey values passed in the embedded fromKey and toKey elements is controlled by the publisher account associated with the authentication token

delete_publisherAssertions

This method deletes a specific assertion about a business relationship from the assertion collection of a particular publisher account. Deleting an assertion effectively invalidates the business relationship based on that assertion. The syntax for this call is shown below.

```
<delete_publisherAssertions generic="2.0" xmlns="urn:uddi-org:api_v2" >
   <authInfo/>
   <publisherAssertion>
      <fromKey/>
      <toKey/>
      <keyedReference/>
   </publisherAssertion>
  [<publisherAssertion/> ...]
</delete_publisherAssertions>
```

The following errors can occur in this call:

❑ E_assertionNotFound: No such matching assertion was found in the publisher's matching collection

❑ E_authTokenExpired: The authentication token value passed in the authInfo argument is no longer valid because the token has expired

❑ E_authTokenRequired: The authentication token value passed in the authInfo argument is either missing or is not valid

get_assertionStatusReport

This method is used to get a status report on publisher assertions. This report helps in managing the publisher assertions.

```
<get_assertionStatusReport generic="2.0" xmlns="urn:uddi-org:api_v2" >
   <authInfo/>
  [<completionStatus/>]
</get_assertionStatusReport>
```

The optional completionStatus element is used to restrict the result set. It can have one of following three possible values:

❑ status:complete returns only the publisher assertions that are complete to be returned, that is: there are matching assertions from both parties involved

❑ status:toKey_incomplete returns only those publisher assertions where the party who controls the businessEntity referenced by the toKey value in an assertion has not made a matching assertion to be listed

❑ status:fromKey_incomplete returns only those publisher assertions where the party who controls the businessEntity referenced by the fromKey value in an assertion has not made a matching assertion to be listed

The errors that can occur in this call are:

❑ E_invalidCompletionStatus: The completionStatus value passed is unrecognized

❑ E_authTokenExpired: The authentication token value passed in the authInfo argument is no longer valid because the token has expired

❑   E_authTokenRequired: The authentication token value passed in the authInfo argument
     is either missing or is not valid

get_publisherAssertions

The get_publisherAssertions method returns the active set of publisher assertions for a publisher.

The syntax for the call is:

```
<get_publisherAssertions generic="2.0" xmlns="urn:uddi-org:api_v2" >
    <authInfo/>
</get_publisherAssertions>
```

The errors that can occur in this call are:

❑   E_authTokenExpired: The authentication token value passed in the authInfo argument is
     no longer valid because the token has expired

❑   E_authTokenRequired: The authentication token value passed in the authInfo argument
     is either missing or is not valid

set_publisherAssertions

set_publisherAssertions is used to save the entire set of publisher assertions. It replaces any
exiting assertions in the registry.

```
<set_publisherAssertions generic="2.0" xmlns="urn:uddi-org:api_v2" >
    <authInfo/>
    <publisherAssertion>
        <fromKey/>
        <toKey/>
        <keyedReference/>
    </publisherAssertion>
  [<publisherAssertion>...]
</set_publisherAssertions>
```

The errors that can occur in this call are:

❑   E_invalidKeyPassed: One of the uuid_key values passed did not match with any known
     businessKey or tModelKey values

❑   E_authTokenExpired: The authentication token value passed in the authInfo argument is
     no longer valid because the token has expired

❑   E_authTokenRequired: The authentication token value passed in the authInfo argument
     is either missing or is not valid

❑   E_userMismatch: Neither of the businessKey values passed in the embedded fromKey and
     toKey elements is controlled by the publisher account associated with the authentication token

UDDI Errors

When any of these UDDI calls result in an error, a description about the error is returned in the form of
a disposition report structure in the SOAP Fault. A typical error message is shown below – this one is for
an expired authorization token:

```
<?xml version="1.0" encoding="UTF-8" ?>
<Envelope xmlns="http://schemas.xmlsoaporg.org/soap/envelope/">
    <Body>
        <Fault>
            <faultcode>Client</faultcode>
            <faultstring>Client Error</faultstring>
            <detail>
                <dispositionReport generic="2.0"
                                operator="www.ibm.com/services/uddi"
                                xmlns="urn:uddi-org:api_v2">
                    <result errno="10110" >
                        <errInfo errCode="E_authTokenExpired">
                            Authorization token expired.
                        </errInfo>
                    </result>
                </dispositionReport>
            </detail>
        </Fault>
    </Body>
</Envelope>
```

Query patterns

The inquiry APIs discussed above are all of the find_xx or get_xx type. A programmer would use a find_xx API call to get a list of all entries of that type and then use a get_xx call to get additional information on a specific entry. For example, a find_business call would first be issued to locate all businesses in a specific category area, and then a get_BusinessDetailExt call would be used to get additional information about a specific business. The UDDI API usage patterns or conventions fall under three broad categories:

❑   The **browse pattern** involves starting from some broad information, such as the business name, or a part of name and performing a search. Then based on the result set of the search, drill-down (the **drill down pattern**) for specific information. The find_xx methods in the inquiry API are of the browse pattern, and the get_xx methods are drill down methods.

❑   The **invocation pattern** deals with invoking a method on a remote Web Service. This call is made using information obtained from the binding template for a service. For performance reasons, the results of a find on the UDDI registry may sometimes be cached locally, so the invocation of the method would first be done based on the cached bindingTemplate, and only if that fails would an effort be made to locate a fresh bindingTemplate.

❑   The binding template data structure discussed earlier contains information about the Web Service. A programmer would need use inquiry API to locate this and then invoke methods on a Web Service based on it. Typical sequences for these kinds of interactions could be:

   a.   Locate a business entity using the UDDI Inquiry API method find_business.

   b.   Drill down for more detail about a business service using get_serviceDetail or request a full business entity structure using the get_businessDetail or get_businessDetailExt method. A business entity contains all information about advertised Web Services and the programmer can select a particular binding template from it.

   c.   The programmer builds a program based on the specifications obtained from the binding template. This information is stored in the tModel keys stored in the service's binding template.

d. The client program so constructed is finally run which invokes the Web Service using the binding template information.

Lets us go over some sample interactions:

First, find a business with the name XMethods.

```
<find_business generic="2.0" xmlns="urn:uddi-org:api_v2">
   <name>XMethods</name>
</find_business>
```

Here the generic attribute specifies the API version number. This call locates all businesses that have the string XMethods in a part of their name. The search is done based on a leftmost match, hence if the name parameter had been just X instead of XMethods, it would have matched Xmethods and Xilinx, as well as all companies with names starting with X.

The response for this message is shown below.

```
<businessList generic="2.0" operator="www.ibm.com/services/uddi"
              truncated="false" xmlns="urn:uddi-org:api_v2">
    <businessInfos>
       <businessInfo businessKey="BA744ED0-3AAF-11D5-80DC-002035229C64">
          <name>XMethods</name>
          <description xml:lang="en">Web services resource site</description>
          <serviceInfos>
             <serviceInfo businessKey="BA744ED0-3AAF-11D5-80DC-002035229C64"
                          serviceKey="D5B180A0-4342-11D5-BD6C-002035229C64">
                <name>XMethods Barnes and Noble Quote</name>
             </serviceInfo>
             <serviceInfo businessKey="BA744ED0-3AAF-11D5-80DC-002035229C64"
                          serviceKey="ED85F000-4345-11D5-BD6C-002035229C64">
                <name>XMethods Pacific Bell SMS Service</name>
             </serviceInfo>
             <serviceInfo businessKey="BA744ED0-3AAF-11D5-80DC-002035229C64"
                          serviceKey="D5921160-3E16-11D5-98BF-002035229C64">
                <name>XMethods Delayed Stock Quotes</name>
             </serviceInfo>
             <serviceInfo businessKey="BA744ED0-3AAF-11D5-80DC-002035229C64"
                          serviceKey="618167A0-3E64-11D5-98BF-002035229C64">
                <name>XMethods Currency Exchange Rates</name>
             </serviceInfo>
          </serviceInfos>
       </businessInfo>
    </businessInfos>
</businessList>
```

The response message above shows the list of all businesses that match the string Xmethods. At this moment, only one does, and hence only one BusinessInfo structure can be seen. This business has multiple services registered as can be seen by the multiple ServiceInfos.

The programmer can then get more information about a specific service. For instance, we can do a find_service to locate a particular service in this business entity:

```
<find_service generic='2.0' xmlns='urn:uddi-org:api_v2'
   businessKey= BA744ED0-3AAF-11D5-80DC-002035229C64'>
   <name>XMethods Currency Exchange</name>
</find_service>
```

This would give back information about the services found that match the given name:

```
<serviceList generic="2.0" operator="www.ibm.com/services/uddi"
            truncated="false" xmlns="urn:uddi-org:api_v2">
   <serviceInfos>
      <serviceInfo businessKey="BA744ED0-3AAF-11D5-80DC-002035229C64"
                  serviceKey="618167A0-3E64-11D5-98BF-002035229C64">
         <name>XMethods Currency Exchange Rates</name>
      </serviceInfo>
   </serviceInfos>
</serviceList>
```

The service keys returned help to uniquely identify the service.

Alternatively, we could have used the service key to drill-down and get the detail information about the service:

```
<get_serviceDetail generic='2.0' xmlns='urn:uddi-org:api'>
   <serviceKey>618167A0-3E64-11D5-98BF-002035229C64</serviceKey>
</get_serviceDetail>
```

The response would have looked something like that given below.

```
<serviceDetail generic="2.0" operator="www.ibm.com/services/uddi"
            truncated="false" xmlns="urn:uddi-org:api_v2">
   <businessService businessKey="BA744ED0-3AAF-11D5-80DC-002035229C64"
                  serviceKey="618167A0-3E64-11D5-98BF-002035229C64">
      <name>XMethods Currency Exchange Rates</name>
      <description xml:lang="en">
         Returns exchange rates between 2 countries&apos;currencies
      </description>
      <description xml:lang="en">
         SOAP binding for currency exchange rates service
      </description>
      <bindingTemplates>
         <bindingTemplate bindingKey="618474E0-3E64-11D5-98BF-002035229C64"
                        serviceKey="618167A0-3E64-11D5-98BF-002035229C64">
            <description xml:lang="en">
               SOAP binding for currency exchange rates service
            </description>
            <accessPoint URLType="http">
               http://services.xmethods.net:80/soap
            </accessPoint>
            <tModelInstanceDetails>
               <tModelInstanceInfo tModelKey="UUID:E092F730-3E63-11D5-98BF-
                                 002035229C64"/>
            </tModelInstanceDetails>
         </bindingTemplate>
      </bindingTemplates>
   </businessService>
</serviceDetail>
```

This is just one sample pattern for browsing – we could very well have done a drill-down using the business key, and obtained the entire business entity; or started the search at a different place by searching by the tModel, and locating businesses that have services implementing the tModel.

API Design principles

The UDDI API is built on some simple design principles. The main ones are discussed below:

Security

Of the two APIs, only the publishing API has a requirement for security since it allows storing, changing, and removing information from the registry. This API requires authenticated access to the registry, however it is the responsibility of the operator node to define the authentication protocol. The requirements of security are simple – a service provider would need to first sign up with one of the operator nodes, and establish user credentials. Using these credentials (these could be as simple as a username/password pair), the service provider can publish and update information in the registry. Only the publisher of an entry in the UDDI registry has rights to modify or delete it. Also, the publisher can modify an entry listing only at the specific operator node where it was originally registered.

Versioning

Versioning is an important requirement in a distributed system as services and their API can change over time. The clients and the service would thus need to know about the version of the API being used, so as not to cause miscommunication. All messages defined in the API are required to be tagged with a version attribute – the message being in XML, this is in the form of an XML attribute. Operator sites have agreements in place on the version number that should be supported. For UDDI version 1.0 for example, the version number sent in the messages is "1.0".

```
<find_business generic="1.0" xmlns="urn:uddi-org:api">
    ...
</find_business>
```

Similarly, a UDDI version 2.0 implementation should send:

```
<find_business generic="2.0" xmlns="urn:uddi-org:api_v2">
    ...
</find_business>
```

SOAP Messaging

SOAP defines a XML based messaging mechanism. All operator sites are required to support SOAP over HTTP as the standard transport for UDDI messages.

Error Handling

UDDI specific error messages are sent back using the SOAP Fault field (see Chapter 3 for more details) in SOAP messages – this has been described in earlier in more detail.

Specifications for UDDI Operators

UDDI v2 has also formalized the requirements for UDDI node operators. These are required to be followed by all operator nodes in the global UDDI registry, but private UDDI registries should also find them useful.

The first specification document, the **UDDI version 2.0 Operator's Specification** defines the behavior and operational requirements from node operators – these including the following:

Managing Directory Information

This lays down policies for information storage, backup and recovery, updates and deletions and resignation of operator nodes.

For example, the backup and recovery section of this specification simply says that this is the responsibility of the operator node, and it should not rely on data stored at other nodes to restore itself after a system failure.

In case of updates and deletes, it states that deletion of a `businessEntity` causes all contained `businessServices` to be deleted, but not the `tModels`, as only the reference to the `tModel` (and not the actual `tModel`) is contained in the `businessEntity`. The same applies to `businessServices` – deletion of a `businessService` will cause the contained `bindingTemplates` to be deleted. Deletion of a `tModel` however, causes it to go into a depreciated state – any `find_tModel` call will not return it; however calls to `get_tModelDetail` will work so as to continue supporting existing services that implement it but preventing new services from using it.

Resignation of an operator node is also considered and policies laid down for transferring data to another operator node and also for notification of businesses that have published data at that operator node.

Security

Three security issues are considered in this specification – unauthorized access, disclosure of information, and Denial of Service. It also specifies what information needs to be logged for audit purposes, and the approved certificate authorities for the operator nodes (namely Verisign and Equifax).

Data Management Requirements

This defines a disparate set of requirements – some for processing of whitespace characters in the published data, and others for publishing restrictions, data type lengths, validations of the schema, UUID encoding etc. It allows for two kinds of users – Tier 1 users with lower limits on the amount of data they can publish and Tier 2 users with significantly higher limits. For example, a Tier 1 user can publish one `businessEntity`, four `businessServices`, two `bindingTemplates` per `businessService`, etc. Tier 2 users would be users with larger requirements, such as large corporations, market makers, registrars of companies etc, and these would need to negotiate limits with operator nodes.

Custody Transfer

The specifications recognize two kinds of transfers of data – intra-operator and inter-operator – and lays down steps for them. Intra-operator transfers could be due to a change in employee responsible for publishing (hence a new publisher account) or merger of businesses (hence merging under a single publisher account).

Inter-operator transfers could be due to unsatisfactory level of service provided by given operator node, change in availability of an operator node (that is: resignation of an operator node) or even business mergers, acquisitions or spin-offs.

UUID Generation Algorithm

As mentioned earlier, the UUID or the Universal Unique Identifiers are guaranteed to be unique. The operator nodes need to provide for these and are expected to implement the DCE UUID generation algorithm. The reference section at the end of this chapter has further information on where details of this algorithm could be found.

Operator Web User Interface

Each operator node is required to provide a HTML 3.2 based web user interface for the basic activities that a user would needs to do – establishing user credentials at the UDDI node, activate the publisher account, change ownership of business entities and tModels and contact the administrator of the operator node.

The second specification document for node operators, the **UDDI Version 2.0 Replication Specification**, describes the protocol used to replicate registry information between the UDDI nodes. It defines messages for replication, changing records and error detection. It also lays down procedures for bringing new operator nodes online, for resignation of operator nodes and auditing and logging requirements related to replication.

UDDI and WSDL

WSDL or **Web Service Definition Language** is an XML format for describing Web Services. A WSDL document for a Web Service defines it in terms of its interface, its protocol bindings, and its deployment details. WSDL allows for separation of the definition of endpoints of a service from their actual network deployment and data structures.

UDDI does not specify any particular format of a service description. However, it recommends using WSDL to describe services as a best practice, as it helps provide a uniform way for describing the service interfaces (see Chapter 4 for more details).

Structure of WSDL Service Description

WSDL has an import directive that allows the separation of the different service element definition into independent documents, which then can be imported as needed. This is useful in writing clearer service definitions, by separating the definitions according to their level of abstraction and also allows for reusability. A typical use of this would be the separation of the service interface description, from those portions that describe the implementation and deployment details. An example of a WSDL service description with this kind of separation is given below.

CapitalService is a simple Web Service that takes as an input the name of the country, and returns its capital city. The following example WSDL service description, was published by the fictitious standards body, foobar.org, at http://foobar.org/capitalService/capitalService.xsd:

```
<?xml version="1.0"?>
<schema targetNamespace="http://foobar.org/capitalService/schemas"
        xmlns="http://www.w3.org/2000/10/XMLSchema">

    <element name="CapitalNameRequest">
        <complexType>
            <all>
                <element name="country" type="string"/>
```

```
            </all>
          </complexType>
      </element>
      <element name="CapitalName">
          <complexType>
              <all>
                  <element name="capital" type="string"/>
              </all>
          </complexType>
      </element>
  </schema>
```

The service interface description at http://foobar.org/capitalService/capitalServiceDefn.wsdl:

```
<?xml version="1.0"?>
<definitions name="CapitalName"
             targetNamespace="http://foobar.org/capitalService/definitions"
             xmlns:tns="http://foobar.org/capitalService/definitions"
             xmlns:xsd1="http://foobar.org/capitalService/schemas"
             xmlns:soap="http://schemas.xmlsoap.org/wsdl/soap/"
             xmlns="http://schemas.xmlsoap.org/wsdl/">

    <import namespace="http://foobar.org/capitalService/schemas"
            location="http://foobar.org/capitalService/capitalService.xsd"/>

    <message name="GetCapitalNameInput">
        <part name="body" element="xsd1:CapitalNameRequest"/>
    </message>

    <message name="GetCapitalNameOutput">
        <part name="body" element="xsd1:CapitalName"/>
    </message>

    <portType name="CapitalNamePortType">
        <operation name="GetCapitalName">
            <input message="tns:GetCapitalNameInput"/>
            <output message="tns:GetCapitalNameOutput"/>
        </operation>
    </portType>
</definitions>
```

And finally the service definition itself, with implementation details at
http://foobar.org/capitalName/capitalService.wsdl:

```
<?xml version="1.0"?>
<definitions name="CapitalName"
             targetNamespace="http://foobar.org/capitalName/service"
             xmlns:tns="http://foobar.org/capitalName/service"
             xmlns:soap="http://schemas.xmlsoap.org/wsdl/soap/"
             xmlns:defs="http://foobar.org/capitalName/definitions"
             xmlns="http://schemas.xmlsoap.org/wsdl/">

    <import namespace="http://foobar.org/capitalName/definitions"
            location="http://foobar.org/capitalName
```

217

```
                     /capitalServiceDefn.wsdl"/>

    <binding name="CapitalNameSoapBinding" type="defs:CapitalNamePortType">
        <soap:binding style="document"
                      transport="http://schemas.xmlsoap.org/soap/http"/>
        <operation name="GetCapitalName">
            <soap:operation soapAction="http://foobar.org/GetCapitalName"/>
            <input>
                <soap:body use="literal"/>
            </input>
            <output>
                <soap:body use="literal"/>
            </output>
        </operation>
    </binding>

    <service name="CapitalNameService">
        <documentation>
            This service takes a country name as input and returns the name of
            its capital city.
        </documentation>
        <port name="CapitalNamePort" binding="tns:CapitalNameBinding">
            <soap:address location="http://foobar.org/capitalName"/>
        </port>
    </service>
</definitions>
```

Authoring the UDDI Service Descriptions

The steps for using WSDL for describing Web Services are given below:

Create and Publish the Service Interface Definitions

Usually a standards body or a consortium of service providers would define a service in one or more service interface definition documents. The interface definition would have service interfaces and protocol bindings and would be made publicly available. These definitions are then registered as UDDI tModels and the overviewDoc field in the tModel points to the corresponding WSDL document. The tModel definition of this is given below. It uses the WSDL service description for the CapitalService described earlier:

```
<tModel authorizedName="..." operator="..." tModelKey="...">
    <name>CapitalName Service</name>
    <description xml:lang="en">
      WSDL description for a Capital Names service
    </description>
    <overviewDoc>
        <description xml:lang="en">
          WSDL source document.
        </description>
        <overviewURL>
            http://foobar.org/capitalName/CapitalService.wsdl
```

```
            </overviewURL>
        </overviewDoc>
        <categoryBag>
            <keyedReference tModelKey="UUID:..."
                            keyName="uddi-org:types"
                            keyValue="wsdlSpec"/>
        </categoryBag>
    </tModel>
```

As can be seen, the `tModel` is classified as being of type `wsdlSpec`, and its overviewURL points to the WSDL document.

Build Implementations of the Service

Programmers at service provider companies could then build implementations of the service based on the WSDL description of it.

Deploy and Register the Service

The developed services would then be deployed and their availability advertised in the UDDI registry. The access points for the services would be advertised in the business service structure. In the example business service structure below, a fictitious service provider company, Acme.com, implements and deploys this service, making it available at the URL http://acme.com/AcmeCapitalService/ (fictitious URL). UDDI does not define how the Web Service should be implemented.

```
<businessService businessKey="..." serviceKey="...">
    <name>StockQuoteService</name>
    <description> (...) </description>
    <bindingTemplates>
        <bindingTemplate>
            (...)
            <accessPoint urlType="http">
                http://acme.com/AcmeCapitalService/
            </accessPoint>
            <tModelnstanceDetails>
                <tModelnstanceInfo tModelKey="...">

                </tModelnstanceInfo>
            </tModelnstanceDetails>
        </bindingTemplate>
    </bindingTemplates>
</businessService>
```

Finally, users of the service would be able to locate the service based on the `tModel` key, which acts as a unique signature for the service. Since the found services implement a known interface, the client can then dynamically bind and invoke methods on the service. For more information on binding with WSDL see Chapter 4.

Other Technologies

In the following sections we discuss some UDDI-related technologies that have attempted to serve a similar purpose to, or compliment UDDI, and assist the creation of business registries.

ebXML

ebXML is an international initiative established by UN/CEFACT (United Nations Center for Trade Facilitation and Electronic Business) and OASIS (Organization for the Advancement of Structured Information Standards).

ebXML predates UDDI. The rationale for ebXML was to develop XML specifications for global business exchanges and create a single electronic marketplace where enterprises of any size and geographical location could meet and conduct business with each other though XML based messaging.

The ebXML architecture has five major components. These are:

Components	Description
Business Process and Information model	A business process is a way of describing the processes of a company in a way that are understandable by other companies. The information model defines re-usable components. These components are used to define data in terms that are meaningful across businesses.
Company Profiles	The company profile includes the business profile with its ebXML capabilities and supported business scenarios.
Messaging Services	The messaging services specifications define common protocols for enabling business applications to exchange data.
Registry and Repository	The registry and repository is used to store company profiles, trading partner specifications and business process definitions. It can also be used to store a library of core components.
Collaborative Partner Agreements	These define the technical parameters of the relationship between partners.

As can be seen, the scope of ebXML is far more ambitious that UDDI, which merely address the registry-related aspects.

A typical ebXML interaction could look like the following:

1. An organization or a standards body would publish business processes and their associated messages

2. An organization would register itself and its business processes in the registry

3. It would build applications that perform the tasks defined in the business processes

4. A partner could browse the repository for appropriate company profiles, business processes, or for the processes that a selected partner supports

5. The two partners then negotiate technical details of their interaction and draw up a Collaborative Partner Agreement (CPA)

6. Finally, the two parties send and receive ebXML messages over a secure and reliable messaging service

It is still not clear how ebXML will interoperate with UDDI – there is an overlap between the ebXML Registry and Repository specifications and UDDI. Recently however, the ebXML Messaging Team agreed to use SOAP as the transport, reversing the earlier decision of using their own messaging protocol. It remains to be seen if some common ground will be found between UDDI and ebXML registries. UDDI itself is evolving, and adding features already there in ebXML. Many software vendors, including Sun, which are pushing ebXML, are now also supporting UDDI. They believe that SOAP can be used as the protocol to discover a particular service within a UDDI repository, and ebXML can be used as the framework for enabling reliable and secure electronic business services.

JAXR

JAXR, or **Java API for XML Registries,** aims to provide a unified API for accessing XML based distributed registries. JAXR does not define any business registry standards, XML messaging standards or XML schema; it merely defines the API for registry access. It is backed by Sun, and was originally intended to provide an API for accessing ebXML business registries, but is now targeted for heterogeneous XML registries – ebXML, UDDI or any other. This is done using "pluggable providers" for different registry types – for instance one for ebXML, one for UDDI and so on.

It also provides for two flavors of API – a Business API that is influenced by the UDDI API and has which fewer capabilities, and a Generic API with more capabilities and targeted to the ebXML Registry specifications.

JAXR's capabilities include support for:

- ❑ Industry standard XML registry functionality

- ❑ Registration of member organizations and enterprises

- ❑ Submission and storing of arbitrary registry content

- ❑ Registry content querying based on defined classification schemes, complex ad hoc queries and keyword based search

- ❑ Sharing of Web Services, business process, schemas and business documents between partners

- ❑ Heterogeneous distributed registries

- ❑ Enabling publish/subscribe XML messaging between parties

The JAXR API is built on top of the JAXM (Java API for XML Messaging) API, which defines an API for XML-based messaging. Reference implementations of JAXR are already available from the Javasoft web site (see the reference section at the end of the chapter) and a final release should be in the first quarter of 2002.

DSML

DSML or **Directory Services Markup Language** is a framework for describing the structure and content of directory service information.

This directory information is represented as an XML document. DSML defines a simple XML Schema for it, which enables directories to publish information that can be shared via standard Internet protocols (for example: HTTP and SMTP). DSML does not specify the attributes of the directory itself, or even how this directory information is accessed. Hence, it can be used on top of standard directory protocols like LDAP.

DSML is supposed to complement UDDI in bridging the gap between directories and XML-based applications. It also can be used for interoperability between different directory services, helping them to search and exchange information between each other.

DSML defines the directory entries and the schema for the entries. For example, let us consider a LDAP directory entry, shown below in the LDIF format. LDIF, or **LDAP Data Interchange Format**, is a means to describe a directory entry in a text format.

```
dn: cn=John Doe,ou=People,o=Wrox Publishing,dc=Wrox,dc=com
objectclass: top
objectclass: person
objectclass: organizationalPerson
objectclass: inetOrgPerson
sn: Doe
mail: john.doe@nospam.wrox.com
givenName:John
cn: John Doe
...
```

This same entry represented as a DSML document, would be:

```
<dsml:dsml xmlns:dsml="http://www.dsml.org/DSML">
    <dsml:directory-entries>
        <dsml:entry dn="cn=John Doe,ou=People,o=Wrox Publishing,
                    dc=Wrox,dc=com">
            <dsml:objectclass>
                <dsml:oc-value>top</dsml:oc-value>
                <dsml:oc-value>person</dsml:oc-value>
                <dsml:oc-value>organizationalPerson</dsml:oc-value>
                <dsml:oc-value>inetOrgPerson</dsml:oc-value>
            </dsml:objectclass>
            <dsml:attr name="sn"><dsml:value>Doe</dsml:value></dsml:attr>
                <dsml:attr name="mail">
                    <dsml:value>john.doe@nospam.wrox.com</dsml:value>
            </dsml:attr>
            <dsml:attr name="givenname">
                <dsml:value>John</dsml:value>
            </dsml:attr>
            <dsml:attr name="cn">
                <dsml:value>John Doe</dsml:value>
            </dsml:attr>
        </dsml:entry>
    </dsml:directory-entries>
</dsml:dsml>
```

The corresponding DSML directory schema for this entry would look like the following:

```
<dsml:dsml xmlns:dsml="http://www.dsml.org/DSML">
    <dsml:directory-schema>
        <dsml:class id="person" superior="#top" type="structural">
        <dsml:name>person</dsml:name>
        <dsml:description>...</dsml:description>
        <dsml:object-identifier>2.5.6.6</dsml:object-identifier>
        <dsml:attribute ref="#sn" required="true"/>
```

```
            <dsml:attribute ref="#cn" required="true"/>
            <dsml:attribute ref="#userPassword" required="false"/>
            <dsml:attribute ref="#telephoneNumber" required="false"/>
            <dsml:attribute ref="#seeAlso" required="false"/>
            <dsml:attribute ref="#givenname" required="false"/>
            <dsml:attribute ref="#description" required="false"/>
        </dsml:class>
        ...
      </dsml:directory-schema>
    </dsml:dsml>
```

The directory server (for example an LDAP based server) would need to produce such DSML documents as an optional output. That way it would be able to share information with other applications and directory servers in a portable manner.

Bowstreet initially proposed the DSML standard. Since then, it has received support from a number of other companies including IBM, Microsoft, Novell, Oracle, and the Sun-Netscape Alliance. It has been submitted to the OASIS standards body, and further information can be obtained from the DSML.org (http://www.dsml.org/) website.

Summary

In this chapter, we took a detailed look at the UDDI 2.0 specification, its data structures and API.

In addition, we also examined some deployment scenarios for UDDI registries. Though the global UDDI registry is important, private registries like those deployed in an Intranet environment or in closed marketplace should play a major role.

UDDI and parts of the ebXML specifications have areas of overlap, and though it in unclear at the moment which of these standards will prevail, UDDI seems to have a lot more momentum. Also, UDDI is adding on features (such as the ability to define business agreements and collaborations) that are present in the ebXML stack, but missing from UDDI.

To summarize, UDDI defines a simple specification for business registries; it does not concern itself with the web services themselves – these are deployed outside and merely advertised in the registry. It does not even store the interface definitions of the services. Instead, these too are kept outside the registry and pointed to by the `tModel`. What it does define is a standard XML API for publishing and finding this information.

References

❑ **UDDI:**
http://www.UDDI.org/
http://xml.coverpages.org/uddi.html

❑ **UDDI mailing lists:**
Technical mailing list: http://groups.yahoo.com/group/uddi-technical/
General mailing list: http://groups.yahoo.com/group/uddi-general/

- ❏ **ebXML:**
  http://www.ebXML.org/

- ❏ **JAXR:**
  http://java.sun.com/xml/xml_jaxr.html
  http://jcp.org/jsr/detail/093.jsp

- ❏ **UUID generation algorithms (Internet Draft):**
  http://www.ics.uci.edu/pub/ietf/webdav/uuid-guid/draft-leach-uuids-guids-01.txt

- ❏ **DSML:**
  http://www.dsml.org/

- ❏ **NAICS:**
  http://www.naics.com/
  http://www.census.gov/epcd/www/naics.html

- ❏ **SIC:**
  http://www.census.gov/epcd/www/sic.html

- ❏ **UNSPSC:**
  http://www.unspsc.org/

- ❏ **Thomas Register of American companies:**
  http://www.thomasregister.com/

- ❏ **Dun & Bradstreet Data Universal Number System (D-U-N-S):**
  http://www.dnb.com/

7

UDDI Implementations

In the previous chapter, we went over details of the UDDI protocol specifications. In this chapter, we will see examples of using the UDDI registry for publishing information about businesses, the services they provide, and how clients can programmatically interact with the registry to search for this information. We will also see an example of a simple Web Service that is deployed in Apache SOAP, published in the UDDI registry and finally discovered by a client program that then invokes methods on this service. This chapter is based on concepts and terms introduced in the previous chapter.

There are a number of UDDI implementations conforming to UDDI 1.0, although most major UDDI implementation still don't (at least at the time this chapter was written) support 2.0. In this chapter we will primarily be using IBM's UDDI4J. In additon, we will briefly look at some other implementations too, including the Microsoft UDDI SDK, HP UDDI (part of HP Web Services Platform) and UDDI::Lite. Regardless of which implementation is used, – the cross platform nature of UDDI's SOAP based API ensures platform independence in publishing and searching for information in the registry.

This chapter's structure is as follows:

❑   We will first take a look at the software to be downloaded and the setup needed on our machine to run the examples contained within this chapter

❑   Next, we will begin with a tutorial introduction to the UDDI4J API, which is explained using sample code for programmatically browsing the UDDI Business Registry

❑   We will then see how to sign up at a UDDI Business Registry operator node. In this example, we sign up with IBM's test registry (instead of the production Business Registry)

❑   The main chapter example follows after this – implementing, deploying, and publishing information about an airline Web Service. We will also take a look at some tools that come with IBM WSTK (Web Service Toolkit)

❑ Finally, we will briefly go over some other UDDI implementations like Microsoft's UDDI SDK, HP UDDI etc, and provide download locations for them

Note that the code examples in this chapter are complete, although they have explanation sections interspersed. These and other examples in this book can be downloaded from http://www.wrox.com/.

Setup

The software that needs to be downloaded for the example in the chapter is given below, along with the setup steps required.

Software Downloads

You need to download the following software products:

❑ IBM's Web Services Toolkit (WSTK), which contains UDDI4J. This is available from http://www.alphaworks.ibm.com/tech/webservicestoolkit, but please note that it is about 38 Megabytes in size, so it will take a while to download. We used WSTK 2.3 in this chapter

❑ A JDK, available from http://java.sun.com/. These particular examples were run using JDK 1.3, although the JDK version should not matter, as long as it is fairly up-to-date

❑ The Xerces XML parser, which may also be downloaded from http://xml.apache.org/. These programs used the xerces version 1.2.3

❑ Tomcat, available from http://jakarta.apache.org/ was used for deploying the Web Service. For these examples, we used version 3.2.1. However, any servlet compliant web server could be used in its place.

❑ The Apache SOAP 2.1 toolkit, available from http://xml.apache.org/soap/index.html was used to build the Web Service and the client code that invokes it. Again, we are not limited to the platform that we use to build or invoke the Web Service

❑ JavaMail, available from http://java.sun.com/product/javamail/. This chapter used Javamail 1.2

❑ The JavaBeans Activation Framework (JAF), which can be downloaded from http://java.sun.com/products/beans. Both JavaMail and JAF are required for Apache SOAP – these may not be required if some other platform is used to build the Web Service

❑ Java Secure Socket Extension (JSSE) which can be downloaded from http://java.sun.com/products/jsse/index-102.html

Setup Instructions

It is assumed that you know how to install and set up Tomcat – additional information for this is available at the Jakarta-Tomcat website http://jakarta.apache.org/. As mentioned earlier, you need not use Tomcat – the SOAP documentation web page (http://xml.apache.org/soap/docs/index.html) has setup steps for a number of other web servers.

Tomcat and Apache SOAP Setup

❑ Add `xerces.jar`, `soap.jar`, `activation.jar` and `mail.jar` to the CLASSPATH in `tomcat.bat`. For this, edit the `tomcat.bat` file and add:

```
set CLASSPATH=c:\xerces-1_2_3\xerces.jar;c:\software\soap-
2_1\lib\soap.jar;c:\javamail-1.2\mail.jar;c:\jaf-
1.0.1\activation.jar;c:\install\wrox\webservices\UDDIImpl;%CLASSPATH
```

Make corresponding changes in `tomcat.sh` for UNIX deployments. Both these files are in the `bin` directory under the Jakarta Tomcat installation. `Xerces.jar` is obtained from the Xerces 1.2.3 software that we downloaded, `actication.jar` from the Java Activation Framework (JAF), `mail.jar` from JavaMail 1.2 and `soap.jar` from Apache SOAP 2.1.

❏ Make sure that you use the right version of Xerces. Version 1.2 or after is fine, but some other versions may not work properly with Apache SOAP.

❏ Ensure that `xerces.jar` is **first** on the `CLASSPATH`, by finding the following line in `tomcat.bat` (or an equivalent one in `tomcat.sh`):

```
set CLASSPATH=%CP%;CLASSPATH
```

and changing it to:

```
set CP=%CLASSPATH%;%CP%.
```

Check the `CLASSPATH` displayed when Tomcat starts up.

❏ Add the following soap context to the `server.xml` file. This file is located in the `conf` directory under the location where Jakarta Tomcat is installed.

```
<!-- SOAP context -->
   <Context path="/soap"
            docBase="c:/soap-2_1/webapps/soap"
            debug="1"
            reloadable="true" >
   </Context>
```

The `docBase` may be different for your system – it contains the full path to the `webapps/soap` directory. In the example above, `c:/soap-2_1` is the SOAP install directory. Also note that this path needs to be in the UNIX convention – that is: using "/" instead of "\".

❏ Start Tomcat using the `tomcat.bat` (`tomcat.sh` on UNIX) batch file, located in the `bin` directory of Tomcat installation, with the following command at the DOS prompt:

> tomcat start

The screen shot of Tomcat starting up is shown below. It also shows the CLASSPATH settings that we set earlier in `tomcat.bat`. Make sure that they are correct.

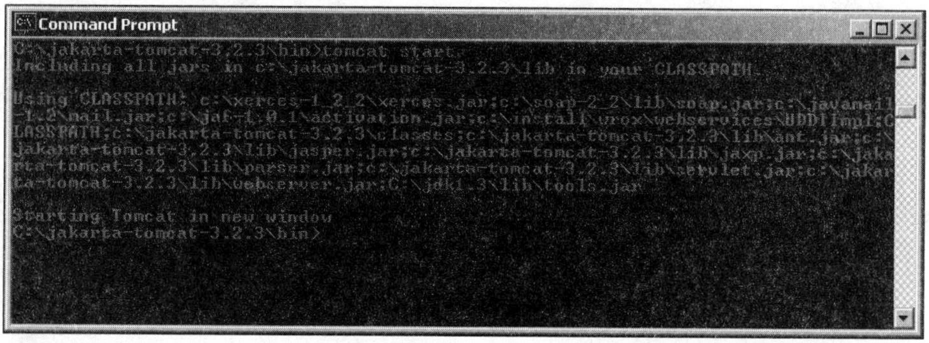

❑ Next, check that Tomcat started properly.

Check this by starting your browser and viewing the URL http://127.0.0 1:8080. Here 8080 is the default port that Tomcat starts on, and 127.0.0.1 is the loopback IP address for your machine (same as localhost).

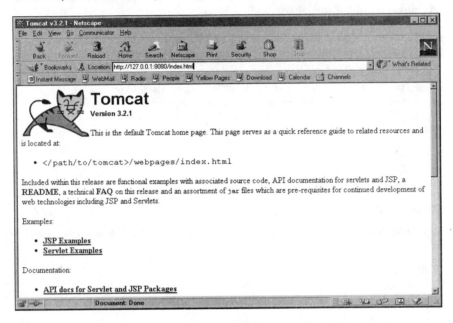

❑ Check that SOAP context settings are correct.

View the URL http://127.0.0.1:8080/soap/index.html in your browser. If you don't get the web page shown below, it means that the soap context settings in server.xml are incorrect.

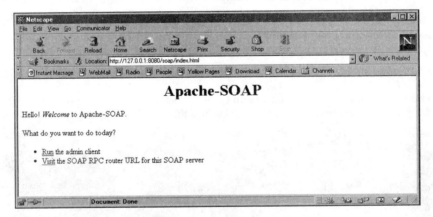

❑ Check to see if the SOAP router can run properly.

Click on the Visit the SOAP RPC router URL for this SOAP server link above. If you don't see the web page below, it means that either the CLASSPATH settings in tomcat.bat are wrong, or you have an incompatible version of Xerces parser. In either case, check your CLASSPATH again.

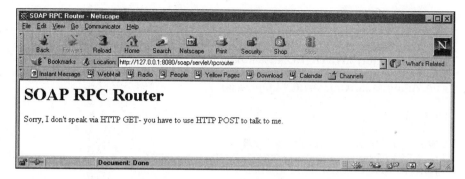

❏ Check if the SOAP Admin client can run properly.

Click on the **Run the admin client** link. Now click on the **List** button on the left hand side to display all deployed services.

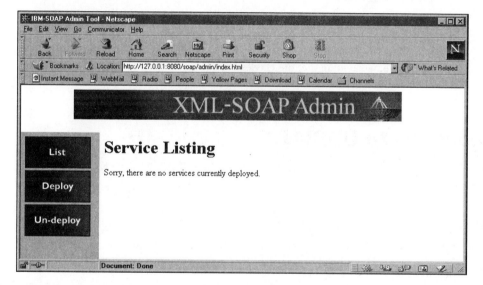

The web page says that no services have been currently deployed, which is correct as we have a fresh installation. In case you see an error instead of this, it means that either your CLASSPATH settings in tomcat.bat are wrong, or that you have an incompatible version of the Xerces parser.

Environment settings

You also need to make the following CLASSPATH and environment-settings settings for building and running your programs:

❏ Make sure JAVA_HOME is defined, and your PATH variable includes %JAVA_HOME%\bin

❏ The required CLASSPATH settings are:

On Windows:

```
> set WSTK_HOME=c:\wstk-2.3
> set CLASSPATH=c:\xerces-
1_2_3\xerces.jar;%WSTK_HOME%\uddi4j\lib\uddi4j.jar;c:\software\soap-
2_1\lib\soap.jar;%WSTK_HOME%\lib\ibmjsse.jar;c:\javamail-1.2\mail.jar;c:\jaf-
1.0.1\activation.jar;c:\install\wrox\webservices\UDDIImpl;c:\jsse1.0.2\lib\jcert.jar;C:\jss
e1.0.2\lib\jnet.jar;C:\jsse1.0.2\lib\jsse.jar
```

On UNIX:

```
$ WSTK_HOME=/somepath/wstk-2.3
$ CLASSPATH=/somepath/xerces-1_2_3/xerces.jar:\
 $WSTK_HOME/uddi4j/lib/uddi4j.jar:\
 /somepath/soap-2_1/lib/soap.jar:$WSTK_HOME/lib/ibmjsse.jar:\
 /somepath/javamail-1.2/mail.jar:/somepath/jaf-1.0.1/activation.jar:\
 /somepath/jsse1.0.2/lib/jcert.jar:/somepath/jsse1.0.2/lib/jnet.jar:\
 /somepath/jsse1.0.2/lib/jsse.jar:/usr/home/wrox/webservices/UDDIImpl
$ export CLASSPATH
```

Set WSTK_HOME (seen above) to the install directory of Web Services Toolkit (c:\wstk-2.3, if you choose the default). You may need to tweak the CLASSPATH above for your particular machine – for example locations of mail.jar, soap.jar, etc. Also, in the CLASSPATH settings above, we assume that the classes have been build in the c:\install\wrox\webservices\UDDIImpl directory

Introduction to UDDI4J

IBM's UDDI4J is packaged along with the Web Services Toolkit (WSTK). The web services toolkit includes:

❑ A UDDI registry implementation. This implementation is useful for private UDDI registry operators. In this chapter we use the publicly hosted UDDI registry nodes

❑ Run time libraries and tools. This includes the UDDI API (uddi4j.jar), service registry API and service proxy API. The UDDI API is covered in greater detail in this chapter, the other two are not

❑ A set of design time tools. These include a UDDI registry browser tool, a tool for generating WSDL descriptions from Java and COM objects, a tool for generating service templates and a tool for building service proxy objects. These tools are described later in the chapter

We could, if we wanted, run a UDDI registry locally on our network and publish to this registry. The UDDI4J registry requires the IBM DB2 database to run – this too is available for an evaluation download.

Such a registry deployment would be private to our organisation and unless other users have access to this registry (and know about it!), we would be unable to publicise our services to the world. Such a deployment may make sense in some cases – see the section on private UDDI deployments in Chapter 6. Some classic examples where we would want to deploy a private registry are:

❑ An Intranet deployment of Web Services

❑ A closed Business-to-Business (B2B) marketplace

Chapter 6 discusses these and other deployment scenarios in more detail.

In this chapter however, we use the publicly accessible UDDI nodes hosted by IBM and Microsoft. These form a part of the UDDI operator "cloud", and any service or business information published on any one of these nodes is accessible at all nodes – albeit with a slight delay before the information gets replicated.

UDDI4J API

To summarize the UDDI data structures in brief:

❑ **Business Entities** contain information about the business, such as name, description, contact information etc. They contain Business Services and there can be one or more (or none) Business Services in a Business Entity.

The `BusinessEntity` class in UDDI4J represents a Business Entity

❑ **Business Services** contain information about the services that a business offers. They can contain one or more (or none) Binding Templates.

The `BusinessService` class in UDDI4J represents a Business Service

❑ A **Binding Template** has information about where the service can be accessed (for example: its entry point). The Binding Template has references to tModels – it contains tModel Keys. The `BindingTemplate` class represents a Binding Template

❑ Finally, a **tModel** defines the technical fingerprint for a service or taxonomy. The `tModel` class in UDDI4J represents a tModel

More detail on these data structures can be found in the previous chapter. The UDDI4J API has "publish" methods that allow us to add, modify, and delete these data structures as well as "inquiry" methods for searching. All operations against the UDDI registry in UDDI4J are done via the `UDDIProxy` object (in the `com.ibm.uddi.client` package). This object represents an UDDI server and has methods corresponding to each of the UDDI Inquiry and Publish API calls. The methods that this class has are given below. This list does not give all the methods – please refer to the UDDI4J javadocs for this.

Constructing a UDDIProxy object

The contructor below constructs a `UDDIProxy` object and sets the inquiry URL (URL to which the UDDI Inquiry requests are sent), publish URL (URL to which the UDDI Inquiry requests are sent), and the transport to use for sending the requests. At present only HTTP (HTTPS in case of publish URL) is supported, so the transport parameter should be set to `Null`.

```
UDDIProxy (URL inquiryURL, URL publishURL,
           org.apache.soap.transport.SOAPTransport transport)
```

The default constructor for a `UDDIProxy` object:

```
UDDIProxy ()
```

In this case, the following "set" methods can be used for setting Inquiry and Publish URLs, and the transport:

```
setInquiryURL (URL url)
setPublishURL (URL url)
setTransport (org.apache.soap.transport.SOAPTransport transport)
```

Getting an authentication token

The publishing calls require to be authenticated. The following calls are used for getting an authetication token and expiring it after use.

The get_authToken() method takes a user ID and credentials (for example: password) and returns an authentication token. This token is used for all publish and delete calls (see below):

```
get_authToken (String userID, String credentials)
```

The discard_authToken() method is used to inform an Operator Site that the authentication token can be discarded:

```
discard_authToken (String authToken)
```

Methods to publish to the UDDI registry

The save_binding() method saves new BindingTemplates (or updates exiting ones). It takes a vector (one dimensional array) of BindingTemplate objects and returns successfully saved Binding Templates back in a BindingDetail object.

```
BindingDetail save_binding (String authInfo, Vector bindingTemplates)
```

The save_business() method saves a new BusinessEntity (or updates an exiting ones). It takes a vector of BusinessEntity objects returns a successfully saved Business Entities back in a BusinessDetail object.

```
BusinessDetail save_business(String authInfo, Vector businessEntities)
```

The save_service() method saves new BusinessServices (or updates exiting ones). It takes a vector of BusinessService objects and returns successfully saved business services back in a ServiceDetail object.

```
ServiceDetail save_service (String authInfo, Vector businessServices)
```

The save_tModel() method saves new tModels (or updates exiting ones). It takes a vector of TModels and returns successfully saved tModels back in a TModelDetail object.

```
TModelDetail save_tModel(String authInfo, Vector tModels)
```

In addition all these methods take the authenication token (authInfo argument) as a parameter.

Methods for deleting from UDDI registry:

```
DispositionReport delete_binding (String authInfo, String bindingKey)
DispositionReport delete_business (String authInfo, String businessKey)
DispositionReport delete_service (String authInfo, String serviceKey)
DispositionReport delete_tModel (String authInfo, String tModelKey)
```

These methods cause a Business Entity, Business Service, Binding Template, or a tModel to be deleted, as specified by the unique keys. These calls require an authentication token (authInfo argument) to be passed as input too – see the get_authToken() method.

All these "delete" methods return a DispositionReport on failure. This contains the cause of the failure – some common error codes are:

❑ E_accountLimitExceeded

The user account limits have been exceeded. UDDI operator nodes set limits on users – for example ordinary users (or Tier 1 users) can publish one businessEntity, four businessServices, and two bindingTemplates per businessService, etc. Tier 2 users would be users with larger requirements, such as large corporations, market makers, registrars of companies etc., and these would need to negotiate this with operator nodes

❑ E_authTokenRequired

The authentication token value passed in the authInfo argument is either missing or is not valid

❑ E_categorizationNotAllowed

Restrictions have been placed by the taxonomy provider on the types of information that should be included at that location within a specific taxonomy

❑ E_invalidCategory

The given keyValue did not correspond to a category within the taxonomy identified by a tModelKey value within one of the categoryBag elements provided

❑ E_invalidKeyPassed

The request cannot be satisfied because one or more uuid_key values specified is not a valid key value

❑ E_keyRetired

The request cannot be satisfied because one or more uuid_key values specified have previously been hidden or removed by the requester

❑ E_operatorMismatch

One or more of the uuid_key values passed refer to data that is not controlled by the Operator Site that received the request for processing

❑ E_userMismatch

One or more of the uuid_key values passed refers to data that is not controlled by the individual who is represented by the authentication token

Getting all Business Entities and tModels published by us

This can be done using the `get_registeredInfo()` method that takes an authentication token and returns all Business Entities and tModels associated with it:

```
RegisteredInfo get_registeredInfo (String authInfo)
```

Inquiry methods

These methods include the `find_business()`, `find_service()`, `find_binding()`, and `find_tModel()` methods that allow us to find a list of Business Entites (`BusinesList` class in UDDI4J), a list of services (`ServiceList` class), or list of tModels (`TmodelList` class). The search can be on the basis of a number of search criteria. Chapter 6 has discussed the find API methods in UDDI in greater detail.

❑ In addtion to the "find" methods, there are "get" methods (`get_businessDetail()`, `get_serviceDetail()`, `get_bindingDetail()`, and `get_tModelDetail()`) that allow users to get further details about a specific Business Entity, Business Service, Binding Template, or tModel.

In general, the use of the inquiry API would follow a pattern of first doing a search (that is: a **browse pattern**) using the "find" methods based on some criteria, such as name of the business, classification, etc. This would return a summarized list of found entities. In the case of `find_business()` we would get a `BusinessList`, in the case of `find_service()`, a `ServiceList` and so on. Following this, users would select one or more entities and get more detail about them using the "get" methods (**drill-down pattern**). This returns the detailed information – for example: a `get_business()` method would return a `BusinessDetail` that contains an array of `BusinessEntities`.

❑ Some of these methods are listed below. For a complete list, please refer to the UDDI4J java docs.

Finding a business: *This can be done using various criteria:*

❑ Search by the name of the business. We can specify a partial name in the search criteria – for instance a find business with the name "I" will match both IBM and Intel. The match for the name is done on the basis of the leftmost matching string. There is also support for a "wild-card" – the character "%" matches any character:

```
BusinessList find_business (String name, FindQualifiers findQualifiers, int
                            maxRows)
```

❑ Search based on the `tModels` that are contained in the Binding Template (as specified by `TModelBag` parameter). This is useful in finding businesses that have services implementing a specific tModel.

```
BusinessList find_business (TModelBag bag, FindQualifiers findQualifiers,
                            int maxRows)
```

❑ Search based on the Category Reference in the Business Entity. These Category References are used to classify the services of a business in various industry taxonomies. The two supported industry and service taxonomies are NAICS (North American Industry Classification System) and UNSPSC (Universal Standard Products and Services Classification). In addition, there is ISO 3166, which is a geographical classification taxonomy. Details of these can be found in the previous chapter.

```
BusinessList find_business (CategoryBag bag, FindQualifiers findQualifiers,
                            int maxRows)
```

❑ Search based on the alternative identifier tags for a business. A business may be tagged using one or more identifier tags – these can be the D-U-N-S number (Dun & Bradstreet Data Universal Numbering System), Thomas Register ID etc. These too are explained in more detail in the previous chapter.

```
BusinessList find_business (IdentifierBag bag, FindQualifiers findQualifiers,
                            int maxRows)
```

The findQualifiers parameter is used to change the default behavior of the search criteria. Some valid Find Qualifiers are – caseSensitiveMatch, exactNameMatch, sortByDateAsc, sortByDateDesc, sortByNameAsc, and sortByNameDesc. The maxRows parameter specifies the maximum number of search result desired by the client – setting it to zero means that no limit is being set.

Finding a service:

The find_service() methods have similar methods. However, these methods take a Business Key. This is because the BusinessService is contained within a BusinessEntity:

```
ServiceList find_service (String businessKey, CategoryBag bag,
                          FindQualifiers findQualifiers, int maxRows)
ServiceList find_service (String businessKey, String name,
                          FindQualifiers findQualifiers, int maxRows)
ServiceList find_service (String businessKey, TModelBag bag,
                          FindQualifiers findQualifiers, int maxRows)
```

Finding a binding template:

The find_binding() method takes a Service Key as a parameter. This is because the BindingTemplate is contained within a BusinessService. This method returns Binding Templates that contain the tModel keys specified in the tModel bag. FindQualifiers and maxRows have the same significance as before:

```
BindingDetail find_binding (FindQualifiers findQualifiers, String serviceKey,
                            TModelBag tmodelbag, int maxRows)
```

Finding a tmodel:

Finally, the find_tModel() methods allow us to search for a tModel based on the name of the tModel, the category references, and the identifiers for the tModel.

```
TModelList find_tModel (CategoryBag bag, FindQualifiers findQualifiers,
                        int maxRows)
TModelList find_tModel (IdentifierBag identifierBag,
                        FindQualifiers findQualifiers, int maxRows)
TModelList find_tModel (String name, FindQualifiers findQualifiers,
                        int maxRows)
```

The methods above give us a list of Binding Template, Business Services, Business Entities or `tModels`. Once we have this list, we can use "get" methods to obtain detailed information on one or more of these.

The `get_bindingDetail()` methods take a `bindingKey` (or a vector of `bindingKeys`) and return a full `BindingTemplate` structure (or a list of `BindingTemplates`) packaged within a `BindingDetail` object:

```
BindingDetail get_bindingDetail (String bindingKey)
BindingDetail get_bindingDetail (Vector bindingKeyStrings)
```

The `get_businessDetail()` methods take a `businessKey` (or a vector of businessKeys) and return a full Business Entity structure (or a list of Business Entities) packaged within a `BusinessDetail` object.

```
BusinessDetail get_businessDetail (String businessKey)
BusinessDetail get_businessDetail (Vector businessKeyStrings)
```

The `get_serviceDetail()` methods take a `serviceKey` (or a vector of `serviceKeys`) and return a full BusinessService structure (or a list of Business Services) packaged within a `ServiceDetail` object.

```
ServiceDetail get_serviceDetail (String serviceKey)
ServiceDetail get_serviceDetail (Vector serviceKeyStrings)
```

The `get_tModelDetail` methods take a `tModelKey` (or a vector of `tModelKeys`) and return a full `TModel` structure (or a list of tModels) packaged within a `TModelDetail` object.

```
TModelDetail get_tModelDetail (String tModelKey)
TModelDetail get_tModelDetail (Vector tModelKeyStrings)
```

Programmatically Browsing the UDDI Registry

In the previous chapter we saw an example of a drill-down query pattern, which involves starting from some broad information about a business service – such as the business name, or a part of the name. Then, based on the search result, drilling down for more information. Lets see how this is done programmatically. We will be writing a client program (`UDDIClient.java`) for a widget retailer, who tries to obtain information about buying widgets from "Foobar Widgets".

This program:

❑   Carries out a find for a business named "Foobar Widgets Inc"

❑   Selects one business from the list of businesses found

❑   Drills down to get all the services that this business provides

❑   From the list of services, selects one named "Buy Widgets"

❑   Drills down in this service to get the Binding Templates, and extracts out the access point from the first Binding Template. The access point contains the access end point for the service, which can be a URL for a Web Service or, as in this case, a phone number. Other possible types for access point include email address and fax number

First, all the imports required for the program – the `com.ibm.uddi.client` package has the

UDDIProxy class that we described in the earlier section. As can be seen, we put this class (and all other classes in this chapter) in a package called wrox.webservices.UDDIImpl.

```
package wrox.webservices.UDDIImpl;

import java.net.*;
import java.text.*;
import java.util.*;
import java.io.*;

import com.ibm.uddi.*;
import com.ibm.uddi.client.*;
import com.ibm.uddi.datatype.binding.*;
import com.ibm.uddi.datatype.business.*;
import com.ibm.uddi.datatype.service.*;
import com.ibm.uddi.datatype.tmodel.*;
import com.ibm.uddi.response.*;
import com.ibm.uddi.util.*;

import org.apache.soap.SOAPException;
import org.apache.soap.transport.http.SOAPHTTPConnection;

/**
 * UDDIClient class uses the UDDI4J Inquiry API to navigate
 * the UDDI registry.
 */
public class UDDIClient {
```

The constants below show the name of the business and the service. We will be browsing the registry to find this business and service.

```
    private final static String BUSINESS_NAME = "Foobar Widget Inc";
    private final static String SERVICE_NAME  = "Buy Widgets";
```

The first step is to construct an UDDIProxy object, seen below

```
    /* Construct a UDDIProxy object - this represents an UDDI server
     * and the actions that can be invoked against it.
     */
    UDDIProxy uddiProxy = new UDDIProxy ();
```

Some users who are behind a firewall may be going out to the Internet through a proxy server. In this case, they may need to specify the proxy settings. The commented code below shows how they can be specified. In order to determine what the settings are in your case, you might need to consult with a system administration. Alternatively, you could see the settings in your web browser. For example, in case of Internet Explorer, select **Tools | Internet Options**, then click on the **Connections** tab. Next, click on **Lan Settings**. This should show you the proxy server settings for your browser. Make the changes in the code below and uncomment. In case you do not have a username/password required for your proxy server, you can remove those lines.

```
/* Setting for the proxy server- in case you are behind a firewall */
    /*
    SOAPHTTPConnection soapHTTPConnection = new SOAPHTTPConnection ();
    soapHTTPConnection.setUserName ("proxy-username");
    soapHTTPConnection.setPassword ("proxy-password");
```

```
        soapHTTPConnection.setProxyHost ("proxyhostname");
        soapHTTPConnection.setProxyPort (8080);
        uddiProxy.setTransport (soapHTTPConnection);
    */
```

We then set the inquiry URL. The inquiry URL is the URL to which UDDI inquiry methods can be posted. This example allows for setting it to either the Microsoft or the IBM UDDI nodes – this can be selected with a command line flag.

```
    /* Select which UDDI node to send the query to */
        if (args.length < 1) {
            System.out.println ("usage: UDDIClient <IBM_PROD|MS_PROD>");
            System.exit (1);
        }

        String inquiryUrl = null;
        if (args[0].equals ("IBM_PROD")) {
          inquiryUrl = UDDIOperatorURLs.IBM_INQUIRY_URL_PRODUCTION;
          System.out.println ("Inquiry URL set to IBM UDDI node ["
                              + inquiryUrl + "]");
        } else { /* MS_PROD */
          inquiryUrl = UDDIOperatorURLs.MICROSOFT_INQUIRY_URL_PRODUCTION;
          System.out.println ("Inquiry URL set to Microsoft UDDI node ["
                              + inquiryUrl + "]");
        }

        try {
          uddiProxy.setInquiryURL (inquiryUrl);
        } catch (MalformedURLException e) {
          System.err.println ("Malformed inquiry URL [" + inquiryUrl + "]");
          System.exit (1); /* fatal error */
        }
```

Next, we search for "Foobar Widgets Inc" by name. We use the find_business() method described earlier in the section on UDDIProxy. This method takes the business name (BUSINESS_NAME constant), the find qualifiers (which in this case are null), and the maximum number of results desired. Passing 0 as the maximum number indicates that the client is not setting any maximum limit, and all found results should be returned. However, the UDDI registry can truncate the results of the search if the number of matches found are too large. The determination of the truncation limit is up to individual registry operators.

```
        /* Find all businesses matching the partial name "Foobar Widgets" */
        BusinessList businessList = null;
        try {
            businessList = uddiProxy.find_business (BUSINESS_NAME, null, 0);
        } catch (UDDIException e) {
          System.err.println ("UDDI error finding business: ["
                              + e.getFaultCode() + "]" + e.getFaultString());
          DispositionReport dispositionReport = e.getDispositionReport ();
          System.err.println ("More error information : "
                              + dispositionReport.getErrCode() + ": "
                              + dispositionReport.getErrInfoText());
          System.exit (1); /* fatal error */
        } catch (SOAPException e) {
          System.err.println ("SOAP error finding business "
                              + e.getFaultCode() + ": " + e.getMessage());
          System.exit (1); /* fatal error */
        }
    }
```

As can be seen in the code above, the UDDI error is sent back in a `DispositionReport` structure. The UDDI errors that can occur as a result of this query are

❑ `E_nameTooLong`: The name of the business passed in the search was too long

❑ `E_unsupported`: One or more find qualifiers passed was not recognized

The complete list of UDDI errors are discussed in Chapter 6. There is also some discussion of errors in the above section, *UDDI4J API*.

The `find_business ()` call should return a `BusinessList` that has brief information about businesses that match the name "Foobar Widgets Inc". The search is done based on a leftmost match – hence if the name parameter had been just "Foo", it would have matched "Foobar Widgets Inc" as well as "Food and Drug Administration". This information is contained in the form of `BusinessInfo` structures. We then extract out this list of `BusinessInfos` using the `getBusinessInfos` method. This method returns a vector of `BusinessInfos` which we obtain using the `getBusinessInfoVector ()` method. The `BusinessInfo` vector contains a summarized list of businesses that match the search criteria – we then print out the name and Business Key of each of the businesses:

```
    Vector businessInfoVector =
        businessList.getBusinessInfos().getBusinessInfoVector();

    System.out.println ("Found " + businessInfoVector.size()
                        + " businesses matching the name" + BUSINESS_NAME
                        + ". These are: \n");

for (int i = 0; i < businessInfoVector.size(); i ++) {
    System.out.println (
        "[" + i + "] "
        + ((BusinessInfo)businessInfoVector.elementAt(i)).getNameString()
        + " [businessKey=" +
        ((BusinessInfo)businessInfoVector.elementAt(i)).getBusinessKey()
        + "]");
    }
```

Then, we select one of these businesses. In this example, we take the first business found and get its business key using the `getBusinessKey()` method. The Business Key is a unique ID for a business assigned by the UDDI registry operator when the business is registered with it. Next, we drill-down to get more information about this business. We use the `get_businessDetail()` method, passing it the Business Key we obtained earlier, to get the entire Business Entity.

```
    /* Taking the first found business */
    String businessKey =
        ((BusinessInfo)businessInfoVector.elementAt(0)).getBusinessKey();

    System.out.println ("Selected: " + BUSINESS_NAME + " with business key " +
                        businessKey);

    /* Drill down for more information about the business */
    Vector businessKeyVector = new Vector ();
    businessKeyVector.addElement (businessKey);

    BusinessDetail businessDetail = null;
    try {
        businessDetail = uddiProxy.get_businessDetail (businessKeyVector);
    } catch (UDDIException e) {
```

```
        System.err.println ("UDDI error finding business detail: ["
                     + e.getFaultCode() + "]" + e.getFaultString()
                     );
    DispositionReport dispositionReport = e.getDispositionReport ();
    System.err.println ("More error information : "
                     + dispositionReport.getErrCode() + ": "
                     + dispositionReport.getErrInfoText());
    System.exit (1); /* fatal error */
} catch (SOAPException e) {
    System.err.println ("SOAP error finding business detail: "
                     + e.getFaultCode() + ": " + e.getMessage());
    System.exit (1); /* fatal error */


}
```

The resulting `BusinessDetail` contains a vector of `BusinessEntity` objects. Since we passed only one Business Key to the `get_businessDetail()` method, we get only one `BusinessEntity`. Hence we can use the `getBusinessEntityVector()` method to get the vector and take the first (and only) element in it.

```
BusinessEntity businessEntity =
    (BusinessEntity) businessDetail.getBusinessEntityVector().elementAt(0);
```

This `BusinessEntity` object has all the published information about a business. In case of error, the `DispositionReport` can be inspected to obtain more information on why the call failed.

Next, we select one service out of the many that a Business Entity provides. In this example, we select a service that matches the name `"Buy Widgets"` – this is the value of the `SERVICE_NAME` constant that we are comparing to the names of the found services. In the code below, we use the `getNameString()` method on each `BusinessService` in the `businessServiceVector` to get the name of the service.

```
    Vector businessServiceVector =
  businessEntity.getBusinessServices().getBusinessServiceVector();

    System.out.println ("Found " + businessServiceVector.size()
                   + " services in this business entity. These are: \n");

    BusinessService businessService = null;
    for (int i = 0; i < businessServiceVector.size(); i++) {
      String serviceName =
((BusinessService)businessServiceVector.elementAt(i)).getNameString();
      System.out.println ("[" + i + "] " + serviceName);
      if (serviceName.equals (SERVICE_NAME)) {
      businessService = (BusinessService)businessServiceVector.elementAt(i);
      }
    }

    if (businessService == null) {
      System.err.println ("No service found matching " +
                       SERVICE_NAME + ". Quitting.");
      System.exit (1);
    }

    System.out.println ("Selected " + SERVICE_NAME +
                       " service with service key " +
                       businessService.getServiceKey());
```

Finally, having got the service that we were looking for, we try to obtain information on how it can be accessed. Specifically, we try and obtain the "Access Point" for the service using the getAccessPoint() method on the BindingTemplate. The access point contains the location to contact for getting the service – it could be a URL, a phone number, an e-mail address, or a fax number. We do this for the very first Binding Template in the service, and hence in the code below we are taking the first element from the bindingTemplateVector.

```
    /* Get the binding templates - information on how to access the service */
    Vector bindingTemplateVector =
        businessService.getBindingTemplates().getBindingTemplateVector();
    /* Find the access point for the first binding template */
    AccessPoint accessPoint =
  ((BindingTemplate)bindingTemplateVector.elementAt(0)).getAccessPoint();
```

We then print out the name and the access point URL for the service. The getText() method for the AccessPoint object gives the actual URL, and the getURLType would contain the type of the URL – this could be http, https, mailto, phone or fax.

```
    System.out.println ("The " + SERVICE_NAME
                        + " service can be accessed via "
                        + accessPoint.getURLType()
                        + ": "
                        + accessPoint.getText());
    }
}
```

This program uses several constants – these come from the UDDIOperatorURLs.java class that is listed a bit later. This class will be used in all subsequent programs too, so it is important to take note of it now. You need to compile this class (from install\wrox\webservices\UDDIImpl) before any other class in this chapter.

> **javac -d . UDDIOperatorURLs.java**
> **javac -d . UDDIClient.java**

Make sure that your CLASSPATH settings are as described earlier in the *Environment Settings* section.

When we run this program (from install\wrox\webservices\UDDIImpl) against IBM's production Business Registry:

> **java wrox.webservices.UDDIImpl.UDDICLient IBM_PROD**

we get the following output:

Oh well. After all this code, all we get is a toll free number to call for further information!

This client program can be downloaded from the Wrox web site (http://www.wrox.com/). It can be run against both the IBM and Microsoft UDDI nodes – and should result in the same information. The code doesn't need to recompiled for this – the command line argument "IBM_PROD" tells the program to use IBM's UDDI node, and "MS_PROD" tells it to use Microsoft's.

> **java wrox.webservices.UDDIImpl.UDDIClient MS_PROD**

If the result is not the same at both nodes, it means that the business entity has been modified on the UDDI node where it was registered, and this information still hasn't been propagated to all other nodes in the UDDI cloud. More about replication between UDDI nodes is discussed in Chapter 6.

The UDDIOperatorsURLs class that we mentioned earlier is listed below. It contains the URLs (publish and inquiry) for the UDDI operator nodes – IBM Production Business Registry, Microsoft Production Business Registry, IBM Test Business Registry, and Microsoft Test Business Registry.

```
package wrox.webservices.UDDIImpl;

/**
 * UDDI operator node URLs
 */
public class UDDIOperatorURLs {

    /* URL for UDDI Inquiry in the Production UDDI registry node at IBM     */
    public final static String IBM_INQUIRY_URL_PRODUCTION = "http://www-
3.ibm.com/services/uddi/inquiryapi";
    /* URL for UDDI Publish in the Production UDDI registry node at IBM     */
    public final static String IBM_PUBLISH_URL_PRODUCTION = "https://www-
3.ibm.com:443/services/uddi/protect/publishapi";

    /* URL for UDDI Inquiry in the Test UDDI registry node at IBM     */
    public final static String IBM_INQUIRY_URL_TEST = "http://www-
3.ibm.com/services/uddi/testregistry/inquiryapi";
    /* URL for UDDI Publish in the Test UDDI registry node at IBM     */
    public final static String IBM_PUBLISH_URL_TEST = "https://www-
3.ibm.com:443/services/uddi/testregistry/protect/publishapi";

    /* URL for UDDI Inquiry in the Production UDDI registry node at Microsoft */
    public final static String MICROSOFT_INQUIRY_URL_PRODUCTION =
"http://uddi.microsoft.com/inquire";
```

```
        /* URL for UDDI Publish in the Production UDDI registry node at Microsoft */
        public final static String MICROSOFT_PUBLISH_URL_PRODUCTION =
."https://uddi.microsoft.com/publish";

        /* URL for UDDI Inquiry in the Test UDDI registry node at Microsoft      */
        public final static String MICROSOFT_INQUIRY_URL_TEST =
    "http://test.uddi.microsoft.com/inquire";
        /* URL for UDDI Publish in the Test UDDI registry node at Microsoft      */
        public final static String MICROSOFT_PUBLISH_URL_TEST =
    "https://test.uddi.microsoft.com/publish";

        /* URL for UDDI Inquiry in the locally installed UDDI registry node      */
        public final static String LOCALHOST_INQUIRY_URL_TEST =
    "http://localhost:8080/uddi/servlet/uddi";
        /* URL for UDDI Publish in the locally installed UDDI registry node      */
        public final static String LOCALHOST_PUBLISH_URL_TEST =
    "http://localhost:8080/uddi/servlet/uddi";

}
```

Browsing the UDDI Registry Using GUI tools

Users can also use GUI tools – both stand-alone programs as well as web-based UDDI browsers to access content in the UDDI registry.

Let's try this same inquiry using the web based UDDI browser at IBM. This can be accessed at http://www-3.ibm.com/services/uddi/find. However, through this interface we are only able to browse data published at the IBM production Business Registry.

First, we search for the business name "Foobar Widgets", as shown below:

The results of the search are shown here:

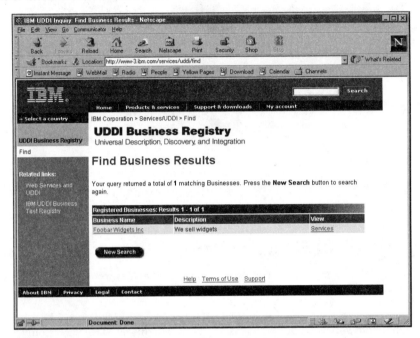

Next, we need to click on the Services link to get the list of services:

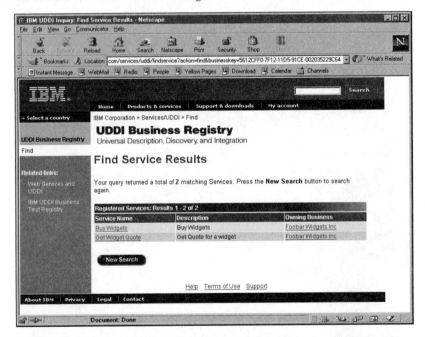

From the list of services, we can select the one named "Buy Widgets", and click on its name to drill-down into it. We now get the Binding Templates – and the access point for the first one. This, as we saw in our programmatic search was the "1-800-WIDGETS" phone number.

Another web interface for browsing the UDDI Business Registry is shown below. This is Microsoft's production UDDI site at http://uddi.microsoft.com/ and this allows us to browse Microsoft's production Business Registry.

Finally, there is another UDDI browser at soapclient.com –
http://www.soapclient.com/uddisearch.html. This browser allows us to search different registry nodes –
such as the production and test UDDI nodes at IBM and Microsoft. This browser has an interesting
feature of displaying the request and response UDDI messages as XML documents, and we will be using
this in our examples.

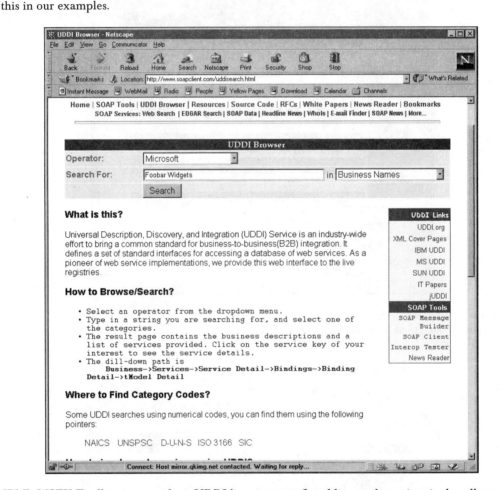

IBM's WSTK Toolkit comes with an UDDI browser, too. In additon to browsing, it also allows
publishing and unpublishing of data from the UDDI registry.

Before you begin using the IBM UDDI browser, you need to set it up to point to the IBM production
Business Registry. This can be done using the wstkconfig.bat script (wstkconfig.sh in case of
UNIX) located in the bin directory under WSTK installation. You then need to enter userid and
password for the UDDI registry. The section on creating an account with the UDDI registry (later in
the chapter) shows how to get these.

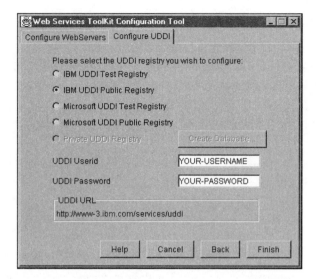

The screenshot below shows the browser being used for finding and viewing UDDI registry content. In this case we are searching for a service provider by the name of the company. This browser.bat (browser.sh in case of UNIX) script located in the bin directory under WSTK installation invokes this browser.

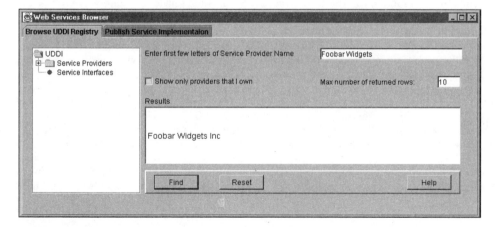

An Airline Web Service

In Chapter 6, we described a common use case scenario for the UDDI Business Registry. To repeat:

1. Standards bodies populate the UDDI Business Registry with descriptions of various kinds of services

2. Businesses (service providers) populate the Business Registry with descriptions of the services that they provide

3. The UDDI Business Registry assigns unique identifiers to each service and business registration

4. Online marketplaces, search engines, and business applications query the registry to discover services

5. Businesses use this data to invoke methods on remote services and integrate with each other over the Web

The description of the kinds of services, or the Service Type Registration is done using tModels in UDDI. In the case of a Web Service, this information would have the kinds of methods that the service exposes, what is the data format expected and so on. This is usually in the form of a WSDL (Web Services Description Language) document – details of WSDL are discussed in Chapter 4. The tModel does not contain the WSDL document – it merely contains a URL that points to it. The tModel could be published by a standards body or an industry consortium, or by the company deploying the Web Service.

Once the tModel has been published, businesses that wish to provide services as defined in the tModel implement Web Services based on the WSDL definition. These services are accessable via a URL, and businesses then publish this information in the UDDI registry – this **service URL** is contained in the Binding Template of the service that the business publishes.

Next, clients can discover these Web Services. The discovery can occur in different ways – the clients could know the service type registration (that is: a known tModel), and find all businesses that implement it. Alternatively, they could do a search based on the name of business, or the industry classification for the business. For example, an airline company is tagged with a NAICS (North American Industry Classification System) code for "Scheduled Passenger Air Transportation", and a client could to do an inquiry in the UDDI registry for all such service providers. NAICS is an industry classification taxonomy supported by UDDI – the others being UNSPSC (Universal Standard Products and Services Classification) and ISO 3166 (geographic classification). In our example Web Service client, we use the first mechanism, that is: search by tModel to locate a Web Service. Once the client discovers the Web service, it can extract out the access point for the service (also called the service URL) from Binding Template.

After the client has discovered a Web Service, it can then invoke methods on it. The client uses the WSDL description for the service that is published in the tModel to get information on how to invoke the service. The service URL gives the location of the Web Service, and based on this (that is: where a Web Service is running, and how to invoke it) a client can invoke the service methods.

In the samples below, this is what we try to do – first publish a tModel, then a Business Entity that provides services as described in it, and finally a client that finds and invokes methods on it. The steps in this are:

1. Create an account at the IBM test registry

2. Write a Web Service and deploy it in Apache SOAP

3. Publish a tModel for the Web Service. We will see how this can be done both programmatically as well as using GUI tools

4. Publish a Business Entity. Again, we will see how this can be done both programmatically as well as using GUI tools

5. Write a client program that searches for the services implementing the tModel, finds one and invokes methods on the service

Creating an Account With the UDDI Registry

For publishing, we use the test UDDI registry – and not the production one. It is advisable to publish to a test registry to iron out any problem with a Web Service before publishing real data in the production UDDI Business Registry. In order to be able to publish information, we need to be registered with the test registry. The IBM test registry has a web-based signup mechanism accessible at http://www-3.ibm.com/services/uddi/testregistry/, as seen below.

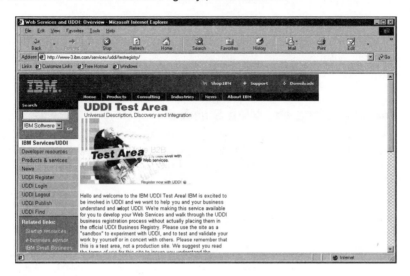

From here, we can navigate to the "Register" screen (shown below), by first clicking on the UDDI Register link (on the left hand side), then clicking First Time? (at the bottom right of the next screen), and then clicking on the Register button that eventually appears near the center of the screen. In this chapter we will be registering a dummy company called "Crashes R'Us Airlines", and will be publishing information about this company.

After filling in all the necessary details on the registration page, press the Continue button at the bottom of this page and again at the bottom of the next one. After agreeing with the terms and conditions, and entering the activation key sent to us by e-mail, we are ready to start publishing our business information on this registry node. Make a note of the user ID and password somewhere, as these will be required for publishing. We will be using IBM UDDI4J in this chapter; however, it is not necessary that we publish to the IBM test UDDI node – we could have just as easily used the one at Microsoft. The Microsoft test registry is at http://test.uddi.microsoft.com/.

When trying out examples in the chapter, create your own account at the test registry instead of using the user ID shown above. You also need to change the USERNAME and PASSWORD constants in the code (mentioned where relevant).

Now that the account has been created, we are ready to start writing our Web Service.

Developing and Deploying the Web Service

The web service class FareService has one public method called getFare() that returns fare information. Our airline (mis)operates two flights – one from San Jose, California to Taipei, Taiwan; and the other to Cancun, Mexico. The getFare() method returns a constant fare for each of the flights.

```
package wrox.webservices.UDDIImpl;

/**
 * The FareService implements a simple web service for our
 * fictitious airline. This service exposes a getFare() method
 * that give fare information for flights.
 */
public class FareService {

    /**
     * getFare returns fare information for a flight. The fare information
     * is in US Dollars.
     * @param source       Airport code for the starting airport
     * @param destination  Airport code for the destination airport
     */
    public float getFare (String source, String destination) {
        /* Our airline has only two flights - one from San Jose (SJC) to
         * Taipei, Taiwan (TPE), and the other to Cancun, Mexico (CAN).
         */
        if (destination.equals ("TPE")) /* Taipei, Taiwan (TPE) */
            return (float) 899.95;
        else /* Cancun, Mexico (CAN) */
            return (float) 349.95;

        /* The starting airport will always be SJC. A more realistic
         * fare quoting service would probably be more complicated
         * than this.
         */
    }

    /** Testing code for the service. No matter how trivial the service,
     * this kind of test code is always useful.
     */
    public static void main (String args[]) {
        FareService fareService = new FareService ();
```

```
        System.out.println ("The fare from San Jose to Taipei is "
                        + fareService.getFare ("SJC", "TPE"));
        System.out.println ("The fare from San Jose to Cancun is "
                        + fareService.getFare ("SJC", "CAN"));
    }

}
```

We now deploy this service in Apache SOAP running on the Tomcat web server.
First you need to compile this service (from `install\wrox\webservices\UDDIImpl`):

> javac -d . FareService.java

Tomcat's classpath should contain the location of this class file. In this case, the CLASSPATH in
`tomcat.bat` should contain `c:\install\wrox\webservices\UDDIImpl`. You should have already
made the setup changes mentioned in the beginning of this chapter.

As, we have already seen in Chapter 5, the default URL of the SOAP admin page is
http://localhost:8080/soap/admin/index.html. Open this URL in a web browser and click on the Deploy button.

The figure below shows SOAP Admin page and service being deployed.

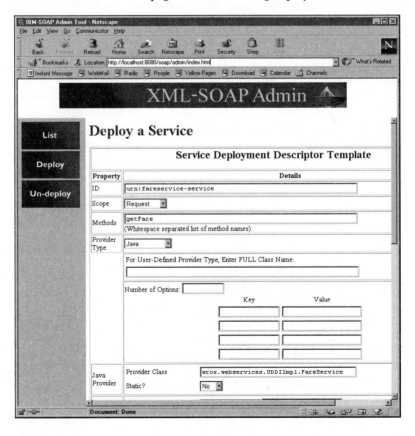

❑ ID

This is a URN (Uniform Resource Name) and is used to uniquely identify the service to the client. The target URI that was used in the client call needs to match this value. So set this field to "urn:fareservice-service". The syntax for this URN field by convention should be of the form urn:*SomeID*

❑ Scope

The scope defines the lifetime of the object serving the invocation request. It can have the possible values of request, session, or application. In case it is request, a new instance of the service object is created for every incoming client request. In the case of session, the service object is available for the entire client session. application scope would mean that successive service invocations belonging to different sessions would share the same service object. This field is not very important for this project, and can be left as "request"

❑ Methods

This field defines the methods that are exposed by the service. Set this field to the method name, that is: getFare

❑ Provider Type

This specifies the language of implementation for the service. Currently the only ones supported are Java, Bean scripts, and user defined provider types. Set this field to "java"

❑ User-Defined Provider Type

This field and the ones next to it on the form can be skipped – it is used for user defined provider types

❑ Java Provider

This is the fully qualified class name of class implementing the service. Enter wrox.webservices.UDDIImpl.FareService as the Provider Class. Select "no" for the Static? field, as the methods are all instance methods

❑ Script Provider

This field can be skipped – because the Provider Type is "Java"

❑ Type Mappings

For basic types like String, default serializers and de-serializers are invoked. For any other type, we need to provide classes that handle serialization of Java types to XML and de-serialization from XML to the Java type. This field can be skipped

❑ Default Mapping Registry Class

This is the fully qualified class name of a customized registry that manages the serializer/deserializers for the service. This field can be skipped

After filling in all this information, click the Deploy button to deploy the service. On success, you should see the following:

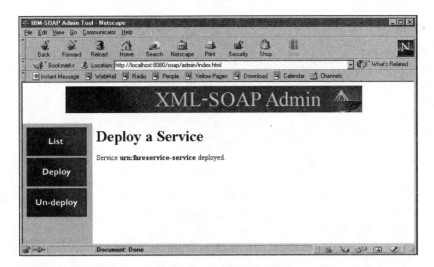

To confirm, click on the List button, and then on the service URN listed. You should see the following:

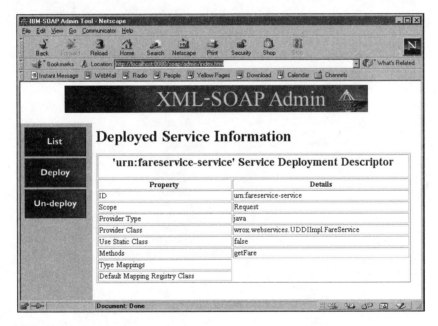

Programmatically Publishing the tModel

A Web Service is described using WSDL as the interface definition language. This is not required, but is recommended as best practice. We will be using WSDL descriptions for our Web Service. These WSDL descriptions were generated using the WSDL generation tool (`wsdlgen.bat`) that came with the IBM WSTK. This tool takes a Java class, an EJB `.jar` file, or even a COM Dispatch interface and generates a WSDL description for it – we could have written this description by hand instead. The tool is shown below, and can be invoked using the `wsdlgen.bat` batch file (`wsdlgen.sh` for UNIX) located in the `bin` directory under WSTK install home.

> wsdlgen.bat

At the WSDL Generation prompt, select the Java Class radio button and click Next.

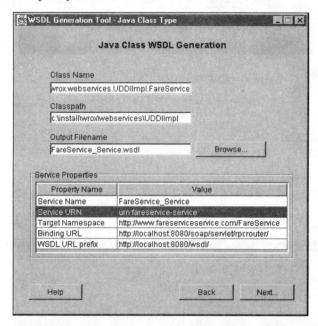

Enter this information (above) and click on the Next... button. A list of the methods that this service implements is shown (below).

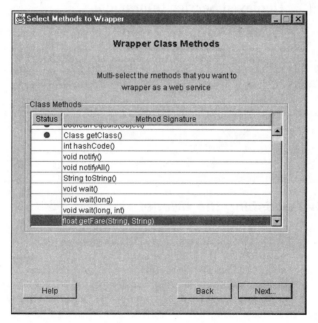

Select float getFare(string, string) and click on Next....

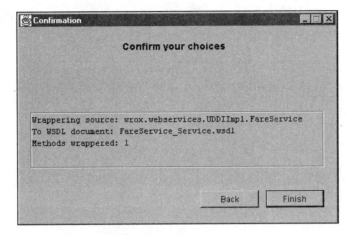

Then select Finish to generate the WSDL files.

The generated WSDL files – FareService_Service.wsdl and FareService_Service-Interface.wsdl – should be copied (from C:\wstk-2.3\bin) to a location that can be accessed via a web browser. In this example, we place it in the local web server itself. In our deployment, the webserver (Jakarta Tomcat) is installed in c:\Jakarta-tomcat-3.2.1, hence we create a directory called wsdl under c:\Jakarta-tomcat-3.2.1\webapps\Root and copy the two wsdl files in it. This location would vary if you have some other Web server instead of Jakarta Tomcat, or if it is installed somewhere else.

The WSDL file is now accessible at http://127.0.0.1:8080/wsdl/FareService_Service.wsdl. Naturally, if we wish to have this available to the world, we should use a URL that can be accessed from outside our machine – 127.0.0.1 is the lookback IP address that maps back to our machine.

This brings us to the interesting question – do we write the WSDL description of service first, or the service itself? In this case we have written the service and used a tool to generate a WSDL description for it. However, there are tools such as WSTK's **servicegen** that can take a WSDL description and generate a template for a service. This can be used by other service providers – they can use this mechanism to build conforming services.

Now we are ready to publish the tModel – the code for this is shown below in the SaveTModel class. First all the package declarations and imports:

```
package wrox.webservices.UDDIImpl;

import java.net.*;
import java.util.*;
import java.io.*;

import com.ibm.uddi.*;
import com.ibm.uddi.client.*;
import com.ibm.uddi.response.*;
import com.ibm.uddi.datatype.*;
import com.ibm.uddi.datatype.tmodel.*;
```

```
import com.ibm.uddi.datatype.business.*;
import com.ibm.uddi.util.*;

import org.apache.soap.SOAPException;
import org.apache.soap.transport.http.SOAPHTTPConnection;

/**
 * The SaveTModel class publishes a TModel description.
 * A tModel acts as a unique signature for a service. Typically
 * standards bodies would publish tModels and individual companies
 * would write implementations conforming to them.
 */
public class SaveTModel {
```

You need to change the lines below with the username and password that you set while creating an account with the UDDI test registry.

```
/* The username and password to interact with the UDDI registry */
private final static String USERNAME = "YOUR-USERNAME";
private final static String PASSWORD = "YOUR-PASSWORD";
```

The name and description strings that are published with the tModel are shown below. We could have more than one description string, and also have description in languages other than English. The WSDL_TMODEL_KEY constant contains the canonical (or defined) tModel Key for WSDL documents. Setting this tModel Key in the category bag of our tModel identifies our tModel as one that supports a WSDL based Web Service.

```
/* The tModel information */
private final static String WSDL_TMODEL_KEY
    = "uuid:C1ACF26D-9672-4404-9D70-39B756E62AB4";
private final static String TMODEL_NAME = "fare_service_tmodel";
private final static String TMODEL_DESC =
    "The fare service provides a programmatic API for getting airline fare
    information";
```

The URL for the WSDL description follows; as mentioned earlier, we need to change this URL to something other than the lookback address if we wish to have it accessable from some other machine.

```
private final static String WSDL_URL =
    "http://127.0.0.1:8080/wsdl/FareService_Service.wsdl";
```

This is a helper method used for constructing single object vectors.

```
/* Helper method for constructing a vector with one element in it */
private static Vector constructVector (Object object) {
    Vector vector = new Vector ();
    vector.addElement (object);
    return vector;
}

public static void main (String args[]) {
```

The publish method calls are transported over SSL, hence the code below:

```
/* Settings for HTTPS, SSL support */
    System.setProperty ("java.protocol.handler.pkgs",
                        "com.ibm.net.ssl.internal.www.protocol");
    java.security.Security.addProvider (new com.ibm.jsse.JSSEProvider ());
```

We now construct an UDDIProxy object. In this case we need to set the publish URL. However, this time we need to set the Publish URL instead of the Inquiry URL (though both could be set). The Publish URL is the URL to which the UDDI publish requests are sent.

```
/* Construct a UDDIProxy object - this represents a UDDI server
 * and the actions that can be invoked against it.
 */
UDDIProxy uddiProxy = new UDDIProxy ();

/* Setting for the proxy server- in case you are behind a firewall */
/*
    SOAPHTTPConnection soapHTTPConnection = new SOAPHTTPConnection ();
    soapHTTPConnection.setUserName ("proxy-username");
    soapHTTPConnection.setPassword ("proxy-password");
    soapHTTPConnection.setProxyHost ("proxyhostname");
    soapHTTPConnection.setProxyPort (8080);
    uddiProxy.setTransport (soapHTTPConnection);
*/

    /* Set the publish URL to the test registry node at IBM */
    try {
       uddiProxy.setPublishURL (UDDIOperatorURLs.IBM_PUBLISH_URL_TEST);
       System.out.println ("Publishing tModel to "
                           + UDDIOperatorURLs.IBM_PUBLISH_URL_TEST);
    } catch (MalformedURLException e) {
    System.err.println ("Malformed publish URL for the UDDI registry ["
                        + UDDIOperatorURLs.IBM_PUBLISH_URL_TEST + "]");
    e.printStackTrace ();
    System.exit (1); /* fatal error */
}
```

Next we call the get_authToken() API call to get an authentication token from the registry. This call takes the username and password that we set when we registered with the registry. The authentication token is used for all subsequent publish API call – this ensures that no one else other that us can delete or modify information that we publish.

```
    /* Get an authentication token */
    AuthToken authToken = null;
    try {
        authToken = uddiProxy.get_authToken(USERNAME, PASSWORD);
    }
    catch (UDDIException e) {
        System.err.println ("UDDI error getting authentication token: ["
                            + e.getFaultCode() + "]" + e.getFaultString()
                            );
    DispositionReport dispositionReport = e.getDispositionReport ();
    System.err.println ("More error information : "
                        + dispositionReport.getErrCode() + ": "
```

```
                                    + dispositionReport.getErrInfoText());
         System.exit (1); /* fatal error */
         } catch (SOAPException e) {
         System.err.println ("SOAP error getting authentication token "
                           + e.getFaultCode() + ": " + e.getMessage());
         System.exit (1); /* fatal error */
      }
```

We now construct a tModel, filling in the name of the tModel (TMODEL_NAME constant), a short description for it (TMODEL_DESC constant), and the URL of the WSDL file that describes the service (WSDL_URL constant). We pass an empty tModel Key to the constructor of the tModel object – this causes a new tModel to be created. If instead we had passed a valid tModel Key, the data already existing in the registry would get modified. We also classify this tModel using the WSDL_TMODEL_KEY tModel Key to specify that this tModel supports a service described using WSDL. The overviewURL would then be interpreted as the URL of a WSDL document.

```
   /* Construct the tModel - the empty tModel key should cause the UDDI
      * registry to assign a (unique) key for the tModel.
      */
   TModel tModel = new TModel ("", TMODEL_NAME);
   tModel.setDefaultDescriptionString (TMODEL_DESC);

   OverviewDoc overviewDoc = new OverviewDoc ();
   overviewDoc.setOverviewURL (new OverviewURL (WSDL_URL));
   overviewDoc.setDefaultDescriptionString ("WSDL Document");
   tModel.setOverviewDoc (overviewDoc);

   KeyedReference keyedReference = new KeyedReference ();
   keyedReference.setKeyName ("uddi-org:types");
   keyedReference.setKeyValue ("wsdlSpec");
   keyedReference.setTModelKey (WSDL_TMODEL_KEY);

   CategoryBag categoryBag = new CategoryBag ();
   categoryBag.setKeyedReferenceVector (constructVector (keyedReference));
   tModel.setCategoryBag (categoryBag);
```

Finally we publish the tModel data using a save_tModel() call. The save_tModel() call takes the authentication token and a vector of tModels and publishes each one of them if authentication succeeds. In case of failure, the Disposition Report would contain the details of the failure. On success, we print out the tModel Key.

```
   /* Publish the tModel in the registry */
   TModelDetail tModelDetail = null;
   try {
      tModelDetail = uddiProxy.save_tModel (authToken.getAuthInfoString (),
                                         constructVector (tModel));
   } catch (UDDIException e) {
      System.err.println ("UDDI error saving tModel: ["
                        + e.getFaultCode() + "]" + e.getFaultString()
                        );
```

```
        DispositionReport dispositionReport = e.getDispositionReport ();
        System.err.println ("More error information : "
                        + dispositionReport.getErrCode() + ": "
                        + dispositionReport.getErrInfoText());
      System.exit (1); /* fatal error */
    } catch (SOAPException e) {
      System.err.println ("SOAP error saving tModel: "
                        + e.getFaultCode() + ": " + e.getMessage());
      System.exit (1); /* fatal error */

    }

    /* Get the tModel key assigned for this tModel */
    Vector tModelVector = tModelDetail.getTModelVector();

    /* Since we saved only one tModel, the resulting tModel
     * detail should have only one tModel in it.
     */
    TModel thisTModel = (TModel) (tModelVector.elementAt(0));
    String tModelKey = thisTModel.getTModelKey ();

    System.out.println ("The " + TMODEL_NAME
                        + " tModel has been successfully updated "
                        + " in the UDDI registry and assigned the tModel Key: "
                        + tModelKey);

  }
}
```

Compile this program (from `install\wrox\webservices\UDDIImpl`):

> **javac -d . SaveTModel.java**

and run it:

> **java wrox.webservices.UDDIImpl.SaveTModel**

the following output should result:

Save the tModel Key (in this example its is UUID:94B5B570-80B5-11D5-A76E-0004AC49CC1E) that is shown on the screen – we will be using it later in the chapter. You will get a different tModel key than the one shown above, as the UDDI registry will assign you a unique tModel Key. You need to use that tModel key (which you get from running SaveTModel) in your examples.

Publishing the tModel Using GUI Tools

Another way to publish a `tModel` is by using a tool to submit this information to the UDDI registry. The screenshot below is of the web interface of the UDDI test registry at IBM being used to submit this information. The URL for the test registry is http://www-3.ibm.com/services/uddi/testregistry/index.html.

Programmatically Publishing the Business Entity

Next, we publish our business listings, using a class that we have elected to call `SaveBusiness`. The imports and package declaration for the `SaveBusiness` class are given below.

```
package wrox.webservices.UDDIImpl;

import java.net.*;
import java.util.*;
import java.io.*;

import com.ibm.uddi.*;
import com.ibm.uddi.client.*;
import com.ibm.uddi.response.*;
import com.ibm.uddi.datatype.binding.*;
import com.ibm.uddi.datatype.business.*;
import com.ibm.uddi.datatype.tmodel.*;
import com.ibm.uddi.datatype.service.*;
import com.ibm.uddi.util.*;

import org.apache.soap.SOAPException;
import org.apache.soap.transport.http.SOAPHTTPConnection;
```

```
/**
    * The SaveBusiness class publishes a Business Listing for a
    * fictitious airline company in the UDDI registry.
 */
public class SaveBusiness {
```

The username and password are the same as in the last example – you should edit this program and add them here too.

```
/* The username and password to interact with the UDDI registry */
private final static String USERNAME = "YOUR-USERNAME";
private final static String PASSWORD = "YOUR-PASSWORD";
```

Next we see the data for the Business Entity that we are about to publish – this includes the name (BUSINESS_NAME), a short description (BUSINESS_DESCRIPTION), contact information (CONTACT_PERSON, CONTACT_EMAIL, CONTACT_PHONE etc.), and the URL for the service (SERVICE_URL – this is the URL of the SOAP server where the Web Service is deployed).

```
/* The business information */
private final static String BUSINESS_NAME       = "Crashes R'Us Airlines";
private final static String BUSINESS_DESCRIPTION =
"Crashes R'Us Airlines aims to provide a memorable flight experience - "
+ "remember to bring a bathing suit on our trans-Pacific flights!";
private final static String CONTACT_PERSON      = "John J. Doe";
private final static String CONTACT_EMAIL       = "john.j.doe@crashesrus.com";
private final static String CONTACT_ADDRESS_LN1 = "123 Airline Ave";
private final static String CONTACT_ADDRESS_LN2 = "San Jose";
private final static String CONTACT_ADDRESS_LN3 = "CA 95192";
private final static String CONTACT_PHONE       = "1-408-555-1234";
private final static String SERVICE_NAME        = "fare_service";
private final static String SERVICE_URL
= "http://127.0.0.1:8080/soap/servlet/rpcrouter";
private final static String SERVICE_DESC        = "SOAP service for fare
quotes";

/* Helper method for constructing a vector with one element in it */
private static Vector constructVector (Object object) {
    Vector vector = new Vector ();
    vector.addElement (object);
    return vector;
}

public static void main (String args[]) {
```

This program takes the tModel Key as a command line input – you should have saved the tModel Key from the previous program (SaveTModel).

```
/* Process command line arguments */
if (args.length != 1) {
    System.out.println
    ("usage: java wrox.webserices.UDDIImpl.SaveBusiness <TMODEL_KEY>");
    System.exit (1);
}

/* Settings for HTTPS, SSL support */
```

```
System.setProperty ("java.protocol.handler.pkgs",
                    "com.ibm.net.ssl.internal.www.protocol");
java.security.Security.addProvider (new com.ibm.jsse.JSSEProvider ());
```

The first step is to create an UDDIProxy object. The Publish URL, as mentioned earlier, is the URL to which the UDDI publish requests should be sent.

```
/* Construct an UDDIProxy object - this represents a UDDI server
 * and the actions that can be invoked against it.
 */
    UDDIProxy uddiProxy = new UDDIProxy ();
```

As before, in case you are behind a proxy server, you would need to set the appropriate values in the code below and uncomment it.

```
/* Setting for the proxy server- in case you are behind one */
/*
    SOAPHTTPConnection soapHTTPConnection = new SOAPHTTPConnection ();
    soapHTTPConnection.setUserName ("proxy-username");
    soapHTTPConnection.setPassword ("proxy-password");
    soapHTTPConnection.setProxyHost ("proxyhostname");
    soapHTTPConnection.setProxyPort (8080);
    uddiProxy.setTransport (soapHTTPConnection);
*/

    /* Set the publish URL to the test registry node at IBM */
    try {
    uddiProxy.setPublishURL (UDDIOperatorURLs.IBM_PUBLISH_URL_TEST);
    System.out.println ("Publishing businessEntity to "
                        + UDDIOperatorURLs.IBM_PUBLISH_URL_TEST);
    } catch (MalformedURLException e) {
    System.err.println ("Malformed publish URL for the UDDI registry ["
                        + UDDIOperatorURLs.IBM_PUBLISH_URL_TEST + "]");
    e.printStackTrace ();
    System.exit (1); /* fatal error */
    }
```

The publish UDDI calls are authenticated calls unlike the inquiry calls. They require an authentication token. The get_authToken() UDDI call is used to obtain an authentication token.

```
    /* Get an authentication token */
    AuthToken authToken = null;
    try {authToken = uddiProxy.get_authToken(USERNAME, PASSWORD);
    }
    catch (UDDIException e) {
        System.err.println ("UDDI error getting authentication token: ["
                            + e.getFaultCode() + "]" + e.getFaultString()
    );
    DispositionReport dispositionReport = e.getDispositionReport ();
    System.err.println ("More error information : "
                        + dispositionReport.getErrCode() + ": "
                        + dispositionReport.getErrInfoText());
    System.exit (1); /* fatal error */
    }
    catch (SOAPException e) {
        System.err.println ("SOAP error getting authentication token: "
                            + e.getFaultCode() + ": " + e.getMessage());
```

```
            System.exit (1); /* fatal error */

    }
```

Next, we create a Business Entity object and fill in its attributes. These include the name of the business (BUSINESS_NAME constant), a short text description (BUSINESS_DESCRIPTION constant), the contact address, phone number, and email address. We add a vector of contacts to a Business Entity, as there can be multiple contacts for a business. In this example however, we have just one contact. In this example too, we pass an empty Business Key and hence a new business entity is created in the UDDI registry.

```
/* Create and populate our business entity object.
   * The business key is passed as an empty string - this causes it to
   * be assigned by the operator node
*/
BusinessEntity businessEntity = new BusinessEntity ("", BUSINESS_NAME);

/* Set Business Description */
businessEntity.setDefaultDescriptionString (BUSINESS_DESCRIPTION);

/* Set Contact Info */
Contact  contact  = new Contact ();
contact.setPersonName (CONTACT_PERSON);

Address address = new Address ();
Vector addressStrings = new Vector ();
addressStrings.addElement (CONTACT_ADDRESS_LN1);
addressStrings.addElement (CONTACT_ADDRESS_LN2);
addressStrings.addElement (CONTACT_ADDRESS_LN3);
address.setAddressLineStrings (addressStrings);
contact.setAddressVector (constructVector (address));

Email email = new Email (CONTACT_EMAIL);
contact.setEmailVector (constructVector (email));

Phone phone = new Phone (CONTACT_PHONE);
contact.setPhoneVector (constructVector (phone));

Contacts contacts = new Contacts ();
contacts.setContactVector (constructVector (contact));
businessEntity.setContacts (contacts);
```

In addition, industry standard classification codes (NAICS, or the North American Industry Classification System in this case) are used to add classification information about this business listing. More information on these classification codes and their use can be found in Chapter 6. IBM's toolkit comes with a "categoryhelper" tool (see screenshot below) that helps determine the NAICS and UNSPSC (Universal Standard Products and Services Classification) classification code for a business or a service (categoryhelper.bat in the bin directoy).

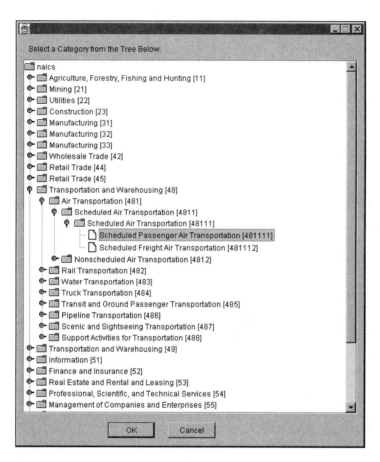

We use the NAICS classification code of 481111 (Scheduled Passenger Air Transportation) for our business.

```
/* Set business classification -
 *   We use NAICS (North American Industry Classification System) codes
 *   to classify this business. The particular code that we use is:
 *     481111 Scheduled Passenger Air Transportation
 *   See www.naics.com for additional details.
 */
KeyedReference keyedReference = new KeyedReference ();
keyedReference.setKeyName ("NAICS: Scheduled Passenger Air Transportation");
keyedReference.setKeyValue ("481111");
keyedReference.setTModelKey (TModel.NAICS_TMODEL_KEY);

CategoryBag categoryBag = new CategoryBag ();
categoryBag.setKeyedReferenceVector (constructVector (keyedReference));
businessEntity.setCategoryBag (categoryBag);

/* Construct the bindingTemplate structure */
String tModelKey = args[0];
TModelInstanceInfo tModelInstanceInfo = new TModelInstanceInfo (tModelKey);
TModelInstanceDetails tModelInstanceDetails = new TModelInstanceDetails();
tModelInstanceDetails.setTModelInstanceInfoVector (constructVector
(tModelInstanceInfo));
```

Next, we first construct the Binding Template, which gives information on how to "bind" to the service. We set the SOAP router URL as "Access Point" in the Binding Template – client programs that desire to interact with the service would need to determine this URL, and post their method invocations to it. In our example, this URL is the URL of the SOAP listener http://127.0.0.1:8080/soap/servlet/rpcrouter/ as specified by the SERVICE_URL constant.

```
BindingTemplate bindingTemplate = new BindingTemplate ();
bindingTemplate.setTModelInstanceDetails (tModelInstanceDetails);
bindingTemplate.setAccessPoint (new AccessPoint (SERVICE_URL, "http"));
bindingTemplate.setDefaultDescriptionString (SERVICE_DESC);

/* Construct the businessService structure */
BindingTemplates bindingTemplates = new BindingTemplates ();
bindingTemplates.setBindingTemplateVector (constructVector(bindingTemplate));
BusinessService businessService = new BusinessService ("",
                         SERVICE_NAME, bindingTemplates);

/* Add to businessEntity */
BusinessServices businessServices = new BusinessServices ();
businessServices.setBusinessServiceVector (constructVector (businessService));
businessEntity.setBusinessServices (businessServices);

/* Create a Vector of business entity objects, and add
 * the BusinessEntity created to it.
 */
Vector businessEntities = new Vector ();
businessEntities.addElement (businessEntity);
```

Finally, we are ready to publish this businessEntity. The save_business() method takes the authentication token and a vector of Business Entities as its parameters and returns the successfully saved business entities in a BusinessDetail object.

```
/* Finally, update this business entity information in the registry */
System.out.println ("Attempting to publish businessEntity for " +
                    BUSINESS_NAME);
BusinessDetail businessDetail = null;
try {
   businessDetail = uddiProxy.save_business (authToken.getAuthInfoString (),
                                       businessEntities);
}
catch (UDDIException e) {
   System.err.println ("UDDI related error while saving business entity: ["
                       + e.getFaultCode() + "]" + e.getFaultString());
   DispositionReport dispositionReport = e.getDispositionReport ();
   System.err.println ("More error information : "
                       + dispositionReport.getErrCode() + ": "
         + dispositionReport.getErrInfoText());
   System.exit (1); /* fatal error */
}
catch (SOAPException e) {
   System.err.println ("SOAP related error saving business entity: "
                       + e.getFaultCode() + ": " + e.getMessage());
   System.exit (1); /* fatal error */
}
```

After the publish call, the UDDI operator site should be informed to invalidate the authentication token. This would cause any subsequent publish call with this token to fail.

```
    /* Finally, invalidate the authentication token */
    try {
       uddiProxy.discard_authToken(authToken.getAuthInfo());
    } catch (Exception e) { /* ignore */ }
```

Since this is a new business listing, we do not set the Business Key (which is a unique identifier for the business). Instead, we examine the `BusinessDetail` structure returned and obtain the Business Key.

```
    /* Get the business key assigned for our company */
    Vector businessEntityVector = businessDetail.getBusinessEntityVector();

    /* Since we saved only one Business Entity, the resulting Business
       * Detail should have only one Business Entity in it
    */
    BusinessEntity thisBusinessEntity = (BusinessEntity)
                                        (businessEntityVector.elementAt(0));
    String businessKey = thisBusinessEntity.getBusinessKey ();

    System.out.println ("The " + BUSINESS_NAME
                        + " Business Entity has been successfully updated "
                        + " in the UDDI registry and assigned the Business Key: "
                        + businessKey);

    }
}
```

Now, after filling in the USERNAME and PASSWORD variables with your own choices (that were chosen in the *Creating an account with the UDDI Registry* section above), save this in the UDDIImpl directory, go to the install\wrox\webservices\UDDIImpl directory, compile this program and run it, using the following commands:

> **javac -d . SaveBusiness.java**

On running this program, we should see something like the following:

Let's run this program once again.

What happened? Well, remember the limit that we mentioned on the number of Business Entities that a Tier 1 user can publish – one! We need to delete the Business Entity before we can publish again – the deletion example is covered later in the chapter. Another alternative is updating the existing Business Entity.

Change the line in the code that sets Business Key to an empty string (thus telling the operator node to assign a new key):

```
BusinessEntity businessEntity = new BusinessEntity ("", BUSINESS_NAME);
```

Put the Business Key that we were assigned in its place. For example:

```
BusinessEntity businessEntity = new
    BusinessEntity ("1D90E780-8ABF-11D5-A4A5-0004AC49CC1E", BUSINESS_NAME);
```

This buiness key will be different for you - the UDDI registry assigns unique business keys for each new business entity.

Now compile and re-run the program, and this error will not occur again.

Lets examine the data that has been published in the registry. We will now use the UDDI browser at soapclient.com (http://www.soapclient.com/uddisearch.html) to find this business by name. Once we find the business, we click on the Business Name to get detailed information about the business. We should see something like this:

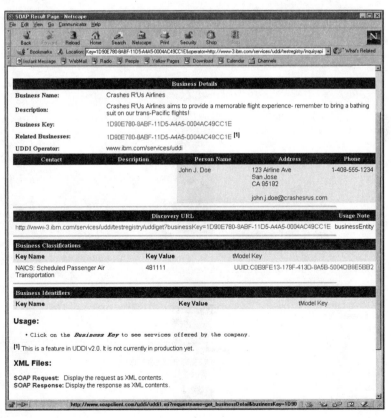

Now click on the **SOAP Response** option at the bottom of the web page to get and see the
BusinessEntity we just published. You should be presented with the following output:

```xml
<?xml version="1.0" encoding="ISO-8859-1"?>
<businessDetail generic="1.0" operator="www.ibm.com/services/uddi"
                truncated="false" xmlns="urn:uddi-org:api">
    <businessEntity authorizedName="100000089X"
                businessKey="1D90E780-8ABF-11D5-A4A5-0004AC49CC1E"
                operator="www.ibm.com/services/uddi">
        <discoveryURLs>
            <discoveryURL useType="businessEntity">
                http://www-3.ibm.com/services/uddi/testregistry
                /uddiget?businessKey=1D90E780-8ABF-11D5-A4A5-0004AC49CC1E
            </discoveryURL>
        </discoveryURLs>
        <name>Crashes R&apos;Us Airlines</name>
        <description xml:lang="en">
            Crashes R&apos;Us Airlines aims to provide a memorable flight experience
            - remember to bring a bathing suit on our trans-Pacific flights!
        </description>
        <description xml:lang="en">SOAP service for fare quotes</description>
        <contacts>
            <contact useType="">
                <personName>John J. Doe</personName>
                <phone useType="">1-408-555-1234</phone>
                <email useType="">john.j.doe@crashesrus.com</email>
                <address sortCode="" useType="">
                    <addressLine>123 Airline Ave</addressLine>
                    <addressLine>San Jose</addressLine>
                    <addressLine>CA 95192</addressLine>
                </address>
            </contact>
        </contacts>
        <businessServices>
            <businessService businessKey="1D90E780-8ABF-11D5-A4A5-0004AC49CC1E"
                        serviceKey="2CCEC810-80B6-11D5-A76E-0004AC49CC1E">
                <name>fare_service</name>
                <description xml:lang="en">SOAP service for fare quotes</description>
                <bindingTemplates>
                    <bindingTemplate bindingKey="2CCF6450-80B6-11D5-A76E-0004AC49CC1E"
                                serviceKey="2CCEC810-80B6-11D5-A76E-0004AC49CC1E">
                        <description xml:lang="en">
                            SOAP service for fare quotes
                        </description>
                        <accessPoint URLType="http">
                            http://127.0.0.1:8080/soap/servlet/rpcrouter
                        </accessPoint>
                        <tModelInstanceDetails>
                            <tModelInstanceInfo tModelKey="UUID:94B5B570-80B5-11D5-A76E-
                                                0004AC49CC1E"/>
                        </tModelInstanceDetails>
                    </bindingTemplate>
                </bindingTemplates>
            </businessService>
        </businessServices>
        <categoryBag>
            <keyedReference keyName="NAICS: Scheduled Passenger Air Transportation"
                        keyValue="481111" tModelKey="UUID:C0B9FE13-179F-413D-
                                8A5B-5004DB8E5BB2"/>
        </categoryBag>
    </businessEntity>
</businessDetail>
```

You will not get the same business, service, binding and tModel keys. All these keys are generated by the UDDI server and are unique.

Chapter 6 described the UDDI data structures in detail – it would be an interesting exercise to go over the published Business Entity data above and understand the various elements.

Publishing the Business Entity Using GUI Tools

Another way to publish a Business Entity is by using a tool to submit this information to the UDDI registry. The screenshot below is of the web interace of the UDDI test registry at IBM being used to submit this information. The URL for the test registry is http://www-3.ibm.com/services/uddi/testregistry/index.html.

Finding and Invoking Methods on the Web Service

Finding and invoking a web service can be done in various ways. In our client example, we examine one typical way for doing this. We have a four-step process:

❑ Get the tModel Key. In this example we assume that we have a well-known tModel

❑ Find businesses that implement services conforming to the tModel

❑ Locate the service within the Business Entity

❑ Bind to and invoke methods on the Web Service

How do we know what methods to invoke on the Web Service when we find it? This is where the WSDL description that we published along with the tModel comes in handy. The WSDL document contains the interface defination for the Web Service, and we can use automated tools to generate the service stubs. IBM WSTK comes with one such tool – **proxygen**. Proxygen takes a WSDL file as input, and generates a "service stub". Clients can invoke methods on this service stub, just as they would on the actual Web service method. Proxygen is also located in the `bin` directory under the WSTK install home like the other tools.

Since this `tModel` is a well-known tModel, we can get to it using either the `tModel` Key or the name, and grab the WSDL document that is refered to in its `"overviewDoc"` field. The screenshot below shows this using the UDDI browser at soapclient.com (http://www.soapclient.com/uddisearch.html) to search for this `tModel`.

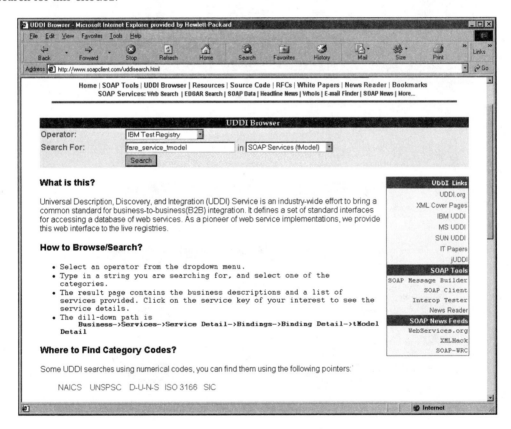

Click on the **Submit** button – you should get all `tModels` that match this name.

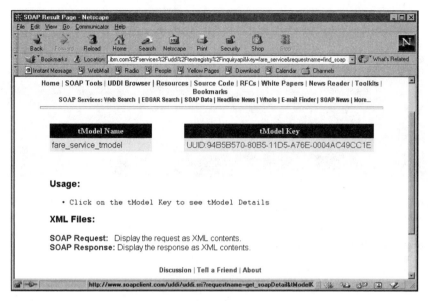

Select one of them (right now it shows only one such `tModel`) and click on the `tModel` key to get the `tModel` detail.

The `tModel` detail is shown below. The OverviewURL gives the URL for the WSDL file that contains the service interface defination of the fare service. Save this WSDL file (at the URL http://127.0.0.1:8080/wsdl/FareService_Service.wsdl). We will use this to generate the client side proxy.

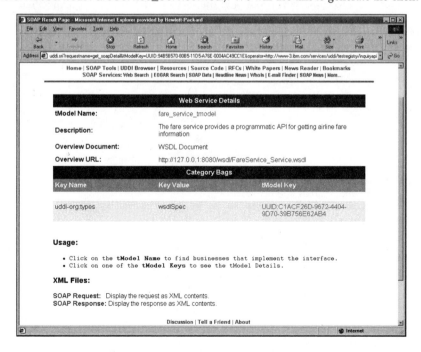

We now invoke proxygen on this saved WSDL file (from \install\wrox\webservices\UDDIImpl) as shown below:

> **c:\wstk-2.3\bin\proxygen FareService_Service.wsdl**

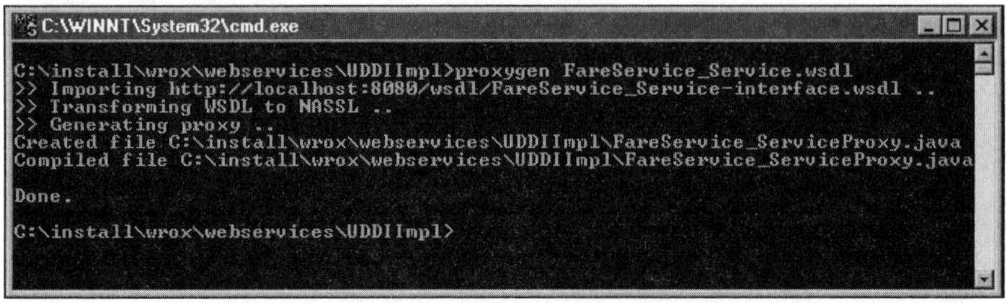

In this example, we'd like to put this proxy in the same package as the rest of the code. So we delete the class file (from install\wrox\webservices\UDDIImpl) for the service stub.

> **del FareService_ServiceProxy.class**

Now we edit the FareService_ServiceProxy.java file and add package wrox.webservices.UDDIImpl; as the first line and recompile the java file.

> **javac -d . FareService_ServiceProxy.java**

If we view this Java file, we can see that it has a setEndPoint() method that sets the service URL and a getFare() method that is the proxy method for the actual Web Service method. Invoking getFare() on the service proxy (that is: on FareService_ServiceProxy object) causes a SOAP request to be sent to the Web Service running at the service URL that we just specified.

Now we are ready to find the service and invoke methods on it – this is demonstrated in the FareClient class below. First, all the imports for the class:

```
package wrox.webservices.UDDIImpl;

import java.net.*;
import java.text.*;
import java.util.*;
import java.io.*;

import com.ibm.uddi.*;
import com.ibm.uddi.client.*;
import com.ibm.uddi.datatype.binding.*;
import com.ibm.uddi.datatype.business.*;
import com.ibm.uddi.datatype.service.*;
import com.ibm.uddi.datatype.tmodel.*;
import com.ibm.uddi.response.*;
import com.ibm.uddi.util.*;

import org.apache.soap.*;
import org.apache.soap.rpc.*;
import org.apache.soap.transport.http.SOAPHTTPConnection;
```

```
/**
 * The FareClient class knows the tModel of the fare quoting
 * service, and finds the service based on that. It then invokes
 * the getFare() method.
 *
 * This example is based on the premise that standards bodies
 * would define and publish tModels and individual  companies
 * would provide implementations.
 */
public class FareClient {
```

Our itinerary – we are interested in the fare for a flight from San Jose to Taipei.

```
/* The flight itinerary - we are flying from
 * FROM_AIRPORT to TO_AIRPORT
 */
private final static String FROM_AIRPORT = "SJC";
private final static String TO_AIRPORT   = "TPE";
public static void main (String args[]) {
```

This program takes the tModel Key as the command line argument. This is because we do a search by tModel, as a tModel Key is unique (unlike a tModel Name).

```
/* Process command line arguments */
   if (args.length != 1) {
       System.out.println
           ("usage: java wrox.webserices.UDDIImpl.FareClient <TMODEL_KEY>");
   System.exit (1);
}
```

As usual we construct an UDDIProxy object. However this time we set the inquiry URL, and not the publish URL.

```
/* Construct a UDDIProxy object - this represents a UDDI server
 * and the actions that can be invoked against it.
 */
UDDIProxy uddiProxy = new UDDIProxy ();

/* Setting for the proxy server- in case you are behind one */
/*
   SOAPHTTPConnection soapHTTPConnection = new SOAPHTTPConnection ();
   soapHTTPConnection.setUserName ("proxy-username");
   soapHTTPConnection.setPassword ("proxy-password");
   soapHTTPConnection.setProxyHost ("proxyhostname");
   soapHTTPConnection.setProxyPort (8080);
   uddiProxy.setTransport (soapHTTPConnection);
*/

/* Set the inquiry URL to the Test registry node at IBM */
try {
   /* Had the business been published to the UDDI global registry
    * instead of the test registry, the inquiry URL could have been
    * set to any UDDI node (such as the one at Microsoft).
```

```
        */
        uddiProxy.setInquiryURL (UDDIOperatorURLs.IBM_INQUIRY_URL_TEST);
        System.out.println ("Inquiry URL : ["
                        + UDDIOperatorURLs.IBM_INQUIRY_URL_TEST + "]");
    }
    catch (MalformedURLException e) {
        System.err.println ("Malformed inquiry URL for the UDDI registry ["
                        + UDDIOperatorURLs.IBM_INQUIRY_URL_TEST + "]");
        e.printStackTrace ();
        System.exit (1); /* fatal error */
    }
```

The first step in our search – we locate a tModel using the tModel Key, which we passed via the command line, and get the tModel detail. We use the `get_tModelDetail` method to get the `tModel` details.

```
/* Assumption: There exists at least one tModel, business, service
 *             that matches each of the searches. No error checking
 *             performed. We simply select the first found - in real
 *             life, there may be some business logic built in to
 *             select based on some other criteria.
 */

/* Step 1: Locate tModel by well known tModel key
 *
 *         The OverviewURL of the tModel would point to the wsdl
 *         description of the service.
 */


String tModelKey = args[0]; /* passed as command line argument */

/* Now that we have the required tModel key, drill down and get the
   tModelDetail */

    TModelDetail tModelDetail = null;
    try {
        tModelDetail = uddiProxy.get_tModelDetail (tModelKey);
    }
    catch (Exception e) {
        System.err.println ("Exception finding tModel detail: "
                        + e.getMessage ());
        e.printStackTrace ();
        System.exit (1); /* fatal error */
    }
```

`TModelDetails` contain a vector of `tModels`. However, since we passed just one `tModel` Key to the `get_tModelDetail()` method, we will have just one `tModel` in the `tModelDetail` object. We get the vector using the `getTModelVector` call and take its first (and only) element.

```
    TModel tModel = (TModel)tModelDetail.getTModelVector().elementAt(0);
```

In case the service had a WSDL description for it, it would be published (or rather the URL pointing to the WSDL document would be) as the "Overview Document" in the `tModel`. We use the `getOverviewDoc` to get the `OverviewDoc` element and extract out the URL of the WSDL file using the `getOverviewURLString()` method.

```
    String overviewURL = tModel.getOverviewDoc().getOverviewURLString();
    System.out.println ("OverviewURL of service is " + overviewURL);
```

The next thing to do is to find businesses that have services implementing this tModel. We do a find by tModel Key (passed in the tModelBag argument). The second argument to find_tModel, which is null here, can have find qualifiers that can modify the search result. Valid find qualifiers include caseSensitiveMatch, exactNameMatch, sortByDateAsc, sortByDateDesc, sortByNameAsc, and sortByNameDesc. The third argument to find_business() is "maxRows" which specifies the maximum number of search results. It is set to zero, which implies that all found results should be returned (subject to truncation by the UDDI registry).

```
    /* Step 2: Find businesses (businessEntity) that have a service that
     *         implements this tModel and and use some business logic to
     *         select one from them.
     */
    Vector tmpTModelVector = new Vector();
    tmpTModelVector.addElement (tModelKey); /* found earlier */
    TModelBag tModelBag = new TModelBag (tmpTModelVector);
    BusinessList businessList = null;
    try {
        businessList = uddiProxy.find_business (tModelBag, null, 0);
    }
    catch (Exception e) {
        System.err.println ("Exception finding business entity: "
                            + e.getMessage ());
        e.printStackTrace ();
        System.exit (1); /* fatal error */
    }

    Vector businessVector =
  businessList.getBusinessInfos().getBusinessInfoVector();
```

Now, from the list of businesses, we need to select one (or more, if so required) business. Usually this would be done based on some business logic – say based on some internal rating, or on the cost of providing the desired service, or geographic location of the business, and so on. Our sample program selects on the basis of the first business found.

```
    /* Select one business out of the list - we select the first one */
    if (businessVector.isEmpty()) {
        System.err.println ("No Business found implemenenting tModel "
                            + tModelKey + ". Sorry!");
        System.exit (1);
    }
    String businessKey =
  ((BusinessInfo)businessVector.elementAt(0)).getBusinessKey ();
```

Next, we search for services within this Business Entity for our service of interest – the one that implements this tModel. We call the find_service() method with the Business Key, a tModelBag containing this tModel, no findQualifiers (set as null) and no limit on the maximum number of search results we are looking for (maxRows set to 0).

```
    /* Now that we have the required business key, we can drill down
     * for additional information  - the businessDetail structure. For
     * now, we dont need to do that.
     */
```

```
/* Step 3: Locate the service (serviceInfo) within the business
 *        entity.
 *
 *        The AccessPoint would have the service URL  - which in
 *        this case is the URL of the SOAP router/listener.
 */

    ServiceList serviceList = null;
    try {
        serviceList = uddiProxy.find_service (businessKey, tModelBag, null, 0);
    }
    catch (Exception e) {
        System.err.println ("Exception finding business service: "
                            + e.getMessage ());
        e.printStackTrace ();
        System.exit (1); /* fatal error */
    }
```

The find_service() method returns a ServiceList object containing a ServiceInfos structure. This has a vector of ServiceInfo objects. The ServiceInfo contains summarized information about a BusinessService. In this example, we simply select the first ServiceInfo.

```
    Vector serviceVector = serviceList.getServiceInfos().getServiceInfoVector();
    /* Taking the first business service matching this search */
    String serviceKey =
((ServiceInfo)serviceVector.elementAt(0)).getServiceKey();
```

We then drill down in the found service to get more information about it. The get_serviceDetail() call takes a Service Key and returns a ServiceDetail object. This contains a vector of BusinessServices – we obtain this using the getBusinessServiceVector method. Since we passed just one Service Key to get_serviceDetail() (we could have passed more than one), we get just one BusinessService object. From this BusinessService object we get the Binding Templates (using the getBindingTemplates call) and extract the "access point" from the first Binding Template contained in it. The access point gives the URL for the service, which in this case is URL of the SOAP listener.

```
    /* Now, drill down to get the ServiceDetail */

    ServiceDetail serviceDetail = null;
    try {
        serviceDetail = uddiProxy.get_serviceDetail (serviceKey);
    }
    catch (Exception e) {
        System.err.println ("Exception finding service detail: "
                            + e.getMessage ());
        e.printStackTrace ();
        System.exit (1); /* fatal error */
    }

    BusinessService businessService =
(BusinessService)serviceDetail.getBusinessServiceVector().elementAt(0);
    BindingTemplates bindingTemplates = businessService.getBindingTemplates();
    BindingTemplate bindingTemplate = (BindingTemplate)
bindingTemplates.getBindingTemplateVector().elementAt(0);
    String accessPoint = bindingTemplate.getAccessPoint().getText();
    System.out.println ("accessPoint of service is " + accessPoint);
```

Now we are all set to invoke the service – this is where the scope of UDDI ends. UDDI does not define anything more than the publishing and the inquiry mechanism. In place of the SOAP listener it could have been just about anything in the access point – such as the URL of a web page with information on how to proceed or a HTML form, an email address, or even a phone number. However, since the tModel that this service implements defines a SOAP-based web service with a "known" interface, the client can proceed and post a SOAP request to that URL.

From the tModel of this service we know that it is a SOAP Web Service, and we have already generated a client proxy object (FareService_ServiceProxy) for it. Now, we set the end point URL in this object (setEndPoint() method) to the service URL we discovered earlier in the binding template, and invoke the getFare() method on the service proxy.

The service proxy has code to form a SOAP request for the getFare() method and send it to the access point URL that we set with the 'setEndPoint()' method. The returned fare information is then deserialized from the SOAP response returned by the Web Service.

```
/* Step 4: Bind and Invoke */

/* Fare request for a flight from San Jose, California
   * to Taipei, Taiwan
*/
float fare = (float) 0.0;
try {
   FareService_ServiceProxy fareServiceProxy =
               new FareService_ServiceProxy();
   fareServiceProxy.setEndPoint (new URL(accessPoint));
   fare = fareServiceProxy.getFare (FROM_AIRPORT, TO_AIRPORT);
}
catch (SOAPException e) {
   System.err.println ("Exception invoking method: "
                     + e.getFaultCode() + ": "
                     + e.getMessage ());
   e.printStackTrace ();
   System.exit (1); /* fatal error */
}
catch (MalformedURLException e) {
   System.err.println ("Malformed service URL ["
                     + accessPoint + "]");
   e.printStackTrace ();
   System.exit (1); /* fatal error */
}

System.out.println ("Requested fare from " + FROM_AIRPORT +
                  " to " + TO_AIRPORT +
                  " is $" + fare);
   }
}
```

When we compile the FareClient class (from install\wrox\webservices\UDDIImpl) and run it, we should see the following output:

```
> javac –d . FareClient.java
> java wrox.webservices.UDDIImpl.FareClient UUID:94B5B570-80B5-11D5-A76E-
   0004AC49CC1E
```

```
C:\WINNT\System32\cmd.exe                                           _ □ ×

C:\install\wrox\webservices\UDDIImpl>java wrox.webservices.UDDIImpl.FareClient U
UID:94B5B570-80B5-11D5-A76E-0004AC49CC1E
Inquiry URL : [http://www-3.ibm.com/services/uddi/testregistry/inquiryapi]
OverviewURL of service is http://127.0.0.1:8080/wsdl/FareService_Service.wsdl
accessPoint of service is http://127.0.0.1:8080/soap/servlet/rpcrouter
Requested fare from SJC to TPE is $899.95

C:\install\wrox\webservices\UDDIImpl>
```

Programmatically Deleting a Business Entity

The UDDI API has delete methods for removing Business Services, Binding Templates, and even entire Business Entities. The code below shows how a business (identified by its Business Key) is removed. This call needs to be issued with care, as the entire Business Entity information, along with the Business Services and Binding Templates contained in it, will be removed.

As usual, we first have the imports for this program, and then the code builds an UDDIProxy object with the publish URL set to the IBM test registry. The DeleteBusiness class that does the required deletion is shown below.

```java
package wrox.webservices.UDDIImpl;

import java.net.*;
import java.util.*;
import java.io.*;

import com.ibm.uddi.*;
import com.ibm.uddi.client.*;
import com.ibm.uddi.response.*;
import com.ibm.uddi.datatype.business.*;

import org.apache.soap.SOAPException;
import org.apache.soap.transport.http.SOAPHTTPConnection;


/**
 * The DeleteBusiness class deletes the business listing for a company.
 * Only the publisher of a businessEntity can remove it, and
 * this can only be done at the node where it was published.
 */
public class DeleteBusiness {

    /* Name of the business */
    private final static String BUSINESS_NAME = "Crashes R'Us Airlines";
```

As before, you would need to change these USERNAME and PASSWORD values to the actual username and password that you had set earlier.

```java
    /* The username and password to interact with the UDDI registry */
    private final static String USERNAME = "YOUR-USERNAME";
    private final static String PASSWORD = "YOUR-PASSWORD";

    public static void main (String args[]) {
```

```
    /* Settings for HTTPS, SSL support */
    System.setProperty ("java.protocol.handler.pkgs",
                    "com.ibm.net.ssl.internal.www.protocol");
    java.security.Security.addProvider (new com.ibm.jsse.JSSEProvider ());

    /* Construct a UDDIProxy object - this represents a UDDI server
     * and the actions that can be invoked against it.
     */
    UDDIProxy uddiProxy = new UDDIProxy ();
/* Setting for the proxy server- in case you are behind one */
/*
    SOAPHTTPConnection soapHTTPConnection = new SOAPHTTPConnection ();
    soapHTTPConnection.setUserName ("proxy-username");
    soapHTTPConnection.setPassword ("proxy-password");
    soapHTTPConnection.setProxyHost ("proxyhostname");
    soapHTTPConnection.setProxyPort (8080);
    uddiProxy.setTransport (soapHTTPConnection);
*/
```

In this program, we set both the Inquiry and Publish URLs in the UDDIProxy. The publish URL is required for the delete_business() method, and we don't need to have the inquiry URL. However we are setting it so that we could extend this program later to show more information about the buiness that we are deleting. We can delete (or for that matter change) a Business Entity or a tModel only at the operator node where it was published.

```
    /* Set the inquiry and publish URLs to the Test registry node at IBM */
    try {
        uddiProxy.setInquiryURL (UDDIOperatorURLs.IBM_INQUIRY_URL_TEST);
        uddiProxy.setPublishURL (UDDIOperatorURLs.IBM_PUBLISH_URL_TEST);
        System.out.println ("Inquiry URL: "
                        + UDDIOperatorURLs.IBM_INQUIRY_URL_TEST + "\n");
        System.out.println ("Publishing URL: "
                        + UDDIOperatorURLs.IBM_PUBLISH_URL_TEST + "\n");
    }
    catch (MalformedURLException e) {
        System.err.println ("Malformed URLs for the UDDI registry ["
                        + UDDIOperatorURLs.IBM_PUBLISH_URL_TEST + ", "
                        + UDDIOperatorURLs.IBM_INQUIRY_URL_TEST + "]");
        e.printStackTrace ();
        System.exit (1); /* fatal error */
    }
```

As before, we get the authentication token to be used for all subsequent publish calls.

```
    /* Get an authentication token */
    AuthToken authToken = null;
    /* The Disposition report contains the return status from the call */
    DispositionReport dispositionReport = null;

    try {
        authToken = uddiProxy.get_authToken(USERNAME, PASSWORD);
    }
    catch (UDDIException e) {
```

```
            System.err.println ("UDDI error getting authentication token: ["
                            + e.getFaultCode() + "]" + e.getFaultString()
                            );
            dispositionReport = e.getDispositionReport ();
            System.err.println ("More error information : "
                            + dispositionReport.getErrCode() + ": "
                            + dispositionReport.getErrInfoText());
            System.exit (1); /* fatal error */
        }
        catch (SOAPException e) {
            System.err.println ("SOAP error getting authentication token "
                            + e.getFaultCode() + ": " + e.getMessage());
            System.exit (1); /* fatal error */

        }
```

The `get_registeredInfo()` call takes the authentication token as input and return a `RegisteredInfo` object that contains all the Business Entities and `tModels` published by us.

```
        /* Get all business entities and tModel published by us */
        RegisteredInfo registeredInfo = new RegisteredInfo ();
        try {
            System.out.println (
            "Getting all business entities and tModels published by us");
            registeredInfo = uddiProxy.get_registeredInfo
                            (authToken.getAuthInfoString());
        }
        catch (UDDIException e) {
            System.err.println
                ("UDDI error getting registered info: ["
                + e.getFaultCode() + "]" + e.getFaultString());
                dispositionReport = e.getDispositionReport ();
                System.err.println ("More error information : "
                            + dispositionReport.getErrCode() + ": "
                            + dispositionReport.getErrInfoText());
        }
        catch (SOAPException e) {
            System.err.println ("SOAP error getting registered info: "
                            + e.getFaultCode() + ": " + e.getMessage());
        }
```

We extract out the Business Infos from the `registeredInfo` object. The Business Info, as mentioned earlier has contains a summary list of all published Business Entities.

```
        Vector businessInfoVector =
    registeredInfo.getBusinessInfos().getBusinessInfoVector();
        Vector tModelInfoVector =
    registeredInfo.getTModelInfos().getTModelInfoVector();

        System.out.println ("Found " + businessInfoVector.size()
                            + " business entities and "
                            + tModelInfoVector.size()
                            + " tModels published by us"
                            );
```

Removing a Business Entity would also remove all Business Services and Binding Templates published inside it. Hence, we ask for confirmation before going ahead and purging the Business Entity.

```
                /* Delete the business entity */
                char reply = 'n';
                if (!businessInfoVector.isEmpty()) {
                    System.out.println ("Remove business entities? [yn]: ");
                    InputStreamReader inputReader = new InputStreamReader (System.in);
                    try {
                        reply = (char) inputReader.read();
                    }
                    catch (Exception e) {/*ignore*/}
                }
```

Tier 1 users (read most users!) are allowed to publish only one Business Entity, and hence we remove the first (and only) Business Entity from the registry. There is another delete_business() method that can remove a vector of Business Entities (specified by a vector of Business Keys). Other than the Business Key, the delete_business() method also takes the authentication token as a parameter.

```
                if (reply == 'y') {
                /* Assuming only one business entity; as that's all you are
                    allowed to publish */
                BusinessInfo businessInfo = (BusinessInfo) businessInfoVector.elementAt(0);
                String businessKey = businessInfo.getBusinessKey ();

                try {
                    System.out.println ("\nAttempting to delete business with businessKey ["
                                        + businessKey + "]");
                    dispositionReport = uddiProxy.delete_business (
                                        authToken.getAuthInfoString(),
                                        businessKey);
                }
                catch (UDDIException e) {
                    System.err.println
                        ("UDDI related error while deleting business entity: ["
                        + e.getFaultCode() + "]" + e.getFaultString());
                    dispositionReport = e.getDispositionReport ();
                    System.err.println ("More error information : "
                                        + dispositionReport.getErrCode() + ": "
                                        + dispositionReport.getErrInfoText());
                }
                catch (SOAPException e) {
                    System.err.println ("SOAP related error deleting business entity: "
                                        + e.getFaultCode() + ": " + e.getMessage());
                }

                if (dispositionReport.success ()) {
                    System.out.println ("Successfully deleted businesEntity for "
                                        + BUSINESS_NAME + "[" + businessKey + "]");
                }
                else {
                    System.err.println ("Error in deleting businesEntity for "
                        + BUSINESS_NAME + "[" + businessKey + "]:"
                        + "Errno (" + dispositionReport.getErrno() + ") "
                        + "ErrCode (" + dispositionReport.getErrCode() + ") "
                        + "ErrText (" + dispositionReport.getErrInfoText() + ") ");
                }
        } /* remove business entity */
    } /* end main */
}
```

Finally, compile and run this program (from install\wrox\webservices\UDDIImpl):

```
> javac –d . DeleteBusiness.java
> java wrox.webservices.UDDIImpl.DeleteBusiness
```

Deleting a Business Entity Using GUI Tools

We can also use the web interface to the UDDI test registry node at IBM, to delete the Business Entity. The screenshot below shows this.

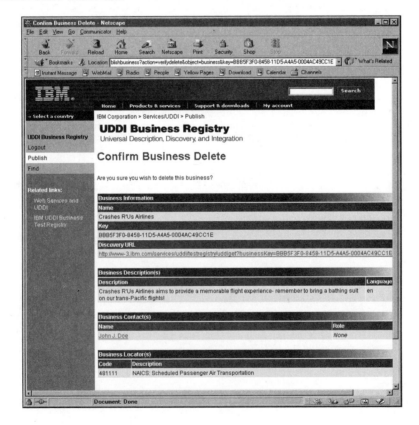

Microsoft UDDI SDK

Microsoft's UDDI SDK provides an API for interacting with the UDDI registry. Programmers using Visual Basic, VBScript, Jscript, C#, or any programming language compliant with COM can use this API. The UDDI API defines an "UDDI Request Manager" object that acts as a proxy for the remote UDDI registry. Client programs format their requests and send it to the Request Manager, which interacts with the registry and returns a response back to the client program.

A brief example of what a client program written using Microsoft's UDDI SDK would look like its given below. This is intended to give you a feel of the API, and not act as a tutorial. The Microsoft UDDI SDK can be downloaded from http://uddi.microsoft.com/developer/, and contains tutorials and examples.

In this example, we try to search for all businesses with the name Foobar Widgets, just as we did in the first UDDI4J sample program (UddiClient.java):

```
BusinessList businessList = null;
    try {
        businessList = uddiProxy.find_business ("Foobar Widgets", null, 0);
    }
    catch (Exception e) {... }
```

The Microsoft UDDI SDK equivalent in Visual Basic is given below:

First the program declares a `RequestManager`, which, as we mentioned earlier, acts as a proxy for the UDDI server.

```
Dim req As New UDDIEnv.RequestManager    ' the request manager
```

Then, we declare `Envelope` objects for the request and response messages. We also declare the `Message` objects for the `find_business` request, the businessList response and for the businessInfo data structure. In the Microsoft UDDI SDK, the `Envelope` objects manage the SOAP details for transmission and the request/response processing. The `Message` objects provide an object-oriented interface to the UDDI data structures.

```
Dim env As New UDDIEnv.Envelope          ' for the request
Dim respEnv As UDDIEnv.Envelope          ' for the response
Dim inqMsg As New UDDI10.find_business   ' Request Document Object
Dim inqRsp As New UDDI10.businessList    ' Response Document Object
Dim result As UDDI10.businessInfo
```

We set up the request document with the request envelope.

```
Set env.Plugin = inqMsg
```

The search criteria – we are searching by the company name "Foobar Widgets".

```
' Search criteria
inqMsg.Name = "Foobar Widgets"
```

Finally, we send the find business request to the UDDI server.

```
    Set respEnv = req.UDDIRequest(env)
    ...
```

Similarly, our program for publishing business listings would look something like this in Microsoft UDDI SDK:

```
    Dim saveBizEntity As New save_business
    Dim bizDetail As New businessDetail
    Dim env As New UDDIEnv.Envelope
    Dim ret As UDDIEnv.Envelope
    Dim req as new UDDIEnv.requestManager
```

Set the username and password for authenticated access to the UDDI registry:

```
    Req.authenticate "YOURNAME", "YOURPASSWORD"
```

Fill in the Business Entity structure:

```
    Set env.Plugin = saveBizEntity
    With saveBizEntity.AddbusinessEntity
        .Name = "Crashes RUs Airlines"
        .Adddescription = " Crashes Rus Airlines aims to provide a memorable flight
    experience"
        With .businessServices.AddbusinessService
            .Name = " fare_service"
            .Adddescription = "SOAP service for fare quotes"
```

Set the access point for the service:

```
        With .bindingTemplates.AddbindingTemplate
            .accessPoint = http://127.0.0.1:8080/soap/servlet/rpcrouter
```

Set the tModel Key to that of the previously saved tModel:

```
        With .tModelInstanceDetails.AddtModelInstanceInfo
            .tModelKey = "UUID:94B5B570-80B5-11D5-A76E-0004AC49CC1E"
            End With
        End With
    End With
    End With
```

Finally, send the save business request to the UDDI server:

```
    Set ret = req.UDDIRequest (env)
    ...
```

HP Web Services Platform

HP's UDDI implementation is packaged along with the HP Web Services Platform (WSP) available from http://www.hp.com/go/webservices/. This includes, among other components, a private registry implementation, an UDDI client SDK, and an UDDI browser tool that allows us to browse as well as publish data. At the time of writing this book, it supports UDDI 1.0 only, but a UDDI 2.0 implementation should be released soon.

HP UDDI Browser

The screenshot below shows the HP UDDI browser finding all businesses matching the name "IBM" in the UDDI Business Registry:

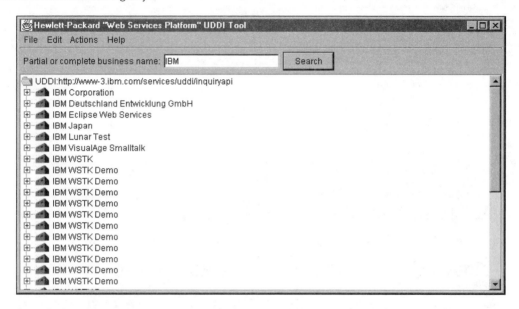

Next, we expand the first business found (that is: IBM Corporation) to drill-down into the Business Entity. We can see all the services that are provided by this Business Entity:

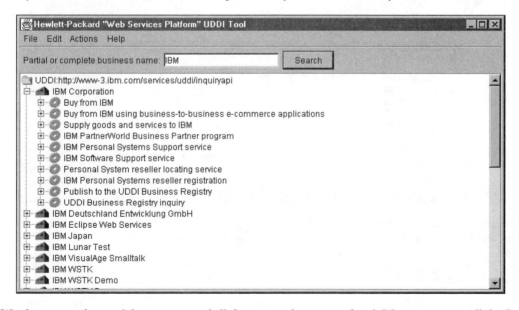

We then expand one of the services to drill-down into the service detail. We can now see all the Binding Templates for the service.

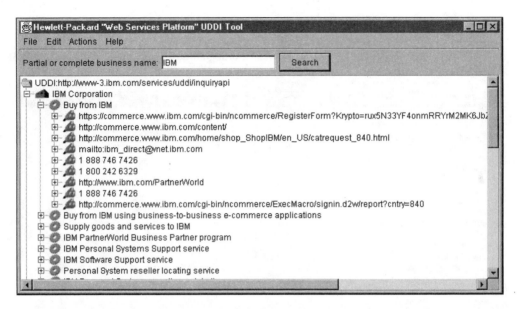

Finally, we expand the Binding Templates themselves to see the tModels they refer to:

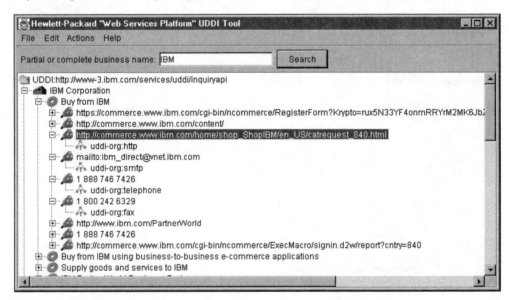

In addition to browsing the registry, the browser tool allows users to publish and edit Business Entities, Business Services, Binding Templates, and tModels.

UDDI Client SDK

The HP UDDI client SDK provides a java API for building UDDI client programs. The sample shown below is intended to give a feel of the API; for more details download the HP Web Service Platform from http://www.hp.com/go/webservices/.

This program (`FindBusiness.java`) takes as a command line argument the UDDI registry to which it should send the inquiry message, and the name of the business. It then does a `find_business()` request to locate all businesses that match the name.

First, we see all the imports required for the program:

```
import com.hp.uddi.api.*;
import java.net.*;

public class FindBusiness {
```

Next, we see the URLs of the production, and test UDDI Business Registries.

```
/* URL for UDDI inquiry in the Production UDDI registry node at IBM       */
public final static String IBM_INQUIRY_URL_PRODUCTION = "http://www-
        3.ibm.com/services/uddi/inquiryapi";

/* URL for UDDI inquiry in the Test UDDI registry node at IBM             */
public final static String IBM_INQUIRY_URL_TEST = "http://www-
        3.ibm.com/services/uddi/testregistry/inquiryapi";

/* URL for UDDI inquiry in the Production UDDI registry node at Microsoft */
public final static String MICROSOFT_INQUIRY_URL_PRODUCTION =
        "http://uddi.microsoft.com/inquire";

/* URL for UDDI inquiry in the Test UDDI registry node at Microsoft       */
public final static String MICROSOFT_INQUIRY_URL_TEST =
        "http://test.uddi.microsoft.com/inquire";

// Print error messsage and die
private static void fatal (String message)
{
    System.err.println ("Fatal: " + message);
    System.exit (1);
}
```

This program, as explained earlier, takes a name (or URL) of the UDDI registry as its first argument. The second argument is the name of the business:

```
public static void main (String args[]) {
    if (args.length != 2)
    fatal (
        "usage: java com.hp.uddi.samples.FindBusiness
        [IBM_PROD|MS_PROD|IBM_TEST|MS_TEST|<url>] <business name>");
    UDDISOAPClient uddiSoapClient = null;

    String inquiryUrl = null;

    if (args[0].equals ("IBM_PROD"))
        inquiryUrl = IBM_INQUIRY_URL_PRODUCTION;
    else if (args[0].equals ("MS_PROD"))
        inquiryUrl = MICROSOFT_INQUIRY_URL_PRODUCTION;
    else if (args[0].equals ("IBM_TEST"))
        inquiryUrl = IBM_INQUIRY_URL_TEST;
```

```
        else if (args[0].equals ("MS_TEST"))
            inquiryUrl = MICROSOFT_INQUIRY_URL_TEST;
        else
            inquiryUrl = args[0];
```

Next, we build the UDDISOAPClient object. This objects represents the UDDI server and is the entry point for all UDDI inquiry and publish methods. We construct the UDDISOAPClient, passing it the UDDI Inquiry URL:

```
    try {
        uddiSoapClient = new UDDISOAPClient (inquiryUrl);
        System.out.println ("Setting URL to " + inquiryUrl);
    } catch (MalformedURLException e) {
        fatal ("Malformed Inquiry URL " + inquiryUrl + ": "
                + e.getMessage());
    }
```

We then construct a "find" request. This is done with a FindBusinessRequest object. Since we are doing a search by name, we use the setName() method to set the business name passed from the command line:

```
    FindBusinessRequest findBusinessRequest = new FindBusinessRequest();
    try {
        findBusinessRequest.setName (args[1]);
    }
    catch (UDDIException e) {
        fatal ("Error setting name : " + e.getErrorCode()
                + ": " + e.getErrorMessage());
    }
```

Finally, we invoke the find business request on the UDDI server and print out the result we obtain:

```
    UDDIResponse uddiResponse = null;
    try {
        System.out.println ("Request is " + findBusinessRequest.toXML());
        uddiResponse = uddiSoapClient.findBusiness (findBusinessRequest);
    }
    catch (UDDIException e) {
        fatal ("Error finding business: " + e.getErrorCode()
                + ": " + e.getErrorMessage());
    }

    System.out.println ("Got message: \n"
                        + uddiResponse.toXML ());
    }
}
```

The screenshot below shows the FindBusiness.java program being invoked on the UDDI test registry at IBM to locate all businesses named "Crashes R'Us Airlines" – this should give the BusinessEntity that we published earlier in the chapter. The Business, Service and Binding Keys that show up in the screenshot below will not match those in your example. This is because each new Business Entity (or Business Service, or Binding Template) gets an unqiue key assigned to it. This is also the reason why the Business Key differs from those in previous examples. We had deleted the Business Entity in a previous example, and had to publish it again to get this example to work!

```
MS Select C:\WINNT\System32\cmd.exe                                    _ □ ✕
C:\install\wrox\webservices\UDDIImpl>java FindBusiness
Fatal: usage: java com.hp.uddi.samples.FindBusiness [IBM_PROD|MS_PROD|IBM_TEST|M
S_TEST|<url>] <business name>

C:\install\wrox\webservices\UDDIImpl>java FindBusiness IBM_TEST "Crashes R'Us"
Setting URL to http://www-3.ibm.com/services/uddi/testregistry/inquiryapi
Request is <find_business generic="1.0" xmlns="urn:uddi-org:api"><name>Crashes R
'Us</name></find_business>
Got message:
<businessList generic="1.0" operator="www.ibm.com/services/uddi" truncated="fals
e" xmlns="urn:uddi-org:api"><businessInfos><businessInfo businessKey="19B56BF0-8
AC8-11D5-A4A5-0004AC49CC1E"><name>Crashes R'Us Airlines</name><description xml:l
ang="en">Crashes R'Us Airlines aims to provide a memorable flight experience- re
member to bring a bathing suit on our trans-Pacific flights!</description><servi
ceInfos><serviceInfo businessKey="19B56BF0-8AC8-11D5-A4A5-0004AC49CC1E" serviceK
ey="19C46010-8AC8-11D5-A4A5-0004AC49CC1E"><name>fare_service</name></serviceInfo
></serviceInfos></businessInfo></businessInfos></businessList>

C:\install\wrox\webservices\UDDIImpl>
```

UDDI Private Registry

The HP WSP also comes with a private registry implementation. The current version of the HP UDDI server supports Windows NT/2000 and Linux, and uses Hypersonic as its backend database. Hewlett Packard has also signed up to be an operator node for the UDDI Business Registry, and this will be operational sometime towards the end of 2001.

UDDI::Lite

UDDI::Lite is a Perl client library for UDDI. It is packaged and distributed as a part of SOAP::Lite and is available as freeware, under the same licensing restrictions as that of Perl itself. It supports both the UDDI v1.0 Inquiry and the Publishing API, and is built on top of SOAP::Lite.

This client library can be downloaded from http://www.soaplite.com/, and this site has additional documentation and sample code for UDDI::Lite.

Revisiting the SaveBusiness and SaveService examples that we had written earlier in UDDI4J, a equivalent UDDI::Lite implementation would look something like this:

```
use UDDI::Lite
    import => ['UDDI::Data'],
    import => ['UDDI::Lite'],
```

Set the publish URL to IBM's test UDDI registry:

```
proxy => "https://www-
3.ibm.com:443/services/uddi/testregistry/protect/publishapi";
```

Set the username and password for authenticated access to the registry. Using this username and password, we obtain an authentication token that is used in all subsequent publishing API calls.

```
my $authToken = get_authToken({userID => 'YOURNAME', cred => 'YOURPASSWORD'})-
>authInfo;
```

Construct a Business Entity structure, filling in the required fields:

```
my $businessEntity= with businessEntity =>
    name("Crashes Rus Airlines"),
    description("Crashes Rus Airlines aims to provide a memorable flight
experience"),
    businessKey(''),
    businessServices with businessService =>
        name("fare_service"),
        description("SOAP service for fare quotes"),
        serviceKey(''),
        bindingTemplates with bindingTemplate =>
            description("None"),
```

Set the access point of the service:

```
        accessPoint('http://127.0.0.1:8080/soap/servlet/rpcrouter'),
        bindingKey(''),
```

Set the tModel Key to that of the previously saved tModel:

```
        tModelInstanceDetails with tModelInstanceInfo =>
            description('fare_service_tmodel'),
            tModelKey('UUID:94B5B570-80B5-11D5-A76E-0004AC49CC1E');
            save_business($authToken, $businessEntity);
```

Users could then search for this business – a piece of sample code demonstrating this is given below that searches for all businesses with names starting with "Crash".

```
use UDDI::Lite
    'UDDI::Lite' => [':inquire'],
    proxy => 'http://www-3.ibm.com/services/uddi/testregistry/inquiryapi';
    print find_business(name => 'Crash')
    -> businessInfos->businessInfo->serviceInfos->serviceInfo->name;
```

Other Implementations

There are a number of other UDDI implementations – Idoox WASP UDDI and jUDDI to name just two.

Idoox provides a distributed DNS like UDDI implementation that allows for hierarchical organization of registries and also for selective replication. It supports both Oracle and PostgreSQL as its backend databases. This can be downloaded from http://www.idoox.com/products/index.html.

jUDDI (pronounced "Judy"), is a freeware implementation of UDDI 1.0 in Java, and is primarily developed by Bowstreet. It contains a private UDDI registry implementation and a toolkit for programmers. It has been released under the BSD licence and can be downloaded from http://www.juddi.org/

pUDDIng (pronounced "pudding") is yet another freeware implementation of the UDDI registry and client in Java, and is the first one to be UDDI 2.0 compliant. pUDDIng uses Oracle as its backend database. It is released under the GNU LGPL licence and can be downloaded from http://www.opensorcerer.org/.

MindElectric's GLUE platform also includes a UDDI server and a client. It can be downloaded from http://www.themindelectric.com/products/uddi/uddi.html.

Summary

In this chapter we saw an end-to-end example of a Web Service – developing the service, publishing information about it in the UDDI registry, programmatically finding it and invoking methods on it. We used IBM's UDDI4J for this, though given the cross platform nature of SOAP and UDDI, we could just as well have written the service using Microsoft SOAP SDK, published it in the registry using a Perl based UDDI program (UDDI::Lite), and then found and invoked methods on it using a java client built on UDDI4J!

In addition, we very briefly covered a few other UDDI implementations such as Microsoft's UDDI SDK and UDDI::Lite.

References

- ❑ **IBM UDDI4J (part of IBM Web Services Toolkit):**
  http://www.alphaworks.ibm.com/tech/webservicestoolkit

- ❑ **Microsoft's UDDI SDK:**
  http://uddi.microsoft.com/developer/

- ❑ **jUDDI from BowStreet:**
  http://www.jUDDI.org

- ❑ **Idoox WASP UDDI:**
  http://www.idoox.com/products/index.html

- ❑ **UDDI::Lite:**
  http://www.soaplite.com/

- ❑ **MindElectric UDDI:**
  http://www.themindelectric.com/products/uddi/uddi.html

- ❑ **pUDDIng:**
  http://www.opensorcerer.org/

8

Microsoft SOAP Toolkit 2.0

SOAP has been presented as the protocol of the future, a technology that will allow communication across languages and platforms. In fact, the future is already happening right now. The authors of the SOAP Specification designed it with the intention that SOAP systems could be built quickly from existing components, and as a result, there are already over 20 different SOAP implementations available to developers. Of all these, the one most likely be used more than any other is Microsoft's **SOAP Toolkit 2.0**, a SOAP implementation for Windows written and supported by Microsoft. This chapter examines the Microsoft SOAP Toolkit 2.0 in detail, looking at the model it uses, and methods for implementing SOAP today using the Toolkit.

SOAP for "Legacy" Windows

Microsoft has made it clear that the future of Windows development lies with the .NET platform, which is founded on the Common Language Run-time that allows all Visual Studio development languages to share library routines and features. XML is tightly integrated into .NET, especially in the implementation of SOAP. If you are running Windows-based servers, you will not find it a difficult task to develop Web Services using the .NET platform.

Now, although the future may be .NET, we are still living in the present. At the time of writing, Visual Studio .NET and the .NET Framework SDK have just entered their second beta phase. This is not to say that the current release of the tools is not powerful and surprisingly stable, which it is, but they are nonetheless still beta code. Microsoft has suggested that Visual Studio .NET may be ready to ship in the latter part of this year, or possibly early 2002, in order to iron out as many teething problems of the new system as possible before commercial release. (If only the rest of us had the luxury of waiting so long to ship a product!)

The point is that the majority of Windows developers are currently working with Visual Studio 6.0 and will not be able to develop new projects with .NET for some time. Even those lucky developers who have embarked on new projects developed exclusively with .NET from the outset will probably have some "legacy" Windows applications written in Visual Studio 6.0 that will need to interface with the .NET applications. In either case, the Microsoft SOAP Toolkit 2.0 will be of benefit.

Did I Miss 1.0?

Since SOAP is such a new technology, many of you will probably wonder how the Microsoft SOAP Toolkit is already on version 2.0. There are no creative versioning tricks or space-time anomalies at work here. Early adopters may know that Microsoft did in fact release the SOAP Toolkit version 1.0 in the summer of 2000. The first version of the toolkit was created by the MSDN team to help introduce SOAP to Windows developers, but it was really for demonstration purposes only. Version 1.0 closely resembled the high level API of the current Toolkit, with a client proxy object and ASP listener. It predated the WSDL specification, and was more a proof of concept than a practicable solution, as it did not support anything other than RPC SOAP over plain HTTP. Version 2.0, which went gold in April of 2001, is a completely different product to 1.0, and, other than the name, they have very little in common.

The core of version 1.0 was implemented by an ActiveX module named ROPE.DLL. This probably gave the MSDN team some cause for mirth, and you can perhaps picture them rolling around on the floor gasping, "We actually got them to use SOAP on a ROPE!" The ROPE.DLL is worth mentioning here just to clear up some of the confusion about the Toolkit that remains as a result of the earlier release. Without fail, every couple of days, there will be a post to the Microsoft SOAP newsgroups that seeks information on ROPE.DLL. If you are using ROPE.DLL, you are using the wrong version of the Toolkit: version 2.0 is a fully supported developer product; version 1.0 and its ROPE.DLL are not.

Downloading the Toolkit

If you want to start working with the Toolkit, you first have to download it. The Microsoft SOAP Toolkit 2.0 SP2 is available for free and can be downloaded from this URL:

http://msdn.microsoft.com/downloads/default.asp?URL=/code/sample.asp?url=/msdn-files/027/001/580/MsdnCompositeDoc.xml

The Toolkit is available as three separate downloads. The first download will give you the full SDK, including APIs, documentation, and utilities. The second download contains a set of sample applications that demonstrate use of the Toolkit's various features. The last download contains just the redistributable files that you will need to deploy your Toolkit solutions. It should be noted that in order to deploy a SOAP server, you need Microsoft's IIS to be installed as well as the Toolkit redistributables. All of the downloads are available from the URL listed above. The above URL also has a link to Microsoft's online documentation for the toolkit.

Microsoft recently announced that they will ship the client-side components of the SOAP Toolkit 2.0 with Windows XP, something to bear in mind when building applications.

The MSTK2 Model

One of the biggest criticisms of the first Toolkit was its inflexibility. For simple RPC-style SOAP, the original Toolkit worked well, but SOAP is much more than that. In order for the Toolkit to be a useful SOAP implementation for all Windows developers, it had to be able to handle SOAP in other ways while still making the RPC-style SOAP as simple as possible. Perhaps this is the reason behind the fact that the Microsoft SOAP Toolkit 2.0 is actually three COM APIs in one, namely:

❑ **High Level** – objects that simplify RPC style SOAP using proxies and stubs, relying heavily on XML meta data. It uses the low level API to do its work, and there are opportunities to build on the high level API using the low level API.

❑ **Low Level** – objects that directly access SOAP message structure and SOAP transport capabilities without relying on XML meta data.

❑ **SMO (Simple Messaging Object) Framework** – objects that make it easier to use SOAP messages containing general XML, rather than RPC-style payloads.

In addition to the three SOAP APIs provided by the Toolkit, there are a couple of other tools and utilities that are a valuable part of a development toolset. They are:

❑ **WSDL Generator** – a wizard for generating XML meta data derived from a COM object, which is extremely useful for the high level API.

❑ **WSDL and WSML API** – an additional COM API for reading and writing XML meta data.

❑ **MSSOAPT** – a debug utility that can trace the progress of SOAP requests and responses.

The following figure shows how all these components fit together to make up the Toolkit:

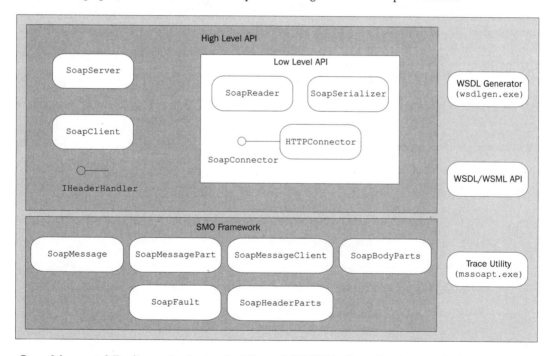

One of the most difficult aspects of using the Microsoft SOAP Toolkit is figuring out which API and tools you are going to need. You can determine which APIs best fit your requirements by looking at your application and the Web Services you will be accessing. We will discuss the approaches for this, and how they can be best applied to real-world problems, later in this chapter.

WSDL Revisited

We have already had a pretty good look at WSDL, the Web Services Definition Language, in Chapter 5, but we now need to consider the role it has to play in Microsoft's SOAP model. WSDL is an XML-based language for describing meta data for Web Services. By providing machine-readable documentation to describe Web Services, WSDL opens up a whole new world of possibilities for tools developers.

In the Microsoft SOAP Toolkit, WSDL plays an important role. Using the WSDL Generator that comes as part of the Toolkit, you can create WSDL documents from an existing COM type library, which are in turn used by the high level API of the Toolkit to produce client proxies for a Web Service. If you have tried out the .NET Framework SDK or Visual Studio .NET, you may know that the tools that come with these packages can also go the opposite direction: given a WSDL document, they can generate a piece of stub code. However, this functionality does not exist in the current version of the SOAP Toolkit, although I think it would make a handy addition.

Introducing WSML

Although the Toolkit uses the standard language for defining services, WSDL, it also introduces a proprietary language called WSML, the Web Services Meta Language. It is unfortunate that the letters of the two acronyms are so close, as it has led some people to believe that Microsoft has subverted WSDL for its own purposes. In truth, WSDL and WSML serve two very different roles in the Toolkit framework, and the proprietary nature of WSML is completely justified when you consider the role it has to play.

If you are developing components using Visual Studio 6.0, you are probably building them as COM components. With SOAP, such COM objects can be exposed as Web Services. It would take a lot of boilerplate code to create a direct mapping from a WSDL Web Service to COM, and the Toolkit sidesteps this with WSML.

WSML is not difficult to read, so let's take a look at a typical WSML document:

```
<?xml version='1.0' encoding='UTF-8' ?>
<!-- Generated 06/21/01 by Microsoft SOAP Toolkit WSDL File Generator, Version
1.00.623.1 -->
<servicemapping name='AVL'>
  <service name='AVL'>
    <using PROGID='AVL.VehicleLocator' cachable='0' ID='VehicleLocatorObject' />
    <port name='VehicleLocatorSoapPort'>
      <operation name='SendMessageToVehicle'>
        <execute uses='VehicleLocatorObject' method='SendMessageToVehicle'
               dispID='1610809345'>
          <parameter callIndex='1' name='strID' elementName='strID' />
          <parameter callIndex='2' name='strMessage' elementName='strMessage' />
        </execute>
      </operation>
      <operation name='GetVehicleLocation'>
        <execute uses='VehicleLocatorObject' method='GetVehicleLocation'
               dispID='1610809344'>
          <parameter callIndex='1' name='strID' elementName='strID' />
          <parameter callIndex='-1' name='retval' elementName='Result' />
        </execute>
      </operation>
    </port>
  </service>
</servicemapping>
```

We can see how WSML documents map WSDL entities to COM objects and methods. Notice that where WSML refers to WSDL, it thankfully uses the same element names: `service`, `port`, `operation`, and `parameter`.

So, inside the Toolkit, WSDL and WSML go hand in hand. The Toolkit provides an ISAPI extension that uses WSDL and WSML documents to map incoming SOAP requests to COM methods, and vice versa. The ISAPI listener looks for the WSDL file and the WSML file of the same name in a single folder, and as long as both these files are in place, the ISAPI listener is able to map incoming SOAP messages to COM methods automatically.

About the Samples

The Microsoft SOAP Toolkit gives us a chance to apply SOAP, and so the rest of this chapter is made up of examples that use the Toolkit APIs. The complete source code for the sample applications of this chapter can be found amongst the code download for the book. We'll be keeping things simple by detailing a single problem to solve, which we then address using the three distinct APIs of the Toolkit. The problem will be to develop a Web Service that provides system information about the machine that it is running on. There is no need to get carried away with the possible capabilities of such a Web Service, although it has the potential of being a handy utility if its functions were to be expanded. For now, we'll just provide three methods: `GetSystemName()`, `GetNumberOfProcessors()`, and `GetOS()`. The listing below shows the declarations for the methods of our Visual Basic object:

```
Public Function GetSystemName() As String

Public Function GetNumberOfProcessors() As Integer

Public Function GetOS() As String
```

The examples in this chapter are written in Visual Basic 6.0. Because all of the Toolkit APIs are provided through COM, the examples could be written in any language that supports the use of COM objects.

Cruising at 10,000 Feet – the High Level API

The majority of developers and companies are not interested in SOAP because it is a cool technology, but because it promises to make a range of programming tasks a whole lot easier. As you might expect, of the three APIs the Toolkit provides, the high level API is the easiest to use, so it makes sense to start here, and work our way down. It hides almost all implementation details of SOAP from the developer, both at the client and the server, through the use of WSDL and WSML.

The high level API is primarily made up of two objects: the `SoapClient` object, and the `SoapServer` object. `SoapClient` serves as a proxy for the Web Service when provided with a WSDL document, while `SoapServer` functions as a mapping tool. Given a pair of WSDL and WSML documents, `SoapServer` can then map SOAP messages to COM methods. We will deal with these two objects in greater detail later, but the figure below shows how they form the basis of the architecture for the high level API:

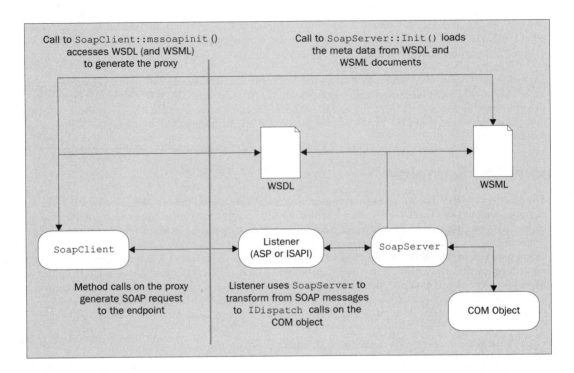

Building The SysInfo Object

To start working with the high level API, we need a COM object. All of our examples will provide the same functionality using alternate approaches, so this COM object will be used in all of them, although the high level API will interact with it the most directly. We shall create a new Visual Basic project, an ActiveX DLL, which will serve as the COM server for our example.

First, launch Visual Basic and select **New Project**. From the list of available project types, select **ActiveX DLL**. Inside of our project, we need to create a new class module called `SystemInfo`, which will contain the implementations of the methods listed earlier in the chapter. This is the object that will be eventually exposed as a Web Service using the toolkit APIs, so we need to bear this in mind when designing the object. In particular, when choosing method and parameter names, we need to be aware that they will be exposed through the Web Services interface.

When we created the new project, Visual Basic generated an empty class named **Class1**, which you can see in the Project Explorer. In the Properties window, rename **Class1** to be `SystemInfo`. The `SystemInfo` class module accesses system information through a couple of Windows API calls. Replace the code for the `SystemInfo` class with the code listed below.

```
' SystemInfoService.cls
'
' This class implements methods that give system information and control.
'

Option Explicit

Private Const MAX_NAME_LEN As Long = 15
```

```
Private Const MAX_OS_LEN As Long = 128

' SYSTEM_INFO - GetSystemInfo()
Private Type SYSTEM_INFO
        dwOemID As Long
        dwPageSize As Long
        lpMinimumApplicationAddress As Long
        lpMaximumApplicationAddress As Long
        dwActiveProcessorMask As Long
        dwNumberOfProcessors As Long
        dwProcessorType As Long
        dwAllocationGranularity As Long
        dwReserved As Long
End Type

' OSVERSIONINFO - GetVersionEx()
Private Type OSVERSIONINFO
        dwOSVersionInfoSize As Long
        dwMajorVersion As Long
        dwMinorVersion As Long
        dwBuildNumber As Long
        dwPlatformId As Long
        szCSDVersion As String * 128      '  Maintenance string for PSS usage
End Type

Private Declare Function GetComputerName Lib "kernel32" Alias "GetComputerNameA"
(ByVal lpBuffer As String, nSize As Long) As Long

Private Declare Sub GetSystemInfo Lib "kernel32" (lpSystemInfo As SYSTEM_INFO)

Private Declare Function GetVersionEx Lib "kernel32" Alias "GetVersionExA"
(lpVersionInformation As OSVERSIONINFO) As Long

Private Declare Function ExitWindowsEx Lib "user32" (ByVal uFlags As Long, ByVal
dwReserved As Long) As Long

' Data members
Private m_si As SYSTEM_INFO

Private m_osvi As OSVERSIONINFO

Private Sub Class_Initialize()

On Error GoTo InitErr

    Dim lRet As Long

    GetSystemInfo m_si

    m_osvi.dwOSVersionInfoSize = 20 + MAX_OS_LEN
    m_osvi.szCSDVersion = Space$(MAX_OS_LEN)

    GetVersionEx m_osvi

    Exit Sub
```

```
InitErr:

   Exit Sub

End Sub

Public Function GetSystemName() As String

   Dim sName As String
   Dim lSize As Long
   Dim lRet As Long

   sName = Space$(MAX_NAME_LEN + 1)
   lSize = Len(sName)
   lRet = GetComputerName(sName, 50)

   GetSystemName = sName
   Exit Function

End Function

Public Function GetNumberOfProcessors() As Integer

   GetNumberOfProcessors = m_si.dwNumberOfProcessors
   Exit Function

End Function

Public Function GetOS() As String

   Select Case m_osvi.dwPlatformId
      Case 1
         If m_osvi.dwMinorVersion = 0 Then
            GetOS = "Windows 95"
         ElseIf m_osvi.dwMinorVersion = 10 Then
            GetOS = "Windows 98"
      End If

      Case 2
         If m_osvi.dwMajorVersion = 3 Then
            GetOS = "Windows NT 3.51"
         ElseIf m_osvi.dwMajorVersion = 4 Then
            GetOS = "Windows NT 4.0"
         ElseIf m_osvi.dwMajorVersion = 5 Then
            GetOS = "Windows 2000"
      End If

      Case Else
         GetOS = "Unknown"
   End Select
   Exit Function

End Function
```

This class module is the only code we need for our ActiveX DLL, so we're ready to build our project. Select the project, **Project1**, in the Project Explorer and rename it to be `SysInfo`. Now, from the menu, select **File/Make SysInfo.dll** and generate the ActiveX DLL. `SysInfo.dll` can now be used in conjunction with the Toolkit's WSDL Generator.

Generating WSDL and WSML

WSDL and WSML perform important roles in the Toolkit framework, but, as you can see from the examples, writing them by hand is unlikely to be a big bag of fun. If the Web Services you are using the Toolkit to create map well to COM objects, then you can use the Toolkit's WSDL Generator to generate both your WSDL and WSML documents automatically.

The WSDL Generator, which we briefly met in Chapters 4 and 5, is a stand alone, wizard-style application that generates the documents needed for a Microsoft SOAP Toolkit-based Web Service. Given the type library information from a COM object, the WSDL Generator can create associated WSDL and WSML documents allowing the object to be used with the high level API.

Let's take another look at the steps involved in using the WSDL Generator, `wsdlgen.exe`. When you launch this application from the **Start** menu, you will be presented with the following Welcome screen:

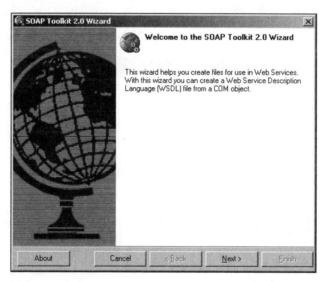

Click **Next** to start the Wizard, whereupon you will be asked to name your service, and to select its COM object implementation. The name of the service is used to derive filenames for the WSDL, WSML, and optional ASP code that the Wizard generates, and is also used within the WSDL and WSML files. For our service, enter `SystemInfoService` in the top box. In addition, this will be used in the `name` attribute of the `service` element to name the service, and also to scope the names of the message's identifiers, as in `SystemInfoService.GetOS()`. To specify the COM module, you can either type in the filename and path, or browse to find it.

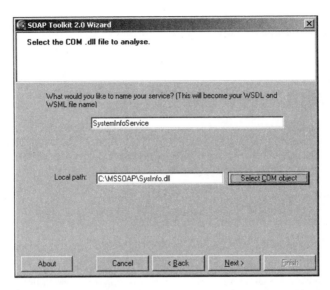

Page three provides an 'option tree' interface that allows you to select what methods of the objects in the module selected on the preceding page are to be exposed by the Web Service. Using the appropriate check boxes, you can select to expose functionality at the object, interface, or method level:

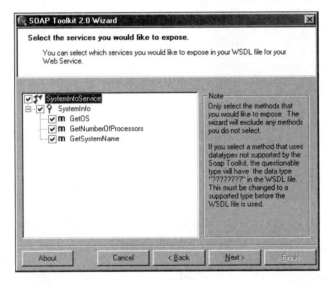

Once all `sysinfo.dll`'s methods have been selected, click Next to move to the next page and specify how the endpoint is to be deployed. First, you must enter a URI for the folder that will contain the endpoint. This URI will be used to define the address of the endpoint itself. There are two choices of listener type available, namely ISAPI or ASP. We will discuss this choice in more detail later, but for now select the ISAPI option. The final option on this page is the XML Schema namespace for the endpoint. The SOAP specification refers to the 1999 schema, while the current schema is dated 2001. This choice can have an impact on what clients are able to access your service, as some may be based on a SOAP implementation that only works with an older namespace. I recommend using the 2001 schema, because implementations will be targeting that as their standard.

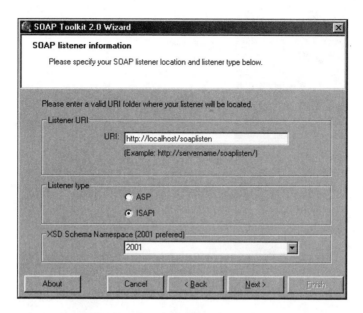

There are two more choices on the next screen, but we're almost home. Firstly, you must select the character encoding that will be used when generating the WSDL file. Secondly, you must enter the path for the folder that the generated files are to be placed in. If you are deploying locally, you can point this directly to the folder that serves as the IIS virtual folder. If not, you will need to use a temporary folder to contain your build until you can upload it to the server.

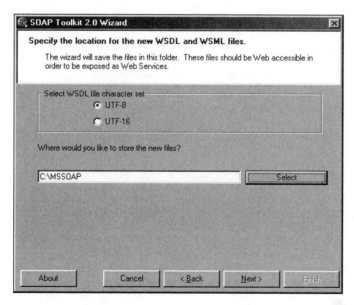

Now we have completed all necessary steps for the program to create our WSDL and WSML documents:

The WSDL Generator should have produced two documents: a WSDL document, and a WSML document. Both documents are named after the service name we selected, which here was `SystemInfoService`.

Below is a listing of `SystemInfoService.wsdl`:

```
<?xml version='1.0' encoding='UTF-8' ?>
<!-- Generated 06/24/01 by Microsoft SOAP Toolkit WSDL File Generator, Version
1.00.623.1 -->
<definitions name='SystemInfoService'
            targetNamespace='http://tempuri.org/wsdl/'
            xmlns:wsdlns='http://tempuri.org/wsdl/'
            xmlns:typens='http://tempuri.org/type'
            xmlns:soap='http://schemas.xmlsoap.org/wsdl/soap/'
            xmlns:xsd='http://www.w3.org/2001/XMLSchema'
            xmlns:stk='http://schemas.microsoft.com/soap-toolkit/wsdl-extension'
            xmlns='http://schemas.xmlsoap.org/wsdl/'>
    <types>
       <schema targetNamespace='http://tempuri.org/type'
          xmlns='http://www.w3.org/2001/XMLSchema'
          xmlns:SOAP-ENC='http://schemas.xmlsoap.org/soap/encoding/'
          xmlns:wsdl='http://schemas.xmlsoap.org/wsdl/'
          elementFormDefault='qualified'>
       </schema>
    </types>
    <message name='SystemInfoService.GetOS'>
    </message>
    <message name='SystemInfoService.GetOSResponse'>
       <part name='Result' type='xsd:string'/>
    </message>
    <message name='SystemInfoService.GetNumberOfProcessors'>
    </message>
    <message name='SystemInfoService.GetNumberOfProcessorsResponse'>
```

```
         <part name='Result' type='xsd:short'/>
   </message>
   <message name='SystemInfoService.GetSystemName'>
   </message>
   <message name='SystemInfoService.GetSystemNameResponse'>
       <part name='Result' type='xsd:string'/>
   </message>
   <portType name='SystemInfoServiceSoapPort'>
       <operation name='GetOS' parameterOrder=''>
           <input message='wsdlns:SystemInfoService.GetOS' />
           <output message='wsdlns:SystemInfoService.GetOSResponse' />
       </operation>
       <operation name='GetNumberOfProcessors' parameterOrder=''>
           <input message='wsdlns:SystemInfoService.GetNumberOfProcessors' />
           <output
               message='wsdlns:SystemInfoService.GetNumberOfProcessorsResponse' />
       </operation>
       <operation name='GetSystemName' parameterOrder=''>
           <input message='wsdlns:SystemInfoService.GetSystemName' />
           <output message='wsdlns:SystemInfoService.GetSystemNameResponse' />
       </operation>
   </portType>
   <binding name='SystemInfoServiceSoapBinding'
           type='wsdlns:SystemInfoServiceSoapPort' >
       <stk:binding preferredEncoding='UTF-8'/>
       <soap:binding style='rpc'
                   transport='http://schemas.xmlsoap.org/soap/http' />
       <operation name='GetOS' >
           <soap:operation
               soapAction='http://tempuri.org/action/SystemInfoService.GetOS' />
           <input>
               <soap:body use='encoded' namespace='http://tempuri.org/message/'
                       encodingStyle='http://schemas.xmlsoap.org/soap/encoding/'
               />
           </input>
           <output>
               <soap:body use='encoded' namespace='http://tempuri.org/message/'
                       encodingStyle='http://schemas.xmlsoap.org/soap/encoding/'
               />
           </output>
        </operation>
       <operation name='GetNumberOfProcessors' >
       <soap:operation
soapAction='http://tempuri.org/action/SystemInfoService.GetNumberOfProcessors'
       />
           <input>
               <soap:body use='encoded' namespace='http://tempuri.org/message/'
                       encodingStyle='http://schemas.xmlsoap.org/soap/encoding/'
               />
           </input>
           <output>
               <soap:body use='encoded' namespace='http://tempuri.org/message/'
                       encodingStyle='http://schemas.xmlsoap.org/soap/encoding/'
               />
           </output>
       </operation>
```

```
        <operation name='GetSystemName' >
            <soap:operation
soapAction='http://tempuri.org/action/SystemInfoService.GetSystemName' />
            <input>
                <soap:body use='encoded' namespace='http://tempuri.org/message/'
                            encodingStyle='http://schemas.xmlsoap.org/soap/encoding/'
                />
            </input>
            <output>
                <soap:body use='encoded' namespace='http://tempuri.org/message/'
                            encodingStyle='http://schemas.xmlsoap.org/soap/encoding/'
                />
            </output>
        </operation>
    </binding>
    <service name='SystemInfoService' >
        <port name='SystemInfoServiceSoapPort'
                binding='wsdlns:SystemInfoServiceSoapBinding' >
            <soap:address
location='http://localhost/mstk2/high/sysinfo/SystemInfoService.WSDL' />
        </port>
    </service>
</definitions>
```

Here is `SystemInfoService.wsml`, which contains the generated WSML. Notice in particular the `using` element, which identifies the COM object by its `PROGID`. For each method that our object implemented, we now have a corresponding operation, just as in the WSDL file.

```
<?xml version='1.0' encoding='UTF-8' ?>
 <!-- Generated 06/24/01 by Microsoft SOAP Toolkit WSDL File Generator, Version
1.00.623.1 -->
<servicemapping name='SystemInfoService'>
    <service name='SystemInfoService'>
        <using PROGID='Sysinfo.SystemInfoService'
                cachable='0'
                ID='SystemInfoServiceObject' />
        <port name='SystemInfoServiceSoapPort'>
            <operation name='GetOS'>
                <execute uses='SystemInfoServiceObject'
                    method='GetOS' dispID='1610809347'>
                    <parameter callIndex='-1' name='retval' elementName='Result' />
                </execute>
            </operation>
            <operation name='GetNumberOfProcessors'>
                <execute uses='SystemInfoServiceObject'
                    method='GetNumberOfProcessors'
                    dispID='1610809346'>
                    <parameter callIndex='-1' name='retval' elementName='Result' />
                </execute>
            </operation>
            <operation name='GetSystemName'>
                <execute uses='SystemInfoServiceObject'
                    method='GetSystemName'
                    dispID='1610809345'>
                    <parameter callIndex='-1' name='retval' elementName='Result' />
```

```
            </execute>
          </operation>
        </port>
    </service>
</servicemapping>
```

Even if the Web Service you are creating does not map perfectly to an existing COM object, we still recommend using the WSDL Generator to create the documents. Once the documents are created, modifying them is easier and less prone to error than writing your own documents from scratch. This allows you to leverage the capabilities of the WSDL Generator while still controlling the end product.

Listeners

When the WSDL Generator generated our WSDL and WSML files, we selected the ISAPI option. This option defines the type of listener that will be used by the endpoint. A **listener** is a component that receives SOAP messages over a particular transport and passes them on to the Toolkit for processing. Currently, both listener options are HTTP listeners. There are two listeners provided by the Toolkit: an ISAPI listener, and an ASP listener. You can select either option, and both will function identically as SOAP endpoints, but there are a couple of differences between them that you should be aware of. If you choose the ISAPI listener, the address of the SOAP endpoint will be the WSDL file, because that is what the ISAPI listener uses to create the mapping. The ISAPI listener is triggered whenever a file with the .wsdl extension is accessed.

For the ASP listener though, the endpoint address is the ASP file that the WSDL Generator generates when the ASP listener option is selected. As mentioned previously, the behavior of the endpoint is exactly the same whether you use the ISAPI listener or ASP, but testing of the endpoints shows that the ISAPI listener is slightly faster, while the ASP endpoint is more easily modifiable. If we rerun the WSDL Generator on SystemInfoService, this time selecting the ASP listener option, we will end up with a file called SystemInfoService.asp in addition to the WSDL and WSML files.

```
<%@ LANGUAGE=VBScript %>
<%
Option Explicit
On Error Resume Next
Response.ContentType = "text/xml"
Dim SoapServer
If Not Application("SoapServerInitialized") Then
    Application.Lock
    If Not Application("SoapServerInitialized") Then
        Dim WSDLFilePath
        Dim WSMLFilePath
        WSDLFilePath = Server.MapPath("SystemInfoService.wsdl")
        WSMLFilePath = Server.MapPath("SystemInfoService.wsml")
        Set SoapServer = Server.CreateObject("MSSOAP.SoapServer")
        If Err Then SendFault "Cannot create SoapServer object. " &
            Err.Description
        SoapServer.Init WSDLFilePath, WSMLFilePath
        If Err Then SendFault "SoapServer.Init failed. " & Err.Description
        Set Application("SystemInfoServiceServer") = SoapServer
        Application("SoapServerInitialized") = True
    End If
    Application.UnLock
End If
Set SoapServer = Application("SystemInfoServiceServer")
```

```
SoapServer.SoapInvoke Request, Response, ""
If Err Then SendFault "SoapServer.SoapInvoke failed. " & Err.Description
Sub SendFault(ByVal LogMessage)
    Dim Serializer
    On Error Resume Next
    ' "URI Query" logging must be enabled for AppendToLog to work
    Response.AppendToLog " SOAP ERROR: " & LogMessage
    Set Serializer = Server.CreateObject("MSSOAP.SoapSerializer")
    If Err Then
        Response.AppendToLog "Could not create SoapSerializer object. " &
        Err.Description
        Response.Status = "500 Internal Server Error"
    Else
        Serializer.Init Response
        If Err Then
            Response.AppendToLog "SoapSerializer.Init failed. " & Err.Description
            Response.Status = "500 Internal Server Error"
        Else
            Serializer.startEnvelope
            Serializer.startBody
            Serializer.startFault "Server", "The request could not be processed due
                to a problem in the server. Please contact the system admistrator."
                & LogMessage
            Serializer.endFault
            Serializer.endBody
            Serializer.endEnvelope
            If Err Then
                Response.AppendToLog "SoapSerializer failed. " & Err.Description
                Response.Status = "500 Internal Server Error"
            End If
        End If
    End If
    Response.End
End Sub
%>
```

The ASP code above uses the `SoapServer` object of the high level API to process the SOAP messages posted to it.

The SoapServer Object

When you build a Web Service out of the high level API, you are building it around a COM object or a set of COM objects. The idea is that the existing functionality of your COM objects can be exposed directly, and the job of the Toolkit is to eliminate the need for tiresome boilerplate code to make that happen – all this boilerplate code is now wrapped up inside the `SoapServer` object.

We can see the `SoapServer` object at work in the ASP we generated for our `SystemInfoService` service. Let's take a more detailed look at that code now and see how `SoapServer` is used.

First, we have our standard ASP opening code. The `ContentType` property of the `Response` object corresponds to the HTTP header `Content-Type`, and so we should set this in accordance with the SOAP specification, which states that SOAP messages over HTTP must use `text/xml` for the response header:

```
<%@ LANGUAGE=VBScript %>
<%
Option Explicit
On Error Resume Next
Response.ContentType = "text/xml"
```

This ASP, as generated by the WSDL Generator, includes code in the next lines that checks to see if `SoapServer` has been cached. A reference to the `SoapServer` object is placed in a variable in the `Application` collection so that we do not have to instantiate and initialize the object every time the page is accessed.

```
Dim SoapServer
If Not Application("SoapServerInitialized") Then
    Application.Lock
    If Not Application("SoapServerInitialized") Then
```

The next four lines of code resolve the relative paths of the WSDL and WSML documents associated with this endpoint, so they can be loaded using `SoapServer`. Like all files accessed by ASP, the `SoapServer` object requires absolute paths to the documents, so we need to use the `Server.MapPath` method to build an absolute path to the WSDL file, as shown below.

```
        Dim WSDLFilePath
        Dim WSMLFilePath
        WSDLFilePath = Server.MapPath("SystemInfoService.wsdl")
        WSMLFilePath = Server.MapPath("SystemInfoService.wsml")
```

Once we have located our meta data, we need to create the `SoapServer` object and initialize it. The next lines do just that. Notice the call to the `SendFault()` function; a function generated as part of the ASP page. `SendFault()` actually uses the low level API of the Toolkit to build a SOAP Fault, which is then returned as the response to the client. We will take another look at `SendFault()` when we discuss the low level API later in this chapter. If the object is initialized successfully, the page caches it.

```
        Set SoapServer = Server.CreateObject("MSSOAP.SoapServer")
        If Err Then SendFault "Cannot create SoapServer object. " & Err.Description
        SoapServer.Init WSDLFilePath, WSMLFilePath
        If Err Then SendFault "SoapServer.Init failed. " & Err.Description
        Set Application("SystemInfoServiceServer") = SoapServer
        Application("SoapServerInitialized") = True
    End If
Application.UnLock
```

Before we move on, let's take a quick look at the `Init()` method.

The Init() Method

The code we've just seen uses the `Init()` method of the `SoapServer` object. This method is the most important of the three methods provided by `SoapServer`. You pass in paths to the WSDL and WSML files that describe the endpoint, and the `SoapServer` object uses the meta data they contain to process any SOAP requests it receives.

```
Sub Init(pUrlWSDLFile As String, bstrWSMLFileSpec As String)
```

Once we have initialized `SoapServer`, we use the `SoapInvoke()` method to handle received SOAP requests. The last line of the ASP file calls the `SendFault()` procedure in the event of an error.

```
Set SoapServer = Application("SystemInfoServiceServer")
SoapServer.SoapInvoke Request, Response, ""
If Err Then SendFault "SoapServer.SoapInvoke failed. " & Err.Description
```

The SoapInvoke() Method

```
Sub SoapInvoke( varInput, pOutputStream As Unknown )
```

The `SoapServer` object can map SOAP messages based on the meta data used to initialize it. The `SoapInvoke()` method is used to process the message. The `varInput` parameter is a `Variant` containing the message. Because it is a `Variant`, messages can be passed to it in a variety of formats: strings, streams, or in the case of ASP, `Request` objects. Similarly, the `pOutputStream` parameter contains the response to the message. You can pass in either a stream (as an `IStream` pointer) or an ASP `Response` object here as well.

When `SoapServer` processes the request successfully, the `pOutputStream` parameter will contain the valid SOAP response message. If there is a problem with the request message, or for some reason processing cannot occur, `pOutputStream` will contain the appropriate SOAP Fault message. Since `SoapInvoke()` puts a fault in the response when necessary, you may wonder why the `SendFault()` procedure of the ASP page needs to exist at all. `SendFault()` is used in the case of errors that occur outside of `SoapServer`, such as when the call to `Init()` fails – possibly the most common error associated with the high level API, which arises from malformed WSDL. `SoapServer` can handle faults during the message processing, but general COM errors must be handled by the ASP or ISAPI listener.

Now that we have seen how we can use `SoapServer` to process the incoming SOAP messages, let's see how we can use the high level API to send the messages in the first place.

The SoapClient Object

Just as `SoapServer` takes care of the bulk of the work for the SOAP endpoint, the `SoapClient` object correspondingly takes care of the work for the client, that is, the application sending the SOAP message. The `SoapClient` object relies on WSDL to generate a **proxy**; a local object with methods that are merely pass-throughs to the Web Service it is representing.

So, how does it work? Basically, you initialize the `SoapClient` object with some WSDL, and then the object uses this meta data to dynamically handle automation through the `IDispatch` interface. Normally, a COM object implements a set of fixed methods and properties. In the case of the `SoapClient` object, `IDispatch` processes the fixed methods and properties of `SoapClient`, but it also allows the methods of the Web Service to be invoked as methods on the object. To see this at work, let's put together a quick client application using Visual Basic.

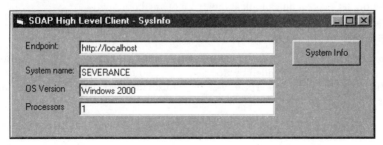

First, create a new project in Visual Basic. Select New Project, and choose the Standard Exe project.

Next, we want to give our project access to the SOAP Toolkit functionality. To use the high level API, either client-side or server-side, we must add a reference to the Toolkit in our application. On the Visual Basic menu, go to Project/References, and check the box next to Microsoft SOAP Type Library to activate mssoapi.dll; the module that contains both the high level and the low level APIs of the Toolkit.

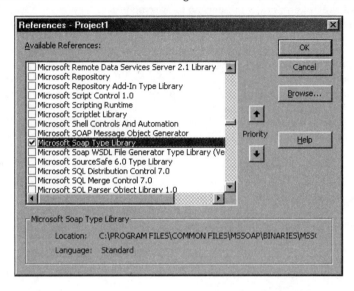

After we have access to the Toolkit, we need to assemble our form. The project created a blank form for us when we created the project. Place four text boxes on the form: one for the endpoint URL, and three for the data fields returned from SysInfo. The text boxes are txtEndpoint, txtName, txtOS, and txtProcCount. In addition to the text boxes, place a command button on the form named cmdSysInfo, which will trigger our call to the SOAP endpoint.

The important code resides in the handler for the System Info button, cmdSysInfo.

```
Private m_client As SoapClient

Private Sub Form_Load()

    Set m_client = New SoapClient

    m_client.mssoapinit txtEndpoint.Text

End Sub

Private Sub cmdSysInfo_Click()

    txtName.Text = m_client.GetSystemName()

    txtOS.Text = m_client.GetOS()

    txtProcCount = m_client.GetNumberOfProcessors()

End Sub
```

313

This is where the strength of the high level API really shows. After calling the `mssoapinit()` method of the SOAP client, the object becomes an active proxy for our Web Service. If you tried to run the code before a call to `mssoapinit()`, you would see the all too familiar "Object doesn't support this property or method" dialog box. This occurs because without meta data detailing how the Web Service method `GetOS()` may be accessed, the `SoapClient` object cannot know what to do when it is invoked.

Working with the `SoapClient` proxy presents an interesting problem for some Visual Basic programmers who are used to the IntelliSense support that the Microsoft development environments provide. IntelliSense is based on type information from the COM infrastructure that provides meta data about an object to a client application. Although the `SoapClient` object provides a dynamic implementation of `IDispatch`, as a standard COM object it cannot provide dynamic type information to Visual Basic. This is because Visual Basic only asks objects for their type information when they are loaded (except for ActiveX designers, a special class of COM object). To make a slightly complicated story short, you don't know what methods were added to the `SoapClient` object after a call to `mssoapinit()` except by looking at the WSDL file or some additional documentation. In order to invoke a method, it must be spelled correctly, and this will not be detected until run-time. So, in the case of our `SystemInfoService` endpoint, this code succeeds:

```
txtProcCount = m_client.GetNumberOfProcessors()    'OK
```

while this code would fail at run-time:

```
txtProcCount = m_client.GetNumProcessors()         'No such method
```

The moral of the story is make sure you run every line of code when testing high level API applications (of course, you test every line of code anyway!), because compilers won't be able to pick up spelling errors or misnamed methods.

In Visual Studio .NET, Microsoft provides full IntelliSense support for Web Services using WSDL as the metadata.

Let's take a look at the `mssoapinit()` method and see the information it uses to build this dynamic method list.

The mssoapinit() Method

Initializing the `SoapClient` object is necessary to create the proxy for the Web Service. You initialize the object using the `mssoapinit()` method (a distinctive if non-standard name for the method). There are four parameters, but only the first is required.

```
Sub mssoapinit(bstrWSDLFile    As String, _
               [bstrServiceName As String], _
               [bstrPort       As String], _
               [bstrWSMLFile    As String])
```

The first, required, parameter is `bstrWSDLFile`, a URL to the WSDL file object to be loaded. The examples below are all valid `mssoapinit()` calls to initialize our Web Service:

```
m_client.mssoapinit "http://localhost/mstk2/high/sysinfo/SystemInfoService.wsdl"

m_client.mssoapinit "c:\sysinfo\SystemInfoService.wsdl"
```

```
m_client.mssoapinit "file://c:\sysinfo\SystemInfoService.wsdl"

m_client.mssoapinit "ftp://localhost/sysinfo/SystemInfoService.wsdl"
```

The other parameters to `mssoapinit()` help define the methods to be accessed in more detail. The string parameter `bstrServiceName` indicates which service element should be used in the WSDL file. The `bstrPort` parameter is a string indicating the WSDL port. In both cases, if the parameters are blank (which they are by default), `SoapClient` will use the first one it finds. The last parameter, `bstrWSMLFile`, is used to help the client translate complex types into COM objects on the client. We'll look at that in more detail when we talk about extending the Toolkit later in the chapter.

SoapClient Extras

We could end our discussion of the `SoapClient` object here, but once you have been using the high level API at the client for a while, you may wish to take things a little bit farther. There are additional properties and methods of `SoapClient` for more closely controlling SOAP messaging, but we need to use the low level API to access this functionality. Fortunately, the high level API is just a nice wrapper around the low level.

The ClientProperty Property

No, that's not an error that occurred during printing, there really is a property of the `SoapClient` object called `ClientProperty`. `ClientProperty` allows you to set and get the values of the properties of `SoapClient`. You access the values of specific properties by parameters, making `ClientProperty` look more like a collection than a property. This is an unusual approach, but it has the benefits of allowing `SoapClient`'s properties to grow in future without having to change the `ISoapClient` interface, and it allows new `SoapClient` implementations to be written. So, should you want to set the value of the `ServerHTTPRequest` property (described below), the code you would need would look like this:

```
m_client.ClientProperty("ServerHTTPRequest") = True     ' ASP Safe
```

There are two properties that are exposed via `ClientProperty`, and they are both important. The first is `ServerHTTPRequest`, a Boolean value indicating whether the server-safe XML HTTP components should be used for connections (the standard `XMLHTTP` object is not safe for server use). This property should be set to `true` whenever you use the `SoapClient` object from an ASP because it uses the Microsoft WinInet API, which has problems when used from ASP. The other property provided by the current version of `SoapClient` is `ConnectorProgID`. By setting this property, you can control what types of connections `SoapClient` uses. We will talk more about Toolkit connections in the later discussion of the low level API.

The HeaderHandler Property

The SOAP Header element, you may recall from Chapter 3, is a placeholder where the message syntax can be extended without changing the payload or the SOAP specification. For example, we might want to add some sort of authentication to our system information service so that a valid user name and password must be provided. What we would like to avoid is the need to change our method signatures so that each call takes additional parameters for this type of information, like `GetOS(username, pwd)`, for example. The ideal approach would be to pass the authentication information with the message, but outside the payload; which is where the Header comes in.

The `HeaderHandler` property of the `SoapClient` object gives us a way to hook into the high level API and use the SOAP Header. You can set the `HeaderHandler` property to reference an object that implements the `IHeaderHandler` interface. This interface is effectively the meeting point between the high and low level APIs: the high level API uses it, but its methods refer to low-level objects. As well as being useful at the client, you can also refer to a `HeaderHandler` object in your WSML file to process the SOAP Header on the server.

Debugging with the Toolkit

Because we are working with distributed applications, it can be tricky to hunt down problems with our SOAP clients and endpoints. Not only are there are additional complexities due to the distribution, but at the same time it becomes harder to determine on which side of the wire the problem lies. For developers there are two techniques readily available: SOAP Fault reports, and tracing.

The Fault Element

In SOAP, error conditions are indicated in the response in the form of a Fault element. SOAP faults contain standard information about the error, such as the type of error, a brief description, and where in the processing chain (if applicable) the error occurred.

> *SOAP messages can be processed along a chain of endpoints. For more information on endpoints and intermediaries, see Chapter 3 for details about SOAP.*

In addition to this standard information, the SOAP specification allows for an open area in the Fault: the `detail` element. The `detail` element can contain application or implementation-specific information in XML. The Toolkit uses this element to hold extended error information from the high level API regarding COM errors that occur on the server. From this, you can better determine the nature of any problems you may be having with your endpoint. The code below shows an example of a fault detail returned by the `SoapServer` object, formatted for readability. Inside the detail, the `mserror:returnCode` element contains the HRESULT (the standard for COM method return codes) for the error, and `mserror:source` contains the module name. These two pieces of information can save you a lot of time, as long as the called COM component is capable of providing such data, of course.

```
<?xml version="1.0" encoding="UTF-8" standalone="no" ?>
<SOAP-ENV:Envelope SOAP-ENV:encodingStyle=
 "http://schemas.xmlsoap.org/soap/encoding/"
 xmlns:SOAP-ENV="http://schemas.xmlsoap.org/soap/envelope/">

  <SOAP-ENV:Body>
    <SOAP-ENV:Fault>

      <faultcode>SOAP-ENV:Server</faultcode>
      <faultstring>
        WSDLOperation: Executing method GetNumberOfProcessors failed
      </faultstring>
      <faultactor>
        http://tempuri.org/action/SystemInfoService.GetNumberOfProcessors
      </faultactor>

      <detail>
        <mserror:errorInfo xmlns:mserror=
          "http://schemas.microsoft.com/soap-toolkit/faultdetail/error/">
```

```
          <mserror:returnCode>-2146828277</mserror:returnCode>

          <mserror:serverErrorInfo>
             <mserror:description>Division by zero</mserror:description>
             <mserror:source>Sysinfo</mserror:source>
          </mserror:serverErrorInfo>

          <mserror:callStack>
             <mserror:callElement>
                <mserror:component>WSDLOperation</mserror:component>
                   <mserror:description>
                      Executing method GetNumberOfProcessors failed
                   </mserror:description>
                <mserror:returnCode>-2147352567</mserror:returnCode>
             </mserror:callElement>
          </mserror:callStack>

       </mserror:errorInfo>
    </detail>

    </SOAP-ENV:Fault>
   </SOAP-ENV:Body>
  </SOAP-ENV:Envelope>
```

Tracing Messages

Tracing can be invaluable when debugging, and no more so than when you are debugging a Web Service. To help you trace your SOAP messages, the Microsoft Toolkit includes the handy trace utility called mssoapt.exe. Using this tool, you can select a port to listen to on the local machine, and then the utility will trace traffic on that port by forwarding all the data on to the host and port of your choice. The utility listens on a predefined destination port, and then retransmits the data on another port. You can then see a history of the request and response messages that traveled through that tunnel, as shown in the following screenshot:

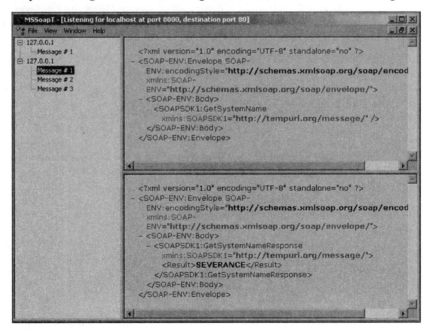

In addition to the Microsoft SOAP Toolkit tracing utility, there is also a great pair of tracing utilities provided by Simon Fell, author of the pocketSOAP Toolkit. The utilities, tcpTrace and proxyTrace, are useful when working with SOAP messages and WSDL. You can download both utilities from the pocketSOAP web site at http://www.pocketsoap.com.

The trace utility is useful for debugging any of the three APIs of the Toolkit, since all of them in the end use HTTP and SOAP messages. Now that we have covered the high level API, let's take a look at a lower level approach that the Toolkit provides for dealing with SOAP.

Drilling Down – The Low Level API

The high level API is great for many developers. If you want to expose COM objects as Web Services, or access endpoints that provide WSDL, the high level API is a powerful tool that can be very simple to use. However, some situations require a more controlled use of SOAP and Web Services than the high level API provides. For those situations, the low level API of the Toolkit allows you to directly compose and transport SOAP messages using a set of COM objects.

There are situations where either the low level or high level APIs would do, so what are the situations where the high level API comes up short?

❑ **No WSDL** – Without WSDL to describe the Web Service, the SoapClient object has no way of knowing how to compose a message, or to generate a COM proxy for the Web Service. In this case, you need to compose the message yourself, something the low level API allows you to do. Most Web Services are likely to provide a WSDL description in the near future, but there's no guarantee of this.

❑ **No COM Objects** – If you do not already have a COM object that is suitable for rendering as a Web Service, you may wish to write a dedicated endpoint. Using the low level API, you can write a SOAP endpoint that handles the incoming messages directly without the need to transform from SOAP to IDispatch calls.

❑ **Blind Exposure Can Be Bad** – Even if you do have a COM object that could serve as your Web Service, perhaps you don't want to blindly expose all of the object's methods to the world. With the low level API, you can write a component that processes SOAP messages and uses the original COM object to perform the real work. This allows your new endpoint to get in-between the message and the COM object to perform additional error checking, logging, etc.

This is not a complete list, but it outlines the fundamental differences between the high level and low level APIs. To sum up, the high level API relies on WSDL and tries to take care of everything for you. So if you want finer-grained control than that provided by the high level API, either on the client or server, you will have to use the low level API.

There are three major components to the low level API: the SoapReader object, the SoapSerializer object, and the SoapConnector interface. Basically, SoapReader and SoapSerializer are used to read and write SOAP messages respectively, and the SoapConnector interface represents a SOAP transport. We will examine each of these in more detail, but the following diagram shows how the low level components fit together:

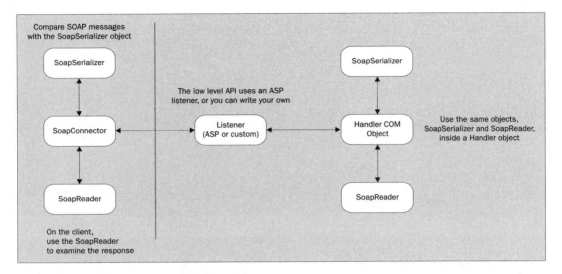

Let's rebuild our previous example using the low level API and see how it lets us exert greater control over SOAP messages and transports.

Déjà vu – SystemInfoService the Hard Way

Again, we shall begin at the server, but this time things are different. We do not have the same requirements for WSDL and WSML as when using the high level API. With the low level API, we need to write our own object to handle incoming requests.

First, we create another ActiveX DLL project, this time called `LowRider`. Inside the project we need to create a new class module called `LowBoy`. This will be our message handler, processing requests and generating responses. Just as we did in the high level client, add a reference to the Microsoft SOAP Type Library to the `LowRider` project.

But how will `LowBoy` get the messages in the first place? The low level API does not have any listeners of its own, so we will write one in ASP. We could write a listener as an ISAPI module, or even a mini-web server, but that's a lot of work when we can just use a couple of lines of ASP. Since we are going to use ASP as the listener, `LowBoy` will provide a method that can interface with the page. To do that, we need to include a reference to the ASP Object Library `asp.dll`, as well as the Toolkit library `mssoap1.dll`, and our original COM object, `SysInfo.dll`.

At The Server

Our new COM object `LowBoy` needs just one method to make it a message processor. That method, of course, is `ProcessRequest`, or something similar. It uses ASP as the listener, so the method needs to accept an ASP `Request` object and an ASP `Response` object. Here is the source code for our object:

```
Option Explicit
' LowBoy
'
' Message Handler Object Using the Low Level SOAP API

Public Sub ProcessRequest(request As ASPTypeLibrary.request, response As
```

```
       ASPTypeLibrary.response)

On Error GoTo ProcessErr

    ' Always text/xml
    response.ContentType = "text/xml"

    ' Read and write SOAP messages
    Dim soapIn As New SoapReader
    Dim soapOut As New SoapSerializer

    ' From our first app, this does the work
    Dim si As New SystemInfoService

    Dim strBodyName As String
    Dim strResult As String

    ' Load the request, write out to the response
    soapIn.Load request
    soapOut.Init response

    strBodyName = soapIn.RPCStruct.baseName

    ' Find the appropriate method to call
    Select Case strBodyName

        Case "GetOS"
            strResult = si.GetOS()

        Case "GetSystemName"
            strResult = si.GetSystemName()

        Case "GetNumberOfProcessors"
            strResult = si.GetNumberOfProcessors()

        Case Else
            Err.Raise 1000, "LowBoy", "Method not found"
        End Select

    ' Write out the response
    soapOut.startEnvelope
    soapOut.startBody
    soapOut.startElement strBodyName & "Response", "http://tempuri.org/message/"
    soapOut.startElement "Result", "http://tempuri.org/message/"
    soapOut.writeString strResult
    soapOut.endElement
    soapOut.endElement
    soapOut.endBody
    soapOut.endEnvelope

    Exit Sub

ProcessErr:
    ' Create a Fault element
    response.Status = 500
```

```
        soapOut.startEnvelope
        soapOut.startBody
        soapOut.startFault "Server", Err.Description
        soapOut.endFault
        soapOut.endBody
        soapOut.endEnvelope

        Exit Sub

   End Sub
```

Let's take a look at some of the objects we are using in this sample to understand the role they play in the low level API. The server object uses two important low level objects: `SoapReader`, and `SoapSerializer`.

> *The low level API objects manipulate SOAP messages as they actually are, rather than hiding the format through proxies and COM mappings. For a review of the SOAP format, refer back to Chapter 3.*

The SoapReader Object

The `SoapReader` object will load a SOAP message and break it down into its constituent parts for ease of processing. In our server sample, we define the variable `soapIn` as an instance of a `SoapReader`. The first thing we do with a `SoapReader` is load the message.

```
    soapIn.Load request
```

The `load()` method of the `SoapReader` functions much like the `load()` method of the MSXML parser (indeed, I suspect it may be little more than a pass-through to that method, since there is also the familiar `loadXML()` method as well). The parameter to the `load()` method could be a URL, a path to a local file, an `IStream` pointer, or an ASP 3.0 `Request` object. After successfully loading the message from the ASP `Request` object, the parts of the message can be accessed as properties of the `SoapReader` object. These properties are exposed using the Microsoft XML model used by the MSXML parser. All the parts of a message are available: `Body`, `Header`, `Fault`, and so on, and every property is of type `XMLDOMElement` or `XMLDOMNodeList` (except for `soapAction`, which is a string). This is helpful because we don't have to traverse the XML to access the payload. If we want to access the XML in the header, we just use the `Header` property of the `SoapReader`. In the case of RPC, the payload is only a property away, namely `RPCStruct`:

```
    strBodyName = soapIn.RPCStruct.baseName
```

> *Be aware that the properties of `SoapReader` that begin with the letters RPC are only valid when you are working with SOAP messages that follow the RPC convention of the SOAP Specification. If you try to read a message that was serialized differently, such as a BizTalk Server message, the RPC properties of `SoapReader` would not apply.*

The value of `RPCStruct` is an `XMLDOMElement`, so it has all the properties and methods accordingly. If you remember from Chapter 3, the RPC convention of SOAP dictates that method calls and responses are represented as `structs`. That means that when working with SOAP RPC, you can count on the name of the method call being the `baseName` of the `RPCStruct`. In this case, that is the value we use to find out what the message is for. The parameters of methods are accessible as child elements of the `RPCStruct` property, or through the `RPCParameter` property of `SoapReader`. For example, if we had a SOAP request that passed a social security number as a parameter, the code to access that parameter's value would look something like this:

```
Dim ssn As String

ssn = soapIn.RPCParameter("ssn").Text
```

Now that we can read a SOAP message, we need to be able to compose a response. For that, the low level API provides the `SoapSerializer` object.

The SoapSerializer Object

Like `SoapReader`, `SoapSerializer` works with a SOAP message in parts: `Envelope`, `Body`, `Fault`, and so on. As you might expect, the difference is that `SoapSerializer` takes those parts and constructs a complete new message that can be serialized to a stream or ASP 3.0 response.

The methods of the `SoapSerializer` object echo those of the SAX event model, as you can see from the example code below. When you compose a message, you do it using pairs of method calls that signify the start and end of a message part, and begin with `start` and `end` respectively. For example, you begin the message with a call to `startEnvelope()`, and you end it with a call to `endEnvelope()`.

```
' Write out the response
soapOut.startEnvelope
soapOut.startBody
soapOut.startElement strBodyName & "Response", "http://tempuri.org/message/"
soapOut.startElement "Result", "http://tempuri.org/message/"
soapOut.writeString strResult
soapOut.endElement
soapOut.endElement
soapOut.endBody
soapOut.endEnvelope
```

You must make the method calls in order and in pairs. If you miss a call, or call one method twice, you will produce an error. Besides the `start~` and `end~` methods, there are methods for writing data values into the message elements. In the code above, the call to `writeString()` actually sets the value for the `Result` element. You can also write binary or XML data using the `writeBuffer()` and `writeXML()` methods respectively.

There is also a method, `SoapAttribute()`, for working with custom XML attributes in the message, and methods for dealing with XML namespaces `SoapNamespace()`, `SoapDefaultNamespace()`, `getPrefixForNamespace()`. These are quite esoteric methods that you are unlikely to need as you are getting started, but it is good to know they are there should the need arise.

Wrapping It Up

With the object in place, all we need now is two lines of ASP to complete the server-side code, which we save as `LowRider.asp`:

```
<%
    Set LowBoy = Server.CreateObject("LowRider.LowBoy")
    LowBoy.ProcessRequest Request, Response
%>
```

Now that the server is correctly set up, we can build a client to test it. As luck would have it, we already have a client – the high level client developed earlier. We could create a new WSDL file following the same steps for the high level API, but because both Web Services implement the same methods, all we need to do is copy the WSDL file from our high level server, and save it as a separate file (`LowRider.WSDL`), with just one modification. Near the end of the document, the WSDL contains an element called `service`. The service element contains the URL address of the endpoint. If we replace that with our new address, we will have a WSDL file that the client can use to interface with our low level code.

First, we update the WSDL to look like this:

```
<service name='SystemInfoService' >
   <port name='SystemInfoServiceSoapPort'
         binding='wsdlns:SystemInfoServiceSoapBinding' >
      <soap:address location='http://localhost/mstk2/ low/sysinfo/LowRider.asp'
      />
   </port>
</service>
```

Then, we give the new WSDL file as the endpoint for the high level client. If we've done everything right, the high level client will work exactly the same with the new low level server.

Low Level Clients

We have already tested our new service using our high level client, but let's see what the client-side code looks like using the low level API. To keep things simple, we'll use our original client application, and just replace our call to `GetOS()` with a low level equivalent. Because the high and low level APIs are both located in the same module, we already have access to all the objects we need.

In order to access the service using the low level client directly, we need to add the following code to our client application, along with a command button to invoke it:

```
Private Sub GetOSWithLowLevelAPI()
On Error GoTo LowErr

    ' Reader and writer
    Dim soapIn As New SoapReader
    Dim soapout As New SoapSerializer

    ' Connector, in this case, HTTP
    Dim conn As SoapConnector
    Set conn = New HttpConnector

    ' Tell it where it needs to go
    conn.Property("EndPointURL") = txtEndpoint.Text
    ' We know the SoapAction from the WSDL file
    conn.Property("SoapAction") =
     "http://tempuri.org/action/SystemInfoService.GetOS"

    ' Initialize the writer
    soapout.Init conn.InputStream

    conn.BeginMessage

    soapout.startEnvelope
```

```
    soapout.startBody

    ' Payload, the code differs here for each method
    soapout.startElement "GetOS", "http://tempuri.org/message/"
    soapout.endElement

    soapout.endBody
    soapout.endEnvelope

    conn.EndMessage

    ' Load the response into the reader
    soapIn.Load conn.OutputStream

    ' If there is no Fault, get the OS value
    If soapIn.Fault Is Nothing Then

        ' The return value is in RPCResult.Text
        txtOS.Text = soapIn.RPCResult.Text

        ' Make it red to show the low level API did it
        txtOS.BackColor = RGB(255, 0, 0)

    Else

        ' If we get a Fault, let's see it
        MsgBox soapIn.faultstring

    End If

    Exit Sub

LowErr:
    MsgBox Err.Description
    Exit Sub

End Sub
```

Does This Look Familiar?

As you can see, the client code has a lot in common with low level server code we developed. Just as we did at the server, we use the `SoapReader` and `SoapSerializer` objects at the client to process messages. The more you work with the low level API, the more you will realize that most of your time is spent reading and writing messages using these two objects. The important parts of the client code are the areas where it differs from the server.

The SoapConnector Interface

The difference between the low level client and server code is the `SoapConnector` interface. At the server, we did not have to worry about how messages were being transported. Our listener was written in ASP, so ASP was responsible for getting the request and for returning the response. On the client, however, we must explicitly send a message as a request.

The means of transporting SOAP messages with the low level API is provided by the `SoapConnector` interface which represents a transport binding as described in the SOAP specification. By implementing this interface, an object sets itself up as a conduit for SOAP messages.

The first thing we need to do is make ourselves a `SoapConnector` interface to work with:

```
' Connector, in this case, HTTP
Dim conn As SoapConnector
Set conn = New HttpConnector
```

`SoapConnector` is our interface, and `HttpConnector` is our object. We'll talk more about `HttpConnector` in a minute. The next step is to configure our connector's custom properties, which we do using the `Property` property in a similar fashion to how we set the parameterized properties of the high level API before. This approach is necessary because, while SOAP transports will share some commonalities, most of their configuration settings will be platform-specific.

```
' Tell it where it needs to go
conn.Property("EndPointURL") = txtEndpoint.Text

' We know the SoapAction from the WSDL file
conn.Property("SoapAction") = "http://tempuri.org/action/SystemInfoService.GetOS"
```

Now that we have configured our connector, we can begin using it. First, we attach the `SoapSerializer` to it so that we can compose our request message. Then, we initiate the message by using the `BeginMessage()` method.

```
' Initialize the writer
soapout.Init conn.InputStream

conn.BeginMessage
```

The next lines actually write the message out to the connector using the `SoapSerializer` object. Once that is done, we can end the message. The call to `EndMessage()` triggers the connector to transport the message, and the application can now wait to receive the response.

```
conn.EndMessage

' Load the response into the reader
soapIn.Load conn.OutputStream
```

The HttpConnector Object

`SoapConnector` is just an interface, albeit an important one. If we are going to be sending and receiving SOAP messages, we need a concrete object that implements the `SoapConnector` interface. If we are working with HTTP as our transport protocol, then the object we will need is `HttpConnector`.

Just as the HTTP binding is the only concrete implementation of the SOAP transport concept, `HttpConnector` is the only concrete implementation of a connector that comes with the toolkit. Like all `SoapConnectors`, `HttpConnector` provides access to custom settings through the `Property` property. The `HttpConnector` object allows you to set values for basic authentication, proxy servers, and SSL. The most important properties, however, are `EndPointURL` and `SoapAction`.

```
' Tell it where it needs to go
conn.Property("EndPointURL") = txtEndpoint.Text

' We know the SoapAction from the WSDL file
conn.Property("SoapAction") = "http://tempuri.org/action/SystemInfoService.GetOS"
```

The `EndPointURL` property tells `HttpConnector` where to send messages, and it corresponds to the `address` element in the WSDL documents. The `SoapAction` property is used to indicate the value of the `SOAPAction` HTTP header. Values for `SoapAction` like the one above are generated by the WSDL Generator, but whatever the implementation of SOAP, you will need both of these pieces of information to connect to an endpoint successfully.

Error Trapping

Now that our `SoapReader` object has been attached to the `SoapConnector`'s `OutputStream` property, we have access to the response message. For the most part, we treat this just as we read the request on the server, using `SoapReader`. This time, the message might contain a SOAP Fault, so we use the `Fault` property of `SoapReader` to check for faults before processing the return. The return value is accessible through a different property called `RPCResult`.

```
' If there is no Fault, get the OS value
If soapIn.Fault Is Nothing Then

    ' The return value is in RPCResult.Text
    txtOS.Text = soapIn.RPCResult.Text
```

The low level API is extremely flexible, and it gives developers a couple of ways to customize and handle processing. Anything you may need to do with SOAP messages should be possible with the low level API. In some cases, where the API doesn't quite support your needs, you can build extensions that fit into the low level model. We will talk about such extensibility in a moment, but first let's take a quick look at the last API of the Toolkit: the SMO Framework.

Documents – The SMO Framework

In both the previous examples, we were working with RPC-style SOAP. SOAP has received a lot of interest from the development community and businesses because it makes RPC over the Internet easier, but SOAP is much more than that. SOAP is a messaging protocol built from XML, so any XML can be transported in a SOAP message. This could be an XML purchase order, an XSL stylesheet, or in our case, system information.

The Toolkit team has provided a third API, the **SOAP Messaging Object (SMO) Framework**, to support SOAP messages that do not use RPC. SMO is designed to make it easier to work with generic XML inside a SOAP payload.

Code Generation

The high and low level APIs provide COM objects and interfaces that we used to build SOAP clients and endpoints. In the SMO Framework, similar objects exist, but the framework uses a code generator approach as well. The core component of the SMO Framework is a Visual Basic add-in that functions as a code generator. The add-in is responsible for reading an XML schema and generating Visual Basic class modules to work with messages conforming to that schema.

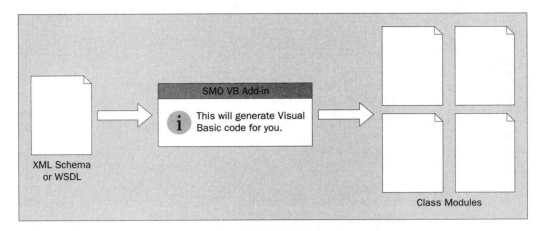

The SMO code generator is aptly named the SMO Generator, and it is located in mssmogen.dll. You can use the SMO Generator from inside Visual Basic by loading it as an add-in to the Visual Basic IDE. Select Add-Ins/Add-In Manager..., and you will see the Microsoft SOAP Messaging Object Generator in the list of available add-ins. Now, the SMO Generator will be available item under the Add-Ins drop down.

In the latest version of the Toolkit, the SMO Generator does not accept either W3 schemas or WSDL as input. Instead, the SMO Generator reads **XML Data Reduced (XDR)** schema documents, Microsoft's proprietary schema format. Future versions of the SMO Framework will support W3 schemas and schema fragments inside WSDL. To show how the SMO Generator works, we will use an XDR document that represents our system information provided by the SysInfo module:

```xml
<?xml version="1.0"?>
<Schema xmlns="urn:schemas-microsoft-com:xml-data" xmlns:dt="urn:schemas-
microsoft-com:datatypes">

   <ElementType name="SystemInformation" content="eltOnly" order="seq">
      <element type="Name"/>
      <element type="OS"/>
      <element type="ProcessorCount"/>
   </ElementType>

   <ElementType name="Name" dt:type="string"/>

   <ElementType name="OS" dt:type="string"/>

   <ElementType name="ProcessorCount" dt:type="string"/>
</Schema>
```

Given this XDR document, the SMO Generator will generate the following class module code:

```vb
' Generated by Microsoft SOAP Message Object Generator v1.0.1
' File: SystemInformation
'
' Wrapper for XML comprising a part of a SOAP message. The
' object implements the ISoapMessagePart interface, allowing the
' object to work in concert with a SoapMessage object.
```

```
'

Option Explicit

Implements ISoapMessagePart
Private m_elementNames(2) As String
Private m_elementNamespaces(2) As String
Private m_NodeBody As IXMLDOMNode

Public Property Get XMLDOMNode_() As IXMLDOMNode
    Set XMLDOMNode_ = m_NodeBody
End Property

Private Sub Class_Initialize()
   m_elementNames(0) = modSYSTEMINFORMATION_.C_NAME
   m_elementNamespaces(0) = modSYSTEMINFORMATION_.C_NAME_NS
   m_elementNames(1) = modSYSTEMINFORMATION_.C_OS
   m_elementNamespaces(1) = modSYSTEMINFORMATION_.C_OS_NS
   m_elementNames(2) = modSYSTEMINFORMATION_.C_PROCESSORCOUNT
   m_elementNamespaces(2) = modSYSTEMINFORMATION_.C_PROCESSORCOUNT_NS
End Sub

Public Property Let ProcessorCount(ByVal xValue As String)
    FindElement(m_NodeBody, modSYSTEMINFORMATION_.C_PROCESSORCOUNT,
modSYSTEMINFORMATION_.C_PROCESSORCOUNT_NS).Text = xValue
End Property

Public Property Get ProcessorCount() As String
    ProcessorCount = FindElement(m_NodeBody,
modSYSTEMINFORMATION_.C_PROCESSORCOUNT,
modSYSTEMINFORMATION_.C_PROCESSORCOUNT_NS).Text
End Property

Public Property Let OS(ByVal xValue As String)
    FindElement(m_NodeBody, modSYSTEMINFORMATION_.C_OS,
modSYSTEMINFORMATION_.C_OS_NS).Text = xValue
End Property

Public Property Get OS() As String
    OS = FindElement(m_NodeBody, modSYSTEMINFORMATION_.C_OS,
modSYSTEMINFORMATION_.C_OS_NS).Text
End Property

Public Property Let Name(ByVal xValue As String)
    FindElement(m_NodeBody, modSYSTEMINFORMATION_.C_NAME,
modSYSTEMINFORMATION_.C_NAME_NS).Text = xValue
End Property

Public Property Get Name() As String
    Name = FindElement(m_NodeBody, modSYSTEMINFORMATION_.C_NAME,
modSYSTEMINFORMATION_.C_NAME_NS).Text
End Property

Private Sub Class_Terminate()

    Set m_NodeBody = Nothing
```

```
End Sub

Public Sub ISoapMessagePart_ResetContent()

    While m_NodeBody.hasChildNodes
        m_NodeBody.removeChild m_NodeBody.firstChild
    Wend

    Dim i As Integer
    i = m_NodeBody.Attributes.length - 1
    While i >= 0
        m_NodeBody.Attributes.removeNamedItem m_NodeBody.Attributes.Item(i).nodeName
        i = i - 1
    Wend
    addElement m_NodeBody, modSYSTEMINFORMATION_.C_NAME,
modSYSTEMINFORMATION_.C_NAME_NS, vbNullString
    addElement m_NodeBody, modSYSTEMINFORMATION_.C_OS,
modSYSTEMINFORMATION_.C_OS_NS, vbNullString
    addElement m_NodeBody, modSYSTEMINFORMATION_.C_PROCESSORCOUNT,
modSYSTEMINFORMATION_.C_PROCESSORCOUNT_NS, vbNullString

End Sub

Public Property Get ISoapMessagePart_Element() As MSXML2.IXMLDOMElement
    Set ISoapMessagePart_Element = m_NodeBody
End Property

Public Property Set ISoapMessagePart_Element(ByVal Element As
MSXML2.IXMLDOMElement)
    Dim body As MSXML2.IXMLDOMNode

    Set m_NodeBody = Element

    If m_NodeBody.baseName <> modSYSTEMINFORMATION_.C_SYSTEMINFORMATION Or
m_NodeBody.NamespaceURI <> modSYSTEMINFORMATION_.C_SYSTEMINFORMATION_NS Then
        Set m_NodeBody = Nothing
        Err.Raise vbObjectError, , "Wrong element assigned to message part object."
    End If

End Property

Public Property Get ISoapMessagePart_NamespaceURI() As String
    ISoapMessagePart_NamespaceURI = modSYSTEMINFORMATION_.C_SYSTEMINFORMATION_NS
End Property

Public Property Get ISoapMessagePart_ElementName() As String
    ISoapMessagePart_ElementName = modSYSTEMINFORMATION_.C_SYSTEMINFORMATION
End Property

Private Property Get ISoapMessagePart_MessagePart() As Object
    Set ISoapMessagePart_MessagePart = Me
End Property
```

If you look at the code above, you will notice that the code frequently refers to values and functions that are not listed here. That is because the SMO Generator generates two other files as well: a constants file containing namespace URIs, element, and method names (in this case, named modSYSTEMINFORMATION.bas); and a utility functions file (called SMOGHelp.bas) that provides helper functions like the FindElement() method shown above. In all, the SMO Generator creates one class module per top level element in the schema, plus two modules containing constants and helper methods respectively.

SMO Objects At Work

The SystemInformation object implements the ISoapMessagePart interface, which is a contract that allows the object to be read from and written to a SOAP message. The SoapMessage object in the SMO Framework represents SOAP messages.

Objects generated by the SMO Generator are usable on both the client and server because of the nature of the SoapMessage object. Any object that implements the ISoapMessagePart interface can be attached to the SoapMessage object, which is the unit of transfer for the SMO Framework (methods pass and return instances of these objects). On the client, you use the SoapMessageClient object, SMO's answer to the SoapClient object of the high level API.

On the server, there is no object that corresponds to the SoapServer. Instead, a SoapMessage object can be initialised from an ASP Request object. Once the message has been initialised, the SMO class can attach to the message and load its state. When the response has been created, the steps are reversed: a SOAP message is attached to the ASP Response object, and the response SMO class is attached to the message.

> The names of the SMO Framework objects can be easily confused with objects from the other two APIs (SoapClient versus SoapMessageClient). The only true overlap between SMO and the other APIs is the common use of SoapConnector, which allows us to address the issue of transport in a unified way for all three APIs.

Why SMO?

There isn't anything that you can do with the SMO Framework that you can't do with the low level API. However, the major advantage of SMO is that it generates a large amount of code to help simplify using XML documents in SOAP messages. In my opinion, the SMO Framework would be more useful if it wrapped the high or low level APIs for its underlying architecture. Instead, the Toolkit provides a whole new set of similar objects that are not related to either the high or low level APIs. If you need to transfer specific XML documents for which a schema exists, the SMO Framework is a great fit. For other uses, I would stick with the combination of high and low level APIs.

Beyond the Basics

The authors of the SOAP Specification designed the protocol to be extensible. In areas such as data representation, protocol extensions, and transport, the SOAP Specification is designed to allow the protocol to grow and adapt to a wide variety of uses. The developers behind the Microsoft SOAP Toolkit took this philosophy to heart when creating the Toolkit. The fact that there are three distinct APIs provided to cover all levels of SOAP use is a testament to that.

Aside from potentially increasing the number of APIs, there is room to extend the Toolkit within the APIs using COM. The Toolkit APIs are built on COM and are well designed, so there are points in the Toolkit where you can plug in your own implementations to extend the Toolkit's capabilities, as we will see in the following couple of examples.

Working with Connectors

Although we have focused on SOAP messages sent over HTTP (which is certainly the primary purpose of the Microsoft SOAP Toolkit), the SOAP Specification allows the use of any type of transport that fits the system. SOAP messages can be transmitted using HTTP, raw sockets, or even some sort of pseudo-transport for testing such as a message log. As we saw before, the concept of SOAP transport in the Microsoft Toolkit is represented by the `SoapConnector` interface. If you need a new transport, the `SoapConnector` interface is what you must implement.

Connectors and SoapClient

When we examined the `SoapClient` object earlier in the chapter, it did all the work for us. Just point it at a WSDL document, and fire off those methods. This all works wonderfully except in special circumstances, such as asynchronous communication. In that case, you need RPC over a protocol other than HTTP, such as SMTP. The `SoapClient` object uses `SoapConnectors` internally, but to customize our transport, we need to gain control over that process.

We can control how `SoapClient` uses a connector in a couple of ways. The simplest way is to access the properties of the `SoapConnector` it is using. We can do this by using the `ConnectorProperty` property of the `SoapClient` object. Like `ClientProperty`, `ConnectorProperty` takes a string parameter indicating which value you would like to set or get.

Let's assume that we wish to use authentication to access the endpoint of our Web Service. If we are using the low level API, we can use the `Property` property of the `HTTPConnector`. If we are working with the `SoapClient` object, we must use `Connector` Property.

```
Dim client as New SoapClient
Dim conn as New HttpConnector

' The next two lines are essentially the same
client.ConnectorProperty("AuthUser") = "chris"

conn.Property("AuthUser") = "chris"
```

What if configuring the connector is not enough? What if, as mentioned earlier, we need a different connector altogether? The `SoapClient` object uses another Toolkit object called the `SoapConnectorFactory` to create `SoapConnectors` based on WSDL information. Unfortunately, there is no way I know of to extend the factory's capabilities to cover new protocols, notwithstanding some future Microsoft update to the Toolkit.

> *For those of you familiar with URL monikers and component categories, you may agree that there could be a better way to build a `SoapConnectorFactory`, so that developers could extend it in a way that was transparent to users of the high level API. However, I shall leave that as an exercise for the braver readers out there!*

So, in this case, we need to force the `SoapClient` to use a particular `SoapConnector` implementation. Luckily, we can, using the `ConnectorProgID` property. If we have an implementation of the `SoapConnector` interface called `MySoapConnector`, then this code would force the `SoapClient` to use it for all its messaging:

```
m_client.ClientProperty("ConnectorProgID") = "MySoap.MySoapConnector"
```

Now let's look at how we can implement `SoapConnector` to create our own custom connector objects.

Custom Connectors

SOAP can be used over any transport, but unfortunately, no one has gotten around to implementing SOAP over every transport available to us. That's where you, the enterprising developer, come in. Armed with your development tools and a need to transport SOAP messages over Protocol X, you can implement your own custom `SoapConnector` and integrate it into the Microsoft SOAP Toolkit.

Of course, not every transport needs to be a wire protocol. The message doesn't need to go anywhere; it just needs to be processed. In fact, we can build a custom `SoapConnector` that serves as a debugging tool by always returning a Fault of our choice. The diagram below shows how such a custom `SoapConnector`, called `FaultyConnector`, might operate. `FaultyConnector` is written as a Visual Basic class.

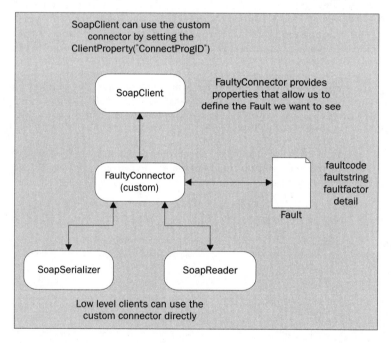

`FaultyConnector` behaves just about the same as the `HttpConnector` object provided by the Toolkit. Instead of passing messages over HTTP, however, it simply returns a Fault. The connector has properties (`faultcode`, `faultstring`, `faultactor`, and `detail`) that allow you to customize the Fault to be generated. The code for the custom connector is shown below, and it is pretty straightforward. We implement the `SoapConnector` interface (first add a reference to the SOAP Type Library `mssoap1.dll`), and stub out the methods. The only methods of importance are `EndMessage()`, which is where we generate the Fault, and the `Property Let()` and `Get()` methods. You will also notice the two variables, `m_xmlIn` and `m_xmlOut`. These two DOMDocuments serve as our `InputStream` and `OutputStream`. We can use the DOMDocument here because it implements the `IStream` interface the serializers are expecting.

```
' FaultyConnector
'
' Custom SoapConnector that always returns a Fault
'

Option Explicit
```

```
' SoapConnector interface
Implements SoapConnector

' DOMDocuments serve as our input and output streams
Private m_xmlIn As MSXML2.DOMDocument
Private m_xmlOut As MSXML2.DOMDocument

Private m_strFaultCode As String
Private m_strFaultString As String
Private m_strFaultActor As String
Private m_xmlDetail As MSXML2.IXMLDOMNodeList

Private Sub Class_Initialize()

    SoapConnector_reset

End Sub

Private Sub SoapConnector_BeginMessage()

    SoapConnector_BeginMessageWSDL Nothing

End Sub

Private Sub SoapConnector_BeginMessageWSDL(ByVal pOperation As
MSSOAPLib.IWSDLOperation)

    'No op

End Sub

Private Sub SoapConnector_Connect()

    SoapConnector_ConnectWSDL Nothing

End Sub

Private Sub SoapConnector_ConnectWSDL(ByVal pPort As MSSOAPLib.IWSDLPort)

    ' No op

End Sub

Private Sub SoapConnector_EndMessage()

    'We always write a Fault
    Dim soapOut As New SoapSerializer

    soapOut.Init m_xmlOut

    soapOut.startEnvelope
    soapOut.startBody

    soapOut.startFault m_strFaultCode, m_strFaultString, m_strFaultActor
    soapOut.startFaultDetail
```

```
        If Not m_xmlDetail Is Nothing Then
            Dim n As IXMLDOMNode
            For Each n In m_xmlDetail
                soapOut.startElement n.baseName, n.namespaceURI
                soapOut.writeString n.xml
                soapOut.endElement
            Next n
        End If
        soapOut.endFaultDetail
        soapOut.endFault

        soapOut.endBody
        soapOut.endEnvelope

End Sub

Private Property Get SoapConnector_InputStream() As MSSOAPLib.IStream

    Set SoapConnector_InputStream = m_xmlIn

End Property

Private Property Get SoapConnector_OutputStream() As MSSOAPLib.IStream

    Set SoapConnector_OutputStream = m_xmlOut

End Property

' RHS is an abbreviation for right hand side
Private Property Let SoapConnector_Property(ByVal pPropertyName As String, ByVal
RHS As Variant)

    Select Case pPropertyName

        Case "faultcode"
            m_strFaultCode = RHS

        Case "faultstring"
            m_strFaultString = RHS

        Case "faultactor"
            m_strFaultActor = RHS

        Case "detail"
            Set m_xmlDetail = RHS

        Case Else
            Err.Description = "Invalid property name"
            Err.Raise 1000

    End Select
    Exit Property

End Property
```

```
    Private Property Get SoapConnector_Property(ByVal pPropertyName As String) As
    Variant

        Select Case pPropertyName

            Case "faultcode"
                SoapConnector_Property = m_strFaultCode

            Case "faultstring"
                SoapConnector_Property = m_strFaultString

            Case "faultactor"
                SoapConnector_Property = m_strFaultActor

            Case "detail"
                SoapConnector_Property = CVar(m_xmlDetail)

            Case Else
                Err.Description = "Invalid property name"
                Err.Raise 1000

        End Select
        Exit Property

    End Property

    Private Sub SoapConnector_reset()

        Set m_xmlIn = New DOMDocument
        Set m_xmlOut = New DOMDocument

        m_strFaultCode = "Server"
        m_strFaultString = "Automatic Fault"
        m_strFaultActor = "uri:FaultyConnector"
        Set m_xmlDetail = Nothing

    End Sub
```

Now we can put `FaultyConnector` to use and plug it into a client application, as shown here:

```
' Use FaultyConnector
m_client.ClientProperty("ConnectorProgID") = "MSTKPLUS.FaultyConnector"

' Initialize the proxy
m_client.mssoapinit "http://localhost/mstk2/high/sysinfo/"

' Plug in our fault string
m_client.ConnectorProperty("faultstring") = "What did you expect?"

' Invoke the method and watch it fail
MsgBox m_client.GetOS()
```

This custom connector makes a good testing tool, but you can implement any connector that you can imagine as long as there is an appropriate listener available. You could apply the same principle to raw sockets or MSMQ, or you could write a more sophisticated connector that serializes and transmits messages from a database. In all these cases, just follow the model used for the `FaultyConnector`, and the rest of the Toolkit should never know the difference.

Working with Complex Types

It is relatively simple for us to build examples that use simple types, like strings and integers, which pass easily from client to server. In the real world, we generally need to deal with complex types, such as arrays and objects. The Microsoft SOAP Toolkit provides methods for dealing with complex types, and for some cases, the Toolkit does most of the work for you. In the other instances, it is up to you to build custom objects to do the work.

Arrays

While arrays in SOAP can be a complicated area to work in, the Toolkit does a good job of handling arrays of basic types. Let's start with a simple COM object that takes an array of integers, and returns the largest. The method signature for the object is listed below:

```
Public Function GetMax(nums() As Integer) As Integer
    Dim iMax As Integer
    Dim iCurr As Integer

    iMax = 0

    For iCurr = 0 To UBound(nums)
        If iMax < nums(iCurr) Then iMax = nums(iCurr)
    Next iCurr

    GetMax = iMax

End Function
```

If we want to use this object in the high level API, we need to run the WSDL Generator against the object. When we do, it produces the following WSDL document:

```
<?xml version='1.0' encoding='UTF-8' ?>
 <!-- Generated 06/28/01 by Microsoft SOAP Toolkit WSDL File Generator, Version
 1.00.623.1 -->
<definitions  name ='MyArrayService' targetNamespace='http://tempuri.org/wsdl/'
             xmlns:wsdlns='http://tempuri.org/wsdl/'
             xmlns:typens='http://tempuri.org/type'
             xmlns:soap='http://schemas.xmlsoap.org/wsdl/soap/'
             xmlns:xsd='http://www.w3.org/2001/XMLSchema'
             xmlns:stk='http://schemas.microsoft.com/soap-toolkit/wsdl-extension'
             xmlns='http://schemas.xmlsoap.org/wsdl/'>
    <types>
       <schema targetNamespace='http://tempuri.org/type'
          xmlns='http://www.w3.org/2001/XMLSchema'
          xmlns:SOAP-ENC='http://schemas.xmlsoap.org/soap/encoding/'
          xmlns:wsdl='http://schemas.xmlsoap.org/wsdl/'
          elementFormDefault='qualified'>
       <complexType  name ='ArrayOfshort'>
          <complexContent>
             <restriction base='SOAP-ENC:Array'>
                <attribute ref='SOAP-ENC:arrayType' wsdl:arrayType='short[]'/>
             </restriction>
          </complexContent>
       </complexType>
```

```
            </schema>
        </types>
        <message name='MaxFinder.GetMax'>
            <part name='nums' type='typens:ArrayOfshort'/>
        </message>
        <message name='MaxFinder.GetMaxResponse'>
            <part name='Result' type='xsd:short'/>
            <part name='nums' type='typens:ArrayOfshort'/>
        </message>
        <portType name='MaxFinderSoapPort'>
            <operation name='GetMax' parameterOrder='nums'>
                <input message='wsdlns:MaxFinder.GetMax' />
                <output message='wsdlns:MaxFinder.GetMaxResponse' />
            </operation>
        </portType>
        <binding name='MaxFinderSoapBinding' type='wsdlns:MaxFinderSoapPort' >
            <stk:binding preferredEncoding='UTF-8'/>
            <soap:binding style='rpc' transport='http://schemas.xmlsoap.org
                                            /soap/http' />
            <operation name='GetMax' >
                <soap:operation soapAction='http://tempuri.org/action/MaxFinder.GetMax'
                />
                <input>
                    <soap:body use='encoded' namespace='http://tempuri.org/message/'
                    encodingStyle='http://schemas.xmlsoap.org/soap/encoding/' />
                </input>
                <output>
                    <soap:body use='encoded' namespace='http://tempuri.org/message/'
                    encodingStyle='http://schemas.xmlsoap.org/soap/encoding/' />
                </output>
            </operation>
        </binding>
        <service name='MyArrayService' >
            <port name='MaxFinderSoapPort' binding='wsdlns:MaxFinderSoapBinding' >
                <soap:address
                location='http://localhost/mstk2/complex/MyArrayService.WSDL' />
            </port>
        </service>
    </definitions>
```

As you can see, the WSDL that is generated here is somewhat different from our previous examples. The
types element, which contains the additional schema for the document, actually contains something now.
The ArrayOfshort complexType has been generated, representing the SOAP Array.

The question is, what does the SoapClient object do with this kind of WSDL? The good news is that it
does just what you would want. SoapClient can understand WSDL that contains SOAP arrays of simple
types, and it can map those straight to arrays in Visual Basic. The client code shown below accesses our
GetMax() method, and the handling of the array is transparent:

```
Private Sub cmdMyMax_Click()

    Dim c As New SoapClient

    c.mssoapinit "http://localhost/mstk2/complex/MyArrayService.wsdl"
```

```
    Dim i(3) As Integer

    i(0) = 1
    i(1) = 32
    i(2) = -6

    Dim iMax As Integer

    iMax = c.GetMax(i)

    MsgBox "The maximum is " & iMax

End Sub
```

Custom Types

So arrays are not too difficult, but in order to work with custom types such as objects, you will have to write a little code. The Toolkit allows you to hook into the type mapping process, that is, the step where Toolkit objects like `SoapClient` decide how to translate between XML and COM data types. The objects that hook into that process must implement a common interface, namely the `ISoapTypeMapper` interface.

The ISoapTypeMapper Interface

Objects that implement the `ISoapTypeMapper` interface are responsible to converting between XML and whatever particular type they represent. There are only four methods in this interface: `Init()`, `read()`, `write()`, and `varType()`. The `Init()` method initializes the mapper with a schema fragment and a `SoapTypeMapperFactory` object, which we will discuss further in a moment. The `read()` and `write()` methods convert XML to data, and data into XML respectively. The `varType()` method simply returns the `VARTYPE` of the data to be mapped (`vbString` for a string, `vbObject` for an object, and so on).

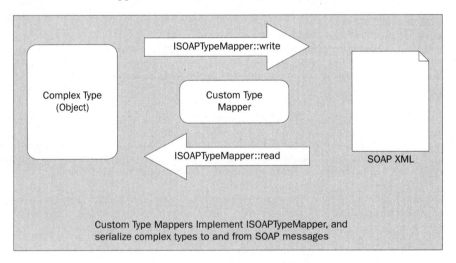

Custom Type Mappers Implement ISOAPTypeMapper, and
serialize complex types to and from SOAP messages

Type mappers are associated with a data type in one of two ways. Firstly, the type can be added to the `SoapTypeMapperFactory`, which we address below. The second method is to include information about the mapper inside the WSDL and WSML documents.

The SoapTypeMapperFactory Object

We now know that we can create custom type mappers for our complex types. The tricky thing about complex types, though, is that they can be nested to make really complex types. Structures and objects can be nested, and so we need a way to leverage type mappers in a recursive format. In order to do that, we need a single object that can contain all the type mappers for any type we may encounter. Luckily, Microsoft has already provided one, aptly named `SoapTypeMapperFactory`.

The `SoapTypeMapperFactory` functions as a registry for implementations of `ISoapTypeMapperFactory`. You can register type mappers by using the `addType()` method. Once a type is registered, you can then access it by name. The biggest advantage of the factory, however, is that mappers for all basic types (`string`, `float`, `date`, etc.) are already registered in the factory. Since all complex data types are composed of simple types, the `SoapTypeMapperFactory` can usually give you all you need to convert between your data and XML, whether it is just a string or a nested `struct`. Inside your own custom mapper, you can use the mappers provided by the factory to serialize the simple types.

WSDL and WSML

The high level API objects `SoapClient` and `SoapServer` can both use WSML to determine the custom type mapper to use when composing and receiving messages. Earlier, we only used the WSML document server-side. With custom mapping, the WSML becomes useful at both ends of the application.

We can use WSDL Generator when working with complex types, but whenever the generator encounters a type it cannot handle (such as a complex type), it generates WSDL message elements that look something like this:

```
<message name='SysInfoDataService.GetSysInfo'>
   <part name='si' type='xsd:???????'/>
</message>
<message name='SysInfoDataService.GetSysInfoResponse'>
   <part name='si' type='xsd:???????'/>
</message>
```

The type of the message parts shown above as `xsd:???????` is not part of the XML Schema, as you probably guessed. It is a placeholder that you, the developer, must fill in with the appropriate type. Before you can refer to the type, however, you have to create it.

Consider our earlier example that provided system information. We can consolidate the three methods into just one that returns a complex type of the following form:

```
<complexType name="SysInfoData">
   <sequence>
      <element name='SystemName' type='string'/>
      <element name='OS' type='string'/>
      <element name='NumberOfProcessors' type='short'/>
   </sequence>
</complexType>
```

That type, `SysInfoData`, then needs to be inserted into the `schema` element of the WSDL document. When inserting it, we place it into a namespace for this document, `typens`. After that is done, the message parts can refer to it as a valid type, as shown here (for brevity, only fragments are shown here, rather than complete documents):

```
<types>
   <schema targetNamespace='http://tempuri.org/type'
      xmlns='http://www.w3.org/2001/XMLSchema'
      xmlns:SOAP-ENC='http://schemas.xmlsoap.org/soap/encoding/'
      xmlns:wsdl='http://schemas.xmlsoap.org/wsdl/'
      elementFormDefault='qualified'>
      <complexType name="SysInfoData">
         <sequence>
            <element name='SystemName' type='string'/>
            <element name='OS' type='string'/>
            <element name='NumberOfProcessors' type='short'/>
         </sequence>
      </complexType>
   </schema>
</types>
<message name='SysInfoDataService.GetSysInfo'>
   <part name='si' type='typens:SysInfoData'/>
</message>
<message name='SysInfoDataService.GetSysInfoResponse'>
   <part name='si' type='typens:SysInfoData'/>
</message>
```

The WSML file that would be generated for our new Web Service would look like this:

```
<?xml version='1.0' encoding='UTF-8' ?>
<!-- Generated 06/28/01 by Microsoft SOAP Toolkit WSDL File Generator, Version
1.00.623.1 -->
<servicemapping name='SysInfoDataService'>
   <service name='SysInfoDataService'>
      <using PROGID='ComplexSysInfo.SysInfoDataService' cachable='0'
             ID='SysInfoDataServiceObject' />
      <port name='SysInfoDataServiceSoapPort'>
         <operation name='GetSysInfo'>
            <execute uses='SysInfoDataServiceObject' method='GetSysInfo'
                     dispID='1610809344'>
               <parameter callIndex='1' name='si' elementName='si' />
            </execute>
         </operation>
      </port>
   </service>
</servicemapping>
```

This describes the endpoint object, but not our new data object. In order to tell the SoapClient and SoapServer objects how to serialize the data, we need to add an additional piece of information to the WSML: the types element as highlighted here:

```
<?xml version='1.0' encoding='UTF-8' ?>
 <!-- Generated 06/28/01 by Microsoft SOAP Toolkit WSDL File Generator, Version
1.00.623.1 -->
<servicemapping name='SysInfoDataService'>
   <service name='SysInfoDataService'>
      <using PROGID='ComplexSysInfo.SysInfoDataService' cachable='0'
             ID='SysInfoDataServiceObject' />
      <using PROGID='ComplexData.SysInfoDataMapper' cachable='0'
             ID='SysInfoDataMapper' />
      <types>
         <type name='SysInfoData' targetNamespace='http://tempuri.org/type'
               uses='SysInfoDataMapper'/>
      </types>
```

```
<port name='SysInfoDataServiceSoapPort'>
    <operation name='GetSysInfo'>
        <execute uses='SysInfoDataServiceObject' method='GetSysInfo'
                dispID='1610809344'>
            <parameter callIndex='1' name='si' elementName='si' />
        </execute>
    </operation>
</port>
    </service>
</servicemapping>
```

Now, on both client and server sides, the high level API will understand that it must use `SysInfoDataMapper` to serialize objects of type `SysInfoData`. By creating a custom type mapper, we have extended the capabilities of the Toolkit greatly simplifying the task of using complex types.

Over-extended

We have only just touched upon how the Toolkit can be extended. Because the high and low level APIs of the Toolkit are pretty well designed COM code, there is great potential to hook into the framework and replace or extend objects, or build onto the model in ways that the original developers never imagined. Microsoft itself is certain to extend the Toolkit's features, but I recommend playing with custom connectors and other objects as a great way of learning how to take advantage of the SOAP Toolkit's features. SOAP is still a growing technology, and there are plenty of Toolkit extensions still possible. I hope that Microsoft will give the Toolkit all the support it needs to succeed, and that they will provide a place for developers to contribute their extensions to help with that success.

Summary

In this chapter, we have learned about the Microsoft SOAP Toolkit 2.0 and how we can use it to work with Web Services using Visual Studio 6.0. Version 2.0 of the Toolkit is a fully supported product that Microsoft has created to help developers transition between current development and the .NET Framework. That transition may take some time, and until then, the Toolkit is a powerful tool with an important role in Web Services development.

We have now examined the three APIs of the Toolkit, starting with the high level API. To recap, the high level API relies heavily on WSDL and WSML to map between COM and SOAP. It uses a client side proxy, and can function with either ISAPI or ASP listeners. The low level API is more flexible and powerful than the high level API, but it gives you greater flexibility. It is helpful to know that the high level API is just a COM-oriented wrapper around the low level objects. The final API, the SMO Framework, is a tool that is potentially valuable when working with XML documents as message payloads. SMO is potentially quite confusing, however, because of the means of code generation and the separate object model.

In general, when the Toolkit doesn't do what we want already, we can extend its capabilities with a little custom code. We looked at how to control the use of `SoapConnectors`, and even how to build a simple `SoapConnector` implementation in Visual Basic. We also learned how to work with complex data types, such as arrays or objects, using the Toolkit.

The Microsoft SOAP Toolkit 2.0 is just one SOAP implementation. It's not even the only COM implementation. It is, however, likely to be the most widely distributed, widely used SOAP implementation, and as a supported Microsoft product, it's a "legacy" Windows developer's greatest asset when working with Web Services.

9

Other SOAP Implementations

Since the introduction of SOAP, dozens of implementations (both open source and commercial) have appeared, and the number continues to grow. These implementations span the gamut of operating systems, languages, and run-times – indeed, any system that can handle HTTP and XML is a viable platform for SOAP.

In this chapter, we take a closer look at the following three SOAP toolkits, each written for a different language. They are:

- ❑ SOAP::Lite (Perl)
- ❑ EasySoap++ (C++)
- ❑ SOAPx4 (PHP)

Each of these implementations is open source and freely distributable. For each toolkit, we will look at:

- ❑ How to acquire and install the toolkit
- ❑ Writing servers with the toolkit
- ❑ Writing clients with the toolkit

The "flavor" of SOAP messaging that we demonstrate for each of these toolkits is RPC SOAP, which utilizes the SOAP encoding of parameters, as defined in section 5 of the SOAP Specification. This form of SOAP messaging has been the most popular amongst the first generation of SOAP toolkits.

There are no conflicts or dependencies between these toolkits, so you can have all three of them installed simultaneously on your machine if you wish.

Before We Get Started

Let's take care of a couple of introductory issues first. In this section we take a look at the common example scenario that we will use throughout the chapter. We also look at **tcpTrace**, a very useful tool for examining SOAP wiredumps.

The Echo Service Example

To illustrate how each of the toolkits works, we will use the example of an "Echo" service. This service is about as simple as it gets – it merely takes an input parameter sent from a client and echoes it back. This service is actually based on the interoperability test suite used by the SOAPBuilders e-group.

> **SOAPBuilders is an e-group housed at Yahoo Groups that provides the developers of SOAP toolkits with a forum for the discussion of SOAP implementation and interoperability issues.**
>
> **One of the group's primary activities has been cross-toolkit testing using an expanded version of the same Echo tests that we will use throughout this chapter. Each toolkit implementor publishes the Echo service that implements the various "Echo" methods for different data types and structures. Once the service has been published, other toolkit implementers build Echo clients with their own toolkits and test whether their clients interoperate with the service.**
>
> **To join the SOAPBuilders group, visit http://groups.yahoo.com/group/soapbuilders.**
>
> **You can also find links to the service endpoints and client results at http://www.xmethods.net/ilab.**

For the purposes of this chapter, we will focus on three methods exposed by the service:

- ❑   echoString() – to illustrate how basic data types (such as strings) are handled and serialized into XML

- ❑   echoIntegerArray() – to illustrate how arrays are handled

- ❑   echoStruct() – to illustrate how SOAP structures (complex types) are handled

A WSDL description for our example service, based on the WSDL description for the SOAPBuilders Echo Tests, is provided below. This is an abstract WSDL description – in other words, it's a generic interface description and contains no information specific to an actual endpoint (such as a URL address). Normally, endpoint-specific information is contained in the **service** element of the WSDL description, but we don't see this element below. See Chapter 4 for more information on how to interpret WSDL.

```
<?xml version="1.0"?>
<definitions name="InteropTest" targetNamespace="http://soapinterop.org/"
xmlns="http://schemas.xmlsoap.org/wsdl/"
xmlns:soap="http://schemas.xmlsoap.org/wsdl/soap/"
xmlns:xsd="http://www.w3.org/2001/XMLSchema"
xmlns:SOAP-ENC="http://schemas.xmlsoap.org/soap/encoding/"
xmlns:tns="http://soapinterop.org/"
xmlns:s="http://soapinterop.org/xsd"
xmlns:wsdl="http://schemas.xmlsoap.org/wsdl/">

<types>
   <schema xmlns="http://www.w3.org/2001/XMLSchema"
           targetNamespace="http://soapinterop.org/xsd">
      <complexType name="ArrayOfint">
         <complexContent>
            <restriction base="SOAP-ENC:Array">
               <sequence>
                  <element name="item" type="int" maxOccurs="unbounded"/>
               </sequence>
               <attribute ref="SOAP-ENC:arrayType" wsdl:arrayType="int[]"/>
            </restriction>
         </complexContent>
      </complexType>
      <complexType name="SOAPStruct">
         <all>
            <element name="varString" type="string"/>
            <element name="varInt" type="int"/>
            <element name="varFloat" type="float"/>
         </all>
      </complexType>
   </schema>
</types>
<binding name="InteropTestSoapBinding" type="tns:InteropTestPortType">
   <soap:binding style="rpc"
                 transport="http://schemas.xmlsoap.org/soap/http"/>
      <operation name="echoString">
         <soap:operation soapAction="http://soapinterop.org/"/>
         <input>
            <soap:body use="encoded"
                       namespace="http://soapinterop.org/"
               encodingStyle="http://schemas.xmlsoap.org/soap/encoding/"/>
         </input>
         <output>
            <soap:body use="encoded"
                       namespace="http://soapinterop.org/"
               encodingStyle="http://schemas.xmlsoap.org/soap/encoding/"/>
         </output>
      </operation>
      <operation name="echoIntegerArray">
         <soap:operation soapAction="http://soapinterop.org/"/>
         <input>
            <soap:body use="encoded"
                       namespace="http://soapinterop.org/"
               encodingStyle="http://schemas.xmlsoap.org/soap/encoding/"/>
         </input>
         <output>
```

```
                <soap:body use="encoded"
                        namespace="http://soapinterop.org/"
                encodingStyle="http://schemas.xmlsoap.org/soap/encoding/"/>
        </output>
    </operation>
    <operation name="echoStruct">
        <soap:operation soapAction="http://soapinterop.org/"/>
        <input>
            <soap:body use="encoded"
                        namespace="http://soapinterop.org/"
                encodingStyle="http://schemas.xmlsoap.org/soap/encoding/"/>
        </input>
        <output>
            <soap:body use="encoded"
                        namespace="http://soapinterop.org/"
                encodingStyle="http://schemas.xmlsoap.org/soap/encoding/"/>
        </output>
    </operation>
  </binding>
  <portType name="InteropTestPortType">
    <operation name="echoString" parameterOrder="inputString">
        <input message="tns:echoStringRequest"
                name="echoString"/>
        <output message="tns:echoStringResponse"
                name="echoStringResponse"/>
    </operation>
    <operation name="echoIntegerArray" parameterOrder="inputIntegerArray">
        <input message="tns:echoIntegerArrayRequest"
                name="echoIntegerArray"/>
        <output message="tns:echoIntegerArrayResponse"
                name="echoIntegerArrayResponse"/>
    </operation>
    <operation name="echoStruct" parameterOrder="inputStruct">
        <input message="tns:echoStructRequest"
                name="echoStruct"/>
        <output message="tns:echoStructResponse"
            name="echoStructResponse"/>
    </operation>
  </portType>
  <message name="echoStringRequest">
    <part name="inputString" type="xsd:string"/>
  </message>
  <message name="echoStringResponse">
    <part name="return" type="xsd:string"/>
  </message>
  <message name="echoIntegerArrayRequest">
    <part name="inputIntegerArray" type="s:ArrayOfint"/>
  </message>
  <message name="echoIntegerArrayResponse">
    <part name="return" type="s:ArrayOfint"/>
  </message>
  <message name="echoStructRequest">
    <part name="inputStruct" type="s:SOAPStruct"/>
  </message>
  <message name="echoStructResponse">
    <part name="return" type="s:SOAPStruct"/>
  </message>
</definitions>
```

Some general points about the service definitions that influence how we build our clients and servers:

- ❏ The SOAPAction namespace used for all methods is `http://soapinterop.org/`
- ❏ The method namespace used for all methods is `http://soapinterop.org/`
- ❏ The SOAP structure `SOAPStruct` is defined within the `http://soapinterop.org/xsd` namespace. It is also defined using the `all` element grouping, indicating that child element order is not important.
- ❏ The version of XML Schema used is 2001.

> One note regarding the use of the 2001 XML Schema: Many of the early SOAP implementations primarily supported the use of the 1999 XML Schema, and in fact two of the three implementations examined in this chapter default to the use of the 1999 XML Schema. Thus, the SOAP envelopes that they produce will not be technically compliant with the WSDL description given above, on this one point.
>
> In practice, the mixing of schema version between clients and servers has had only limited impact on cross-toolkit interoperability, as only a few toolkits throw an exception upon receiving a different version of the schema from the one it natively uses.
>
> In any case, now that the XML Schema is an official W3C Recommendation, many of the toolkits based on the 1999 Schema are now migrating to the 2001 Schema as the default, and we'll start to see this discrepancy less and less.

Examining SOAP Wiredumps with tcpTrace

For our examples, we provide wiredumps of the HTTP request and response between the client and the server. Within those wiredumps, you can examine both the HTTP headers as well as the SOAP envelope XML.

In practice, the ability to examine the wiredumps is absolutely critical to your ability to debug SOAP calls, so having a tool that allows you to do this is highly recommended. There are a few tools out there – for example, the **tcpTunnelGUI** tool (which you can see in action in Chapter 1), written in Java and bundled with Apache SOAP, is a popular choice. The tool that we used to generate our wiredumps in this chapter was **tcpTrace** version 0.4, which is available at http://www.pocketsoap.com/tcptrace. tcpTrace is a native Windows tool.

tcpTrace is a "tunnel" application that sits between your SOAP client and service. Rather than sending its request directly to the service, the client sends it to tcpTrace, which listens on a separate host/port combination. tcpTrace then forwards the request to the actual service and the service response is tunneled back to the client. Since tcpTrace is in the middle, it has visibility of the SOAP envelopes being passed between client and server and makes them available for your viewing. The following diagram should illustrate this more clearly.

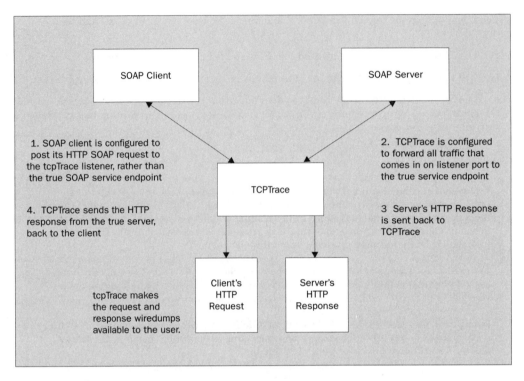

The download link for the tcpTrace zip file is found on the tcpTrace homepage at
http://www.pocketsoap.com/tcptrace. The executable file tcptrace.exe is simply extracted from the
archive and is ready to run out of the box.

As an example, let's say that we have a service running on an endpoint URL of http://localhost:8080/ and
we wish to have tcpTrace record the request and response envelopes to and from the service. We will pick
port 8081 to host the tcpTrace listener.

When we start tcpTrace we see the following startup configuration window – configure it with the following
parameters:

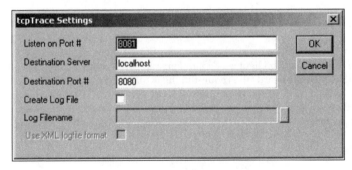

Now click OK. Note that if you want to have the request and response envelopes logged to a file as well, you
can indicate that here, too.

With this configuration, we configure the client to use the endpoint URL http://localhost:8081/. All requests that are sent to port 8081 are then forwarded to the true service on port 8080. When a request comes through, we see the request/response pair logged in tcpTrace:

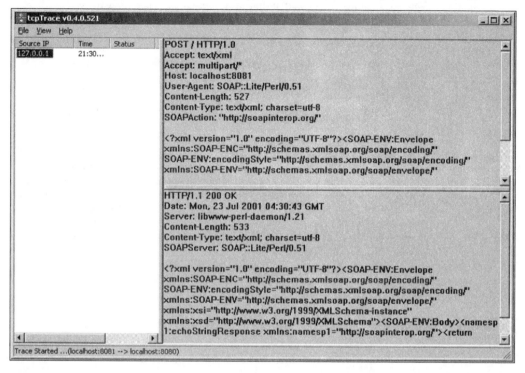

As you send more requests through the tcpTrace tunnel, they are indexed in the left windowpane and you can browse through a history. A very handy feature! Now we will get onto the first of our alternative SOAP implementations, SOAP::Lite for Perl.

SOAP::Lite for Perl

SOAP::Lite, a package written by Paul Kulchenko, is a full-featured and easy-to-use implementation of SOAP for the Perl programming language. It provides the developer with a set of Perl objects that make building SOAP servers and clients easy.

For more information on SOAP::Lite as well as a list of its latest features, visit http://www.soaplite.com. This chapter was written using version 0.50 of SOAP::Lite.

Installing SOAP::Lite

SOAP::Lite is distributed as a standard Perl package, so the normal procedures for Perl package installation apply. The following steps guide you through the installation process. It is applicable for both Windows and UNIX installations except where otherwise noted. An understanding of how to use Perl and how to install Perl packages is assumed.

> **Automating the istallation: If you have the `CPAN.pm` module installed and configured, you can automate the steps described below, from download of the package all the way through installation and testing. An added benefit is that packages that SOAP::Lite is dependent on are automatically installed for you as well, if they aren't already present on your system. Just type**
>
> **> perl –MCPAN –e 'install SOAP::Lite'**
>
> **from the command line.**

Prerequisites

SOAP::Lite requires Perl 5.004 or higher. If you do not have Perl installed already, you can download the **ActivePerl** distribution from ActiveState, http://www.activestate.com. In fact, the ActivePerl distribution comes bundled with SOAP::Lite, so that you don't have to explicitly install it; if so, you can skip this SOAP::Lite installation section. ActiveState provides ActivePerl distributions for both UNIX/Linux and Windows.

SOAP::Lite can be downloaded on its own from the http://www.soaplite.com website. Alternatively, you can download it from your favorite CPAN mirror.

There are two versions available, a tarred and gzipped version for UNIX and a zipped version for Windows. Download and extract your package of choice to a temporary working directory.

Preparing the Makefile

Once you have extracted the SOAP::Lite distribution, change to the distribution directory and run the following:

> **perl Makefile.PL**

You should see something like the following output:

This command creates the `Makefile`, in preparation for the build process. Examine the following prompt found in the screenshot above:

During "make test" phase we may run tests with several SOAP servers that may take long and may fail due to server/connectivity problems.

Do you want to perform these tests in addition to the core tests? [no]

If you decide to override the testing option default so that the SOAP server tests are run, you may see many errors when the tests are run as part of the installation process. This does not necessarily indicate a problem with the installation; there are a large number of these tests, and any or all of them may fail if the remote SOAP server is down or if you cannot connect to the remote servers for a networking reason. These errors do not indicate an actual installation problem!

As you can see, SOAP::Lite provides a wide range of installation options. Which options you choose will determine which Perl packages will be considered prerequisite. Note that if you proceed without having all of your prerequisite modules installed, you will experience an error message like the one seen at the bottom of the following screenshot:

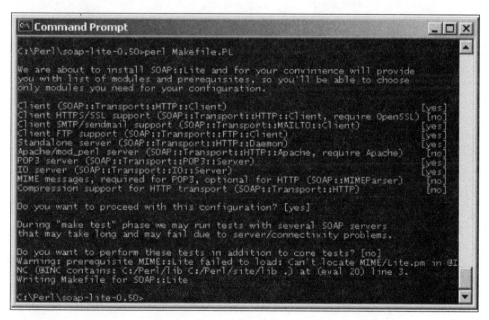

This warning indicates that our system is missing one of the dependencies that SOAP::Lite needs. Please check the `README` file to determine the latest package dependencies. If you are missing any external Perl packages, please install them first before proceeding.

Builiding, Testing, and Installing the Package

Once the `Makefile` has been created, you now need to execute the "make". Build the package by executing the following command in the same directory:

> **make**

Next, you can test the package with

> **make test**

and then install it with

> **make install**

Please note that if you are using the Microsoft development tools, the version of the make program is actually called nmake, so you should do the appropriate substitution in the commands above.

A quick test you can use to verify successful installation is to use the command

> **perl –e "use SOAP::Lite"**

If you receive no error messages, your SOAP::Lite installation is complete. If on the other hand, you receive an error message like this:

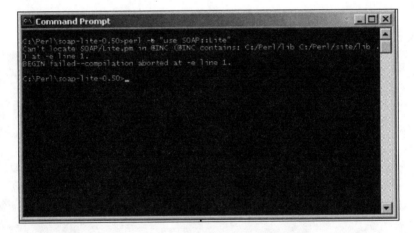

then the SOAP::Lite package has not been installed properly. Please go back and retry the installation, paying special attention to any errors you may come across.

Implementing the Echo Services with SOAP::Lite

Let's walk through the process of building the Echo service, as described in the previous section, as well as the Echo clients

Implementing the echoString Server and Client

First, let's build a server that is compliant with the WSDL service description for the Echo services. We will build a standalone server, using a file that we will now create, called Echo.pl. Let's walk through this code:

```perl
#!/usr/bin/perl

use SOAP::Lite;
use SOAP::Transport::HTTP;
```

```
my $soapServer = SOAP::Transport::HTTP::Daemon
    -> new (LocalPort => 8080)
    -> dispatch_to(qw(echoString echoIntegerArray echoStruct))
    -> on_action (sub {
        die "SOAPAction should be \"http://soapinterop.org/\"\n"
        unless $_[0] eq '"http://soapinterop.org/"'; });
```

This code creates a SOAP service that listens for requests on port 8080. This service is self-contained and runs standalone, with its own integrated HTTP listener in "daemon" mode. **Daemon** processes are persistent-lived processes that handle service requests or take care of housekeeping tasks. Note that SOAP::Lite servers can also be run as CGI applications, Apache mod_perl modules and so on, as well. For information on how to do this, see the SOAP::Lite user guide at http://guide.soaplite.com .

There's a couple of things to pay attention to here.

First of all, the dispatch_to() method either takes a package name or a set of methods, if the methods are defined locally. See the section on service dispatching below for more information on how dispatching works with SOAP::Lite. In this particular example, incoming requests are dispatched to one of three methods defined in the local package.

Secondly, the on_action() method allows you to register a subroutine for validation of SOAPAction. In this example, we strictly validate for the value specified in the WSDL description, http://soapinterop.org/. Note that if we didn't really care to validate, and wanted to accept any SOAPAction value, the subroutine we would pass into on_action() would be an empty one, that is "{ }".

```
print "Starting SOAP server on URL:  " . $soapServer->url ."\n";
$soapServer->handle;
```

This last line is the line that actually kicks off the daemon. The remainder of the source code is the definition of the methods that the server will dispatch to.

```
sub echoString {
    # Receives a string and echoes it back
    my ($class, $inputString) = @_;
    die "no input provided\n" if !$inputString;
    return SOAP::Data->name('return')->type('string')->value($inputString);
}
```

Here, we wrap the returned variable with a SOAP::Data object. The use of SOAP::Data objects allows us to easily fine tune how the parameter is serialized in the SOAP envelope.

Also, we see an illustration of how to throw SOAP faults here. It's very easy; simply throw a Perl exception by executing die() and SOAP::Lite will generate a SOAP fault parameterized as follows:

Fault Parameter	Setting
faultcode	"SOAP-ENV:Server"
faultstring	(text of exception message)
faultactor	Server URL

We now run our code; you should see something like the following:

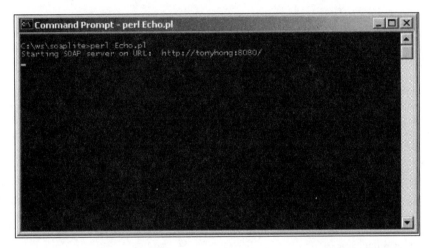

At this point, we have a running server, and you will not see the command prompt return. This is normal, since the server stays running, listening for requests. Now, let's build a client that can utilize the service we just created. The code for the echoString.pl client is shown below:

```perl
#!/usr/bin/perl

use SOAP::Lite;

$inputString="Hello";
$inputSoapParam = SOAP::Data
    ->name('inputString')
    ->type('string')
    ->value($inputString);

$response=SOAP::Lite
    -> proxy('http://localhost:8080/')
    -> uri('http://soapinterop.org/')
    -> on_action( sub { '"http://soapinterop.org/"' })
    -> echoString ($inputSoapParam);
```

This last call is the heart of the SOAP::Lite client. It configures and executes the SOAP remote method invocation. A SOAP::Lite response object is returned and referenced by the $response variable; this object is used to check for any SOAP fault that may have occurred, and to obtain the return value sent back from the server if there was not fault.

The proxy() method defines the SOAP endpoint URL, the HTTP URL that receives our SOAP request. The service publisher also provides this value to the client developer.

The uri() method essentially sets the service identifier for the call; the server uses this identifier to dispatch the call to the proper server-side object. The service publisher must provide this value to the client developer.

The on_action() method allows us to set the SOAPAction sent by the client. By default, the SOAP::Lite client sends a SOAPAction value of form:

```
"[Method Namespace URI]#[Method]"
```

Without this call, our client would be sending a SOAPAction value of
`"http://soapinterop.org/#echoString"`, which, of course, is inconsistent with the WSDL service
definition of the Echo service, which calls for it to be simply `http://soapinterop.org/`. `on_action()`
accepts a subroutine that returns the proper SOAPAction value.

Note that the SOAPAction values must always be explicitly double quoted. The SOAP specification
mandates that these quotes exist for non-null SOAPAction values.

Finally, the `echoString()` method is the server method being invoked. In this case, the `$inputString`
variable, which holds the string we wish to have echoed, is passed to the method. SOAP::Lite takes the name
of this method and uses this as the name of the method in serializing the call into the SOAP envelope, as we
will see.

Let's continue with our program – the fault handling is next.

```
if($response->fault) {
print "SOAP Fault received. \n\n";
print "Fault Code    : " . $response->faultcode   . "\n";
print "Fault String : " . $response->faultstring . "\n";
print "Fault Actor : " . $response->faultactor . "\n";
die;
}
```

If a SOAP fault results, the `$response->fault` will hold a reference to a SOAP::Lite `Fault` object.
Information about the fault itself is provided through a set of methods on the `$response` object.

Fault Info Accessor	Description
$response->faultcode	Returns fault code of the returned fault. Faults sent back from the server are coded as "SOAP-ENV:Server". Faults originating on the client are coded "SOAP-ENV:Client"
$response->faultstring	Returns diagnostic text for the returned fault; corresponds to the `faultstring` text in the SOAP Fault envelope.
$response->faultdetail	Perl string or hash holding additional fault information.
$response->faultactor	Returns information about who threw the fault; derived from the `faultactor` element in the SOAP Fault envelope.

If a network fault is encountered, which may result, for example, if the client is unable to bind to the TCP
socket of the SOAP endpoint, then the program will die immediately with an error message.

If no fault resulted and the call was successful, the return value from the remote method is accessed via the
variable `$response->result`, as is shown below in the final line of our client program:

```
print "Sent '".$inputString."', received '".$response->result ."'\n"
```

The complete versions of all the code files in this chapter can be found in this book's code download,
available from http://www.wrox.com/.

If we run the client program with $inputString set to "Hello", we get the following output:

```
Sent 'Hello', received 'Hello'
```

As you may remember, the server checks the echoString input parameter to see if it is an empty string, and if so, an exception is throw via the die() method. The SOAP::Lite server libraries translate this exception into a SOAP fault.

If we run this program with $inputString set to empty string (""), we receive the SOAP fault from the server. In our client program, this fault is detected by checking $response->fault, and printing the fault information, as follows:

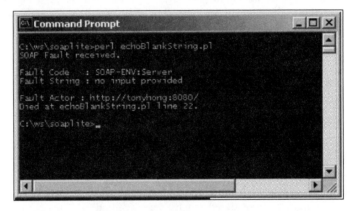

Finally, let's take a look at the request and response SOAP envelopes generated by the client and server for a successful echoString call. The client request is:

```
POST / HTTP/1.0
Accept: text/xml
Accept: multipart/*
Host: tony.xmethods.net:8080
User-Agent: SOAP::Lite/Perl/0.50
Content-Length: 512
Content-Type: text/xml; charset=utf-8
SOAPAction: "http://soapinterop.org/"

<?xml version="1.0" encoding="UTF-8"?>
<SOAP-ENV:Envelope
    xmlns:SOAP-ENC="http://schemas.xmlsoap.org/soap/encoding/"
    SOAP-ENV:encodingStyle="http://schemas.xmlsoap.org/soap/encoding/"
    xmlns:xsi="http://www.w3.org/1999/XMLSchema-instance"
    xmlns:SOAP-ENV="http://schemas.xmlsoap.org/soap/envelope/"
    xmlns:xsd="http://www.w3.org/1999/XMLSchema">
    <SOAP-ENV:Body>
        <namesp1:echoString xmlns:namesp1="http://soapinterop.org/">
            <inputString xsi:type="xsd:string">hello</inputString>
        </namesp1:echoString>
    </SOAP-ENV:Body>
</SOAP-ENV:Envelope>
```

The server response is:

```
HTTP/1.1 200 OK
Date: Sat, 16 Jun 2001 10:49:50 GMT
Server: libwww-perl-daemon/1.24
Content-Length: 533
Content-Type: text/xml
SOAPServer: SOAP::Lite/Perl/0.50

<?xml version="1.0" encoding="UTF-8"?>
<SOAP-ENV:Envelope
   xmlns:SOAP-ENC="http://schemas.xmlsoap.org/soap/encoding/"
   SOAP-ENV:encodingStyle="http://schemas.xmlsoap.org/soap/encoding/"
   xmlns:xsi="http://www.w3.org/1999/XMLSchema-instance"
   xmlns:SOAP-ENV="http://schemas.xmlsoap.org/soap/envelope/"
   xmlns:xsd="http://www.w3.org/1999/XMLSchema">
   <SOAP-ENV:Body>
      <namesp1:echoStringResponse xmlns:namesp1="http://soapinterop.org/">
         <return xsi:type="xsd:string">hello</return>
      </namesp1:echoStringResponse>
   </SOAP-ENV:Body>
</SOAP-ENV:Envelope>
```

> **SOAP::Lite has an easy built-in way for you to examine the request and response SOAP envelopes when running a SOAP::Lite client – just use the "+ trace" modifier on the package import for SOAP::Lite within the client program file, like so:**
>
> **> use SOAP::Lite +trace ;**

The only way these envelopes are non-compliant with the WSDL description is that SOAP::Lite by default uses the 1999 schema for its XML encoding, as opposed to using the 2001 version. In the 0.50 version of SOAP::Lite used for this writing, this is not configurable, but by the time you read this, the latest version of SOAP::Lite will have support for the 2001 XML Schema incorporated.

Note also here that the name of the server response element is `echoStringResponse`. The SOAP::Lite server by default uses the name of the method with the string "Response" appended to it, as is suggested by the SOAP Specification.

Implementing the echoIntegerArray Server and Client

In the simple client example above we showed how the client was able to invoke a remote method with a basic type (string) as a parameter. Now, let's see how we handle passing arrays with SOAP::Lite.

Let's add the method `echoIntegerArray()` to the server we built in the last example.

```perl
#!/usr/bin/perl

use SOAP::Lite;
use SOAP::Transport::HTTP;

my $soapServer = SOAP::Transport::HTTP::Daemon
   -> new (LocalPort => 8080)
```

```
    -> dispatch_to(qw(echoString echoIntegerArray echoStruct))
    -> on_action (sub {
          die "SOAPAction should be \"http://soapinterop.org/\"\n"
          unless $_[0] eq '"http://soapinterop.org/"'; });

print "Starting SOAP server on URL:  " . $soapServer->url ."\n";
$soapServer->handle;

sub echoString  {
   # Receives a string and echoes it back
   my ($class, $inputString) = @_;
   die "no input provided\n" if !$inputString;
   return SOAP::Data->name("return")->type("string")->value($inputString);
}
```

```
sub echoIntegerArray {
   my($class,$inputIntegerArray)=@_;

   # Create our results Array, an array of SOAP::Data objects
   my @resultsArray;
   foreach $inputInteger (@{$inputIntegerArray}) {
      push @resultsArray,
         SOAP::Data->name('item')->type('int')->value($inputInteger);
   }

   return SOAP::Data->name('return')->value(\@resultsArray);
}
```

Here, we return an array of SOAP::Data objects, each of which wraps a single integer. As you can see in the code that creates the array, each array element parameter is named item, consistent with the definition of the array in the schema definition of the WSDL types. As was the case in the echostring example, we return the array itself wrapped in a SOAP::Data object with a name of "return", to be consistent with the WSDL definition of the return parameter.

> **Hint:** While the SOAP 1.1 specification states that names of the array elements are inconsequential, it's good practice to make sure that the array element names match up to any XML Schema definitions of the array that may be published in a WSDL file, in case the server implementation does strict validation of the parameter encoding against a schema.

The client code to invoke the echoIntegerArray() method is shown below:

```
#!/usr/bin/perl

use SOAP::Lite;

@intarray=(
   SOAP::Data->name('item')->type('int')->value(0),
   SOAP::Data->name('item')->type('int')->value(1),
   SOAP::Data->name('item')->type('int')->value(2)
);
```

Here, we pass in our array of `SOAP::Data` objects as an argument for the SOAP call:

```
$response=SOAP::Lite
    -> proxy('http://localhost:8080/')
    -> uri('http://soapinterop.org/')
    -> on_action( sub { '"http://soapinterop.org/"' })
    -> echoIntegerArray(
    SOAP::Data->name("inputIntegerArray")->value(\@intarray)
    );
```

Now, let's check our results. If the call was successful, we print out the returned array. Note here that by the time we call the `result()` method, the deserializer has "unwrapped" the response parameters so that only native Perl variables, not `SOAP::Data` objects, are returned to us.

```
if($response->fault) {
    print "SOAP Fault received. \n\n";
    print "Fault Code   : " . $response->faultcode   . "\n";
    print "Fault String : " . $response->faultstring . "\n";
    print "Fault Actor : " . $response->faultactor . "\n";
    die;
}
else {
    @retArray=@{$response->result};
    print "RECEIVED: \n";
    foreach $returnVal (@retArray){
        print "Integer Array Element: ".$returnVal."\n";
    }
}
```

Running this program results in the following output:

Let's look at the request/reply envelopes that this client and server generate:

```
POST / HTTP/1.0
Accept: text/xml
Accept: multipart/*
Host: tony.xmethods.net:8080
User-Agent: SOAP::Lite/Perl/0.50
Content-Length: 675
Content-Type: text/xml; charset=utf-8
SOAPAction: "http://soapinterop.org/"
```

```
<?xml version="1.0" encoding="UTF-8"?>
<SOAP-ENV:Envelope
      xmlns:SOAP-ENC="http://schemas.xmlsoap.org/soap/encoding/"
      SOAP-ENV:encodingStyle="http://schemas.xmlsoap.org/soap/encoding/"
      xmlns:xsi="http://www.w3.org/1999/XMLSchema-instance"
      xmlns:SOAP-ENV="http://schemas.xmlsoap.org/soap/envelope/"
      xmlns:xsd="http://www.w3.org/1999/XMLSchema">

  <SOAP-ENV:Body>
    <namesp1:echoIntegerArray xmlns:namesp1="http://soapinterop.org/">
      <SOAP-ENC:Array SOAP-ENC:arrayType="xsd:int[3]"
                    xsi:type="SOAP-ENC:Array">
        <item xsi:type="xsd:int">0</item>
        <item xsi:type="xsd:int">1</item>
        <item xsi:type="xsd:int">2</item>
      </SOAP-ENC:Array>
    </namesp1:echoIntegerArray>
  </SOAP-ENV:Body>
</SOAP-ENV:Envelope>
```

The server response is:

```
HTTP/1.1 200 OK
Date: Sat, 16 Jun 2001 10:56:06 GMT
Server: libwww-perl-daemon/1.24
Content-Length: 675
Content-Type: text/xml
SOAPServer: SOAP::Lite/Perl/0.50

<?xml version="1.0" encoding="UTF-8"?>
<SOAP-ENV:Envelope
      xmlns:SOAP-ENC="http://schemas.xmlsoap.org/soap/encoding/"
      SOAP-ENV:encodingStyle="http://schemas.xmlsoap.org/soap/encoding/"
      xmlns:xsi="http://www.w3.org/1999/XMLSchema-instance"
      xmlns:SOAP-ENV="http://schemas.xmlsoap.org/soap/envelope/"
      xmlns:xsd="http://www.w3.org/1999/XMLSchema">

  <SOAP-ENV:Body>
    <namesp3:echoIntegerArrayResponse
    xmlns:namesp3="http://soapinterop.org/">
      <return SOAP-ENC:arrayType="xsd:int[3]"
            xsi:type="SOAP-ENC:Array">
        <item xsi:type="xsd:int">0</item>
        <item xsi:type="xsd:int">1</item>
        <item xsi:type="xsd:int">2</item>
      </return>
    </namesp3:echoIntegerArrayResponse>
  </SOAP-ENV:Body>
</SOAP-ENV:Envelope>
```

The serialization of the array parameter is consistent with the WSDL definition of the array and the return parameter.

Implementing the echoStruct Server and Client

Now, we turn our attention to the third and final method, `echoStruct()`. In this example, we see how we handle the passing of SOAP structures, which map to and from Perl hashes. Let's start with our additions to the `Echo.pl` source file, highlighted below:

```perl
#!/usr/bin/perl

use SOAP::Lite;
use SOAP::Transport::HTTP;

my $soapServer = SOAP::Transport::HTTP::Daemon
    -> new (LocalPort => 8080)
    -> dispatch_to(qw(echoString echoIntegerArray echoStruct))
    -> on_action (sub {
          die "SOAPAction should be \"http://soapinterop.org/\"\n"
          unless $_[0] eq '"http://soapinterop.org/"'; });

$soapServer->serializer->maptype({SOAPStruct =>
'http://soapinterop.org/xsd'});
```

The standard Echo WSDL definition of the `SOAPStruct` complex type occurs within the namespace `http://soapinterop.org/xsd`. SOAP::Lite maintains its own internal registry of SOAP types and the namespaces associated with those types. We need to associate this namespace with the `SOAPStruct` type so that the server's serializer associates the namespace with the type in the serialized parameter when echoing the structure back – `maptype()` is used for this purpose.

> In XML Schemas, user-derived types (SOAP structures) are defined within a namespace. When a `SOAP::Data` object wrapping a Perl hash is serialized into a SOAP structure during the SOAP envelope creation process, the XML element that represents the parameter is declared within this namespace.
>
> Of course, this namespace information is not carried with the Perl hash itself. SOAP::Data objects can be associated with the hash to specify name and type, but they do not carry the namespace value that is associated with the XML Schema definition for the type. In order to allow SOAP::Lite to attach the proper namespace, the `maptype()` method is used. This method can be used on both the client and server.

Continuing with the code....

```perl
print "Starting SOAP server on URL:  " . $soapServer->url ."\n";
$soapServer->handle;

sub echoString  {
   # Receives a string and echoes it back
   my ($class, $inputString) = @_;
   die "no input provided\n" if !$inputString;
   return SOAP::Data->name("return")->type("string")->value($inputString);
}

sub echoIntegerArray {
   my($class,$inputIntegerArray)=@_;
```

```
    # Create our results Array, an array of SOAP::Data objects
    my @resultsArray;
    foreach $inputInteger (@{$inputIntegerArray}) {
        push @resultsArray,
            SOAP::Data->name('item')->type('int')->value($inputInteger);
    }

    return SOAP::Data->name('return')->value(\@resultsArray);
}
```

```
sub echoStruct {
    my ($class, $inputStruct) = @_;
    return SOAP::Data->name('return')->type('SOAPStruct')
->value($inputStruct);
}
```

We wrap the return SOAPStruct hash in a SOAP::Data object, setting the name of the parameter and associating the parameter with the SOAPStruct type. Remember, the maptype() method has already mapped the proper namespace to this particular type. Between the SOAP::Data object and the namespace associated with the type in the type mapping registry, the serializer has everything it needs to generate the proper serialization of the parameter.

Note that by the time the server method receives the structure $inputStruct, it has already been "unwrapped" into it's basic Perl hash representation.

Now, here's the client:

```
#!/usr/bin/perl

use SOAP::Lite;

my %SOAPStruct = (
        varString => "test string",
        varInt => 5,
        varFloat => 6.2
    );

$response=SOAP::Lite
    -> uri('http://soapinterop.org/')
    -> proxy('http://localhost:8080/')
    -> on_action( sub { '"http://soapinterop.org/"' })
    -> maptype({SOAPStruct => 'http://soapinterop.org/xsd'})
    -> echoStruct(
    SOAP::Data->name("inputStruct")->type('SOAPStruct')->value(\%SOAPStruct)
    );

if($response->fault) {
        print "SOAP Fault received. \n\n";
        print "Fault Code    : " . $response->faultcode   . "\n";
        print "Fault String : " . $response->faultstring . "\n";
        print "Fault Actor : " . $response->faultactor . "\n";
        die;
}
```

```
    else {
        print "RECEIVED: \n";
        print "varString : ".$response->result->{varString}."\n";
        print "varInt : ".$response->result->{varInt}."\n";
        print "varFloat : ".$response->result->{varFloat}."\n";
    }
```

Here we see that we also need to use `maptype()` on the client to ensure that the proper namespace gets attached to the `SOAPStruct` type, and that we pass in a `SOAP::Data` object into the `echoStruct` method call. Also note that, like in the case of the Integer Array client, we pass in the scalar reference to the hash, not the actual hash itself.

Running the client, we see the following:

which is our expected result.

Let's look at the envelopes now. First the client request:

```
POST / HTTP/1.0
Accept: text/xml
Accept: multipart/*
Host: tony.xmethods.net:80
User-Agent: SOAP::Lite/Perl/0.50
Content-Length: 711
Content-Type: text/xml; charset=utf-8
SOAPAction: "http://soapinterop.org/"

<?xml version="1.0" encoding="UTF-8"?>
<SOAP-ENV:Envelope
    xmlns:SOAP-ENC="http://schemas.xmlsoap.org/soap/encoding/"
    SOAP-ENV:encodingStyle="http://schemas.xmlsoap.org/soap/encoding/"
    xmlns:xsi="http://www.w3.org/1999/XMLSchema-instance"
    xmlns:SOAP-ENV="http://schemas.xmlsoap.org/soap/envelope/"
    xmlns:xsd="http://www.w3.org/1999/XMLSchema"
    xmlns:namesp1="http://soapinterop.org/xsd">

    <SOAP-ENV:Body>
        <namesp2:echoStruct xmlns:namesp2="http://soapinterop.org/">
            <inputStruct xsi:type="namesp1:SOAPStruct">
                <varFloat xsi:type="xsd:float">6.2</varFloat>
                <varString xsi:type="xsd:string">test string</varString>
                <varInt xsi:type="xsd:int">5</varInt>
            </inputStruct>
        </namesp2:echoStruct>
    </SOAP-ENV:Body>
</SOAP-ENV:Envelope>
```

The server response is:

```
HTTP/1.1 200 OK
Date: Sat, 16 Jun 2001 11:03:14 GMT
Server: libwww-perl-daemon/1.24
Content-Length: 717
Content-Type: text/xml
SOAPServer: SOAP::Lite/Perl/0.50

<?xml version="1.0" encoding="UTF-8"?>
<SOAP-ENV:Envelope
    xmlns:SOAP-ENC="http://schemas.xmlsoap.org/soap/encoding/"
    SOAP-ENV:encodingStyle="http://schemas.xmlsoap.org/soap/encoding/"
    xmlns:xsi="http://www.w3.org/1999/XMLSchema-instance"
    xmlns:SOAP-ENV="http://schemas.xmlsoap.org/soap/envelope/"
    xmlns:xsd="http://www.w3.org/1999/XMLSchema"
    xmlns:namesp1="http://soapinterop.org/xsd">

    <SOAP-ENV:Body>
        <namesp2:echoStructResponse xmlns:namesp2="http://soapinterop.org/">
            <return xsi:type="namesp1:SOAPStruct">
                <varFloat xsi:type="xsd:float">6.2</varFloat>
                <varString xsi:type="xsd:string">test string</varString>
                <varInt xsi:type="xsd:int">5</varInt>
            </return>
        </namesp2:echoStructResponse>
    </SOAP-ENV:Body>
</SOAP-ENV:Envelope>
```

Pay special attention to the serialization of the SOAPStruct structure. As you see, it adheres to the standard WSDL description of the service.

One other note of interest here – as you can see from the serialized structure, Perl does not maintain order when it serializes a hash into a structure. When we created the hash in the code, we defined the fields in the following order:

1. varString

2. varInt

3. varFloat

but as we see in the envelope, the structure's child elements appear in this order:

1. varFloat

2. varString

3. varInt

This is due to the fact that Perl hashes are not ordered. In the case of this service definition, that's OK – the structure is defined using the all element grouping:

```
<complexType name="SOAPStruct">
   <all>
      <element name="varString" type="string"/>
      <element name="varInt" type="int"/>
      <element name="varFloat" type="float"/>
   </all>
</complexType>
```

This means that a specific child element order is not mandated. Had it been defined with sequence, which **does** mandate order, our client may not be able to reliably bind to the service if the service strictly validates a specific order.

More SOAP::Lite Basics

To round off this section on SOAP::Lite, let's take a look at some additional basic features of SOAP::Lite.

Fault Handlers for SOAP::Lite Clients

We've seen that a SOAP::Lite client's default behavior is to throw an exception immediately if it encounters a network fault, but to continue execution if a SOAP fault is sent back from the server, storing the fault details in the SOAP response object.

We can change this default behavior. The on_fault() method defines a subroutine that is executed if either a network fault or a SOAP fault occurs during the method call. The scope of a fault handler may be a single SOAP::Lite invocation, or global for all the invocations, depending on where we define the on_fault() to register the new fault handler.

Local Definition of Fault Handler

```
my $response = SOAP::Lite
        -> uri('urn:Echo')
        -> proxy('http://localhost:8080')
        -> on_fault(sub {
        my($soap, $res) = @_;
        die ref $res ? $res->faultstring : $soap->transport->status;
     })
        -> echoString($inputString);
```

Let's look at exactly what we are doing here. Upon the occurrence of any fault, the subroutine defined by on_fault() is executed. The $res variable holds the SOAP::Lite response object with the faultcode and faultstring information, provided the fault occurred at the SOAP level. Otherwise, the fault occurred at the transport level and $res will be undefined. In this case, the variable $soap->transport->status holds the transport error information.

Global Definition of Fault Handler

The on_fault() method can be defined globally instead of at the level of the single method invocation. This is done by specifying the method on the package import, rather than at the object level.

As an example, examine the following package import statement:

```
use SOAP::Lite
        on_fault => sub { my($soap, $res) = @_;
        die ref $res ? $res->faultstring : $soap->transport->status, "\n"; };
```

The default handler will be in effect for all SOAP::Lite method invocations made within the file.

Client Configuration via WSDL Binding

Our examples assume that no WSDL service description for our server is available. However, SOAP::Lite clients can also bind to WSDL documents that describe a service. The WSDL binding process configures everything that the service needs to invoke the method, including proper SOAPAction value, parameter names, parameter types, method namespace values, and so on. Binding to services via WSDL can greatly simplify things for the client.

To bind to a WSDL file, we use the `service()` method. Here's an example:

```
my $service = SOAP::Lite
    -> service("http://localhost/soaplite/EchoService.wsdl");
```

This method gives you back a `service` object. To invoke the method, simply call the method using the `service` object:

```
my $retString = $service->echoString($inputString);
```

An important point to note here is that when binding via WSDL, clients may forego entirely the use of `SOAP::Data` objects and instead pass in the native Perl variables. In other words, rather than using

```
$retString= $service -> echoString (
    SOAP::Data->name("inputString")
            ->type("string")
            ->value("Hello"));
```

we can instead simply use:

```
$retString= $service -> echoString ("Hello");
```

Why is this? Remember, the `SOAP::Data` object is important because the serializer needs to have meta information about how to serialize native language parameters into SOAP, and `SOAP::Data` allows you to attach that meta-information to your Perl variables. When binding via WSDL, the serializer looks to the WSDL description for this meta information instead.

The variable returned into `$retString` is the actual return value from the remote method. This is somewhat different from the return value of the remote method invocation using the conventional configuration approach described earlier; in that case, a response object is returned and to actually retrieve the return value of the call, you call the `result()` method on that object.

To access a fault from the object, by using the service object's `call()` method:

```
$service->call->fault
```

holds the pointer to the fault object, if a fault occurs, and

```
$service->call->faultcode
$service->call->faultstring
$service->call->faultdetail
```

are used to access the fault information.

Service Dispatching

The first thing that a SOAP::Lite server needs to do with an incoming SOAP request message is to figure out which Perl object holds the method being invoked. Let's take a closer look at how SOAP::Lite servers perform this dispatching of incoming requests.

The key to dispatching is the **method namespace URI** of the SOAP Envelope (abbreviated as **URI** hereon). On the client side, the URI is set by the uri() method. SOAP::Lite expects the URI to be in one of two different forms:

- ❑ urn:CLASS
- ❑ http://urltext/CLASS

where CLASS is the name of the Perl class being targeted for method invocation.

In our specific example, we saw that our server used the dispatch() command to direct incoming requests directly to methods in our local package. Actually, as it turns out for this example, the fact that the methods were in the same package as the server code was a requirement. Why?

The WSDL description of the service mandated a method namespace value of http://soapinterop.org/. As you can see, there is no CLASS value here. So SOAP::Lite dispatcher was not able to route the request to an external package based on the method namespace URI.

Had the mandated method namespace been http://soapinterop.org/interop, then we would have used the following:

```
my $soapServer = SOAP::Transport::HTTP::Daemon
    -> new (LocalPort => 8080)
    -> dispatch_to('interop')
    -> on_action (sub {
        die "SOAPAction should be \"http://soapinterop.org/\"\n"
        unless $_[0] eq '"http://soapinterop.org/"'; });
```

In addition, we would have placed our server methods into a Perl package called interop.

In general, if the name of the target class derived from the URI doesn't match the class indicated in the dispatch_to() method, an exception is thrown on the server and a SOAP Fault will be returned to the client.

SOAP::Lite servers can also be configured to dispatch to one of a set of packages; this is done by specifying more than one class name in the dispatch_to() method. There is also an option to specify a directory that holds Perl packages, rather than specifying the classes themselves.

Character Set Encoding

SOAP::Lite by default uses UTF-8 character set encoding. To change the encoding declaration on the SOAP envelope, use the encoding() method. As an example, the following code fragment shows how to force the envelope to specify the use of the ISO-8859-1 character set encoding rather than UTF-8:

```
my $response = SOAP::Lite
    -> proxy (...)
    -> uri (...)
    -> encoding('iso-8859-1')
    -> echoString($string);
```

Of course, the actual encoding of the parameters that you are passing must match the value that you specify within the encoding() method.

Now, let's turn our attention to the next toolkit, EasySoap++.

EasySoap++

EasySoap++ is a SOAP toolkit for C++. With it, you can build both SOAP clients and SOAP servers on a variety of platforms, including Linux/UNIX and Windows. It is an open-source project housed at SourceForge, a website that is home to a number of open source projects. EasySoap's homepage at SourceForge is http://sourceforge.net/projects/easysoap.

This chapter was written using the latest release of EasySoap++, version 0.4, on a Linux system. However, we will attempt to accommodate MS users in this section too (see below)!

Installing EasySoap++

> **MS Visual C++ 6 Users:**
>
> While our look at EasySoap++ is UNIX/Linux/GNU-focused, an EasySoap++ DLL can be easily built with Windows Visual C++. We'll provide some side notes throughout this installation section to explain how.

Prerequisites

EasySoap++ has dependencies on two packages – one required, one optional:

❑ **Expat** is required. It is a widely used open-source XML parser that is housed on SourceForge at http://sourceforge.net/projects/expat. EasySoap++ uses Expat for its basic XML processing needs. If you don't have Expat installed on your system already then don't worry – we take you through the installation process below.

❑ **OpenSSL** is an optional package, necessary only if you want to create clients that utilize SSL to connect to servers via HTTPS. The OpenSSL project is housed at http://www.openssl.org. Since it is only optional and we do NOT assume that you have it installed for our examples, we will not walk through how to install it. Please visit the OpenSSL website for more details if you are interested.

In general, it's a good idea to check the EasySoap++ README file included with the distribution for the latest installation notes.

Obtaining and Installing Expat

Since Expat is a required prerequisite package, we'll walk through how to install it. As of this writing, the latest release of Expat is version 1.95.2, which is downloadable at http://download.sourceforge.net/expat/expat-1.95.2.tar.gz.

MS Visual C++ 6 Users:

There is a Windows installer available for Expat 1.95.2 – download and run
http://prdownloads.sourceforge.net/expat/expat_win32bin_1_95_2.exe. When
the installer prompts you for the installation directory, please create a directory with the
name **expat-1.95.2** in the same directory that will hold the EasySoap++-0.4 directory.
for example, if you are planning to install EasySoap++0.4 at **c:\easysoap++-0.4,** you
would want the installer to install expat at **c:\expat-1.95.2.** The reason for this is that
the Windows build file for EasySoap++ 0.4 is hardwired to look for the expat distribution
in a directory called **expat-1.95.2** at the same level as the EasySoap++-0.4 directory.
For more information, consult the EasySoap++ README file.

Once you've done this, jump to the next section on installing EasySoap++.

Download and unpack the distribution into the directory of your choice with the command:

> gunzip –c expat-1.95.2.tar.gz | tar xvf –

You'll see the directory expat-1.95.2 produced from the archive extraction. Move into this directory and
run the executable configure script. In any case, you should see a display like the following:

```
[tony@concord expat-1.95.2]$ ./configure
loading cache ./config.cache
checking host system type... i686-pc-linux-gnu
checking build system type... i686-pc-linux-gnu
checking for ranlib... (cached) ranlib
checking for gcc... (cached) gcc
checking whether the C compiler (gcc ) works... yes
checking whether the C compiler (gcc ) is a cross-compiler... no
checking whether we are using GNU C... (cached) yes
checking whether gcc accepts -g... (cached) yes
checking for ld used by GCC... (cached) /usr/bin/ld
checking if the linker (/usr/bin/ld) is GNU ld... (cached) yes
checking for BSD-compatible nm... (cached) /usr/bin/nm -B
checking whether ln -s works... (cached) yes
checking for object suffix... o
```

The configure script analyzes your system in preparation for building the Expat libraries, and generates the
Makefile for your upcoming Expat build.

NOTE: By default, the expat build process places the expat library files into
/usr/local/lib and the expat header file into **/usr/local/include**. If you want to
have the files placed elsewhere, use the command

./configure -prefix=PREFIX_PATH

where **PREFIX_PATH** is the path to where you want the installation to occur. The build
process will then place the library and the include file into **PREFIX_PATH/lib/** and
PREFIX_PATH/include/, respectively.

Finally, move back to the top of the `expat` directory and build the libraries with the command

> make

If the build completes properly, the last step you have to perform is to install the libraries. Run the command

> make install

> If you stayed with the defaults when you ran the configure program, you may need to have root permissions to install into the `/usr/local/lib` and `/usr/local/include` directories. The default build process will produce both static and shared object libraries.

Obtaining and Installing EasySoap++

EasySoap++ is available at http://www.sourceforge.net/projects/easysoap. It is distributed as a tar/gzipped file. Unpack it, and you'll see a directory called `easysoap`. That is the root directory for the distribution.

If you were with us in the preceeding section to install Expat, you'll find that the installation process for EasySoap++ is very similar.

Move into the `easysoap` directory and run the `configure` program, as seen below:

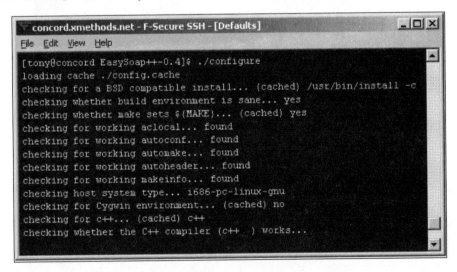

The configure program generates the appropriate `Makefile` for the build we are about to do of EasySoap++.

> NOTE: By default, the EasySoap++ build process places the EasySoap++ library file into
> `/usr/local/lib/`, and the header files into `/usr/local/include/easysoap/`. If
> you want to have the files placed elsewhere, use the following command:
>
> `./configure -prefix=PREFIX_PATH`
>
> Where `PREFIX_PATH` is the path to where you want the installation to occur. The build
> process will then place the library and the include file into `PREFIX_PATH/lib/` and
> `PREFIX_PATH/include/easysoap/`, respectively.
>
> Also, if you installed Expat into a non-standard location in the previous section, you may
> need to pass in the location of the directories holding the Expat library and include files to
> the configure program. To do this, `set` (and on UNIX systems, `export`) the
> environmental variables `LIBS` for the library path and `CPPFLAGS` for the include path for
> the Expat libraries. For example, if you are running the Bash shell on a Linux system you
> might use the following:
>
> `export CPPFLAGS="-I/path/to/include/dir"`
> `LIBS="-L/path/to/libs/dir"`
>
> before running the configure program.

The next step is to run the build. Run the command

> **make**

to kick it off. Once the make process has completed successfully, you can run

> **make install**

to install it. EasySoap++ will copy the library and header files into `/usr/local/lib/` and
`/usr/local/include/easysoap/` by default, unless you specified otherwise in the configure step (see
the note above).

> **MS Visual C++ 6 Users:**
>
> To build EasySoap++ under Visual Studio, open the visual workspace file `easysoap.dsw`
> located in top level of the EasySoap++ directory. By hitting F7 or selecting **Build
> easysoap.dll** from the **Build** menu, you will build the `easysoap.dll` and
> `easysoap.lib` files, which will reside in directory `win32\ReleaseSymbols`.
>
> Remember that for this to work, you must have installed Expat in the same parent
> directory that the EasySoap++-0.4 directory is installed. See the Windows installation
> notes for Expat in the previous section.

Building the Echo Service and Clients

In this next section, we'll look at how we build the Echo services and clients. As you can see from the Makefiles that we are working with, we use the compiler flags for the Linux/GNU environment, so you should adjust accordingly if you are building in a different environment.

> **MS Visual C++ Users:**
>
> The Visual development environments don't use Makefiles, so you can ignore any talk of them in the examples below. However, you need to be sure to configure your Visual environment to link in the EasySoap++ and Expat **DLL** and **lib** files we created in the installation section.

echoString

Let's look at how to build the `echoString` service and the client that exercises it. Let's start with the following `Makefile`:

```
# The directory $EXPAT/lib should hold your expat library
EXPAT := /usr/local

# The  easysoap distribution
EASYHOME := /usr/local
```

Be sure to replace the `EASYHOME` value with the correct path for your installation!

```
EASYDIR := $(EASYHOME)/lib
EASYSOAPLIB := $(EASYDIR)/libeasysoap.a
CPPFLAGS := -I$(EASYHOME)/include/easysoap

# Linux Flags
CXXFLAGS := -g -Wall
LDFLAGS := -L$(EXPAT)/lib -L$(EASYDIR) -leasysoap -lexpat

# SunOS Flags
#CXXFLAGS := -g -Wall
#LDFLAGS := -L$(EXPAT)/lib -L$(EASYDIR) -leasysoap -lexpat -lsocket -lnsl

# Cygwin Flags
#CXXFLAGS := -g -Wall
#LDFLAGS := -L$(EXPAT)/lib -L$(EASYDIR) -leasysoap -lexpat -lwsock32
```

Make sure that the appropriate flags for your operating system are uncommented.

```
all : Echo.cgi

Echo.cgi : Echo.o $(EASYSOAPLIB)
# The line below is a TAB, not 8 spaces
        g++ -g -static -o $@ $< $(LDFLAGS)

$(EASYSOAPLIB) :
```

```
# The line below is a TAB, not 8 spaces
        cd $(EASYHOME)/src; make

clean:
# The line below is a TAB, not 8 spaces
        rm -f *.o Echo.cgi
```

If you are typing this `Makefile` in by hand, please take note of the TAB comments.

Let's create our simple server next. Create a new file in the project directory and name this file `Echo.cpp`, the name that is consistent with the `Makefile`. First, some includes:

```
#include <SOAP.h>
#include <SOAPCGIServer.h>
```

As you can see, building a simple EasySoap++ Soap server in CGI form requires only two includes. `SOAP.h` is the core include file that houses most of the necessary EasySoap++ definitions. The `SOAPCGIServer.h` file is used specifically for CGI servers.

First, we define the method `EchoHandler`. This is the handler that processes the incoming SOAP request, taking care of dispatching the request to the appropriate method.

```
class EchoHandler : public SOAPDispatchHandler<EchoHandler>
{
public:
    EchoHandler()
    {
        const char * ns = "http://soapinterop.org/";
        DispatchMethod("echoString", ns, &EchoHandler::echoString);
    }

    ~EchoHandler() {}

    EchoHandler * GetTarget(const SOAPEnvelope& request)
    {
        return this;
    }
```

Here, we see that in the constructor for the handler, each of the methods we wish to have published is registered with the `DispatchMethod()` method. The method name, method namespace, and the pointer to the method are all provided as arguments.

Now, we get to the `echoString()` method itself.

```
    void echoString(const SOAPMethod& request, SOAPMethod& response)
    {
        SOAPString val;
        request.GetParameter("inputString") >> val;
        if(!strcmp(val,"")) {
            throw SOAPException("error - no input provided");
        response.AddParameter("return") << val;
    }
};
```

As you can see, two arguments are provided to the `echoString()` method, which are both handles to SOAPMethod objects. The first SOAPMethod object, `request`, carries the input parameters as well as any header information carried with the request. The method then adds the `return` parameter into the response SOAPMethod object.

SOAPMethod objects hold representations of SOAP envelopes, including header information, parameters, etc. In the `echoString()` method, we simply take the response object that the server has instantiated for us and add to it the return parameter that we will stream back to the client. We do this by calling the `AddParameter()` method and configuring the resulting new parameter object with the basic `SOAPString` variable; the mapping is managed by the definition of the overloaded operator <<. For a more detailed look at how this works, see the *Parameter Serialization* section below.

Moving on, we show the `main()` for the CGI server next:

```
int main(int argc, char* argv[], char *env[])
{
    SOAPCGIServer cgi;
    EchoHandler echohandle;
    return cgi.DispatchTo(&echohandle).Handle();
}
```

In the last line above, two things are happening. First, the appropriate handler is registered with the CGI to process incoming requests using the `DispatchTo()` method. After the registration, the `Handle()` method sends the incoming request to the handler.

That's it for the code. Let's compile the source code to produce the executable by running

> **make**

which produces the CGI executable `Echo.cgi`. We then copy it to an appropriate CGI directory on our web server.

As you can see, we've just created a version of the Echo server we know and love. Let's now turn our attention to the corresponding Echo client. We'll build the client, `echoString`, in the same build directory as the server. Let's modify our `Makefile` to accommodate the new addition:

```
# The directory $EXPAT/lib should hold your expat library
EXPAT := /usr/local

# The  easysoap distribution
EASYHOME := /usr/local

EASYDIR := $(EASYHOME)/lib
EASYSOAPLIB := $(EASYDIR)/libeasysoap.a
CPPFLAGS := -I$(EASYHOME)/include/easysoap


# Linux Flags
CXXFLAGS := -g -Wall
LDFLAGS := -L$(EXPAT)/lib -L$(EASYDIR) -leasysoap -lexpat

# SunOS Flags
#CXXFLAGS := -g -Wall
#LDFLAGS := -L$(EXPAT)/lib -L/$(EASYDIR) -leasysoap -lexpat -lsocket -lnsl
```

```
# Cygwin Flags
#CXXFLAGS := -g -Wall
#LDFLAGS := -L$(EXPAT)/lib -L/$(EASYDIR) -leasysoap -lexpat -lwsock32


all : Echo.cgi echoString


Echo.cgi : Echo.o $(EASYSOAPLIB)
# The line below is a TAB, not 8 spaces
        g++ -g -static -o $@ $< $(LDFLAGS)


echoString : echoString.o $(EASYSOAPLIB)
# The line below is a TAB, not 8 spaces
        g++ -g -static -o $@ $< $(LDFLAGS)


$(EASYSOAPLIB) :
# The line below is a TAB, not 8 spaces
        cd $(EASYHOME)/src; make


clean:
# The line below is a TAB, not 8 spaces
        rm -f *.o Echo.cgi echoString
```

Next, we create our client source code file, echoString.cpp:

```
#include <iostream>
#include <SOAP.h>
#include <SOAPSocket.h>

using namespace std;
```

SOAP.h is the same core include that we see in building the server. The SOAPSocket.h include files are used here for exception handling:

```
int main()
{

    const char * httpproxy = 0;
    SOAPString msg;
    try
    {
        SOAPProxy proxy ("http://localhost/cgi/Echo.cgi", httpproxy);
```

As you can see from the URL, we are running the client on the same machine as the server, however you should adjust the URL for your own environment.

As you can see, this method invocation is taking place within a try/catch block, since a wide variety of exceptions may occur within the block.

The `SOAPProxy` object manages the actual call to the SOAP service. The constructor shown here takes two URLs; the first one is the SOAP endpoint URL, while the second is the URL for any HTTP Proxy server that may exist for your network. In this case, we set the proxy URL to NULL.

Here we instantiate the `SOAPMethod` object that will handle our method invocation to the server:

```
SOAPMethod method(
    "echoString",
    "http://soapinterop.org/",
    "http://soapinterop.org/",
    0);
```

The arguments used in the `SOAPMethod` constructor are described in the table below:

Argument name	Type	Description
name	char *	The name of the method being invoked.
ns	char *	The namespace that the method is defined within
SOAPAction	char *	SOAPAction base value
Append flag	boolean	SOAPAction method append flag; append the name of the method, separated by a hash (#), to the SOAPAction base value if set to `true`

Next, we create a new SOAP `Parameter` object and hang it off the `SOAPMethod` object we just created. The `AddParameter` method on the `SOAPMethod` object instantiates a SOAP `Parameter` object and attaches it to the `SOAPMethod` object. This is the parameter that we will send to the server as the method argument.

```
SOAPString inputValue = "hello";
method.AddParameter("inputString") << inputValue;
```

Finally, we invoke the RPC:

```
const SOAPResponse& response = proxy.Execute(method);
```

As you can see, the `SOAPMethod` object that we have instantiated is passed as an argument to the `SOAPProxy` object, and a `SOAPResponse` object is returned, encapsulating the single return value from the server.

Like the `SOAPMethod` object, the `SOAPResponse` object is a representation of the SOAP envelope, albeit without SOAP header information and a bit more simplified. SOAP headers are not supported on EasySoap++ RPC response docs. It holds the SOAP return value sent back from the server, which is extracted by a provided accessor:

```
response.GetReturnValue() >> msg;
```

The value will take on one of the SOAP types; in this case, a `SOAPString` class is extracted from the response, and we use the `msg` object pointer to print it:

```
        cout << msg << endl;
    }
```

This ends our `try` block. If an exception occurs, we `catch` it and print it out. The `SOAPSocketException` exception is thrown for TCP-level socket binding errors:

```
    catch (SOAPSocketException& ex)
    {
        cout << "Socket Exception: " << ex.What() << endl;
    }
```

The `SOAPFaultException` exception is thrown when the server returns a SOAP Fault. The `What()` method on the `SOAPFaultException` exception returns the SOAP Fault detail:

```
    catch (SOAPFaultException& ex)
    {
        cout << "SOAP Fault: " << ex.What() << endl;
```

`SOAPFaultException` is really a subclass of the more general `SOAPException`, which can be thrown for such things as serialization errors, etc.

```
    }
    catch (SOAPException& ex)
    {
        cout << "SOAP Exception: " << ex.What() << endl;
    }
```

For all other exceptions, we print out a generic error message.

```
    catch (...)
    {
        cout << "Unknown error" << endl;
    }
}
```

Now, let's build it. Running **make** will generate the `echoString` client executable. Let's run that executable:

Let's look at the SOAP envelopes generated by the `echoString` client and server. Here is the client request envelope:

```
POST /cgi/Echo.cgi HTTP/1.1
Host: localhost:80
User-Agent: EasySoap++/0.2
Content-Type: text/xml; charset="UTF-8"
SOAPAction: "http://soapinterop.org/"
Content-Length: 414

<E:Envelope xmlns:E="http://schemas.xmlsoap.org/soap/envelope/"
xmlns:A="http://schemas.xmlsoap.org/soap/encoding/"
xmlns:s="http://www.w3.org/2001/XMLSchema-instance"
xmlns:y="http://www.w3.org/2001/XMLSchema"
E:encodingStyle="http://schemas.xmlsoap.org/soap/encoding/">
    <E:Body>
        <m:echoString xmlns:m="http://soapinterop.org/">
            <inputString s:type="y:string">Hello</inputString>
        </m:echoString>
    </E:Body>
</E:Envelope>
```

and the response from the server:

```
HTTP/1.1 200 OK
Date: Wed, 27 Jun 2001 06:10:43 GMT
Server: Apache/1.3.14 (Unix) tomcat/1.0 PHP/4.0.1pl2
SOAPServer: EasySoap++/0.2
Cache-Control: s-maxage=60, proxy-revalidate
Content-Length: 420
Content-Type: text/xml; charset="UTF-8"

<E:Envelope xmlns:E="http://schemas.xmlsoap.org/soap/envelope/"
xmlns:A="http://schemas.xmlsoap.org/soap/encoding/"
xmlns:s="http://www.w3.org/2001/XMLSchema-instance"
xmlns:y="http://www.w3.org/2001/XMLSchema"
E:encodingStyle="http://schemas.xmlsoap.org/soap/encoding/">
    <E:Body>
        <m:echoStringResponse xmlns:m="http://soapinterop.org/">
            <return s:type="y:string">Hello</return>
        </m:echoStringResponse>
    </E:Body>
</E:Envelope>
```

Here, we see that the values we've attached to the `SOAPMethod` and `SOAPParameter` objects for SOAPAction, method namespace, method name, parameter name, and parameter type all conform to the WSDL definition of the service.

This example touched on how to generate a request/response pair utilizing a basic type as an argument. Now, let's take a look at how arrays are handled, with the `echoIntegerArray()` method.

echoIntegerArray

Let's update our server by adding to the Echo.cpp file, like so:

```
#include <SOAP.h>
#include <SOAPCGIServer.h>

class EchoHandler: public SOAPDispatchHandler<EchoHandler>
{
public:
    EchoHandler()
    {
        const char * ns = "http://soapinterop.org/";
        DispatchMethod("echoString", ns, &EchoHandler::echoString);

        DispatchMethod
        ("echoIntegerArray", ns, &EchoHandler::echoIntegerArray);
    }

    ~EchoHandler()
    {
    }

    EchoHandler * GetTarget(const SOAPEnvelope& request)
    {
        return this;
    }

    void echoString(const SOAPMethod& request, SOAPMethod& response)
    {
        SOAPString val;
        request.GetParameter("inputString") >> val;
        if(!strcmp(val,""))
            {throw SOAPException("no string value supplied");}
                response.AddParameter("return") << val;
    }

    void echoIntegerArray (const SOAPMethod& request, SOAPMethod&
                            response)
    {
        SOAPArray<int> val;
        request.GetParameter("inputIntegerArray") >> val;
        response.AddParameter("return") << val;
    }
};

int
main(int argc, char* argv[], char *env[])
{
    SOAPCGIServer cgi;
    EchoHandler echohandle;

    return cgi.DispatchTo(&echohandle).Handle();
}
```

We see that we use the SOAPArray class as the basic type for arrays, and that the overloaded operator << is used to map SOAPArray to SOAPParameter.

The GetParameter method is mapped the request SOAP Parameter "inputIntegerArray" into the integer array through the use of the overloaded operator >>.

For the array, as for all of the built-in basic types, the operator overloading is defined in the include/SOAPParameter.h file.

When we recompile by running make, a new Echo.cgi server results. We then put that in place of the original in our web server CGI directory.

Next, let's update the Makefile for our client echoIntegerArray:

```
# The directory $EXPAT/lib should hold your expat library
EXPAT := /usr/local

# The  easysoap distribution
EASYHOME := /usr/local

EASYDIR := $(EASYHOME)/lib
EASYSOAPLIB := $(EASYDIR)/libeasysoap.a
CPPFLAGS := -I$(EASYHOME)/include/easysoap

# Linux Flags
CXXFLAGS := -g -Wall
LDFLAGS := -L$(EXPAT)/lib -L$(EASYDIR) -leasysoap -lexpat

# SunOS Flags
#CXXFLAGS := -g -Wall
#LDFLAGS := -L$(EXPAT)/lib -L/$(EASYDIR) -leasysoap -lexpat -lsocket -lnsl

# Cygwin Flags
#CXXFLAGS := -g -Wall
#LDFLAGS := -L$(EXPAT)/lib -L/$(EASYDIR) -leasysoap -lexpat -lwsock32


all : Echo.cgi echoString echoIntegerArray

Echo.cgi : Echo.o $(EASYSOAPLIB)
# The line below is a TAB, not 8 spaces
        g++ -g -static -o $@ $< $(LDFLAGS)

echoString : echoString.o $(EASYSOAPLIB)
# The line below is a TAB, not 8 spaces
        g++ -g -static -o $@ $< $(LDFLAGS)

echoIntegerArray : echoIntegerArray.o $(EASYSOAPLIB)
# The line below is a TAB, not 8 spaces
        g++ -g -static -o $@ $< $(LDFLAGS)

$(EASYSOAPLIB) :
# The line below is a TAB, not 8 spaces
        cd $(EASYHOME)/src; make

clean:
# The line below is a TAB, not 8 spaces
        rm -f *.o Echo.cgi echoString echoIntegerArray
```

Finally, we create the `echoIntegerArray` client with a new file called `echoIntegerArray.cpp`:

```cpp
#include <iostream>
#include <SOAP.h>
#include <SOAPSocket.h>

using namespace std;

int main(int argc, char ** argv)
{
    const char * httpproxy = 0;
    SOAPArray<int> inputArray;
    SOAPArray<int> outputArray;

    SOAPProxy proxy ("http://localhost/cgi/Echo.cgi", httpproxy);

    try
    {
        // Build the array
        for(int i=1;i<=5; ++i)
            {
                inputArray.Add(i);
            }

        // Build the request SOAPMethod object
        SOAPMethod method("echoIntegerArray",
                          "http://soapinterop.org/",
                          "http://soapinterop.org/",
                          0);
        SOAPParameter& param=method.AddParameter("inputIntegerArray");
        param << inputArray;

        // Manually set the parameter array type in case we have
        // zero length array and cannot derive array type
        param.SetArrayType("int");

        // Execute the method
        const SOAPResponse& response=proxy.Execute(method);

        // Pull the return parameter out and map into results array
        response.GetReturnValue() >> outputArray;

        // Print the results
        for(int i=0; i<(int)outputArray.Size(); ++i)
        {
            cout << "Integer Array Element: " <<
            outputArray.GetAt(i) << endl;
        }
    }
    catch (SOAPSocketException& ex)
    {
        cout << "Socket Exception: " << ex.What() << endl;
    }
    catch (SOAPFaultException& ex)
    {
        cout << "SOAP Fault: " << ex.What() << endl;
```

```
        }
        catch (SOAPException& ex)
        {
            cout << "SOAP Exception: " << ex.What() << endl;
        }
        catch (...)
        {
            cout << "Unknown error" << endl;
        }
    }
```

To compile our new client, we execute make echoIntegerArray. The make process should produce the echoIntegerArray executable.

When we run the executable, we should get the following output:

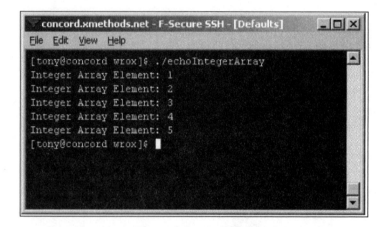

The client request generated by the echoIntegerArray client is show below:

```
POST /cgi/Echo.cgi HTTP/1.1
Host: localhost:80
User-Agent: EasySoap++/0.2
Content-Type: text/xml; charset="UTF-8"
SOAPAction: "urn:soapaction"
Content-Length: 525

<E:Envelope xmlns:E="http://schemas.xmlsoap.org/soap/envelope/"
xmlns:A="http://schemas.xmlsoap.org/soap/encoding/"
xmlns:s="http://www.w3.org/2001/XMLSchema-instance"
xmlns:y="http://www.w3.org/2001/XMLSchema"
E:encodingStyle="http://schemas.xmlsoap.org/soap/encoding/">
    <E:Body>
        <m:echoIntegerArray xmlns:m="http://soapinterop.org/">
            <inputIntegerArray s:type="A:Array" A:arrayType="y:int[5]">
                <item>1</item>
                <item>2</item>
                <item>3</item>
                <item>4</item>
                <item>5</item>
```

```
                </inputIntegerArray>
            </m:echoIntegerArray>
        </E:Body>
    </E:Envelope>
```

and the `echoIntegerArray` response from the server:

```
HTTP/1.1 200 OK
Date: Thu, 28 Jun 2001 10:06:42 GMT
Server: Apache/1.3.14 (Unix) tomcat/1.0 PHP/4.0.1p12
SOAPServer: EasySoap++/0.2
Cache-Control: s-maxage=60, proxy-revalidate
Content-Length: 519
Content-Type: text/xml; charset="UTF-8"

<E:Envelope xmlns:E="http://schemas.xmlsoap.org/soap/envelope/"
xmlns:A="http://schemas.xmlsoap.org/soap/encoding/"
xmlns:s="http://www.w3.org/2001/XMLSchema-instance"
xmlns:y="http://www.w3.org/2001/XMLSchema"
E:encodingStyle="http://schemas.xmlsoap.org/soap/encoding/">
    <E:Body>
        <m:echoIntegerArrayResponse xmlns:m="http://soapinterop.org/">
            <return s:type="A:Array" A:arrayType="y:int[5]">
                <item>1</item>
                <item>2</item>
                <item>3</item>
                <item>4</item>
                <item>5</item>
            </return>
        </m:echoIntegerArrayResponse>
    </E:Body>
</E:Envelope>
```

One thing to note here – EasySoap++ by default sets its array item element names to `item`, which happens to match our WSDL. This not currently changeable in EasySoap++ without updating the EasySoap++ source code and then recompiling. However, the SOAP 1.1 specification states that array item element names are not validated and are thus irrelevant. Most servers do not validate on this name. However, practical experience shows that some implementations **do** validate the array item element names against an XML Schema, so there could potentially be an issue for an EasySoap++ client if a server strictly validates the array item name and the schema sets it to a value other than `item`.

Finally, let's see how structures are defined and handled in EasySoap++.

echoStruct

First, let's define the structure that we will be passing. We create a header file, `Echo.h`, to hold the definition:

```
struct SOAPStruct
{
    SOAPString    varString;
    int           varInt;
    float         varFloat;
```

```
    SOAPStruct()
    {
       varInt = 0;
       varFloat = 0.0;
    }

    SOAPStruct(const char *str, int i, float f)
    {
       varString = str;
       varInt = i;
       varFloat = f;
    }

    static const char * soap_name;
    static const char * soap_namespace;
};

const char *SOAPStruct::soap_name = "SOAPStruct";
const char *SOAPStruct::soap_namespace = "http://soapinterop.org/xsd";

//  Define how we serialize the struct
inline SOAPParameter&
operator<<(SOAPParameter& param, const SOAPStruct& val)
{
    param.SetType(val.soap_name, val.soap_namespace);
    param.SetIsStruct();

    param.AddParameter("varString") << val.varString;
    param.AddParameter("varInt") << val.varInt;
    param.AddParameter("varFloat") << val.varFloat;

    return param;
}

// Define how we de-serialize the struct
inline const SOAPParameter&
operator>>(const SOAPParameter& param, SOAPStruct& val)
{
    param.GetParameter("varString") >> val.varString;
    param.GetParameter("varInt") >> val.varInt;
    param.GetParameter("varFloat") >> val.varFloat;

    return param;
}
```

In addition to the definition of the three primary fields, the structure definition also holds the fields soap_name and soap_namespace, which store the name and XML Namespace of the structure. These values are used when the structure is serialized into its XML form, and they are defined as constant values in the structure definition.

As we've seen before, the << and >> operators are programmed to map between SOAP Parameter objects and their structures. The SOAP Parameters are what are actually serialized; these operators allow the explicit transformation from the structure to the SOAP Parameter and back again within the client and server programs.

Next, lets turn our attention to the server. Add the following highlighted lines to create the new echoStruct() method and register it with the dispatcher.

```cpp
#include <SOAP.h>
#include <SOAPCGIServer.h>
#include "Echo.h"


class EchoHandler : public SOAPDispatchHandler<EchoHandler>
{
    public:
        EchoHandler()
        {
            const char * ns = "http://soapinterop.org/";
            DispatchMethod("echoString", ns, &EchoHandler::echoString);

            DispatchMethod ("echoIntegerArray", ns,
                            &EchoHandler::echoIntegerArray);
            DispatchMethod("echoStruct", ns, &EchoHandler::echoStruct);
        }

        ~EchoHandler()
        {
        }

        EchoHandler * GetTarget(const SOAPEnvelope& request)
        {
            return this;
        }

        void echoString(const SOAPMethod& request, SOAPMethod& response)
        {
            SOAPString val;
            request.GetParameter("inputString") >> val;
            if(!strcmp(val,""))
                {throw SOAPException("no string value supplied");}
                response.AddParameter("return") << val;
        }

        void echoIntegerArray (const SOAPMethod& request, SOAPMethod&
                               response)
        {
            SOAPArray<int> val;
            request.GetParameter("inputIntegerArray") >> val;
            response.AddParameter("return") << val;
        }

        void echoStruct(const SOAPMethod& request, SOAPMethod& response)
        {
            SOAPStruct val;
            request.GetParameter("inputStruct") >>  val;
            response.AddParameter("return") << val;
        }

};
```

```
int
main(int argc, char* argv[], char *env[])
{
    SOAPCGIServer cgi;
    EchoHandler echohandle;

    return cgi.DispatchTo(&echohandle).Handle();
}
```

Now, on to our `echoStruct` client:

```
#include <iostream>
#include <SOAP.h>
#include <SOAPSocket.h>
#include "Echo.h"

using namespace std;

int main(int argc, char ** argv)
{
    const char * httpproxy = 0;
    SOAPString msg;

    SOAPProxy proxy ("http://localhost/cgi/Echo.cgi", httpproxy);
    try
    {
        SOAPStruct returnStruct;

        // Build our input structure
        SOAPStruct inputStruct = SOAPStruct("test string", 5, 6.2);

        // Build the method object to represent our RPC invocation
        SOAPMethod method("echoStruct",
                          "http://soapinterop.org/",
                          "http://soapinterop.org/",
                          0);

        // .. and attach a new SOAP Parameter to the method argument list
        SOAPParameter & param=method.AddParameter("inputStruct");

        //... map the input structure into the parameter
            param << inputStruct;

        // Execute the RPC method invocation
        const SOAPResponse& response=proxy.Execute(method);

        // Take the response object and extract out the return parameter
        response.GetReturnValue() >> returnStruct;

        // and print the fields.
        cout << "Received SOAPStruct with values:" << endl;
        cout << "varString: " << returnStruct.varString << endl;
        cout << "varInt: " << returnStruct.varInt << endl;
        cout << "varFloat: " << returnStruct.varFloat << endl;
    }
```

```
      catch (SOAPSocketException& ex)
      {
         cout << "Socket Exception: " << ex.What() << endl;
      }
      catch (SOAPFaultException& ex)
      {
         cout << "SOAP Fault: " << ex.What() << endl;
      }
      catch (SOAPException& ex)
      {
         cout << "SOAP Exception: " << ex.What() << endl;
      }
      catch (...)
      {
         cout << "Unknown error" << endl;
      }
}
```

Next, the appropriate modifications to the Makefile to build the echoStruct client:

```
# The directory $EXPAT/lib should hold your expat library
EXPAT := /usr/local

# The  easysoap distribution
EASYHOME := /usr/local

EASYDIR := $(EASYHOME)/lib
EASYSOAPLIB := $(EASYDIR)/libeasysoap.a
CPPFLAGS := -I$(EASYHOME)/include/easysoap

# Linux Flags
CXXFLAGS := -g -Wall
LDFLAGS := -L$(EXPAT)/lib -L$(EASYDIR) -leasysoap -lexpat

# SunOS Flags
#CXXFLAGS := -g -Wall
#LDFLAGS := -L$(EXPAT)/lib -L/$(EASYDIR) -leasysoap -lexpat -lsocket -lnsl

# Cygwin Flags
#CXXFLAGS := -g -Wall
#LDFLAGS := -L$(EXPAT)/lib -L/$(EASYDIR) -leasysoap -lexpat -lwsock32


all : Echo.cgi echoString echoIntegerArray echoStruct

Echo.cgi : Echo.o $(EASYSOAPLIB)
# The line below is a TAB, not 8 spaces
        g++ -g -static -o $@ $< $(LDFLAGS)

echoString : echoString.o $(EASYSOAPLIB)
# The line below is a TAB, not 8 spaces
        g++ -g -static -o $@ $< $(LDFLAGS)

echoIntegerArray : echoIntegerArray.o $(EASYSOAPLIB)
# The line below is a TAB, not 8 spaces
```

```
        g++ -g -static -o $@ $< $(LDFLAGS)

echoStruct : echoStruct.o $(EASYSOAPLIB)
# The line below is a TAB, not 8 spaces
        g++ -g -static -o $@ $< $(LDFLAGS)

$(EASYSOAPLIB) :
# The line below is a TAB, not 8 spaces
        cd $(EASYHOME)/src; make

clean:
# The line below is a TAB, not 8 spaces
        rm -f *.o Echo.cgi echoString echoIntegerArray echoStruct
```

Run make to generate the echoStruct client executable – now when we run the new client, we get the following output:

A successful invocation. Finally, let's look at the echoStruct request and response envelopes. First, the request:

```
POST /cgi/Echo.cgi HTTP/1.1
Host: localhost:80
User-Agent: EasySoap++/0.2
Content-Type: text/xml; charset="UTF-8"
SOAPAction: "urn:soapaction"
Content-Length: 587

<E:Envelope xmlns:E="http://schemas.xmlsoap.org/soap/envelope/"
xmlns:A="http://schemas.xmlsoap.org/soap/encoding/"
xmlns:s="http://www.w3.org/2001/XMLSchema-instance"
xmlns:y="http://www.w3.org/2001/XMLSchema"
E:encodingStyle="http://schemas.xmlsoap.org/soap/encoding/">
    <E:Body>
        <m:echoStruct xmlns:m="http://soapinterop.org/">
            <inputStruct s:type="ns1:SOAPStruct"
                xmlns:ns1="http://soapinterop.org/xsd">
                <varFloat s:type="y:float">6.19999981</varFloat>
                <varString s:type="y:string">test string</varString>
```

```
              <varInt s:type="y:int">5</varInt>
           </inputStruct>
        </m:echoStruct>
     </E:Body>
  </E:Envelope>
```

and then the server response:

```
HTTP/1.1 200 OK
Date: Thu, 28 Jun 2001 07:20:22 GMT
Server: Apache/1.3.14 (Unix) tomcat/1.0 PHP/4.0.1pl2
SOAPServer: EasySoap++/0.2
Cache-Control: s-maxage=60, proxy-revalidate
Content-Length: 593
Content-Type: text/xml; charset="UTF-8"

<E:Envelope xmlns:E="http://schemas.xmlsoap.org/soap/envelope/"
xmlns:A="http://schemas.xmlsoap.org/soap/encoding/"
xmlns:s="http://www.w3.org/2001/XMLSchema-instance"
xmlns:y="http://www.w3.org/2001/XMLSchema"
E:encodingStyle="http://schemas.xmlsoap.org/soap/encoding/">
   <E:Body>
      <m:echoStructResponse xmlns:m="http://soapinterop.org/">
         <return s:type="ns1:SOAPStruct"
                 xmlns:ns1="http://soapinterop.org/xsd">
            <varFloat s:type="y:float">6.19999981</varFloat>
            <varString s:type="y:string">test string</varString>
            <varInt s:type="y:int">5</varInt>
         </return>
      </m:echoStructResponse>
   </E:Body>
</E:Envelope>
```

Note here that the SOAPStruct serialization, including the type name, type namespace, and its child element names conform to the WSDL definition of the structure.

More EasySoap++ Basics

Now let's take a look under the covers to see how you can modify aspects of envelope creation.

Parameter Serialization

Let's take a closer look at how EasySoap++ manages the serialization/deserialization of parameters to and from XML form. The following diagram gives us a simplistic view of the serialization process:

We've discussed how the basic types, arrays, and structs are serialized into SOAP parameter objects. Now let's look at the other piece of the picture – how parameter objects are serialized into XML.

When we built our basic `echoString` client, we constructed a `SOAPMethod` object, which represented the SOAP RPC call and the associated `SOAPParameter()` method arguments. We then passed it into the `SOAPProxy` object's `execute()` method, as is shown below:

```
SOAPMethod method(
"echoString",
"http://soapinterop.org/",
"http://soapinterop.org/",
0);
method.AddParameter("inputString") << "Hello"
const SOAPResponse& response = proxy.Execute(method);
```

The `AddParameter` call on the `SOAPMethod` object creates the `SOAPParameter` object from the C++ basic type. The `SOAPParameter` holds all the information needed to generate the XML, including parameter name, type information, value, parameter attributes, whether the parameter is actually an array or a structure, and so on. In this case, the name of the parameter, the value of the parameter, and the type of the parameter are all set on the new `SOAPParameter`.

The `SOAPProxy` constructs the SOAP Envelope, and as part of this process, it serializes each of the `SOAPParameter` objects into XML form.

On the server side, deserialization works in just the opposite way. The XML is used to reconstruct the `Method` object, including the objects attached to the parameter that represent the method arguments. The objects are constructed with all the appropriate information from the XML and then passed into the called method by the server.

The following types are already converted to and from `SOAPParameter` objects. This conversion is done via the overloaded operators `>>` and `<<` (see `include/SOAPParameter.h` for more details), which are defined "out of the box" by EasySoap++.

- ❑ `bool`
- ❑ `int`
- ❑ `float`
- ❑ `double`
- ❑ `SOAPBase64`
- ❑ `SOAPString`
- ❑ `SOAPArray`
- ❑ `struct`

Serialization/deserialization mechanisms may also be defined for any type through the `<<` and `>>` operators, including user-defined types and standard types such as `std::vector`, `std::map`, etc.

Let's take a closer look at how EasySoap++ handles structures. When serializing SOAP structures, you must pay attention to a couple of extra things that you don't need to worry about with basic parameters – namely setting the type name of the structure and namespace.

To illustrate this, the type name and namespace of the `SOAPStruct` element sent in the `echoStruct` **client** request is highlighted below:

```
POST /cgi/Echo.cgi HTTP/1.1
Host: tony.xmethods.net:80
User-Agent: EasySoap++/0.2
Content-Type: text/xml; charset="UTF-8"
SOAPAction: "urn:soapaction"
Content-Length: 587

<E:Envelope xmlns:E="http://schemas.xmlsoap.org/soap/envelope/"
xmlns:A="http://schemas.xmlsoap.org/soap/encoding/"
xmlns:s="http://www.w3.org/2001/XMLSchema-instance"
xmlns:y="http://www.w3.org/2001/XMLSchema"
E:encodingStyle="http://schemas.xmlsoap.org/soap/encoding/">
   <E:Body>
      <m:echoStruct xmlns:m="http://soapinterop.org/">
         <inputStruct s:type="ns1:SOAPStruct"
            xmlns:ns1="http://soapinterop.org/xsd">
               <varFloat s:type="y:float">6.19999981</varFloat>
               <varString s:type="y:string">test string</varString>
               <varInt s:type="y:int">5</varInt>
         </inputStruct>
      </m:echoStruct>
   </E:Body>
</E:Envelope>
```

In the `echoStruct` example above, we saw that the type name and namespace of the SOAP structure are included in the definition of the struct itself, and these values are used in the definition of the << operator to set those values on newly created SOAP parameter objects that represent structures. Below, we highlight the lines in the definition of `SOAPStruct` structure (found in the `Echo.h` header file) that set the type name and namespace for the structure:

```
struct SOAPStruct
{
    SOAPString      varString;
    int             varInt;
    float           varFloat;

    SOAPStruct()
    {
       varInt = 0;
       varFloat = 0.0;
    }

    SOAPStruct(const char *str, int i, float f)
    {
       varString = str;
       varInt = i;
       varFloat = f;
    }

    static const char *    soap_name;
    static const char *    soap_namespace;
```

```
};
const char *SOAPStruct::soap_name = "SOAPStruct";
const char *SOAPStruct::soap_namespace = "http://soapinterop.org/xsd";

//  Define how we serialize the struct
inline SOAPParameter&
operator<<(SOAPParameter& param, const SOAPStruct& val)
{
    param.SetType(val.soap_name, val.soap_namespace);
    param.SetIsStruct();

    param.AddParameter("varString") << val.varString;
    param.AddParameter("varInt") << val.varInt;
    param.AddParameter("varFloat") << val.varFloat;

    return param;
}

// Define how we de-serialize the struct
inline const SOAPParameter&
operator>>(const SOAPParameter& param, SOAPStruct& val)
{
    param.GetParameter("varString") >> val.varString;
    param.GetParameter("varInt") >> val.varInt;
    param.GetParameter("varFloat") >> val.varFloat;

    return param;
}
```

The values of both the name of the type and type's namespace are passed into the `SetType()` method. By setting these values, the resulting XML is appropriately generated.

XML Schema Version and Character Set Encoding

EasySoap++ by default uses the 2001 XML Schema. Also by default, the EasySoap++ string class `SOAPString` assumes that the strings it holds are already UTF-8 (that is, the class does not do the conversion from the local codepage to UTF-8). In addition, `wchar_t` strings in UTF-16 are also supported. The following code fragment illustrates this:

```
SOAPParameter p;
p << L"My Unicode string with strange characters.";
```

Next, we move onto our third and final SOAP implementation, SOAPx4 for PHP.

SOAPx4

SOAPx4 is an implementation built for PHP, the popular server-side web scripting language. You can read more about PHP at http://www.php.net/. SOAPx4 provides both client and server SOAP capabilities.

On the client side, SOAPx4 is ideal for providing PHP-driven web pages with SOAP client capabilities. For example, you may generate a web page that calls a stock quote service. Each time the page is invoked, the PHP server executes the SOAP call, retrieves the result, and displays the quote in HTML.

On the server side, you'll find that building SOAP services with PHP is as fast, easy, and powerful as building browser-oriented PHP web pages. An added benefit is that you can take the same PHP libraries you've built to support web site development and reuse them for SOAP services.

In this chapter, we'll install SOAPx4 and then look at how to build our Echo SOAP service with it, entirely in PHP. Then, we'll create a PHP-driven web page with embedded SOAP client capabilities to access the service.

This chapter was written using version 0.5 of SOAPx4 on a webserver with PHP 4.06.

Installing SOAPx4

Now we will have a look at what we need to set up to run our PHP SOAP examples.

Prerequisites

As you might expect, you must first have a PHP-enabled web server installed before using SOAPx4. PHP is an "add-on" module that can be integrated into such web servers as Apache and IIS. If you don't have PHP installed already on your web server, download it from http://www.php.net/downloads.php. This page provides all the information and links you'll need to get PHP installed and running. SOAPx4 requires at least PHP version 4.04.

For the purposes of this chapter, we'll assume that the .php extension is used for PHP files. Which extensions are used for PHP files is set at PHP install time – if your web server/PHP installation utilizes a different extension (such as .php4, a common alternative), modify the file names accordingly in our examples below.

Download and Installing the SOAPx4 Package

The SOAPx4 package is downloadable from the SOAPx4 website, http://dietrich.ganx4.com/soapx4/. SOAPx4 is distributed as a set of PHP files, archived as a zip file. SOAPx4 can be used on any platform that supports PHP, including Windows and Linux. Fundamentally, there are only two files from the zip that implement the SOAP functionality: one file implements the server functionality (class.soap_server.php), and the other implements the client functionality (class.soap_client.php). The files can be placed anywhere you like on your web server as long as you can import the files using the standard PHP "include" mechanism.

For example, if you place the files in the directory /usr/local/soapx4, you can include the files in the following way:

```php
<?php
    include ("/usr/local/soapx4/class.soap_client.php");
    include ("/usr/local/soapx4/class.soap_server.php");
?>
```

The path of the file passed in as the argument to "include" may be either absolute or relative. How's that for easy installation?

Now that the SOAPx4 files are installed, let's create our first SOAPx4 server and client pair. Again, we'll use the familiar Echo service as the foundation for our examples.

Building the Echo Service and Clients

In the client examples below, we utilize the SOAPx4 "high-level" API, a very simple and intuitive interface way to make our SOAP calls. There is also a lower-level set of APIs that allow finer-grained control of SOAP data structures and envelopes, at the expense of greater complexity. Please consult the examples and documentation that come with the SOAPx4 distribution for more information on how to utilize the lower-level APIs.

echoString

To start, we create a PHP file on our web server called `Echo.php`.

```php
<?php

include("class.soap_client.php");
include("class.soap_server.php");
```

Notice that these include directives imply that the two SOAPx4 library files are in the same directory as the `Echo.php` file, based on the relative file paths. Even though it is a SOAP server we are building, the client library file is needed as well as it contains PHP function definitions that are used by the server.

Next, we instantiate the core server object and register our method with it, so it knows how to dispatch calls to the method:

```php
$server = new soap_server;

$server->add_to_map(
       "echoString",               // function name
       array("string"),            // array of input types
       array("string")             // array of output types
);
```

As part of this `add_to_map()` call, we register the name of the method and define an array of types to indicate what the server should expect as input. We also define another array of types to indicate what the server should expect to return.

Now, on to the actual function we want to publish:

```php
function echoString($inputString){
     if(! $inputString)
   {
```

This first block is simply executing the check for an empty input value to the **echoString** function.

```php
         $params = array(
            "faultcode" => "Server",
            "faultstring" => "Empty Input",
            "detail" => "No string detected."
```

```
        );

        $faultmsg = new soapmsg(
            "Fault",
            $params,
            "http://schemas.xmlsoap.org/soap/envelope/"
        );
        return $faultmsg;
    }
```

The code above illustrates how SOAPx4 servers throw faults – we construct a `soapmsg` object and parameterize it with the appropriate fault fields.

Next, we get to the part of the method that performs the echo.

```
    $returnSoapVal = new soapval("return","string", $inputString);
    return $returnSoapVal;
}
```

You can see here that we use a `soapval` object to hold our SOAP parameters. The `soapval` class serves a purpose very similar to SOAP::Lite's `SOAP::Data` class and the EasySoap++ `SOAPParameter` class. It is used to represent SOAP data and structures, with defined mappings to and from "native" PHP data.

Finally, the last bit of PHP code completes our server.

```
$server->service($HTTP_RAW_POST_DATA);

?>
```

This is the line that actually processes the incoming SOAP request. Once this request is handled, the PHP engine outputs the SOAP response, which is passed back through the web server to the client.

That's all there is to it – we now have a fully functional SOAP server written in PHP! Now, let's look at the corresponding client.

This client is going to be different from the other clients we've created in this chapter. Since PHP is a server-side web scripting language, our soap client is a PHP file with the soap code embedded in HTML. Let's create a file, `echoString.php`. The first PHP code loads the SOAPx4 client library.

```
<html>
<body>

<h1>echoString client</h1>

<? include ("class.soap_client.php");
```

Now, we create our SOAP parameter that we will pass as an argument to the server. We take a basic PHP variable and wrap it with a `soapval` object.

```
$inputString="hello!";
$inputSoapVal=new soapval ("inputString","string",$inputString );
```

Now we create the object that manages the sending of the client request, parameterized with the server endpoint URL; we use the endpoint for the service we just created in the previous section:

```
$client = new soapclient("http://localhost/soapx4/Echo.php");
```

Finally, we execute the `call()` method to invoke the remote method. The `call()` method takes the following arguments, in order:

- ❑ Method name
- ❑ An array of `soapval` objects, one for each parameter
- ❑ Method namespace
- ❑ SOAPAction value

The `call()` method returns a scalar value or handle to an array, representing the result of the method invocation.

```
if($returnVal = $client->call( "echoString", array($inputSoapVal),
        "http://soapinterop.org/", "http://soapinterop.org/" )) {

        print "<strong>Sent:</strong> ".$inputString."<BR>\n";
        print "<strong>Got Back:</strong> ".$returnVal;
    }
?>

</body>
</html>
```

Now let's try running our client against the server. Pointing our browser to the URL of the `echoString.php` page we just created, we get:

Our call was successful!

Let's look at the wire-dump of the request and reply envelopes. First the request, generated by our client:

```
POST /soapx4/Echo.php HTTP/1.0
User-Agent: SOAPx4 v0.13492
Host: tonyhong
Content-Type: text/xml
Content-Length: 554
SOAPAction: "http://soapinterop.org/"

<?xml version="1.0"?>
<SOAP-ENV:Envelope  xmlns:SOAP-ENV="http://schemas.xmlsoap.org/soap/envelope/"
xmlns:xsi="http://www.w3.org/1999/XMLSchema-instance"
xmlns:xsd="http://www.w3.org/1999/XMLSchema" xmlns:SOAP-
ENC="http://schemas.xmlsoap.org/soap/encoding/"
xmlns:si="http://soapinterop.org/xsd" xmlns:ns6="http://soapinterop.org/" SOAP-
ENV:encodingStyle="http://schemas.xmlsoap.org/soap/encoding/">
    <SOAP-ENV:Body>
        <ns6:echoString>
            <inputstring xsi:type="xsd:string">hello!</inputstring>
        </ns6:echoString>
    </SOAP-ENV:Body>
</SOAP-ENV:Envelope>
```

and the server response:

```
HTTP/1.1 200 OK
Date: Sun, 01 Jul 2001 03:08:51 GMT
Server: Apache/1.3.14 (Unix) tomcat/1.0 PHP/4.0.6
Cache-Control: s-maxage=60, proxy-revalidate
X-Powered-By: PHP/4.0.6
Status: 200
Connection: Close
Content-Length: 548
Content-Type: text/xml; charset=UTF-8

<?xml version="1.0"?>
<SOAP-ENV:Envelope  xmlns:SOAP-ENV="http://schemas.xmlsoap.org/soap/envelope/"
xmlns:xsi="http://www.w3.org/1999/XMLSchema-instance"
xmlns:xsd="http://www.w3.org/1999/XMLSchema" xmlns:SOAP-
ENC="http://schemas.xmlsoap.org/soap/encoding/"
xmlns:si="http://soapinterop.org/xsd" xmlns:ns6="soapinterop" SOAP-
ENV:encodingStyle="http://schemas.xmlsoap.org/soap/encoding/">
    <SOAP-ENV:Body>
        <ns6:echoStringResponse>
            <return xsi:type="xsd:string">hello!</return>
        </ns6:echoStringResponse>
    </SOAP-ENV:Body>
</SOAP-ENV:Envelope>
```

As you can see, these envelopes conform to our standard WSDL description for the Echo service, except for the fact that SOAPx4 uses the 1999 version of the schema (currently), instead of 2001.

Finally, let's talk a bit about client fault handling. The high-level SOAPx4 API automatically defaults to printing out the fault information if a fault occurs on the web page. Our echoString service faults if an empty input value is passed in, so let's update our echoString client to force a fault to occur this way and see what we get back:

In the client echoString.php we modify the following line:

```
<html>
<body>

<h1>echoString client</h1>

<? include ("class.soap_client.php");

$inputString="";
$inputSoapVal=new soapval ("inputString","string",$inputString );
$client = new soapclient("http://localhost/soapx4/Echo.php");
if($returnVal = $client->call( "echoString", array($inputSoapVal),
        "http://soapinterop.org/", "http://soapinterop.org/" )) {
    print "<strong>Sent:</strong> ".$inputString."<BR>\n";
    print "<strong>Got Back:</strong> ".$returnVal;
}
?>
```

When we point our browser to this client, we get the following result:

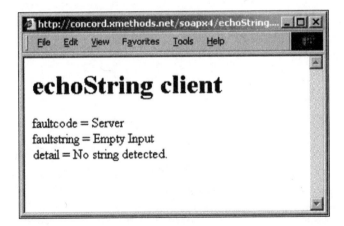

As you can see, these fault values match the fault parameter values set in the Echo.php server code.

echoIntegerArray

Now let's look at how we implement the echoIntegerArray server. We start by adding the following lines to the Echo.php server file:

```php
<?php
include("class.soap_client.php");
include("class.soap_server.php");

$server = new soap_server;

$server->add_to_map(
    "echoString",          // function name
    array("string"),       // array of input types
    array("string")        // array of output types
);
$server->add_to_map(
    "echoIntegerArray",    // function name
    array("array"),        // array of input types
    array("array")         // array of output types
);

function echoString($inputString){
    if(! $inputString)
    {
        $params = array(
            "faultcode" => "Server",
            "faultstring" => "Empty Input",
            "detail" => "No string detected."
        );

        $faultmsg  = new soapmsg(
            "Fault",
            $params,
            "http://schemas.xmlsoap.org/soap/envelope/"
        );
        return $faultmsg;
    }
    $returnSoapVal=new soapval("return","string",$inputString);
    return $returnSoapVal;
}
function echoIntegerArray($inputIntegerArray) {
    $returnSoapVal=new soapval("return","array",$inputIntegerArray);
    return $returnSoapVal;
}
$server->service($HTTP_RAW_POST_DATA);

?>
```

The added code implements the echoIntegerArray function and registers it with the server. If you look at the function, you'll see that we return a SOAP parameter created from the input array, named return.

Now let's create our corresponding echoIntegerArray client:

```html
<html>
<body>

<h1>echoIntegerArray client</h1>

<? include ("class.soap_client.php");
```

Here, we create the SOAP parameter object. We create it from a PHP array of integers, assigning it a name of inputIntegerArray and a type of array.

```
$inputIntegerArray=array(-1,0,1,2,3,4,5);
$inputSoapVal=new soapval("inputIntegerArray","array", $inputIntegerArray);
$client = new soapclient("http://localhost/soapx4/Echo.php");
```

Now we make the actual call:

```
if($returnVal = $client->call("echoIntegerArray", array($inputSoapVal),
        "http://soapinterop.org/","http://soapinterop.org/" )){
```

and if we received the return array value (which should be the case as long as we didn't fault), we print out both the sent array and the array received back:

```
        print "<strong>Sent:</strong>\n";
        for($index=0; $index < count($inputIntegerArray); $index++)
        print $inputIntegerArray[$index]." ";
        print "<BR>\n";

        print "<strong>Got Back:</strong>\n";
        for($index=0; $index < count($returnVal); $index++)
        print $returnVal[$index]." ";
        print "<BR>\n";
    }
?>

</body>
</html>
```

Now, when we point our browser to this new client PHP file (echoIntegerArray.php), we see the successful invocation of our new method:

Let's take a look at the envelopes that we just generated. First the request generated by the client:

```
POST /soapx4/Echo.php HTTP/1.0
User-Agent: SOAPx4 v0.13492
Host: tonyhong
Content-Type: text/xml
Content-Length: 856
SOAPAction: "http://soapinterop.org/"

<?xml version="1.0"?>
<SOAP-ENV:Envelope  xmlns:SOAP-ENV="http://schemas.xmlsoap.org/soap/envelope/"
xmlns:xsi="http://www.w3.org/1999/XMLSchema-instance"
xmlns:xsd="http://www.w3.org/1999/XMLSchema" xmlns:SOAP-
ENC="http://schemas.xmlsoap.org/soap/encoding/"
xmlns:si="http://soapinterop.org/xsd" xmlns:ns6="http://soapinterop.org/" SOAP-
ENV:encodingStyle="http://schemas.xmlsoap.org/soap/encoding/">
    <SOAP-ENV:Body>
        <ns6:echoIntegerArray>
            <inputIntegerArray xsi:type="SOAP-ENC:Array"
                               SOAP-ENC:arrayType="xsd:int[7]">
                <item xsi:type="xsd:int">-1</item>
                <item xsi:type="xsd:int">0</item>
                <item xsi:type="xsd:int">1</item>
                <item xsi:type="xsd:int">2</item>
                <item xsi:type="xsd:int">3</item>
                <item xsi:type="xsd:int">4</item>
                <item xsi:type="xsd:int">5</item>
            </inputIntegerArray>
        </ns6:echoIntegerArray>
    </SOAP-ENV:Body>
</SOAP-ENV:Envelope>
```

and the response from the server:

```
HTTP/1.1 200 OK
Date: Sun, 01 Jul 2001 04:40:34 GMT
Server: Apache/1.3.14 (Unix) tomcat/1.0 PHP/4.0.6
Cache-Control: s-maxage=60, proxy-revalidate
X-Powered-By: PHP/4.0.6
Status: 200
Connection: Close
Content-Length: 838
Content-Type: text/xml; charset=UTF-8

<?xml version="1.0"?>
<SOAP-ENV:Envelope  xmlns:SOAP-ENV="http://schemas.xmlsoap.org/soap/envelope/"
xmlns:xsi="http://www.w3.org/1999/XMLSchema-instance"
xmlns:xsd="http://www.w3.org/1999/XMLSchema" xmlns:SOAP-
ENC="http://schemas.xmlsoap.org/soap/encoding/"
xmlns:si="http://soapinterop.org/xsd" xmlns:ns6="soapinterop" SOAP-
ENV:encodingStyle="http://schemas.xmlsoap.org/soap/encoding/">
    <SOAP-ENV:Body>
        <ns6:echoIntegerArrayResponse>
            <return xsi:type="SOAP-ENC:Array"
                    SOAP-ENC:arrayType="xsd:int[7]">
```

401

```
            <item xsi:type="xsd:int">-1</item>
            <item xsi:type="xsd:int">0</item>
            <item xsi:type="xsd:int">1</item>
            <item xsi:type="xsd:int">2</item>
            <item xsi:type="xsd:int">3</item>
            <item xsi:type="xsd:int">4</item>
            <item xsi:type="xsd:int">5</item>
        </return>
      </ns6:echoIntegerArrayResponse>
    </SOAP-ENV:Body>
</SOAP-ENV:Envelope>
```

As expected, you can see that the array serialization takes the form specified by the standard WSDL description of the service.

echoStruct

Finally, let's look at how structures are handled. Let's add one more method to the server, the echoStruct() method.

```php
<?php

include("class.soap_client.php");
include("class.soap_server.php");

$server = new soap_server;

$server->add_to_map(
      "echoString",          // function name
      array("string"),       // array of input types
      array("string")        // array of output types
);
$server->add_to_map(
      "echoIntegerArray",    // function name
      array("array"),        // array of input types
      array("array")         // array of output types
);
$server->add_to_map(
      "echoStruct",          // function name
      array("SOAPStruct"),   // array of input types
      array("SOAPStruct")    // array of output types
);

function echoString($inputString){

    if(! $inputString)
    {
        $params = array(
           "faultcode" => "Server",
           "faultstring" => "Empty Input",
           "detail" => "No string detected."
        );

        $faultmsg  = new soapmsg(
           "Fault",
```

```
        $params,
        "http://schemas.xmlsoap.org/soap/envelope/"
    );
    return $faultmsg;
}

$returnSoapVal=new soapval("return","string",$inputString);
return $returnSoapVal;
}


function echoIntegerArray($inputIntegerArray) {
    $returnSoapVal=new soapval("return","array",$inputIntegerArray);
    return $returnSoapVal;
}

function echoStruct($inputStruct) {
    $returnSoapVal=new soapval(
        "return",
        "SOAPStruct",
        $inputStruct,
        "",
        "http://soapbuilders.org/xsd");

    return $returnSoapVal;
}

$server->service($HTTP_RAW_POST_DATA);
?>
```

Look carefully at how we create our SOAP parameter in the echoStruct() method. In the previous examples, we have only had three arguments passed into the soapval constructor: parameter name, type, and value. Here, we see that the method can optionally take two more arguments: parameter namespace and type namespace.

In most cases you come across, parameters are unqualified, so the parameter namespace argument will usually be null. However, for the structure we have defined for our Echo tests, a user-defined type named SOAPStruct, which is defined in the http://soapbuilders.org/xsd namespace, we need to attach the type namespace information.

Now, let's build the client PHP page, echoStruct.php:

```
<html>
<body>
<h1>echoStruct client</h1>

<? include ("class.soap_client.php");
```

Here we define our basic structure, in the form of a PHP associative array:

```
// Define our input structure
$inputStruct=array(
    "varString" => "test string",
    "varInt" => 5,
    "varFloat" => 6.2);
```

and now that we have the basic value, let's map it into the SOAP parameter equivalent:

```
$inputStructSoapVal=new soapval("inputStruct","SOAPStruct",$inputStruct,"",
                        "http://soapbuilders.org/xsd");
```

Here, we see that we've attached the proper namespace to our user-defined type, SOAPStruct, as we did when creating the echoStruct function on the server. It looks similar to the previous echoString and echoIntegerArray client examples, except for the way we print our results.

```
$client = new soapclient("http://localhost/soapx4/Echo.php");

if($returnVal = $client->call("echoStruct",array($inputStructSoapVal),
"http://soapinterop.org/","http://soapinterop.org/")){

    print "<strong>Sent:</strong><BR>\n";
    print "varString: ".$inputStruct["varString"]."<BR>\n";
    print "varInt: ".$inputStruct["varInt"]."<BR>\n";
    print "varFloat: ".$inputStruct["varFloat"]."<BR>\n";
    print "<P>\n";
    print "<strong>Received:</strong><BR>\n";
    print "varString: ".$returnVal["varString"]."<BR>\n";
    print "varInt: ".$returnVal["varInt"]."<BR>\n";
    print "varFloat: ".$returnVal["varFloat"]."<BR>\n";
}
?>
</body>
</html>
```

When we point our browser to this file, we see that the round trip invocation is successful:

Finally, let's look at the request and response wiredumps generated by our client and server. First the request:

```
POST /soapx4/Echo.php HTTP/1.0
User-Agent: SOAPx4 v0.13492
Host: tonyhong
Content-Type: text/xml
Content-Length: 738
SOAPAction: "http://soapinterop.org/"

<?xml version="1.0"?>
<SOAP-ENV:Envelope  xmlns:SOAP-ENV="http://schemas.xmlsoap.org/soap/envelope/"
xmlns:xsi="http://www.w3.org/1999/XMLSchema-instance"
xmlns:xsd="http://www.w3.org/1999/XMLSchema" xmlns:SOAP-
ENC="http://schemas.xmlsoap.org/soap/encoding/"
xmlns:si="http://soapinterop.org/xsd" xmlns:ns6="http://soapbuilders.org/xsd"
xmlns:ns7="http://soapinterop.org/" SOAP-
ENV:encodingStyle="http://schemas.xmlsoap.org/soap/encoding/">
    <SOAP-ENV:Body>
        <ns7:echoStruct>
            <inputStruct xsi:type="ns6:SOAPStruct">
                <varString xsi:type="xsd:string">test string</varString>
                <varInt xsi:type="xsd:int">5</varInt>
                <varFloat xsi:type="xsd:float">6.2</varFloat>
            </inputStruct>
        </ns7:echoStruct>
    </SOAP-ENV:Body>
</SOAP-ENV:Envelope>
```

and the subsequent server response:

```
HTTP/1.1 200 OK
Date: Sun, 01 Jul 2001 05:58:48 GMT
Server: Apache/1.3.14 (Unix) tomcat/1.0 PHP/4.0.6
Cache-Control: s-maxage=60, proxy-revalidate
X-Powered-By: PHP/4.0.6
Status: 200
Connection: Close
Content-Length: 732
Content-Type: text/xml; charset=UTF-8

<?xml version="1.0"?>
<SOAP-ENV:Envelope  xmlns:SOAP-ENV="http://schemas.xmlsoap.org/soap/envelope/"
xmlns:xsi="http://www.w3.org/1999/XMLSchema-instance"
xmlns:xsd="http://www.w3.org/1999/XMLSchema" xmlns:SOAP-
ENC="http://schemas.xmlsoap.org/soap/encoding/"
xmlns:si="http://soapinterop.org/xsd" xmlns:ns6="http://soapbuilders.org/xsd"
xmlns:ns7="soapinterop" SOAP-
ENV:encodingStyle="http://schemas.xmlsoap.org/soap/encoding/">
    <SOAP-ENV:Body>
        <ns7:echoStructResponse>
            <return xsi:type="ns6:SOAPStruct">
                <varString xsi:type="xsd:string">test string</varString>
                <varInt xsi:type="xsd:int">5</varInt>
                <varFloat xsi:type="xsd:float">6.2</varFloat>
            </return>
        </ns7:echoStructResponse>
    </SOAP-ENV:Body>
</SOAP-ENV:Envelope>
```

As you can see, the SOAPStruct structure is serialized in a way consistent with its XML Schema WSDL definition.

More SOAPx4 Basics

Now that we've looked at how to use SOAPx4 to implement our basic Echo service, let's have a look at some other basic SOAPx4 details that you will find useful.

Valid Data Types in Parameter Serialization

soapval objects, which represent SOAP parameters, are used as a bridge between native PHP variables/arrays and serialized SOAP representations of basic types, arrays, and structures. The $soapTypes array in the class.soap_client.php file defines those variables that are recognized as basic types:

- ❏ i4
- ❏ int
- ❏ boolean
- ❏ string
- ❏ double
- ❏ float
- ❏ timeInstant
- ❏ dateTime
- ❏ base64Binary
- ❏ base64

SOAPx4 understands how to translate between native PHP variables and SOAP parameters of these types automatically, in addition to arrays and user-defined structures, which we saw in the previous examples.

XML Schema Version and Character Set Encoding

At the time of writing, SOAPx4 uses the 1999 version of the XML Schema and the UTF-8 character set encoding. Both the upgrade to the 2001 XML Schema and support for other character set encodings are planned for the near future.

Client Configuration via WSDL Binding

In the previous examples, we saw how to call services without the benefit of a WSDL service description. Binding to a service with SOAPx4 is even easier.

Let's revisit our echoString client, with a couple of changes:

```
<html>
<body>

<h1>echoString client</h1>

<? include ("class.soap_client.php");

$inputString="hello";
$client = new soapclient("http://localhost/soapx4/Echo.wsdl", "wsdl");
```

The call to instantiate our `soapclient` object now takes two arguments. The first is the URL to the WSDL file and the second is a literal, "wsdl".

```
if($returnVal = $client->call( "echoString", array($inputString))) {
```

As you can see, we do not need to specify the method namespace or SOAPAction values anymore, since that's all taken care of, specified by the WSDL service description.

Also, notice that in the input parameter array, we pass in `$inputString`. Before, when we weren't using WSDL to configure our client, we had to instantiate a `soapval` object and pass that in instead, requiring the extra object instantiation step. Why is it that we don't have to use a `soapval` object this time? Remember, to fully describe a parameter using SOAP encoding, we specify the name, type, and value of the parameter; in SOAPx4, without WSDL, we do this with a `soapval` object. However, when our client binds to a WSDL document, the WSDL document itself specifies the expected name and type of the parameter. So all our application code needs to do is pass the value of the parameter, and the parameter will be serialized correctly.

The rest of the file is unchanged:

```
        print "<strong>Sent:</strong> ".$inputString."<BR>\n";
        print "<strong>Got Back:</strong> ".$returnVal;
}
?>

</body>
</html>
```

We create the `Echo.wsdl` file by taking the WSDL description that we examined at the beginning of this chapter and adding the following `service` element to it:

```
<service name="InteropTest">
  <port name="InteropTestPort" binding="tns:InteropTestSoapBinding">
        <soap:address location="http://localhost/soapx4/Echo.php"/>
  </port>
</service>
```

When we point our browser at the new WSDL-enabled client, we get the following output:

So we see that the client's WSDL binding worked!

407

Summary

In this chapter, we've looked at three different SOAP implementations based on different languages (Perl, C++, and PHP), demonstrating SOAP RPC messaging using parameter encoding defined by section 5 of the SOAP Specification. While the languages are very different, common patterns in how the toolkits worked were seen. For example, in all three cases, the concept of the SOAP parameter object as a representation of the SOAP-encoded parameter, and its mapping to and from the native language data representations, was important. Each toolkit's SOAP parameter object extended the native variables and structures, attaching meta information such as parameter name, XML Schema type, and namespace information that allowed the native data to be serialized properly into the common-ground representation.

Any language on any platform, scripted or compiled, can be a participant in a SOAP-encoded message exchange as long as its internal structures and design can be mapped into SOAP-encoded parameters. The mapping to this common space serves as the foundation for SOAP interoperability. No doubt, as SOAP (newest version 1.2) continues to gain traction, we'll see more and more implementations, on a diverse set of platforms, appearing and integrating with each other.

10

Java Web Service Implementations

In this chapter we will adopt a slightly different style as we take a very in-depth, detailed view of a Web Services implementation using Java, SOAP, WSTK, and UDDI. We will deliver our Java-based Web Service through Apache/Tomcat, then a UDDI-based test site (courtesy of IBM), using SOAP as the information transfer medium. So, let us enter the world of Organized Campgrounds, and the mission of one man, Derek Smalls, to get their proposed Web Services plan off the ground.

Note that the code examples in the chapter have whitespace added to them to enhance readability. Be careful to remove it when trying them out, if you are copying from the chapter, as they may affect running of the code. Better still, download all the code from http://www.wrox.com/, and you will have fully working versions straight away.

Introduction

This is the story of Organized Campgrounds and their effort to provide a Web Service to facilitate the reservation of campsites at campgrounds around the world. Organized Campgrounds is a trade organization of campground operators. The members of Organized Campgrounds are independent operators of campgrounds who belong to Organized Campgrounds in order to promote the campground industry. Being a forward-looking group, they understand the value of Web Services and have recently decided to undertake the development of a network of Web Services to permit campground customers to learn about and reserve campsites at member campgrounds from the comfort of their desktop computers. Active development on the project began with the employment of Derek Smalls, a consultant familiar with Web Services. Derek was given a brief description of the vision of the Web Service and then asked to prepare a proposal on how to proceed with the project.

This vision consisted of the following:

> *A user who is considering visiting any of the participating member campgrounds will use the Campground Browser application to browse the various available destinations. By browsing, they'll be able to learn about the campgrounds and make reservations for specific campsites within the campgrounds.*

Derek knew that a single, centralized, server would be impractical for this application. The necessary resources for computing and administration dictated by a single, central, server would be beyond the budget of Organized Campgrounds. Further, it would introduce a level of bureaucracy that would frustrate member campgrounds. It would be better to let the members manage their own servers and somehow organize them into a federation that customers could browse via the Internet. The challenge would be to provide a standard interface to all the servers so that the Campground Browser application could use a single protocol to communicate with the various campground servers of the members. Also, it would be necessary to make some kind of directory available so that the Campground Browser could easily find all of the member servers.

Finally, Derek realized that these kinds of interactions between the client and server (server delivering campground data to client, client requesting a reservation from the server, etc.) could be easily expressed as remote procedure calls, and designing them that way would facilitate development of the Campground Browser client. In fact, he quickly devised a simple object-oriented design consisting of a Campground object, resident on the server, on which the client application would invoke methods to effect the browsing.

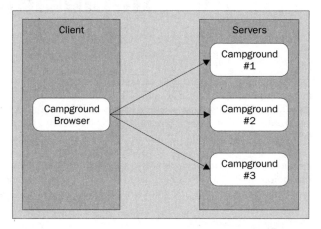

Although by no means an expert, Derek had enough experience of **SOAP** and **UDDI** to know that these technologies were ideal for a problem such as the one he faced. He then outlined a proposal for a system design that used SOAP and UDDI, to be implemented in Java. The proposal described a client/server system consisting of the Campground Browser, a client application that runs on the customer's desktop computer, and a federation of servers, one per member campground, which the Campground Browser contact's via the Internet. The member servers would each run on a machine managed by the corresponding organization member campground. The member servers would adhere to a standard Campground API so that the client application could interact with all of them in the same way. In addition, the member servers would all be registered with a UDDI registry so that the Campground Browser could find the participating member servers and present the list to the customer as part of the browsing operation. Each member campground could join the federation by obtaining a description of the Campground API, creating a server that implements that API, and then registering their server with the UDDI registry.

Since he had not had as much experience with SOAP and UDDI as he would perhaps have liked at this stage, Derek chose an iterative approach to the project. He would learn about these technologies stepwise, starting with basic principles and only proceeding to more advanced topics when he felt confident with the preceding topics. By using this technique, he hoped to avoid the all-too-common syndrome where a project is designed as a whole and implemented in a single large step, only to discover at the end of that single step that a fundamental problem exists with the design (by which time it is usually too late to remedy the problem). Instead, he would make incremental progress through a number of steps, each of which would result in a functioning, although limited, system.

His progress objectives were to:

1. Design an API for the member servers

2. Build one or two prototype member servers

3. Build a Campground Browser, which would be installed on a customer's desktop computer

When launched, the Campground Browser would search for participating Organized Campground member servers. It would then find each member that the customer wishes to learn more about, and potentially make campsite reservations with, and interact with their servers. Because the member servers all implement the same standard API, the Campground Browser can use a single protocol to communicate with all the servers. The one or two prototype member servers that Derek would implement would serve as an example of how members could implement their own servers and incorporate them in the Organized Campgrounds federation.

Organized Campgrounds then accepted the proposal, and Derek proceeded to assemble the tools he would need for the job. Strictly speaking, SOAP is a protocol, but it is generally considered to consist of two concrete components as well. The first is a library of code that enables programmers to produce and parse SOAP XML messages, and the second is a webapp that acts as the end point for SOAP communication at a server, which then uses objects to deliver the requested service. In addition, the webapp provides some administrative tools for deploying Web Services.

Installation

> Derek's setup is very similar to the Java/Apache/Tomcat/SOAP setups already used in Chapters 5 and 7. If you are comfortable with this setup already, then you might think you are fairly safe to skip to the *Simple First Demo* section – however, make sure you create your `install` directory tree and `config.bat` file first (see below). Either that, or download all you need from **http://www.wrox.com/**

Derek chose the Apache Software Foundation as the source for his SOAP toolkit. Apache is a non-profit organization, which supports various open-source software projects, including a high quality, widely used, and free SOAP toolkit. He found the toolkit at http://xml.apache.org. IBM has developed the SOAP toolkit for the most part, but IBM has donated the toolkit to the Apache organization, making it freely available. To run applications such as the ones detailed in this chapter (the likes of which were also seen in Chapters 5 and 7), Apache SOAP requires the following, which must be downloaded separately:

1. The Xerces XML parser, which may also be downloaded from http://xml.apache.org. SOAP makes use of XML namespaces, so a namespace-capable XML package is required. Any version of Xerces above 1.2 will suffice.

2. The Javabeans Activation Framework (version 1.0.1 or later), which may be downloaded from http://java.sun.com/products/beans/

3. Javamail (version 1.2 or later), which may be downloaded from http://java.sun.com/products/javamail/

4. Next, Derek needed a servlet container. This is a framework, or container, for running servlets. Almost any servlet container will do, but Derek chose Tomcat since it is also freely available at apache.org. Tomcat was originally developed by Sun Microsystems, but has been donated to the Jakarta project at Apache, and can be found at http://jakarta.apache.org "/". For his application, Derek chose version 3.2.2.

5. A Java development kit. He already had a Java development environment for his NT workstation. Version 1.2.2 or above is required, so Derek used 1.2.2 since he was using that for another project. His environment was configured so that JAVA_HOME was defined and his PATH variable included %JAVA_HOME%\bin.

Note that Derek performed his development work on a Windows NT workstation, but Windows 2000 Professional or Server would have worked just as well. Also, he could have used Unix: in that case the steps he followed would have been very similar to what is described here, merely substituting / for \, .sh for .bat, and tar for zip.

After downloading and unzipping these files into their default locations, they were arranged like so:

- The SOAP toolkit tree was located at C:\soap-2_2 (since he downloaded version 2.2). The lib subdirectory contained a soap.jar file

- Xerces was located at C:\xerces-1_4_0, and contained a xerces.jar file

- The Javabeans Activation Framework was in a directory C:\jaf-1.0.1, and contained a file named activation.jar

- The javamail package was in a directory named javamail-1.1.3 and contained a mail.jar file

- Since Derek downloaded version 3.2.2 of Tomcat, it was unzipped into C:\jakarta-tomcat-3.2.2

His first step after downloading was to configure Tomcat so that it would run the SOAP webapp. To begin with, this means defining the TOMCAT_HOME variable to point to the jakarta-tomcat-3.2.2 directory. The SOAP servlet, rpcrouter, uses soap.jar, xerces.jar, activation.jar, and mail.jar, so it is important to put those files into the CLASSPATH variable before starting Tomcat. In addition, it is important that Xerces be used by SOAP for XML parsing, so it is necessary to put xerces.jar at the front of the CLASSPATH variable. He also put Tomcat's bin directory into his PATH. This is a lot to set up, considering it would have to be performed multiple times, so to make it quicker and easier, Derek wrote the following file, config.bat, to make all these settings using a simple one-word command:

```
set TOMCAT_HOME=c:\jakarta-tomcat-3.2.2
set CLASSPATH=.;c:\soap-2_2;c:\soap-2_2\lib\soap.jar;c:\xerces-
1_2_2\xerces.jar;c:\jaf-1.0.1\activation.jar;c:\javamail-1.2\mail.jar
set path=%TOMCAT_HOME%\bin;%path%
```

He would be using command prompt windows to run Tomcat, deploy Web Services, compile Java, and run Java applications. Whenever opening a command window, he first ran `config.bat` before issuing any other commands drive. The next thing that Derek did was to create a directory called `install` on his `C:` drive, where all his application code was to be installed. Next, he placed the `config.bat` file in the root of `install`.

Since Tomcat appends things to `CLASSPATH`, it is important to make a minor adjustment to make sure that `xerces.jar` is used: edit the following line (which can be found about 100 lines down) in `jakarta-tomcat-3.2.2\bin\tomcat.bat` file and replace

```
set CP=%CP%;%CLASSPATH%
```

with the following line:

```
set CP=%CLASSPATH%;%CP%
```

This ensures that `xerces.jar` will appear near the beginning of `CLASSPATH`, and will therefore be used by SOAP for XML parsing instead of the XML classes in Tomcat. Finally, configure Tomcat so that it can find SOAP, by inserting the following into the `Context` element inside the `jakarta-tomcat3.2.2\conf\server.xml` file:

```
<Context
    path="/soap"
    docBase="C:/soap-2_2/webapps/soap"
    reloadable="true">
</Context>
```

Derek placed it immediately following the similar `/examples` context. Note that `docBase` should contain the full path, in UNIX style (forward slashes) to the `webapps/soap` directory, wherever it was installed. This instructs Tomcat to run the specified webapp when it receives a URL containing `/soap`.

After performing these tasks, Derek opened a command window, ran `config.bat`, and issued the **tomcat run** command. He then tested that it was running properly by entering http://localhost:8080/soap into his web browser (This may not work when using a proxy server). By default, Tomcat listens on port 8080, so it should respond to that URL. If it has been configured to find SOAP properly, it should display the following default page:

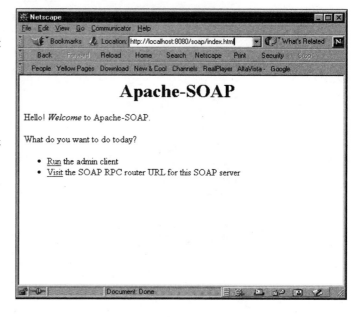

This indicated that the SOAP context was properly configured for Tomcat. He then clicked on the Visit link and saw this:

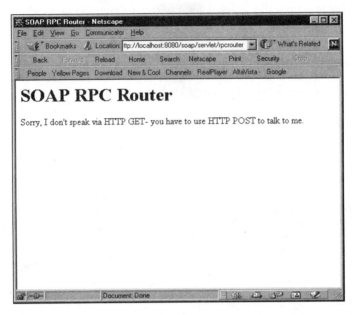

This means that the rpcrouter is running properly. The rpcrouter servlet is designed to communicate with SOAP clients instead of a web browser, and he received a message informing him of that. Next, he clicked on his browser's Back button and clicked on the Run link instead. He then saw the following:

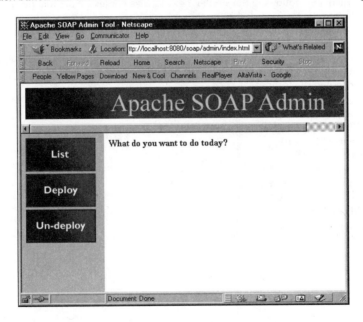

Lastly, he clicked on the List link and saw this:

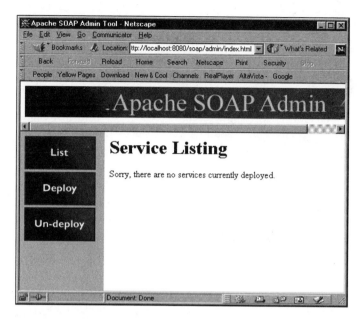

This meant that the list JSP was working properly, and as expected – since he hadn't installed any applications yet, it indicated that no services are deployed. Derek sighed with relief: he now had SOAP installed properly, and was ready to begin with his first prototype web service.

Simple First Demo

To get his feet wet with SOAP, Derek wanted to begin with a simple example that demonstrated a client, which invokes a method on an object implemented on a server. In this simple initial case however, both client and server would be running on his desktop computer, but in different processes. Keeping in mind that the client and server would eventually be on different machines across the Internet, he chose a design that could eventually grow into what he wanted for the production campground system.

The Server

He created a directory called `cg1` inside his `install` directory, into which the Java app was to be placed. He chose an interface called `Campground`, which would be defined by `OrganizedCampgrounds`, to be implemented by the member servers. As he progressed with the project, he would add more methods to this interface, but to begin with, `Campground` had only a single method, `computePrice()`:

```
package com.organizedCampgrounds;

public interface Campground{
    public int computePrice(int dayOfWeek);
}
```

This interface was placed into the `com.organizedCampgrounds` package (into the directory `C:\install\com\organizedCampgrounds`). This package would be maintained by Organized Campgrounds and would be made available to members, to be used when developing their Web Services.

For this initial example, he chose a member, Borrego Campground, to serve as a prototype server. The `BorregoCampground` class would implement the `Campground` interface, in the same way that all member servers eventually would. The example server would need to implement the single method, `computePrice()`, defined in the `Campground` interface. The simple implementation of `computePrice()` computes the daily price to stay at Borrego Campground. A value of 0 for day indicates Sunday, 1 is Monday, right up to 6 for Saturday. Since weekends are particularly popular at Borrego Campground, Sunday and Saturday prices are $15, while all other days are $10. `BorregoCampground.java` looks like this:

```
package com.borregoCampground;
import com.organizedCampgrounds.*;

public class BorregoCampground implements Campground{

    public int computePrice(int day) throws IllegalArgumentException{
        switch(day){
            case 0:
            case 6:
                return 15;
            case 1:
            case 2:
            case 3:
            case 4:
            case 5:
                return 10;
            default:
                throw new IllegalArgumentException("Invalid day of week: " + day);
        }
    }
}
```

Unlike the `Campground` interface, this is code that would be maintained by the member, so he put it into the `com.borregoCampground` package (`C:\install\cg1\borregoCampground`), corresponding to the `BorregoCampground.com` domain name reserved by the Borrego Campground member. For this prototype he would be switching back and forth between two roles. In the first role he would be an Organized Campgrounds developer, putting code into the `com.organizedCampgrounds` package to be used by all members. In the second role he would be emulating a member and putting code into the `com.borregoCampground` package, to be maintained by the Borrego Campground member.

With the server-side code written and in place, the next step was to open a command window, run `config.bat`, then navigate to the root of `cg1` and compile the files using the following commands:

> **javac com\organizedCampgrounds\Campground.java**
> **javac com\borregoCampground\BorregoCampground.java**

Now that the server code was built, it was time to deploy it, meaning make it available to clients. He opened another command window, ran `config.bat`, changed directory to `cg1`, and started Tomcat:

> **tomcat run**

Next, he visited the SOAP admin servlet with his web browser at http://localhost:8080/soap/admin. Clicking on the Deploy button, he was presented with the following form (as we saw in Chapters 5 and 7):

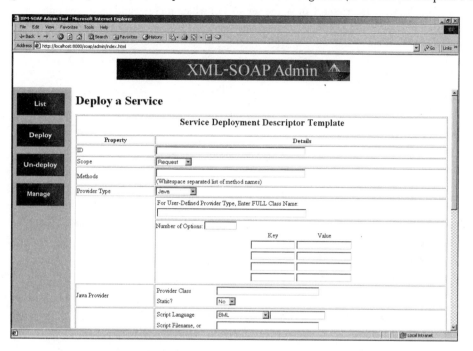

This form permitted him to specify how he would like the BorregoCampground service deployed. Filling in the following fields in the form, he left the other fields blank or with their default values:

❑ ID – urn:Campground

❑ Scope – Application

❑ Methods – computePrice

❑ Provider Type – Java

❑ Provider Class – com.borregoCampground.BorregoCampground

The ID is the unique identifier for the BorregoCampground on this server (the server may offer many services simultaneously). The Scope indicates how often the BorregoCampground object will be instantiated. Generally it will either be instantiated once for the lifetime of the Tomcat server (Application), once per client session (Session), or every time a client request is received (Request). For this case, Derek chose the former, indicated by Application. Since BorregoCampground is implemented in Java, he chose Java for Provider type (Javascript is also an option), and gave the name of the class for Provider Class. Finally, in Methods, he indicated that the computePrice() method is available for clients. When complete, he pressed the Deploy button at the bottom of the form (not the Deploy button on the left). This had the effect of telling SOAP how to serve requests from clients for BorregoCampground. Note that the deployment information is stored in a file (the DeployedServices.ds file in the C:\soap-2_2\webapps\soap directory) so it is persistent – in other words there is no need to re-enter the information the next time SOAP is launched by Tomcat.

419

The Client

Next, it was time to write the client. Unlike the servers, of which there would be many, one per member campground, there would only be one client application, provided by Organized Campgrounds. For this reason, the `Client` application would go into the `com.organizedCampgrounds` package:

```
package com.organizedCampgrounds;

import java.net.*;
import org.apache.soap.*;
import org.apache.soap.rpc.*;

    public class Client {
        public static void main( String[] args ) throws Exception {
            /*
             * Define the location where the campground may be found and
             * the identifier for the campground object.
             */
            URL url = new URL( "http://localhost:8080/soap/servlet/rpcrouter" );
            String urn = "urn:Campground";

        /*
         * Set up the call
         */
            Call call = new Call();
            call.setTargetObjectURI( urn );
            call.setMethodName( "computePrice" );
            call.setEncodingStyleURI( Constants.NS_URI_SOAP_ENC );
            java.util.Vector params = new java.util.Vector();
            params.addElement( new Parameter( "dayOfWeek",
                                Integer.class, new Integer(args[0]), null ) );
            call.setParams( params );

            try {
                System.out.println("Contacting campground");
                System.out.println(" URL: " + url);
                System.out.println(" URN: " + urn);

            /*
             * Make the call
             */
                Response response = call.invoke( url, "" );

            if( !response.generatedFault()) {
                Parameter result = response.getReturnValue(); // response was OK
                int price = ((Integer)(result.getValue())).intValue();
                System.out.println( "Daily price= " + price );
            }
            else {
                /*
                 * Error from the campground object
                 */
            Fault f = response.getFault();
                System.err.println("Campground error: ");
                System.err.println(" " + f.getFaultCode());
```

```
                    System.err.println(" " + f.getFaultString());
                }
        }
        catch( SOAPException e ) {
            /*
              * Error trying to make the call
              */
            Throwable target = e.getTargetException();
            System.out.println("Call error: " + target.getMessage());
            target.printStackTrace();
            System.err.println("SOAPException: ");
            System.err.println(" " + e.getFaultCode());
            System.err.println(" " + e.getMessage());
        }
    }
}
```

He then created a second command window, and after running `config.bat`, compiled the client:

> **javac com\organizedCampgrounds\Client.java**

He was then ready to run the client with the following command to compute the daily price for Sunday:

> **java com.organizedCampgrounds.Client 0**

This resulted in the following output:

Seeing the correct price for Sunday, he then tried the Monday case:

> **java com.organizedCampgrounds.Client 1**

The output was as follows:

This successful execution of the client and server components of the system meant that he was able to contact the server from the client, compute the price properly, and return the value back to the client. Finally, he tried an invalid day of week to force an exception to occur:

```
Command Prompt                                          _ □ ×
C:\install\cg1> java com.organizedCampgrounds.Client 9
Contacting campground
  URL: http://localhost:8080/soap/servlet/rpcrouter
  URN: urn:Campground
Campground error:
  SOAP-ENV:Server
  Exception from service object: Invalid day of week: 9

C:\install\cg1>_
```

Most errors that occur at this stage are attributable to class name or classpath errors. For example, when first trying this example, Derek forgot to put '.' in his classpath in the window from which he ran Tomcat. The result was that the SOAP rpcrouter servlet was unable to find the `BorregoCampground` class to carry out the wishes of the client. Here's what that error looked like:

```
Command Prompt                                          _ □ ×
C:\install>cd cg1
C:\install\cg1>java com.organizedCampgrounds.Client 0
Contacting campground
  URL: http://localhost:8080/soap/servlet/rpcrouter
  URN: urn:Campground
Campground error:
  SOAP-ENV:Client
  Deployment error in SOAP service 'urn:Campground': class name 'com.organized
pgrounds.Campsite' could not be resolved: com.organizedCampgrounds.Campsite
```

Passing Objects

As Derek considered his next step in exploration of SOAP, he wondered how he would pass objects between the client and the server. In particular, he wanted to send a `Campsite` object from the server to the client. The `Campsite` object would contain information that describes a single site within a campground. For example, it would have a description of the site, the size in square feet, and a shade factor which indicates how much or how little sun a site receives. This would be used to present a description of the campsite to the customer, who could then use that information when choosing which campsite to reserve.

SOAP uses a serialization scheme to define how to marshall an object – which means produce a representation of an object which may be transmitted across the network. In the case of SOAP, this data stream will be formatted using XML. The sender of the object includes a description of how it serialized the object in the XML when it transmits the object. The receiver then uses the reverse partner of that serialization scheme when it receives the object in order to instantiate it.

This means that the sender and receiver must already have both members of the serializer/deserializer pair (implemented as a Serializer class). That wouldn't be a problem with the campground application since OrganizedCampgrounds.com will already be distributing the Campground interface, so distributing a small number of classes to members would not be a problem. However, Apache SOAP already includes a very useful serializer/deserializer pair for Java developers: the **BeanSerializer**. The BeanSerializer uses reflection to formulate the XML to be transmitted when passing the object and to rebuild the object after it is received. It makes one requirement on the object to be passed: it must be bean-like. This simply means that it should have a series of public `get()`/`set()` methods, one for each attribute. It will use the `get()` methods when building the XML, and the `set()` methods when reconstructing the object at the receiver. In addition it must have a public default constructor.

Implementing Campsite Objects

Derek chose to take advantage of the BeanSerializer and designed the `Campsite` class according to its requirements. He put the `Campsite` class into the `com.organizedCampgrounds` package, since it would be made available to implementers of the various member services. Note that it includes a `get()`/`set()` pair of methods for each attribute. Note also that the BeanSerializer will attempt to call all of the `get()` methods when serializing and all of the `set()` methods when deserializing, so he was careful not to have extra `get()`/`set()` methods that do not correspond to attributes. He began by cloning `cg1` and naming this new directory `cg2`, and set about making the enhancements for his second prototype. `Campsite.java` now looks like this:

```java
package com.organizedCampgrounds;

public class Campsite{
    private String description; // comments that describe the site
    private int size;           // in square feet
    private int shade;          // 1-10, where 1 is full sun, 10 is no sun

    public Campsite(){
    }

    public Campsite(String _descr, int _size, int _shade){
        description = _descr;
        size = _size;
        shade = _shade;
    }

    public String getDescription(){
        return description;
    }
    public void setDescription(String _descr){
        description = _descr;
    }

    public int getSize(){
        return size;
    }
    public void setSize(int _size){
        size = _size;
    }

    public int getShade(){
        return shade;
    }
    public void setShade(int _shade){
        shade = _shade;
    }
}
```

Next, he added new methods to the `Campground` interface for querying campsites and making reservations. The campsite querying methods include a method for querying the number of campsites and one for getting a specific campsite, specified by campsite number, where the numbers range from 0 for the first one to n-1 where n is the number of campsites. For input, the reservation method takes a day of the week, interpreted as the next occurrence of that day of week (so 0 means next Sunday), and a campsite number. For this prototype reservations can only be made one week in advance and for only one day at a time. Finally, the reservation method takes the name of customer making the reservation. `reserveCampsite()` returns true if the reservation was made successfully, false if the specified campsite is already reserved for that day of the week. The new `Campground.java` look like this:

```
package com.organizedCampgrounds;

public interface Campground{
    public int computePrice(int dayOfWeek);
    public int getNumberOfCampsites();
    public Campsite getCampsite(int campsiteNumber);
    public boolean reserveCampsite(int dayOfWeek, int campsiteNumber, String name);
}
```

Next, he enhanced his BorregoCampground prototype member service to implement the new methods of the Campground interface. He used a simple case for the prototype, which only contained two campsites, and a simple schedule scheme that uses a two dimensional matrix of campsites/day-of-week. Each element of the matrix is null if the corresponding campsite is available for that day of the week. If it is reserved, the matrix element contains the name of the customer. Obviously, the production version would need to be more robust, but this would suffice for the prototype:

```
package com.borregoCampground;

import com.organizedCampgrounds.*;

public class BorregoCampground implements Campground{
    private Campsite[] campsites = {
        new Campsite("Very nice view",   500,  8),
        new Campsite("On the riverbank", 450, 10)
    };
    private String schedule[][];

    public BorregoCampground(){
        /*
         * Intialize the schedule. A null for a campsite on a day of
         * week means it is available. When it is reserved, it will
         * contain the name of the person holding the reservation.
         */
        schedule = new String[7][]; // For each day of the week
        for(int i=0; i<schedule.length; i++)
            schedule[i] = new String[campsites.length]; // For each site
        for(int dow=0; dow<7; dow++)
        for(int site=0; site<campsites.length; site++)
            schedule[dow][site] = null;

    }

    public int computePrice(int day) throws IllegalArgumentException{
        switch(day){
            case 0:
            case 6:
                return 15;
            case 1:
            case 2:
            case 3:
            case 4:
            case 5:
                return 10;
            default:
                throw new IllegalArgumentException("Invalid day of week: " + day);
```

```
      }
   }

   public int getNumberOfCampsites(){
      return campsites.length;
   }

   public Campsite getCampsite(int campsiteNumber){
      return campsites[campsiteNumber];
   }

   public boolean reserveCampsite(int dayOfWeek, int campsiteNumber, String name){
      if (schedule[dayOfWeek][campsiteNumber] == null){
         schedule[dayOfWeek][campsiteNumber] = name;
         return true;
      }
      else{
         return false;
      }
   }
}
```

After changing directory to cg2, he compiled Campsite.java and Campground.java in
cg2\com\organizedCampgrounds, and BorregoCampground.java in
cg2\com\borregoCampground. He was now ready to deploy the service, which he did by stopping the
previous Tomcat by pressing *Ctrl-c* (or entering the tomcat stop command in a new window after running
config.bat), changing directory to cg2, and restarting Tomcat with tomcat run. He undeployed the
previous Campground service by visiting http://localhost:8080/soap/admin in his web browser,
choosing Undeploy, and clicking on urn:Campground. In general, it was necessary for Derek to redeploy his
service whenever he changed the deployment attributes. If he modified a server class file, but left the
deployment attributes the unchanged, it was only necessary to restart Tomcat. Next, he clicked on the deploy
button again, and this time entered the following information into the deploy form:

❑   ID – urn:Campground

❑   Scope – Application

❑   Methods – computePrice getNumberOfCampsites getCampsite
            reserveCampsite

❑   Provider Type – Java

❑   Provider Class – com.borregoCampground.BorregoCampground

❑   Number of mappings – 1

This is similar to before, but now the Number of mappings is set to 1, indicating that one type of object will
be passed between the client and server. He then filled in the top row of the Type Mapping section as
follows to specify how this type of object is to be passed:

❑   Encoding style – SOAP

❑   Namespace URI – http://proxy.organizedCampgrounds.com

❑   Local part – Campsite

❑   Java type – com.organizedCampgrounds.Campsite

❑ Java to XML serializer – `org.apache.soap.encoding.soapenc.BeanSerializer`

❑ XML to Java deserializer – `org.apache.soap.encoding.soapenc.BeanSerializer`

The Namespace URI defines the scope of the names used in the mapping of the Campsite object to the corresponding XML to be used when it is enroute from the server to the client. The Java type identifies the Java class for this mapping, and the BeanSerializer is identified as the serializer/deserializer to be used. It was now ready to deploy, so he pressed the Deploy button at the bottom of the form.

He then turned his attention to the client. To begin with, he would only add the ability to query the number of campsites, and then print out a description of each campsite. Note that a mapping is defined for the getCampsite() method that looks much like the deployment type mapping. The updated Client.java file is as follows:

```java
package com.organizedCampgrounds;

import java.net.*;
import org.apache.soap.*;
import org.apache.soap.rpc.*;
import org.apache.soap.encoding.*;
import org.apache.soap.encoding.soapenc.*;
import org.apache.soap.util.xml.QName;

public class Client {
    public static void main( String[] args ) throws Exception {
        /*
         * Define the location where the campground may be found and
         * the identifier for the campground object.
         */
        URL url = new URL( "http://localhost:8080/soap/servlet/rpcrouter" );
        String urn = "urn:Campground";
        int nCampsites=0;
        Response response;
        /*
         * Set up the call
         */
        Call call = new Call();
        call.setTargetObjectURI( urn );
        call.setEncodingStyleURI( Constants.NS_URI_SOAP_ENC );
        java.util.Vector params = new java.util.Vector();

        try {
            System.out.println("Contacting campground");
            System.out.println(" URL: " + url);
            System.out.println(" URN: " + urn);

            /*
             * Call computePrice
             */
            call.setMethodName( "computePrice" );
            params.addElement( new Parameter( "dayOfWeek", Integer.class,
            new Integer(args[0]), null ) );
            call.setParams( params );
            response = call.invoke( url, "" );
            if( !response.generatedFault()){
```

```
         Parameter result = response.getReturnValue(); // response was OK
         int price = ((Integer)(result.getValue())).intValue();
         System.out.println( "Daily price = " + price );
      }
else {
   Fault f = response.getFault();
   System.err.println("Campground error: \n " +
   f.getFaultCode() + "\n " + f.getFaultString());
}


   /*
      * Call getNumberOfCampsites
   */
call.setMethodName( "getNumberOfCampsites" );
params.clear();
call.setParams( params );
response = call.invoke( url, "" );
if( !response.generatedFault()){
   Parameter result = response.getReturnValue(); // response was OK
   nCampsites = ((Integer)(result.getValue())).intValue();
   System.out.println( "Number of campsites = " + nCampsites );
}
else {
   Fault f = response.getFault();
   System.err.println("Campground error: \n " +
   f.getFaultCode() + "\n " + f.getFaultString());
}


   /*
      * Call getCampsite for each campsite
   */
call.setMethodName( "getCampsite" );
SOAPMappingRegistry registry = new SOAPMappingRegistry();
QName qname = new QName( "http://proxy.organizedCampgrounds.com",
                        "Campsite" );

BeanSerializer serializer = new BeanSerializer();
registry.mapTypes( Constants.NS_URI_SOAP_ENC, qname, Campsite.class,
                   serializer, serializer );
call.setSOAPMappingRegistry( registry );

for(int i=0;  i<nCampsites; i++){
   params.clear();
   params.addElement( new Parameter( "campsiteNumber", Integer.class,
   new Integer(i), null ) );
   call.setParams( params );
   response = call.invoke( url, "" );
   if( !response.generatedFault()){
      Parameter result = response.getReturnValue(); // response was OK
      Campsite campsite = ((Campsite)(result.getValue()));
      System.out.println( "Campsite " + i + ": " +
      campsite.getDescription() + "\n Size: " +
      campsite.getSize() + " square feet, Shade(1-10):  " +
      campsite.getShade());
   }
```

```
        else {
            Fault f = response.getFault();
            System.err.println("Campground error: \n " +
            f.getFaultCode() + "\n " + f.getFaultString());
        }
    }
}
    catch( SOAPException e ) {
        /*
         * Error trying to make the call
         */
        Throwable target = e.getTargetException();
        System.out.println("Call error: " + target.getMessage());
        target.printStackTrace();
            System.err.println("SOAPException: ");
            System.err.println("  " + e.getFaultCode());
            System.err.println("  " + e.getMessage());
    }
  }
}
```

After compiling Client.java in cg2\com\organizedCampgrounds, he was ready to try it out, using the same command as before:

Using the Tunneler

The above display looked correct, but Derek is the kind of person who is not satisfied simply to see successful results. To truly become comfortable with a technology, he prefers to know how it works. That's when he discovered the tunneler that is included with the Apache SOAP toolkit. Opening another window, setting his directory to cg2, and running config.bat, Derek then entered the following command to launch the tunneler:

> **java org.apache.soap.util.net.TcpTunnelGui 8070 localhost 8080**

This launched the tunneler, like so:

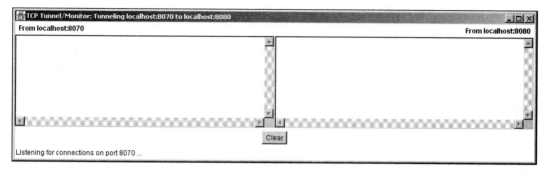

The tunneler captures messages sent to port 8070 (any unused port will do) and forwards them to port 8080, where Tomcat would receive and process them. Since it is capturing the messages that flow back and forth, it can display them, thus permitting Derek to inspect the XML that passed between the client and the server. The messages from the client are displayed in the left pane, messages from the server in the right.

He then made a slight modification to this line in `Client.java`, replacing port 8080 with port 8070:

```
URL url = new URL( "http://localhost:8070/soap/servlet/rpcrouter" );
```

This would send messages from the client to the tunneler (instead of directly to rpcrouter), which would display them in the left panel, then forward them to the server. The process would be reversed for messages from the server, with the messages displayed in the right pane before being forwarded to the client. He left the tunneler open and listening. Next, opening another command window, running `config.bat`, and changing to the `cg2` directory, he recompiled `Client.java` and ran it once more, using the following commands:

> **javac com\organizedCampgrounds\Client.java**
> **java com.organizedCampgrounds.Client 0**

This produced the following display in the tunneler. He scrolled both panes to the top and inspected the results:

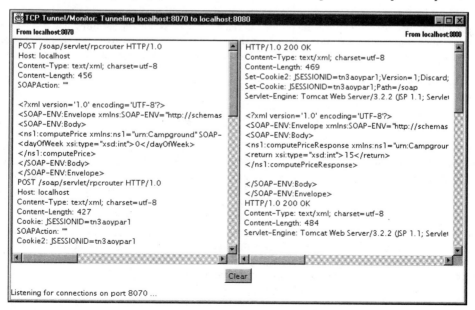

This clearly showed the request from the client for the `computePrice()` call and the response from the server.

The request was encapsulated in an HTTP POST. The SOAP message was contained in a SOAP envelope, with the details of the call to `computePrice()` in the body. Within the body he noticed the name of the `computePrice()` method, and the `dayOfWeek` parameter, which included both the value of 0 and an indication that it was an integer.

The response, likewise, was in a SOAP body and showed the value of 15, again with an indication that it was an integer.

This provided Derek with some valuable insight into how SOAP works. The rpcrouter servlet receives this XML, including the `urn:Campground` identifier. It then uses the deployment information that was provided to realize that a `BorregoCampground` object is to be used for this request. Since the scope was specified as "Application" when deployed, a single `BorregoCampground` object was constructed when rpcrouter started, and used for all subsequent requests. The rpcrouter servlet then determined from the XML that a `computePrice()` method is to be invoked on that `BorregoCampground` object, passing the specified value.

Armed with the knowledge that he now understood what was happening with SOAP behind the scenes, he felt more confident about proceeding.

Anyway, things were running very nicely, and the server passed the `Campsite` object properly, but he couldn't help noticing that the code in the client to make each call was rather cumbersome. He dreaded writing a client in which each call to the `Campground` object would require 10-20 lines of code in the client. He was accustomed to only needing a single line of code in Java to invoke a method on an object. There must be a better way.

Wrapping Strategies

That's when it occurred to Derek that a proxy design pattern would be very useful. A proxy is a class that is a surrogate for another class. It exports the public interface of the class it is representing while encapsulating the complexities of accessing that other class. This shifting of the complexity from the client to the proxy makes the complexity easier to manage since it is localized in the proxy, resulting in a simplified client.

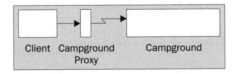

Client Campground   Campground
        Proxy

In this example, he could have a `CampgroundProxy` class, resident on the client, which would have the same public interface as `Campground`, but would handle all of the complexities of dealing with SOAP to access the true `Campground` class on the server. This would permit him to write the main logic of his client application without getting bogged down in code that deals with SOAP.

Here is his `CampgroundProxy` class. It is very similar to the previous `Client`, except that it exports the `Campground` interface. He made a copy of the cg2 directory tree, named cg3, created a `cg3\com\organizedCampgrounds\proxy` directory, and created a new `CampgroundProxy.java` file in the `cg3\com\organizedCampgrounds\proxy` directory.

```
package com.organizedCampgrounds.proxy;

import java.net.*;
import org.apache.soap.*;
import org.apache.soap.rpc.*;
import org.apache.soap.encoding.*;
import org.apache.soap.encoding.soapenc.*;
import org.apache.soap.util.xml.QName;

    public class CampgroundProxy implements Campground {
        private URL;
        private String urn = "urn:Campground";
        private Call call;

        public CampgroundProxy() throws Exception {
            /*
             * Define the identifier for the campground object.
             */

            call = new Call();
            call.setTargetObjectURI( urn );
            call.setEncodingStyleURI( Constants.NS_URI_SOAP_ENC );
        }

        public void setEndPoint(URL _url){
            this.url = _url;
        }

        public int computePrice(int dayOfWeek){
            int price=0;
            java.util.Vector params = new java.util.Vector();

        try {
            System.out.println("Contacting campground");
            System.out.println(" URL: " + url);
            System.out.println(" URN: " + urn);

            /*
             * Call computePrice
             */
            call.setMethodName( "computePrice" );
            params.addElement( new Parameter( "dayOfWeek", Integer.class, new
                             Integer(dayOfWeek), null ) );
            call.setParams( params );
            Response response = call.invoke( url, "" );
            if( !response.generatedFault()){
                Parameter result = response.getReturnValue();
                // response was OK
                price = ((Integer)(result.getValue())).intValue();
            }
            else {
                Fault f = response.getFault();
                System.err.println("Campground error: \n " +
                f.getFaultCode() + "\n " + f.getFaultString());
            }
        }
```

```
     catch( SOAPException e ) {
        /*
            * Error trying to make the call
        */
        Throwable target = e.getTargetException();
        System.out.println("Call error: " + target.getMessage());
        target.printStackTrace();
           System.err.println("SOAPException: ");
           System.err.println(" " + e.getFaultCode());
           System.err.println(" " + e.getMessage());
        }
        return price;
   }

   public int getNumberOfCampsites(){
      int nCampsites=0;
      java.util.Vector params = new java.util.Vector();
      try{
      /*
         * Call getNumberOfCampsites
      */
      call.setMethodName( "getNumberOfCampsites" );
      params.clear();
      call.setParams( params );
      Response response = call.invoke( url, "" );
      if( !response.generatedFault()){
         Parameter result = response.getReturnValue(); // response was OK
         nCampsites = ((Integer)(result.getValue())).intValue();
      }
      else {
         Fault f = response.getFault();
         System.err.println("Campground error: \n " + f.getFaultCode()
                            + "\n " + f.getFaultString());
      }
   }
      catch( SOAPException e ) {
         /*
            * Error trying to make the call
         */
         Throwable target = e.getTargetException();
         System.out.println("Call error: " + target.getMessage());
         target.printStackTrace();
         System.err.println("SOAPException: ");
         System.err.println(" " + e.getFaultCode());
         System.err.println(" " + e.getMessage());
      }
      return nCampsites;
   }

   public Campsite getCampsite(int campsiteNumber){
      Campsite campsite=null;
      java.util.Vector params = new java.util.Vector();
      try{
      /*
         * Call getCampsite for specified campsite
      */
```

```
      call.setMethodName( "getCampsite" );
      SOAPMappingRegistry registry = new SOAPMappingRegistry();
      QName qname = new QName( "urn:Campsite", "Campsite" );
      BeanSerializer serializer = new BeanSerializer();
      registry.mapTypes( Constants.NS_URI_SOAP_ENC, qname,
                         Campsite.class, serializer, serializer );
      call.setSOAPMappingRegistry( registry );

      params.clear();
      params.addElement( new Parameter( "campsiteNumber", Integer.class,
                         new Integer(campsiteNumber), null ) );
      call.setParams( params );
      Response response = call.invoke( url, "" );
      if( !response.generatedFault()){
         Parameter result = response.getReturnValue(); // response was OK
         campsite = ((Campsite)(result.getValue()));
      }
      else {
         Fault f = response.getFault();
         System.err.println("Campground error: \n " +
                   f.getFaultCode() + "\n " + f.getFaultString());
      }
   }

   catch( SOAPException e ) {
      /*
         * Error trying to make the call
      */
      Throwable target = e.getTargetException();
      System.out.println("Call error: " + target.getMessage());
      target.printStackTrace();
      System.err.println("SOAPException: ");
      System.err.println(" " + e.getFaultCode());
      System.err.println(" " + e.getMessage());
   }
   return campsite;
}

public boolean reserveCampsite(int dayOfWeek, int campsiteNumber,
String name){
boolean success=false;
java.util.Vector params = new java.util.Vector();

try {
/*
   * Call reserveCampsite
*/
call.setMethodName( "reserveCampsite" );
params.addElement( new Parameter( "dayOfWeek", Integer.class,
                  new Integer(dayOfWeek), null ) );
params.addElement( new Parameter( "campsiteNumber", Integer.class,
                  new Integer(campsiteNumber), null ) );
params.addElement( new Parameter( "name", String.class, name,
                  null ) );
call.setParams( params );
Response response = call.invoke( url, "" );
```

```
        if( !response.generatedFault()){
            Parameter result = response.getReturnValue(); // response was OK
            success = ((Boolean)(result.getValue())).booleanValue();
        }
        else {
            Fault f = response.getFault();
            System.err.println("Campground error: \n " +
                        f.getFaultCode() + "\n " + f.getFaultString());
        }
    }
    catch( SOAPException e ) {
    /*
        * Error trying to make the call
    */
    Throwable target = e.getTargetException();
    System.out.println("Call error: " + target.getMessage());
    target.printStackTrace();
        System.err.println("SOAPException: ");
        System.err.println(" " + e.getFaultCode());
        System.err.println(" " + e.getMessage());
    }
    return success;
    }
}
```

He recognized that there was still quite a bit of SOAP complexity, but when he saw how streamlined his `Client.java` became, he felt it was a good design, so he enhanced the client to include a call to the `reserveCampsite()` method. He still needed to decide how to handle errors (should the proxy class throw exceptions in these cases which would be caught by the client?), but he made a note to resolve that later.

```
package com.organizedCampgrounds;

import java.io.*;
import java.net.*;

    public class Client {
    public static void main( String[] args ) throws Exception {
        /*
            * Define the location where the campground may be found.
        */
        com.organizedCampgrounds.proxy.CampgroundProxy campground =
        new com.organizedCampgrounds.proxy.CampgroundProxy();
        campground.setEndPoint(new
        URL("http://localhost:8080/soap/servlet/rpcrouter"));

        System.out.println("Price: " +
        campground.computePrice(Integer.parseInt(args[0])));
        int nCampsites=campground.getNumberOfCampsites();
        for(int i=0; i<nCampsites; i++){
            Campsite campsite = campground.getCampsite(i);
            System.out.println( "Campsite " + i + ": " + campsite.description +
            "\n Size: " + campsite.size + " square feet, Shade(1-10):  " +
            campsite.shade);
```

```
    }
    System.out.println("Choose campsite: " );
    BufferedReader keyboardInput =
    new BufferedReader(new InputStreamReader(System.in));
    String site = keyboardInput.readLine();
    if (site.length() > 0){
        boolean success =
        campground.reserveCampsite(Integer.parseInt(args[0]),
        Integer.parseInt(site), "Derek");
        System.out.println("Success: " + success);
    }
  }
}
```

After compiling these files, he left his cg2 server running. That would suffice for this demo since he hadn't made any server side changes. He also left the tunneler running in case he needed it for debugging since he had noticed that sometimes the tunneler provided additional details when something went wrong. Whenever he wanted to use the tunneler he would modify the client to use port 8070 instead of 8080. Derek then ran the cg3 demo client. He ran the client twice, reserving campsite 1 both times in his name. As expected, the first time he ran it the reservation succeeded. When he ran it the second time, as expected, the reservation failed since site 1 had previously been reserved:

He was satisfied at this point that the proxy approach was a good one. However, he could foresee that creating the proxy code might become tedious, particularly if he needed to add a lot of methods to Campground or other server classes to be accessed from the client.

Proxy Generation With WSTK

Derek knew that the Web Services Toolkit (WSTK) from IBM included an automatic proxy generator, so he decided to try it out. Taking note of the fact that the WSTK is about 38 megabytes in size, he began to download it from http://www.alphaworks.ibm.com/tech/webservicetoolkit, then went to get himself a well-earned coffee. When he got back, it had finished, so he ran the installer. The noteworthy steps he had to follow during the installation are as follows:

❑ Enter the path to the JAVA_HOME directory – Derek entered C:\jdk1.2.2 (at least version 1.2.2 is required by WSTK).

❑ Choose a web server – Derek was careful to choose Tomcat for his web server, and he specified his TOMCAT_HOME (the jakarta-tomcat-3.2.2 directory) directory went prompted to do so.

This produced a directory tree named wstk-2.3 (he had downloaded version 2.3). He then went to his working directory and made a copy of the cg3 directory tree, naming it cg4 (note that WSTK has problems with directory names that contain spaces, so be sure to avoid such names when choosing a place to install it). He would use WSTK to create his proxy this time, so he deleted CampgroundProxy.java and CampgroundProxy.class from the cg4\com\organizedCampgrounds\proxy directory.

WSTK uses a number of environment variables, which are defined by running the wstk-2.3\bin\wstkenv.bat script, so Derek began his work on cg4 by running that command. Creating a proxy with WSTK is a 2-step process:

1. In the first step, a pair of **WSDL (Web Services Description Language)** files are created. This is accomplished with the wsdlgen command. wsdlgen uses reflection to learn about the public interface to a Java class, and then builds the XML that describes the class, and prompts for information about how it will be deployed, and also includes that information in the WSDL file.

2. In the second step, the WSDL files are used to generate and compile the proxy class. This is done with the proxygen command.

Derek changed to the cg4 directory, ran wsdlgen, and was presented with a series of screens, the first of which is as follows:

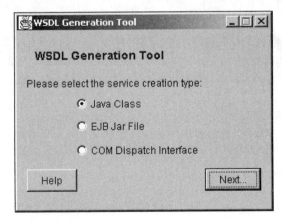

Derek selected **Java Class**, indicating that a Java `class` file would be the source of the information for the WSDL file, then pressed **Next**...The next screen required entry of numerous properties and identifiers:

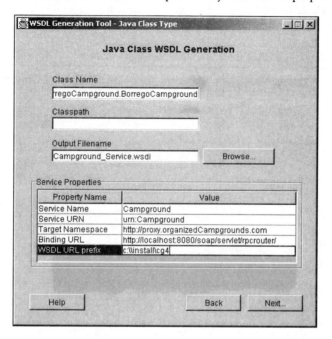

The specific class Derek used was `com.borregoCampground.BorregoCampground`, so he entered that as the class name. Note that the client actually deals with the `Campground` interface, but a concrete class is required for `wsdlgen`, so `BorregoCampground` was used instead of `Campground`.

Leaving the classpath empty (this is used to tell `wsdlgen` where to find the class if it is not already in `CLASSPATH`), he entered `Campground_Service.wsdl` as the name of the WSDL file to be created. Actually, two files will be created – the name of the second one will be derived from the name entered in this field by appending `-interface` onto it.

He set the **Service Name** to `Campground`, and as in his earlier prototypes, the **Service URN** was set to `urn:Campground`.

The **Target Namespace** serves a dual purpose in `wsdlgen`, indicating both the namespace to be used in any mappings, and to indicate where to put any generated Java source and class files. In this case, since his system passed an object between client and server (`Campsite`), `wsdlgen` would be creating some `Campsite` files. The target namespace of `http://proxy.organizedCampgrounds.com` specifies to put them in a convenient place: a new directory named `com\organizedCampgrounds\proxy`, which had the purpose of holding the files of the `com.organizedCampgrounds.proxy` package, a package that held these automatically generated files.

The **Binding URL** indicates the URL to be used to contact the rpcrouter servlet.

A pair of WSDL files will be generated, and one will "import" the other. It is thus necessary to indicate where it can find the other file so it may be imported. This is done by entering the full path to the `cg4` directory, which is where both of the WSDL files will be created, into the **WSDL URL prefix** field.

Note that version 2.3 of WSTK has a problem with entering service properties. It is necessary to change focus after entering the last value before pressing the Next button. For example, after entering the WSDL URL prefix, click on the Binding URL field to ensure the WSDL URL prefix is accepted before pressing Next

The next screen requires selection of the methods to be wrappered:

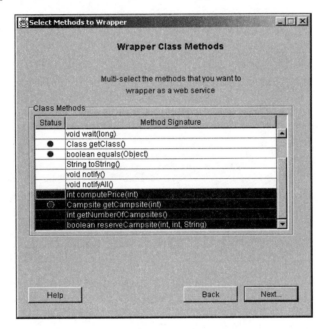

Since he was not interested in serving any of the methods inherited from Object, he multi-selected only the 4 Campground methods at the bottom of the list. The getCampsite() method was marked with a red dot, indicating that this method returns a complex type (Campsite).

On the next screen he selected Campsite, indicating that his server would return Campsite objects from the getCampsite() method:

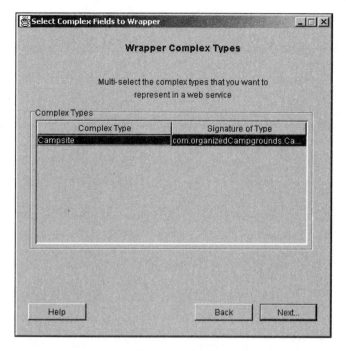

Finally, he received a confirmation screen and pressed the Finish button:

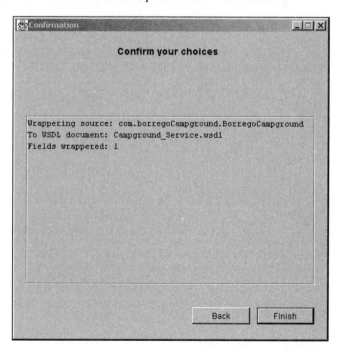

After a few moments, a confirmation alert was presented which indicated that the WSDL files had been successfully created:

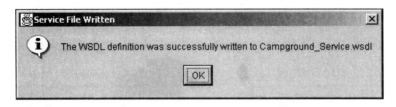

Examining the contents of the `cg4` directory, Derek noticed that the 2 WSDL files had indeed been created. The `Campground_Service.wsdl` file was rather small:

```xml
<?xml version="1.0" encoding="UTF-8"?>
<definitions name="Campground"
    targetNamespace="http://proxy.organizedCampgrounds.com"
    xmlns="http://schemas.xmlsoap.org/wsdl/"
    xmlns:soap="http://schemas.xmlsoap.org/wsdl/soap/"
    xmlns:tns="http://proxy.organizedCampgrounds.com"
    xmlns:xsd="http://www.w3.org/1999/XMLSchema">

<import
    location="c:\\install\cg4/Campground_Service-interface.wsdl"
    namespace="http://proxy.organizedCampgrounds.com-interface">
</import>

<service name="Campground-Borrego">
    <documentation>
        IBM WSTK 2.0 generated service definition file
    </documentation>
    <port binding="CampgroundBinding" name="CampgroundPort">
        <soap:address
            location="http://localhost:8080/soap/servlet/rpcrouter"/>
    </port>
</service>

</definitions>
```

It contained information, including the URL to the rpcrouter servlet, and an import tag with a location attribute referring to the other WSDL file. The interface file was a bit larger and contained information describing the Campground interface and the Campsite class:

```xml
<?xml version="1.0" encoding="UTF-8"?>
<definitions name="Campground"
    targetNamespace="http://com.organizedCampgrounds.com-interface"
    xmlns="http://schemas.xmlsoap.org/wsdl/"
    xmlns:soap="http://schemas.xmlsoap.org/wsdl/soap/"
    xmlns:tns="http://com.organizedCampgrounds.com"
    xmlns:xsd="http://www.w3.org/1999/XMLSchema">

<types>
    <xsd:schema targetNamespace="http://com.organizedCampgrounds.com"
            xmlns="http://www.w3.org/1999/XMLSchema/">
    <xsd:complexType   name="Campsite">
        <xsd:element name="description" type="xsd:string"/>
        <xsd:element name="size" type="xsd:int"/>
        <xsd:element name="shade" type="xsd:int"/>
```

```
      </xsd:complexType>

    </xsd:schema>
</types>

<message name="IncomputePriceRequest">
    <part name="meth1_inType1" type="xsd:int"/>
</message>

<message name="OutcomputePriceResponse">
    <part name="meth1_outType" type="xsd:int"/>
</message>

<message name="IngetCampsiteRequest">
    <part name="meth2_inType1" type="xsd:int"/>
</message>

<message name="OutgetCampsiteResponse">
    <part name="meth2_outType" type="tns:Campsite"/>
</message>

<message name="IngetNumberOfCampsitesRequest"/>

<message name="OutgetNumberOfCampsitesResponse">
    <part name="meth3_outType" type="xsd:int"/>
</message>

<message name="InreserveCampsiteRequest">
    <part name="meth4_inType1" type="xsd:int"/>
    <part name="meth4_inType2" type="xsd:int"/>
    <part name="meth4_inType3" type="xsd:string"/>
</message>

<message name="OutreserveCampsiteResponse">
    <part name="meth4_outType" type="xsd:boolean"/>
</message>

<portType name="Campground">
    <operation name="computePrice">
       <input message="IncomputePriceRequest"/>
       <output message="OutcomputePriceResponse"/>
    </operation>

    <operation name="getCampsite">
       <input message="IngetCampsiteRequest"/>
       <output message="OutgetCampsiteResponse"/>
    </operation>

    <operation name="getNumberOfCampsites">
       <input message="IngetNumberOfCampsitesRequest"/>
       <output message="OutgetNumberOfCampsitesResponse"/>
    </operation>

    <operation name="reserveCampsite">
       <input message="InreserveCampsiteRequest"/>
```

```
            <output message="OutreserveCampsiteResponse"/>
        </operation>
    </portType>

    <binding name="CampgroundBinding" type="Campground">
        <soap:binding style="rpc"
                       transport="http://schemas.xmlsoap.org/soap/http"/>
        <operation name="computePrice">
        <soap:operation soapAction="urn:Campground"/>
        <input>
            <soap:body encodingStyle="http://schemas.xmlsoap.org/soap/encoding/"
                       namespace="urn:Campground"
                       use="encoded"/>
        </input>
        <output>
            <soap:body encodingStyle="http://schemas.xmlsoap.org/soap/encoding/"
                       namespace="urn:Campground"
                       use="encoded"/>
        </output>
        </operation>
        <operation name="getCampsite">
        <soap:operation soapAction="urn:Campground"/>
        <input>
            <soap:body encodingStyle="http://schemas.xmlsoap.org/soap/encoding/"
                       namespace="urn:Campground"
                       use="encoded"/>
        </input>
        <output>
            <soap:body encodingStyle="http://schemas.xmlsoap.org/soap/encoding/"
                       namespace="urn:Campground"
                       use="encoded"/>
        </output>
        </operation>
        <operation name="getNumberOfCampsites">
        <soap:operation soapAction="urn:Campground"/>
        <input>
            <soap:body encodingStyle="http://schemas.xmlsoap.org/soap/encoding/"
                       namespace="urn:Campground"
                       use="encoded"/>
        </input>
        <output>
            <soap:body encodingStyle="http://schemas.xmlsoap.org/soap/encoding/"
                       namespace="urn:Campground"
                       use="encoded"/>
        </output>
        </operation>
        <operation name="reserveCampsite">
        <soap:operation soapAction="urn:Campground"/>
        <input>
            <soap:body encodingStyle="http://schemas.xmlsoap.org/soap/encoding/"
                       namespace="urn:Campground"
                       use="encoded"/>
        </input>
        <output>
            <soap:body encodingStyle="http://schemas.xmlsoap.org/soap/encoding/"
```

```
                    namespace="urn:Campground" use="encoded"/>
    </output>
    </operation>
</binding>

</definitions>
```

He noticed a pair of message tags for each `Campground()` method: one describing the input parameters, and one describing the return type. He could now see that this was exactly the kind of information that would be necessary to produce the proxy class, so he proceeded to use the `proxygen` command to create the proxy.

First of all, Derek recalled something that he had read about in some WSTK documentation: In version 2.3 of WSTK, `proxygen.bat` does not take any input parameters other than the WSDL file name, even though the underlying command which the script runs has some important options. For example, `-override on` indicates to overwrite files from any previous `proxygen` invocations (important if you run `proxygen` a second time). Also, `-package` indicates the package to which the proxy will belong. For Derek's case, he wanted to specify both of these options, so he copied `proxygen.bat` from the `wstk-2.3\bin` directory to the `cg4` directory and edited it to add the following:

```
-override on -package com.organizedCampgrounds.proxy
```

This was added to the line near the bottom where the command is run (the line that begins with `%JAVA_CMD%`). The result was a line that looks like this:

```
"%JAVA_CMD%" -cp "%WSTK_CP%" com.ibm.wsdl.Main -in %WSDL_DOC% -override on -
package
```

He then ran the `proxygen` command:

> proxygen Campground_Service.wsdl

This created and compiled the `CampgroundProxy` class into the `cg4\com\organizedCampgrounds\proxy` directory. He inspected the `CampgroundProxy.java` file and saw that it was roughly equivalent to the `CampgroundProxy.java` file that he had created manually in the cg3 prototype. This would be a real time-saver!

If the Campground interface did not have any complex types (such as `Campsite`) he would now be ready to go. However, there was one problem. He noticed that `proxygen` had generated its own version of `Campsite.java`. This was unfortunate since he already had his own implementation of Campsite. This is a limitation of WSTK 2.3, but not a difficult one to work around.

He needed to edit two files: `cg4\DeploymentDescriptor.xml` and `cg4\com\organizedCampgrounds\proxy\CampgroundProxy.java`, and he needed to make the same two edits to each file:

1. His `Campsite` class uses the BeanSerializer instead of the one that `proxygen` created, so he replaced the 2 instances of `com.organizedCampgrounds.proxy.CampsiteSerializer` with `org.apache.soap.encoding.soapenc.BeanSerializer`.

443

2. His `Campsite` class is in the `com.organizedCampgrounds` package, so he replaced the instances of `com.organizedCampgrounds.proxy.Campsite` with `com.organizedCampgrounds.Campsite`.

After making these two edits in each of the two files, he noticed one other difference between the generated proxy and the proxy he had created earlier. The generated proxy's class declaration did not specify that it implemented the `Campground` interface. Doing so would have the benefit of providing some compile-time protection when building `Client.java`. He made a note to consider that as a future enhancement and proceeded to compile the proxy:

> **javac com\organizedCampgrounds\proxy\CampgroundProxy.java**

He was now ready to run. He stopped any Tomcat processes that were running, changed to the `cg4` directory, and then proceeded to restart Tomcat.

Before deploying, he learned of an alternative to the web browser SOAP admin interface, which he could use to deploy and undeploy. From another command window he ran the following:

> **java org.apache.soap.server.ServiceManagerClient**
> **http://localhost:8080/soap/servlet/rpcrouter undeploy urn:Campground**

This command, which he put into a script named `undeploy.bat` (in the `install` directory) so he could easily rerun it later, invokes the `ServiceManagerClient` application that may be used to undeploy and deploy. In this case, since he specified `undeploy`, which undeployed Campground. He then ran the following command to deploy:

> **java org.apache.soap.server.ServiceManagerClient**
> **http://localhost:8080/soap/servlet/rpcrouter deploy DeploymentDescriptor.xml**

This command, which he put into a script named `deploy.bat` (also in the `install` directory), deploys a service according to the information contained within `DeploymentDescriptor.xml` (This file was thoughtfully produced by `wsdlgen`). This made sense to Derek, since he had provided nearly all the information necessary to deploy when he ran `wsdlgen` (although he had to edit it to correct the serializer). Using this command would be a real time saver compared to using the web browser interface. He then ran `deploy.bat` from the `cg4` directory:

> **..\deploy.bat**

Not being the trusting sort, he then went to the web browser admin interface at http://localhost:8080/soap/admin and listed the Campground service to verify the deployment information. It looked fine, so he proceeded to run his client using the following:

> **java com.organizedCampgrounds.Client 0**

It ran correctly, so he now had a tool that could generate proxies automatically. Armed with this, he could easily imagine how member servers would be written for campgrounds by developers all over the world. Since these servers would all implement the `Campground` interface, his client could be distributed to customers, and it would work with any of the member servers.

But how would a customer find the member servers?

UDDI

A similar issue had been nagging Derek for a while. His client code had the following line:

```
campground.setEndPoint(new URL("http://localhost:8080/soap/servlet/rpcrouter"));
```

If there were only one member server, then, when deployed to the general public, this URL would be changed to point to a public web server where the member campground server is resident. However, what if that server moves? It would be a disaster to hardcode the URL in the client. How would he update the client application? Wouldn't it be better to lookup the location of the server in some directory service, hosted at a location that would not be subject to change? If he could do that, then updating the URL for the campground server would simply be a matter of modifying the public directory.

While the campground client application he had been prototyping would actually be contacting multiple servers, he could foresee other Organized Campgrounds applications which might need such a directory lookup capability to find a single service, so he decided to explore this technique. After mastering that, he would proceed to working with multiple services.

He had some experience of UDDI, and it seemed like just the kind of directory service he was looking for. UDDI, the Universal Description Discovery and Integration system is a standard XML protocol that is used as an interface to UDDI directory servers, called **operator sites**. A UDDI operator site acts like a phone book, performing searches for services on a number of different criteria. . When performed at run-time by the client, such a search is "just in time", or JIT. These searches are the "discovery" in UDDI, and permit a client to discover the location of a particular service of interest…just the kind of thing Derek had in mind.

If he were going to prototype an application that used UDDI, he would need a sandbox in which to work, so he visited http://www-3.ibm.com/services/uddi/testregistry/index.html. This test area web site is provided by IBM as a place to register Web Services for use during application development. He followed the instructions there to obtain a user id and password. After registering, he logged into the server with his web browser to verify that his user id and password were correct.

He edited the wstkProperties.xml file in wstk2.3\lib so that his client application would know how to contact a UDDI server (the UDDI library reads this file at run time):

```
<!-- Default UDDI registry name -->
   <uddi.registry.name>ibmtest</uddi.registry.name>

   <!--IBM Test Area -->
   <uddi.inquiry.ibmtest>
      http://www-3.ibm.com/services/uddi/testregistry/inquiryapi
   </uddi.inquiry.ibmtest>
   <uddi.publish.ibmtest>
      https://www-3.ibm.com/services/uddi/testregistry/protect/publishapi
   </uddi.publish.ibmtest>
   <uddi.userid.ibmtest>Derek</uddi.userid.ibmtest>
   <uddi.cred.ibmtest>passwordForDerek</uddi.cred.ibmtest>
```

The uddi.registry.name element indicates that the ibmtest UDDI server is to be used. The following elements indicate how to contact that server. In particular, he put his UDDI user name in the uddi.userid.ibmtest element and his password in the uddi.cred.ibmtest element.

He was now ready to start using the UDDI directory server to eliminate the hardcoded URL in his client application.

The first step would be to put the URL on the directory server. He noticed from the web site that it was possible to do this interactively from his web browser. However, from his past experience with deploying his campground server with SOAP, he preferred a programmatic approach where he could issue a command to perform the operation. For this purpose, he chose to use a library that is included in the WSTK. The WSTK actually provides UDDI access in a pair of `.jar` files: `wstk2.3\uddi4j\lib\uddi4j.jar` is a low-level library for UDDI access, and `wstk2.3\lib\wstk.jar` is a higher-level library that builds on `uddi4j.jar` to provide more convenient access. He could have simply appended these to his classpath, but WSTK includes a copy of SOAP and, when using WSTK libraries, it is best to use the version of SOAP that is included with it. So, he created a special command window just for the purpose of running applications that communicate with the UDDI server (that will include the `BorregoCampgroundRegister` and the client application, and later, the `PalomarCampgroundRegister`) and set his `CLASSPATH` in this new window with the following commands:

```
> call %WSTK_HOME%\bin\wstkenv.bat
> set CLASSPATH=%WSTK_CP%;%WSTK_HOME%\uddi4j\lib\uddi4j.jar
```

> All following commands that register services with UDDI, and build and run clients that use UDDI were run in command windows initialized by issuing these commands after running **config.bat**. Command windows, which deployed Web Services and ran Tomcat, were initialized as before, by simply running **config.bat**.

For convenience, he put these two commands into a file named `configuddi.bat` in the install directory.

He then created a new directory tree, `cg5`, by cloning `cg4`. Next, he wrote a small program to register his service and put it in `com\borregoCampground\BorregoCampgroundRegister.java`. This task would be how the developers of future campground servers would register their servers so customers can find them:

```java
package com.borregoCampground;

import com.ibm.wstk.service.registry.ServiceRegistryProxy;
import com.ibm.wstk.service.definition.ServiceDefinition;
import com.ibm.wstk.service.definition.ServiceImplementation;
import com.ibm.wstk.service.definition.ServiceInterface;
import com.ibm.wstk.service.definition.soap.SOAPServiceDefinition;
import com.ibm.wstk.soap.SOAPServiceManagerProxy;
import com.ibm.wstk.service.util.CategoryList;
import com.ibm.wstk.uddi.TModelKeyTable;
import com.ibm.wstk.service.provider.ServiceProvider;

public class BorregoCampgroundRegister {

    public static void main(String[] args) throws Exception {

    /**
     * Set up a proxy to use to communicate with the UDDI service.
     */
        ServiceRegistryProxy srp = new ServiceRegistryProxy();
        String soapRouterURL = args[3];
```

```
/**
 * Specify the category for the service. As a campground,
 * it fits under category 90.
 */
    CategoryList categoryList = new CategoryList();
    categoryList.addCategory(TModelKeyTable.UNSPSC_TMODEL_KEY,
                             "Travel, Food, Lodging and Entertainment
                             Services","90");

/*
 * Register the Service Provider, i.e. the business Borrego Campground
 */
    String providerName = "BorregoCampground";
    String providerDesc = "Borrego Campground";

    ServiceProvider serviceProvider =
        new ServiceProvider(providerName,providerDesc,categoryList);
    serviceProvider = srp.publish(serviceProvider);
    System.out.println("\tProvider Business Key: " +
                       serviceProvider.getBusinessKey());

/**
 * Register the Service Interface, to specify the API to the
 * Campground service.
 */
    String interfaceWSDL = args[0];
    ServiceInterface serviceInterface =
        new ServiceInterface(interfaceWSDL, categoryList);
    serviceInterface = srp.publish(serviceInterface);
    System.out.println("\tInterface tModel Key: " +
                       serviceInterface.getTModelKey());

/**
 * Register the Service Implementation, which indicates specifically
 * how to contact the Borrego Campground web service.
 */
    String implementationWSDL = args[1];
    String deploymentDescriptor = args[2];
    SOAPServiceDefinition ssd =
        new SOAPServiceDefinition(implementationWSDL,
                                  categoryList,
                                  deploymentDescriptor,
                                  soapRouterURL);
    ServiceDefinition sd = srp.publish(serviceProvider, ssd);
    System.out.println("\tImplementation Service Key: " +
                       sd.getServiceImplementation().getServiceKey());
    }
}
```

This program has 5 steps:

1. Establish a proxy to communicate with the UDDI server or operator site. This proxy class, `ServiceRegistryProxy`, is provided as part of the WSTK UDDI library to facilitate access to the UDDI server. He was familiar with this technique, having used it himself in his client. It would serve to provide access to the UDDI server while hiding the gory details of that access. The information in the `wstkProperties.xml` file (including his user name and password) would be used by the proxy to contact the UDDI server.

2. Choose a category for the Web Service. Categories serve to organize services along functional lines in order to facilitate browsing or searching for a particular kind of service. UDDI includes a number of categorization schemes, any or all of which may be used simultaneously to categorize a service in a number of ways. He reviewed the UNSPC categories on the UDDI web site and selected one that was appropriate for a campground: Number 90, "Travel, Food, Lodging and Entertainment Services".

3. Register the service provider. The service provider is the business that offers the Web Service, in this case Borrego Campground. The UDDI spec refers to this as a "business entity".

4. Register the service interface. This describes the API that the Web Service, that is, the BorregoCampground class, supports. The UDDI API uses WSDL files to describe this API and he had generated an interface WSDL file in prototype 4, so he would use that file (specifying it on the command line when running this program). In UDDI terms, this is the "tModel" (for technical model).

5. Register the service implementation. This describes, among other things, the location (generally via URL) to one particular member server. Unlike the service interface, the implementation would vary from member server to member server. In UDDI terms, this is the "binding template". For more in-depth information UDDI terminology mentioned here, see Chapters 6 and 7.

This table lists the various UDDI data structures for the Campground case, and which party they are maintained by:

Maintained by each member campground (for example, Borrego Campground)	Maintained by Organized Campgrounds
Service Provider ("Borrego Campground")	Service Interface (The Campground.java interface)
Service Implementation (URL to the Web Service)	

The BorregoCamgroundRegister.java program was compiled with the following command (ensuring that the CLASSPATH was set as indicated earlier to include wstk.jar and uddi4j.jar):

> javac com\borregoCampground\BorregoCampgroundRegister.java

It now became clear to Derek why wsdlgen had produced two WSDL files. The interface, which will be shared among all member servers goes into one file: Campground_Service-interface.wsdl. The implementation, which will be specific to each member server, goes into Campground_Service.wsdl. He immediately saw that the best way to deploy this would be to have OrganizedCampgrounds.com provide an interface file on their web server that all member services could share. He recalled that when running wsdlgen in prototype cg4, he entered a WSDL URL prefix. He specified the path on his file system where the WSDL files resided (the cg4 directory). It was now obvious that in future, when developers of member servers run wsdlgen, they should enter the URL to an interface file that resides on the OrganizedCampgrounds.com web server. Also, the service interface registration that he included in BorregoCampgroundRegister.java for the prototype would actually be performed by Organized Campgrounds in the production environment.

In order to emulate this configuration for his development environment, Derek performed the following steps:

- ❑ Since Tomcat acts as a simple web server as well as a servlet container, he would use Tomcat as the web server that would deliver the WSDL files. To do so, he created a `wsdl` directory in `jakarta-tomcat-3.2.2\webapps\Root`.

- ❑ He could have rerun `wsdlgen` using the URL http://localhost:8080/wsdl, but Derek chose to simply edit `Campground_Service.wsdl`, replacing

  ```
  location="c:\\install\cg4/Campground_Service-interface.wsdl"
  ```

  with

  ```
  location="http://localhost:8080/wsdl/Campground_Service-interface.wsdl"
  ```

  This would import the interface file from the web server when reading the implementation file.

- ❑ Looking ahead to the possibility of having multiple campgrounds deployed he gave this implementation a unique name by replacing this line in `Campground_Service.wsdl`

- ❑ `<service name="Campground">`

  with this:

  ```
  <service name="Campground-Borrego">
  ```

  This would serve to register his implementation with a name to distinguish it from other campgrounds.

- ❑ Copy the two WSDL files into the `jakarta-tomcat-3.2.2\webapps\Root\wsdl` directory that he created in the first step.

Now he could serve up access to the implementation and interface WSDL files in his development environment just like the future developers of member servers would do. The only difference was that, while he had both files on one web server, in the production environment, the single interface file would be on the central **OrganizedCampgrounds.com** web server and the various implementation files would be on the many member web servers. He tested that the WSDL files were deployed properly by entering the following URL into his web browser:

http://localhost:8080/wsdl/Campground_Service.wsdl (Tomcat was still running from prototype 4).

When the WSDL files were properly implemented, this showed the implementation WSDL file, and he used this to verify that the location for the import was
`location="http://localhost:8080/wsdl/Campground_Service-interface.wsdl"`

He was now ready to register his service with the UDDI server, so he ran his `CampgroundRegister` program. The register program takes four input parameters:

- ❑ The name of the interface file
- ❑ The name of the implementation file

449

❏   The name of the deployment descriptor file

❏   The URL to the rpcrouter servlet

Running from the cg5 directory, he entered the following at the command prompt:

```
> java com.borregoCampground.BorregoCampgroundRegister
Campground_Service-interface.wsdl Campground_Service.wsdl DeploymentDescriptor.xml
http://localhost:8080/soap/servlet/rpcrouter
```

When run successfully, it reported a Provider Business Key, an interface tModel Key, and an Implementation Service Key. When an entity is registered with a UDDI operator site, a globally unique identifier, a key, is assigned to the entity. The output of the command showed that the entities had been successfully registered and assigned keys. Derek had just performed the task that each future developer of a member service would perform: he had registered a member service with a UDDI registry so that the client application could find it. Now it was time to enhance his client application to use the UDDI registry. To ensure that the registration had succeeded, he logged into the IBM UDDI test area with his web browser and verified that the web service was indeed registered. He saw the business name, which corresponds to the service provider in the BorregoCampgroundRegister application, the service, which corresponds to the ServiceImplementation, and the service type, which corresponds to the ServiceInterface. The display he got looked like the following:

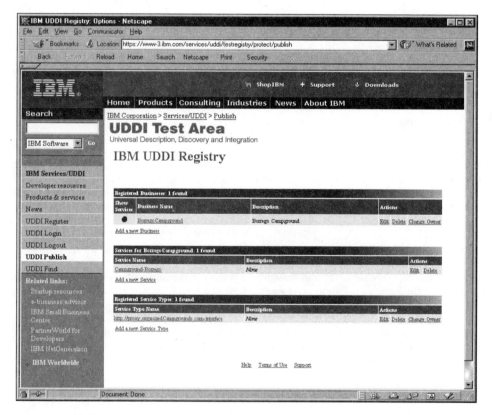

It was now time to enhance his client to use the UDDI registry to eliminate the hard-coded URL to the Web Service. First, he needed a utility to perform the UDDI lookup (UDDI.java):

```java
package com.organizedCampgrounds;

import java.util.Vector;

import com.ibm.uddi.datatype.binding.*;
import com.ibm.wstk.service.definition.*;
import com.ibm.wstk.service.registry.*;
import com.ibm.uddi.util.*;

/**
 * Provide access to a UDDI registry.
 */
public class UDDI{
   /**
    * Use a UDDI registry to find the end point for a service, given
    * a name of the service and the name of the binding port.
    */
   public static String getServiceEndPoint(String serviceName, String
      portName){
   try {
      ServiceRegistryProxy serviceRegistry = new ServiceRegistryProxy();
      ServiceDefinition[] def = serviceRegistry.findServices(serviceName,
      true);
      ServiceImplementation impl = def[0].getServiceImplementation();

      /*
       * Of the potentially multiple binding templates, find the one
       * that matches the specified portName.  First, find the position
       * of the specified port in the portNames array....
       */
      String[] portNames = impl.getPortNames();
      int portIndex=0;
      boolean found = false;
      for (int i = 0;  i < portNames.length; i++) {
         if (portNames[i].equals(portName)) {
         portIndex = i;
         found = true;
         break;
      }
   }

      if (found == false)
      return(null);

      /*
       * ... Next, use that index to look up the BindingTemplate in
       * the BindingTemplate Vector.
       */
      Vector v = impl.getBindingTemplateList();
      BindingTemplate template = (BindingTemplate)
         impl.getBindingTemplateList().elementAt(portIndex);
      return(template.getAccessPoint().getText());

      } catch (ServiceRegistryProxyException ex) {
         System.err.println("Registry lookup error: " + ex.getMessage());
      }
      return null;
   }

}
```

This utility takes the name of a service and retrieves the URL to be used by SOAP to contact a specific instance of that Web Service. The `ServiceRegistryProxy` class offers many ways to find service interfaces and service implementations. For example, given an interface, it can find all services that support that interface. For this prototype, Derek chose to search for services by name. In order to keep his prototype simple, he used the second argument to the `findServices` call to indicate to only search his own area of the UDDI operator site (Most published URLs on the UDDI test server, like Derek's, include localhost, so each one is only useful to the developer who registered it).

After compiling this (again, in a command window in which the `configuddi.bat` command had been run) this with the command:

> **javac com\organizedCampgrounds\UDDI.java**

he then modified `Client.java` to replace the hard-coded URL in the line that calls `setEndPoint()` with a call to the `UDDI.getServiceEndPoint` method:

```
String url = UDDI.getServiceEndPoint("Campground", "CampgroundPort");
System.out.println("URL from UDDI: " + url);
campground.setEndPoint(new URL (url));
```

This would find the service that begins with the string "Campground" (the `findServices` method is essentially a wild card search, so it returns services which begin with "Campground") and return the URL. Compiling the client with:

> **javac com\organizedCampgrounds\Client.java**

he was now ready to try it out:

> **java com.organizedCampgrounds.Client 0**

It displayed the following, when run twice identically:

This showed that the URL to the web service had been retrieved from the UDDI server.

Derek had now successfully used UDDI to eliminate the hardcoded URL in his client. If the Borrego Campground server moved to a new URL, Borrego Campground would only have to update the UDDI registry and the client would continue to function properly.

The UDDI directory had served this important purpose, but there was a second way in which he wanted to use it. There would be many member servers in the production system and he wanted to prototype the ability to find all of these servers. This meant he needed to emulate the existence of multiple servers. In this next prototype he wanted to have the client find multiple servers, present the list to the user, who would then choose a campground, and then be presented with the list of campsites for that selected campground. This meant he would have to create a second web service and register it with the UDDI server.

Setting Up Another Web Service

However, he only had one development machine. So, to create a second Web Service on the same machine as the first server, he performed the following steps:

❑ Implement a second campground web service. He created a `cg6` directory, which was a clone of the `cg5` directory, except he replaced references to the Borrego campground with Palomar campground.

❑ Clone the `soap-2_2` directory tree. This would emulate a second Web Service. He named this clone `soap-palomar`.

❑ Clone the `jakarta-tomcat-3.2.2` directory tree. He would run a second instance of Tomcat, this one listening on port 8090, instead of listening on 8080 like the first one does. This would emulate the existence of a second member server. He named this clone `tomcat-8090`, and then edited the `server.xml` file in the `conf` directory of the clone to change the soap context to use `soap-palomar`. He did this by modifying the `docBase` attribute of the `Context` element he added earlier. This means he replaced this line in the palomar version of `server.xml`:

```
docBase="C:/soap-2_2/webapps/soap"
```

with

```
docBase="c:/soap-palomar/webapps/soap"
```

He also modified any `Connector` elements that were not commented out and changed the port values so that they would not conflict with the port in use by the original Tomcat. He found them and changed them as follows from 8007 to 8008 (any unused port will do):

```
<Parameter name="port" value="8008"/>
```

The final change you need to make to this file is to change the connection port from 8080 to any unused port. Derek chose 8090. Search `server.xml` for its one instance of 8080, and change it to 8090.

❑ Next, he created a new command window, set the directory to `cg6`, ran the `..\config.bat` command, entered the `set TOMCAT_HOME=c:\\tomcat-8090` command to refer to the cloned Tomcat directory, and entered tomcat run. In his web browser he entered http://localhost:8090/soap/admin to visit the admin page for the palomar server. When he performed a List, he saw a service deployed since this soap context was copied from the Borrego server, which had one service deployed. He then used the Undeploy button to remove this service.

❑ He created a `cg6\com\palomarCampground` directory, which contained a Palomar Campground service very similar to the Borrego Campground, except with different campsite information (the source for this service may be found in the `cg6\com\palomarCampground` directory of the code download for this chapter at http://www.wrox.com/)

❑ He ran `wsdlgen` as before, substituting `palomar` for `borrego` and port `8090` for `8080`. Here are the values he entered into the "Java Class WSDL Generation" form:

Class Name	`com.palomarCampground.PalomarCampground`
Output Filename	`Campground_Service.wsdl`
Service Name	`Campground`
Service URN	`urnCampground`
Target Namespace	`http://proxy.organizedCampgrounds.com`
Binding URL	`http://localhost:8090/soap/servlet/rpcrouter`
WSDL URL Prefix	`http://localhost:8090/wsdl`

❑ He then made the same two edits to the `com\organizedCampgrounds\proxy\CampgroundProxy.java` and `DeploymentDescriptor.xml` that he had made before:

1. His `Campsite` class uses the BeanSerializer instead of the one that `proxygen` created, so he replaced the 2 instances of `com.organizedCampgrounds.proxy.CampsiteSerializer` with `org.apache.soap.encoding.soapenc.BeanSerializer`.

2. His `Campsite` class is in the `com.organizedCampgrounds` package, so he replaced the instances of `com.organizedCampgrounds.proxy.Campsite` with `com.organizedCampgrounds.Campsite`.

❑ He edited `Campground_Service.wsdl` as before, to give this implementation a unique name in the UDDI registry (within the scope of his business), replacing

```
<service name="Campground">
```

with

```
<service name="Campground-Palomar">
```

❑ As before, he then copied the two `.wsdl` files into the `tomcat-8090\webapps\Root\wsdl` directory. Again, he verified the proper implementation of these by entering the following URL into his web browser:

http://localhost:8090/wsdl/Campground_Service.wsdl

As expected, this showed a service element with the name "Campground-Palomar".

❏   Now it was time to actually deploy the new service, with the following commands:

> **..\config.bat**
> **java org.apache.soap.server.ServiceManagerClient**
>   **http://localhost:8090/soap/servlet/rpcrouter deploy DeploymentDescriptor.xml**

He now had two web servers, one listening on port 8080 and the other on 8090. The one on 8080 had Borrego Campground deployed and the one listening on port 8090 had Palomar Campground deployed.

He was now ready to register Palomar with the UDDI server. Here he had to make a concession to working in a development environment. The IBM UDDI test server only permits one business per account. So, instead of creating a second business for Palomar, as would be the case in the production environment, he would add Palomar as a second service to Borrego. He used a slightly modified version of `BorregoCampgroundRegister.java`, named `PalomarCampgroundRegister.java`:

```
package com.palomarCampground;

import com.ibm.wstk.service.registry.ServiceRegistryProxy;
import com.ibm.wstk.service.definition.ServiceDefinition;
import com.ibm.wstk.service.definition.ServiceImplementation;
import com.ibm.wstk.service.definition.ServiceInterface;
import com.ibm.wstk.service.definition.soap.SOAPServiceDefinition;
import com.ibm.wstk.soap.SOAPServiceManagerProxy;
import com.ibm.wstk.service.util.CategoryList;
import com.ibm.wstk.uddi.TModelKeyTable;
import com.ibm.wstk.service.provider.ServiceProvider;

public class PalomarCampgroundRegister {

    public static void main(String[] args) throws Exception {

    /**
        * Set up a proxy to use to communicate with the UDDI service.
    */
    ServiceRegistryProxy srp = new ServiceRegistryProxy();
    String soapRouterURL = args[3];
    SOAPServiceManagerProxy ssmp =
        new SOAPServiceManagerProxy(soapRouterURL);

    /**
        * Specify the category for the service. As a campground,
        * it fits under category 90.
    */
    CategoryList categoryList = new CategoryList();
    categoryList.addCategory(TModelKeyTable.UNSPSC_TMODEL_KEY,
        "Travel, Food, Lodging and Entertainment Services","90");

    /*
        * For test purposes, find the existing Service Provider,
        * BorregoCampground, instead of creating a new one.
    */
    ServiceProvider[] serviceProviders =
        srp.findServiceProviders("BorregoCampground", true);
    ServiceProvider serviceProvider = serviceProviders[0];
    System.out.println("\tProvider Business Key: " +
```

```
                serviceProvider.getBusinessKey());

    /**
        * Register the Service Implementation, which indicates specifically
        * how to contact the Palomar Campground web service.
    */
    String implementationWSDL = args[1];
    String deploymentDescriptor = args[2];
    SOAPServiceDefinition ssd =
        new SOAPServiceDefinition(implementationWSDL,
                                  categoryList,
                                  deploymentDescriptor,
                                  soapRouterURL);
    ServiceDefinition sd = srp.publish(serviceProvider, ssd);
    System.out.println("\tImplementation Service Key: " +
        sd.getServiceImplementation().getServiceKey());

    }
}
```

This modified version did not register a Service Provider (a business), even though in production it would. It did not register a service interface (service type) either, which correctly emulated the production environment since only Organized Campgrounds would register the single service interface that all the member servers would share. It did, however, register a service, named `Campground-Palomar` (this name is specified in the `Campground_Service.wsdl` file). He then created a command window in which he ran `wstkenv.bat` and added the `uddi4j` `jar` files to his classpath (as described earlier, using the `configuddi.bat` script in the `install` directory). Lastly, he compiled it using

> javac com\palomarCampground\PalomarCampgroundRegister.java

He then ran it similarly to the `BorregoCampgroundRegister` he ran earlier, with the slight difference that this service would be located at port 8090:

> java com.palomarCampground.PalomarCampgroundRegister
Campground_Service-interface.wsdl Campground_Service.wsdl DeploymentDescriptor.xml
http://localhost:8090/servlet/rpcrouter

He then verified the registration by visiting his UDDI test area web page and saw that indeed, there were now two services registered: one at port 8080, and a second one, Campground-Palomar, at port 8090. (He examined the port numbers by clicking on each service name to see the service details, something that you can try yourself). The UDDI site now looks like this:

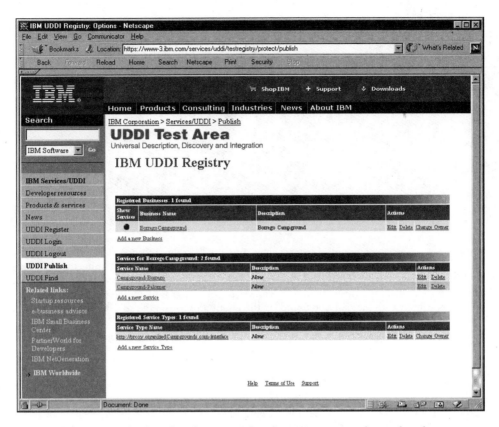

He now had two services deployed and registered and it was time to enhance his client to present a list of services to the user. First, he enhanced the `UDDI.getServiceEndPoints()` method to return a `ServiceDescriptor` array instead of a string. Each descriptor would contain a URL and the name of a service:

```
package com.organizedCampgrounds;

public class ServiceDescriptor{
    public String url;
    public String description;
    public ServiceDescriptor(String _url, String _desc){
        url = _url;
        description = _desc;
    }
}
```

He then modified the client to present a menu of the descriptions, and connected to the service at the corresponding URL (the source for this version of the `Client.java`, `UDDI.java`, and `ServiceDescriptor.java` files may be found in the `cg6\com\organizedCampgrounds` directory of the code download for this chapter at http://www.wrox.com/). After compiling these three files, he ran the client and observed the following:

```
Command Prompt                                                        _ □ ×
C:\install\cg6>java com.organizedCampgrounds.Client 0
Campgrounds:
(0) Campground-Borrego
(1) Campground-Palomar
Enter campground number:
1
URL from UDDI: http://localhost:8090/soap/servlet/rpcrouter
Price: 25
Campsite 0: Mountain top campsite with a view of the entire valley.
  Size: 500 square feet, Shade(1-10):  8
Campsite 1: This campsite is very popular since it is so secluded.
  Size: 450 square feet, Shade(1-10):  10
Campsite 2: This is a nice, big site that gets plenty of sunshine and has a lot
of room for setting up several tents.
  Size: 950 square feet, Shade(1-10):  3
Choose campsite:
0
Success: true

C:\install\cg6>
```

As you will observe, he saw a menu of two services, one for Borrego and one for Palomar. Choosing Palomar, he saw a different set of campsites to choose from than he saw when connecting to Borrego. Success! Not only had he used the UDDI server to store the URL for the service, he had used it as a searchable database of campground Web Services. As new campgrounds were implemented and registered, they would automatically be found by the client and presented to the user as campgrounds at which they could reserve a campsite.

End Game

Derek had now:

- ❑ Created two prototype Web Services and published their existence on a UDDI server
- ❑ Created a client that used the UDDI server to find the Web Services
- ❑ Used the information from the UDDI server to bind the client to the Web Services so that the client could employ the servers to perform a useful task

Before proceeding to fill out the Campground interface and the client to be more complete, he explored two other techniques: writing his own serializer, and using servlet containers other than Tomcat.

Writing a Serializer

Derek was concerned about the potential size of the XML that would be transmitted from the server to the client. Information such as the descriptions could potentially be quite lengthy and some clients could possibly be bandwidth constrained. For example, a client running on a wireless handheld device would have a low bandwidth connection to the Internet, and a voluminous SOAP message due to a long campsite description string could pose a problem. One solution that he investigated was writing his own serializer. If he had his own serializer for Campsite objects, he could do things like performing compression on the description string so that it would be shorter during transmission. Once received by the client, the serializer would uncompress the string so that it could be presented to the user in its original form. The code for the serializer is as follows:

```java
package com.organizedCampgrounds.proxy;

import java.io.*;
import java.util.zip.*;

import org.w3c.dom.*;
import org.apache.soap.*;
import org.apache.soap.encoding.soapenc.*;
import org.apache.soap.rpc.*;
import org.apache.soap.util.*;
import org.apache.soap.util.xml.*;

/**
   Serializer for Campsite class which compresses the description string.
*/
public class CampsiteCompSerializer implements Serializer, Deserializer{

    public void marshall(String inScopeEncStyle, Class javaType,
        Object src, Object context, Writer sink,
        NSStack nsStack, XMLJavaMappingRegistry xjmr,
        SOAPContext ctx)
            throws IllegalArgumentException, IOException{

        nsStack.pushScope();

        /*
         * Start the Campsite element.
         */
        SoapEncUtils.generateStructureHeader(inScopeEncStyle, javaType,
        context,
        sink, nsStack, xjmr);

        sink.write(StringUtils.lineSeparator);

        com.organizedCampgrounds.Campsite src2 =
            (com.organizedCampgrounds.Campsite)src;
        Parameter param;

        /*
         * The description string is compressed before inserting it into the
         * Parameter.
         */
        param = new Parameter("description", java.lang.String.class,
            compressIt(src2.description), null);
        xjmr.marshall(inScopeEncStyle, Parameter.class, param, null,
            sink, nsStack, ctx);
        sink.write(StringUtils.lineSeparator);

        /*
         * Size is an integer.
         */
        param = new Parameter("size", int.class, new Integer(src2.size),
        null);
            xjmr.marshall(inScopeEncStyle, Parameter.class, param, null,
            sink, nsStack, ctx);
            sink.write(StringUtils.lineSeparator);
```

```
      /*
       * Shade is an integer.
       */
      param = new Parameter("shade", int.class, new Integer(src2.shade),
      null);
      xjmr.marshall(inScopeEncStyle, Parameter.class, param, null,
         sink, nsStack, ctx);
      sink.write(StringUtils.lineSeparator);

      sink.write("</" + context + '>');

      nsStack.popScope();
   }

   public Bean unmarshall(String inScopeEncStyle, QName elementType,
      Node src, XMLJavaMappingRegistry xjmr,
      SOAPContext ctx)
      throws IllegalArgumentException{

      Element root = (Element)src;
      Element tempEl = DOMUtils.getFirstChildElement(root);
      com.organizedCampgrounds.proxy.Campsite target;

      try{
         /*
          * Create a Campsite object.
          */
         target =
(com.organizedCampgrounds.proxy.Campsite)com.organizedCampgrounds.Campsite.class.n
ewInstance();
      }
      catch (Exception e){
         throw new IllegalArgumentException("Error constructing object: "
         + e.getMessage());
      }

      while (tempEl != null){
         Bean paramBean = xjmr.unmarshall(inScopeEncStyle,
         RPCConstants.Q_ELEM_PARAMETER,
         tempEl,
         ctx);
         Parameter param = (Parameter)paramBean.value;
         String tagName = tempEl.getTagName();

         /*
          * Decompress the description string.
          */
         if (tagName.equals("description")){
            target.description_Elem =
            decompressIt((java.lang.String)param.getValue());
         }

         /*
          * Size is an integer.
          */
```

```
        if (tagName.equals("size")){
            target.size_Elem = ((Integer)param.getValue()).intValue();
        }

        /*
         * Shade is an integer.
         */
        if (tagName.equals("shade")){
            target.shade_Elem = ((Integer)param.getValue()).intValue();
        }

        /*
         * Get the next parameter.
         */
        tempEl = DOMUtils.getNextSiblingElement(tempEl);
    }

    return new Bean(com.organizedCampgrounds.Campsite.class, target);
}


/*
 * Compress a string.
 */
private String compressIt(String in){
    byte[] uncompressedBytes = in.getBytes();
    System.out.println("Original length: " + uncompressedBytes.length);
    Deflater def = new Deflater();
    def.setInput(uncompressedBytes);
    def.finish();
    byte outbuf[] = new byte[uncompressedBytes.length];
    int len = def.deflate(outbuf);
    System.out.println("Compressed length: " + len);
    byte[] compressedBytes = new byte[len];
    for(int i=0; i<len; i++)
    compressedBytes[i] = outbuf[i];
    return new String(compressedBytes);
}

/*
 * Decompress a string.
 */
private String decompressIt(String compressedBytes){
    Inflater inf = new Inflater();
    inf.setInput(compressedBytes.getBytes());
    byte infbuf[] = new byte[inf.getRemaining()*3];
    try{
        System.out.println("Inflated length: " + inf.inflate(infbuf));
    }
    catch(DataFormatException e){
        System.err.println("Err: " + e.getMessage());
    }
    return new String(infbuf);
}
}
```

His custom serializer implements the `Serializer` and `Deserializer` interfaces, which require the `marshall()` and `unmarshall()` methods, respectively. These methods mirror each other: `marshall()` takes each attribute of the Campsite and serializes it, while `unmarshall()` deserializes each attribute.

Serialization consists of some boilerplate code to emit the proper XML (for example the `generateStructureHeader` and `sink.write` calls) along with creation of Parameter objects and passing of the Parameters to the `XMLJavaMappingRegistry`. One Parameter object is built for each attribute to be transmitted (although sometimes it is convenient to have multiple Parameters per attribute). Since the type-mapping registry will have serializers defined for the object forms of all the Java primitives, the task of writing a custom serializer is reduced to assembling a set of Parameter objects, each of which contains a primitive object. For example, the Parameter for the `shade` attribute contains an Integer.

Deserialization is the reverse process – a series of elements are retrieved, and the value is retrieved from each one. The `Campsite` object is then constructed from those values.

Using this technique, Derek was able to specialize his serialization. When deploying his Web Services, he specified his custom `CampsiteCompSerializer` instead of the Bean serializer like he had done before.

Using an Alternative Servlet Container

While Tomcat worked fine as a servlet container for his prototypes, he felt the need for a more advanced servlet container as he approached the release of the project. He learned about JRun (see http://www.allaire.com/ for information, and download a trial version of JRun 3.1 from http://www.macromedia.com/software/jrun/trial), a popular servlet container, and found that in some cases it would be a useful alternative to Tomcat. For example, JRun provides more control over partitioning Web Services into multiple JVM (Java virtual machine) instances. This can be useful in a production environment where a failure in one JVM shouldn't impair other Web Services. However, JRun can be more complex to configure and run, so Derek continued to use Tomcat when prototyping. Using JRun with SOAP was not difficult and involved the same two steps that he had performed with Tomcat to configure it to work with SOAP.

First, he modified the CLASSPATH variable so that the Xerces XML library would be at the front, so that would supersede any other XML libraries, which might occur in the CLASSPATH. Also, he added `soap.jar` to the CLASSPATH. JRun offers a number of ways to modify CLASSPATH, and you would normally append to the CLASSPATH in a local properties file, but Derek was again faced with the dilemma of how to put `xerces.jar` at the front, so he chose the straightforward approach of modifying `java.classpath` in the `global.properties` in the `lib` directory of the JRun folder (JRUN_HOME) as follows:

```
jrun.classpath=c:\\soap\\soap-2_2\\lib\\soap.jar;d:\\install\\xerces-
1_4_0\\xerces.jar;c:\\jdk1.2.2\\jaf-1.0.1\\activation.jar;c:\\jdk1.2.2\\javamail-
1.1.3\\mail.jar;{jrun.rootdir}/lib/ext;{jrun.rootdir}/lib/jrun.jar;{jrun.rootdir}/
lib/install.jar
```

Second, for his prototype, he chose to add the SOAP application to the default server in JRun. To accomplish this, he modified the `soap-app.rootdir`, `soap-app.class`, and `webapp.mapping` lines of the `local.properties` file in the JRun `servers\default` directory:

```
soap-app.rootdir=c:\\install\\soap-2_2\\webapps\\soap
soap-app.class={webapp.service-class}
webapp.mapping./soap=soap-app
```

Also in this file, he added soap to the list of applications in the default server:

```
servlet.webapps=default-app,demo-app,etx-app,soap-app
```

With this configuration he was able to run SOAP within the JRun servlet container, in the same way that he had done earlier with Tomcat, but he was now able to take advantage of the additional features of JRun.

Epilog

At this point he had learned all the new technologies he would require to complete the project, and felt confident in his ability to use them. He then proceeded onto the less daunting tasks of refining the servers and the client. For example, he added more methods to the server to provide more information to the user about the campgrounds and campsites, and to make the reservation process more complete. Geographic information was added to the Campground interface so a customer could find campgrounds in a particular area of interest. He also added persistence to the reservations so they would remain intact between instantiations of the Campground object, and enhanced the reservations so they could be made more than seven days in advance and for more than one day at a time. He changed the UDDI searching so that, instead of searching by name, the client searched to find all servers implementing the campground interface and implemented a GUI for the client.

When it was time to deploy the client application, Derek faced a choice: he could continue to implement it as an application, which would be installed on the user's computer. This worked fine, but it would be simpler for the customer if no installation was required. That suggested a second possibility: make the client a servlet that runs on Organized Campgrounds' web server. In that scenario, the customer uses their web browser to contact the servlet at www.OrganizedCampgrounds.com and the servlet generates HTML forms, which are displayed in the customer's web browser to perform the same tasks as the client application. The servlet alternative was attractive since it meant that nothing from Organized Campgrounds needed to be installed on the customer's computer. The advantage to the application was that it could have a richer user interface since it wasn't limited to HTML. In the end, both alternatives were implemented and it was the customer's choice whether to use one or the other.

After the Campground interface and client application were complete, it was time for the member campgrounds to begin implementing their own Web Services. They used Derek's prototypes as examples and deployed them on their own server machines and registered them with a UDDI registry. When the system went live, relatively few member servers were published, but the number grew over time and, through the magic of publish-find-bind, the client application/servlet automatically discovered these new member campgrounds as they were added and presented them to customers.

Summary

At this point we leave Derek and his world of campground Web Services. By the time you have worked through all the examples listed here (the code for which can all the downloaded from http://www.wrox.com/), you should be able to do the following:

- ❑ Implement a Java-based server-client web service application through Apache and Tomcat, using SOAP to access and transmit objects.

- ❑ Monitor the passing of these SOAP objects through the serialization/deserialization process using a tunneler.

- ❑ Add a proxy class to the application to deal with the SOAP complexities, making the Java code easier to implement.

- ❑ Use the IBM WSTK to automatically generate the proxy class.

- ❑ Register the web service and add additional services to our application through the use of a UDDI site, thus enabling the client to discover the presence and location of Web Services.

- ❑ Begin to explore the ideas of writing custom serializers, and using alternate servlet containers to Tomcat.

11
.NET Web Services

Microsoft has made it clear: the future of Windows development is .NET. With .NET, Microsoft recognizes what we, fans of Web Services, already know: the future of software lies in applications integrating code and data living across the Internet. Moreover, with .NET, Microsoft provides a new framework to facilitate these distributed, collaborative applications. The term .NET describes the whole enchilada – Microsoft's corporate-wide strategy to develop new products and services, and retool existing products to support this future. Over the next few years all of Microsoft's flagship products – the operating systems, the Office suite, the enterprise servers – will be folded into the .NET vision. In addition, Microsoft is developing several .NET "building block services". These are Web Services to which developers can subscribe. Passport – a service that provides user authentication – is one of these Microsoft building block services that exist today. Another example is the recently announced HailStorm (http://www.microsoft.com/net/hailstorm.asp), a Web Service implementation that makes a user's preferences, address book entries, inbox, calendar, and other personal data available over the web. Hailstorm is pre-Beta at the time of writing, but in the future applications will be able to authenticate a user and then query profile information from HailStorm. This prevents a user from having to continually re-enter personal data. The Microsoft-provided building block Web Services exemplify the .NET vision (for more on Hailstorm, refer to Chapter 1).

While .NET refers to the vision, the **.NET Framework** refers to specifics: the run-time environment in which .NET applications execute, and the .NET class libraries with which .NET applications are built. If there is a theme to this chapter, and to the .NET Framework itself, it is that XML Web Services are extremely important in .NET. Consequently, the .NET Framework class libraries and .NET tools make building and deploying Web Services, and clients that use them, shockingly easy. Remarkably, only a year or so ago, the SOAP Toolkit was considered a proof of concept. Web services in the .NET Framework are not an experiment – they are fundamental.

While the SOAP Toolkit 2.0 will remain an important tool for developers for some time, developers adopting .NET will enjoy .NET's integrated support and range of options for developing Web Services. At the time of writing, .NET is still in Beta, although developers have had their hands on it since the autumn of 2000, and most have been surprised by its present stability. It's important to note that the .NET Framework is not COM-based; .NET Framework classes are not COM components. However, .NET provides rich COM interoperability services that allow developers to generate wrappers and use so-called "legacy" COM components. .NET's rich Web Service integration may even compel developers to explore .NET's web service support coupled with .NET's interoperability services, if only to deploy a Web Service interface for existing COM components.

In this chapter we will look at Web Services in .NET, including:

❑   A **.NET Primer**. Understanding a few .NET Framework concepts will give us context for the rest of the chapter. In this section, we'll introduce the basic features of a .NET application and we'll briefly discuss .NET code execution.

❑   An **ASP.NET Web Service**. As we have already promised, developing Web Services in .NET is simple, particularly with ASP.NET – Microsoft's .NET rewrite of its Active Server Pages. In this section, we will describe an example web service to retrieve up-to-date area codes. We start by looking at the prototype application class that provides this functionality. Then, using only `Notepad.exe` and the magic of three additional lines of code, we will transform our .NET class into a deployable web service. We will then use ASP.NET's built-in support to test our service and view it's WSDL description.

❑   **ASP.NET Web Services with Visual Studio .NET**. Visual Studio .NET (VS.NET) is Microsoft's .NET-generation development environment. The application templates in VS.NET, create more sophisticated deployments of Web Services. In this section, we will walk through the steps of creating a web service using VS.NET. This will give us an opportunity to discuss additional options we have in deploying our web service.

❑   **Building Web Service Proxies**. Once we have deployed our web service, both with and without VS.NET, we will turn to creating a client application. In this section, we will cover generating and using a client proxy. Walking through the steps of creating a web service proxy, we will get to see **Web Service Discovery** (**DISCO**) at work. This gives us an excuse to introduce a few DISCO basics.

❑   **.NET Remoting**. While ASP.NET makes writing and deploying Web Services a walk in the park, the .NET Framework gives us other mechanisms to create Web Services. In this section, we will introduce .NET Remoting. We will discuss how and why .NET Remoting could be used to create a web service. We won't cover .NET Remoting in depth because this chapter is meant to provide an overview only. Additionally, the most commonplace method for creating Web Services in .NET will be through the use of ASP.NET.

Getting Started with Web Services for .NET

To start working with .NET, we must, minimally, obtain the Microsoft .NET Framework SDK Beta 2. To create a .NET Web Service we are not, strictly speaking, required to install the Microsoft Visual Studio .NET Beta 2. However, in this chapter we will use VS.NET extensively. With its project templates, debugging environment, resource editors, and editing features like IntelliSense, VS.NET is an indispensable tool for the .NET developer.

> Note that installing VS.NET Beta 2, automatically installs the .NET Framework SDK Beta 2.
>
> At the time of writing, the .NET Framework Beta 2 and Visual Studio .NET Beta 2 had just been released. Be warned that this section describes the Beta 2 implementations. There could quite possibly be major changes in the Release Candidate. Also, the following download instructions only apply to Beta 2.

Acquiring the Visual Studio .NET Beta 2

A set of CDs or DVDs containing the VS.NET Beta 2 for education and evaluation can be ordered for a shipping and handling fee. US, and Canadian customers refer to this URL:

http://developerstore.com/devstore/product.asp?productID=7627&store=TOOLBOX_NA

International customers should refer to this URL:

http://developerstore.com/devstore/product.asp?productID=7629&store=TOOLBOX_INTL

MSDN Universal subscribers automatically receive the Visual Studio .NET Beta 2, or can download it from the MSDN subscriber page at this URL:

https://login.passport.com/login.asp?id=6078&ru=https%3A%2F%2Fmsdn%2Eone%2Emicrosoft%2E com%2FPublic%2FPassportReturn%2Easp&tw=3600&fs=1&kv=1&ct=994582804&ems=1&ver=1.99 0.1052.1

Note that the VS.NET Beta 2 may update the several components on your system including Internet Explorer 6.0, Microsoft Data Access Components (MDAC) 2.7, the new Windows Installer (fancy new installer package).

Acquiring the .NET Framework SDK Beta 2

The Microsoft .NET Framework SDK Beta 2 is available for free and can be downloaded from this URL:

http://msdn.microsoft.com/downloads/default.asp?url=/downloads/sample.asp?url=/msdn-files/027/000/976/msdncompositedoc.xml

Or, a CD can be ordered containing the Microsoft .NET Framework SDK Beta, for a shipping fee, from this URL:

http://developerstore.com/devstore/product.asp?productID=7625&store=TOOLBOX_NA

Downloading the .NET Framework Redistributable

The .NET Framework will be built into future releases of Windows operations systems. Until then, we must minimally install the .NET Framework Redistributable Beta 2 to all machines to which we distribute our web service, or any .NET application. The .NET Framework Redistributable can be downloaded from:

http://msdn.microsoft.com/downloads/default.asp?url=/downloads/sample.asp?url=/msdn-files/027/000/976/msdncompositedoc.xml

Note the Microsoft Internet Explorer and Microsoft Information Server version dependencies, and Microsoft Data Access Component version recommendations that are described by this web page.

A .NET Primer

Windows and the technologies we use to develop for it have undergone a complex evolution over the past decade. Most Windows development in the past 5 years has been based on COM/DCOM/MTS/COM+ Services technologies. Remarkably, these services have their roots in OLE2 (Object Linking and Embedding), a technology introduced in 1994, before we had really begun to even think about developing powerful and dynamic web applications. These COM-based technologies were often difficult, required developer's to write reams of COM plumbing code, and most importantly to us, provided no standard firewall-proof way to programmatically expose functionality over the web.

.NET and the .NET Framework represent a radical departure from this tradition. .NET is Microsoft's rewrite – a new framework and a new run-time – for programming Windows applications. With the new run-time come a number of useful new services, and we will mention a few of these next. However, this section will serve to touch on the .NET basics and introduce enough .NET terminology to get us through the rest of the chapter.

The Common Language Runtime

The **Common Language Runtime** (**CLR**) forms the foundation of the .NET Framework. It manages the execution of .NET code and provides a number of services.

In a nutshell, all .NET compilers produce what is called **Microsoft Intermediate Language** (**MSIL**) code, a CPU-independent tokenized set of instructions. When MSIL code is executed, the CLR is invoked. The CLR includes **just-in-time** (**JIT**) **compilers**, which compile the MSIL code to native code as the code is loaded. The native code is then cached for later use. It is important to note that the CLR always executes native code – not interpreted code (a key distinction, between .NET code and Java code, to which the .NET run-time is often compared). .NET compilers generate MSIL code, and the CLR's JIT compilers produce native code.

Microsoft provides several **.NET compilers**:

- ❑ **VB.NET.** The next generation version of Visual Basic
- ❑ **C++ with Managed Extension**. C++ with extensions to support .NET
- ❑ **JScript.NET.** A .NET compatible version of Jscript

❑   **C#.** A new C++-derived (and Java-like) language created specifically for .NET development

Additionally, Microsoft provides the Common Language Specification – a specification that describes a minimal set of features that other languages can support to be .NET compliant. This allows third parties to develop compilers to target .NET. At this time 30 or so non-Microsoft .NET-compatible compilers are under development, including versions of Python, Perl and Java .NET compilers. All code created to target .NET is referred to as "managed code", meaning that is managed by the CLR.

The CLR does much more than just compile MSIL code to native code. It verifies that code is type-safe, enforces a new layer of security called **Code Access Security,** implements an infrastructure to ensure version compatibility between application components, and manages memory and threads. Most of these services are outside of the scope of this chapter. However, understanding a bit of the memory management services will be important for reading code samples in this chapter. In managing memory, the CLR performs automatic garbage collection, that is, it deallocates memory used by an application's objects for us. The CLR counts references to our code's objects, and when an object is no longer referred to within the code, it is freed automatically. Notice that throughout our C# code samples we allocate objects with the new keyword, but we do not explicitly de-allocate them as we would in C++ with the delete keyword. Be assured that the CLR is doing this for us behind the scenes.

Common Type System

The Common Type System (CTS) defines a subset of common data types in the .NET Framework, and describes how new data types can be declared and used, whereas COM provided a standard for producing components that were binary compatible – but each language still had it's own language-specific type system. CTS replaces this with a run-time type system – all languages share a basic set of types and rules for extending types.

The CTS and the Common Language Specification are the mechanisms by which .NET can support cross language integration. In addition, this cross-language integration is exciting stuff. Constructs like class properties, exceptions, and events are dealt with uniformly across languages. With cross-language integration, it's possible for example, to create and compile a C# class called FooBase into a library. We can then create a VB.NET application that refers to the FooBase library. In our VB.NET project, we create a VB.NET class that directly derives from the FooBase class.

Assemblies

We will use the term **assembly** throughout the chapter. Assemblies are the building blocks of .NET applications. Physically, an assembly is a portable executable (PE) – a DLL or EXE. An assembly is not necessarily always a single DLL or EXE – there are such things a multiple file assemblies. In multiple file assemblies the contents of an assembly are spread out over multiple compiled modules. However, the logistics and advantages of multiple file assemblies are outside the scope of this chapter. All the assemblies we build in this chapter will be single file assemblies – that is single DLLs or EXEs.

Assemblies are the unit of versioning, security, deployment, and type scoping. **Meta data** contained within assemblies makes them completely self-describing. To provide a DLL assembly for third parties to use, we do not need to also distribute a separate type library, IDL description, include file or static library. We simply deploy the assembly. The meta data in our assembly gives our clients everything they need to know about its contents. .NET tools and utilities also use the meta data. For example, by adding a reference to our assembly in Visual Studio .NET, the development environment helps use the meta data in the assembly to display the types our assembly exports in its IntelliSense typing feature, and the Solution Explorer window pane.

To the untrained eye, a .NET assembly might look like any other Windows DLL or EXE. But don't be fooled. It's their contents that distinguish them. Assemblies contain the following elements:

❑ The **PE Header**. This is simply a standard part of all EXEs or DLLs

❑ The **unmanaged stub**. This is a small bit of unmanaged code (natively compiled) that invokes the CLR with a pointer to the MSIL, and then turns over execution control to the CLR. Unlike a non-.NET DLL or EXE, this is the only native code

❑ **Meta data**. The meta data, again, is the information that makes an assembly completely self-describing. It is saved in a COFF (Common Object File Format) header in binary format

❑ **MSIL (Microsoft Intermediate Language) code**. MSIL is the compiler-generated intermediate language. Assemblies can contain only application resources. In these cases, there is no MSIL in the assembly

❑ **Resources**. Optionally, assemblies can contain .NET application resources, such as localized strings

Reflection is the process by which other applications can programmatically discover information about an assembly – information like the assembly's version number, and the types it implements.

.NET Framework Class Library

The .NET Framework class library is an object-oriented library of classes and other types included with the .NET Framework SDK. The Framework class library functionality is the foundation of all .NET applications, regardless of the language or the application type. Classes in the library provide functionality to do everything from rendering Windows controls to manipulating XML documents. In the past, Windows developers had at their disposal a vast assortment of Microsoft frameworks (MFC, ATL, or VB, for example) and component libraries (ADO, SOAP Toolkit, MS XML, etc.) to do a vast assortment of tasks. The .NET Framework class library provides access to system functionality and envelops the functionality provided by all of these prior frameworks and component libraries. The .NET Framework library is vast – it includes hundreds and hundreds of classes and types. Most importantly to us, the framework class library implements the classes upon which .NET Web Services are built.

All .NET classes, including the ones we implement, are organized hierarchically in **namespaces**. All .NET Framework class library types belong to the **system namespace** or a namespace nested within the system namespace. For example, in this chapter we will use a number of web service classes that are defined in a namespace called `System.Web.Services`.

C#

With the .NET Framework, Microsoft introduces a new language called C#. Languages like VB.NET have been (rather radically in many developer's opinions) retooled to support .NET. However, C# was created and designed by Microsoft specifically for .NET development. C# can be viewed as a simplified C++. Certainly it has its syntax roots in C++; however, many arcane, confusing, and dangerous aspects of C++ have been removed or simplified. As a C++ programmer, the author has found the transition to C# to be rather smooth. For this reason, and the fact that it's a great language for .NET development, the sample code given in this chapter is in C#.

C++ and Java programmers should not have too difficult a time reading the C# code in this chapter. However, listed here are a few notable differences between C# and C++ syntax:

❑ **Simplified Member Access Syntax.** C++ uses the "->" operator to refer to class or struct members when an object is heap-allocated, and the "." to refer to class or struct members when the object is stack-allocated. C# always uses the "." syntax to refer to class members like data and methods. For example:

```
myObj.SomeMethod();
```

calls the SomeMethod() method of the class given by myObj.

❑ **Parameter Attributes**. Parameters can be attributed with the keywords **ref** and **out**. By default, if a parameter does not have the ref or out attribute, the parameter is passed by value. By annotating a parameter with ref, the parameter is passed by reference. By annotating a parameter with out, the parameter is also passed by reference, however it's assumed to be set when the method is invoked. For example, in the following method the out attribute is used to indicate that the strNewPhoneNumber is passed by reference and assumed to be invalid upon method invocation:

```
public bool CheckForSplit(string strPhoneNum, out string strNewPhoneNum);
```

❑ **Common type system types**. C# uses shared types implemented in the common type system. Many of these types have been mapped to familiar C++ keywords. For example, the common type system's System.Int32 type is mapped to the C# int keyword, and is used like the C++ int type. Notable exceptions are strings and arrays, which have a different syntax than C++ programmers are used to. To read the chapter's sample code, it should be enough to understand that string is a built-in type, and that arrays must be declared with brackets following the type. After declaration, an array is then allocated and sized using the new keyword. For example:

```
int[] myArray;
myArray = new int[3];
```

❑ **Everything is an object**. C# allows us to treat everything, including primitive types, as objects. There are even a few methods we can call on all types. ToString() is one of these. This means we can do the following:

```
int myInt = 7;
string myString = myInt.ToString();
```

❑ **Static class members syntax**. Static members of a class are referred to by class name and not an instance name. For example, if class Foo implements the following static method:

```
public static DoSomething()
```

We call the method DoSomething() using this syntax:

```
Foo.DoSomething;
```

❑ **The using keyword**. There are two methods we can use to access a data type that is implemented in another namespace. First, we can refer to the data type with its fully qualified name in our source code. That is the name of data type prefixed by the namespace to which it belongs. For example, if our implementation used a .NET Framework class library class called Random, which is implemented in the System namespace, our code could always refer to the class as System.Random, as shown:

```
System.Random r;
r = new System.Random();
```

Always prefixing the data type with its namespace can get longwinded. Luckily, we have an alternative. We can add a `using` statement to our implementation file, which references the namespace containing the data type of interest to us. If we do this, we can refer to the data type without prefixing it with its namespace. So, to get access to the `Random` class, for example, we would add the following line to our source file:

```
using System;
Random r;
r = new Random();
```

❑ **No deletes**. Recall that .NET automatically does the garbage collection for us

ASP.NET

Active Server Pages (**ASP**) is Microsoft's web development platform for scripting dynamic, interactive web applications. ASP web applications run on top of Microsoft Internet Information Server (IIS). The .NET Framework SDK includes a complete .NET rewrite of ASP called **ASP.NET**. ASP.NET applications are common language run-time managed applications, which can be written in any .NET-compatible language. ASP.NET requires Microsoft Internet Information Server 5.0, which the .NET Framework SDK installs for us.

ASP.NET now provides integral support for Web Services.

For readers familiar with ASP, we will mention a few of ASP.NET's new features and the major changes between ASP and ASP.NET. ASP.NET introduces server-side form controls, new user authentication and authorization options, a built-in web page caching mechanism, built-in debugging and tracing features, and new options to save session state. High on our list of favorite improvement is that ASP.NET code can now be written with any full-featured .NET language, including Microsoft's VB.NET, C#, Jscript, or any other .NET language. The late-bound scripting languages that ASP required – like VBScript – go away. Good riddance, in the author's opinion! Also this code executes as natively compiled code, vastly improving performance. In addition, ASP.NET has complete access to the .NET Framework class library and all its functionality.

ASP.NET *web site* development is a book length topic, which we will not cover in this chapter. The important point to remember for users new to ASP.NET is that Web Services have much in common with all web applications. As web applications and Web Services are built upon HTTP, which is a stateless protocol, both are stateless. Among other implications, this means that, we can't set properties in a web service class – the property value would be lost between calls. Because state is not supported at the protocol level, web applications have had to come up with mechanisms to keep state. Web server tools, like ASP.NET and ASP before it, can give us this functionality. To keep state in ASP.NET web sites or web service applications we can use something called the `Session` object. Security is a second issue that web site applications have long had to deal with. ASP.NET, and IIS below it, give us a number of methods to perform authentication and authorization. Additionally, ASP.NET lets us cache the results of a web page, or the results of a web service method call. We won't discuss keeping state or security options in this chapter – they are advanced ASP.NET topics. However, be aware that by building Web Services with ASP.NET we are able to leverage the infrastructure that provides these goodies.

For those new to ASP/ASP.NET, don't worry. As we will see, the platform allows us focus on our application logic without worrying too much about the underlying details. We will see that next.

An ASP.NET Web Service

So without further ado, let's code-up and deploy our first ASP.NET web service! In this section, we will describe and code a class to provide area code update functionality. Then we will step through the process of transforming our class into a deployable ASP.NET web service.

In the next section, we will use the VS.NET development environment to test and enhance our Web Service. In this section, we'll see that all we really need is the source code for our class, and `Notepad.exe` (or any text editor).

An Area Code Update Service

However, before we get started, let's discuss the example we will be implementing.

The Problem

Between my husband and myself we have a total of seven phone numbers associated with us, covering our home phone, office phones, pager, cell phones, modem and fax lines (please be clear, we are not proud of this). We represent the cause of an explosion of new area codes over the last five years in North America. Because of the ever-increasing demand for phone numbers causing existing area codes to run out of available numbers, over 150 new area codes have been added since 1995. For the non-North American readers, area codes are the first 3 digits of a US or Canadian phone number. When it becomes apparent that an area will run out of phone numbers, the phone company assigns a new area code, and the existing area code is "split". Phone numbers belonging to some of the exchange prefixes (the 3 digits in a phone number following the area code) are shifted to the new area code. As a result, hundreds of thousands of phone numbers are changed.

New area codes represent a constant headache for organizations that keep phone number data. This is where our Web Service comes in. In this chapter, we will design and prototype a service that businesses could subscribe to, and use to update phone number data.

The AreaCodeService Class

We begin by implementing a class, the `AreaCodeService` class, which clients can use to determine whether or not a phone number is currently valid. We will look at the entire implementation in a few paragraphs, but for now let's talk about a few specifics.

First, we declare this class and a helper class within the `DotnetServices` namespace. To declare a namespace we use the C# keyword `namespace` followed by the namespace name. The contents of the namespace are enclosed in the brackets which follow. Our namespace declaration looks like this:

```
namespace DotnetServices
{
// implementation here
}
```

The one important public method that our class implements is called `CheckForSplit()`. Its method signature is shown below:

```
public string CheckForSplit(string strPhoneNumber)
```

Applications that use the class simply create an instance of our class and call this method. It is possible that the given phone number's area code was split, creating a new area code, and the given phone number was assigned to the new area code. If this is the case, the phone number has changed and the method returns the new phone number. If the number is unchanged, `CheckForSplit()` returns null. We will see in the code listing below that our prototype uses hard-coded data.

Let's look at the implementation: first there is a helper class called `AreaCodeSplitInfo`. It contains four `public` data members that describe a single area code split:

```
// Area code split descriptor class
public class AreaCodeSplitInfo
{
    public int iOldAreaCode;
    public int iNewAreaCode;
    public DateTime dtStartSwitch;
    public int[] listExchanges;
}
```

The `iOldAreaCode` member, not surprisingly, stores the pre-switch area code. The `iNewAreaCode` member stores the newly assigned area code. The `dtStartSwitch` is a system `DateTime` data member that contains the date that the new area code becomes valid. When an area code is split, there is generally what is called a "permissive dialing period" – a several month-long time span during which both the new and the old area codes are valid. At the end of this period, only the new area code will work. For our prototype, we will only worry about the date marking the beginning of the permissive dialing period. Lastly, the `listExchanges` data member holds an array of the exchange prefix numbers that are affected by the area code split.

The `AreaCodeService` class has a single data member, a `private` instance of the `AreaCodeSplitInfo` class:

```
private AreaCodeSplitInfo acSplitInfo;
```

The `AreaCodeService` class implements a constructor and the following private methods:

❑ `InitializeData()`. This method initializes the hard-coded data, and is called by the constructor. This data describes an actual area code split taking place in Arizona this year. In the code below, we have omitted the full list of 324 affected exchanges for the sake of brevity

❑ `ParsePhoneNumber()`. This method parses a 10-digit phone number into an area code, an exchange prefix, and the final 4 digits. For the prototype, we are a little sloppy: we assume the parameter passed in is in the expected format – our real implementation will contain format verification code

The following code (`Chapter12\ApplicationLogic\AreaCodeService.cs` in the download) shows the entire implementation:

```
using System;

namespace DotNetServices
{
    // Area code split descriptor class
    public class AreaCodeSplitInfo
    {
```

```
    public int iOldAreaCode;
    public int iNewAreaCode;
    public DateTime dtStartSwitch;
    public int[] listExchanges;
}


// Area code service class
public class AreaCodeService
{
    private AreaCodeSplitInfo acSplitInfo;

    public AreaCodeService()
    {
        InitializeData();
    }

    private void InitializeData()
    {
        // Hardcode some sample data
        acSplitInfo = new AreaCodeSplitInfo();
        acSplitInfo.iOldAreaCode = 520;
        acSplitInfo.iNewAreaCode = 928;
        acSplitInfo.dtStartSwitch = DateTime.Parse("June 23, 2001");
        acSplitInfo.listExchanges = new int[]
        {
            200, 201, 203, 204, 210, 213, 214, 217, 220, 221,
            222, 223, 226, 227, 231, 233, 234, 236, 244, 246,
            // ... Full list omitted for brevity
            970, 978
        };

    }

    private void ParsePhoneNum(string strPhoneNumber,
        out int iAreaCode,
        out int iExchange,
        out int iLastPart)
    {
        // Parse a 10-digit phone number into 3 parts:
        // areacode, exchange, and final 4 digits

        // Expects a 10 digit string - if string contains other
        // characters or is not 10 digits, an exception is thrown
        iAreaCode = Int32.Parse(strPhoneNumber.Substring(0, 3));
        iExchange = Int32.Parse(strPhoneNumber.Substring(3, 3));
        iLastPart = Int32.Parse(strPhoneNumber.Substring(6, 4));
    }

    public string CheckForSplit(string strPhoneNumber)
    {
        int iAreaCode;
        int iExchange;
        int iLastPart;

        ParsePhoneNum(strPhoneNumber, out iAreaCode,
                out iExchange, out iLastPart);
```

```
                  // Query against hardcoded data
                  if (iAreaCode == acSplitInfo.iOldAreaCode &&
                     DateTime.Now >= acSplitInfo.dtStartSwitch)
                  {
                     // If matches split area code, compare exchange to list of
                     // all affected changes
                     for (int i = 0; i < acSplitInfo.listExchanges.Length; i++)
                     {
                        if (iExchange == acSplitInfo.listExchanges[i])
                        {
                           // If a match found, format and return new number
                           return acSplitInfo.iNewAreaCode.ToString()
                              + iExchange.ToString()
                              + iLastPart.ToString();
                        }
                     }
                  }
                  return null;
            }
      }
}
```

Our `CheckForSplit()` method first parses the phone number parameter. In a real implementation, we would create a database to track area code split information. Incidentally, this type of data is generally collected from announcements made by an organization called the North American Numbering Plan Administration (http://www.nanpa.com/). Our `CheckForSplit()` method would query against this database. However, for our prototype, we simply compare the phone number parameter to the hard-coded data describing a single area code split. We compare today's date with the hard-coded start date. If the area codes match, and it is after the switch date, the exchange prefix is compared to the list of affected prefixes to determine if the area code has changed. If the phone number has changed, the new number is formatted and returned. If the phone number has not changed, `null` is returned.

AreaCodeService ASP.NET Web Service

So that is it for our prototype implementation logic. We will save our class to a C# source file named `AreaCodeService.cs`. Note that `.cs` is the extension for C# source files. We could then compile an assembly DLL with the C# compiler (`csc.exe`). To do this we enter the following at the DOS prompt:

>csc.exe /target:library AreaCodeService.cs

In the sample code, refer to the `Chapter12\ApplicationLogic\AreaCodeService.cs` file.

This generates a library named `AreaCodeService.dll`. The `/target:library` option indicates a DLL library. By default the library will have the same name as the source file with the `.dll` extension. Use the `/out:` option to override the default library name.

If this were our completed database-enabled implementation, we could then package this library with an area code update database and ship it to our customers. In fact, there are companies making money by doing just this. The problem is that every time the area code data changes – several times a year – the updates need to be propagated to the customers – by download or via some physical media. How tiresome, how Twentieth Century!

With a Web Service solution the data is only updated at the Web Service server. This type of solution – providing access to dynamic data – represents one of the most common and important types of problem that Web Services solve.

With that in mind, lets transform our AreaCodeService implementation into a Web Service. Luckily, transforming a class implementation into a web service can be done with only four minor modifications to the code shown above. We'll quickly mention each modification, and then go back and discuss what each one does. The modifications are:

❑   Instead of saving the file to a `.cs` file, we save our implementation to a file with the `.asmx` extension in a URI-addressable location.

   To deploy our prototype in particular, we need to save the code listed above with the file name `AreaCodeService.asmx` to the root of our default IIS web site. The default location, used by most systems is the `C:\Inetpub\wwwroot\` directory.

❑   We add the use of the `System.Web.Services` namespace towards the top of the `AreaCodeService.asmx` file, as shown:

```
using System;
using System.Web.Services;
```

❑   We add a line of code called the Web Service directive to the top of the file `AreaCodeService.asmx`.

   For our prototype, we add this line specifically:

```
<%@ WebService Language="c#"
            Class="DotNetServices.AreaCodeService" %>
```

❑   We prefix our `CheckForSplit()` method with a special tag called an attribute. The attribute we add is the `[WebMethod]` attribute. Here is what the attributed method looks like:

```
[WebMethod]
public string CheckForSplit(string strPhoneNumber)
```

As we can see, it takes very little code modification to change our class into a Web Service. You will notice that the application logic itself is unchanged. The modifications are minor but they pack a punch. We do these four steps and we have transformed our AreaCodeService implementation into a web service *and* deployed it. Let's discuss what each steps does.

.asmx Files

ASP.NET Web Service files are simply files with the `.asmx` extension put in a URI-addressable directory. ASP.NET provides support for Web Services with the new `.asmx` file type. An `.asmx` file is simply a text file containing code, like any other ASP.NET script file.

The System.Web.Services namespace

ASP.NET Web Services must include the use of the `System.Web.Services` namespace. This namespace and the classes it contains are part of the .NET Framework class library. This namespace, in particular, contains the classes and attributes that we use to implement Web Services. Among other things, the `[WebMethod]` attribute is defined within this namespace.

The WebService Directive

In ASP.NET directives are used to specify settings or characteristics of the page. For ASP.NET Web Services, the WebService directive is required. It is used to identify which class implements the web service functionality. For our prototype, this is the DotNetServices.AreaCodeService class.

Directives are enclosed in <%@ %> brackets. Directives can include one or more attributes (paired with values). Language="C#" is an example of an optional attribute to the WebService directive. The general form of a directive is as shown:

```
<%@ DirectiveName Attribute="Value" [Attribute=Value] %>
```

The Class Attribute

The Class attribute is a required clause. It is used to indicate the class that implements the web service. Specifically the fully qualified class name prefixed with the namespace that implements it.

In our example, the class name is AreaCodeService and the namespace is DotnetServices, so the fully qualified class name is DotnetServices.AreaCodeService.

The Language Attribute

The Language attribute is a clause attribute of the Web Service directive. It indicates to ASP.NET which language the named class is implemented in.

The default language is VB.NET, so we set Language="c#" to proclaim our language of choice.

The WebMethod Attribute

Annotating a method with the [WebMethod] tag in an .asmx file tells ASP.NET to expose the method as a callable web service operation. Note that this method must be public.

Attributes

In all .NET languages, an attribute is a descriptive declaration that can be used to annotate code elements such as classes, fields, and methods. Nevertheless, don't be fooled by their simple appearance! In .NET, attributes can be wildly powerful. For example when we tack on the .NET Framework's [WebMethod] attribute, we add in a great deal of functionality. Behind the scenes, the [WebMethod] attribute adds all the plumbing code to serialize and deserialize SOAP messages and map these messages to types and return values. No small potatoes!

Attributes often have optional properties. Setting an optional property affects the operation of attributes. Setting an attribute property has this general syntax:

```
[AttributeName(PropertyName="Value")]
```

The [WebMethod] attribute, for example, has the Description property. We'll discuss its use later in the chapter. However, as an example of how properties are specified we show its use here:

```
[WebMethod(Description="Returns the updated phone number, or null if the phone
number has not changed.")]
```

The AreaCodeService.asmx

Here is our entire `AreaCodeService.asmx` web service implementation, with the modifications described above. We have omitted the method implementations because they have not changed.

AreaCodeService.asmx

```
<%@ WebService Language="c#" Class="DotnetServices.AreaCodeService" %>

using System;
using System.Web.Services;

namespace DotnetServices
{

    AreaCodeInfo class implementation not shown, same as above

    // Area code service class
    public class AreaCodeService
    {
        complete class implementation omitted, same as above

        [WebMethod]
        public string CheckForSplit(string strPhoneNumber)
        {
            method implementation not shown, same as above
        }
    }

}
```

Testing AreaCodeService

So, that's all we need to do! We have transformed our AreaCodeService into a web service, and by saving it to an URI-addressable location on our server, we have deployed it, too.

ASP.NET gives us built-in support to test our Web Service too. With ASP.NET's built-in help page we don't need to code-up a client application to test our Web Service, then worry about debugging the web service, and client application at the same time. The help page lets us test the web service the second it's deployed.

If you are following along with the sample code, copy the file `Chapter12\AreaCodeService.asmx` (from the code download) to the root directory of your IIS Default Web Site. On default installations this will be `\inetpub\wwwroot`.

Now if we open our browser and request our `AreaCodeService.asmx` page – at the URL http://localhost/AreaCodeService.asmx – we see the following ASP.NET-generated help page:

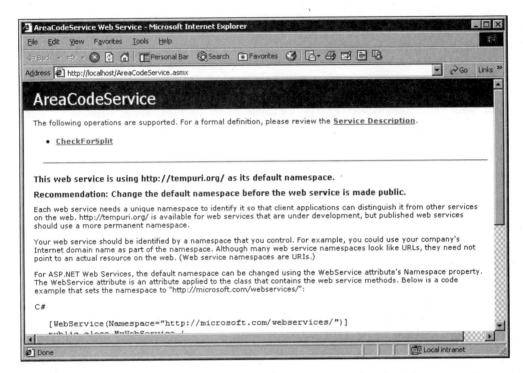

When we request the `AreaCodeService.asmx` page, ASP.NET dynamically generates this page based on what it knows about our service. Notice the **AreaCodeService** service name, listed at the top, and the name of our web-callable method, `CheckForSplit()`. If our service exposed additional methods, they would also be listed.

Notice the informational message at the bottom of the help page recommending that we change the default namespace. We should do this, and in a few more pages, we will explain the issue and change the namespace (once again relying on the power of attributes).

With this built-in help page we do two types of actions:

1. We can view and test our exposed methods. In our example, we have only one exposed method – the `CheckForSplit()` method. If our Web Service exposed more than one method, these too would be shown. To test our AreaCodeService's method we click the CheckForSplit link.

2. We can also retrieve the WSDL description of our service by clicking the Service Description link.

Let's test our method, and click the CheckForSplit link. ASP.NET generates the page shown below – a form with which we can test our web service:

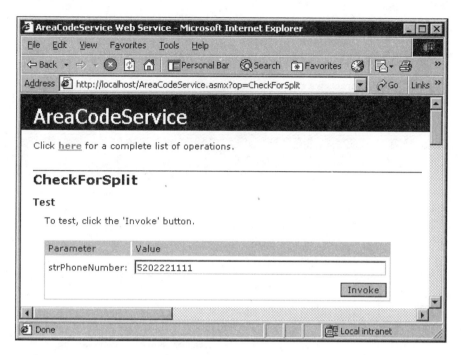

We type in the strPhoneNumber value. We set it to 5202221111 – a phone number we know has changed. If we refer back to our hard-coded data we see that 520 is a split area code that our data describes, and 222 is included in the affected exchange prefix list. Notice that we are careful not to add spaces or punctuation to our phone number. Recall our prototype CheckForSplit() implementation expects a 10-digit numeric string.

By clicking the Invoke button, we invoke our web service method with the parameter we entered. We now see the method results in the following Web Service response:

Indeed, we see that the method has correctly returned the changed phone number as XML. Could it be any easier?

Looking closely though, we can see that the response is XML, but not SOAP-encoded XML. In fact, it is a simple HTTP GET response. We will discuss why this is in the *ASP.NET Protocol Support* section.

Retrieving the WSDL

The ASP.NET help page will also return the WSDL contract for the Web Service.

To retrieve the WSDL contract, we can click on the Service Description link from the ASP.NET-generated help page at http://localhost/AreaCodeService.asmx. Doing this we see the following WSDL contract for the AreaCodeService.

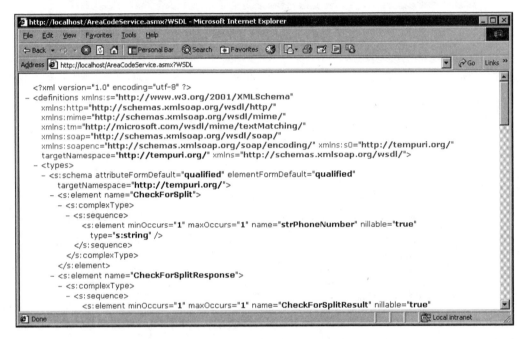

```
<?xml version="1.0" encoding="utf-8" ?>
- <definitions xmlns:s="http://www.w3.org/2001/XMLSchema"
    xmlns:http="http://schemas.xmlsoap.org/wsdl/http/"
    xmlns:mime="http://schemas.xmlsoap.org/wsdl/mime/"
    xmlns:tm="http://microsoft.com/wsdl/mime/textMatching/"
    xmlns:soap="http://schemas.xmlsoap.org/wsdl/soap/"
    xmlns:soapenc="http://schemas.xmlsoap.org/soap/encoding/" xmlns:s0="http://tempuri.org/"
    targetNamespace="http://tempuri.org/" xmlns="http://schemas.xmlsoap.org/wsdl/">
  - <types>
    - <s:schema attributeFormDefault="qualified" elementFormDefault="qualified"
        targetNamespace="http://tempuri.org/">
      - <s:element name="CheckForSplit">
        - <s:complexType>
          - <s:sequence>
              <s:element minOccurs="1" maxOccurs="1" name="strPhoneNumber" nillable="true"
                type="s:string" />
            </s:sequence>
          </s:complexType>
        </s:element>
      - <s:element name="CheckForSplitResponse">
        - <s:complexType>
          - <s:sequence>
              <s:element minOccurs="1" maxOccurs="1" name="CheckForSplitResult" nillable="true"
```

In fact, to retrieve the WSDL for any ASP.NET web service, we can simply request the Web Service name followed by ?WSDL. For our example, we would enter:

http://localhost/AreaCodeService.asmx?WSDL

ASP.NET Protocol Support

Notice that when we invoked the Web Service above (to check 5202221111), the web service method was actually invoked with the following HTTP GET:

http://localhost/AreaCodeService.asmx/CheckForSplit?strPhoneNumber=5202221111

The parameter name and value are given as query string parameters. Check the URL shown in the response screenshot on the previous page. Notice also in Figure 3 that our result was returned as XML over the HTTP GET protocol.

ASP.NET Web Services will automatically support the HTTP GET, HTTP POST, and SOAP protocols. Examining the WSDL for the AreaCodeService, retrieved from querying http://localhost/AreaCodeService.asmx?WSDL, we notice the following binding information describing protocol support:

```
<binding name="AreaCodeServiceSoap" type="s0:AreaCodeServiceSoap">
    <soap:binding transport="http://schemas.xmlsoap.org/soap/http"
                  style="document" />
    <operation name="CheckForSplit">
        <soap:operation soapAction="http://tempuri.org/CheckForSplit"
                        style="document" />
        <input>
            <soap:body use="literal" />
        </input>
        <output>
            <soap:body use="literal" />
        </output>
    </operation>
</binding>
<binding name="AreaCodeServiceHttpGet" type="s0:AreaCodeServiceHttpGet">
    <http:binding verb="GET" />
    <operation name="CheckForSplit">
        <http:operation location="/CheckForSplit" />
        <input>
            <http:urlEncoded />
        </input>
        <output>
            <mime:mimeXml part="Body" />
        </output>
    </operation>
</binding>
<binding name="AreaCodeServiceHttpPost" type="s0:AreaCodeServiceHttpPost">
    <http:binding verb="POST" />
    <operation name="CheckForSplit">
        <http:operation location="/CheckForSplit" />
        <input>
            <mime:content type="application/x-www-form-urlencoded" />
        </input>
        <output>
            <mime:mimeXml part="Body" />
        </output>
    </operation>
</binding>
```

HTTP GET and HTTP POST

The HTTP GET is interesting to us because this is the protocol that the help page supports to test our web service methods.

It is possible to modify the help test page to support HTTP POST. The ASP.NET help file is generated by the ASP.NET page `DefaultWsdlHelpGenerator.aspx`. The beta .NET Framework SDK version we installed, put this in the `\WINNT\Microsoft.NET\Framework\<version>\Config` directory. On other systems and with other SDK versions, this could install to a different directory, so you may need to search around. We can edit this file, like any ASP.NET page. In this file, set the following `showPost` flag to `true` (near the top of the file), as shown, and the help page will support POST.

```
bool showPost = true;
```

This will cause the help page for all Web Services on our system to support POST. While using the help page to test invoking our method via HTTP POST may seem like a fun thing to try (depending on your idea of fun), it's not really very useful, or easy. Here's why: the ASP.NET listener expects the body of an HTTP document to be an XML document. The POST submitted by the browser will send parameters as (incompatible) name-value pairs.

The important thing to keep in mind is that HTTP POST and HTTP GET are supported to help us test simple HTML applications, like our ASP.NET's help page. SOAP is a more flexible and robust protocol. The .NET Framework SDK included a utility to generate web service client proxies. We will discuss this utility soon. These utility-generated proxies will always use the richer SOAP protocol, never the HTTP GET or HTTP POST protocols.

SOAP

SOAP is a much richer protocol for Web Service transport. For example, imagine we had decided to implement our `CheckForSplit()` method with the following method signature:

```
public bool CheckForSplit(string strPhoneNum, out string strNewPhoneNum);
```

This method exposes the same functionality as our current version of `CheckForSplit()`, but with slightly different semantics. If the area code changed for the given `strPhoneNum`, this method returns `true` and sets `strNewPhoneNum` parameter to the new number. If the area code did not change, this method would return `false` and the value of `strNewPhoneNum` would be undefined.

Generating a web service with this method we would quickly find that the web service could no longer support HTTP GET and HTTP POST. HTTP GET and HTTP POST cannot support OUT parameters. SOAP, on the other hand, would come through for us.

Imagine we decide to add a new method to our web service. This method has the following signature:

```
public AreaCodeSplitInfo[] GetSplitInfo(DateTime dtStart, DateTime dtEnd)
```

This method takes a date range, and returns descriptors for area code splits that occur within the given date range. The method returns an array of `AreaCodeSplitInfo` objects. Refer back to our web service code to see this class defined. Again, HTTP GET and HTTP POST are unable to handle this more complex class – they really only deal with very simple inputs and outputs. SOAP, on the other hand, is adept at transferring rich, even nested data types.

Creating a Web Service from a WSDL Description

In the section above, we generated a Web Service, and then used ASP.NET to generate a WSDL description of our service. However, we could have just as easily approached the assignment in the opposite direction.

Imagine that we had implemented our AreaCodeService with another web service framework. We then decide to recreate the application with ASP.NET. The .NET Framework SDK includes a utility, called the Web Services Description Language Utility (`wsdl.exe`) that can help us out. This utility will generate an abstract base class for a web service, given a WSDL file.

> In object oriented-languages, abstract classes are classes that cannot be instantiated directly. However, other classes can derive from them. Abstract classes define one or more abstract method or property, which derived classes are required to implement. Additionally, abstract classes can contain members with implementations.

The generated abstract base class will contain an abstract method with the correct signature for each exposed web service operation. Then, to implement the Web Service, all we need to do is derive a class from the abstract base, and provide the implementation for each of the abstract methods. The wsdl.exe utility-generated abstract base class guarantees that we will implement the Web Service's exposed web methods with method signatures that match those described in the WSDL contract.

It's not as complicated as it sounds. Let's look at an example. Imagine that we started with only a WSDL description for our class, in the file AreaCodeService.wsdl. We could then execute the following at the DOS prompt:

> **> wsdl.exe AreaCodeService.wsdl /server**

This file can be found in the sample code in the Chapter12\WebServiceTemplate directory (in the download). The first argument is the name of our WSDL file, AreaCodeService.wsdl, followed by the /server option. The /server option causes wsdl.exe to generate the abstract base class for a web service server. Without this option, the wsdl.exe default is to generate a client proxy. We will get a chance to do this later in the chapter.

By default, that wsdl.exe generates C# source code. wsdl.exe can also generate VB.NET or JavaScript source code. To generate VB.NET or JavaScript code, we would use the /language option and set it to vb or js, respectively. The following shows the command line parameters to make wsdl.exe generate VB.NET code from the AreaCodeService.wsdl:

> **> wsdl.exe AreaCodeService.wsdl /server /language:vb**

For the AreaCodeService WSDL description, wsdl.exe generates the following C# code, saved to the file AreaCodeService.cs

```
//---------------------------------------------------------------------------//
<autogenerated>
//    This code was generated by a tool.
//    Runtime Version: 1.0.2914.16
//
//    Changes to this file may cause incorrect behavior and will be lost if
//    the code is regenerated.
// </autogenerated>
//---------------------------------------------------------------------------
//
// This source code was auto-generated by wsdl, Version=1.0.2914.16.
//
using System.Diagnostics;
using System.Xml.Serialization;
using System;
using System.Web.Services.Protocols;
using System.Web.Services;
```

```
[System.Web.Services.WebServiceBindingAttribute(Name="AreaCodeServiceSoap",
Namespace="http://tempuri.org/")]
public abstract class AreaCodeService : System.Web.Services.WebService
{
    [System.Web.Services.WebMethodAttribute()]
[System.Web.Services.Protocols.SoapDocumentMethodAttribute("http://tempuri.org/Che
ckForSplit", Use=System.Web.Services.Description.SoapBindingUse.Literal,
ParameterStyle=System.Web.Services.Protocols.SoapParameterStyle.Wrapped)]
    public abstract string CheckForSplit(string strPhoneNumber);
}
```

Deciphering this code we see that it defines an abstract class named `AreaCodeService`. This class
defines the abstract method `CheckForSplit()` with the method signature we expect:

```
public abstract string CheckForSplit(string strPhoneNumber);
```

The `[WebMethod]` annotates the `CheckForSplit()` method, although using a syntax we are not
familiar with (`[System.Web.Services.WebMethodAttribute()]`).

ASP.NET Web Services with Visual Studio .NET

Now that we have seen the very minimal number of steps needed to transform a class into a Web
Service, we will recreate our AreaCodeService with VS.NET's ASP.NET web service template project.
VS.NET makes it even easier – it creates an `.asmx` file with a skeleton class for us. However, we will
see that using the template creates a deployment with some interesting additional functionality. This will
give us a springboard to talk about deployment options we have with ASP.NET. We will finish this
section by looking at how we can use web service attributes to add functionality.

Unlike previous versions of Microsoft's Visual Studio, in VS.NET: VB.NET, C++, ASP.NET, and now
C# share a development environment. (Finally, with .NET's common type system and this shared
environment, debugging multi-language applications – even ASP.NET applications – is no longer a
headache-inducing proposition.)

Using Visual Studio .NET's ASP.NET Web Service Template

Let's get started. If you are starting with the provided sample code, ignore the following procedure.
Instead, copy the `Chapter12\AreaCodeService2` directory (from the code download) and its
contents to the root directory of your IIS Default Web Site. This is typically the `\inetpub\wwwroot`
directory. Within the Internet Information Services configuration create a new Virtual Directory with
the alias `AreaCodeService2`. Set the directory to point to the `AreaCodeService2` directory you just
copied into your root directory. Use the default permissions.

However, we will go through the steps of creating this project from scratch, as it will give us a chance
to see how the VS.NET template works.

Open VS.Net, and from the VS .NET "start" page click the New Project button, or select New | Project
from the File menu. Then select Visual C# Projects in the Project Types box, and select the ASP.NET
Web Service in the Templates box. We will name this version of our web service,
`AreaCodeService2`, as shown:

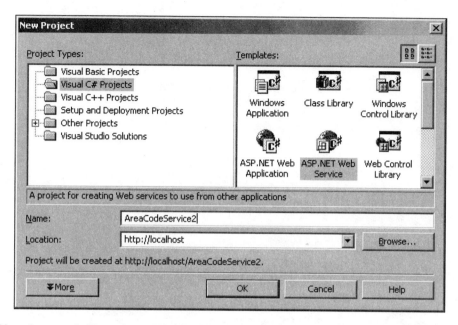

Hit **OK**, and we are halfway there. VS.NET will churn away for a few seconds, generating a virtual directory (assuming you have the correct permissions to create a virtual directory in IIS) for the application and creating the files needed to support our web service.

In the Solution Explorer window (View | Solution Explorer), notice that the template has created a file named Service1.asmx. To be consistent with the previous version of our application, we rename the Service1.asmx file to AreaCodeService2.asmx. To do this, we *right-click* on the Service1.asmx file and select the **Rename** item from the pop-up menu. With the AreaCodeService.asmx file selected in the Solution Explorer window, we hit *F7* to open the source file to edit our service.

The following shows the code the VS.NET template generates for us:

```
using System;
using System.Collections;
using System.ComponentModel;
using System.Data;
using System.Diagnostics;
using System.Web;
using System.Web.Services;

namespace AreaCodeService3
{
    /// <summary>
    /// Summary description for Service1.
    /// </summary>
    public class Service1 : System.Web.Services.WebService
    {
        public Service1()
        {
            //CODEGEN: This call is required by the ASP.NET Web Services Designer
```

```
        InitializeComponent();
    }

    #region Component Designer generated code
    /// <summary>
    /// Required method for Designer support - do not modify
    /// the contents of this method with the code editor.
    /// </summary>
    private void InitializeComponent()
    {
    }
    #endregion

    /// <summary>
    /// Clean up any resources being used.
    /// </summary>
    protected override void Dispose( bool disposing )
    {
    }

    // WEB SERVICE EXAMPLE
    // The HelloWorld() example service returns the string Hello World
    // To build, uncomment the following lines then save and build the project
    // To test this web service, press F5

//      [WebMethod]
//      public string HelloWorld()
//      {
//          return "Hello World";
//      }
    }
}
```

Notice the commented out method `HelloMethod()` (at the bottom of the file). Notice also that it is annotated with `[WebMethod]`. Doing nothing else, we could deploy a (rather useless) web service by running through the template and then un-commenting these lines and compiling – about 60 seconds worth of work. Building Web Services *really* doesn't get any easier than this.

However, we'll forge on with our AreaCodeService (because we like useful Web Services!). We edit this file, cutting and pasting in code from our previous `AreaCodeService.asmx` implementation. We are careful not to remove any of the template-generated code, except the commented-out `HelloWorld()` method. Moreover, we are careful to rename the class and its constructor to `AreaCodeService2` instead of `AreaCodeService`.

When we are done, the implementation looks like this:

```
using System;
using System.Collections;
using System.ComponentModel;
using System.Data;
using System.Diagnostics;
using System.Web;
using System.Web.Services;
```

```
namespace DotnetServices
{
    // Area code split descriptor class
    public class AreaCodeSplitInfo
    {
        public int iOldAreaCode;
        public int iNewAreaCode;
        public DateTime dtStartSwitch;
        public int[] listExchanges;
    }


    /// <summary>
    /// Summary description for Service1.
    /// </summary>
    public class AreaCodeService2 : System.Web.Services.WebService
    {
        private AreaCodeSplitInfo acSplitInfo;

        public AreaCodeService2()
        {
            //CODEGEN: This call is required by the ASP.NET Web Services Designer
            InitializeComponent();
            InitializeData();
        }

        #region Component Designer generated code
        /// <summary>
        /// Required method for Designer support - do not modify
        /// the contents of this method with the code editor.
        /// </summary>
        private void InitializeComponent()
        {
        }
        #endregion

        /// <summary>
        /// Clean up any resources being used.
        /// </summary>
        protected override void Dispose( bool disposing )
        {
        }

        private void InitializeData()
        {
            // Hardcode some sample data
            acSplitInfo = new AreaCodeSplitInfo();
            acSplitInfo.iOldAreaCode = 520;
            acSplitInfo.iNewAreaCode = 928;
            acSplitInfo.dtStartSwitch = DateTime.Parse("June 23, 2001");
            acSplitInfo.listExchanges = new int[]
            {
                200, 201, 203, 204, 210, 213, 214, 217, 220, 221,
                222, 223, 226, 227, 231, 233, 234, 236, 244, 246,
                // ... full list omitted for brevity
                970, 978
            };
```

```
            }

            private void ParsePhoneNum(string strPhoneNumber,
                out int iAreaCode,
                out int iExchange,
                out int iLastPart)
            {
                // Parse a 10 digit phone number into 3 parts:
                // areacode, exchange and final 4 digits

                // Expects a 10 digit string - if string contains other
                // characters or is not 10 digits, an exception is thrown
                iAreaCode = Int32.Parse(strPhoneNumber.Substring(0, 3));
                iExchange = Int32.Parse(strPhoneNumber.Substring(3, 3));
                iLastPart = Int32.Parse(strPhoneNumber.Substring(6, 4));
            }

            [WebMethod]
            public string CheckForSplit(string strPhoneNumber)
            {
                int iAreaCode;
                int iExchange;
                int iLastPart;

                ParsePhoneNum(strPhoneNumber, out iAreaCode, out iExchange, out
    iLastPart);

                // Query against hardcoded data
                if (iAreaCode == acSplitInfo.iOldAreaCode &&
                    DateTime.Now >= acSplitInfo.dtStartSwitch)
                {
                    // If matches split area code, compare exchange to list of
                    // all affected changes
                    for (int i = 0; i < acSplitInfo.listExchanges.Length; i++)
                    {
                        if (iExchange == acSplitInfo.listExchanges[i])
                        {
                            // If a match found, format and return new number
                            return acSplitInfo.iNewAreaCode.ToString() +
                                iExchange.ToString() +    iLastPart.ToString();
                        }
                    }
                }
                return null;
            }
        }
    }
```

Next, we compile and are ready to go. "Compile?" you ask. "Since when do we compile ASP.NET .asmx files?." A good question, and we are getting to that next.

Using Codebehind

Web services created with the VS.NET Web Services template *do* need to be compiled. Let's get to the bottom of this.

From the Project menu, select the Show All Files option. Something like the following should be visible in VS.NET's Solution Explorer window:

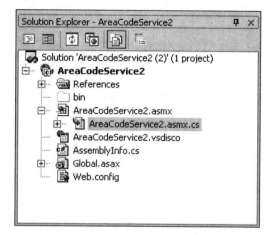

Notice that when we select to view the contents of AreaCodeService2.asmx in the main window, VS.NET does something a little tricky – it instead displays the contents of a file named AreaCodeService2.asmx.cs – a regular C# source file. To examine the contents of the *real* AreaCodeService2.asmx file, open this file with MS Notepad.

The AreaCodeService2.asmx file itself contains only the following line, the WebService directive.

```
<%@ WebService Language="c#" Codebehind="AreaCodeService2.asmx.cs"
            Class="DotnetServices.AreaCodeService2" %>
```

Notice the Codebehind attribute – it is key.

The Codebehind attribute tells ASP.NET that the web service class is implemented in the named file, in our example this is the AreaCodeService.asmx.cs file. When we compile our application, by pressing *Ctrl-Shift-B*, this file is compiled into an assembly DLL. This DLL must reside in the ASP.NET application's bin directory. VS.Net automatically creates this directory and deploys the referenced assembly to this directory.

In our example, AreaCodeService2.asmx.cs contains the implementation. When we compile the web service, AreaCodeService.asmx.cs is compiled into the file AreaCodeService.dll, which resides in the AreaCodeService2\bin directory.

Without the Codebehind attribute, .asmx code is considered **inline**. In inline implementations the web service code resides in the .asmx file – it is completely self-contained. Our first implementation of AreaCodeService was an example of an inline implementation.

By default, all VS.NET projects use the Codebehind attribute configuration. The advantage to using the Codebehind attribute is that it protects our source code from being viewed, and allows the code to be shared with other ASP.NET applications. This disadvantage is that using the Codebehind attribute adds additional files and subdirectories to the web service. In addition, it requires that we compile the web service assembly DLL each time we make a change. With self-contained, inline configurations, ASP.NET automatically detects any change we make to the .asmx file and reloads the latest version.

Template-generated Files

While we are on the topic of files that the VS.NET template creates, let's look at the others, shown in previous screenshot.

Dynamic Discovery and .VSDISCO Files

Web Service discovery is the process of finding Web Service descriptions. Web service discovery is supported through .vsdicso XML documents. Files of type .vsdisco give ASP.NET's dynamic discovery process hints about where finding Web Services and their WSDL contracts.

We will discuss the dynamic discovery process in more detail later in this chapter.

Our example file AreaCodeService2.vsdisco, is shown below:

```
<?xml version="1.0" ?>
<dynamicDiscovery xmlns="urn:schemas-dynamicdiscovery:disco.2000-03-17">
    <exclude path="_vti_cnf" />
    <exclude path="_vti_pvt" />
    <exclude path="_vti_log" />
    <exclude path="_vti_script" />
    <exclude path="_vti_txt" />
    <exclude path="Web References" />
</dynamicDiscovery>
```

The exclude path lines tell the dynamic discovery process to exclude the named group of application subdirectories. The named _vti_* subdirectories are Microsoft Front Page Extensions that VS.NET automatically creates for every ASP.NET application. They contain files to support Front Page projects and never Web Services, so sensibly they are excluded. Notice that the \bin subdirectory, the directory to which we deploy our web service assembly, is not in the exclude list. Thus our AreaCodeService2 web service will be discovered.

Later in this chapter when we use VS.NET to create our client proxy, we will see how delightfully helpful these are.

AssemblyInfo.cs, Global.asax, Global.asax.cs, and Web.config

Additionally, the VS.NET ASP.NET web service template creates the following files:

❑ AssemblyInfo.cs. This file contains attributes that allow us to (optionally) specify characteristics of the AreaCodeService.dll assembly, such as the version

❑ Global.asax and Global.asax.cs. The Global.asax is a standard ASP.NET application file. Like, .asmx files, .asax files can use code-behind files to contain application logic. In this case the code-behind file is the Global.asax.cs file. These files can contain global application code, including event handler methods that respond to session or application start and stop events that ASP.NET raises. These events are outside the scope of this chapter, but note that the default implementation does nothing in response to these events, as shown:

```
public class Global : System.Web.HttpApplication
{
    protected void Application_Start(Object sender, EventArgs e)
```

```
        {
        }
        protected void Session_Start(Object sender, EventArgs e)
        {
        }
        protected void Application_BeginRequest(Object sender, EventArgs e)
        {
        }
        protected void Application_EndRequest(Object sender, EventArgs e)
        {
        }
        protected void Session_End(Object sender, EventArgs e)
        {
        }
        protected void Application_End(Object sender, EventArgs e)
        {
        }
    }
```

The code-behind source is compiled to the `AreaCodeService.dll` assembly also. This pair of files is optional

- ❑ `Web.config`. In this XML file we can configure application settings. Very powerful and helpful ASP.NET application debugging and tracing features can be turned on and off through settings in this file. A full discussion of the application properties that can be configured within this file is outside of the scope of this chapter. The inline comments within this file itself give a good introduction to the application properties that can be configured

The important thing to remember is that because, ASP.NET Web Services are ASP.NET applications, Web Services get all the built-in functionality available to any other ASP.NET application including the ASP.NET-fired application and session start and end events.

The WebService Class

When the VS.NET ASP.NET template creates a web service, it declares the class differently than in our initial simple AreaCodeService implementation. Looking at our VS.NET implementation below, notice that our `AreaCodeService2` class derives from a system class called `System.Web.Services.WebService`:

```
    public class AreaCodeService2 : System.Web.Services.WebService
    {
    }
```

Inheriting from `System.Web.Services.WebService` gives us easy access to ASP.NET built-in objects called intrinsics. Intrinsics include the `Session` object mentioned in the *.NET Primer* section. Recall, we can use the `Session` object to keep state. Other ASP.NET intrinsic objects can give us information about the current user and context. Again, it's important to realize that because our web service is an ASP.NET application, like all others it thereby has access to all these ASP.NET constructs.

More About WebMethod and WebService Attributes

Before we move on to creating proxies, we will end this section by discussing the attributes in the `System.Web.Services.Webservice` namespace in more depth. We've already introduced the `[WebMethod]` attribute – the attribute we tag our methods with to expose them.

The `[WebService]` attribute is also in this namespace –it can be used to change characteristics of the web service class itself.

Do not confuse the `[WebService]` attribute with the `System.Web.Services.WebService` base class, discussed in the last section. The `[WebService]` attribute is an attribute we can optionally use to annotate our web service class; the `System.Web.Services.WebService` class is a class we can optionally derive from. Both can be used with our Web Service class, and both are optional, but they are otherwise unrelated.

We aren't required to use the `[WebService]` attribute – as we saw in our first example, the only attribute required to deploy a web service is the `[WebMethod]` attribute. Understand that applying the `[WebService]` attribute does not result in class methods being exposed – we will still need to use the `[WebMethod]` attribute to expose our methods.

Using Attributes to Document our Web Service

Both the `[WebService]`, and `[WebMethod]` attributes have a `Description` property. With it we can associate a bit of documentation with our web service. This is a good practice and habit to get into right away. When we create our client proxy class, we will see how this can help out our users.

The WebMethod Decription Property

To document our `CheckSplit()` method, we add a `Description` property to our `[WebMethod]` attribute, and set it to a short description of the method. This code in the `AreaCodeService2.asmx.cs` file now looks like this:

```
[WebMethod(Description="Returns the updated phone number, or null if the
            phone number has not changed.")]
    public string CheckForSplit(string strPhoneNumber)
```

The WebService Decription Property

The `[WebService]` attribute also has a `Description` property. We can use it describe the Web Service itself. For example, the following shows the `[WebService]` attribute with the `Description` property set, applied to our `AreaCodeService2` class in the `AreaCodeService2.asmx.cs` file:

```
[WebService(Description="This class contains methods to check area codes.")]
    public class AreaCodeService2 : System.Web.Services.WebService
```

Viewing WebMethod and WebService Documentation

Let's now look at how these `Description` properties can be helpful. After adding the `Description` properties to both the `[WebMethod]` and `[WebService]` attributes as shown above, let's request the help page. Remember, because we have changed the code-behind source, we must recompile our application. To recompile and open our browser to http://localhost/AreaCodeService2/AreaCodeService2.asmx, we hit *F5*. Below is what we see:

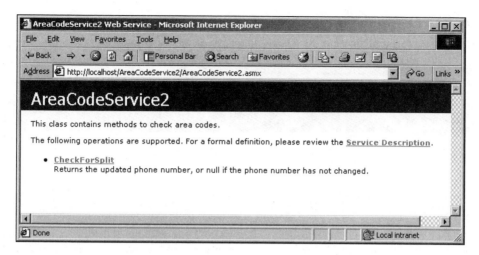

Notice our AreaCodeService2 description, shown under the web service name, and the method documentation listed under the **CheckForSplit** link. Nice! This `Description` property information becomes part of the WSDL description of our class. Viewing the WSDL by requesting http://localhost/AreaCodeService2/AreaCodeService2.asmx?WSDL from within our browser, we see that the `[WebService]` Description property information is included as a new `documentation` element in the `service` element:

```
<service name="AreaCodeService2">
   <documentation>
      This class contains methods to check area codes.
   </documentation>
   ...
</service>
```

Notice also that the `[WebMethod]` Description property is added as a new `documentation` element within each `portType` element:

```
<portType name="AreaCodeService2Soap">
   <operation name="CheckForSplit">
      <documentation>
         Returns the updated phone number, or null if the phone number has
         not changed.
      </documentation>
      <input message="s0:CheckForSplitSoapIn" />
      <output message="s0:CheckForSplitSoapOut" />
   </operation>
</portType>
```

Changing the Default Namespace

By this point, the recommendation that shows up on the default help page starts to be annoying:

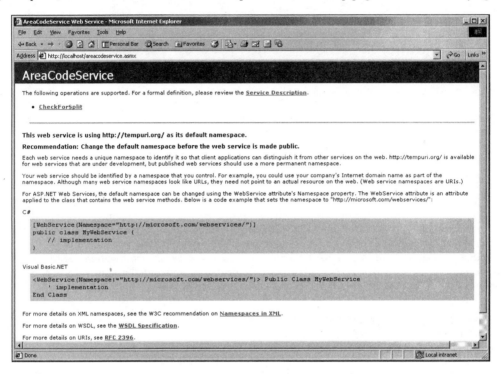

So, what is this about? Moreover, how do we follow the recommendation to change the default namespace?

If we look at the WSDL our service contract generates (below), we notice that names which are specific to our web service – s0:CheckForSplit, s0:CheckForSplitResponse, etc, are qualified with the s0 namespace. The namespace s0 is set to http://tempuri.org/.

```xml
<?xml version="1.0" encoding="utf-8"?>
<definitions xmlns:s="http://www.w3.org/2001/XMLSchema"
             xmlns:http="http://schemas.xmlsoap.org/wsdl/http/"
             xmlns:mime="http://schemas.xmlsoap.org/wsdl/mime/"
             xmlns:tm="http://microsoft.com/wsdl/mime/textMatching/"
             xmlns:soap="http://schemas.xmlsoap.org/wsdl/soap/"
             xmlns:soapenc="http://schemas.xmlsoap.org/soap/encoding/"
             xmlns:s0="http://tempuri.org/"
             targetNamespace="http://tempuri.org/"
             xmlns="http://schemas.xmlsoap.org/wsdl/">
    ...
   <message name="CheckForSplitSoapIn">
      <part name="parameters" element="s0:CheckForSplit" />
   </message>
   <message name="CheckForSplitSoapOut">
      <part name="parameters" element="s0:CheckForSplitResponse" />
   </message>
    ...
</definitions>
```

Defining this namespace for our markup vocabulary ensures that our `CheckForSplit` element can be distinguished from any other organization's `CheckForSplit` element. However, the namespace http://tempuri.org/ – the default – is simply a placeholder. We need to set our namespace to a unique URI, and to ensure its uniqueness; it should be a URI that we have control over.

We do this by setting `Namespace` property of the `[WebService]` attribute to a URL of our choice. For our service, let's set it to http://kusadasi/webservices. Setting the `Namespace` property looks like this:

```
[WebService(Namespace = "http://kusadasi/webservices")]
public class AreaCodeService2 : System.Web.Services.WebService
{
...
}
```

`kusadasi` is the name of my server, and is a unique name on my Intranet. If we were to deploy our Web Service to the Internet, we would need to use a URI that included a complete Internet domain to ensure uniqueness. The `webservices` part is added to be descriptive.

Be clear that the URI http://kusadasi/webservices **does not** refer to a real resource on a system. That isn't required. The Namespace value simply needs to be a unique URI. Refer to the W3C specification on XML schemas for more info about this.

After making this change we recompile by hitting *Ctrl-Shift-B*.

Viewing the WSDL by requesting http://localhost/AreaCodeService2/AreaCodeService2.asmx?WSDL from within our browser, we see that our namespace has changed, as shown:

```
<?xml version="1.0" encoding="utf-8" ?>
<definitions xmlns:s="http://www.w3.org/2001/XMLSchema"
          xmlns:http="http://schemas.xmlsoap.org/wsdl/http/"
          xmlns:mime="http://schemas.xmlsoap.org/wsdl/mime/"
          xmlns:tm="http://microsoft.com/wsdl/mime/textMatching/"
          xmlns:soap="http://schemas.xmlsoap.org/wsdl/soap/"
          xmlns:soapenc="http://schemas.xmlsoap.org/soap/encoding/"
          xmlns:s0="http://kusadasi/webservices"
          targetNamespace="http://kusadasi/webservices"
          xmlns="http://schemas.xmlsoap.org/wsdl/">
    ...
```

And viewing the help page at http://localhost/AreaCodeService2/AreaCodeService2.asmx?WSDL, we notice the recommendation message no longer pesters us. Setting the namespace is another one of those good habits to adopt right away.

Renaming a Web Service or a Web Service Method

Imagine that we decided to extend our area code Web Service to include a second method. Our second method is an overloaded version of `CheckForSplit()`.

An overload method means that multiple methods share the same name, but have different formal parameter lists. Each overloaded method must have a different number of parameters or have parameters of different types than other instances of the overloaded method. Many programming languages support method overloading, including C#, C++, VB.NET.

It does the same operation as our first one – determines if a phone number has changed by comparing the area code and exchange against the area code split data. However, our new method has a different signature:

```
public int CheckForSplit(int iAreaCode, int iExchange)
```

Below is the earlier one:

```
public string CheckForSplit(string strPhoneNumber)
```

Instead of a `string` phone number parameter, we pass it an area code and an exchange prefix. It returns an updated area code, or 0 if the area code has not changed for the given exchange. C# allows method overloading, however web service protocols don't. SOAP requires that methods within a given service have unique names. We can rename the exposed version of our `CheckForSplit()` method using the `MessageName` property of the `[WebMethod]` attribute. Here we show documenting of this method, and renaming the exposed method to `CheckForSplit2`:

```
[WebMethod(MessageName="CheckForSplit2",
          Description="Returns the updated area code, or 0 if the phone
          number has not changed.")]
public int CheckForSplit(int iAreaCode, int iExchange)
{
...
}
```

Problem solved! The method is still overloaded in our implementation, but the exposed method is known by a different name.

Similarly, the Web Service name that is exposed is the class name by default. Much like exposing a method with a non-default name, we can rename the web service itself. To do this we use the `Name` property of the `[WebService]` attribute.

For example, if we decided to include our company name, "Acme" (what else?), in our service name, we could rename `AreaCodeService2` to `AcmeAreaCodeService`, as shown:

```
[WebService(Name = "AcmeAreaCodeService")]
public class AreaCodeService2 : System.Web.Services.WebService
{
```

Let's recompile and test the two previously described changes, that is, adding a new, overloaded `CheckForSplit()` method and renaming the exposed second version to `CheckForSplit2()`, and renaming our web service to AcmeAreaCodeService. We recompile and open our browser to http://localhost/AreaCodeService2/AreaCodeService2.asmx by hitting *F7*. The below screenshot, is what we see:

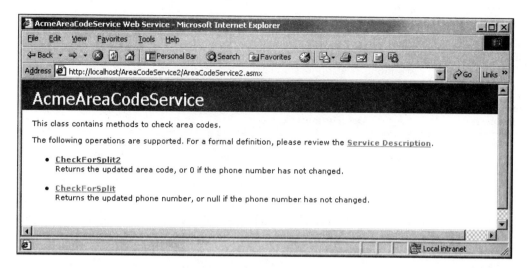

Navigating our browser to http://localhost/AreaCodeService2/AreaCodeService2.asmx?WSDL, we notice a few changes to our WSDL contract. First, we see our new `CheckForSplit()` method, referred to as CheckForSplit2:

```
<s:element name="CheckForSplit2">
   <s:complexType>
      <s:sequence>
        <s:element minOccurs="1" maxOccurs="1"
                   name="iAreaCode" type="s:int" />
        <s:element minOccurs="1" maxOccurs="1"
                   name="iExchange" type="s:int" />
      </s:sequence>
   </s:complexType>
</s:element>
<s:element name="CheckForSplit2Response">
   <s:complexType>
      <s:sequence>
        <s:element minOccurs="1" maxOccurs="1"
                   name="CheckForSplit2Result" type="s:int" />
      </s:sequence>
   </s:complexType>
</s:element>
<s:element name="string" nillable="true" type="s:string" />
<s:element name="int" type="s:int" />
```

Notice also that our Web Service is now known by the name of AcmeAreaCodeService:

```
<service name="AcmeAreaCodeService">
   ...
</service>
```

Other WebMethod Attribute properties

The [WebMethod] attribute, in particular, demonstrates how powerful attributes in .NET can be. Moreover, we have just scratched the surface of what this attribute can do for your web service. We'll briefly mention the [WebMethod] attribute's other properties to give an idea of how you can put this attribute to work:

Property:	Description:
CacheDuration	This property allows us to cache a method's return value for the number of seconds specified. During the cache duration, the method is not executed if invoked with the same parameters; instead the cached result is returned. Every executed parameter combination gets cached, so this property must be used wisely.
TransactionOption	ASP.NET Web Services can participate in COM+ transactions. This property specifies how the web service method participates in the transaction.
EnableSession	By default, ASP.NET session state is disabled. This property can be used to enable the ability to save session state. Be aware that this will cause HTTP cookies to be used, which has additional overhead.
BufferResponse	By default, a web service result will not be transmitted until the response is completely buffered. When a method returns a large response, or a response that formed slowly, this property can be set to allow ASP.NET to start the transmission of the response before it is fully buffered.

Building Web Service Proxies

At this point we have seen how to build Web Services with and without the aid of VS.NET. In both scenarios, ASP.NET's infrastructure and the .NET Framework classes do the heavy lifting for us. What .NET does for creating Web Services, it also does for creating client applications that use Web Services. In this section we will look at VS.NET's support for discovering Web Services, creating client proxies for them, and fine-tuning their use.

When we create our client test application we will see how helpful Web Service Discovery can be. So before we jump into discussing our client test application, let's take a moment to talk more in depth about this process.

An Introduction to Web Service Discovery and DISCO

Web Service Discovery is the process of finding Web Service descriptions. Dynamic discovery is the process of finding particular Web Services automatically, without requiring the web service implementer to take any special registration steps. DISCO refers to the XML schema that dynamic discovery processes use to describe the Web Services that are found.

In ASP.NET, dynamic web service discovery is supported through an HTTP handler for .vsdisco XML documents. To learn about which Web Services exist and how to use them, a client can point a browser at a .vsdisco file.

The .NET Framework installs the file.`default.vsdisco` to the root of the default web site (with a default IIS install this is at `\inetput\wwwroot`). Files of type `.vsdisco` assist the dynamic discovery process. The `default.vsdisco` file contains the following:

```
<?xml version="1.0" ?>
<dynamicDiscovery xmlns="urn:schemas-dynamicdiscovery:disco.2000-03-17">
    <exclude path="_vti_cnf" />
    <exclude path="_vti_pvt" />
    <exclude path="_vti_log" />
    <exclude path="_vti_script" />
    <exclude path="_vti_txt" />
</dynamicDiscovery>
```

This tells the dynamic discovery process which subdirectories to exclude in the dynamic discovery process.

If we navigate to a `.vsdisco` file from a browser, the dynamic discovery process searches for additional `.vsdisco` files and Web Services in the directory in which the `.vsdisco` file resides, and all non-exluded directories and virtual directories one level below, for additional `.vsdisco` files and Web Services. The dynamic discovery process doesn't return the content of the `.vsdicso` file. It instead returns an XML document with information about the Web Services and additional `.vsdisco` files it found. Specifically, it returns the following types of elements:

❏ **discoveryRef** elements. The `discoveryRef` element contains the URL of `.vsdisco` files either in the current directory or in a directory one subdirectory below

❏ **contractRef** elements. The `contractRef` element contains the URL of a WSDL contracts for a web service

These elements are defined in the DISCO XML schema.

On the author's system, navigating to http://localhost/default.disco returns the two following `discoveryRef` elements:

```
<?xml version="1.0" encoding="utf-8" ?>
<discovery xmlns="http://schemas.xmlsoap.org/disco/">
    <discoveryRef ref="http://localhost/HelloService/HelloService.vsdisco" />
    <discoveryRef ref="http://localhost/AreaCodeService2
                       /AreaCodeService2.vsdisco" />
</discovery>
```

By navigating to http://localhost/AreaCodeService2/AreaCodeService2.vsdisco, the dynamic discovery process locates the AreaCodeService web service, and returns the following:

```
<?xml version="1.0" encoding="utf-8" ?>
<discovery xmlns="http://schemas.xmlsoap.org/disco/">
    <contractRef ref="http://localhost/AreaCodeService2
                      /AreaCodeService2.asmx?wsdl"
                 docRef="http://localhost/AreaCodeService2
                         /AreaCodeService2.asmx"
                 xmlns="http://schemas.xmlsoap.org/disco/scl/" />
</discovery>
```

The reference to a WSDL contract for the AreaCodeService gives us enough information to go ahead and use our service. Here we are beginning to see the real power of Web Service Discovery. Using Web Service Discovery, clients can worm through layers and layers of servers and virtual directories, dynamically finding Web Services. In the next section we will see how VS.NET uses dynamic discovery to make creating web service proxies very easy.

Our Client Test Application

In this section we'll create a simple client application to test our web service programmatically. It will be a bare bones .NET Windows application, called AreaCodeClient. AreaCodeClient has the following user interface.

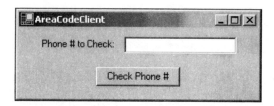

The user will enter a phone number and then click the **Check Phone #** button. This will invoke our Web Service's CheckForSplit() method. The result of our method will display in a pop-up message box.

We won't go through the steps of creating the UI, since creating Windows .NET applications is outside the scope of this chapter. Be assured that creating .NET Windows applications is much like creating Windows applications with VB, Microsoft MFC, and many other frameworks. VS.NET includes VB.NET and C# Windows application templates which generate all of the skeleton code. We used the VS.NET C# Windows Application template to create our client application. In VS.NET, a form designer tool allows us to easily drag and drop controls onto our form and create skeleton window event handlers. The full implementation can be found in the Chapter12\AreaCodeClient (in the code download) directory.

The following show the skeleton code for the Check Phone # button event that the was generated for us:

```
private void button1_Click(object sender, System.EventArgs e)
{
}
```

It is within this method that we will add the code, which calls the CheckForSplit() method of our Web Service. However, before we can do that, we will need to create a proxy class.

Creating a Proxy with Visual Studio.NET

In Chapter 10, we introduced the idea of a client proxy in discussing wrapping strategies.

Recall, a proxy class is a class that includes methods that correspond to the methods that the Web Service exposes. The proxy methods have the same name and signature as the Web Service methods. The proxy class takes care of packaging the parameters to SOAP, and sending the information over the wire to the correct Web Service endpoint, and then unpackaging the returned SOAP response into method return values. This allows our client to access the Web Service as if it were a local resource – without being bogged down dealing with the transport code and SOAP formatting.

Visual Studio .NET has great integral support for creating Web Service proxies. In fact, if you weren't paying close attention you might not even realize you were creating a proxy class. Within a VS.NET project the action of creating a Web Service proxy is referred to as "adding a web reference". VS.NET uses terminology and makes the process as conceptually simple as looking for and then adding a reference to a local library. When we "add a web reference" a proxy class source code file is in fact generated, and it is added to the client project. However, by default this file doesn't show in the project's Solution Explorer file list, as we will see shortly. This is VS.NET trying hard to abstract away the messy details, allowing us to think of Web Services as simply another code resource.

To add a proxy class to our AreaCodeClient from within our AreaCodeClient project, we need to open the **Project** menu. We then select the **Add Web Reference** menu item. Below is the dialog box we see:

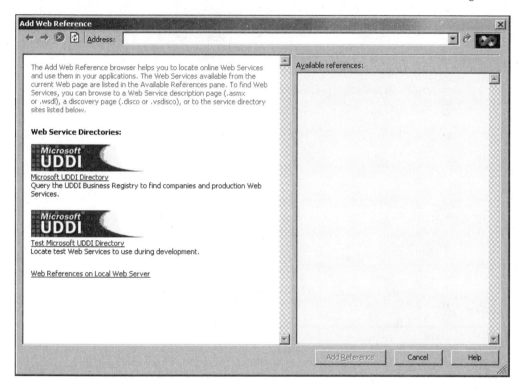

Notice that from this dialog box we can choose to find a web service from a number of sources. We can select one of the following:

- ❑ **Microsoft UDDI Directory**. Selecting this option presents a screen, which allows us to query against Microsoft's production UDDI server. Descriptions of all the Web Services that match our query are displayed. When we find the web service for which we want to create a proxy, we select it's WSDL link and continue

- ❑ **Microsoft Test UDDI Directory**. Selecting this option takes us through the same steps as selecting Microsoft's UDDI Directory, except we are querying against a test directory

- ❑ **Web References on Local Web Server**. Selecting this option uses causes the tool to query our local web server's to discover the Web Services we expose system. Web Services are exposed

❑   **Web References on Another Server**. By entering the URL of some other web service at the top of the screen, we can invoke Web Services discovery on an alternate server

At the moment it seems to be impossible to query against a non-Microsoft UDDI directory, such as IBM's, from this interface.

To build our client proxy, we select Web References on Local Web Server. The Add Web Reference tool then shows us this screen:

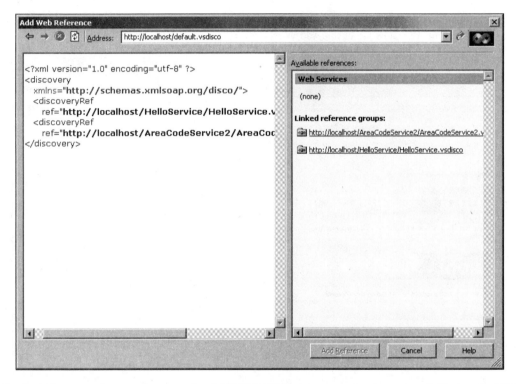

On the left we see the root directory level DISCO XML document that is returned. Notice the URL that is given at the top of the screen – http://localhost/default.vsdisco. There are no Web Service WSDL files given within this DISCO configuration – notice the (none) at the top right of the screen. However two more .vsdisco files are referenced in the DISCO document: the http://localhost/HelloService/HelloService.vsdisco file, and our very own http://localhost/AreaCodeService/AreaCodeService2.vsdisco file. This same information is given in the right panel, in a more readable format. We click on the http://localhost/AreaCodeService/AreaCodeService.vsdisco link select this Web Service.

After clicking on the http://localhost/AreaCodeService2/AreaCodeService2.vsdisco link, we see that our http://localhost/AreaCodeService2/AreaCodeService2.vsdisco file references our actual WSDL contract. Here is what this screen looks like:

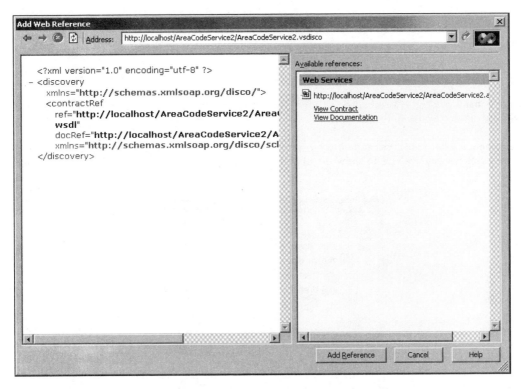

From here we can select the View Contract link on the right panel. This will display the WSDL contract. Alternatively, we can select the View Documentation link. We would then see the documentation we added to AreaCodeService (and it's a good thing we did!). With the WSDL contract at hand, the tool now enables the Add Reference button for us. We can click this to complete the process. Let's do it.

The reference is now added, what a piece of cake! As we mentioned in the introduction to this section, VS.NET will hide the details of the proxy class. All we really need to know to jump right in and use the proxy, we can discern by looking at the Class View window. To open the Class View window, select Class View from the View menu. Here is what we see:

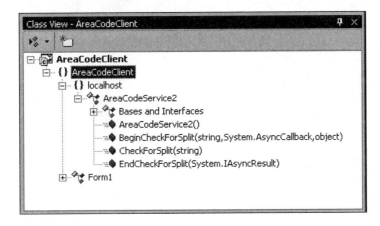

This tells us that our project now contains a class called `AreaCodeService2` in the `AreaCodeClient.localhost` namespace. This class has a constructor and a method with the following signature:

```
public bool CheckForSplit(string strPhoneNum, out string strNewPhoneNum);
```

Notice that `AreaCodeClient.localhost.AreaCodeService2` implements two other methods – we will discuss these later in this chapter.

Let's look at what really was added to our project. Again, from the Projects menu, select Show All Files. If we explicitly set VS.NET to show the hidden proxy files, here's what VS.NET's Solution Explorer shows:

Notice the Solution Explorer shows all of the AreaCodeClient application source files – however the client UI code is not really interesting to us. We care about the Web Reference. Look specifically at the newly-added Web References group. Here is where it gets interesting. Notice a category has been added for localhost – our system. Under this category the following four things have been added:

❑ AreaCodeService2.disco. A DISCO file referencing the AreaCodeService's WSDL contract and the URL of the SOAP endpoint:

```xml
<?xml version="1.0" encoding="utf-8"?>
<discovery xmlns:xsi="http://www.w3.org/2001/XMLSchema-instance"
           xmlns:xsd="http://www.w3.org/2001/XMLSchema"
           xmlns="http://schemas.xmlsoap.org/disco/">
  <contractRef ref="http://localhost/AreaCodeService2
                    /AreaCodeService2.asmx?wsdl"
               docRef="http://localhost/AreaCodeService2
                      /AreaCodeService2.asmx"
               xmlns="http://schemas.xmlsoap.org/disco/scl/" />
  <soap address="http://localhost/AreaCodeService2/AreaCodeService2.asmx"
```

```
        xmlns:q1="http://kusadasi/webservices"
        binding="q1:AreaCodeService2Soap"
        xmlns="http://schemas.xmlsoap.org/disco/soap/" />
</discovery>
```

- ❏ **AreaCodeService2.wsdl**. A local copy of the WSDL contract
- ❏ **Reference.map**. ASP.NET helper file mapping the WSDL and DISCO information to their sources
- ❏ **AreaCodeService2.cs**. Here it is – our proxy implementation file. Because our AreaCodeClient is a C# project, our proxy is also a C# source file

Let's look at the proxy code in `AreaCodeService2.cs`. We double click on this file in the Solution Explorer.

The following `AreaCodeService2.cs` excerpt shows the namespace declaration, the proxy class, the proxy class constructor, and the `CheckForSplit()` method in the proxy class:

```
//------------------------------------------------------------------------------
// <autogenerated>
//    This code was generated by a tool.
//    Runtime Version: 1.0.2914.16
//
//    Changes to this file may cause incorrect behavior and will be lost if
//    the code is regenerated.
// </autogenerated>
//------------------------------------------------------------------------------

namespace AreaCodeClient.localhost {
  using System.Diagnostics;
  using System.Xml.Serialization;
  using System;
  using System.Web.Services.Protocols;
  using System.Web.Services;


  [System.Web.Services.WebServiceBindingAttribute(Name="AreaCodeService2Soap",
Namespace="http://kusadasi/webservices")]
  public class AreaCodeService2 :
System.Web.Services.Protocols.SoapHttpClientProtocol {

    [System.Diagnostics.DebuggerStepThroughAttribute()]
    public AreaCodeService2() {
      this.Url = "http://localhost/AreaCodeService2/AreaCodeService2.asmx";
    }

    [System.Diagnostics.DebuggerStepThroughAttribute()]

[System.Web.Services.Protocols.SoapDocumentMethodAttribute("http://kusadasi/webser
vices/CheckForSplit", RequestNamespace="http://kusadasi/webservices",
ResponseNamespace="http://kusadasi/webservices",
Use=System.Web.Services.Description.SoapBindingUse.Literal,
ParameterStyle=System.Web.Services.Protocols.SoapParameterStyle.Wrapped)]
```

```
    public string CheckForSplit(string strPhoneNumber) {
      object[] results = this.Invoke("CheckForSplit", new object[] {
          strPhoneNumber});
      return ((string)(results[0]));
    }
  ...
  }
}
```

Let's look at each of these four:

❑ **AreaCodeClient.localhost** namespace declaration. The namespace that the proxy specifies is constructed from the project namespace (for our test client this is AreaCodeClient) followed by the name of the host (localhost).

```
namespace AreaCodeClient.localhost
```

❑ **The proxy class**. The proxy class is given the same name as the web service name, AreaCodeService2. It derives from a system class called System.Web.Services.Protocols.SoapHttpClientProtocol. The AreaCodeService2 class is marked with the [WebServiceBinding] attribute. This attribute maps this proxy class to our service's binding and namespace given in the WSDL

```
[System.Web.Services.WebServiceBindingAttribute(Name="AreaCodeService2Soap",
Namespace="http://kusadasi/webservices")]
public class AreaCodeService2:
System.Web.Services.Protocols.SoapHttpClientProtocol
{
  ...
}
```

❑ **The proxy class constructor**. This constructor sets a derived data member, URL, to the URL of our Web Services. The [System.Diagnostics.DebuggerStepThroughAttribute()] attribute controls how debugging responds. We will see shortly how we can override this value.

```
[System.Diagnostics.DebuggerStepThroughAttribute()]
public AreaCodeService2()
{
  this.Url = "http://localhost/AreaCodeService2/AreaCodeService2.asmx";
}
```

❑ The **CheckForSplit()** method. The proxy class contains methods with the exact signature and semantics of our area code Web Service's CheckForSplit() method. We won't worry about the details, but know that the [System.Web.Services.Protocols.SoapDocumentMethodAttribute] attribute just maps the method to the server's listener.

```
[System.Web.Services.Protocols.SoapDocumentMethodAttribute("http://kusadasi/webser
vices/CheckForSplit", RequestNamespace="http://kusadasi/webservices",
ResponseNamespace="http://kusadasi/webservices",
Use=System.Web.Services.Description.SoapBindingUse.Literal,
ParameterStyle=System.Web.Services.Protocols.SoapParameterStyle.Wrapped)]
public string CheckForSplit(string strPhoneNumber)
{
```

```
        object[] results = this.Invoke("CheckForSplit", new object[] {
                strPhoneNumber});
        return ((string)(results[0]));
    }
```

Now that we have our proxy, let's use it in our client application. To do this we first add a `using` statement to use the `AreaCodeClient.localhost` namespace, the namespace that implements the proxy class:

```
    using AreaCodeClient.localhost;
```

Next we add a `private` data member reference to the class that implements our client application logic:

```
        private AreaCodeService2 acs;
```

In our client application class's constructor we add a line to create an instance of our proxy:

```
        acs = new AreaCodeService2();
```

Finally, in our button's click event handler, the `button1_Click()` method, we add a call to our proxy's `CheckForSplit()` method:

```
        // Invoke web service proxy CheckForSplit method
        string strNew = acs.CheckForSplit(textBox1.Text);
```

Our client saves the returned result to a `string` instance. Then our client displays the results in a message box.

The following shows the code together. The VS.NET project containing this code can be found in the `Chapter11\AreaCodeClient` subdirectory (in the code download). Note that some of the unrelated template-generated UI code has been omitted for brevity:

```
using System;
using System.Drawing;
using System.Collections;
using System.ComponentModel;
using System.Windows.Forms;
using System.Data;

namespace AreaCodeClient
{
    /// <summary>
    /// Summary description for Form1.
    /// </summary>
    public class Form1 : System.Windows.Forms.Form
    {
        private System.Windows.Forms.TextBox textBox1;
        private System.Windows.Forms.Label label1;
        private System.Windows.Forms.Button button1;
        /// <summary>
```

```
        /// Required designer variable.
        /// </summary>
        private System.ComponentModel.Container components = null;
        private localhost.AreaCodeService2 acs;

        public Form1()
        {
            //
            // Required for Windows Form Designer support
            //
            InitializeComponent();

            acs = new localhost.AreaCodeService2();

        }

// Some template-generated code not shown

        private void button1_Click(object sender, System.EventArgs e)
        {
            // Invoke web service proxy CheckForSplit method
            string strNew = acs.CheckForSplit(textBox1.Text);

            // Display results
            if (strNew == null)
                MessageBox.Show("Phone # unchanged",
                    "AreaCodeService2.CheckForSplit complete");
            else
                MessageBox.Show("New phone # is " + strNew,
                    "AreaCodeService2.CheckForSplit complete");
        }
    }
}
```

That's it. Let's compile our `AreaCodeClient` application and run it (by hitting *F5*), to test it against our Web Service.

Running our application, we see this screen:

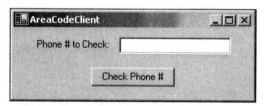

If we enter a phone number that we know is affected by our hard-coded data (again we use `5202221111`, being careful not to include extra spaces or punctuation), and hit **OK**, we see:

Voila! Our proxy and Web Service are working like a charm.

Creating an Asynchronous Proxy

It's easy and it works great – what more could we ask? Well, let me tell you a story. Long ago when I was an intern, I was tasked with writing a GUI application to test an FTP API library. I toiled away for a few hours until I had enough code to log into an FTP server, request a directory listing and populate a listbox. I compiled and started testing. I quickly discovered that making FTP API calls that crawled across the Internet was tricky business. An FTP call could take microseconds or minutes. And making these calls from the thread that controlled the user interface was bad policy. My UI could freeze for seconds at a time, or even hang completely. Not good. I quickly learned to create a new, background thread for calling the FTP API functions. This saved my UI from freezing unpredictably, but devising mechanisms to communicate state information between the background thread and the UI thread complicated my code immensely. Not trivial, and not fun!

This lesson holds true for Web Services: the Internet is an unpredictable entity and it's never safe to assume that a call over the internet will return in a reasonable time span.

Luckily, the folks who brought us the proxy generator are well aware of this little issue. Instead of requiring us to code up the infrastructure to make non-blocking calls to our Web Service, they prefabricate it for us in the proxy.

Notice the VS.NET-generated proxy `AreaCodeService2` class in `AreaCodeService2.cs` also includes these two methods:

```
[System.Diagnostics.DebuggerStepThroughAttribute()]
 public System.IAsyncResult BeginCheckForSplit(string strPhoneNumber,
System.AsyncCallback callback, object asyncState)
{
   return this.BeginInvoke("CheckForSplit", new object[] {
          strPhoneNumber}, callback, asyncState);
}

[System.Diagnostics.DebuggerStepThroughAttribute()]
 public string EndCheckForSplit(System.IAsyncResult asyncResult)
{
   object[] results = this.EndInvoke(asyncResult);
   return ((string)(results[0]));
}
```

For each exposed Web Service method, VS.NET will kindly create two extra methods to support asynchronous operation. Let's discuss these methods:

❑   `BeginMethodName()`. We can use this method to begin an asynchronous invocation of a web service method. The `BeginMethodName()` method has the same parameter list as the original method, followed by two additional asynchronous-related parameters: a `System.AsyncCallback` parameter and an `object` parameter. `System.AsyncCallback` is a delegate, that is, a reference to a method. We set this to a method in our client application. When the asynchronous Web Service finishes, the infrastructure invokes this method. We can use the `object` parameter to associate context information with the asynchronous result.

This method always returns a `System.IAsyncResult`. In our proxy code we see the `BeginCheckForSplit()` has the string `strNumber` parameter, followed by the `System.AsyncCallback` and `object` parameters:

```
System.IAsyncResult BeginCheckForSplit(string strPhoneNumber, System.AsyncCallback
callback, object asyncState)
```

We use this method to begin the web service. When we call it, it will always return immediately.

❑   End*MethodName*(). We use this method to gather the Web Service's return value when we
know our asynchronous method has completed. It has the same return type as the original
CheckForSplit() method. This method always takes a System.IAsyncResult parameter.

Our web service proxy class has this method:

```
public string EndCheckForSplit(System.IAsyncResult asyncResult)
```

Notice it shares the same return type as the synchronous version.

So let's see how these work. We will change our client code so that clicking the button simply starts an
asynchronous call to our CheckForSplit() method.

We add a new "callback" method. This is the method that will be invoked when the asynchronous call is
completed. The method is an instance of the AsyncCallback delegate. Delegates are a C# entity that
we can think of delegates as a type-safe function pointer.

Our AsyncCallback delegate must have the following method signature:

```
public static void AsyncCallback(IAsyncResult ar)
```

We will implement an instance of the AsyncCallback delegate that has this method signature:

```
public static void CheckNumberCallback(IAsyncResult ar)
```

We modify the button click event handler to create a new instance of the AsyncCallback delegate,
setting it to our CheckNumberCallback() method. Our event handler then calls the
BeginCheckForSplit() method with the instance of the AsyncCallback. We pass our instance of
the AreaCodeService2 as the second parameter. We will see why we do this shortly. So our
button1_Click() method now looks like this:

```
private void button1_Click(object sender, System.EventArgs e)
{
    //Instantiate an AsyncCallback delegate
    AsyncCallback callback = new AsyncCallback(Form1.CheckNumberCallback);

    // Begin web service proxy BeginCheckForSplit() method
    acs.BeginCheckForSplit(textBox1.Text, callback, acs);
```

Let's look at what happens in our CheckNumberCallback() method. Here is the implementation:

```
// Callback method invoked by the proxy class when
// the async method completes
public static void CheckNumberCallback(IAsyncResult ar)
{
    // We passed the current instance of AreaCodeService2
```

```
    // parameter to BeginCheckForSplit(), so it will be
    // accessible in the AsyncState property.
    localhost.AreaCodeService2 acs = (localhost.AreaCodeService2) ar.AsyncState;

    // Get the completed results
    string strNew = acs.EndCheckForSplit(ar);

    //Display results
    if (strNew == null)
       MessageBox.Show("Phone # unchanged",
          "AreaCodeService2.CheckForSplit complete");
    else
       MessageBox.Show("New phone # is " + strNew,
          "AreaCodeService2.CheckForSplit complete");
 }
```

This method gets a reference to our `localhost.AreaCodeService2` and then uses it to call the `EndCheckForSplit()` method. This collects the web service return value. The method then displays a message box with the return value, exactly like the synchronous version of client did. Let's look at this line of code in a little more detail:

```
    // We passed the current instance of AreaCodeService2
    // parameter to BeginCheckForSplit(), so it will be
    // accessible in the AsyncState property.
    localhost.AreaCodeService2 acs = (localhost.AreaCodeService2) ar.AsyncState;
```

To get a reference of our `localhost.AreaCodeService2`, we cast the `AsyncState` member of the `IAsyncResult` parameter.

Why can't we just access the private data member acs directly? Notice that `CheckNumberCallback()` is a static method. Static methods don't have access to instance data, including the acs data member. We instead associated our instance of `localhost.AreaCodeService2` with the `IAsyncResult`. We did this when we called the `BeginCheckForSplit()` method, by passing it in as the object parameter:

```
    // Begin web service proxy BeginCheckForSplit() method
    acs.BeginCheckForSplit(textBox1.Text, callback, acs);
```

Here's the complete code starting and ending the asynchronous call.

```
   private void button1_Click(object sender, System.EventArgs e)
   {
      //Instantiate an AsyncCallback delegate
      AsyncCallback callback = new AsyncCallback(Form1.CheckNumberCallback);

      // Begin web service proxy BeginCheckForSplit() method
      acs.BeginCheckForSplit(textBox1.Text, callback, acs);
   }

   // Callback method invoked by the proxy class when
   // the async method completes
   public static void CheckNumberCallback(IAsyncResult ar)
   {
      // We passed the current instance of AreaCodeService2
```

```
        // parameter to BeginCheckForSplit(), so it will be
        // accessible in the AsyncState property.
        localhost.AreaCodeService2 acs = (localhost.AreaCodeService2) ar.AsyncState;

        // Get the completed results
        string strNew = acs.EndCheckForSplit(ar);

        //Display results
        if (strNew == null)
            MessageBox.Show("Phone # unchanged",
                "AreaCodeService2.CheckForSplit complete");
        else
            MessageBox.Show("New phone # is " + strNew,
                "AreaCodeService2.CheckForSplit complete");
    }
```

The beauty of these asynchronous proxy methods is that they will be generated for any and all Web
Services – there is nothing special required of the Web Service. The infrastructure to support
asynchronous invocation exists on the client side.

We compile our asynchronous version of our client, and run:

Notice that when we run this version of the client, the dialog box responds to mouse events while the
web service method executes. We can move the dialog box, minimize, and maximize it, without it
freezing. Perfect!

Using the Web Services Description Language Utility to Generate a Proxy

In the last section we have seen how to find Web Services and create proxy classes with VS.NET.
However, the .NET Platform SDK gives us the utilities we need to do these tasks without VS.NET.

Recall that earlier in this chapter we learned how we could use the Web Services Descriptive Language
utility (wsdl.exe) to generate a web service abstract base class from a WSDL file. This gave a head
start in implementing a web service to match a given WSDL description.

Similarly, we can use `wsdl.exe` to create a proxy class implementation from the command line. To create a proxy class for the web service described in `AreaCodeService.wsdl`, we can use the following:

```
wsdl.exe AreaCodeService.wsdl /out:AreaCodeServiceProxy.cs
```

With the `/out` option we specify the file name for our proxy class.

The default is to create a C# source file. We can use the `/language:vb` option to override this and create a VB.NET source file as shown:

> **wsdl.exe AreaCodeService2.wsdl /out:AreaCodeService2Proxy.vb /language:vb**

Without a WSDL file, we can simply point `wsdl.exe` at our `.asmx` web service page to create our proxy class, like this:

>**wsdl.exe http://kusadasi/AreaCodeService2/AreaCodeService2.asmx /out:AreaCodeService Proxy.cs**

This proxy class will have the same implementation as the one we generated from Add Web Reference dialog within VS.NET – including support for asynchronous operation. However, the `wsdl.exe`-generated proxy class will not set a namespace.

We can also compile our proxy class from the command line. Let's use the C# compiler (`csc.exe`) to build an assembly DLL from our C# proxy class source file `AreaCodeServiceProxy.cs`. To do this we enter the following at the command line:

> **csc.exe /target:library AreaCodeServiceProxy.cs**

This generates a library named `AreaCodeServiceProxy.dll`. The `/target:library` option indicates a DLL library. By default the library will have the same name as the source file with the `.dll` extension. Use the `/out:` option to override the default library name.

Building a Web Service with .NET Remoting

As we have seen in the last two sections, ASP.NET makes building Web Services very simple. The support for Web Services is integral. However, the .NET Framework offers a second option for creating more complex Web Services. In this section we will briefly discuss how we can use .NET Remoting to build Web Services.

All .NET applications execute in the context of an application domain. An application domain, like an application process, provides execution isolation from other applications. The distinction is that multiple application domains can exist within a single process – thereby improving performance. .NET Remoting describes the .NET Framework's general-purpose mechanism for communicating between components in different application domains. Think, DCOM for .NET. Whereas DCOM gave us a COM-based mechanism for inter-process communication, .NET Remoting is the .NET-based mechanism for inter-application domain communication.

The .NET applications using Remoting communicate over something called channels. Channels are responsible for transporting messages. .NET Remoting supports three built-in types of channels: HTTP, SMTP, and TCP. Third parties can implement other channel types. .NET Formatters are responsible for encoding and decoding the messages. .NET Remoting includes two types of formatters: binary, and XML using SOAP. Binary formatting over TCP gives applications an optimized and efficient mechanism for communicating in closed, intranet environment where firewalls are not an issue. However, by registering an HTTP channel endpoint with a SOAP formatter, a host application can expose objects as Web Services.

To discuss the relative limitations of .NET Remoting Web Services let's contrast some of the benefits of creating Web Services with ASP.NET:

❑ ASP.NET includes support for SOAP over HTTP, HTTP GET, and HTTP POST. Remoting supports SOAP over HTTP only

❑ ASP.NET hosts our Web Service. Using .NET Remoting we must create our own application to host our objects. This can be any application – a console application, an NT service, or a GUI application

❑ With ASP.NET we have access to ASP.NET intrinsic objects including the `Session` object to save state. Using .NET Remoting for a generic Web Service, we must devise our own mechanisms to save state

❑ ASP.NET is built on IIS Security. Using .NET Remoting we must devise our own authentication method

❑ Built in test page

However, with .NET Remoting we do get a few things that ASP.NET doesn't provide. .NET Remoting gives us a choice of activation models, remote access to server side objects, and the ability to use all type-system features (like constructors and events) instead of just XSD supported types. However, to take full advantage of all activation models and use of custom types our client must also be implemented using .NET Remoting. That is to say, even though .NET Remoting objects may be SOAP and HTTP-based, taking advantage of some Remoting features may preclude non-.NET Framework clients.

.NET Remoting does have its place, particularly in Intranet applications, but for general purpose Web Services, ASP.NET is both easier to develop and offers a number of persuasive benefits.

ATL Server

At this point we have discussed how we can build Web Services with ASP.NET and .NET Remoting. It is worth mentioning that Visual Studio .NET introduces a third technology for building Web Services. This is ATL Server. ATL Server extends the Active Template Library by providing classes to build ISAPI Web Services for IIS. It is important to note that despite the fact that ATL Server is introduced with Visual Studio .NET, ATL Server is a C++ framework – ATL Server applications are not managed .NET applications. They are regular, natively compiled code. ATL Server offers a powerful and highly optimized option for creating Web Services. However, because they are not .NET Framework-based, they won't be discussed further in this chapter.

Summary

In this chapter we have seen how very serious Microsoft has become about Web Services.

The .NET Framework class library gives us classes and attributes that contain all the web service plumbing.

ASP.NET adds integral support with the new .asmx file type. With this new file type we can deploy our application logic under ASP.NET by simply adding a few attributes and a new page directive. We get the full power of the ASP.NET platform – ASP.NET hosting, the ability to save state using the ASP.NET intrinsic objects, authentication and authorization options, and caching. ASP.NET also includes the help page template to give developers a built in mechanism for testing Web Services using the HTTP GET or HTTP POST protocols.

Moreover, with VS.NET, developing Web Services and web service clients is a simple task. The tools and templates take care of churning out skeleton code and setting up our IIS deployment. With web service project templates we can create and deploy a simple "HelloWorld" web service in a matter of seconds. For creating client applications, VS.NET gives us an easy mechanism to find Web Services via DISCO or UDDI and generate client proxies. While ASP.NET will probably be the more popular option for creating .NET Web Services, .NET Remoting offers a second option for creating more complex Web Services applications.

12

Developing Web Services With Python

Python is a very high-level language. It combines strong object-oriented features with other powerful tools such as dynamic programming, introspection and functional programming support. The popularity of Python is currently on the increase. This is perhaps because of its focus on readability, flexibility and developer productivity. It also has a broad and deep standard library and a vast array of third-party modules, tools and applications. All these factors make it an excellent language for Web Services development.

Python is open source, and versions following 2.1.1 use a licence that is fully compatible with the GNU Public License (GPL) as well. It's free for all uses, including commercial. Python 2.1.1's license is at http://www.python.org/2.1.1/license.html.

Python is an especially apt language for Web Services development for several reasons. It has a very strong standard library for Web communications and data formats, and for XML and HTML manipulation. These are all quite effective for implementing Web Services from first principles. Naturally, given this foundation, there are already a growing number of libraries and tools emerging that provide direct Web Service technology to the developer and end user. One of the reasons XML is so important in Web Services is its extensibility. This is an important feature in the fluid and dynamic business scenarios for which Web Services are typically well suited. Like XML, Python is well known for its flexibility and maintainability. It allows several approaches to programming, including object-oriented, functional and dynamic. The ability to use the dynamic approach especially makes Python quite extensible. It is a strong, application-level companion to XML data format in Web Services development.

As well as being reliable for production implementations of Web Services, Python is strong in scenarios where prototypes need to be developed rapidly. In fact, in the public proof of concept demonstration of e–business Web Service interoperability, at least two of the major participants (Bowstreet and Tie Commerce) used Python to develop their prototype implementations.

In this chapter we will examine some tools and techniques for Web Service development in Python. Only basic knowledge of Python is required to understand this chapter. Please see http://www.python.org/ for introductory resources on Python, including various tutorials. From there you can also download Python itself in source and binary forms (alternatively see Python's SourceForge page http://python.sourceforge.net/). Further useful Python resources are included at the end of the chapter, if you want to take this further.

In this chapter we will explore:

❑   The tools that come with Python, which are useful for Web Services development and deployment.

❑   The third–party Python tools that are available for our purposes.

❑   How to install the major software for the chapter examples.

❑   How to send and receive SOAP messages using Python.

❑   How to manage and process WSDL documents using Python.

❑   How to implement Web Services using 4Suite Server, a Python enabled web server with built–in Web Services features.

Standard Python Library Modules of Interest to Web Services Developers

The current version of Python is 2.1.1. PythonLabs (the core of developers who maintain Python) has scheduled the release of a new Python version every six months or so, so new versions might be available by the time you read this. Throughout its development the Python standard library has accumulated modules at an impressive rate, and now there are many modules useful for Internet programming in general, most of which come in very handy for Web Services development. The modules listed here are all relevant to the examples that will be presented later in the chapter.

This discussion of built–in modules, and the discussion of third–party modules that follows, should illustrate to the reader without a background in Python why it is such a well–suited language for Web Services development.

Detailed documentation of the Python standard library comes with Python itself, or can be found on–line at http://www.python.org/doc/current/lib/lib.html. Other aspects of Python are documented at http://www.python.org/doc/current/.

Web Architecture Modules

One of the hallmarks of the Web Services initiative is its foundation on inexpensive and pervasive Internet transport protocols. Python is an effective language for implementing both Internet clients and servers because of its broad protocol support, and the many approaches that can be taken to building layers on top of the core libraries. The following modules allow the core development of web servers and clients, based on Python's low–level, cross–platform networking support and powerful string handling.

BaseHTTPServer, SimpleHTTPServer and CGIHTTPServer

`BaseHTTPServer` provides the classes to implement a full-blown Web server. An instance of `BaseHTTPServer.HTTPServer` dispatches incoming HTTP requests on a given socket to a given handler object. Typically, we would create such a handler by subclassing `BaseHTTPServer.BaseHTTPRequestHandler`, which provides conveniently named methods invoked by the server instance according to the HTTP request method. Examples of these methods are do_GET and do_POST. These methods are invoked when an HTTP server receives a request of the corresponding type. When an HTTP GET is sent, for instance by the end user entering the address in a browser URL line, the do_GET method is invoked. Of course, if `BaseHTTPServer.BaseHTTPRequestHandler` has been subclassed, we can provide a specialized do_GET method that provides our choice of handler. The idea is the same for the do_POST method, which would be invoked if, say, the end user triggered an HTTP POST by clicking the submit button on an HTML form.

Other library modules such as `SimpleHTTPServer` and `CGIHTTPServer` provide, respectively, specialized servers and handlers for serving data from the local file system and for supporting Common Gateway Interface (CGI) programs.

To handle secure HTTP (HTTPS), we build our Python server with secure sockets layer (SSL) support. Building Python with SSL support requires the OpenSSL library (http://www.openssl.org/), which is available for UNIX and Windows. The Python installation will detect these libraries and enable the SSL support accordingly. If this is done, Python Web Services can use HTTPS to implement security against tampering and eavesdropping based on the Public Key Infrastructure (PKI).

urllib and urllib2

`urllib` provides functions useful for accessing remote resources using URLs, in a client. These functions include:

- ❑ urlopen, which reads a stream of data from a URL.
- ❑ basejoin, which joins a base URL to a relative URL.
- ❑ urlencode, which encodes arbitrary text data in a form syntactically suitable for use in URLs (and encoded HTTP message bodies).

It also provides a couple of classes, `urllib.URLOpener` and `urllib.FancyURLOpener`, which allow for more customized retrieval of resources.

`urllib2` provides classes and more generalized functions that allow URLs to be accessed in extensible ways, for instance, the class `urllib2.HTTPBasicAuthHandler` allows the developer to pass user authentication in HTTP requests that require it.

httplib

httplib provides the HTTP class, which is a lower level tool for requesting data from HTTP servers. It exposes all aspects of the HTTP header and body directly.

Internet Data Format Modules

Once we have the tools to implement the client and server side of Web Services protocols, we need to construct and interpret the data formats that are transported over these protocols. Python provides extensive tools for XML, MIME format processing and common data encoding.

xml.parsers.expat

Expat is one of the most popular open source XML parsers available, and has been used to provide efficient XML support to many programming languages and platforms. The xml.parsers.expat module exposes the Expat API to callbacks and handlers written in Python.

More details on Expat are available from http://sourceforge.net/projects/expat/.

xml.dom

The Document Object Module (DOM) is a standard low–level API for manipulating XML and HTML documents. Python has many DOM implementations, two of which come in the core library:

❑ **Minidom** (xml.dom.minidom) provides a lightweight DOM implementation suitable for many basic processing tasks.

❑ **Pulldom** is a specialized DOM implementation that allows the developer to access XML subtrees on an as–needed basis, allowing for high efficiency when dealing with large documents.

The xml.dom module itself includes both these implementations, and also provides standardized class structure and constants for the various types of nodes that make up the DOM in minidom and pulldom. This also applies for 4DOM, the DOM implementation that is part of PyXML (which we shall discuss soon). Its structure is also used in other third–party DOM implementations such as ParsedXML (http://dev.zope.org/Wikis/DevSite/Projects/ParsedXML/FrontPage/), developed as part of the Zope Python application server (http://zope.org/).

xml.sax

This module provides the open community standard SAX interface to XML parsers. It allows us to develop SAX handlers and callbacks in Python to be used with any of the Python library or third–party XML parsers that have a SAX driver written for them.

mimetools and MimeWriter

The mimetools module provides a specialized class Message for handling e–mail messages that are formatted in MIME. This class can also be used to interpret MIME data from any source, such as SOAP with attachments. Manipulating mimetools.Message objects exposes MIME parts and headers in a natural Python idiom. The MimeWriter.MimeWriter class allows the reverse operation, generating MIME content programmatically.

uu, base64, md5 and sha

The uu and base64 modules provide facilities for encoding and decoding data using the most common Internet forms. They are generally used to allow binary data to be transmitted over protocols that allow only textual data, such as RFC–822 (the standard format for e–mail). The md5 and sha modules allow us to create a digest of a character string. We can use these for security and authentication purposes in Web Services. This capability is a core aspect of Internet security: digests are designed so that tampering with the source text, even by the most devious interloper, would cause a change in the digest. This provides the basis of a digital signature.

Third–party Python Modules and Tools of Interest to Web Services Developers

Python's growing popularity and ease of development has resulted in a rich collection of third–party enhancements, tools and modules, several of which are of particular interest to developers of Web Services.

The software presented in this section is all freeware and open source. We will use some, but not all of it, in our examples later in the chapter.

> Note: several Python SOAP libraries emerged at about the same time so they have names that are confusingly similar. For instance, two separate and quite different packages are called SOAP.py and SOAPy.

SOAP.py

SOAP.py , initially developed by Cayce Ullman and Brian Matthews, is a complete implementation library for SOAP clients and servers over HTTP and HTTPS for Python. It is very easy to use and offers solid interoperability with other SOAP implementations, Python or otherwise. SOAP.py version 0.9.7 doesn't yet handle WSDL, even behind the scenes. WSDL support is planned, but for now the SOAP.py client directly translates Python methods and keyword parameters into SOAP messages, and vice versa for the server. HTTPS support in the client is provided where:

- ❑ SSL has been compiled into Python.
- ❑ HTTPS support in the server is provided.
- ❑ the separate M2Crypto package (http://www.pobox.org.sg/home/ngps/m2/) is installed.

You can download and find out more about SOAP.py from http://sourceforge.net/projects/pywebsvcs/.

SOAPy

SOAPy is a distinct package from SOAP.py, but because of the similar names confusion is inevitable. SOAPy is a tool that reads WSDL 1.0 descriptions, and constructs objects for accessing the corresponding Web Service in a very Python friendly manner. To enable it to do this SOAP 1.1 support and some basic support for W3C XML Schema Descriptions (XSD) are built in. SOAPy provides support for SSL, allowing access to secure Web Services. The package is still in the early stages of development, but already it has the ability to access many of the more popular prototype Web Services available, such as the BabelFish Web Service at http://xmethods.org/detail.html?id=14, which we will use in our SOAPy example later. BabelFish translates words from one language to another.

Further details and the download can be found at http://soapy.sourceforge.net/.

soaplib.py

soaplib.py was developed by Secret Labs AB (http://www.pythonware.com/), the same outfit that developed the popular xmlrpclib.py. It is a SOAP library that provides a Python–friendly interface for SOAP requests and responses. This was one of the first SOAP implementations for Python, but development on this package appears to have stalled at the time of writing.

For downloading and further investigation, visit http://www.pythonware.com/products/soap/.

Orchard

Orchard is a fresh offshoot of Casbah, a project to develop tools for rapid application programming (work on Casbah has recently slowed). Orchard is a module that provides a high–efficiency XML processing system with Web Services features and Python and Perl support. As part of this it includes **Orchard.SOAP**, a module for converting Python objects to and from the SOAP serialization. This is called "SOAP pickling" because it is analogous to the Python library's pickling facilities, converting objects to and from compact binary form.

For more on Orchard, visit http://orchard.sourceforge.net/ and Orchard.SOAP http://casbah.org/~kmacleod/orchard/soap.html.

Lye

Lye is a project by Andrew Dalke to provide a dynamic mapping from Windows COM requests to SOAP requests using soaplib.py. It comes from Secret Labs and is an experimental gateway between the Microsoft Component Object Module (COM) and SOAP. With a bit of work this could be a gentle easing of Windows/Python users into the world of .NET services. .NET communicates between distributed application modules in a similar way to the older Microsoft Distributed COM (DCOM). Lye could be the basis of a migration for traditional COM programmers and code to .NET services.

For more on Lye, goto http://www.biopython.org/~dalke/lye/.

PyXML

This package, maintained by the Python XML Special Interest Group (http://python.org/sigs/xml-sig/), is the main place to go for tools for XML processing in Python. With contributions from a large and active group of developers, its inclusions are many and varied. Briefly, it incorporates additional Python parsers and DOM libraries, including 4DOM, an implementation of DOM level 2 Core, HTML, Traversal and Events. It also contains tools for canonical XML and marshaling Python objects to other formats, amongst other things.

Further details of the functionality you can achieve with PyXML and the download can be found at http://sourceforge.net/projects/pyxml/.

4Suite

4Suite is a package that adds XML processing and object database processing to the core built into Python. Included in 4Suite are:

❑   PyXML.

❑   An XPath library, allowing arbitrary XPath expressions to be evaluated against DOM nodes.

❑   Lightweight DOM implementations in C and Python for efficient processing when XPath is chosen as the primary method for accessing nodes from parsed XML.

❑   A complete XSLT 1.0 processor with many extended features, including the EXSLT community's XSLT extensions (http://exslt.org/).

❑   A Resource Description Framework (RDF) library with support for persistent storage, querying, RDF schemata and a parser and serializer. RDF is a system for managing extensible metadata of web resources, which also makes it useful in several ways for implementing Web Services, as we shall see in an example later.

❑   An XPointer resolver and XLink processor. XPointer and XLink are standards that allow sophisticated links between XML resources.

❑   An object database system that implements most of the Object Database Management Group (ODMG) 3.0 standard in Python, supporting several back ends for actual object storage.

The 4Suite site is at http://www.4suite.org/, and comprises useful documentation, discussion groups and downloads.

4Suite Server

4Suite Server is an XML processing platform and data server built on 4Suite. It cannot be installed without prior installation of 4Suite. It provides:

❑   An XML repository and persistent RDF model, with processing of XSLT, XPath, XLink, XPointer and RDF. It also processes XUpdate, used for efficient update of large XML documents (http://xmldb.org/xupdate/index.html), and RDF Inference Language (RIL) for rules and logically complex processing.

❑   A great number of ways to leverage these tools: HTTP, FTP, SOAP, Web Distributed Authoring and Versioning (WebDAV – http://www.webdav.org/), CORBA (including wrappers for Java) and XPCOM.

4Suite Server supports Web Services through its SOAP support, and add–ons for managing WSDL descriptions and using RDF to support Web Service organization. You can find out more about this package and download it from the 4Suite site given above. Installation instructions for both Windows and UNIX are available in the code download for this chapter.

The remaining sections of the chapter will take you through a number of examples, beginning with applications using basic Python modules and progressing to using some of the third party add–ons we've just discussed. We'll look at Python with SOAP and WSDL and then move on to look at a Python server for Web Services. The code for each example is available for download from http://www.wrox.com/, to save you typing it in. We'll begin by looking at how to install the main software you'll need.

Installing the Required Software

The examples in this chapter require Python 2.1.1, PyXML 0.6.5 and 4Suite 0.11.1b3, or more recent versions of these. We'll look at how to install each of them here, in the required order. Further installations will be needed for some of the later examples, but these are the main ones.

> **Wrox have tested the 3rd party installations and code in this chapter using Windows 2000 Professional and various flavours of UNIX\LINUX. Whilst we have endeavoured to give accurate installation instructions, you may find that there are differences for your system or for more recent releases of the software used.**

Python

Firstly, we need to install Python itself. Download Python 2.1.1 or later from http://www.python.org/.

Windows users: just run the `.exe` file and follow the onscreen instructions.

Please note: Windows users will need to add the directory where Python is installed, along with the directory where it keeps its scripts, to their system variables path statement. This can be done either via the control panel or in `autoexec.bat`. For example in `autoexec.bat`, you would add the line:

```
set C:\python21;C:\python21\scripts
```

This enables the python command when running python scripts at the DOS command line. Adding the scripts directory allows you to run the various batch files you will install during the chapter from any directory.

UNIX users download the `.tgz` file, unpack and make in the normal manner.

> *LINUX users should note that with the most recent versions of Python, such as 2.1.1, it may be necessary to download the source and compile it.*

PyXML

Download the current version, 0.6.5, or later from http://sourceforge.net/projects/pyxml/. Windows users will need to get the installer to match their version of Python and execute it, following the on screen instructions as they appear.

UNIX users need to download the relevant file or files and follow the detailed instructions available at http://py-howto.sourceforge.net/xml-howto/node4.html.

4Suite

4Suite can be downloaded from http://www.4suite.org/. 0.11.1b3 or higher is needed for the examples in this chapter. A Windows binary with an installer is available for Windows users. Run the .exe file and follow the onscreen instructions. You will need to add the Python Scripts directory to your systems variables path statement or autoexec.bat file to run 4Suite commands on the command line in the DOS window if you have not already done so.

UNIX users need to unpack the archive and run:

$ python setup.py install

Now you have these installed, lets move on and look at those examples.

Python and SOAP

SOAP has become the favorite communications protocol for Web Services, as discussed in Chapters 3, 8 and 9. Basic SOAP support was available in Python even before the structure of Web Services emerged, in the shape of various projects implementing Remote Procedure Call (RPC) methods with XML. Moving to the present day, there are currently several well–developed SOAP implementations for Python, some of which we outlined above. We'll now look at a few practical approaches in use currently, although there are others in development that aim to offer improved general SOAP interoperability.

SOAP From First Principles

As we have seen before, the "S" in "SOAP" stands for "Simple", and this is indeed largely the case. With capable HTTP and XML tools, we can create SOAP clients and servers using basic general Python libraries. We'll now explore an example of implementing a SOAP server and a SOAP client. The SOAP server will be presented in the first section, and the SOAP client in the following section.

Basic Python SOAP Server

We can use Python's standard BaseHTTPServer module to implement a SOAP server. All we need to do is set up a server listening on the port of choice with a handler that can process HTTP POST requests (for more on HTTP POST, see Chapter 2). The Python code for implementing such a server is listed below. It is an echo server, the likes of which we have already seen in Chapters 5 and 9. To execute the code, you'll want to save the whole listing as a file basicpythonsoapserver.py or get it from the code download for the book.

In the first section of our code, we import the required modules, string and BaseHTTPServer, from the standard library, and PyExpat and ext from 4DOM (in PyXML). string provides many basic string manipulation functions, and we have already discussed the HTTP server support in BaseHTTPServer above. ext provides routines for turning DOM nodes to XML text, among other things. PyExpat contains the Reader class, which encapsulates the process of generating DOM nodes from read in XML. In the last line we create an instance of a PyExpat reader object for later use.

```
import string, BaseHTTPServer
from xml.dom.ext.reader import PyExpat
from xml.dom import ext
reader = PyExpat.Reader()
```

Next we set up some global constants with namespaces important to the Web Service:

```
SOAP_ENV_NS = 'http://schemas.xmlsoap.org/soap/envelope/'
ECHO_NS = 'http://uche.ogbuji.net/ws/eg/echo-soapser'
```

The server is implemented in the `SoapHandler` class, a specialization of `BaseHTTPServer.BaseHTTPRequestHandler`. This handles HTTP POST messages with its `do_POST` method and starts off performing basic checks on the HTTP headers. Specifically, it checks that there is a `content-length` header, and it prints a message that it returns if not. `BaseHTTPServer.BaseHTTPRequestHandler` returns an HTTP 500 response if the customized handler does not send back any HTTP response information, in a manner that we shall see later in this listing:

```
class SoapHandler(BaseHTTPServer.BaseHTTPRequestHandler):
    def do_POST(self):
        clen = self.headers.getheader('content-length')
        if clen:
            clen = string.atoi(clen)
        else:
            print 'POST ERROR: missing content-length'
            return
```

In the following section of the file, we check that the HTTP request URL comes to the path we expect, and send a 404 (Not found) code if not. Then we read in the HTTP body, using the special `rfile` file–like object that is set up by `BaseHTTPServer.BaseHTTPRequestHandler`. The `read` method on Python file–like objects reads data from the source and returns a string. It accepts an optional argument giving the maximum length to read, which we provide here using the content length given by the HTTP header. We then use the reader object we already set up to convert it to DOM nodes:

```
        if self.path != '/eg/ws/echo-soapser':
            self.send_error(404)
            return
        input_body = self.rfile.read(clen)
        doc = reader.fromString(input_body)
```

In the next section of the script, the comments explain how we retrieve the SOAP body, whose children are the elements implementing the SOAP message parts. The echo server only expects one part, and so grabs the first child. If the local name of this child is `echo` then we pass it on to the `_echo()` method, otherwise we throw an exception.

```
        #This removes extra whitespace from the document, which will
        #Make our task easier
        ext.StripXml(doc)

        #getElementsByTagNameNS returns a list of elements that match
        #the namespace and local name.
```

```
        #The "[0]" gets the first item in the list
        #The effect is to retrieve the node representing the SOAP:Body
                                                         element
        soap_body = doc.getElementsByTagNameNS(SOAP_ENV_NS, 'Body')[0]

        request_element = soap_body.firstChild
        if request_element.localName == 'echo':
            self._echo(request_element)
        else:
            raise ValueError("Unexpected SOAP method: ('%s',
            '%s')"%(request_element.namespaceURI,
              request_element.localName))
        return
```

The _echo() method first extracts the message parameter element from the request element and uses this to build a response. It does this by combining a template with the message text. The triple quotes in Python allow us to define a single string that includes multiple lines. The % operator allows us to treat the string as a template and substitute variable values where we wish. For instance, in this case, we substitute another string value into the place marked by the %s specifier.

```
    def _echo(self, requestElem):
        msg_element = requestElem.getElementsByTagNameNS('', 'msg')[0]

        #The message element should have its child as a text node
        #with the message.
        #The data attribute of a text node is its string value
        msg = msg_element.firstChild.data

        #Build the response
        response_body = """\
<?xml version='1.0' encoding='utf-8'?>
<SOAP-ENV:Envelope
  xmlns:SOAP-ENV="http://schemas.xmlsoap.org/soap/envelope/"
  SOAP-ENV:encodingStyle="http://schemas.xmlsoap.org/soap/encoding/"
>
  <SOAP-ENV:Body>
    <e:echoResponse xmlns:e="http://uche.ogbuji.net/ws/eg/echo-soapser">
      <msg><![CDATA[%s]]></msg>
    </e:echoResponse>
  </SOAP-ENV:Body>
</SOAP-ENV:Envelope>
"""%msg

        self._sendResponse(200, 'OK', response_body)
        return
```

The _sendResponse() method puts together an HTTP response message. First it sets up the response code and status message. Then it sets up four HTTP headers. Finally, it writes the text that we provided into the HTTP body.

```
    def _sendResponse(self, code, msg, body):
        self.send_response(200, 'OK')
        self.send_header('Content-type','text/html; charset=utf-8')
        self.send_header("Connection", "close")
```

```
            self.send_header("Accept-Ranges", "bytes")
            self.send_header('Content-length', len(body)-1)
            self.end_headers()
            self.wfile.write(body)
            return
```

In the above code fragment, you may notice that both double and single quotes have been used. This is perfectly acceptable in Python.

We have defined the class we need to implement the server, so all we need to do is initialize it. When this script is run from Python, it will execute all the top–level statements, including the class definition. The statements that kick off the server are those ones at the bottom of the file. First we set the port and then set up the server network address as a **tuple**, which is a Python data structure that allows one value to contain multiple other values without needing to define a data structure. The tuple consists of the server address and port.

Then we create an instance of the HTTP server, passing in the address and our specialized handler. We print out a status message, and then start the server listening for requests using the `serve_forever()` method. This method instructs the server to listen to multiple requests until the process is terminated.

```
thisport = 8888
server_address = ('127.0.0.1', thisport)
httpd = BaseHTTPServer.HTTPServer(server_address, SoapHandler)
print "Listening on port", thisport
httpd.serve_forever()
```

After installing the relevant software listed at the start of this chapter we can set our server going.

On Windows, the code above should be copied to the file `basicpythonsoapserver.py`, and a new DOS prompt opened up, at which we enter:

> **python basicpythonsoapserver.py**

Now we should get the following line displayed at the prompt:

Listening on port 8888

On UNIX, you should copy the listing to file `basicpythonsoapserver.py` and start up the server in the background as follows:

$ **python basicpythonsoapserver.py &**

You should now get the following output:

[1] 11398
Listening on port 8888

Note that [1] 11398, where the second number is likely to be different for you, is the command shell reporting the process we have placed in the background; and the text Listening on port 8888 *is put out by the server process.*

Note also that in the above command prompts, > signifies the Windows command prompt, and $ signifies the UNIX/Linux command prompt. From now on we will only use > to signify command prompts, except in cases where the commands are UNIX/Linux specific.

Leave the server running, as we'll need it to test the client that we'll be creating next.

Basic Python SOAP client

The basic Python SOAP client just uses the standard `httplib` module to create a specialized HTTP POST request. This could also be done in Python versions after 2.0 with a customized `urllib2` class. The code below is a program that sends a request to the SOAP Echo server we created above. To execute the code, you'll want to save the sections of the listing as a file `basicpythonsoapclient.py` or download it from the Wrox web site.

Again, we start out by importing needed modules from the standard library: `sys` includes many useful functions for accessing system particulars, including the arguments passed in on the command–line. `httplib` contains classes for making requests to HTTP servers. We also set up some global constants, including a template string for the SOAP request. The request is made to the local machine on port 8888, which is how the server was set up.

```
import sys, httplib
from xml.dom.ext.reader import PyExpat
from xml.dom import ext

SERVER_ADDR = '127.0.0.1'
SERVER_PORT = 8888
ECHO_NS = 'http://uche.ogbuji.net/ws/eg/echo-soapser'

BODY_TEMPLATE = """<SOAP-ENV:Envelope
        xmlns:SOAP-ENV="http://schemas.xmlsoap.org/soap/envelope/"
        xmlns:s="http://uche.ogbuji.net/eg/ws/echo-soapser"
        SOAP-ENV:encodingStyle="http://schemas.xmlsoap.org/soap/encoding/"
        >
        <SOAP-ENV:Body>
         <s:echo>
             <msg><![CDATA[%s]]></msg>
         </s:echo>
    </SOAP-ENV:Body>
</SOAP-ENV:Envelope>"""
```

The `Echo` class first prompts the user for the message to send (the `raw_input()` method puts out the given string as a prompt and then reads the user's input until a carriage return, returning the result as a string). Then we substitute this message into the string template we set up, and prepare the HTTP request. The `httplib.HTTP` object represents the request, and is initialized with the network address and port of the remote server. We specify a POST request to the correct path using the `putrequest` method and add HTTP headers using the `putheader` method. Note carefully the setting of the `SOAPAction` header. Remember that without this header an HTTP message cannot be a valid SOAP message. When we've added all our headers we indicate this and then send the HTTP request, including the body we've prepared.

```
def Echo():
    msg = raw_input("Message to send: ")
    body = BODY_TEMPLATE%(msg)
    blen = len(body)
```

```
requestor = httplib.HTTP(SERVER_ADDR, SERVER_PORT)
requestor.putrequest('POST', '/eg/ws/echo-soapser')
requestor.putheader('Host', SERVER_ADDR)
requestor.putheader('Content-Type', 'text/plain; charset="utf-8"')
requestor.putheader('Content-Length', str(blen))
requestor.putheader('SOAPAction', "http://uche.ogbuji.net/eg/ws/echo-
                                                    soapser")

requestor.endheaders()
requestor.send(body)
```

Since we're getting a SOAP response, the HTTP body is XML, which we parse. Next we retrieve the text of the echoResponse element and print out the message and return status to the console:

```
reader = PyExpat.Reader()
doc = reader.fromString(reply_body)
ext.StripXml(doc)

echo_resp = doc.getElementsByTagNameNS(ECHO_NS, 'echoResponse')[0]
msg_elem = echo_resp.firstChild
msg = msg_elem.firstChild.data

print "status code:", status_code
print "status message:", message
print "HTTP reply body:\n", reply_body
print "SOAP response value:", msg
```

Next, we simply invoke the Echo() function.

```
Echo()
```

To run this example, copy the code to a file basicpythonsoapclient.py and execute it. In either UNIX or Windows, we need to type in:

>**python basicpythonsoapclient.py**

The following session shows the result of executing this client in Windows against the server we already launched. We typed in Hello World at the Message to send: prompt, but you could type anything you like:

```
Command Prompt                                                    _ □ X
Microsoft Windows 2000 [Version 5.00.2195]
(C) Copyright 1985-1999 Microsoft Corp.

C:\>cd python_tests

C:\python_tests>python basicpythonsoapclient.py
Message to send: Hello World
status code: 200
status message: OK
HTTP reply body:
<?xml version='1.0' encoding='utf-8'?>
<SOAP-ENV:Envelope
  xmlns:SOAP-ENV="http://schemas.xmlsoap.org/soap/envelope/"
  SOAP-ENV:encodingStyle="http://schemas.xmlsoap.org/soap/encoding/"
>
  <SOAP-ENV:Body>
    <e:echoResponse xmlns:e="http://uche.ogbuji.net/ws/eg/echo-soapser">
      <msg><![CDATA[Hello World]]></msg>
    </e:echoResponse>
  </SOAP-ENV:Body>
</SOAP-ENV:Envelope>

SOAP response value: Hello World

C:\python_tests>
```

The server console is likely to print lines as follows, but the text might differ, or might not appear at all, depending on the set–up:

```
localhost.local - - [18/Jun/2001 00:32:31] "POST /eg/ws/echo–soapser HTTP/1.0" 200 -
```

These examples demonstrate the basics. More features are likely to need to be added for real–world usage. For instance, error handling is quite limited in these examples.

SOAP.py as SOAP client

SOAP.py basically allows the user to set up a proxy object for the remote Web Service with a constructor that takes the SOAP end–point URL and other optional arguments such as the namespace of the SOAP method element (the main request element of the SOAP body). It then dynamically interprets methods invoked on the proxy object, translates them to a SOAP message with the Python method name as SOAP method name, and translates any keyword arguments into parameter elements in the SOAP request.

> Note that a proxy object is a general construct in distributed programming where a local object is set up with the same interface as the actual remote object of interest, with the special property that it forwards all invocations to the remote object for actual handling.

First of all, SOAP.py doesn't come with any installation instructions, but luckily enough, it should be a simple process. Firstly, download the latest, appropriate version from http://sourceforge.net/projects/pywebsvcs/.

The Windows version comes as a .zip file. Extract the contents to a directory of your choice and then copy the SOAP.py file to the directory where you installed Python (this directory is already either on your system variables path or in your autoexec.bat file if you followed the earlier instructions, so Python will be able to find SOAP.py from there).

For UNIX users, after downloading and unpacking, simply copy the file SOAP.py to a spot in your PYTHONPATH. You can determine which directories are in your own path by running:

```
$ python –c "import sys; print sys.path"
['', '/home/uogbuji/lib', '/usr/local/lib/python', '/home/uogbuji/lib/narval', '/usr/local/src/omni/lib/python',
'/usr/local/src/omni/lib/i586_linux_2.0_glibc2.1', '/usr/local/lib/python2.1',
'/usr/local/lib/python2.1/plat–linux2', '/usr/local/lib/python2.1/lib–tk', '/usr/local/lib/python2.1/lib–
dynload', '/usr/local/lib/python2.1/site–packages']
```

Copy SOAP.py to one of the directories listed when you try this command yourself.

Once you have SOAP.py installed, it's quite easy to use. The example below makes a call to Tom Chamberlain's IWordsForCheck Web Service (http://xmethods.com/detail.html?id=103), which translates numbers into English words such as one might use in writing a bank check. To run the code, copy the fragments to a file iwordsforcheck.py or get it from the download on the Wrox web site.

```python
#!/usr/bin/env python

import sys

#Import the SOAP.py machinery
import SOAP
```

```
server = SOAP.SOAPProxy(
    'http://powerofzen.com/cgi-bin/wordsforchecks.exe/soap/IWordsForCheck',
    namespace='urn:UIWordsForChecks-IWordsForCheck'
)
```

Note the namespace keyword argument to the SOAPProxy initializer. This is used as the default XML element namespace when translating Python method invocations to SOAP method invocations. The user can also specify a "namespace" argument to each Python method invocation to override this default. The http://powerofzen.com/cgi-bin/wordsforchecks.exe/soap/IWordsForCheck parameter specifies the precise URI to which the HTTP POST will be sent bearing the SOAP request in its body.

```
try:
        num = float(sys.argv[1])
except IndexError:
        num = 117.25

words = server.getWordsForCheck(Value=num)
print "The number %s in words is %s"%(num, words)
```

The num variable becomes the parameter to the SOAP method. It is set to a Python floating-point value. This is because the proxy will transmit the type information with the SOAP message according to the type of the actual Python object used as argument, and the IWordsForCheck service is expecting a floating–point value for the Value parameter.

The getWordsForCheck() Python method invocation to the proxy dynamically creates a SOAP invocation to the end point set up in the proxy. Since there is no namespace argument, the default element namespace set up in the proxy object is used. The Value keyword argument is turned into a parameter element of that name (in the null namespace according to SOAP encoding custom) and the floating point num value that is passed in becomes the value of this parameter. The return value to the Python method invocation of the proxy is constructed from the SOAP response from the Web Service, in this case a string with the number expressed in English words. Note that a SOAP method can return multiple or compound values generally, which are automatically translated to appropriate Python data constructs by SOAP.py.

In Windows or UNIX, run the code by executing:

> **python iwordsforcheck.py 129.99**

The following should be displayed as a result, if you run it on Windows:

```
Command Prompt                                                    _ □ ×
Microsoft Windows 2000 [Version 5.00.2195]
(C) Copyright 1985-1999 Microsoft Corp.

C:\>cd python_tests

C:\python_tests>python iwordsforcheck.py 129.99
The number 129.99 in words is ONE HUNDRED TWENTY NINE DOLLARS AND 99 CENTS

C:\python_tests>
```

Note that there is a WSDL file for the IWordsForCheck service (http://powerofzen.com/cgi-bin/wordsforchecks.exe/wsdl/IWordsForCheck). SOAP.py doesn't yet use this to construct the SOAP proxy object or for any validation or checking, but it is a useful guide to the client developer.

SOAPy as a SOAP client, Using WSDL

SOAPy is a different project that implements a SOAP client for Python. One major distinction is that SOAPy is designed to work from a WSDL specification. You have already seen WSDL at work in Chapter 4. It's not just a formal description for the developer to read in order to understanding the interface of the Web Service, it can also be used to effect introspection of the Web Service: SOAP clients can dynamically determine interfaces for invoking the Web Service. Given a WSDL instance, SOAPy sets up a proxy object that can be invoked in order to access the remote object.

SOAPy's operation is very simple. To use it, we need to write a Python script such as the one below, which uses SOAPy to access xmethods' BabelFish Web Service (http://xmethods.org/detail.html?id=14). This particular Web Service makes a request from AltaVista's BabelFish service (http://babelfish.altavista.com/) to translate text from one language to another.

```python
#!/usr/bin/env python

import sys

#Import the SOAPy machinery
import soap

#Follow the Web Service description and use it to create a proxy object
#That represents a remote object transparently

server = soap.get_proxy('http://www.xmethods.net/sd/BabelFishService.wsdl')

if len(sys.argv) > 2:
    tm = sys.argv[1]
    s = sys.argv[2]
else:
    tm = "en_es"
    s = "The rain in spain stays mainly in the plain"

result = server.BabelFish(translationmode=tm, sourcedata=s)
print '"%s" translated with mode %s:\n\n%s'%(s, tm, result)
```

Let's look at the first part of the script:

```python
#!/usr/bin/env python

import sys

#Import the SOAPy machinery
import soap

#Follow the Web Service description and use it to create a proxy object
#That represents a remote object transparently

server = soap.get_proxy('http://www.xmethods.net/sd/BabelFishService.wsdl')
```

After the imports, the `soap.get_proxy` function accepts the URI of a WSDL instance, which it retrieves, interprets and uses to create a SOAP proxy object. This proxy is a Python object created using dynamic programming by SOAPy. It has a Python method for each SOAP message defined in the WSDL, and appropriate parameters for each. Therefore the following fragment of the WSDL that our example retrieves from the Babel Fish Service:

```
<message name="BabelFishRequest">
    <part name="translationmode" type="xsd:string"/>
    <part name="sourcedata" type="xsd:string"/>
</message>
<message name="BabelFishResponse">
    <part name="return" type="xsd:string"/>
</message>
<portType name="BabelFishPortType">
    <operation name="BabelFish">
        <input message="tns:BabelFishRequest" name="BabelFish"/>
        <output message="tns:BabelFishResponse" name="BabelFishResponse"/>
    </operation>
</portType>
```

translates into a Python method, `BabelFish`, on the proxy object.

> *The full `BabelFishService.wsdl` file can either be found in the code download for this book or you could get it directly from http://www.xmethods.net/sd/BabelFishService.wsdl.*

In the second and final part of our script keyword arguments are set up in proxy methods with the same names as the parts from the WSDL:

```
if len(sys.argv) > 2:
    tm = sys.argv[1]
    s = sys.argv[2]
else:
    tm = "en_es"
    s = "The rain in spain stays mainly in the plain"

result = server.BabelFish(translationmode=tm, sourcedata=s)
print '"%s" translated with mode %s:\n\n%s'%(s, tm, result)
```

A keyword argument is a way of specifying arguments to Python functions that allow you to specify the name of the argument being passed, rather than relying strictly on order in the argument list. In this case there are `translationmode` and `sourcedata` arguments to the `BabelFish` method.

To run this example, we need to install SOAPy. This is easy enough – just download the most recent, appropriate version from http://soapy.sourceforge.net/. The Windows package comes with an installer that you should run after reading the following important note:

> **There is one very unfortunate gotcha for Windows users. SOAP.py required us to copy a file called `SOAP.py` to a directory in the PYTHONPATH – we placed ours in the python21 directory for the last example. The installer for SOAPy installs a file called `soap.py` to this same directory. These two filenames are identical except for case, but since the Windows file system is case–insensitive, this causes a conflict. Until the developers of SOAP.py and SOAPy sort this out, you will need to move the `SOAP.py` file out of the python21 directory before installing SOAPy.**

UNIX users simply need to unpack the archive and execute:

$ python setup.py install

which is the standard command for installing Python software on either UNIX or Windows.

Next copy the code to `soapybfclient.py` (or download it from the WROX site) and then run the following for either Windows or UNIX:

> python soapybfclient.py

You will see the following output on Windows:

You can specify alternative translation modes and strings for translation as command line arguments. See the Web Service documentation at http://xmethods.org/detail.html?id=14 for a list of supported translation modes. Note that if your string to be translated has spaces or other characters reserved by the command shell, you'll need to use quotation marks.

In the next section, we'll look at further uses of Python and WSDL for Web Services, before exploring the capabilities of 4Suite Server in the final, major section of the chapter.

Python and WSDL

WSDL is a basic facility for Web Services because it provides formal descriptions of the technical aspects of a Web Service. There are several approaches to using Python to interpret, manage and generate WSDL descriptions. We have already seen how SOAPy uses WSDL to generate a proxy SOAP object tailored for the desired interaction. We can also directly manipulate WSDL using **wsdl4py** (http://oss.software.ibm.com/developerworks/projects/wsdl4py/).

Processing WSDL With wsdl4py

wsdl4py is an open source Python library for reading and manipulating WSDL descriptions in a Python-friendly manner. Developed by me (Uche Ogbuji) and Mike Olson, it allows us to create a Python object with methods and attributes representing the various parts of a WSDL document. wsdl4py consists of a single file, `wsdllib.py`.

Reading in and Querying Existing WSDL Documents

wsdl4py allows you to start your processing with an initial WSDL document. It provides three factory functions for this purpose:

- ❑ ReadFromStream() – accepts a file–like object, which is read from the WSDL source.

- ❑ ReadFromString() – accepts a string containing the full WSDL source.

- ❑ ReadFromUri() – accepts a URI, which is resolved and whose contents are read for the WSDL source. Note that this can be a local file object, using the "file:" URL scheme.

Each of these functions returns an object of class Wsdl that represents the source document. As an example of this process, and the API to the resulting WSDL object, the following is a script that reads in a WSDL file and prints out all the messages and message parts:

```
import sys
import wsdllib

def SummarizeMessages(url):
    wsdl = wsdllib.ReadFromUri(url)
    for mname, message in wsdl.messages.items():
        print "Message: %s"%mname
        for pname, part in message.parts.items():
            print "\tPart: %s"%pname
    return

if __name__ == "__main__":
    if len(sys.argv) > 1:
        wsdluri = sys.argv[1]
    else:
        #Use the Babelfish Web Service WSDL as an example if the
        #user does not specify one
        wsdluri = "http://www.xmethods.net/sd/BabelFishService.wsdl "
    SummarizeMessages(wsdluri)
```

This program accepts a URI to WSDL source data on the command line, from which the messages and message parts are displayed. After the command line is interpreted, the ReadFromUri factory function is invoked to return a WSDL object. Among other attributes and methods, this object has a messages attribute that is a dictionary–like object. It has a key, the name of each message and a value, which is a sub–object of class Message. The name of each message is printed and then the parts attribute is accessed, which is another dictionary–like object containing all the parts for the message, indexed by part name.

To run this example, we need to install wsdl4py by downloading its single file (wsdllib.py) from http://oss.software.ibm.com/developerworks/projects/wsdl4py/ and copying it to a location on our PYTHONPATH, as we did with the SOAP.py file when installing SOAP.py. This install and run process is the same for both Windows and UNIX.

Next copy the code to a file wsdlmessageandparts.py (or download it from the Wrox site), and run:

>python wsdlmessageandparts.py

The output is as follows:

```
Command Prompt                                              _ □ ×
Microsoft Windows 2000 [Version 5.00.2195]
(C) Copyright 1985-1999 Microsoft Corp.

C:\>cd python_tests

C:\python_tests>python wsdlmessageandparts.py
Message: getRateRequest
        Part: country1
        Part: country2
Message: getRateResponse
        Part: Result

C:\python_tests>_
```

Our output shows the WSDL messages and parts for the Babel Fish Web Service (which we looked at earlier) because this is given as the default in the script. If we want to do the same for another Web Service, we just need to add the URI for its WSDL file on the command line, after python wsdlmessageandparts.py.

Creating and Manipulating WSDL

The wsdllib.Wsdl class, from wsdl4spy, can also be directly instantiated creating an empty WSDL description that can then be built up. Just as there are attributes and methods for accessing elements of the WSDL description, there are also methods for adding elements. For instance, the addPortType() method adds a port type specification to the description.

The following script creates an empty WSDL description, adds a message, and a part to the message, and prints out the rest:

```python
import wsdllib
from xml.dom.ext import PrettyPrint

def GenerateExampleWsdl():
    wsdl = wsdllib.Wsdl()
    msg = wsdl.messages.addMessage("GetLastTradePriceInput")
    msg.documentation = "Determine the last available trading price for a listing"
    part = msg.addPart("body", "xsd1:TradePrice")
    return wsdl

wsdl = GenerateExampleWsdl()
doc = wsdl.toDom()
PrettyPrint(doc)
```

We import PrettyPrint(), which is a function for printing DOM documents as XML text with indentation. This is useful because wsdl4py allows the export of Wsdl objects in DOM form representing the WSDL source that matches its current state. An empty Wsdl object is created and a message is added. A documentation string is added to the message, using the simple attribute set up for the purpose, and a part is also added to the message. Finally the toDom() method is used to export the WSDL description to DOM, and PrettyPrint() used to turn this into friendly XML text.

To run this program, copy the code to genwsdl.py (or download it) and at a Windows or UNIX command prompt run

>**python genwsdl.py**

The following figure shows a screen-shot of the resulting session running on Windows:

```
Command Prompt                                                    _ □ ×
Microsoft Windows 2000 [Version 5.00.2195]
(C) Copyright 1985-1999 Microsoft Corp.

C:\>cd python_tests

C:\python_tests>python genwsdl.py
<?xml version='1.0' encoding='UTF-8'?>
<wsdl:definitions xmlns:wsdl='http://schemas.xmlsoap.org/wsdl/'>
  <wsdl:types/>
  <wsdl:message name='GetLastTradePriceInput'>
    <wsdl:documentation>Determine the last available trading price for a listing
</wsdl:documentation>
    <wsdl:part name='body' element='xsd1:TradePrice'/>
  </wsdl:message>
</wsdl:definitions>

C:\python_tests>
```

Processing WSDL Using RDF

Web Service descriptions are aptly named. In particular, they are brief descriptions of resources marked by their URIs. The W3C has already developed a framework for managing such descriptions, known as the Resource Description Framework (RDF – http://www.w3.org/RDF/) but WSDL was not originally designed to work with it. There is actually a significant amount of debate that formats such as WSDL should have been designed to use RDF in the first place, and use the standard forms of XML serialization of RDF for interchange. Even though this did not happen, it is possible to use the many tools and capabilities of RDF for managing Web Services descriptions, and we present an example here alongside a discussion of the use of RDF to provide WSDL management facilities.

Note that this section uses several concepts not otherwise introduced in this book: XSLT and RDF. Enough information is given for the user to try out the basic techniques presented, but for further information, you could consult *Professional XML 2nd Edition*, by Mark Birbeck et al (ISBN: 1-861005-05-9) from Wrox Press. On-line resources include my own introduction to RDF (http://www-106.ibm.com/developerworks/xml/library/w-rdf/?dwzone=xml&dwzone=xml) and there are also many RDF resources, including further tutorials at http://www.ilrt.bris.ac.uk/discovery/rdf/resources/.

XSLT is a handy tool for many XML processing chores, not least adapting one data format to another. One quick way to process WSDL descriptions using RDF processing tools is to use an XSLT transform to convert the WSDL source to RDF serialized form. Then the RDF serialized form can be parsed for the RDF processing. There is already work in progress on standardizing such manipulation in the RDF/Web Services special interest group (http://rdfinference.org/index.html#rdfws)

To explore this further, let's look at the code that forms the core of a proposed XSLT transform for converting WSDL to RDF. In the first section, the root element defines the many important namespaces to WSDL descriptions, and a few namespaces for RDF and the RDF representation. Then we specify that the output will be indented XML. In the last line we define a template that specifies that if the processor doesn't have specific instructions for an element, no output at all should be generated for that element. This is necessary because XSLT provides default behavior that outputs all the text contained within an element, if there are no other matching instructions. This would cause a lot of unwanted text to be added to the output.

```
<?xml version="1.0"?>
<xsl:stylesheet
    version='1.0'
```

```
    xmlns:xsl="http://www.w3.org/1999/XSL/Transform"
    xmlns:wsdl="http://schemas.xmlsoap.org/wsdl/"
    xmlns:soap="http://schemas.xmlsoap.org/wsdl/soap/"
    xmlns:mime="http://schemas.xmlsoap.org/wsdl/mime/"
    xmlns:http="http://schemas.xmlsoap.org/wsdl/http/"
    xmlns:rdf="http://www.w3.org/1999/02/22-rdf-syntax-ns#"
    xmlns:xsd="http://www.w3.org/1999/XMLSchema"
    xmlns:x="http://xmlns.rdfinference.org/tools"
    xmlns:rxsd="http://schema.rdfinference.org/xsd"
  >

    <xsl:strip-space elements='*'/>
    <xsl:output method='xml' indent='yes'/>

    <!-- do nothing on unknown elements in general -->
    <xsl:template match='*' priority='-100'/>
```

The next section takes care of any XML schema definitions in the types section of the WSDL. The first template matches any xsd:schema element and puts out the outline of an RDF description of that element (defined by the rdf:Description element). The next template matches XSD element declarations and creates a description of that element itself, also adding a statement that it is an element defined within the xsd:schema already established. Statements are also added specifying the element's type and parent, if it has a parent. The last part of the template processes any children of the element, asserting itself as their parent. The penultimate template matches xsd:all instructions and simply passes the processing on to the children of the xsd:all and the final template similarly deals with complexType declarations and passes on the processing.

```
    <!-- limited XML schema processing -->


    <xsl:template match='xsd:schema'>
      <rdf:Description ID='xsd:{@targetNamespace}'>
        <rxsd:targetNamespace><xsl:value-of
  select='@targetNamespace'/></rxsd:targetNamespace>
        <xsl:apply-templates/>
      </rdf:Description>
    </xsl:template>

    <xsl:template match='xsd:element'>
      <xsl:param name='parent' select=''/>
      <rxsd:element>
        <rdf:Description ID='xsd.{@name}'>
          <xsl:if test='@type'>
            <rxsd:type><xsl:value-of select='@type'/></rxsd:type>
          </xsl:if>
          <xsl:if test='$parent'>
            <rxsd:parent><xsl:value-of select='$parent'/></rxsd:parent>
          </xsl:if>
        </rdf:Description>
      </rxsd:element>
        <xsl:apply-templates>
          <xsl:with-param name='parent' select='@name'/>
        </xsl:apply-templates>
```

```
    </xsl:template>

  <xsl:template match='xsd:all'>
    <xsl:param name='parent' select=''/>
    <xsl:apply-templates>
      <xsl:with-param name='parent' select='$parent'/>
    </xsl:apply-templates>
  </xsl:template>

  <xsl:template match='xsd:complexType'>
    <xsl:param name='parent' select=''/>
    <xsl:apply-templates>
      <xsl:with-param name='parent' select='$parent'/>
    </xsl:apply-templates>
  </xsl:template>
```

The third section handles the specialized WSDL elements. First of all we set up some useful top–level variables. The first template handles the `wsdl:definitions` at the root and puts out an RDF definition wrapper (`rdf:RDF`), then proceeds to all the top–level WSDL elements. The next template passes processing of `wsdl:types` to the XSD templates discussed above. The remaining templates handle the main named WSDL elements. The main processing is to convert the WSDL `name` attributes to RDF IDs, which gives them a formalized global identity. Most other elements and attributes are copied over as is by invoking the `copy-over` mode, shown in the fourth section.

```
    <!-- on to the WSDL -->

  <xsl:variable name='rdf-ns' select='"http://www.w3.org/1999/02/22-rdf-syntax-
ns#"'/>
  <xsl:variable name='wsdl-rdfs' select='"http://rdfinference.org/wsdl.rdfs#"'/>
  <xsl:variable name='def-name' select='/wsdl:definitions/@name'/>

  <xsl:template match='wsdl:definitions'>
    <rdf:RDF>
      <xsl:copy>
        <xsl:attribute name='rdf:ID' namespace='{$rdf-ns}'>
          <xsl:value-of select='@name'/>
        </xsl:attribute>
        <rwsdl:targetNamespace>
          <xsl:value-of select='@targetNamespace'/>
        </rwsdl:targetNamespace>
      </xsl:copy>
      <xsl:apply-templates/>
    </rdf:RDF>
  </xsl:template>

  <xsl:template match='wsdl:types'>
    <xsl:apply-templates/>
  </xsl:template>

  <xsl:template match='wsdl:message|wsdl:portType|wsdl:service'>
    <xsl:copy>
      <xsl:attribute name='rdf:ID' namespace='{$rdf-ns}'>
        <xsl:value-of select='@name'/>
      </xsl:attribute>
```

```
        <rwsdl:defined-by rdf:resource="#{$def-name}"/>
        <xsl:apply-templates select='*'/>
    </xsl:copy>
</xsl:template>

<xsl:template match='wsdl:part'>
    <xsl:copy>
        <xsl:attribute name='rdf:ID' namespace='{$rdf-ns}'>
            <xsl:value-of select='@name'/>
        </xsl:attribute>
        <xsl:attribute name='rdf:type' namespace='{$rdf-ns}'>
            <xsl:value-of select='concat($wsdl-rdfs, "part")'/>
        </xsl:attribute>
        <xsl:apply-templates select='@*' mode='copy-over'/>
    </xsl:copy>
</xsl:template>

<xsl:template match='wsdl:portType/wsdl:operation'>
    <xsl:copy>
        <xsl:attribute name='rdf:ID' namespace='{$rdf-ns}'>
            <xsl:value-of select='@name'/>
        </xsl:attribute>
        <xsl:attribute name='rdf:type' namespace='{$rdf-ns}'>
            <xsl:value-of select='concat($wsdl-rdfs, "operation")'/>
        </xsl:attribute>
        <xsl:apply-templates/>
    </xsl:copy>
</xsl:template>

<xsl:template match='wsdl:input|wsdl:output|wsdl:fault'>
    <xsl:copy>
        <xsl:attribute name='rdf:parseType' namespace='{$rdf-ns}'>
            <xsl:value-of select='"resource"'/>
        </xsl:attribute>
        <rwsdl:message>
            <xsl:value-of select='@message'/>
        </rwsdl:message>
    </xsl:copy>
</xsl:template>

<xsl:template match='wsdl:binding'>
    <xsl:copy>
        <xsl:attribute name='rdf:ID' namespace='{$rdf-ns}'>
            <xsl:value-of select='@name'/>
        </xsl:attribute>
        <rwsdl:defined-by rdf:resource="#{$def-name}"/>
        <xsl:apply-templates select='@*'/>
        <xsl:apply-templates select='*' mode='copy-other'/>
    </xsl:copy>
</xsl:template>
```

The `copy-over` templates copy over the context element and all its attributes and child elements with one exception: they don't copy over attributes called `name`, since these have already been converted to `rdf:ID` attributes.

```
<xsl:template match='*|@*' mode='copy-over'>
  <xsl:if test='not(name() = "name")'>
    <xsl:copy/>
  </xsl:if>
</xsl:template>

<xsl:template match='*' mode='copy-over'>
  <xsl:copy>
    <xsl:apply-templates select='@*|*' mode='copy-over'/>
  </xsl:copy>
</xsl:template>

</xsl:stylesheet>
```

We can use any compliant XSLT 1.0 processor to apply this transform. First we need to copy the code to a file `wsdl2rdf.xslt` (or download it). We will be using an XSLT processor called **4XSLT**, which comes as part of the 4Suite package we installed earlier. Using the command **4xslt** on the command line calls this processor.

None of the examples of WSDL in this chapter so far exercise the schema elements, so we shall illustrate this transform using the example WSDL file included in Section 1.2 of the WSDL 1.1 specification (http://www.w3.org/TR/wsdl). Copy this source to `w3c-eg.wsdl` (or download it from the Wrox web site), and apply the transform under Windows or UNIX by executing:

> **4xslt w3c–eg.wsdl wsdl2rdf.xslt**

The result of the transform from WSDL to RDF serialized form is output to the console. For this example, here is the resulting RDF, copied directly from the screen:

```
<?xml version='1.0' encoding='UTF-8'?>
<rdf:RDF xmlns:soap='http://schemas.xmlsoap.org/wsdl/soap/'
xmlns:wsdl='http://schemas.xmlsoap.org/wsdl/'
xmlns:x='http://xmlns.rdfinference.org/tools'
xmlns:xsd='http://www.w3.org/2000/10/XMLSchema'
xmlns:rwsdl='http://rdfinference.org/wsdl.rdfs#'
xmlns:mime='http://schemas.xmlsoap.org/wsdl/mime/'
xmlns:rdf='http://www.w3.org/1999/02/22-rdf-syntax-ns#'
xmlns:rxsd='http://rdfinference.org/xsd.rdfs#'
xmlns:http='http://schemas.xmlsoap.org/wsdl/http/'>
  <definitions rdf:ID='StockQuote' xmlns:xsd1='http://example.com/stockquote.xsd'
xmlns:tns='http://example.com/stockquote.wsdl'
xmlns='http://schemas.xmlsoap.org/wsdl/'>

<rwsdl:targetNamespace>http://example.com/stockquote.wsdl</rwsdl:targetNamespace>
  </definitions>
  <rdf:Description ID='xsd:http://example.com/stockquote.xsd'>
    <rxsd:targetNamespace>http://example.com/stockquote.xsd
</rxsd:targetNamespace>
    <rxsd:element>
      <rdf:Description ID='xsd.TradePriceRequest'/>
    </rxsd:element>
    <rxsd:element>
      <rdf:Description ID='xsd.tickerSymbol'>
        <rxsd:type>string</rxsd:type>
```

```
              <rxsd:parent>TradePriceRequest</rxsd:parent>
            </rdf:Description>
          </rxsd:element>
          <rxsd:element>
            <rdf:Description ID='xsd.TradePrice'/>
          </rxsd:element>
          <rxsd:element>
            <rdf:Description ID='xsd.price'>
              <rxsd:type>float</rxsd:type>
              <rxsd:parent>TradePrice</rxsd:parent>
            </rdf:Description>
          </rxsd:element>
      </rdf:Description>
      <message rdf:ID='GetLastTradePriceInput'
xmlns='http://schemas.xmlsoap.org/wsdl/'>
          <rwsdl:defined-by rdf:resource='#StockQuote'/>
          <part rdf:ID='body' element='xsd1:TradePriceRequest'
rdf:type='http://rdfinference.org/wsdl.rdfs#part'/>
      </message>
      <message rdf:ID='GetLastTradePriceOutput'
xmlns='http://schemas.xmlsoap.org/wsdl/'>
          <rwsdl:defined-by rdf:resource='#StockQuote'/>
          <part rdf:ID='body' element='xsd1:TradePrice'
rdf:type='http://rdfinference.org/wsdl.rdfs#part'/>
      </message>
      <portType rdf:ID='StockQuotePortType'
xmlns='http://schemas.xmlsoap.org/wsdl/'>
          <rwsdl:defined-by rdf:resource='#StockQuote'/>
          <operation rdf:ID='GetLastTradePrice'
rdf:type='http://rdfinference.org/wsdl.rdfs#operation'>
              <input rdf:parseType='resource'>
                <rwsdl:message>tns:GetLastTradePriceInput</rwsdl:message>
              </input>
              <output rdf:parseType='resource'>
                <rwsdl:message>tns:GetLastTradePriceOutput</rwsdl:message>
              </output>
          </operation>
      </portType>
      <binding rdf:ID='StockQuoteSoapBinding'
xmlns='http://schemas.xmlsoap.org/wsdl/'>
          <rwsdl:defined-by
rdf:resource='#StockQuote'/>StockQuoteSoapBindingtns:StockQuotePortType
</binding>
      <service rdf:ID='StockQuoteService'
xmlns='http://schemas.xmlsoap.org/wsdl/'>
          <rwsdl:defined-by rdf:resource='#StockQuote'/>
      </service>
</rdf:RDF>
```

This output could be saved to a file and parsed for RDF processing. For more on parsing RDF, see *Professional XML Meta Data*, by Kal Ahmed et al (ISBN: 1-861004-51-6), also by Wrox Press.

Next we'll move back to looking at applications using Python and SOAP, but this time using the powerful 4Suite Server. This will move us on from discussion of client–side Web Services access to server–side implementation.

Web Services Implementation in 4Suite Server

4Suite Server is designed to maximize the simplicity of managing XML content and exchange, including exchange through SOAP and other HTTP–based mechanisms. This makes it a handy tool for developing Web Service implementations.

As an example, we'll look at a simple Web Service that returns the current version of various software packages.

WSDL Description of the Software Version Web Service

Firstly, we'll quickly run the through the WSDL description of the Service we'll create. This is purely for your information as WSDL is not necessary for using SOAP.

First come the root element and namespace declarations. These are followed by the XML schema definition that defines the SOAP message elements. getCurrentVersion, getCurrentVersionResponse, and getCurrentVersionFault are each elements with a single child element with text content.

```
<?xml version="1.0"?>
<definitions
  name="getSoftwareVersion"
  targetNamespace="http://uche.ogbuji.net/eg/ws/softver-soapser.wsdl"
  xmlns:tns="http://uche.ogbuji.net/eg/ws/softver-soapser.wsdl"
  xmlns:xsd="http://uche.ogbuji.net/eg/ws/softver-soapser.xsd"
  xmlns:soap="http://schemas.xmlsoap.org/wsdl/soap/"
  xmlns="http://schemas.xmlsoap.org/wsdl/"
>

  <types>
    <schema
      targetNamespace="http://uche.ogbuji.net/eg/ws/softver-soapser"
      xmlns="http://www.w3.org/1999/XMLSchema"
      xmlns:xs="http://www.w3.org/2001/XMLSchema"
    >
    <element name="getCurrentVersion">
      <complexType>
        <all>
          <element name="packageName" type="xs:string"/>
        </all>
      </complexType>
    </element>
    <element name="getCurrentVersionResponse">
      <complexType>
        <all>
          <element name="versionString" type="xs:string"/>
        </all>
      </complexType>
    </element>
    <element name="getCurrentVersionFault">
      <complexType>
        <all>
          <element name="errorMessage" type="xs:string"/>
        </all>
      </complexType>
    </element>
    </schema>
  </types>
```

Moving on to the next section, the `getCurrentVersion` message is the request and requires a child element or part named `packageName`, which is a case-insensitive string identifying the software package of interest. The `getCurrentVersionResponse` message is the response from the Web Service, with a part, `versionString`, which is a string representing the current version number of the requested package. Finally the `getCurrentVersionFault` message can be used to send any error messages back from the Web service. This collection of messages defines the port type for the Web Service.

```
<message name="getCurrentVersion">
  <part name="body" element="xsd:getCurrentVersion"/>
</message>

<message name="getCurrentVersionResponse">
  <part name="body" element="xsd:getCurrentVersionResponse"/>
</message>

<portType name="PortType">
  <operation name="getCurrentVersion">
    <input message="tns:getCurrentVersion"/>
    <output message="tns:getCurrentVersionResponse"/>
  </operation>
</portType>
```

In the final section, the binding specifies that the communication with the Web Service will occur using SOAP. It gives SOAP parameters for each message. Lastly, the service specification gives the network location of the Web Service.

```
<binding name="SoapBinding" type="tns:PortType">
  <soap:binding style="document"
transport="http://schemas.xmlsoap.org/soap/http"/>
  <operation name="getCurrentVersion">
    <soap:operation soapAction="http://uche.ogbuji.net/eg/ws/softver-soapser"/>
    <input>
      <soap:body use="literal" namespace="http://uche.ogbuji.net/eg/ws/softver-
soapser" encodingStyle="http://schemas.xmlsoap.org/soap/encoding/"/>
    </input>
    <output>
      <soap:body use="literal" namespace="http://uche.ogbuji.net/eg/ws/softver-
soapser" encodingStyle="http://schemas.xmlsoap.org/soap/encoding/"/>
    </output>
  </operation>
</binding>

<service name="translate">
  <port name="Port" binding="tns:SoapBinding">
    <soap:address location="http://uche.ogbuji.net/eg/ws/softver-soapser"/>
  </port>
</service>

</definitions>
```

The SOAP Handler Code

4Suite Server allows the developer to define SOAP handlers, which are simple Python modules that receive the SOAP request details and prepare a response for the server to dispatch. The handler code for the Software Version Web Service is quoted and explained below. You'll need to either copy it into a file called `SoftverHandler1.py` or download it from the Wrox web site later.

```
import string
from xml import xpath
from FtServer.Protocols.Http import SoapHandler

SOFTVER_SOAP_NS = 'http://uche.ogbuji.net/eg/ws/softver-soapser'

VERSION_MAPPINGS = {
    "4suite": "0.11.1",
    "4suiteserver": "0.11.1",
    "pyxml": "0.6.5",
    }
```

In the first section of the code, we import `xpath` in order to retrieve any required information from the SOAP message. Importing `SoapHandler` makes available a parent class from which SOAP handler classes derive. This ensures that all the machinery is set up and the handler class only has to perform the specific actions necessary to satisfy the request. The namespace of the message elements in the SOAP body are of particular importance, as well as the local name. A SOAP handler can handle multiple message element namespaces and local names. A dictionary is set up to define the dispatch method invoked to handle each message, as we shall see soon. To make all this easier the SOAP message element namespace is set in a global constant variable, `SOFTVER_SOAP_NS`.

The function of this example Web Service, once again, is to return a version string for a given software package name. For this purpose we set up a global constant dictionary, `VERSION_MAPPINGS` with the current mappings from package to version. Of course in a real Web Service, such data would probably be stored in a less volatile location such as a database, but the dictionary should suit this simple example.

Then we get to the actual function that implements our example Web Service:

```
def GetSoftwareVersion(repository, requestbody, responsebody):
    context = xpath.Context.Context(requestbody)
    packageName = xpath.Evaluate('string(packageName)', context=context)
    ver = VERSION_MAPPINGS[string.lower(packageName)]
```

`GetSoftwareVersion` is invoked by the server with three parameters:

- ❑ `repo` – is an instance of the 4Suite Server XML repository which can be used, for instance, to read or update existing data in the system in order to satisfy the SOAP request.

- ❑ `reqbody` – This is a DOM node representing the `SOAP-ENV:body` element in the request. It can be accessed to view all the message parts, parameters, structures, etc.

- ❑ `respbody` – is a DOM node representing the `SOAP-ENV:body` element to be used in generating the response. It can be mutated in order to add the message body content for the response.

We use XPath to access the parameters, because it is an easy way to access portions of an XML document such as the SOAP request. We set it up to use XPath by creating an XPath context that refers to the request element body. Then we use an XPath expression to extract the `s:packageName` node from the request body. The result is the software package for which the version is requested. The version is simply looked up in the `VERSION_MAPPINGS` dictionary, and the result kept in a variable.

The next step is generating the response message:

```
result = responsebody.ownerDocument.createElementNS(
    SOFTVER_SOAP_NS, 's:getCurrentVersionResponse'
    )
ver_param = responsebody.ownerDocument.createElementNS(
    None, 'versionString'
    )
ver_text = responsebody.ownerDocument.createTextNode(ver)
ver_param.appendChild(ver_text)
result.appendChild(ver_param)
responsebody.appendChild(result)
return 1
```

This is accomplished by manipulating the `respbody` element to insert the `s:getCurrentVersionResponse` response element and set the appropriate text body to the version string.

When all this processing is complete, 1 is returned to signal to the server that the SOAP handler successfully handled the request.

All that remains is a couple of registration chores for setting up the SOAP handler:

```
class SoftVerSoapHandler(SoapHandler.SoapHandler):
    NS_TO_HANDLER_MAPPING = {
        SOFTVER_SOAP_NS: {'getCurrentVersion': GetSoftwareVersion,
                          },
        }
```

In the above section, we define a handler class that simply sets up a special dictionary mapping message element namespaces and local names to functions for handling the message. Usually this is all a SOAP handler class has to do in 4Suite Server, although more complex hooks can be used for highly specialized processing.

```
def Register(props):
    handler = SoftVerSoapHandler()
    return [(handler.handle, 'POST')]
```

Finally a registration function is defined which is invoked whenever the HTTP server is started up. It creates an instance of the SOAP handler class and registers this as a candidate handler of HTTP POST request, which is how SOAP requests are received.

Setting up the SOAP Handler

We will implement this service using **4Suite Server**. Version 0.11.1b3 or more recent is required, and we'll need to download the relevant version from (http://www.4Suite.org/). Windows users should follow the appropriate installation instructions available from the code download for this book (`4sswininstall.txt`) and return to this chapter when they have been completed. UNIX users should follow the instructions available from the book code download in the file `4ssunixinstall.txt`.

Once we have installed 4Suite Server, we now need to install the Software Version Web Service. To do this, we need to download the files in the softver directory of the code download for this book (at http://www.wrox.com/) and place them in a separate directory somewhere on your system. The included files are:

File Name	Description
SoftverHandler1.py	Implements the back-end SOAP handler for the Software Version Web Service
__init__.py	A standard Python file to signal that this directory is a Python package
setup.py	The installation script for this code
soappysoftver.py	The test client for the Software Version Web service
softver-soapser.wsdl	The WSDL for the Software Version Web Service
softver-soapser.xsd	The schema for SOAP messages in the Software Version Web Service
wsdl.docdef	A 4Suite Server definition file for WSDL documents

Ensure that you have set the paths to the configuration file and the database given in the installation instructions for 4Suite Server and then both Windows and UNIX users run the following to install the Service:

> python setup.py install

Once you have done this, the SOAP handler has to be set up in the 4Suite Server configuration file (4ss.cfg) in order to be recognized.

For Windows users, you should find this file in your **Windows** or **WINNT** folder, having placed it there during the installation of 4Suite Server. You now need to replace this file with the 4ss.cfg file from the code download for the book, which will add the sections described below and set up the SOAP handler.

UNIX users should already have used the configuration file with the SOAP handler settings when setting up 4Suite Server according to the instructions in 4ssunixinstall.txt. The following description of the SOAP handler settings is for information only. If you'd like to check your 4ss.cfg file, you can find it by checking the FTSERVER_CONFIG_FILE environment variable.

The 4ss.cfg file that sets up the SOAP handler adds the following to the basic configuration file supplied with 4Suite Server:

```
<rdf:Description ID='SoftVerSoapHandler'>
    <rdf:type
 resource='http://xmlns.4Suite.org/4ss/properties#HttpHandler'/>
    <Priority>40</Priority>
    <Module>FtServer.Share.SoftverHandler1</Module>
  </rdf:Description>

  <rdf:Description ID='SoapHandler'>
    <rdf:type
 resource='http://xmlns.4Suite.org/4ss/properties#HttpHandler'/>
    <Priority>20</Priority>
    <Module>FtServer.Protocols.Http.SoapHandler</Module>
  </rdf:Description>
```

This puts our handler module in line to handle HTTP requests with a priority of 40 and sets up the generic 4Suite Server handler. The higher the priority, the earlier the handler is in the queue. It also adds the following to the Python HTTP server section in the configuration file:

```
<Handler resource='#SoftVerSoapHandler'/>
<Handler resource='#SoapHandler'/>   <!-- optional/multiple -->
```

We now need to restart 4Suite Server to round out the configuration process. In Windows or UNIX, we run 4ss_manager restart from the command line.

Testing the SOAP Implementation With SOAP.py

Once we are all set up, with a configured 4Suite Server instance running, it is a simple matter to test the SOAP server using SOAP.py.

Note that unfortunately, SOAPy was unable to handle this example because of interoperability bugs, but by the time you read this SOAPy may have been updated for better interoperability.

The SOAP.py client script for accessing this Web Service is as follows:

```python
#!/usr/bin/env python

import sys

#Import the SOAP.py machinery
import SOAP

server = SOAP.SOAPProxy(
    'http://localhost:8080/eg/ws/softver-soapser',
    namespace='http://uche.ogbuji.net/eg/ws/softver-soapser'
)

try:
    package = sys.argv[1]
except IndexError:
    package = '4Suite'

version = server.getCurrentVersion(packageName=package)
print "The current version of %s is %s"%(package, version)
```

Copy this to a file named soappysoftver.py (or download it) and execute using the now familiar method:

> **python soappysoftver.py**

The response should be the following:

As you can see, the client has received a response to its request to the server to give the version number for the 4Suite software, indicating that our service is up and running. You can change the package named in the client code to be any of the other software names stored in our dictionary earlier, and return a similar result.

Testing the SOAP Implementation with the Basic Python Library

As another test, and a further illustration of the technique, the following is a simple test program using Python's HTTP and XML tools to access our Web Service on 4Suite Server. The method used is similar to that in our earlier example, where we tested against an existing Service on the Web:

```python
import sys, httplib

SERVER_ADDR = '127.0.0.1'
SERVER_PORT = 8080

BODY_TEMPLATE = """<SOAP-ENV:Envelope
  xmlns:SOAP-ENV="http://schemas.xmlsoap.org/soap/envelope/"
  xmlns:s="http://uche.ogbuji.net/eg/ws/softver-soapser"
  SOAP-ENV:encodingStyle="http://schemas.xmlsoap.org/soap/encoding/"
>
  <SOAP-ENV:Body>
    <s:getCurrentVersion>
      <packageName><![CDATA[%s]]></packageName>
    </s:getCurrentVersion>
  </SOAP-ENV:Body>
</SOAP-ENV:Envelope>"""

def GetSoftwareVersion(name=None):
    if not name:
        name = raw_input("Software package name: ")
    body = BODY_TEMPLATE%(name)
    blen = len(body)
    requestor = httplib.HTTP(SERVER_ADDR, SERVER_PORT)
    requestor.putrequest('POST', '/eg/ws/softver-soapser')
    requestor.putheader('Host', SERVER_ADDR)
    requestor.putheader('Content-Type', 'text/plain; charset="utf-8"')
    requestor.putheader('Content-Length', str(blen))
    requestor.putheader('SOAPAction', "http://uche.ogbuji.net/eg/ws/softver-
soapser")
    requestor.endheaders()
    requestor.send(body)
    (status_code, message, reply_headers) = requestor.getreply()
    reply_body = requestor.getfile().read()
    print status_code
    print message
    print reply_body

if __name__ == "__main__":
    name = None
    if len(sys.argv) > 1:
        name = sys.argv[1]
    GetSoftwareVersion(name)
```

Copy this to a file named `basicsoftvertest.py` (or download it) and execute it in the usual way:

> **python basicsoftvertest.py**

You will be prompted to give a software package name, at which point you should type in one of the software names that we stored in our library earlier.

The following is the result of running the client and typing in 4suiteserver in Windows:

```
C:\python_tests>python basicsoftvertest.py
Software package name: 4suiteserver
200
OK
<?xml version='1.0' encoding='UTF-8'?>
<!DOCTYPE SOAP-ENV:Envelope>
<SOAP-ENV:Envelope xmlns:SOAP-ENV='http://schemas.xmlsoap.org/soap/envelope/' xm
lns:s='http://uche.ogbuji.net/eg/ws/softver-soapser' SOAP-ENV:encodingStyle='htt
p://schemas.xmlsoap.org/soap/encoding/'>
  <SOAP-ENV:Body>
    <s:getCurrentVersionResponse>
      <versionString>0.11.1</versionString>
    </s:getCurrentVersionResponse>
  </SOAP-ENV:Body>
</SOAP-ENV:Envelope>

C:\python_tests>
```

Summary

As you can see, there are many tools and techniques for Web Services programming in Python. Not all of these are mature in their development yet, but of course with Python's famous transparency and ease of use there are few roadblocks beyond the ability of the average developer to repair.

Other facilities for Web Services in Python are already on their way: UDDI, ebXML registry/repository and semantic web support for agent processing are just some of them.

In this chapter we have discussed and tried out:

- ❑ A selection of modules that come with Python and are useful for Web Services development and deployment.

- ❑ Third-party Python tools and modules that are available for Web Services development and deployment.

- ❑ Sending and receiving SOAP messages using facilities in the core Python library as well as SOAP.py.

- ❑ Sending SOAP messages using SOAPy.

- ❑ Managing and processing WSDL documents using Python with wsdl4py.

- ❑ Implementing Web Services using 4Suite Server.

If this has given you a flavor for Python and Python Web Services, check out some of the further resources overleaf.

Further Resources

- ❑ Daily Python – http://www.pythonware.com/daily/
- ❑ Dr. Dobb's Journal Python – http://www.ddj.com/topics/pythonurl/
- ❑ Starship Python – http://starship.python.net/
- ❑ Python Developer Shed – http://www.devshed.com/Server_Side/Python/.

13

Web Services Security

In this chapter we will introduce the topic of security in general and discuss the security of Web Services. We will describe the various methods of handling this very important and often complex aspect of developing an application. More specifically:

❑ We will start with a brief introduction to some of the most important points related to the general topic of security. We will discuss the often-practiced approach of security as an afterthought versus the more appropriate approach of understanding and handling security as part of a continuous process that includes systems security and business practices and policies.

❑ Then, we will look at Web Services and see how security applies to this new paradigm of building distributed applications.

❑ Next, we will focus on the two main levels where we can apply security in applications with Web Services: the **transport level** and the **application level**. We will show practical code examples and configuration guidelines on how we can implement security with applications that utilize Web Services.

❑ Finally, we will look into some of the XML security related technologies that are coming out in the near future. The technologies covered include the security extensions to SOAP, along with some of the new security related XML initiatives.

At a high level, you will notice that this chapter starts by introducing you to security and the most important security concepts, terminology, and technology. It is extremely important that you understand these before continuing on to the second part of the chapter, which focuses on Web Services security and provides some practical suggestions for implementing security in your Web Services applications. The final part of the chapter focuses on upcoming technologies and standards related to the XML Web security. The entire area of Web Services security is very new and has not yet been implemented widely enough for the technologies and standards associated with it to stabilize. With this in mind, this chapter provides information that you can use to implement Web Services security with existing technologies.

Security and XML Web Services

It would be wonderful if we did not have to worry about security. We would be able to avoid a lot of work if we could all just get along. Until this happens, however, we have to be concerned about security. Security involves protecting **valuable assets**. These can be items such as money and goods in general, but also intangible things such as reputation, brand name, and ideas. Security is important in business, where being able to protect sensitive information, such as financial data, is critical to business operations. It is also critical in the exchange of this highly valuable information. Furthermore, security and the related area of privacy are very important to individuals, especially where personal information such as medical records is being accessed, exchanged or stored.

Security was important to a certain degree when we were building standalone applications. Once applications become distributed across networks, even local networks, security becomes significantly more important. The situation arose where more than one user could access a single application without having to sit down at the actual computer on which the application was installed. When we started building Web applications, the importance of security increased exponentially. The highly exposed nature of the Web means that just about anybody can attempt to break into a Web application and compromise its security. Web Services act as building blocks any number of applications. This makes them critical components, and like any valuable resource, they tend to attract hackers.

Security as an Afterthought

Often, applications are built without much regard for security until everything else is in place, just before the application is put into production. Even worse, security is frequently not looked at until the application is in the production environment and someone reports a hole in the security, or a hacker attacks the site.

This practice of handling security as an afterthought to the design and development process is driven by the attitude that security is unnecessary work that offers no financial return. In addition, security can be seen as an inconvenience, because it can affect the ease of use of a system. For example, a strong password policy that requires users to remember long and complicated passwords could be seen as an inconvenient system "feature" that should be avoided if at all possible. What has been overlooked in such a situation is that implementing computer system security is similar to purchasing insurance against losing some of the valuable assets that we described in the above section. In the short term, implementing a strong security policy may seem inconvenient and costly. However, in the long term the users and the owner of the system will reap the rewards of such a policy, especially in the case of a malicious attack directed the system.

Note that it is possible to have excessive security in a particular situation. Not all scenarios require top-level security. Rather, the level of security required depends on the level of sensitivity of the data and other risk factors that vary for each individual business, application, or situation. Understanding that security is not an "all-or-nothing" choice, but that it has to be carefully assessed for each particular situation, makes security a complex challenge.

Another reason for treating security as an afterthought is that implementing security is often more complex than implementing other parts of the system. An **integrated approach** is required, whereby security concerns are analyzed at all levels of the system. This includes examining all the components of the system, as well as business policies and processes in general. If security were compromised at any of these levels, then the system as a whole would be compromised. Take the example of a system that has strong security implemented at the levels of all modules. If an employee with administrator privileges writes down their username and password in an area accessible to a number of other individuals, those individuals can potentially misuse the administrator's account. In this situation, no matter how strong the security is at the technology level, it can be compromised by a simple failure to follow good security procedures at the human level. The well-known phrase that "a chain is only as strong as its weakest link" applies particularly to computer system security. All that a potential hacker needs is a single weak point.

Security as a Process

When faced with the complexity of the task of addressing security, building secure applications can seem daunting. However, following a few simple steps makes this task more manageable.

We must understand that implementing security is little different from implementing the other features of an application. Implementing security takes the form of a **process** that covers all the different levels of the business as described above. This process has to be continually revised and updated as new threats, security bugs, and holes are found.

In this chapter, we focus on the part of the security process that is related to the unique technical implementation of security for Web Services and the applications that offer or consume these services. We will not be covering the entire process of building and implementing security. In particular, we will not be discussing the aspects of appropriate business policies, business procedures, and risk analysis. However, these are things that we should keep in mind as we address security in Web Services.

For more information on the overall process that is taken when addressing system security, the following resources may be useful:

- ❑ The **CERT Coordination Center (CERT/CC)**, a center for Internet security expertise, located at the Software Engineering Institute (SEI) and federally funded research and development center operated at Carnegie Mellon University: http://www.cert.org/.

- ❑ The **Internet Engineering Task Force (IETF)** provides a Site Security Handbook that is intended to serve as a guide for developing security policies and procedures for organizations that have systems on the Internet: http://www.ietf.org/rfc/rfc2196.txt.

- ❑ The paper *Towards a Secure System Engineering Methodology,* presents a methodology for assessing system vulnerabilities and selecting measures to best handle these vulnerabilities, with a look at risk analysis: http://www.counterpane.com/secure-methodology.html.

You may also find some useful resources at the **NIST (National Institute of Standards and Technology)** Computer Security Resources Center at http://csrc.ncsl.nist.gov/, where you can follow the links for the Risk Management Guide, Technical Models for IT Security, and other helpful resources for looking at the overall process of implementing security in your organization.

Key Security Concerns

We now continue our discussion by covering the main security concerns that we need to have when building secure Web Services. These concerns will provide a framework for us to continue on to the practical approaches of addressing Web Services security. They will also equip us with a standard vocabulary that we can use in discussing security.

When people talk about having a system that is secure, they are typically referring to having properly addressed some, if not most, of the following categories of security.

Authentication

Authentication is the process by which a user, computer, or application verifies to another user, computer, or application that they are who or what they claim to be. This is typically achieved through providing credentials such as a password, a PIN (Personal Identification Number) or a smart card. These credentials are evaluated and determined to be correct or incorrect.

In the case of Web Services, authentication is typically between applications, and the credentials provided are typically in the form of a password or a certificate. Certificates will be explained later in this section, after we become familiar with a few more key security points. We will provide more details about authentication methods in Web Services later in this chapter.

Authorization

As soon as a user, computer, or application is successfully authenticated, they will request access to a resource such as a file, database, or an XML Web Service. The access level of the calling user, computer, or application is checked against a list of resource access rights.

The actual implementation of the access control varies across different operating systems and applications. However, the principles described below apply to most situations:

❑ The access level of the calling entity is assigned to appropriate roles or groups.

❑ The level of access allowed to the requested resource is mapped to these roles or groups. The resource will typically have assignments for the level of access that is allowed for each role or group, because not every access is at the same level (some can have read access, others can have write access, etc.).

Once the calling entity's access level is compared to the access level of the resource, access is granted or denied. When access is granted, it is granted at an appropriate level. At this point, we can say that the calling entity has been given **authorization** to act upon the resource.

To illustrate: when the calling application is successfully authenticated by an Web Service, it is checked to see if it is authorized to run the operation that it was asking to perform. If authorization is granted, the request will be serviced by the Web Service. Authorization usually takes place for each operation or method within a Web Service. However, there may be times when authorization for a Web Service as a whole is appropriate, for example where a high granularity of security is not critical. This can simplify the security implementation significantly.

Auditing and Logging

Computer systems can carry out **auditing** and **logging** in order to collect information about attempts to access resources, and the operations performed on those resources. Logging is an excellent tool for gathering information when troubleshooting a system.

Auditing and logging can be carried out at different levels in a system, such as at the operating system level, at the level of the web server, or the database server. We are interested in logging at the level of the Web Services and at the level of the transport layer that is being used for accessing the particular Web Service. For example, if HTTP was being used as the transport layer, we would be interested in the web server's audit and log. Note that the SOAP Protocol that is one of the building blocks of Web Services can also work over other protocols in addition to HTTP, such as SMTP, etc. (see Chapter 1 for more on Web Services architecture).

Integrity and Encryption

Integrity refers to being able to ensure that data remains uncorrupted while in transit or in storage. **Encryption** helps us to achieve integrity and to prevent others from reading data. Since encryption and encryption techniques are very important aspects of security, let's take a closer look at some of the main concepts related to encryption.

Encryption and Related Techniques

Encryption is the scrambling of data in such a way that it can only be unscrambled with the use of the correct cryptographic key or password. The encrypted data can be placed in a message, such as a message exchanged via SOAP, or it can be stored. The theory behind encryption is deeply mathematical, and is beyond the scope of this chapter. However, we will very briefly define some of the main encryption algorithms.

> *For more information on encryption and the related technologies described here, you may want to look at some of the additional resources listed at the end of this section.*

There are two main types of encryption techniques or algorithms:

❑ **Symmetric** algorithms, sometimes called **conventional** algorithms, where the encryption key is usually the same as the decryption key.

❑ **Asymmetric** or **public key** algorithms, where the encryption key is completely different and cannot be derived from the decryption key. One of the keys is called the **private key**, and is kept by the owner of the key. The second key is the **public key**, which is available to others.

Another cryptographic algorithm, which is related to digital signatures, is the technique of **hash**, or **digest,** functions. We'll cover digital signatures in a later section. However, we will take a brief look at hash functions, because they are used in addressing the integrity of data. Hash functions typically create a fixed length value from the bytes that comprise the data. The original data cannot be derived from this value (simply called the "hash" or "digest"). In addition, the hash/digest is sensitive to changes in the original data. A small change in the original data creates significant change in the resulting hash. Another useful feature is that it is not feasible to create data that exactly matches a specific hash, which prevents data tampering. It is interesting to note that techniques similar to hash or digest algorithms (but less complex) have been used in telecommunications for error detection and correction.

Now that we have described the basic ideas behind public key algorithms and hash/digest functions, we can discuss **digital certificates**. Recall that we stated that certificates could be used for authentication. So, what exactly are certificates and why are they important? When decrypting a message that was encrypted with the private key of the sender, we use the public key of the sender, which, as we said, is available for others to use. We need a way of verifying the validity of the public key. Certificates were introduced to address this issue. A certificate is a binary structure that contains information about the holder of a public key. Conceptually, we can think of a certificate as a structure that wraps around the public key, and holds information describing the public key. Some of the information contained in the certificate includes the certificate issuer name, validity period, and the hashed content of the certificate that was encrypted with the certificate issuer's private key (that is, a digital signature provided by the certificate issuer – we'll describe digital signatures soon). The most common format for digital certificates is the **X.509** certificate.

> *To find more information about public certificates and X.509 you can visit the Internet Engineering Task Force (IETF) and the official X.509 certificate specification at*
> http://www.ietf.org/rfc/rfc2459.txt

Before continuing with our discussion of key security concerns, lets look at a few important security-related algorithms.

A Few Words about Encryption Algorithms

When dealing with security, you may encounter a number of terms referencing various security techniques, algorithms, or technologies. We will briefly introduce some of the main terms in this section. Most of the terminology described is related to algorithms, which are different to the commercial programs that implement them. Algorithms are mathematical constructs that can be implemented in various technologies.

There are two main encryption algorithms being used today in public-key cryptography. Both are based on well-known hard-to-solve mathematical problems. One is the **Rivest, Shamir**, and **Adleman** (**RSA**) algorithm, created by three mathematicians at MIT. The RSA algorithm randomly generates a very large prime number or public key. Then, it uses this public key to derive another very large prime number or a private key, through some complex mathematical functions. Users can employ the keys to encrypt and decrypt messages or documents. Various key lengths can be used with RSA, such as 512-bit, 2048-bit and even 4096-bit.

The other major public key algorithm is the **Diffie-Hellman** algorithm. This algorithm is also based on large prime numbers. Systems based on the Diffie-Hellman algorithm depend on the difficulty of computing discrete logarithms in a finite field generated by a large prime number. Various key lengths can be used with the Diffie-Hellman technique.

Another hard-to-solve problem in mathematics is the problem of elliptic curves. These are rich mathematical structures that can be used in encryption. **Elliptic curve** algorithms show promise and may reduce the processing requirements on encryption without lowering the security of systems. This means an opportunity to use shorter keys and achieve encryption levels that would require much higher key lengths with other encryption algorithms. However, more research needs to be done before elliptic curve algorithms can become widely used in the technology world.

When handling symmetric cipher (shared single key) types of encryption, the **Data Encryption Standard** (**DES**) and a stronger version of it called **Triple-DES** are used. Another symmetric key algorithm is the **International Data Encryption Algorithm** (**IDEA**). It was developed in Switzerland, uses a 128-bit key and is generally considered very secure, susceptible only to brute force attacks (attacks where all combinations are tried; such attacks require huge computing power, running over a very long time).

When creating hash/digest functions, the **RSA-MD2** (**Message Digest 2**) and **RSA-MD5** (**Message Digest 5**) are well-known algorithmic approaches. However, many cryptographers consider the **Secure Hash Algorithm** (**SHA**) to be the strongest hash algorithm currently available. "Fingerprinting" data with SHA to verify that it has not been altered is typically achieved by creating a 160-bit message digest or hash. SHA was incorporated by **NIST** (**National Institute of Standards and Technology**) in their **DSS** (**Digital Signature Standard**). Some of the digital signatures algorithms are based on the **Digital Signature Algorithm** (**DSA**), which is utilized with the DSS provided by NIST and the **National Security Agency** (**NSA**), both US government organizations. We'll talk more about digital signatures a little later in this chapter, but keep in mind that hash functions are a primary part of digital signature implementations.

In terms of actual technology or products that implement the various security algorithms, examples include: **PGP** (**Pretty Good Privacy**), Microsoft's **CryptoAPI**, **Java Cryptography Extensions (JCE)** for the Java 2 SDK v.1.4., etc.

If you would like to learn more about the mathematics of encryption, and to find a more in-depth discussion of the many security concepts described in the previous section, you may want to review the Applied Cryptography, Second Edition, Protocols, Algorithms, and Source Code in C, by Bruce Schneier, John Wiley & Sons (ISBN 0-471-11709-9).

The following resource covers some of the history of encryption and provides more information on the various encryption technologies (in less technical details and depth then the previous resource): ICSA Guide to Cryptography, by Randall K. Nichols, McGraw-Hill Professional Publishing (ISBN 0-07-913759-8).

Privacy and Encryption

Privacy means being able to keep information confidential, so that other parties are not able to read it. It is typically accomplished via encryption. However, there is much more to privacy than just encryption. Privacy also has to do with data use policies, as well as respecting individual's preferences as to how data about them should be used. Privacy is a very important concern for users, particularly in the online world. Users like to know that their data is safe and confidential. This is especially the case with the transfer of data such as credit card details, passwords, or other sensitive information.

Web Services, particularly ones that deal with very sensitive data, have to address the privacy issue appropriately. There are various ways to do this. We will discuss privacy further later in this chapter.

Availability (Load Balancing, Failover, Backup)

Although **availability** is not a term associated with security at first glance, it is an integral element of implementing security. Failing all other attempts to compromise the security of a system, a hacker might attempt to bring the system down by simply overloading it. **Denial of Service (DoS)** attacks are quite well known on the Internet today, and even some of the best-protected and largest web sites are susceptible. In these attacks, an attacker tries to overload the system with methods such as sending a flood of requests to a server. Doing this, the attacker may try to crash the system, or at least make it unavailable to valid users for a certain period of time.

To ensure availability, the following practices have to be in place:

❏ **Load Balancing** – the ability to distribute heavy workloads and assuring access to resources, when unpredictably high requests come in, such as when an attacker may try to overload the system.

- ❑ **Packet Filtering** – provides methods of filtering network or Internet traffic based on various criteria such as port number, source address, destination address, IP protocol, and other criteria. Packet filtering at the firewall or proxy server level can lower the load to the actual application server by filtering many of the malicious packets that could be sent to the server.

- ❑ **Virus Checking** – extends packet filtering, to enable filtering for viruses, such as e-mail attachment viruses. However, virus scanning and control goes beyond packet filtering. Users can bring files on a disk that are infected with viruses, so virus control both on desktop systems and on servers is required.

- ❑ **Failover** – the ability to switch or redirect requests for a service to a backup resource if the main one were to fail.

- ❑ **Backup** – backup and restore are operations that ensure that if the system were either compromised or overloaded or failed beyond recovery, it could be quickly brought back online.

Web Services are positioned as the building blocks for creating the next generation of distributed applications. As such, each Web Service would be used by a number of other applications. This makes it very important that Web Services have very high availability. High availability would increase the **Quality of Service (QoS)** of the offered Web Services, and is a characteristic on which customers are likely to place even more emphasis in the future.

Nonrepudiation and Digital Signatures

Nonrepudiation provides mechanisms that prove that an action has occurred. prevents a party (user, computer, or application) from reneging on a promise by claiming that a transaction had never occurred. It involves multiple security techniques, such as authentication, auditing and logging, and integrity. Nonrepudiation has legal connotations as well, and it requires the party to be informed that the action they are trying to take is legally binding. This is where digital signatures come into play.

Digital signatures are unique values that are attached to a file or a message. There are two aspects to digital signatures. One is the hash/digest generated out of the data in the message. This ensures the integrity of the data, as modifications to the data would be noticeable in the hash or digest. We described hash or digest functions earlier in this chapter. The other aspect is the process in which the signing program encrypts the hash using the sender's private key. This encrypted hash is the digital signature and it is written to the message or file.

In order to verify the signature, the receiving program first decrypts the hash with the public key of the sender. The public key can be obtained in different ways, such as by e-mail or from a central repository on the Web. Only the public key of the sending party would be able to decrypt the hash that was encrypted with the corresponding private key. This is how we ensure that the message is coming from the source that we think it is coming from. Next, the receiving program creates the same type of hash from the message or file. Comparing this newly created hash with the hash that came with the message tells us about the integrity of the message. If the hashes match, it means that the message was not tampered with or modified while in transport.

In addition to adding a digital signature to a message, the message itself can optionally be encrypted. One could use the public key of the recipient to encrypt the message content. Only the corresponding private key can decrypt the message, ensuring that no one but the recipient (the owner of the private key) can decrypt it.

There are some specifications that are being worked on at the W3C in the context of Web Services, specifying how to encrypt SOAP messages and how to add digital signatures to them. More details about these upcoming specifications are provided later in this chapter, under the heading *XML Security Related Extensions*.

We have covered most of the important terms and concepts related to application security. During our discussion we looked at the implications of each of the security concepts for Web Services. Next, we will look at the main approaches that we can take when securing Web Services.

Approaches to Web Services Security

Web Services can address the issue of security at two primary levels: at the **transport level** and at the **application level**. There are a number of ways in which to do this within each level. Furthermore, we can extend the application level approach by utilizing the SOAP extensions and other XML security related specifications and standards. We will look at these options towards the end of the chapter.

> *If you have not had a chance to look over the Web Services architecture described in Chapter 1, you may wish to do so. It will help you to understand how Web Services are structured and how the various parts such as the transport layer and message or wire building blocks fit into the overall picture of Web Services.*

In this chapter, we are covering key aspects of security, as well as providing some practical guidance for implementing secure Web Services. Because of this large scope, we will take a pre-built Web Service application and describe how we can secure it. We will not describe how this Web Services application was built and we will not go into describing its non-security related code. We shall make the assumption that you are familiar with creating basic Web Services applications, and will proceed directly to addressing their security. If you are not familiar with the techniques and technologies involved in building Web Services applications, please review the previous chapters dedicated to SOAP, WSDL, and UDDI.

You will find the code for the sample Web Services application on the Wrox web site (http://www.wrox.com/), along with more detailed requirements and installation instructions. If you are interested in learning more about the specific Web Services application utilized in this chapter with complete details about building its code, you can take a look at the following Wrox title: *Professional XML 2nd Edition* (ISBN: 1-861005-05-9), and review the SOAP chapter.

The sample application is a simple implementation of an invoice Web Service, with a few different client types calling it (some via HTTP and some via SMTP). The diagram below illustrates this:

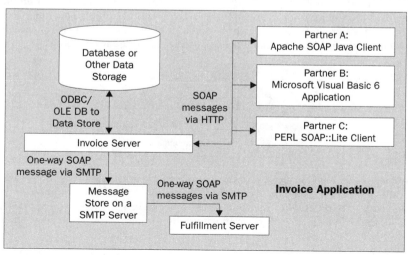

We have an Invoice Server that has a Web Service available to partners that enables them to submit invoices to it via HTTP. The Web Service was implemented using Microsoft technologies (Visual Basic 6 and COM+, with the SOAP Toolkit 2.0). The partners use three different technologies:

- ❏ Java (utilizing the Apache SOAP Toolkit 2.1, which is also part of the IBM Web Services Toolkit 2.2)

- ❏ Visual Basic (this utilizes Visual Basic 6 and COM+ with the SOAP Toolkit 2.0)

- ❏ PERL (utilizing the SOAP::Lite SOAP implementation)

The Invoice Server itself (which is based in Microsoft technologies) acts as a client, and sends XML messages to a Fulfillment Server (which is Java based) asynchronously via SMTP. We will focus on securing the HTTP-based part of this application (that is, the Invoice Server Web Service and communication with the various clients located at our partner sites). We will only briefly cover securing the SMTP-based Web Service hosted on the Fulfillment Server. This is because HTTP is used much more frequently than SMTP in implementing and deploying Web Services. However, keep in mind that most application level approaches to securing Web Services apply equally to HTTP and SMTP, or any other transport protocol for that matter.

We'll start by addressing Web Services security at the transport level. We will only consider the two most popular Internet standard transport protocols: HTTP and SMTP. Of course, HTTP could be used internally, within the corporate firewall communication, as well as outside on the Internet. For securing other transport protocols, you can check your particular technology documentation or consider applying some of the application level security approaches described later in this chapter.

Transport Level Security

Transport level security consists of utilizing the built-in security features of the transport layer of the given protocol that the particular Web Service is utilizing. This is possible because the SOAP message is usually encapsulated directly within the particular packaging mechanism provided by the transport layer.

It is important to remember that transport level security is **point-to-point security**, as far as Web Services are concerned. Point-to-point security refers to being able to secure the communication from one point (such as one computer or application) directly to another point. This implies that the connection is direct with no intermediaries in between. Intermediaries such as routers on the Internet are not considered intermediaries for the purposes of Web Services applications.

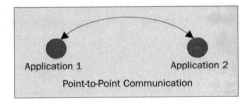

Point-to-Point Communication

From the perspective of Web Services, point-to-point security is sufficient when the consumer application calls the Web Service directly, without having any SOAP intermediaries in between the two. SOAP intermediaries are different to the routers and other Internet-type intermediaries that act on HTTP or SMTP traffic, which can still be used with point-to-point types of security, such as transport level security.

If we want to implement full **end-to-end security**, even when SOAP intermediaries are used, we have to look into application level security techniques, including some of the new XML based security technologies that are described later in this chapter. End-to-end security refers to security implemented in communication that does not have to be direct from one point such as a computer or application to another point. End-to-end security can be implemented across indirect communication lines between applications, where there are SOAP intermediaries involved (see the diagram below).

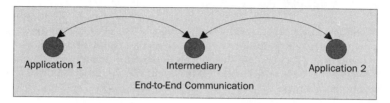

It is interesting to note that transport level security can be implemented at a lower level, that is, at the network level, such as that of the IP (Internet Protocol). IP is part of TCP/IP (Transmission Control Protocol/Internet Protocol), the protocol on which just about all Internet traffic runs. HTTP and SMTP are protocols that run on top of TCP/IP.

For more on Web Services architecture please see Chapter 1. For a more in-depth introduction of TCP/IP you can go to: http://www.hill.com/library/publications/tcpip.shtml, *or to* http://www.cisco.com/warp/public/535/4.html.

Implementing transport level security at the network level consists of securing IP traffic via technologies such as **IPSec (Internet Protocol Security)**. IPSec uses cryptography and implements IP authentication, privacy, and data integrity.

For more information on IPSec, you can go to the Internet Engineering Task Force (IETF) site and look at the Security Architecture for Internet Protocol specification at http://www.ietf.org/rfc/rfc2401.txt. *Most vendors provide specific guides on how they implement IPSec within their own products. You should be able to find this and other documentation at the particular vendor's web site.*

Since we just reviewed what transport level security entails, let's take a closer look at how we can handle security with HTTP.

HTTP

HTTP or Hypertext Transfer Protocol is the most popular Internet protocol, on top of which most Web traffic flows. HTTP is a synchronous protocol, which means that when a request is sent, the client must receive a reply before continuing. The request is a message that is wrapped in HTTP headers, and the reply is a message formatted in a similar fashion, but sent back to the caller. The request/response messages are human-readable text messages. HTTP is a stateless protocol, which means that each request and response pair is an individual event not connected to other request/response pairs. Sessions do not need to be established between the client and server; rather, each request is treated as a separate communication instance. There are some technologies that have been applied to HTTP in order to provide state (or a way of keeping sessions), such as setting cookies via the browser, but such solutions are separate from HTTP itself, and they operate within the client, within the server, or both. Stateless communication has its benefits in that it is quite efficient and highly scalable for very large distributed systems such as the Internet.

There are many products that support HTTP, and their number is bound to increase. Building web access and web support within products is becoming an important selling feature of the vast majority of products, including all types of server-side software, client-side or desktop applications, and even home entertainment software such as games.

> *For more information on HTTP, take a look at its specification at*
> *http://www.ietf.org/rfc/rfc2616.txt, located at the Internet Engineering Task Force (IETF).*

With such an ubiquitous presence, addressing the security of HTTP is crucial for the widespread use of the Internet. Some native HTTP features are used, such as **basic authentication**, which we will describe next. Additional features and technologies have been designed to seamlessly integrate with HTTP and improve its security, such as **SSL** or **Secure Sockets Layer**. We will describe these technologies in further detail later in this chapter.

Basic Authentication

Basic authentication is a simple authentication protocol defined within the HTTP protocol specification. Virtually all web servers and browsers support basic authentication. In addition, basic authentication works quite well through most firewalls and proxy servers. Almost all SOAP toolkits support this authentication method as well. This widespread availability and support is a major advantage.

On the negative side, however, basic authentication sends passwords in the Base64 encoding format, which is very easy to decode, thus making it virtually equivalent to clear text. The way to address this issue is to combine basic authentication with **SSL (Secured Sockets Layers)** . We will describe this in the sections that follow.

When a web page or a resource is designated for basic authentication, the browser will display a dialog box to capture the user name and password and then send these values to the server. Let's familiarize ourselves with what basic authentication looks like and how we can set up a web server to request basic authentication. Then, we will see how Web Services can utilize basic authentication.

XML Web Service Configuration for Basic Authentication

Setting up basic authentication is quite easy. We will show you how to do this on Microsoft's web server, IIS 5.0 (Internet Information Server), as our sample Web Services application was created in Visual Basic and COM+.

> *In order to be able to cover all the main points about Web Services security in one chapter, we will*
> *have to limit our Web Server configuration examples to one server only – in this case IIS 5.0. If you*
> *have a different web server, please check with your web server documentation on specific steps for*
> *enabling Basic Authentication. Basic Authentication operates in a standard way, as it is part of the*
> *HTTP 1.1 protocol specification – therefore there are many conceptual similarities in setting up*
> *Basic Authentication on any web server. If you have IIS 4.0 (on Windows NT 4.0) then you should*
> *be able to get this application to run on it as well, by slightly modifying the instructions provided*
> *(refer to our earlier discussion about the pre-built application and how to obtain it).*

First, we will set up our web server to require basic authentication when resources are accessed within our Web Service directory.

If you have not downloaded this sample Web Services application and have not installed it by following the included directions, please go ahead now and create the soap *virtual directory and make it point to the* Web *folder in your files that you have downloaded. Before installing and configuring the Web Services application, you need to know that you need to have IIS 5 running on your computer (that would require Windows 2000 Professional or Server) and you would need to have the MS SOAP Toolkit 2.0 installed. This is available from:*

http://msdn.microsoft.com/downloads/default.asp?URL=/code/sample.asp?url=/msdn-files/027/001/580/msdncompositedoc.xml

As we mentioned earlier, we will not go into the details of setting up the Web Services application, but we will only focus on implementing security to this application. If you have your own Web Services application that you like to secure with Basic Authentication, you should be able to apply the same concepts described in this section.

Start by opening the **Internet Services Manager** (which is just an instance of the Microsoft Management Console or MMC). You can do this going to your Start button, then Programs | Administrative Tools | Internet Services Manager. Once the Internet Services Manager opens up, you are able to expand the branch next to your server name (by clicking on the plus sign), and then open the web site that you would like to manage (in the picture below we have selected the Default Web Site). At this level, you can either select the entire web site, a directory, or a file, on which you can set the authentication level. You can select it, right-click on it, and select Properties, as shown on the figure below. In this case, we are selecting the virtual directory called soap (where most of our Web Services files are placed), for which we will set the security.

This will open up a **Properties** window. You can set various properties in this window that relate to the resource that you have selected. If you select the **Directory Security** tab, you will see some options that allow you to set authentication levels, as well as some other security settings, such as IP address restrictions and security communications via certificates.

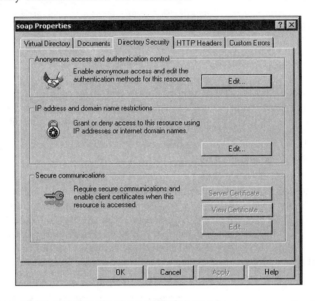

Click on the **Edit** button in the **authentication control** section.

The next window that appears will show the various authentication options that Windows and IIS provide. Different web servers provide slightly different authentication options. However, virtually all of them support basic authentication. You can see in the next screenshot that we have checked the **Basic Authentication** checkbox and cleared all of the other ones. This will force IIS to authenticate the user trying to access this resource using basic authentication. Notice that IIS warns you that basic authentication is not safe, due to the fact that it sends the username and password in clear text.

Also, you can provide a default domain or realm, if you like, by clicking on the Edit button next to the basic authentication option shown on the above screen. At this point, you can click OK and OK again to close the Properties windows.

If you try to access this resource now (or any of the resources within, if it is a folder or an entire web site) via your browser (and you can do this by typing in its address in the URL bar) you will be prompted to authenticate with a dialog box. This dialog box requires you to enter a username and password (as shown in the following picture).

As you can see with this configuration example, it is quite easy to set up basic authentication for any resource such as a web site, directory, or file.

In order to create a particular username and set its password on your system, you should first add the username to the list of users on your system, set its password, and then give it the appropriate permissions. When using IIS 5.0, you can do this within Active Directory if your machine is a member of an Active Directory Domain; otherwise, you can add the username and set its password within the local list of user on your computer. If you are using a different web server and operating system, please check its documentation for instructions for adding users to your system. Another general, but important piece of advice about usernames and passwords is to avoid using administrator level accounts for accessing your Web Services; although administrator level accounts are fine for testing purposes, they should not be used for any production level systems.

So, how can we make our Web Service require basic authentication and then call it from our clients? There are two permission-configuration items that we need to set at the server side. First, we need to set the authentication method for the virtual directory (or entire web site if that is more appropriate in your situation) to require basic authentication, and disable anonymous and any other authentication methods that may have been enabled before. In the case of IIS, that configuration is exactly as shown in the previous configuration example. The second configuration item is to allow anonymous access to our WSDL file (the Web Service description file), because not all clients know how to easily authenticate while obtaining the WSDL file. Our client service needs to be able to read this file before it can connect to the Web Service. In our example, that file is `InvoiceSubmit.WSDL` (available in the code download from Wrox).

Now that we have configured the server side of the Web Service, we will look at modifying our client code so that it can properly authenticate itself and call the Web Service, which now requires basic authentication for us to access it.

Chapter 13

Remember that we are using a pre-built Web Services application in order to illustrate how to add security to Web Services applications. Both the server and the client code of this pre-built application come ready-made in the download. We are only describing how to secure this code in this chapter.

Visual Basic Client Code Modifications

The code modifications that we need to make to the Visual Basic client are quite small. This is a Visual Basic 6 application that utilizes the sample Web Service. Our Visual Basic client uses the Microsoft SOAP Toolkit 2.0 to make SOAP calls, read the WSDL files, etc. The following code sample highlights those modifications that are made to introduce basic authentication:

```
. . .
'Visual Basic code

'Create the soapClient object
Dim soapClient As SoapClient
Set soapClient = New SoapClient

'In a case of an error go to the error handler
On Error GoTo ErrorHandler

'Initiate the soapClient with the correct WSDL file
'and tell it the service name

'SECURITY: WSDL file must be left to have anonymous access
soapClient.mssoapinit txtWSDLFile.Text, "InvoiceSubmit", "", ""

'SECURITY: Specify the connector property
'(in this case that is the HTTP Connector)
'for username and password
'Change these credentials to match yours
soapClient.ConnectorProperty("AuthUser") = "wroxuser"
soapClient.ConnectorProperty("AuthPassword") = "password"

'Initiate the particular method by passing it the needed parameters
'Submit text box values and place the result in the text box
txtResult.Text = CStr(soapClient.InvoiceAdd(txtInvoiceID, txtCustomerID, _
    CDate(txtInvoiceDate), txtNotes, txtDeliveryAddress, txtPaymentTerms, _
    txtPaymentReceived))

'Cleanup
Set soapClient = Nothing

Exit Sub
. . .
```

From the above code you can see that we had to specify two HTTP connector properties, the `AuthUser`, that has the value of the username that we would like this Web Service to be called from, and `AuthPassword`, the password of that username. The same type of code modifications above will apply to clients implemented with ASP or WSH (Windows Scripting Host), both being VBScript based approaches.

Java Client Code Modifications

The modifications required to get our Java-based Web Service client (built using JDK 1.3 and Apache SOAP 2.1) to work with basic authentication are quite simple as well:

574

```
. . .
//Java code

String strProxyHost = null;
String strUserName = new String("wroxuser");
String strPassword = new String("password");
int intProxyPort = -1;

SOAPHTTPConnection oHTTPConn = new SOAPHTTPConnection();
if (strProxyHost != null) {
    oHTTPConn.setProxyHost(strProxyHost);
    oHTTPConn.setProxyPort(intProxyPort);
    }

oHTTPConn.setUserName(strUserName);
oHTTPConn.setPassword(strPassword);
. . .
```

In this code modification, we set up a couple of additional string variables, one holding the username and the other the password or the user that this client should provide to authenticate to our Web Service. Then, we are calling the setUserName() method of the SOAPHTTPConnection class to set the username and the setPassword() method to set the user's password. Everything else remains the same.

PERL Client Code Modifications

The code modifications to our PERL client are once again simple. Our PERL client uses ActivePerl 5.6 and the SOAP::Lite module 0.48. So, basic authentication requires that we override the get_basic_credentials function in the class SOAP::Transport::HTTP::Client with the appropriate username and password:

```
. . .
# PERL code
# Override the get_basic_credentials function with proper username and password
sub SOAP::Transport::HTTP::Client::get_basic_credentials {
    return 'wroxuser' => 'password';
}
```

If you wish to run your PERL examples within your browser, you may have to configure your web server after you install ActivePerl. For information on this topic, follow the references provided earlier about our pre-built Web Services application, and also check the ActivePerl help files and its FAQ section.

With this, we covered basic authentication. Now, we'll review another popular type of authentication found in many web applications.

Forms-based Authentication

Login forms, usually written in HTML, authenticate users based on their login names and passwords. Once the user enters their username and password, these credentials along with any additional information are sent to the server via HTTP. This is a considerable security risk, as HTTP traffic is in plain text. In essence, login forms are very similar to basic authentication. The difference is that the look of an HTML form can be customized, and we have the freedom to choose the type of information we collect. We will look at how we can address the plain text issue in the next section. For now, however, let's look at how login forms work.

When a login form is loaded, it will look something like the one shown in the screenshot below. Of course, we are not required to have an HTML form as our login form. We can have a Java applet, a Java application form, or a Visual Basic form. As long as these forms submit their information to the processing resource using HTTP, everything works in a very similar way.

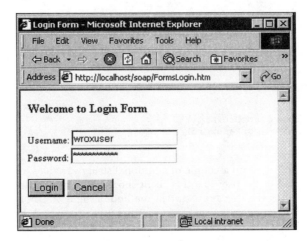

Once the user enters their username and password, they click on the Login button. At this point, the browser submits the information to the back-end process, which will authenticate the user and reply to say if the authentication was successful or not. This is shown in the next image:

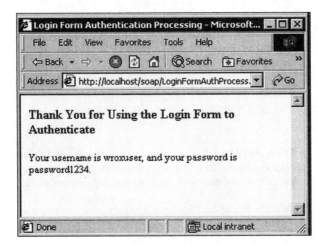

Let's take a quick look at the code that makes this happen (the simple HTML and ASP code that illustrates how forms-based authentication works is included in the code download from the Wrox web site). In this sample scenario, we have two files: one presents the user with the login form (the HTML file) and the other processes the credentials and does all the necessary back-end connecting work (the ASP file). The first file is an HTML form that asks the user to enter their username and password. Additional information can be collected, if needed. The following is the code for the HTML form:

```
<html>
   <head>
      <title>Login Form</title>
   </head>
   <body>
      <form method="POST" action="LoginFormAuthProcess.asp">
         <h3>Welcome to Login Form</h3>
         <p>
            Username: <input type="text" name="txtUsername" size="20"><br \>
            Password: <input type="password" name="txtPassword" size="20">
         </p>
         <p>
            <input type="submit" value="Login" name="btnLogin">
            <input type="reset" value="Cancel" name="btnCancel">
         </p>
      </form>
   </body>
</html>
```

As you can see, besides the standard <html> opening tags, the key part is the section within the <form> tags. Within this element, we have attributes that specify the form method of POST, meaning that the data will be submitted within the body of the HTTP message. The other alternative is to use GET, which appends the values of the form to the end of the URL (Uniform Resource Locator) that specifies the action of this form. The URL in the action attribute specifies the resource that will receive and process the form submission. This will be a web page or component that can process the data submitted by the form. In the case of authentication, this means that the action resource should check the credentials submitted by cross referencing them with some kind of data repository, such as a directory (a LDAP directory, for example), a file with a list of usernames, or a database. The following is the code of the processing resource:

```
<%
'Active Server Pages (ASP)/VB Script Code
Dim strUsernameProvided, strPasswordProvided
Dim strPasswordStored

'Retrieve submitted values from the request collection
strUsernameProvided = Request.Form ("txtUsername")
strPasswordProvided = Request.Form ("txtPassword")

'Include code that connects to a directory such as LDAP,
'   or code that connects to a database
'   or code that simply reads a file that contains user information
'Validate the submitted credentials with the ones from your
'   data repository and if correct, authenticate the user
'In our simple code we will simply hard-code the values
strPasswordStored = "password1234"
```

In the code above, there are two main steps: we set some variables and retrieve the values that were submitted to us via the login form (username and password), and we connect to our back-end storage (such as directory/LDAP source, database, or file) and verify that the submitted credentials are indeed valid. After the comparison of the submitted credentials to the ones we find in our data store, we authenticate the user. This is shown in the following section of our code:

```
'Now validate if the passwords match
If strPasswordProvided = strPasswordStored Then
%>
<html>
   <head>
   <title> Login Form Authentication Processing </title>
   </head>
   <body>
      <p><h3>Thank You for Using the Login Form to Authenticate</h3></p>
      <p>Your username is <% Response.Write strUsernameProvided %>,
      and your password is <% Response.Write strPasswordProvided %>.</p>
   </body>
   </html>
<%
Else
%>
<html>
   <head>
   <title> Login Form Authentication Processing </title>
   </head>
   <body>
      <p><h3>Your credentials are invalid.</h3></p>
   </body>
   </html>
<%
End If
%>
```

Assuming that we have successfully verified the credentials, what should we do next? Once the user credentials have been checked, a session should be set showing that this particular user has successfully logged in. In this way, subsequent attempts to request resources will not require going through the process of logging in. The session information can be kept on the application server itself as a session variable, stored in memory as part of the some of the running processes, or stored in a directory or database. The session key can be kept on the client side, such as within a cookie, passed behind the URL as a parameter, or kept within a hidden HTML field. The session information itself can be kept in a central location, such as a database or a directory, thus allowing the system to easily scale across multiple servers, and then simply send the session ID to the client in the form of a cookie, for example.

It is interesting to note that various technologies, platforms and products have built-in support for forms-based authentication. For example, the Java servlet specification supports forms-based authentication, and Microsoft's Site Server has this kind of support under its Personalization and Membership features. These implementations are very similar to what we have described here, the only difference being that the products may provide additional modules, classes, or objects that can make development work easier.

So, how does forms-based authentication relate to Web Services? First of all, forms-based authentication is very popular in many Web-based applications, second only to basic authentication. There may be situations where we need to connect to a Web Service within a larger Web-based application that is protected with forms-based authentication. In such cases, we need to understand the implications of forms-based authentication when creating Web Services. Your Web Service toolkit is unlikely to have extensive support (if any) for forms-based authentication.

There is little you can do to utilize forms-based authentication, except for sending credentials directly to the resource that is processing the login form input (like the ASP page in our example). However, even if you do this, it is a challenge to get the client service to act as if it were an actual browser and hold state by accessing the Web Service that is behind this forms-based authentication. A better solution to this problem is to recommend enabling Basic Authentication to the Web Service, instead of the forms login-authentication (if this is possible in your particular situation). A second possibility is to ensure that the forms login processing resource accepts a redirection input (for example a URL), to which it should redirect you after it has processed the credentials properly and your client service has been authenticated. If the processing recourse can redirect your service request on the server-side without sending a redirection request to the browser, this option may work as well (for example this could be done under IIS 5.0 with the use of the `Server.Execute()` method).

Now that you are familiar with forms-based authentication and its challenges as it relates to Web Services, we can proceed with addressing one of the most challenging issues that both basic authentication and forms-based authentication face: the transfer of credentials in clear text.

Adding SSL to Basic Authentication

The main concern with using basic authentication (or login form authentication) over HTTP is that the credentials are being sent in plain text. **SSL** (**Secure Sockets Layer**) addresses this concern by encoding transmissions between two points on a network, encrypting the traffic between the client and the server. When applied to HTTP, SSL turns HTTP into **HTTPS**, or **HTTP Secured**. SSL secures end-to-end communication, meaning that communication can be via routers. However, we are talking about TCP/IP routers here, not SOAP routers or intermediaries. SSL only provides point-to-point security for Web Services with XML intermediaries.

Netscape originally designed SSL. However, SSL is now an open and non-proprietary protocol. It provides data encryption, server authentication, and message integrity. SSL works well with firewalls and it is compatible with tunneling technologies such as dial-up connections and **VPN** (**Virtual Private Network**) connections.

SSL requires the use of digital certificates installed on the server side. This is how the server is authenticated to the client. Note that the server does not receive any certificates from the client, although we could optionally require that this be done (we'll explain client-side certificates in the next section). Digital certificates can be obtained from third-party **Certification Authority** (**CA**) companies such as VeriSign or Thawte, but any company can generate them internally with their own certificate server (for example, Microsoft has the Certificate Services that are included with Windows 2000 Server, which can be used to generate your own certificates; iPlanet Certificate Management System provided by the Netscape/Sun Microsystems alliance also provides the capability to generate and manage our yown certificates).

You can find more about VeriSign at http://www.verisign.com/, and Thawte at http://www.thawte.com/.

Before continuing into the discussion of obtaining and installing certificates, let's briefly describe how CAs work, and how they are typically organized into certification hierarchies. In essence, CAs act as agents that can be trusted by the involved parties to issue public key certificates and can guarantee the accuracy of the information contained in the certificates that they issue. CAs typically organize the domains that they serve into hierarchical structures. You can think of this as analogous to the Internet domain names. For example, we have domains that end in .com and .org depending on the purpose of the organization; the country of the organization could determine the domain name, for example French domains end in .fr. Organizations that manage these domains can add more domains below the top level domains. For example, wrox.com was created by adding wrox to the .com domain. CAs have their own domains, and build hierarchical certificate domains similar to this. The top level certificate domain is commonly referred as the **root authority**. The root authority typically issues certificates to lower level domains that act as agents and issue certificates to other entities that may be end users or may be agents themselves. The advantage of this hierarchical system of trust is that it enables the system to scale easily and it also protects the higher-level trusts in such a way that if a lower-level trust is compromised, it can be more easily replaced without impacting the entire system than if we only had a single trust authority.

> *Note that SSL places a noticeable toll on the performance of Web Services. SSL is highly recommended for critical Web Services. However, for situations that require a lesser degree of security or where the network can be easily controlled (such as in an Intranet), the other authentication methods described later in this chapter may provide better performance.*

Obtaining and Installing an SSL Certificate

How exactly do we secure web sites and Web Services with SSL? The first step is to obtain a digital certificate for the web site where the endpoints of our Web Services will be hosted. As we said, we can do this by generating a digital certificate ourselves or by obtaining one from a third party. In this example, we will use VeriSign to obtain our digital certificate.

The entire process starts by generating a **Certificate Signing Request** (**CSR**) at your web server. The instructions for doing this are different depending on the type of web server. We will look at how to do this with IIS 5.0 and then we will submit the CSR to VeriSign (We are selecting IIS 5.0 here due to our sample Web Services application having its server-side implemented and hosted on IIS 5.0.) For other types of web servers, you can go to VeriSign and obtain specific configuration instructions (you can find this at the following address: http://www.verisign.com/support/csr/).

Open the Internet Services Manager, and right-click on the web site for which you would like to obtain a digital certificate (you need to right-click on the web site itself, probably called Default Web Site, and not on a sub-directory or virtual directory such as soap). Select Properties. Within the Properties window, select the Directory Security tab. Click on the Server Certificate button, under the Secure Communications section of the screen. This is shown in the screenshot opposite:

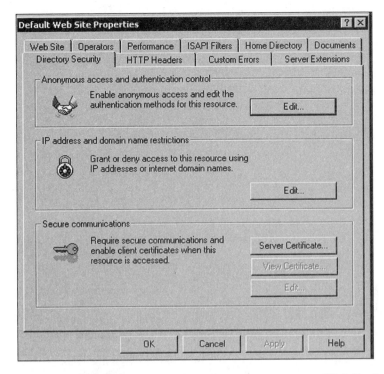

The Web Server Certificate Wizard will open up with a welcome screen. Click Next.

In the screen below, select the option to create a new certificate and click Next.

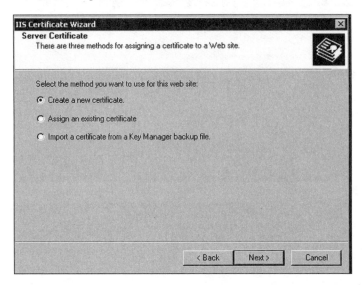

Within the following screen, you can select the option to prepare the request, but choose to send it later. This will generate a file that you can paste into your browser during the registration process with VeriSign. If you were to choose the second option, you would have to be connected to the Internet, and you would be able to skip some of the steps presented in this section.

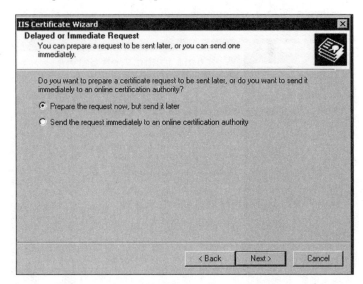

Within the Name and Security Settings screen, you can enter the name of the certificate and the bit length of the certificate. The name of the certificate can be anything, but it is recommended that you select something that is easy to remember. For bit length, you are not recommended to choose a larger value than 1024 for web sites due to the amount of processing overhead that it would create (sometimes you may not see anything larger than 1024 bit length due to US export restrictions). In addition, it is not recommended to use a bit length lower than 1024 (such as 512 due) to the limited security capability of short bit lengths.

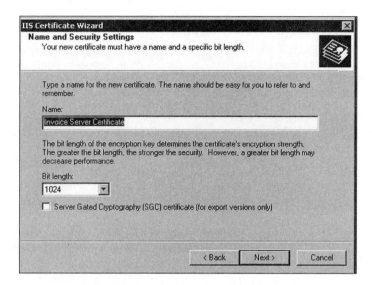

In the next screen, enter the Organization, such as your company name, and then the Organization Unit, such as the branch name or office name. Remember not to use any special characters, such as &, within your organization name, but to fully spell them out.

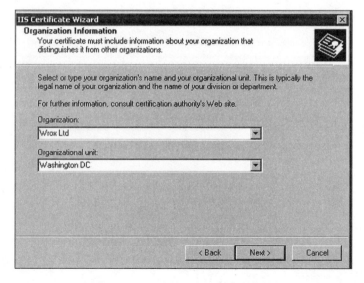

The following screen will ask you about the common name that you would like to associate with your certificate. It is important that you enter the proper common name here, because the only way to change it at a later date is to get a new certificate. The common name has to match the name of the server, as it will be accessed by users. It can be a valid DNS (Domain Name Server) name in the format of domain.com, such as www.wrox.com, or a computer name that may be appropriate for internal use, such as your computer name or its NetBIOS name. When using a computer name, you have to make sure that your web server resolves the computer name to the particular web site (so when you type http://computer_name into your browser you should get the target web site that is hosting your Web Services application).

Keep in mind that your certificate will only be valid for one domain name, the domain where the endpoint to the Web Service is located. So, if the previous domain name is used in our certificate (domain.com), attempting to use this certificate in the domain secure.domain.com will force the browser to report a warning message about this mismatch. Web Services clients will not work properly if the Common Name and the full domain name of the web site do not match (you will see how this works when we describe the code modifications to our Web Services clients, later in this chapter).

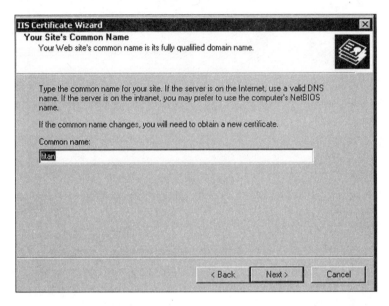

In the next screen, when entering the state, don't forget to avoid abbreviating and write out the complete name of the state.

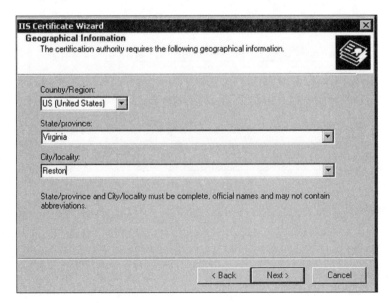

The final three screens (not shown here), will simply guide you through the process of saving the certificate file and they confirm the selections that you have made.

The Certificate Signing Request (CSR) will look like the text shown in the following picture. You should open the certificate file in Notepad – avoid using word processing programs, as some add control characters that when pasted into the sign up form may invalidate your CSR. During the next step, you will be required to copy the text from this file and paste it into an HTML form.

Next, you proceed with filling out a form with VeriSign about yourself and your company. During the enrollment process you will be asked to provide your Certificate Signing Request (CSR) that was generated by your web server (through the process that we had just described). Once you complete the enrolment process, you will be notified that your certificate will arrive in your e-mail box. You should receive your confirmation e-mail within two hours, according to VeriSign. The actual certificate may take up to 5 working days to be issued and delivered to your e-mail account. However, in our experience this often is done much faster, even in a matter of hours.

You can decide to use a free 14-day trial certificate from VeriSign for testing purposes. Follow the same steps to obtain this certificate as with regular certificates. The only difference is that you will not have to provide your credit card information, and you will have to install a certificate to your root certificate store on the computer where you are opening the browser to connect to the secured web site or where the Web Services client service is located. Instructions on how to install the new root to your browser will come with your certificate from VeriSign. To obtain a free test certificate from VeriSign, you can go to http://www.verisign.com and look for a link for a free trial SSL ID.

VeriSign offers a few different production certificates that would enable SSL on your server (for example you have Commerce Site Services, Secure Site Services, etc.) Any of them would work fine for our purpose in this chapter. You may want to read the guides provided by VeriSign before you make a decision as to which one would be best for your particular situation.

Note that SSL servers and clients use S/MIME (Secure MIME or Multipurpose Internet Mail Extensions). We will describe S/MIME in more details in one of our next sections.

Once you get the certificate via the e-mail message from VeriSign, you should save it into a simple text file (or you could name it with the .cer extension). Then, you should go back to your web site in Internet Services Manager that you are trying to enable with SSL, right-click on it, and select Properties. That would bring you the familiar Properties screen, where you should select the Directory Security tab, as shown in the following picture.

Since you have a pending certificate request, when you click the Server Certificate button this time, you will get a slightly different screen. Select to process a pending request and install the certificate.

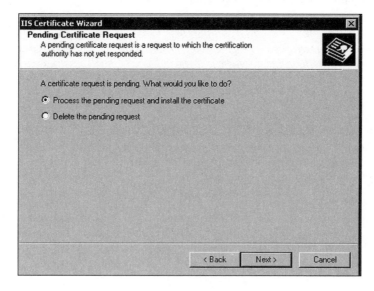

You will be allowed to point to the certificate file, which will install it on your web server.

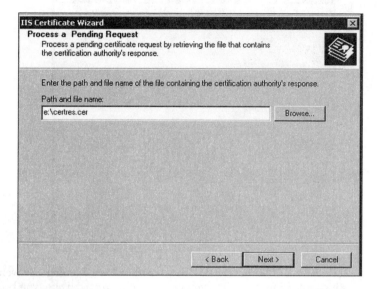

Enabling SSL on Your Web Server

In order to use SSL with your Web Service after you installed the server side certificate, you should enable SSL by implementing the settings as shown on the following screen, which you get to in default Web Site Properties | Secure Communication section | Edit button. Make sure that you check the Require Secure Channel (SSL) checkbox.

> *Optionally, you can check the box stating Require 128-bit Encryption, if you know that all of your client services calling your XML Web Service will have 128-bit support (most new browser versions have this support for example and you may have to check if the support exist in your Web Services toolkit or SOAP Toolkit that is being used on the client-side of the Web Service). 128-bit certificates are more secure than 48-bit or 56-bit ones, so it is recommended that you use them whenever possible.*

You can click OK, confirming that you are requiring a secure channel (or SSL) for the access to the particular resource. You may get a screen asking you if want to overwrite any settings set on the directories below the one that you are currently configuring. This would only happen if you had previously modified certain settings in the directories or files below the current level.

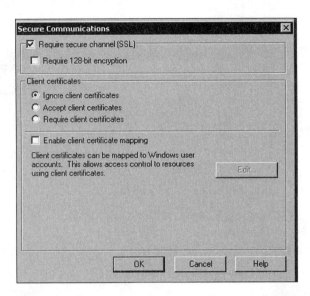

To verify the proper installation of the server side SSL certificate, try opening any web page from the protected web site within your browser. When you connect to a protected site, you browser will show an icon depicting a key that is not broken (Netscape Navigator) or a locked padlock (Internet Explorer/Opera). Depending on your browser settings, you may be prompted with a warning message box telling you that you are entering a secure site.

Another point to remember in terms of proper Web Service configuration under SSL is that the **WSDL file** should still remain accessible at anonymous levels (some Web Services toolkits allow you to keep your WSDL file password protected, but you have to check with the particular toolkit to see if this works correctly). However, you need to modify the `<soap:address>` element and its `location` attribute to point to the secure version of the web site, with the `https` prefix. In our case this is `https://titan/soap/InvoiceSubmit.ASP` instead of the previous one that references `localhost` and uses `http`. Here's the section of the WSDL that changed due to having introduced SSL. You have to implement the same type of change for the `<soap:operation>` element and its `soapAction` attribute. However, the namespace references do not have to be modified to `https` or to the domain name found on the certificate.

> *For more information on WSDL files or Web Services Description Language in general, please see Chapter 4 on WSDL. This chapter is also useful with regard to using WSDL files with different Web Services Toolkits. Otherwise, the WSDL file used in our example is part of the earlier described pre-built Web Services application to which we are applying security in this chapter.*

```
. . .
<binding name="InvoiceSubmitSoapBinding" type="wsdlns:InvoiceSubmitSoapPort">
    <stk:binding preferredEncoding="UTF-8"/>
    <soap:binding style="rpc" transport="http://schemas.xmlsoap.org/soap/http"/>
    <operation name="InvoiceAdd">
        <soap:operation soapAction="https://titan/soap/InvoiceSubmit.ASP"/>
        <input>
            <soap:body use="encoded"
                namespace="http://localhost/soap/InvoiceSubmit.xsd"
                encodingStyle="http://schemas.xmlsoap.org/soap/encoding/"/>
```

```
                </input>
                <output>
                    <soap:body use="encoded"
                        namespace="http://localhost/soap/InvoiceSubmit.xsd"
                        encodingStyle="http://schemas.xmlsoap.org/soap/encoding/"/>
                </output>
            </operation>
        </binding>
        <service name="InvoiceSubmit">
            <port name="InvoiceSubmitSoapPort" binding="wsdlns:InvoiceSubmitSoapBinding">
                <soap:address location="https://titan/soap/InvoiceSubmit.ASP"/>
            </port>
        </service>
        . . .
```

Every time you modify the WSDL file, make sure that you restart IIS (right-click on the web server name within the **Internet Information Manger** and select **Restart IIS**) or unload the web application hosting the Web Service (right-click on your web site, select **Properties**, then the **Home Directory** tab, then click on the **Unload** button). The WSDL file is cached, so the old version should be removed from the cache to make sure that the new file with the new settings will be loaded.

Visual Basic Client Code Modifications

The modifications to the Visual Basic client in order to enable it to support basic authentication over SSL, are small. We have to make sure that we reference our WSDL properly at this time. The correct reference to the WSDL file includes `https` in the address. Also, the name of the service should match the name stated on the server certificate. If it does not, the service will not be able to respond properly to the security notice given. This means that if your certificate was issued to `secure.wrox.com`, then the path to your WSDL file should state `https://secure.wrox.com/soap/myDesc.wsdl`.

```
. . .
'Visual Basic code sample
'For SSL change the WSDL reference to the following:
txtWSDLFile.Text = "https://titan/soap/InvoiceSubmit.wsdl"
. . .
soapClient.ConnectorProperty("UseSSL") = True
. . .
```

In our case, the WSDL reference is to `https://titan/soap/InvoiceSubmit.wsdl`. The additional item that we set is the `UseSSL` property of the `SoapClient` object, and we set it to `True`. Since we specified `https` within our WSDL file, setting the `UseSSL` property is optional (please check the SOAP documentation for more information on the usage of this property).

The client code for ASP and WSH works in a very similar way to the Visual Basic client code.

Java Client Code Modifications

There are a few more steps in getting Java to work with SSL on the client side than with our Visual Basic client. This is partly due to the design decision of our Web Service client to build the Java client without the use of WSDL.

First, save the certificate that you received from VeriSign and installed on your web server as a file in the X.509 format, which is one of the most popular certificate formats. Then, use this file to import your certificate into your Java certificate database. You need to export the certificate and then import it into your Java certificate database only if it is not already trusted. This is always the case for test certificates provided by VeriSign, but it may not be necessary for production certificates, in which case you will be able to skip this import/export process and proceed directly to the Java code modifications later in this section.

You can export the certificate that you have in the following way (these are instructions for IIS 5.0, as that is where the Web Services server-side portion of our application is located). Open the Internet Services Manager, and expand the various servers and web sites, until you find the web site where your Web Services application directory is located. View the Properties of this directory, by right-clicking on the Web Services application virtual directory (in our example this is called soap). Within this window, select the Directory Security tab, as shown in the next image:

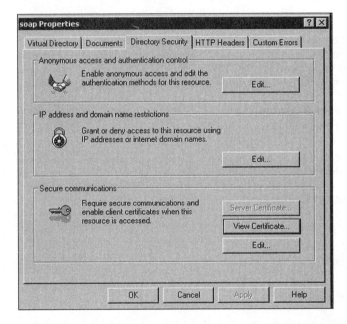

Within this screen, select View Certificate and then click on the Details tab. This is shown in the next screenshot:

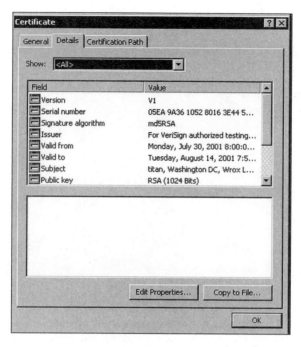

In this screen, you will see the Copy to File button. This will start the Certificate Export Wizard that will help you to export your certificate. The first screen is just an introduction to the wizard screen, so select Next. Next, you will get a screen that asks if you want to export the private key or just the public key. We want to only export the public key, so select the option to not export the private key.

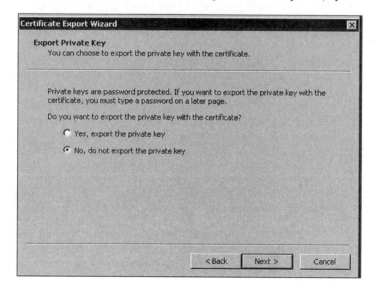

In the screen that follows choose X.509 Base64 encoded file.

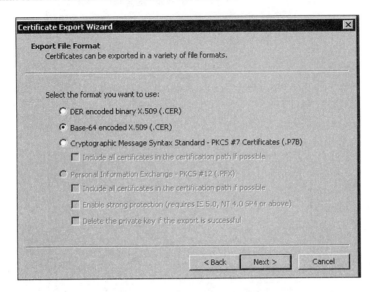

The next two screens will simply ask you for the name of the file and they will confirm the selections that you made. Then, execute the following command that will import the web server certificate into your Java certificate database, allowing our Java client to recognize and trust to use this certificate:

> keytool -import -file E:\cert.cer -keystore E:\jdk1.3\jre\lib\security\cacerts

Don't forget to change the path from E:\cert.cer to your certificate file and the path to your certificate database cacerts. When you run this command, it will likely ask for a password, for which you can use changeit as the standard password for preinstalled certificates with Java certificate stores.

Next, you will have to make sure that you have the following files referenced in your CLASSPATH: jsse.jar, jcert.jar, and jnet.jar, all part of the **JSSE** or **Java Secure Socket Extension** (version 1.0.2 is used in our example). The JSSE will be included with the version of J2SDK v.1.4, but if you have a previous version of Java, then you should download JSSE from the Sun Microsystems web site at http://www.java.sun.com/products/jsse/.

In terms of the modification to the Java client code, you have to add the following references in order to support SSL and HTTPS:

```
//Java code
//Additions for SSL and HTTPS
import java.security.Security;
import java.security.KeyStore;
import javax.security.cert.X509Certificate;
import javax.net.ssl.SSLSocketFactory;
import javax.net.ssl.*;
import com.sun.net.ssl.*;
. . .
```

This code adds support for HTTPS and SSL:

```
   . . .
   //Java code (cont.)
   //Start optional proxy server code
   String strProxyHost = null;
   String strUserName = new String ("wroxuser");
   String strPassword = new String ("password");
   int intProxyPort = -1;
   SOAPHTTPConnection oHTTPConn = new SOAPHTTPConnection();
   if (strProxyHost != null) {
       oHTTPConn.setProxyHost(strProxyHost);
       oHTTPConn.setProxyPort(intProxyPort);
       }
   oHTTPConn.setUserName(strUserName);
   oHTTPConn.setPassword(strPassword);

   //Specify the location of your certificate store
   System.setProperty("javax.net.ssl.trustStore",
       "E:\\jdk1.3\\jre\\lib\\security\\cacerts");

   //HTTPS protocol support
   System.setProperty("java.protocol.handler.pkgs",
       "com.sun.net.ssl.internal.www.protocol");

   //SSL provider support
   java.security.Security.addProvider(new com.sun.net.ssl.internal.ssl.Provider());
   . . .
```

As you can see from the code above, in addition to the code modifications that we added earlier for basic authentication support, we add a few more lines for HTTPS and SSL support. First, we specify the location of our Java certificate store. Make sure that you modify this path to match the path that you have locally on your machine. Then, we specify support for the HTTPS protocol and for the SSL provider.

Finally, we are able to specify the end-point properly, so that it uses `https` and the full domain name of our Web Service:

```
   . . .
   //Java code (cont.)
   //Set the end point, service URL
   String strServiceURL = new String ("https://titan/soap/InvoiceSubmit.ASP");
   URL oURL = new URL(strServiceURL);
   . . .
```

In our case this is: `https://titan/soap/InvoiceSubmit.ASP`. Make sure that you change this to the correct address on your server.

PERL Code Modifications

The code modification to our PERL client is not very different from the modifications we made to it when we enabled it to support basic authentication. The basic authentication setting remains unmodified. However, we need to change our WSDL file and service end-point URLs to include HTTPS instead of HTTP.

```
. . .
# PERL code
. . .
$strWSDL = "https://titan/soap/InvoiceSubmit.wsdl";
$strEndPoint = "https://titan/soap/InvoiceSubmit.ASP";
. . .
# Override the get_basic_credentials function with proper username and password
sub SOAP::Transport::HTTP::Client::get_basic_credentials {
    return 'wroxuser' => 'password';
}
```

As a reminder, if you would like to run your PERL examples within your browser, you may have to configure your web server after you install ActivePerl. For information on this topic, follow the references provided earlier about our pre-built Web Services application, and also check the ActivePerl help files and its FAQ section. Also, you may also like to visit the SOAP::Lite web site for a wealth of information on implementing Web Services with PERL and SOAP, at http://www.soaplite.com/.

We have now covered basic authentication. Next, we'll review another popular type of authentication found in many web applications.

Client Certificates

In addition to using server-side certificates with SSL, client certificates (such as the X.509 type, which is the most widely used specification for using digital certificates) could be used.

Using client-side certificates allows the client to be authenticated to the server in addition to the server being authenticated to the client. In other words, when a client comes to a web site (or in our case when a client requests a service from a Web Service) then using a server-side certificate certifies to the client that the server is truly the one that it claims to be. In addition, this allows us to exchange information under an encrypted channel, such as SSL. However, the server may need a way of knowing for sure that the client is truly the one that it claims to be (providing a username and password may not be considered sufficient in a highly secure scenario). Client certificates allow clients to authenticate to the server above and beyond simply providing a proper username and password – in the case of client certificates we have a third party like a CA (Certificate Authority) guaranteeing the identity of the client. Client certificates are appropriate in highly secure scenarios where it is critical that we are absolutely sure that the client is what it claims to be. In most situations, however, having the client provide a username and password (such as when we have basic authentication) over a secure line (like SSL) is sufficient. An additional benefit of using client certificates, which are part of the Public Key Infrastructure (PKI), is that they offer a way for others to send encrypted messages to the client that only the client can read. This is useful when we have asynchronous communications (for example, you can think of e-mail via SMTP or asynchronous Web Services where the messages are sent not via HTTP, but via SMTP).

Now, a few words about the X.509 specification: this is not a standard yet, so vendor implementations exist that are not compatible with each other. This means that certificates generated on Netscape servers are not fully compatible with certificates generated on Microsoft servers. Also, certificates intended for Microsoft's IE browsers will not work properly in the Netscape browser or in Lotus Notes. This is one of the reasons why client certificates are not widely used. On the other hand, browsers can accept server side certificates from any vendor web server.

You can find more information about public certificates and X.509 by visiting the Internet Engineering Task Force (IETF) at http://www.ietf.org/rfc/rfc2459.txt

We will not look in-depth at using and installing client side certificates with Web Services in this chapter because they are not widely used at this time. However, we will provide some general help and direction on this topic, in case you wish to further explore this option.

When using client-side certificates, you still have to install server-side certificates as described in the previous section. You can obtain client side certificates from CAs such as VeriSign or Thawte. Thawte offers free personal or client side certificates, and you can obtain as many as you want (one for each browser, one for each e-mail address that you have, etc.) If you go to the Thawte site, simply follow the instructions that they have for obtaining a Personal E-mail Certificate.

If you choose to use the Thawte free client-side certificate offer, you can obtain the personal certificate by going to the following page for a step-by-step guide to the enrollment:

https://www.thawte.com/getinfo/products/personal/join.html.

Enrollment takes the form of first getting a username and password for Thawte. You need to link your user profile to your driver license number, passport number, social security number, or other important information about yourself (this is the case within the US; it may be slightly different for other countries, you are still required to link your account to personal information). After you enroll, you will be able to obtain as many personal certificates as you need.

On the server side, you have to enable the request for client-side certificates on the server. In the case of IIS, in the Internet Information Services Manager select the web site or virtual directory to which you would like your web servers to request client-side certificates. Right-click on this and select **Properties**, go to the **Directory Security** tab, and click on the **Edit** button within the **Secure Communications** section of the window. At this time you will get the following screen:

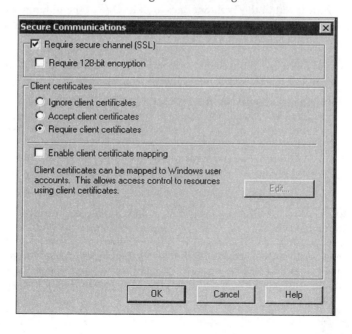

Within this Secure Communications screen, select Require client certificates. Some web servers allow you to actually map client-side certificates to user accounts, which is a useful feature (this maps a particular client certificate to a user account). The final step of the process is to modify your client-side Web Services code to enable the support for client-side certificates. As we said earlier, we will not go into the details of how to do this with various client technology implementations.

> *For more on implementing client certificates in your Web Services application with your Web Services toolkit please check the toolkit documentation.*

There are not many problems with client-side certificates. One that we mentioned is the way that X.509 is implemented by various vendors, creating the need to obtain different client-side certificates for each browser or e-mail client that you have. Another is that they need to be installed on the client machine itself, and they are quite difficult to move around from one machine to another. Smart cards are positioned to alleviate this problem, but their use is not very widespread, at least at this time (smart cards are plastic cards, just like credit cards, with a computer chip inside that can be used to store digital certificates, and used for easy authentication). Until the time when smart card readers (similar to credit card readers you see in stores that accept smart cards) become as common to computers and other devices as CD ROM drives, client-side certificates will struggle to come into use at a much wider level.

Other Authentication Options

There are some other types of authentication that are either less widely used than the ones presented or that are proprietary to a particular vendor:

❑ **Digest Authentication** is similar to basic authentication, but it is not as widely used. However, Microsoft's web server, IIS 5.0, the later versions of W3C Jigsaw open-source server, and the Apache web server do support it. In order to use digest authentication, both the server and the client need to support it. The server side of our Web Service would need to support this type of authentication within the web server, and the client side of our Web service would have to have support for it within the Web Services toolkit. One of the differences between digest authentication and basic authentication is that in digest authentication passwords are transmitted in an encrypted form.

In order to find out more about digest authentication and if it is implemented in your web server, please see your web server documentation.

❑ **Windows Integrated Authentication/NT Challenge Response (NTLM)** are methods proprietary to Microsoft and its web servers and Internet Explorer browsers. In these authentications the password is not sent across the wire at all. Instead, a hash value of the password is sent.

For more on using this type of authentication, please see the IIS documentation, as well as the MS SOAP Toolkit 2.0 documentation or the documentation that of Microsoft's Web Services platform, .NET.

Because these methods of authentication are not as widely used or are proprietary, they are less than ideal choices for implementing the authentication aspect of security in Web Services. If you have an Intranet environment where you can control the types of clients that will be connecting to your Web Service, then some of these authentication methods may be a good choice for your situation. However, for Web Services that will be exposed on the Internet and that will serve a wider selection of users, these authentication methods are not the best ones to use. Therefore, we will not review them in any further detail.

SMTP

SMTP or **Simple Mail Transfer Protocol** is the most popular asynchronous protocol on the Internet today. The majority of today's e-mail works on top of SMTP, and e-mail is one of the most critical features of the Internet today. We might ask the question: why even consider SMTP, when we can use HTTP for Web Services? When we look at various systems and their requirements, HTTP can handle most of those requirements. However, sometimes there are situations when the request/response nature of HTTP is not the most appropriate choice. In the sample application that we described earlier in this chapter, we mentioned that our Invoice Server would be sending SOAP messages to the Fulfillment Server via SMTP. This is an appropriate choice for situations when we have a slow connection between servers, or a server that processes requests asynchronously and cannot get back to us immediately. Sometimes even the business process itself may require human intervention or delayed response, in which case using SMTP's message forwarding nature may be more appropriate.

> *To learn about more SMTP, see its specification at the Internet Engineering Task Force (IETF) at* http://www.ietf.org/rfc/rfc0821.txt

How does SMTP fare in terms of security features? It really does not have much security built in. It is relatively easy to fake e-mail messages and make them appear that they are coming from somebody else. One way around the security challenges with SMTP is to use S/MIME. Another potentially better way is to apply some of the application level security options provided later in this chapter.

S/MIME

S/MIME or **Secured/Multipurpose Internet Mail Extensions** is a specification for encoding any content, including non-**ASCII** (**American Standard Code for Information Exchange**) content, into ASCII character representation. ASCII is a coding system for representing English characters as numbers (we specify English characters here, because most international characters and characters from other languages cannot be represented in ASCII). S/MIME is an open standard.

> *If you are interested in more information for S/MIME, you may want to see the S/MIME message specification at* http://www.ietf.org/rfc/rfc2633.txt *and the S/MIME certificate handling specification at* http://www.ietf.org/rfc/rfc2632.txt.

S/MIME provides message privacy and integrity by encrypting the content of the message and using a secure hashing function. Furthermore, S/MIME allows for authentication with digital signatures. When an e-mail message is sent with S/MIME, the content is digitally signed and encrypted. The message is signed with the sender's private key. The sender's public key is the only one that can verify this, thus validating that our message is coming from the particular sender. The message can be encrypted with the recipient's public key, making it unreadable to all but the recipient who has the private key corresponding to the public key used in the encryption. The public keys used with S/MIME are wrapped in digital certificates (as is the case with most public keys used within the Public Key Infrastructure or PKI – this includes the keys used for establishing SSL connections), in order to certify that the public keys are truly the ones that we think we have. The process of obtaining these digital certificates is as described in the earlier section on client certificates.

Depending on your particular situation, S/MIME may or may not be suitable when using SMTP. Because S/MIME uses client-side digital certificates, it suffers from the problems peculiar to those certificates, such as having to be installed on the client machine. An even more serious issue with client-side certificates and their use in Web Services is that they cannot have **transitive trusts**. In other words, we cannot easily delegate trust to another agent such as a server to act on our behalf. Other application-based technologies, such as ticket-based security schemas, which we will describe in the next section, do allow transitive trusts.

597

We will now provide some general guidelines for implementing S/MIME in SMTP-based Web Services. Rather than covering this in detail, we will look at ticket-based and other application-based security approaches that address security regardless of the transport protocol used later in the chapter.

There are no server configuration modifications that need to be made in order to support S/MIME. Modifications are only made on the client side of the Web Service that connects to the SMTP server to send the e-mail messages with SOAP content in them, and on the server side of the Web Service that connects to the POP3 (Post Office Protocol 3) server to retrieve the messages.

> *Fore more information on POP3, please see its specification at*
> *http://www.ietf.org/rfc/rfc1939.txt, and its updates at http://www.ietf.org/rfc/rfc1957.txt*
> *and http://www.ietf.org/rfc/rfc2449.txt.*

In our application example, in the case of SMTP, we used Microsoft's **CDONTS (Collaboration Data Objects for NT Services)** to send out e-mail with SOAP messages. CDONTS does not have support for S/MIME, so we have to relay to another component to do this. Whenever selecting components for Web Services, keep in mind that we are always looking for components that have been developed and tested for use with the heavier loads of a server, and not for components intended for use in client applications. Good third-party components for sending S/MIME within the environment of IIS would be AspEncrypt and AspE-mail offered by Persits Software (http://persits.com/). Similarly, on the Java side, you would need a mail library that supports reading S/MIME e-mail messages. There are third party extension libraries for Sun's JavaMail that provide S/MIME functionality. Examples include the Java Crypto and Security Implementation (http://security.dstc.edu.au/projects/java/release2.html), the Phaos S/MIME Toolkit (at http://www.phaos.com), and the ISNetworks S/MIME Provider for Java (at http://www.isnetworks.com/smime/). Using some of these third party software modules, you can easily add S/MIME support to the SMTP implementation provided with our sample Web Services application.

Application Level Security

Setting security at the transport level frequently involves dealing with various configurations within the particular transport protocol such as HTTP or SMTP. Security at this level does not impact the SOAP message at all, but it requires configuration of the server and client software, as well as modification of the client software so that it can, for example, make the appropriate authentication calls.

When applying security at the application level, we modify the SOAP message itself. A message modified in this way can be sent via any protocol, and special configuration changes do not have to be made to the server or client-side system software. However, the particular implementation of application level security needs to be supported by both the client and the server that are exchanging Web Services messages.

In this section, we'll take a look at handling security at the application level, and how to submit authentication credentials within SOAP messages. We'll also consider how we can combine some of the transport level approaches like SSL with some of the application level approaches in order to address security more completely. Finally, we'll see how Kerberos and its ticket-based exchanges can be applied to handling security, as well as how some of the new XML security specifications can enhance security at the application level of Web Services.

Credentials in SOAP Messages

For the purposes of authentication, we can submit our username and password credentials within the message of the request that we are sending to the Web Service. In this way, the Web Service can authenticate us every time we make a request. This approach is very easy to implement, and even though it increases the transmission load a little it is quite efficient. In its most basic format, all we would have to do is add two more parameters in every Web Service operation that we have, one being the username and the other being the password.

Here's an example of this approach. Consider the VB Web Service client code shown below:

```
. . .
  'VB Code
txtResult.Text = CStr(SoapClient.InvoiceAdd("wroxuser", "password", _
    txtInvoiceID, txtCustomerID, CDate(txtInvoiceDate), txtNotes, _
    txtDeliveryAddress, txtPaymentTerms, txtPaymentReceived))
. . .
```

As you can see, we are including the username and password credentials as the first two parameters. Once our Web Service receives this input, it queries the appropriate data source where the list of users is stored and authenticates the user. The data store could be a directory/LDAP, database, or even a file. The Web Service checks the requester's credentials with the data store in order to determine if the particular user is authorized to perform the operation requested.

Instead of submitting credentials with each request, we could have an operation within our Web Service that deals only with authentication. Once a user is authenticated, this operation could return a session key that we would submit with each one of our subsequent Web Service requests. Here's some sample code that illustrates this slightly modified approach:

```
. . .
'VB Code
txtSessionKey.Text = CStr(SoapClient.Auth("wroxuser", "password"))

txtResult.Text = CStr(SoapClient.InvoiceAdd(txtSessionKey.Text, _
    txtInvoiceID, txtCustomerID, CDate(txtInvoiceDate), txtNotes, _
    txtDeliveryAddress, txtPaymentTerms, txtPaymentReceived))
. . .
```

The example shown above places the credentials within the body of the SOAP message. Optionally, you could place the credentials within the header section of the SOAP message. However, this is more difficult to access in the current versions of most Web Services toolkits. Some of the XML security related specifications and their adoptions by the XML Protocol may change this in the near future.

We will not provide any further examples in other programming languages, as it is quite simple to modify any of the code to implement this approach.

The message containing the authentication credentials can be submitting via any protocol, and will work fine, as long as the Web Service expects the credentials submitted with the request. However, we are sending our credentials in plain text. One way to address this is by applying some of the methods that we have already learned in this chapter, for example adding SSL to the mix in cases where HTTP is the transport protocol. You can simply follow the instructions that we had provided earlier for you about how to enable SSL for a Web Service, and apply them to a service that stores its credentials within the SOAP body.

An interesting way of implementing SSL would be to create an **authentication Web Service** that is protected with SSL. After authentication, it provides the user with a unique session key with an expiration date. Then, you could use this session key to call Web Services over regular HTTP instead of HTTPS. Depending on the level of security that your application requires, this approach may prove to be faster than the approach of encrypting all of the messages sent between the client and the Web Service. Don't be surprised to see the current early generation of Web Services using this approach.

Kerberos and Ticket-Based Authentication

Kerberos and **ticket-based authentication** are important concepts used in some implementations of Web Services. Microsoft's **Passport** (single sign-on system) and the user-centric collection of Web Services codenamed **HailStorm** use Kerberos and ticket-based authentication in the implementation of its security (for more information on HailStorm, please see Chapter 1).

Ticket-based authentication occurs at the application level. This means that it can be used with any transport protocol. In general, ticket-based authentication uses digital signatures, digital certificates, and shared-key or public key encryption technologies (all covered earlier in this chapter). Within the application, we would include code to do the authentication, perform the encryption of the content, and digitally sign or validate the digital signature of the messages being sent and received. So, it often involves more work to perform ticket-based authentication (at least for the Web Services toolkit releases available at the time of writing), but it provides more flexibility. Although the support for ticket-based encryption is limited at the time of writing, we are confident that this will increase with some of the newer versions of Web Services toolkits and Web Services implementation frameworks.

Kerberos is often used in ticket-based authentication, so we'll review it in further detail.

Kerberos

Kerberos was developed at MIT (Massachusetts Institute of Technology), primarily as an authentication service. It is based on the principal that only a limited number of machines can ever be very secure, thus Kerberos treats the entire network as insecure (except for one machine, and we'll describe that in a moment). Kerberos allows for **mutual authentication** where users and/or services can authenticate each other, which is not very typical of other authentication techniques. Furthermore, other authentication schemas do not allow for **easy delegation**, the ability of a process to delegate a user or service identity to another process. Kerberos uses symmetric key encryption, so the keys to encrypt the message and to decrypt the message are the same (or easily derivable from one another – we covered symmetric and asymmetric key encryption algorithms at the beginning of this chapter).

The following sequence diagram provides us with more details as to how Kerberos works. We have a user service that requests contact with a resource service (such as a Web Service). The other two actors are the **Authentication Server** (**AS**) and the **Ticket Granting Service** (**TGS**), collectively called the **KDC** or the **Key Distribution Center**. The AS and TGS can be on the same computer running as separate services, or they can run on separate computers.

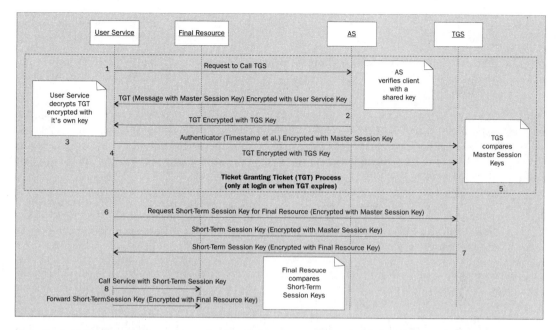

Note that all the keys in the process depicted above are private (and therefore secret) keys, in other words they are not public keys. The authentication with Kerberos happens in the following way (the numbers in the diagram correspond to the steps below):

1. Before accessing any service, the user service requests a ticket to contact the Ticket Granting Server (TGS), as if it were any other service. This request is sent to the Authentication Service (AS).

2. The AS creates a master session key and makes two copies of it. It places one copy in a message (along with other elements, such as data stamps) and encrypts it with the key belonging to the user service. This message is the **Ticket Granting Ticket (TGT)**. The AS places the second copy of the session key into another message that is encrypted with a key belonging to the TGS. It sends both of these copies to the user service. The AS stores data about the clients and servers in its realm, which is how it has access to the various private keys.

3. The user service receives the two messages from the AS. The user service can open the message encrypted with its own key. However, the user service cannot open the message intended for the TGS because it was locked with the TGS key.

4. The user service creates a new message and places a timestamp, possibly with a few optional items, such as an additional session key. This message is sometimes called the **authenticator**. Then, it encrypts the message with the master session key. It sends the message originally provided by the AS and encrypted with the TGS secret key along with the new authenticator message with the timestamp to the TGS.

5. The TGS receives the two messages and it opens the message containing the master session key (remember the AS encrypted this message with the TGS secret key, so only the TGS can open this message). The TGS uses the master session key to open the other message sent to it by the user service, where it finds the timestamp and other information. This proves to the TGS the identity of the user service. Now, the user service and the ticket granting service can communicate with each other using the master session key.

601

6. The user service requests a short-term ticket from the TGS. The user service has to obtain a short-term ticket from the TGS for contacting any resource on the network.

7. The TGS replies back with a short-term session key for accessing the destination resource service. This short-term key is encrypted with the master session key found in the TGT, not with the user service secret key. The TGS also sends the client a copy of the short-term session key encrypted with the key of the final resource. The short-term session key is valid for a very short time, sometimes only for one request. The TGT itself is valid for a relatively short period of time, as well, typically eight hours. So, if stolen, the TGT can be replaced easily and it expires in a relatively short period of time. In contrast, passwords, which are the base for the user service secret key, are changed much less frequently, and if stolen can be much more damaging to overall security of the systems.

8. Now the user service can contact the destination resource using the short-term session key, and also sends it the ticket encrypted with the key of the resource. The final resource decrypts this ticket to obtain the short-term key, which it then uses to decrypt the request from the user service.

If you consider that the TGT and the other tickets or encrypted messages sent by the servers can be exchanged via special blocks of XML that are Base64 encoded and placed within certain XML tags, you can see that these tickets can be exchanged across the Web for authentication by Web Services. It does not matter what kind of operating system, language environment, or object model the client services have. All they have to be able to do is to exchange well-structured XML and support the encryption standards utilized. This gives us the advantage of highly scalable and secure authentication systems that support delegation, encryption, and signatures, and are designed to work on networks that are inherently insecure.

> *For more information on Kerberos you can go to MIT at http://web.mit.edu/kerberos/www/.*
> *You may also fine useful information in the Kerberos specification at*
> *http://www.ietf.org/rfc/rfc1510.txt.*

Ticket-based authentication and Kerberos are among some of the more advanced and secure methods for implementing application level security for Web Services. At the time of writing, there is little support for ticket-based authentication and Kerberos within current Web Services toolkits and frameworks, although this is likely to change (Kerberos support within operating systems, such as Windows 2000, and other applications has existed for some time, but this is not the same as Kerberos support at the level of Web Services). Another difficult issue is that there are no specific guidelines for how ticket-based authentication and Kerberos should be implemented in XML or in SOAP messages. For example, should the signature be stored in the header, under what element, etc. This should be partly addressed by some of the XML-related security specifications.

XML Security Related Specifications

There are a few security related specifications that are being developed at the W3C by various member companies that are intended to address a number of the security needs of Web Services, particularly in providing a standard way of applying security to XML documents, and by extension to SOAP messages. Addressing security in a standard way would enable implementations that are independent of the transport protocol chosen, and which would work across intermediaries, including SOAP intermediaries. The work of the XML Protocol Working Group addresses some of the ways that these XML security related techniques can extend the SOAP message in a standard way. A number of these extensions are likely to be deployed through the addition of standard `Header` entries within the SOAP message. We will show some examples of this approach later in the chapter.

It's important to keep in mind that XML security-related extensions do not tie you down to specific security implementations. They only provide a standard way of handling various aspects of security within XML and Web Services. As the work on these specifications nears completion, we are likely to see support in for them in the various Web Services implementations that are offered by vendors.

This section is forward-looking, covering technologies and specifications that are in the process of development at the time of writing this book. These are exciting technologies and we will try to briefly describe them for you along with some simple code examples. However, if you are interested in learning more about these technologies and specifications, you should follow the references and links provided throughout this section.

We'll start by looking at some of the work on XML Digital Signatures and XML Encryption.

XML Signature

XML Signature is at the status of Candidate Recommendation (a call to the industry to implement the specification so far and give feedback) at the time of writing this book, and it should become an actual Recommendation very soon. The XML Signature Specification provides syntax and processing rules for creating and representing digital signatures. In general, digital signatures can be applied to any digital content, including XML data itself. Architecturally, digital signatures can envelop the content itself, or they can be detached from the actual content and simply reference it.

XML Signature specifies methods of associating keys with referenced data. However, it does not specify how keys are associated with persons or organizations. This means that this specification is an important component of secure XML applications, but is not sufficient to specify security/trust concerns (as digital certificates do for example) and other security aspects.

XML Signatures are used in the following way: data objects being signed are digested (a hash value is calculated from them); the resulting value is placed in an XML element with some additional information, then that element is digested in turn, and cryptographically signed. The specification defines a set of algorithms, their URIs, and the requirements for their implementation. These algorithms include SHA1 for hash generation, Base64 for encoding binary data, DSA with SHA1 (DSS) for signatures, and Canonical XML for canonization. We defined SHA and DSA earlier in this chapter. We will talk more about Canonical XML in the following section on XML *Digital Signatures extensions for SOAP*, where we will also look over an example of XML Signature.

You can find the most current XML Signatures specification at http://www.w3.org/TR/xmldsig-core/ and you can find out more about the workings of the XML Digital Signatures Working Group at http://www.w3.org/Signature/

XML Encryption

XML Encryption is a specification that is a W3C Working Draft, meaning that it is not a Recommendation, or even stable as of yet. This specification is intended to describe how to use XML to represent digitally encrypted Web resources (including XML itself). The XML Encryption specification is intended to be used together with the XML Digital Signatures specification, so that we can sign and encrypt content at the same time. Support for various encryption algorithms present the possibility of easily extending the specification to other or new algorithms.

Here's a very brief example of using XML Encryption, taken from the XML Encryption Syntax and Processing Working Draft (link provided in the resources overleaf):

```
<EncryptedData xmlns='http://www.w3.org/2001/04/xmlenc#'
    Type='http://www.w3.org/2001/04/xmlenc#Element'/>
    <EncryptionMethod Algorithm='http://www.w3.org/2001/04/xmlenc#3des-cbc '/>
    <ds:KeyInfo xmlns:ds='http://www.w3.org/2000/09/xmldsig#'>
        <ds:KeyName>John Smith</ds:KeyName>
    </ds:KeyInfo>
    <CipherData>
        <CipherValue>DEADBEEF</CipherValue>
    </CipherData>
</EncryptedData>
```

The data that is encrypted is enclosed within the `<EncryptedData>` tag, with the actual encrypted value being stored within the `<CipherValue>` tag. The encryption method is stated by specifying the particular algorithm used (for a list of algorithms, please see the specification – a link is provided below). With this example we want to give an overall feel for what XML Encryption is all about. For more detailed description of the syntax and the definition of the various elements, attributes, and other syntax rules, please follow the resources below.

> *For the workings of the XML Encryption Working Group at the W3C, please see http://www.w3.org/Encryption/2001/. The XML Encryption requirements can be found at http://www.w3.org/TR/xml-encryption-req, and the syntax and processing part can be found at http://www.w3.org/TR/xmlenc-core/. For the list of encryption algorithms specified by the XML Encryption specification you can see http://www.w3.org/TR/xmlenc-core/#sec-Algorithms (keep in mind that this list is extensible). IBM, Microsoft, and Entrust did one of the original works on the XML Encryption. It can be found at:*
>
> *http://lists.w3.org/Archives/Public/xml-encryption/2000Dec/att-0024/01-XMLEncryption_v01.html*
>
> *This resource contains some examples as well.*

Now that we have briefly looked at the XML Digital Signatures (XML DSIG) and the XML Encryption efforts, let's take a look at one example of how SOAP messages can be extended in a standard way in order to support security technologies of this type.

Digital Signatures Extensions to SOAP

In the search for a standard way to add XML Digital Signatures to SOAP messages, IBM and Microsoft submitted the **SOAP Security Extensions - Digital Signature** specification to the W3C. This specification is in the format of a Note, meaning that it will not become a Recommendation, but that it is intended for discussions only. The XML Protocol Working Group is likely to address these extensions further within the overall XML Protocol architecture (see Chapter 1 for more on the architecture of Web Services and XML Protocol).

These extensions provide standard ways of adding digital signatures to SOAP messages, and therefore address message integrity. The specification is intended to be extensible in order for it to allow other security standards to be added and made to work together (such as XML Encryption, described earlier, which would address the confidentiality of the message). The SOAP Security Extensions: Digital Signature specification (http://www.w3.org/TR/SOAP-dsig/) defines specific `Header` elements that can be used in a standard way in order to accomplish the addition of digital signatures.

Below is an example of applying digital signatures within a SOAP message, according to the SOAP Security Extensions: Digital Signature specification:

```
<SOAP-ENV:Envelope xmlns:SOAP-ENV="http://schemas.xmlsoap.org/soap/envelope/">
    <SOAP-ENV:Header>
        <SOAP-SEC:Signature
            xmlns:SOAP-SEC="http://schemas.xmlsoap.org/soap/security/2000-12"
            SOAP-ENV:actor="some-URI"
            SOAP-ENV:mustUnderstand="1">
          <ds:Signature xmlns:ds="http://www.w3.org/2000/09/xmldsig#">
             <ds:SignedInfo>
                <ds:CanonicalizationMethod Algorithm="http://www.w3.org/TR/2000
                                                      /CR-xml-c14n-20001026">
                </ds:CanonicalizationMethod>
                <ds:SignatureMethod Algorithm="http://www.w3.org/2000/09
                                               /xmldsig#dsa-sha1"/>
```

The body in this example is signed and the resulting signature `<ds:Signature>` is added to the `<SOAP-SEC:Signature>` header entry. The `SOAP-SEC:Signature` is an element that is present within the `SOAP-ENV:Header` element. It has its own namespace, and it specifies the `actor` for whom this signature is intended (for example, the final recipient or one of the intermediaries). It also specifies that the recipient must understand this header attribute, or it should not process the message. The signature section starts up by specifying the **canonization** method (specified by a URI) and the signature method (DSA-SHA1 in this case). Canonization is a standard way of formatting XML files or messages, and is important for properly validating the signature and avoiding small XML differences that different tools can introduce which invalidate the signature (such as adding whitespace in different ways) .

> *For more information on Canonical XML, please see the Canonical XML recommendation at http://www.w3.org/TR/xml-c14n*

Further, we see the `<Reference>` tag that points to the `<Body>` tag as the one that is being signed. The transform algorithm is specified next with a URI. The digest or hash method is defined with the `<ds:DigestMethod>` tag and it points to the SHA1 algorithm. Finally, we have the digest or hash value. A few lines later, we have the actual signature value itself:

```
            <ds:Reference URI="#Body">
               <ds:Transforms>
                  <ds:Transform Algorithm= "http://www.w3.org/TR/2000
                                            /CR-xml-c14n-20001026"/>
               </ds:Transforms>
               <ds:DigestMethod Algorithm="http://www.w3.org/2000
                                           /09/xmldsig#sha1"/>
               <ds:DigestValue>j6lwx3rvEPO0vKtMup4NbeVu8nk=</ds:DigestValue>
            </ds:Reference>
          </ds:SignedInfo>
          <ds:SignatureValue>MC0CFFrVLtRlk=...</ds:SignatureValue>
        </ds:Signature>
      </SOAP-SEC:Signature>
    </SOAP-ENV:Header>
    <SOAP-ENV:Body xmlns:SOAP-SEC="http://schemas.xmlsoap.org/soap
                                   /security/2000-12"
                   SOAP-SEC:id="Body">
      <m:GetLastTradePrice xmlns:m="some-URI">
```

```
            <m:symbol>IBM</m:symbol>
        </m:GetLastTradePrice>
    </SOAP-ENV:Body>
</SOAP-ENV:Envelope>
```

The SOAP Security Extensions: Digital Signature is not yet widely supported by the various SOAP or Web Services toolkits offered by various vendors. However, as Web Services become more widely used, the need for security will grow dramatically, so the support for the various security techniques and extensions is likely to grow as well.

Privacy Via P3P

The **Platform for Privacy Preferences (P3P)** is a W3C activity in which a number of companies are taking part. Some of the participating companies are: America Online, AT&T, Citigroup, HP, IBM, Microsoft, NCR, NEC, and Nokia. The P3P activity is geared to enable web sites to express their privacy-related practices, such as what data is being collected about the user and how it is being used, in a standardized format (XML in this case). These privacy practices can be automatically retrieved and interpreted by user agents, such as web browsers or a Web Service that is set up to run as an agent on the user's behalf. The ultimate goal is to keep users informed about web site practices by simplifying the process of reading privacy policies. Privacy policies and other legal agreements are all too often very lengthy and full of legal terms that few of us read very carefully or with full understanding. This leads to users not really knowing and understanding what information is being collected about them and how exactly this information is being used.

With P3P, users would not need to read the privacy policies for every site that they visit. Rather, key information about the data that is collected by the web site could be automatically conveyed to a user and discrepancies between the site's practices and the user's preferences can be automatically flagged. P3P is intended to work alongside the legislative and self-regulatory programs that help enforce web site policies, rather than to replace them. For example, P3P does not provide a mechanism for ensuring web sites act according to their policies, as that would be part of the complementary legislative and self-regulatory programs that help enforce policies. In addition, P3P does not provide any details about transferring or securing privacy data. P3P deals with security as far as it is involved with privacy, but it does not address many other security concerns such as encryption, and others. These other issues are to be taken care of by other complementary technologies and standards, such as XML Signatures and XML Encryption. In addition, P3P may have some points of contact with **CC/PP (Composite Capabilities/Preference Profiles)** specification that is being developed within the W3C. CC/PP is a **RDF (Resource Description Framework)** based framework for the management of device profile information. These devices can include any connected device, from cell phones to in-car computers. RDF, if you recall from our earlier chapters, is an application of XML that is used for encoding meta data (data describing other data).

> *For more information on RDF, please see Professional XML (2nd Edition) by Wrox Press (ISBN:1-861005-05-9). In addition, you can see the resources at the W3C: http://www.w3.org/RDF/ and CC/PP: http://www.w3.org/Mobile/CCPP/.*

The P3P specification is at the level of a Candidate Recommendation at the time of writing. This means that it is still a work in progress, even though it is quite detailed and the specification is relatively stable. The P3P specification is intended to go to the Proposed Recommendation stage and then to the Recommendation stage by the end of 2001 or early 2002. In addition to having a number of companies involved in the development of P3P, there have already been announcements of implementing P3P in various products. For instance, Internet Explorer 6 will support P3P as the standard for privacy policies in a machine-readable way, as well as for standard discovery and transfer methods.

P3P specifies that policies are expressed in an XML file (for example `Policy1.xml`), and placed in a particular directory of the web site (the actual language for writing policies is called **APPEL, A P3P Preferences Exchange Language** and is an application of XML). When a user visits a particular web site, they would either retrieve this policy from a default directory or from the directory that the web site has specified and provide this link via some kind of a meta data. In addition, a web site can have multiple policies for various sections of the site.

We will show you a couple of brief code examples of applying P3P, however this is not meant to be an in-depth study of P3P, its structure and all of its tags. The P3P specification is much more extensive and you are encouraged to follow the links provided at the end of this section if you wish to obtain further information on P3P.

The following is an example of a policy reference file, as shown within the P3P specification (slightly modified for brevity). A policy reference file specifies the policies that are relevant within a particular web site and where and how they apply within the site:

```
<META xmlns="http://www.w3.org/2000/12/P3Pv1">
    <POLICY-REFERENCES>
        <EXPIRY max-age="172800"/>
        <POLICY-REF about="/P3P/Policy1.xml">
            <INCLUDE>/*</INCLUDE>
            <EXCLUDE>/catalog/*</EXCLUDE>
        </POLICY-REF>
        <POLICY-REF about="/P3P/Policy2.xml">
            <INCLUDE>/catalog/*</INCLUDE>
        </POLICY-REF>
    </POLICY-REFERENCES>
</META>
```

The policy reference file specifies or references the policies that are available, and to which resources they apply. In our example, we have two policies, `Policy1.xml` and `Policy2.xml`. The first policy applies to all files and directories within the root of the web site. However, it excludes the `catalog` subfolders and everything below it. The `catalog` subfolder has a different policy applied to it and that is the `Policy2.xml`. A policy preference file can contain much more information than the information shown above. It can specify more about the handling of cookies, links to other web sites, expiration of policies, and much more (please follow the links provided at the end of this section to learn more about the details of policy reference files).

The next code example shows an example policy file. The file starts with a `<POLICY>` tag that, besides its namespace, provides a link to the human readable privacy policy with the `discuri` attribute. The `ENTITY` element gives a precise description of the legal entity making the representation of the privacy practices. The `<DATA>` tag specifies the type of data that is being collected in the site or within the particular parts of the web site. The `<ACCESS>` tag shows how much of the user data is accessible by the user directly. The `<nonident/>` tag specifies that no identifiable information is used.

```
<POLICY xmlns="http://www.w3.org/2000/12/P3Pv1"
        discuri="http://www.catalog.example.com/PrivacyPracticeBrowsing.html">
<ENTITY>
    <DATA-GROUP>
        <DATA ref="#business.name">CatalogExample</DATA>
        <DATA ref="#business.contact-info.postal.street">4000 Lincoln Ave.</DATA>
        <DATA ref="#business.contact-info.postal.city">Birmingham</DATA>
```

```
            <DATA ref="#business.contact-info.postal.stateprov">MI</DATA>
            <DATA ref="#business.contact-info.postal.postalcode">48009</DATA>
            <DATA ref="#business.contact-info.postal.country">USA</DATA>
            <DATA ref="#business.contact-info.online.e-
  mail">catalog@example.com</DATA>
            <DATA ref="#business.contact-info.telecom.telephone.intcode">1</DATA>
            <DATA ref="#business.contact-info.telecom.telephone.loccode">248</DATA>
            <DATA ref="#business.contact-info.telecom.telephone.number">3926753</DATA>
      </DATA-GROUP>
    </ENTITY>
    <ACCESS><nonident/></ACCESS>
```

In the next piece of the policy file, the <DISPUTES> element provides instructions of the dispute resolution procedures that should be followed for disputes about the services privacy practices:

```
    <DISPUTES-GROUP>
        <DISPUTES resolution-type="independent"
                service="http://www.PrivacySeal.example.org"
                short-description="PrivacySeal.example.org">
          <IMG src="http://www.PrivacySeal.example.org/Logo.gif"
              alt="PrivacySeal's logo"/>
        <REMEDIES><correct/></REMEDIES>
        </DISPUTES>
    </DISPUTES-GROUP>
```

The final section of the policy file provides a <STATEMENT> tag that describes the data practices applied to the particular data that is being collected. For example the <PURPOSE> section states that the data is to be used for administration, development, or other purposes (this applies when we are talking about clickstream data, data about the movement of the user around the site). The <RETENTION> describes the policy about the retention of the data. <stated-purpose> means that the purpose is stated in the human readable part of the policy (link specified earlier). <DATA-GROUP> and <DATA> reference the type of the data being collected within the site.

```
    <STATEMENT>
        <PURPOSE><admin/><develop/></PURPOSE>
        <RECIPIENT><ours/></RECIPIENT>
        <RETENTION><stated-purpose/></RETENTION>
        <DATA-GROUP>
            <DATA ref="#dynamic.clickstream"/>
            <DATA ref="#dynamic.http"/>
        </DATA-GROUP>
    </STATEMENT>
</POLICY>
```

This completes our brief description of P3P policy. As we mentioned earlier, the P3P specification is quite extensive, so for further information please check the references provided at the end of this section.

Keep in mind that P3P does not solve all privacy issues on the Web, but it is a part of a larger and more comprehensive set of technical and legal solutions. It only focuses on the *disclosure* of web site privacy practices and gives a *choice* to the user as to what to do about them. Its purpose is to help users find out what the privacy practices of a particular site are, and how these practices compare with their privacy preferences. P3P's guiding principle is that user agents (such as web browser or clients of Web Services) should not be configured by default to transfer personal information to a service provider without the users consent. Furthermore, P3P is complementary technology to cookie blocking and anonymity tools. Vendors are incorporating P3P support within these tools.

For more information on P3P, you can go to http://www.w3.org/P3P/ or you can read the FAQ page about P3P at http://www.w3.org/P3P/p3pfaq.html. You can examine the latest P3P specification at http://www.w3.org/TR/P3P/

The topic of our chapter has been the growing need for Web Services security. Along with this, the need for a standard way of handling privacy concerns will grow as well. The relationship between Web Services and privacy policies and preferences is a fairly new development, but one that is likely to receive more attention in the near future.

Digital Rights Management

Digital Rights Management (DRM) is a subject new to XML standards bodies such as the W3C. When we say DRM, we are talking about the digital management of rights, not the management of digital rights. This implies that DRM methods and future standards should work both on- and off-line (meaning on the Web and in disconnected systems).

During 2000 and 2001, the W3C starting collecting opinions and papers from participating organizations about the role that W3C should have within DRM and what specifications and standards would help to this field. There is an interest in creating a rights language by the W3C (probably based on XML). The current W3C response has been to create a DRM Workgroup that will review these issues, coordinate with various groups, and work on proposing a DRM Framework, with work likely to be split among a few different standards bodies.

Considering the emergence of new technologies, such as electronic books and the wider use of digital music and other digital content, DRM is likely to generate strong interest from a number of parties.

To learn more about the early work on DRM by the W3C, please check http://www.w3.org/2000/12/drm-ws/.

Summary

In this chapter we discussed some of the most important security concepts, particularly those related to building secure applications utilizing Web Services. We described some important ways of handling security in Web Services. None of these approaches offers the ideal way to handle security; all of them having their individual strengths and weaknesses. In particular:

❑ We covered some important concepts about security, including security as a process, the key security aspects of authentication, authorization, auditing and logging, integrity, privacy, encryption, availability, nonrepudiation, and digital signatures.

❑ We looked at ways to implement Web Services security at the transport layer, particularly with HTTP and SMTP. We covered techniques such as basic authentication, certificates, and SSL and showed Web Service application examples of how this can be done.

❑ Next, we discussed some of the options available for implementing Web Services security at the application level. We looked at how to combine credentials within the SOAP message and how you can combine these methods with transport level technologies such as SSL.

❑ Ticket-based security technologies such as Kerberos were described.

❑ Finally, we looked at the future of XML security standards including XML Signatures, XML Encryption, and P3P.

Having completed this chapter, you should have a good understanding of the key issues surrounding application and Web Services security, as well as the options available for implementing security within Web Services, and an understanding of some of the new security related developments within XML and Web Services. Security is a complex area, with many aspects to consider, and many issues to analyze. This is why we need a process to handle security appropriately. In order to create the most appropriate security process for our situation, we need to understand the key components of the security process and the workings of the key technologies involved. Only then can we implement a working security process.

Case Study: A Java Filesystem Web Service

So far in this book, we've seen how Web Services provide a powerful way to expose business functionality over the Internet. Now, let's take a look at a practical implementation of a unique Web Service using the Apache SOAP Toolkit and Java. This case study describes the tools and the object model of the Apache SOAP Toolkit, and then demonstrates an implementation of a functional Filesystem Web Service. All the required source code for this chapter is available from the Wrox web site at: http://www.wrox.com/.

The Filesystem Web Service

The Filesystem Web Service implements a virtual filesystem over HTTP. Using SOAP Messaging with Attachments to wrap binary and text files, distributed applications can manipulate files and directories with location transparency and security. The benefits to this Web Service are:

- ❑ Secure remote storage and retrieval of files without investing in quickly outdated hardware
- ❑ Virtual archive and automated/unattended backups
- ❑ Access to data anywhere in the world
- ❑ Virtually unlimited file storage
- ❑ Cross-platform interoperability
- ❑ Operating system and location transparency

Some target users for this Web Service may be:

❑   Wireless application providers and wireless device users who have no local storage

❑   Organizations that want to provide a personal backup solution to their users but cannot afford to install zip/tape drives in every computer

❑   Internet/Application Service Providers (ISPs, ASPs) who want to provide paid services to their customers

❑   Intranet users who require self-service backup/restore capabilities

❑   People who travel, and need access to their files on the road

❑   Individuals with no local backup devices

❑   Users who need data archived in a secure manner

❑   Individuals who require additional disk space due to small local hard drives

❑   Telecommuters

❑   Organizations that require remote backup/disaster recovery

With such a broad range of possible applications in mind, one concern for a Web Service such as this is security.

Why Do We Need Security for Web Services?

When developing web services, specifically those that transact sensitive data, you should verify that only authorized individuals utilize your web service. It makes sense that a Web Services protocol, like SOAP should provide a method for verifying the identity of its user.

Upon inspection of the SOAP specification, you will notice there is no mention of security. Why create a protocol that intentionally omits one of the prime facets of distributed computing? SOAP is actually incomplete by design. Because the SOAP specification doesn't currently address issues related to security, we utilize the built-in security features of the underlying transport protocols that are used to deliver SOAP messages. Since most Web Services rely on the HTTP protocol, we can use any of its various security implementations. Web servers, firewalls, and the like can use the information provided by HTTP to validate usernames and passwords (authentication) and grant or deny their access to resources based on the caller's identity (authorization). With SOAP on top of HTTP, we can pass username and password information in the HTTP header. The HTTP 1.1 Specification (http://www.ietf.org/rfc/rfc2616.txt) defines several challenge response authentication mechanisms, which can be used by a server to challenge a client request and by a client to provide authentication information. The general framework for access authentication, and the specification of **basic** and **digest** authentication, are defined in *"HTTP Authentication: Basic and Digest Access Authentication"* (http://www.ietf.org/rfc/rfc2617.txt).

Ultimately, a future SOAP specification should provide support for many of the available standard transport layer security mechanisms, such as basic, digest, and cryptographic messages over SSL (Secure Socket Layers, see http://home.netscape.com/eng/ssl3/index.html). The server invoking the Web Service should perform authentication and authorization, as opposed to relying on the web server or other hardware. In this fashion, we will have a robust framework through which we expose our services. These issues are especially important if you deal with sensitive information, or wish to charge a fee for your Web Services.

Apache SOAP and the Pluggable Provider

The Apache SOAP project implements a SOAP Web Services framework using Java. The bridge between the SOAP engine and the service being invoked is called the **provider**. The following diagram shows how messages flow through Apache SOAP, and where the pluggable provider fits in:

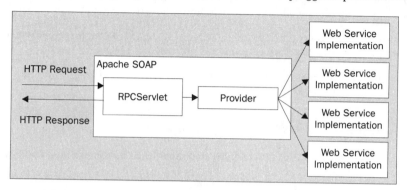

The provider is responsible for:

❑ Locating, loading, and invoking the service

❑ Converting the result from the service into a SOAP envelope

❑ Implementing specialized functionality outside the scope of the SOAP specification

Here, our specialized functionality will be security. By default the SOAP engine will use the `RPCJavaProvider` class as the provider for RPC services, and the `MsgJavaProvider` class for Message services. `RPCJavaProvider` simply loads the appropriate class, invokes the desired method and converts any result into a SOAP envelope. Our pluggable provider will use the Java Database Connectivity (JDBC) interface to authenticate and authorize users against the SOAP service before invoking it. The pluggable provider demonstrated in this chapter will implement authentication and authorization through the use of a JDBC interface to a database of user profiles and Web Services. The user profiles contain username/password pairs for authentication, and a mapping of usernames to Web Services for authorization. The use of a SQL datasource will be a familiar paradigm for Java developers who already make use of database-driven security.

Setting Up The Server

In Chapter 10, we learned how to configure Apache SOAP and Tomcat. The examples in this chapter run unmodified on Apache Tomcat (available from http://jakarta.apache.org/tomcat/index.html). Remember to install the Xerces-J XML parser (http://xml.apache.org/xerces-j/). You will also need JavaMail (available from http://java.sun.com/products/javamail/; remember to specify the location of `mail.jar` on your classpath) and the JavaBeans Activation Framework (available from http://java.sun.com/products/javabeans/glasgow/jaf.html; you'll need to set `activation.jar` on your classpath). These two packages are necessary to handle the file attachment and MIME-encoding mechanisms of this example. To compile the servlet classes, you will need the Java 2 SDK Enterprise Edition (see http://java.sun.com/j2ee/index.html). Some samples that come with Apache SOAP, such as

the Calculator sample, require the Bean Scripting Framework (from
http://oss.software.ibm.com/developerworks/projects/bsf) and JavaScript (which is available with
Mozilla Rhino from http://www.mozilla.org/rhino/). If you would like to try these as well, place
`bsf.jar` and `js.jar` in your classpath. Don't forget to add `soap.jar` to the classpath as well. Ensure
that the `.jar` files are not only referenced in the classpath environment variable, which allows them to
be utilized at compilation time, but that copies of them are placed in Tomcat's `/lib` folder, so that they
are on the server's classpath as well. In a nutshell, here's how to hook it all up:

Some systems require you to set the `TOMCAT_HOME` (or `CATALINA_HOME` for Tomcat 4.0) environment
variable, which points to the directory containing Tomcat.

Set Tomcat's classpath with `xerces.jar` at the front. In `bin/tomcat.bat`, find the `:setClasspath`
section, and modify it to look like this:

```
:setClasspath
set CP=<path to Xerces-J>\lib\xerces.jar;%TOMCAT_HOME%\classes
```

On Unix systems, find the `export CLASSPATH` statement in `bin/tomcat.sh`, and add this line right
before it:

```
CLASSPATH=<path to Xerces-J>/lib/xerces.jar:${CLASSPATH}
```

Next, make sure Tomcat is running on port 8080. You can do this by verifying that `conf/server.xml`
contains a section like this:

```
<Connector className="org.apache.tomcat.service.PoolTcpConnector">
    <Parameter name="handler"
        value="org.apache.tomcat.service.http.HttpConnectionHandler"/>
    <Parameter name="port" value="8080"/>
</Connector>
```

Finally, add a server context for Apache SOAP. Inside the `<ContextManager>` tag, add the
following section:

```
<Context path="/soap"
    docBase="c:/soap-2_2/webapps/soap"
    crossContext="true"
    debug="0"
    reloadable="true"
    trusted="false" >
</Context>
```

The `<Context>` section maps to a path within Tomcat in which a web application exists.

The attributes in the above element are described below:

Attribute	Description
path	The prefix of an HTTP request, instructing Tomcat which application context to use. This attribute always begins with a forward slash ("/").
docBase	Points to a directory which will be the root of this web application.
reloadable	During development, setting this value to true enables Tomcat to reload changes to your source code. This is time consuming, and reportedly error-prone. In a production environment, this should be set to false.

Attribute	Description
`trusted`	Enables access to Tomcat's internal objects. Most applications will set this to false.
`debug`	A value of `"0"` suppresses all console output. A value of `"9"` implies verbose mode.

If you set up everything correctly, running `bin/tomcat start` should display this console:

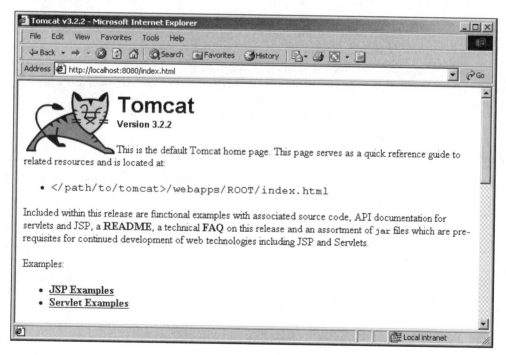

Point your browser to http://localhost:8080/ to verify that everything is up and running. You should see the following page:

To stop Tomcat, run `bin/shutdown`, or just kill the command window.

Setting Up The Database

For authentication and authorization, we will use a SQL database. Specifically, I've chosen MySQL (freely available from http://sourceforge.net/projects/mysql/), although any SQL database will work. MySQL, aside from being free, is very fast, and runs on both Windows and Linux. There is an excellent article on About.com entitled *How to install and configure MySQL for Windows*. The URL for this is http://perl.about.com/library/weekly/aa111400a.htm. For this example, when you are setting up MySQL, please set both the username and password to mysql.

This type of database-driven authentication should be familiar if you've ever set up any type of security on a web site. Our database schema is relatively simple: a table to store our principals and credentials (usernames and passwords), a table to store our Web Service identifiers (URNs), and a table to map the principals and Web Services. We use a many-to-many relationship between principals and Web Services. We want to relate many users to many Web Services. In order to decrease the duplication of data, we'll create a table consisting of nothing but primary keys from the two other tables, called principal_webservice_map. Here we adhere to the Fourth Normal Form (4NF), sometimes referred to as Boyce-Codd Normal Form (BCNF). This form is often overlooked, but it's important when dealing with many-to-many relations. In a nutshell, this means that any given relation may not contain more than one multivalued attribute. This concept is beyond the scope of this chapter, so I leave it as an exercise to the reader to discover its implications. Most of these rules were defined in a paper by E.F. Codd entitled *Further Normalization of the Data Base Relational Model* (this can be found in the book *Data base systems*, R. Rustin, ed., Prentice-Hall, 1972). Mathematicians later developed other normalization rules, such as 4NF, 5NF, etc. There is a good tutorial on database schema normalization at:

http://www.phpbuilder.com/columns/barry20000731.php3.

For the data definition language (DDL) in our example, we will use MySQL's syntax. This DDL can easily be ported to any SQL database with minor changes. To create our database using MySQL, place the file FileSystem.ddl in the bin folder of your MySQL directory (by default this is C:\mysql\bin). Change the current directory to the bin folder of your MySQL directory, and start the server with this command:

>mysqld

Then, execute the following command from the command prompt to create the database using the DDL:

>mysql < FileSystem.ddl

The following command will display that the new database structure was created successfully:

>mysqlshow filesystem

Whenever you restart MySQL, navigate to the MySQL bin folder in the command prompt, start the server, and enter the command:

>mysql -u mysql/mysql filesystem

Where **mysql/mysql** are your username and password. This ensures that the filesystem database is accessible from the database server. To check that it is accessible, enter:

>select * from principal;

at the mysql prompt, which will display the `principal` table of the `filesystem` database:

```
Command Prompt - mysql -u mysql/mysql filesystem
C:\mysql\bin>mysql -u mysql/mysql filesystem
Welcome to the MySQL monitor.  Commands end with ; or \g.
Your MySQL connection id is 2 to server version: 3.23.40-nt

Type 'help;' or '\h' for help. Type '\c' to clear the buffer.

mysql> select * from principal;
+----+----------+-----------+------------------+
| id | username | password  | homedir          |
+----+----------+-----------+------------------+
|  1 | markr    | Jsdh8qSD  | c:/users/markr   |
|  2 | johns    | iJ823hdV  | c:/users/johns   |
|  3 | linust   | js89PndVs | c:/users/linust  |
|  4 | larryw   | 58Jnfjh4g | c:/users/larryw  |
+----+----------+-----------+------------------+
4 rows in set (0.35 sec)

mysql>
```

Let's walk through the DDL for some further explanation of the schema (`FileSystem.ddl` in the code download for this book):

The first line creates an empty database structure, simply called "filesystem", assuming one does not already exist with the same name:

```
CREATE DATABASE IF NOT EXISTS filesystem;
```

Under Unix, database names are case-sensitive (unlike SQL keywords), so you must always refer to your database as `filesystem`, not as `Filesystem`, `FILESYSTEM`, or some other variant. This is also true for table names. Under Windows, this restriction does not apply, although you must refer to databases and tables using the same case throughout a given query.

Creating a database does not select it for use; you must do that explicitly. To make `filesystem` the current database, we `USE` the database:

```
USE filesystem;
```

The hardest part of creating a database is choosing a sound structure. What tables and columns best suit our application? Our users, or **principals**, require a table of their own:

```
'CREATE TABLE principal (
  id int(11) NOT NULL auto_increment,
  username varchar(32) NOT NULL default '',
  password varchar(32) default '',
  homedir varchar(255) NOT NULL default '',
  PRIMARY KEY (id),
  UNIQUE KEY username (username)
) TYPE=MyISAM;
```

We need some way to index and uniquely identify the principals. To that end, we create a **primary key** called id, which we set to auto_increment (also called identity on many systems). We also create two fields for username and password, which are self-explanatory, and a third called homedir, which will contain the physical directory on the web server which will host this user's files. Users also need to be unique, so we assign a UNIQUE KEY to the username field. Finally, we tell MySQL to use the MyISAM database type. This is the default, but you may choose from other database types, such as BerkeleyDB, or InnoDB. These other types support transactions with locking mechanisms, which are not necessary here, since our application is mostly read-only.

Next, let's create a few users for our Web Service by performing an INSERT into the table we just created:

```
INSERT INTO principal VALUES (1,'markr',''Jsdh8qSD'','c:/users/markr');
INSERT INTO principal VALUES (2,'johns','iJ823hdV','c:/users/johns');
INSERT INTO principal VALUES (3,'linust','js89PndVs','c:/users/linust');
INSERT INTO principal VALUES (4,'larryw','58Jnfjh4g','c:/users/larryw');
```

The passwords can be anything you like. Here, we've just used dummy data. Next, we need to create a table to hold references to our deployed Web Services. Since Apache SOAP uses a URI to uniquely identify Web Services, it makes sense for us to use the same identifiers in our database. In the webservice table, we create two columns: id and uri. This pair is also unique, so we create a **composite** primary key consisting of both columns. You will notice below that the PRIMARY KEY clause contains both columns as parameters. Again, we use the default MyISAM database type:

```
CREATE TABLE webservice (
    id int(11) NOT NULL auto_increment,
    uri varchar(64) NOT NULL default '',
    PRIMARY KEY (id,uri)
) TYPE=MyISAM;
```

Next, we insert the URI for our Web Service, urn:filesystem:

```
INSERT INTO webservice VALUES (1,'urn:filesystem');
```

We can also insert some of the Web Services that come with Apache SOAP:

```
INSERT INTO webservice VALUES (2,'urn:AddressFetcher');
INSERT INTO webservice VALUES (3,'urn:AddressFetcher2');
INSERT INTO webservice VALUES (4,'urn:xml-soap-demo-calculator');
INSERT INTO webservice VALUES (5,'urn:sum-COM');
INSERT INTO webservice VALUES (6,'urn:adder-COM');
INSERT INTO webservice VALUES (7,'urn:po-processor');
INSERT INTO webservice VALUES (8,'urn:mimetestprocessor');
INSERT INTO webservice VALUES (9,'urn:mimetest');
INSERT INTO webservice VALUES (10,'urn:xmltoday-delayed-quotes');
INSERT INTO webservice VALUES (11,'urn:ejbhello');
INSERT INTO webservice VALUES (12,'urn:soap-unauthorized');
```

Finally, we need to create a relationship between our principals and our Web Services. Since we have a many-to-many relationship (many principals can access many Web Services), we need a **map** table (sometimes called a **join** table) to link the two. Each record in the table is the unique intersection of a principal and a Web Service. Here, the columns are foreign keys to the two other tables, represented by p_id and ws_id (principal id, and Web Service id, respectively). This pair is also a primary key to the principal_webservice_map table, as shown below:

```
CREATE TABLE principal_webservice_map (
  p_id int(11) NOT NULL default '0',
  ws_id int(11) NOT NULL default '0',
  PRIMARY KEY (p_id,ws_id)
) TYPE=MyISAM;
```

The insertion of a record into this table logically defines permissions. That is, the Web Services to which a particular principal has access. For example, let's grant user `markr` (principal id: 1) access to Web Service `urn:filesystem` (webservice id: 1):

```
INSERT INTO principal_webservice_map VALUES (1,1);
```

Let's go ahead and grant this user access to all other Web Services as well:

```
INSERT INTO principal_webservice_map VALUES (1,2);
INSERT INTO principal_webservice_map VALUES (1,3);
INSERT INTO principal_webservice_map VALUES (1,4);
INSERT INTO principal_webservice_map VALUES (1,5);
INSERT INTO principal_webservice_map VALUES (1,6);
INSERT INTO principal_webservice_map VALUES (1,7);
INSERT INTO principal_webservice_map VALUES (1,8);
INSERT INTO principal_webservice_map VALUES (1,9);
INSERT INTO principal_webservice_map VALUES (1,10);
INSERT INTO principal_webservice_map VALUES (1,11);
```

We can also define permissions for other users:

```
INSERT INTO principal_webservice_map VALUES (2,1);
INSERT INTO principal_webservice_map VALUES (2,4);
INSERT INTO principal_webservice_map VALUES (2,7);
INSERT INTO principal_webservice_map VALUES (2,11);
INSERT INTO principal_webservice_map VALUES (3,1);
INSERT INTO principal_webservice_map VALUES (3,5);
INSERT INTO principal_webservice_map VALUES (3,9);
INSERT INTO principal_webservice_map VALUES (4,1);
INSERT INTO principal_webservice_map VALUES (4,2);
INSERT INTO principal_webservice_map VALUES (4,4);
INSERT INTO principal_webservice_map VALUES (4,7);
INSERT INTO principal_webservice_map VALUES (4,11);
```

The next step in setting up our database is to configure our JDBC datasource. We can use either a native driver or the JDBC-ODBC bridge driver. In this case, we use the bridge driver (sun.jdbc.odbc.JdbcOdbcDriver) to make our provider a little more portable. Ideally, we want to use a native, or Type 4, driver. This is a pure Java driver that uses a native protocol to convert JDBC calls into the database server network protocol. Using this type of driver, the application can make direct calls from a Java client to the database. Type 4 drivers, such as the MySQL JDBC Driver, are typically offered by the database vendor. The native JDBC driver for MySQL is available from http://www.mysql.com/downloads/api-jdbc.html. Because the driver is written purely in Java, it requires no configuration on the client machine other than telling the application where to find the driver. When using a Type 4 driver, just remember to add it to the classpath of your server. In Windows 2000's Control Panel, I've created a System DSN called `filesystem` using the MySQL ODBC driver (which is available from http://www.mysql.com/downloads/api-myodbc.html). The following screenshot shows the configuration options for the ODBC driver on Windows:

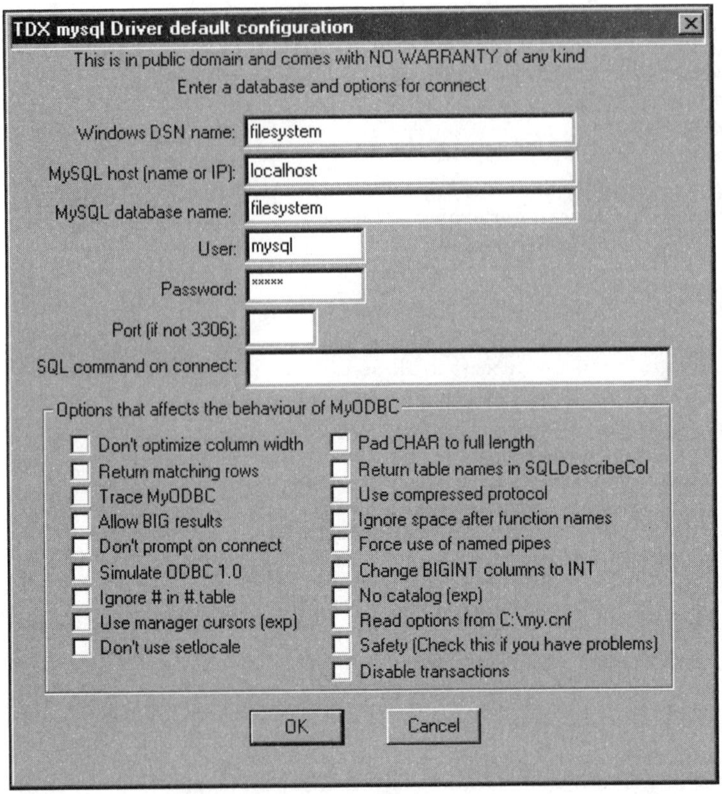

Make sure that you set both the username and password to mysql. That's all there is to setting up the SQL database. Let's move on to writing our pluggable provider's implementation.

Writing a Pluggable Provider

Since the default Java provider does not implement security in any way, we need to create our own pluggable provider. To do this, we implement the `org.apache.soap.util.Provider` interface, as all Apache SOAP providers do. This interface is as follows:

```
package org.apache.soap.util;

import javax.servlet.*;
import javax.servlet.http.*;
import org.apache.soap.*;
import org.apache.soap.rpc.*;
import org.apache.soap.server.*;

public interface Provider {
    public void locate(DeploymentDescriptor dd,
                       Envelope            env,
                       Call                call,
                       String              methodName,
```

```
                        String          targetObjectURI,
                        SOAPContext     reqContext)
            throws SOAPException;
    public void invoke(SOAPContext req, SOAPContext res) throws SOAPException;
}
```

The `locate()` method will be called to allow the provider to verify that the service exists and is
available to process the request. If an error occurs this method should throw a `SOAPException`. After a
successful call to `locate()` the SOAP engine will then call `invoke()` to actually call the service. You
may notice that the invoke method does not have any parameters explicitly pertaining to the Web
Service; they are extracted using the SOAP envelope passed to the `RPCRouterServlet` via HTTP.

The `invoke()` method is also responsible for converting any response from the service into a SOAP
envelope and placing it in the `res` parameter (a `SOAPContext`). This response is then sent back to the
client via HTTP.

Now, let's walk through the implementation of `FilesystemProvider`, our pluggable provider:

```java
import org.apache.soap.rpc.* ;
import org.apache.soap.server.* ;
import org.apache.soap.server.http.* ;
import org.apache.soap.util.* ;

public class FilesystemProvider implements Provider
{
```

Variables are declared, followed by the `locate()` method. Here, we need to grab the HTTP Basic
Authentication information from the headers. This can be obtained from the `HttpServletRequest` object:

```java
public void locate( DeploymentDescriptor dd,
    Envelope env,
    Call call,
    String methodName,
    String targetObjectURI,
    SOAPContext reqContext)
throws SOAPException {

    HttpServlet servlet = (HttpServlet)reqContext.getProperty(
    Constants.BAG_HTTPSERVLET );
    HttpSession session = (HttpSession)reqContext.getProperty(
    Constants.BAG_HTTPSESSION );
    HttpServletRequest req =
(HttpServletRequest)reqContext.getProperty(Constants.BAG_HTTPSERVLETREQUEST);
```

HTTP encodes the authentication header using Base64 encoding. This string is in the form:

```
Authorization: Basic username:password
```

Where `username:password` has been encoded in Base64. Now, let's extract the authentication information:

```
String authorization = req.getHeader("authorization");
authorization = authorization.substring(authorization.indexOf(" "));
byte[] bytes = Base64.decode(authorization);
String decoded = new String(bytes);
int i = decoded.indexOf(":");
String username = decoded.substring(0,i);
String password = decoded.substring(i+1,decoded.length());
```

Next, we need to connect to our database so we can perform the authentication. I've created a separate data access class called `FilesystemProviderDAO` to manage the database connection and abstract out the authentication and authorization queries. We'll use the `isAuthenticated()` and `isAuthorized()` methods of this class to evaluate the caller's credentials. Our first query validates the user's password. If this function returns true, we perform our second query, which evaluates his authorization to the Web Service requested (`FilesystemProviderDAO.java`):

```
public boolean isAuthenticated(String username, String password) {
  try {

    // Create our Statement object
    Statement stmt = con.createStatement();

    // Execute the dynamic query
    ResultSet rs = stmt.executeQuery("SELECT password FROM " +
      "principal WHERE username = '" + username + "'");

    // Get the first (and hopefully only) record:
    if (rs.next()) {
      // Validate the password
      if(rs.getString("password").equals(password)) {
        return true;
      }
    }
    return false;
  }
  catch (SQLException e)  {
    return false;
  }
}
```

Here, we dynamically create the query string by concatenating the `username` and `password` parameters with the `SELECT` statement. While this works, it's not very efficient under load. The next method, `isAuthorized()`, demonstrates the use of a **prepared statement** to perform its query.

```
public boolean isAuthorized(String username, String uri) {
    try {
    // Create a Prepared Statement object

    PreparedStatement pstmt =
      con.prepareStatement("SELECT p.username FROM " +
      "principal_webservice_map pwm, " +
      "principal p, webservice ws " +
      "WHERE pwm.p_id = p.id " +
      "AND pwm.ws_id = ws.id " +
      "AND p.username = ? AND ws.uri = ?");
```

Notice the question marks – these are placeholders for the parameters to the query. Unlike the previous example, we do not dynamically build a query string for prepared statements. We set parameters like this:

```
pstmt.setString(1,username);
pstmt.setString(2,uri);
```

Next, we execute the query, and compare the password field as before:

```
ResultSet rs = pstmt.executeQuery();
if (rs.next()) {
  if(rs.getString("username").equals(username)) {
    return true;
  }
}
return false;
}
catch (SQLException e)  {
  System.err.println("SQLException: " + e.getMessage());
  return false;
}
}
```

Usually, using a `PreparedStatement` is preferable, since many database servers can pre-compile or cache this type of query, improving performance. The database query can be done either way; I just wanted to demonstrate both techniques. If this function returns `true`, we can grant the caller access to the Web Service!

Next, the `FilesystemProvider` class resolves the Web Service, which is referred to as the **target object**. Apache SOAP's Service Manager performs this lookup.

```
ServletConfig  config  = servlet.getServletConfig();
ServletContext context = config.getServletContext();
ServiceManager serviceManager =
    ServerHTTPUtils.getServiceManagerFromContext(context);
```

Did we perform a call on a valid method name? Let's check. If not, we need to throw an exception in the form of a SOAP Fault:

```
if (!RPCRouter.validCall (dd, call)) {
  throw new SOAPException (Constants.FAULT_CODE_SERVER,
    "Method '" + call.getMethodName () + "' is not supported."); }
```

Now that we've successfully located the Web Service, let's set a reference to it as our target object:

```
Object targetObject = ServerHTTPUtils.getTargetObject(serviceManager,
    dd, targetObjectURI, servlet, session, context);
```

Once our target object has been referenced, we can invoke the service:

```
    public void invoke(SOAPContext reqContext, SOAPContext resContext)
    throws SOAPException {
```

First, we perform the actual call on the target object:

```
        Response resp = RPCRouter.invoke(dd, call, targetObject, resContext);
```

Next, we build our SOAP Envelope object. This will contain our response:

```
        Envelope env = resp.buildEnvelope();
```

We need an `IOWriter` object with which to construct our XML declarations. A `StringWriter` is passed to the `marshall()` method to accomplish this:

```
        StringWriter  sw = new StringWriter();
        env.marshall(sw, call.getSOAPMappingRegistry(), resContext);
```

Our last bit of logic sets the root part of our SOAP response to the `StringWriter` object we just created, using our standard UTF-8 encoding:

```
    resContext.setRootPart(sw.toString(),
            Constants.HEADERVAL_CONTENT_TYPE_UTF8);
    }
```

Here, the `Provider` class invokes the Web Service as identified by the target object and builds a SOAP Response envelope to encapsulate our return value, encoded in SOAP's XML Envelope format.

Writing the Filesystem Web Service

Coding the actual Web Service is the simple part of this exercise. Here, we will write a Web Service that exposes several methods, exposing some of the functionality of the `java.io.File` class as a Web Service. Since we are using the HTTP Header information in the SOAP context for authentication information, we need to have access to that information in our Web Service implementation. You will notice each public method has a parameter of type `SOAPContext`. These method signatures do not match those expected by the `FilesystemProxy` class (shown later in this chapter). If a service's public method with a matching signature is not found, a second search is done by our `FilesystemProvider` for a method with an initial parameter of type `SOAPContext`.

> *You should be forewarned that using the SOAP context information in your Web Service implementation will bind you to Apache SOAP. This is one published issue in the Apache SOAP release notes, and you are advised to use this technique carefully.*

Having access to the incoming `SOAPContext` provides you with access to the following objects via the `SOAPContext.getProperty()` method:

- ❑ HttpServlet, using the key org.apache.soap.Constants.BAG_HTTPSERVLET

- ❑ HttpSession, using the key org.apache.soap.Constants.BAG_HTTPSESSION

- ❑ HttpServletRequest, using the key
     org.apache.soap.Constants.BAG_HTTPSERVLETREQUEST

- ❑ HttpServletResponse, using the key
     org.apache.soap.Constants.BAG_HTTPSERVLETRESPONSE

If the original SOAP request was in the SOAP Attachments form, then you can reference the MIME-encoded attachments using the getBodyPart() method.

Using SOAP Attachments

In this section, you will see how SOAP Attachments are used to send and receive file attachments as part of the createNewFile() and getFile() methods in our Web Service. Apache SOAP allows data to be passed along with the XML message without having to embed the data in the XML itself. Since our SOAP message take the form of a MIME multipart message (this is defined in the specification – see http://www.w3.org/TR/SOAP-attachments), entities such as files can be embedded inside.

Below is our Web Service implementation. (This is the file Filesystem.java from the code download):

```java
package com.markrichman.filesystem;

import java.io.*;
import java.sql.*;
import java.util.Date;
import java.util.Enumeration;
import javax.activation.*;
import javax.mail.internet.*;
import javax.servlet.* ;
import javax.servlet.http.* ;
import org.apache.soap.encoding.soapenc.Base64;
import org.apache.soap.rpc.SOAPContext;
import org.apache.soap.util.mime.*;
import org.apache.soap.util.xml.*;

/**
 * @author Mark A. Richman
 * @version 1.0
 */
public class Filesystem {
```

We will go through each of the methods, explaining how the whole attachment mechanism works. Many of the method names will remind you of those from java.io.File. This is intentional, as our Web Service should behave as transparently as possible from a developer's point of view. In fact, most of these methods simply wrap the File class methods entirely.

The `copyTo()` method simply copies a file to a new location:

```
public void copyTo(SOAPContext ctx, String sourcePath, String destPath) throws
Exception {
        File fnew = new File(getHomedir(getUsername(ctx)) + "/" + destPath);
        File fold = new File(getHomedir(getUsername(ctx)) + "/" + sourcePath);

        InputStream in = null;
        OutputStream out = null;
        try {
            in = new FileInputStream(fold);
            out = new FileOutputStream(fnew);
            while (true) {
                int data = in.read();
                if (data == -1) {
                    break;
                }
                out.write(data);
            }
            in.close();
            out.close();
        }
        finally {
            if (in != null) {
                in.close();
            }
            if (out != null) {
                out.close();
            }
        }
    }
```

Note the two methods below, which are used throughout this class:

❏   getHomedir – Gets a user's home directory from the database via the `FilesystemDAO` class

❏   getUsername – Gets the username from the SOAP Context object

`createNewFile` creates a new file, relative to the user's home directory (see the DDL above):

```
public void createNewFile(SOAPContext ctx, String filePath) throws Exception {

        File fnew = new File(getHomedir(getUsername(ctx)) + "/" + filePath);

        if(!fnew.createNewFile()) {
            throw new Exception("File already exists: " + filePath);
        }
```

Next, we must create two objects: a `MimeBodyPart` object to get at the SOAP attachment, and a `DataHandler` object to get an `InputStream` for reading. The JavaMail API provides this functionality for us:

```
        MimeBodyPart mbp;
        DataHandler dh;
        Object o;
        InputStream is;
        FileOutputStream fos = new FileOutputStream(fnew);

        try {
            mbp = ctx.getBodyPart(1);
            dh = mbp.getDataHandler();
            is = dh.getInputStream();
```

Now, we simply write out the file on the server:

```
        int c;
        while ((c = is.read()) != -1)
            fos.write(c);
    }
    catch(Exception e) {
        throw new Exception(e.getMessage());
    }

    return;
}
```

The `delete`, method deletes a file:

```
public boolean delete(SOAPContext ctx, String filePath) throws Exception {
    File fnew = new File(getHomedir(getUsername(ctx)) + "/" + filePath);
    return fnew.delete();
}
```

We can also check the existence of a file on the server using the `exists`, method:

```
public boolean exists(SOAPContext ctx, String filePath) throws Exception {
    File f = new File(getHomedir(getUsername(ctx)) + "/" + filePath);
    return f.exists();
}
```

This method uses the JavaMail API in the reverse way of the `createFile`, method. Here, we send a file back to the client using the `DataHandler`:

```
public DataHandler getFile(SOAPContext ctx, String filePath) throws Exception {
    File f = new File(getHomedir(getUsername(ctx)) + "/" + filePath);
    if(!f.exists())
        throw new Exception("File not found.");

    try {
        DataSource ds = new ByteArrayDataSource(new File(f), null);
        DataHandler dh = new DataHandler(ds);
```

629

```
            return dh;
        }
        catch(Exception e) {
            System.err.println(e.getMessage());
        }
    }
```

`length`, gets a file's length in bytes:

```
public long length(SOAPContext ctx, String filePath) throws Exception {
    File f = new File(getHomedir(getUsername(ctx)) + "/" + filePath);
    return f.length();
}
```

`getParent`, gets a file's parent directory:

```
public String getParent(SOAPContext ctx, String filePath) throws Exception {
    File f = new File(getHomedir(getUsername(ctx)) + "/" + filePath);
    return f.getParent();
}
```

`isDirectory`, asks if a file descriptor is a directory.

```
public boolean isDirectory(SOAPContext ctx, String filePath) throws Exception {
    File f = new File(getHomedir(getUsername(ctx)) + "/" + filePath);
    return f.isDirectory();
}
```

`isFile`, tests to see whether the file is a **normal** file. A file is normal if:

❑   It is not a directory

❑   It satisfies other operating system-dependent criteria (i.e. symbolic links on Unix)

Any non-directory file created by a Java application is guaranteed to be a normal file.

```
public boolean isFile(SOAPContext ctx, String filePath) throws Exception {
    File f = new File(getHomedir(getUsername(ctx)) + "/" + filePath);
    return f.isFile();
}
```

`lastModified`, returns the time that the file denoted by the filePath was last modified:

```
public long lastModified(SOAPContext ctx, String filePath) throws Exception {
    File f = new File(getHomedir(getUsername(ctx)) + "/" + filePath);
    return f.lastModified();
}
```

`list` returns an array of strings naming the files and directories in the directory, assuming the filename we give represents a directory. This again simply encapsulates the functionality of `java.io.File`:

```
public String[] list(SOAPContext ctx, String filePath) throws Exception {
    File f = new File(getHomedir(getUsername(ctx)) + "/" + filePath);
    return f.list();
}
```

`mkdir` creates a directory on the server, given a parent directory specified by `filePath`:

```
public boolean mkdir(SOAPContext ctx, String filePath) throws Exception {
    File f = new File(getHomedir(getUsername(ctx)) + "/" + filePath);
    return f.mkdir();
}
```

`mkdirs` creates the directory named by the `filePath`, including any necessary parent directories that do not already exist:

```
public boolean mkdirs(SOAPContext ctx, String filePath) throws Exception {
    File f = new File(getHomedir(getUsername(ctx)) + "/" + filePath);
    return f.mkdirs();
}
```

`renameTo` renames a file:

```
public boolean renameTo(SOAPContext ctx, String filePath, String newName) throws
Exception {
    File f = new File(getHomedir(getUsername(ctx)) + "/" + filePath);
    return f.renameTo(new File(getUsername(ctx) + "/" + newName));
}
```

`setLastModified` sets the last-modified time of a file or directory:

```
public boolean setLastModified(SOAPContext ctx, String filePath, long time) throws
Exception {
    File f = new File(getHomedir(getUsername(ctx)) + "/" + filePath);
    return f.setLastModified(time);
}
```

Here is our `getUsername()` method. It's important to understand how the HTTP header information is extracted, so we'll go into some detail here. We are particularly interested in the `Authorization` field in the HTTP headers. We can access this simply by calling `getHeader()` on the request object:

```
protected String getUsername(SOAPContext ctx) {
    HttpServletRequest req =
(HttpServletRequest)ctx.getProperty("HttpServletRequest");
    String authorization = req.getHeader("Authorization");
```

For HTTP Basic Authorization, the authorization header is of the form:

```
Authorization: Basic {Base64-encoded username & password}
```

Where the username and password look like "username:password" prior to encoding with the Base64 algorithm. Using some fancy substring manipulation, we get the encoded username and password string:

```
        authorization = authorization.substring(authorization.indexOf(" ")); //
    strip "Basic "
```

Next, decode it using `Base64.decode()`:

```
        byte[] bytes = Base64.decode(authorization);
        String decoded = new String(bytes);
```

The username is what we're after here. It's on the left side of the colon:

```
        int i = decoded.indexOf(":");
        String username = decoded.substring(0,i);
        return username;
    }
```

`getHomedir` gets the user's home directory via the `FilesystemDAO` data access object:

```
    /**
     * Gets the user's home directory via the FilesystemDAO
     * data access object.
     */
    protected String getHomedir(String username) throws Exception {
        FilesystemDAO dao = new FilesystemDAO();
        try {
            return dao.getHomedir(username);
        }
        catch (Exception e) {
            throw new Exception(e.getMessage());
        }

    }

}
```

Once compiled, you can add `Filesystem.class` to your classpath, either under the `com/markrichman/filesystem/` path, or in a `.jar` file containing this package structure. We'll cover packaging a bit later.

Deploying Web Services Using Pluggable Providers

Web Services can be deployed via the command line or through the Apache SOAP Web Admin. Make sure your web server is running, and launch http://localhost:8080/soap/ from your browser. Click Run the admin client when you see the welcome screen. You should then see the following screen:

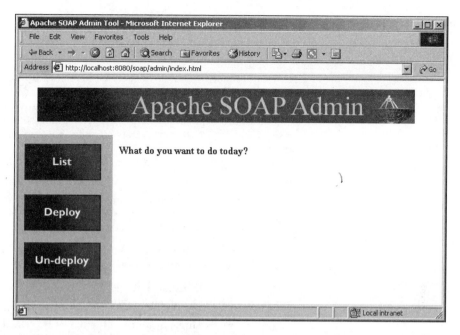

This screen shows the three options that allow you to list, deploy, and un-deploy your Web Services. Since we have no Web Services deployed yet, go ahead and click Deploy. You will be presented with the following screen:

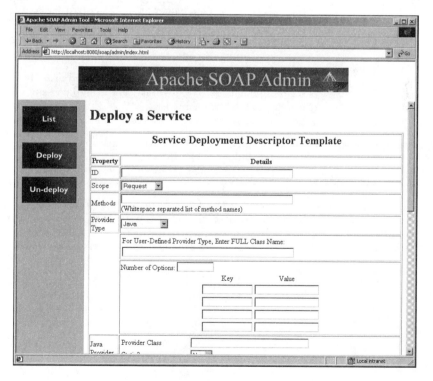

Let's look at each property in the deployment screen:

Property	Description
ID	A URN that uniquely identifies the service to clients. It must be unique among the deployed services, and be encoded as a URI. We commonly use the format: "urn:UniqueServiceID". It corresponds to the target object ID, in the terminology of the SOAP specification. I chose urn:filesystem, but you can really pick any locally unique string you like. See http://www.ietf.org/rfc/rfc2141.txt for a full description of the URN syntax.
Scope	Defines the lifetime of the object serving the invocation request. This corresponds to the scope attribute of the <jsp:useBean> tag in JSP. This tag can have one of the following values: ❑ Request – a new object is created for each request, and is available for the complete duration of the request. ❑ Session – a single instance of the object is created and available for the complete duration of the session. ❑ Application – a single instance of the object is created and available for the complete duration of the application. That is, until the server is shut down.
Method list	Defines the names of the method that can be invoked on this service object. We have the following methods: copyTo, createNewFile, delete, exists, getFile, getParent, isDirectory, isFile, lastModified, length, list, mkdir, mkdirs, renameTo, and setLastModified.
Provider type	Indicates whether the service is implemented using Java or a scripting language. We obviously are using Java, and our provider's full class name is: com.markrichman.filesystem.FilesystemProvider.
Provider class (for Java services)	Fully specified class name of the target object servicing the request. Our pluggable provider is called com.markrichman.filesystem.Filesystem.

We can skip the rest of the options for the purposes of this chapter. Once you've entered the fields, scroll down and click the Deploy button at the bottom of the window. You should see a screen that indicates that the service has been deployed. If you click on the List button, you'll see the URN of your Web Service is listed. Click on its link and you should see the deployed service information screen:

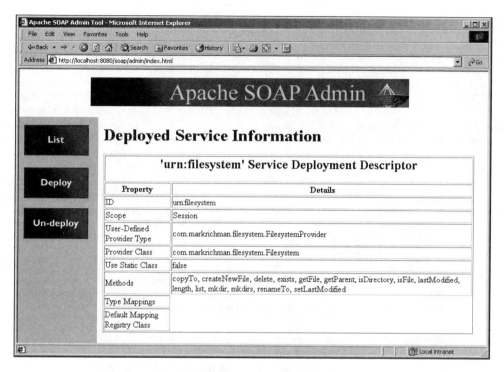

Alternatively, we can deploy the Web Service from the command prompt. To do this, we use a deployment descriptor in XML format. The pluggable provider is simply placed as the full classname in the deployment descriptor's type attribute (DeploymentDescriptor.xml):

```
<isd:service xmlns:isd="http://xml.apache.org/xml-soap/deployment"
             id="urn:filesystem">
  <isd:provider type="com.markrichman.filesystem.FilesystemProvider"
             scope="Session"
             methods="copyTo createNewFile delete exists getFile getParent
isDirectory isFile lastModified length list mkdir mkdirs renameTo
setLastModified">
    <isd:java class="com.markrichman.filesystem.Filesystem"/>
  </isd:provider>
</isd:service>
```

Use the deployment descriptor above to fully describe the service. To deploy the Web Service from the command line:

```
java org.apache.soap.server.ServiceManagerClient
http://localhost:8080/soap/servlet/rpcrouter deploy DeploymentDescriptor.xml
```

The ServiceManagerClient is SOAP client provided with the distribution that communicates with the ServiceManager. Your Web Service will be configured and registered by the Service Manager automatically.

Writing the Filesystem Proxy Class

Invoking a Web Service using the Apache SOAP client API is relatively straightforward. Here, we have created a client proxy class called `FilesystemProxy` to help abstract out a lot of the SOAP internals. You will use this class from your client applications to interact with the Filesystem Web Service. Apache SOAP Web Services are invoked using the `Call` object (`org.apache.soap.rpc.Call`). This object is configured with the endpoint's URL, the target object's URI, method name, and any parameters. In this example, the URL we connect to will be `http://localhost:8080/soap/servlet/rpcrouter`. Remember earlier in this chapter, we configured the server to look for SOAP services on port 8080, with context `/soap`. This URL is bound to `org.apache.soap.server.http.RPCRouterServlet` on the server (see `/webapps/soap/WEB-INF/web.xml`). We also construct a `SOAPHTTPConnection` object to capture the HTTP basic authentication information. The URI of the method call element is used as the object ID on the remote side. Since our Filesystem service takes no parameters, our `params` object is empty (you will notice, however, that the Filesystem Web Service captures the `SOAPContext` parameter transparently). We can now call the `invoke()` method of our `Call` object, which returns a `Response` object. If any exceptions were thrown on the server, the `Fault` object will contain those details. The `resp` object will encapsulate the SOAP response. Calling the `Response.getReturnValue().getValue()` will display the return value of an object. All other types must be cast from object to their expected types. The following code is available from the download as `FilesystemProxy.java`. With the Java Activation Framework and JavaMail on your classpath, you can compile the code with the following command:

```
javac com/markrichman/filesystem/FilesystemProxy.java
```

Again, let's walk through this class's implementation. As the majority of the functions in this section are fairly repetitive, I will just display the most interesting ones:

```
package com.markrichman.filesystem;

import java.io.*;
import java.net.URL;
import java.util.Vector;
import javax.activation.*;
import javax.mail.internet.*;
import org.apache.soap.Constants;
import org.apache.soap.rpc.Call;
import org.apache.soap.Fault;
import org.apache.soap.rpc.Parameter;
import org.apache.soap.rpc.Response;
import org.apache.soap.transport.http.SOAPHTTPConnection;
import org.apache.soap.util.mime.*;


public class FilesystemProxy {
```

The `createNewFile()` method sets up our `Call` object as usual. Notice the `attach()` method. This is responsible for the MIME functionality used in the SOAP with Attachments specification.

```
public boolean createNewFile(String filePath, File file) throws Exception {
    Call call = new Call ();
    call.setTargetObjectURI(targetObjectURI);
    call.setMethodName("createNewFile");
    SOAPHTTPConnection hc = new SOAPHTTPConnection();
    hc.setUserName(username);
    hc.setPassword(password);
    call.setSOAPTransport(hc);
    call.setEncodingStyleURI(Constants.NS_URI_SOAP_ENC);
    Vector params = new Vector ();
    params.addElement (new Parameter("filePath", String.class, filePath, null));
    call.setParams(params);

    System.out.println("Attaching file: " + file.getName());
    attach(file,call);    // MIME Attachment

    Response resp = call.invoke (new URL(url), "");

    if (resp.generatedFault()) {
        Fault fault = resp.getFault ();
        System.out.println ("Ouch, the call failed: ");
        System.out.println ("  Fault Code    = " + fault.getFaultCode ());
        System.out.println ("  Fault java.lang.String = " + fault.getFaultString
());
        throw new Exception(fault.getFaultString());
    }
    else {
        return true;
    }
}
```

Here is the code to actually perform the download. We get the file using the DataHandler. We use a protected utility function called detach() to assist us:

```
public void getFile(String filePath, String local) throws Exception {
    Call call = new Call ();
    call.setTargetObjectURI(targetObjectURI);
    call.setMethodName("getFile");
    SOAPHTTPConnection hc = new SOAPHTTPConnection();
    hc.setUserName(username);
    hc.setPassword(password);
    call.setSOAPTransport(hc);
    Vector params = new Vector ();
    params.addElement (new Parameter("filePath", String.class, filePath, null));
    call.setParams (params);

    Response resp = call.invoke (new URL(url), "");

    if (resp.generatedFault ()) {
```

```
                Fault fault = resp.getFault ();
                System.out.println ("Ouch, the call failed: ");
                System.out.println ("   Fault Code      = " + fault.getFaultCode ());
                System.out.println ("   Fault java.lang.String = " + fault.getFaultString
    ());

                throw new Exception(fault.getFaultString());
            }
        else {
                Parameter result = resp.getReturnValue ();
                System.out.println ( result.getValue() );
                File f = new File(local);
                detach(resp,f);
            }
        }
```

Another interesting method – here we pass back a string array. Apache SOAP handles this for us automatically. List all the files in a directory, returned as a string array:

```
    public String[] list(String filePath) throws Exception {
        Call call = new Call ();
        call.setTargetObjectURI(targetObjectURI);
        call.setMethodName("length");
        SOAPHTTPConnection hc = new SOAPHTTPConnection();
        hc.setUserName(username);
        hc.setPassword(password);
        call.setSOAPTransport(hc);
        Vector params = new Vector ();
        params.addElement (new Parameter("filePath", String.class, filePath, null));
        call.setParams (params);

        Response resp = call.invoke (new URL(url), "");

        if (resp.generatedFault ()) {
            Fault fault = resp.getFault ();
            System.out.println ("Ouch, the call failed: ");
            System.out.println ("   Fault Code      = " + fault.getFaultCode ());
            System.out.println ("   Fault java.lang.String = " + fault.getFaultString
    ());

            throw new Exception(fault.getFaultString());
        }
        else {
            Parameter result = resp.getReturnValue ();
            System.out.println ( result.getValue() );
            String[] s = (String[])result.getValue();
            return s;
        }
    }
```

Here is our utility function for attaching a file to our Call object. This should look very familiar, however we add one line of code to add the MimeBodyPart to the Call object. The SOAP framework will marshall the binary attachment for us:

```
protected void attach(File file, Call call) {
   try {
      DataSource ds = new ByteArrayDataSource(file,null);
      DataHandler dh = new DataHandler(ds);
      MimeBodyPart part = new MimeBodyPart();
      part.setDataHandler(dh) ;
      call.addBodyPart(part);
   }
   catch(Exception e) {
      System.err.println(e.getMessage());
   }


}
```

Now, we can detach the MIME attachment. We simply get at the MimeBodyPart; since we only have one attachment in this instance, we pass getBodyPart() a parameter of 1. The attachment is saved to a local file, specified by f.

```
protected void detach(Response resp, File f) {
   // Write the data
   try {
      MimeBodyPart mbp;
      DataHandler dh;
      Object o;
      InputStream is;
      FileOutputStream fos = new FileOutputStream(f);

      mbp = (MimeBodyPart)resp.getBodyPart(1);
      dh = mbp.getDataHandler();
      is = dh.getInputStream();

      int c;
      while ((c = is.read()) != -1)
         fos.write(c);
   }
   catch(Exception e) {
      System.err.println(e.getMessage());
   }
}
}
```

Writing the Filesystem Client Class

The Filesystem client class is relatively simple. It simply instantiates the FilesystemProxy class, and exercises a few of its functions. Feel free to modify this implementation to test on your own. You'll want to specify a file on your local system, represented here as a.gif. The following code is available in the code download as FilesystemClient.java:

```
package com.markrichman.filesystem;

public class FilesystemClient {

    public static void main (String[] args) {
        try {
            FilesystemProxy fs = new FilesystemProxy();
            fs.setUsername("markr");
            fs.setPassword("Jsdh8qSD");

            for(int i=0;i<10;i++) {
                if(fs.exists(i+"a.gif"))
                    continue;
                fs.createNewFile(i+"a.gif", new java.io.File("a.gif"));
                System.out.println("Last Modified: " +
fs.lastModified(i+"a.gif"));
```

We specify the new last-modified time, measured in milliseconds since the epoch (00:00:00 GMT, January 1, 1970):

```
                fs.setLastModified(i+"a.gif", 153055769);
                System.out.println("New Last Modified: " +
fs.lastModified(i+"a.gif"));
                System.out.println(fs.length(i+"a.gif"));
                fs.copyTo(i+"a.gif", i+"xa.gif");
                fs.delete(i+"a.gif");
                fs.delete(i+"xa.gif");
            }
        }
        catch(Exception e) {
            System.err.println(e.getMessage());
        }
    }
}
```

Packaging the .jar File

I prefer to use a .jar file, so I can package my Web Service, pluggable provider, and database classes all together. We create our .jar file as follows:

```
jar cvf Filesystem.jar com/markrichman/filesystem/*.class
```

The resulting .jar file will be structured like this:

```
META-INF/MANIFEST.MF
com/markrichman/filesystem/Filesystem.class
com/markrichman/filesystem/FilesystemClient.class
com/markrichman/filesystem/FilesystemDAO.class
com/markrichman/filesystem/FilesystemProvider.class
com/markrichman/filesystem/FilesystemProxy.class
```

Dropping this .jar file into Tomcat's /lib folder automatically adds it to the classpath on startup.

Trying It Out

There are a few minor prerequisites before you fire up the client. You need to create a folder called `C:\users`. This is the `homedir` value in the `principal` table specified in `Filesystem.ddl`. The test file `a.gif` will be uploaded and saved there by the web service. The `a.gif` file is a test file - you can alter `FilesystemClient.java` to point to whichever file you like on your hard drive.

To execute the `FilesystemClient`, run the following at the command prompt:

>java com.markrichman.filesystem.FilesystemClient

If all goes well, the client will be authenticated against the `Filesystem` Web Service. You should also see some informational text in the web server's console. Now, test out what happens when you use the wrong password, or delete the reference in the `principal_webservice_map` table in the database. There is a Web Service called `urn:soap-unauthorized` in the database for which no user has permissions. Try using this as the parameter for `call.setTargetObjectURI()`. Bad username/password combinations generate the fault string Bad password, and authorization failures generate a User not authorized fault. I'll leave it as an exercise to the reader to explore the strength of this mechanism.

Summary

I hope you enjoyed this tour of the features and facilities offered by the Apache SOAP Toolkit. The intention throughout this case study has been to provide a solid starting point for you to explore the areas of Web Service development that are of interest to you. Hopefully, this chapter has inspired you to develop unique Web Services of your own with Apache SOAP and Java.

For further work, here are some suggestions on how to build on this case study:

- ❑ Implement the data access in LDAP, as opposed to JDBC.

- ❑ Create a wireless device application that performs the client and proxy functionality. One application here is virtual local storage for handheld devices with no local storage of their own.

- ❑ Implement an offsite backup solution via SOAP and HTTP.

- ❑ Build upon this service to add versioning for your own configuration management system.

15

Case Study: Wrox Online Auction Domain

The goal of this chapter is to demonstrate a set of skills and techniques that will enable you to design and implement a Web Services interface to an existing application. With this in mind, we'll work through a case study on the **Wrox Online Auction Domain** (**WOAD**) using SOAP, WSDL and UDDI to design, build and publish the Web Services layer of an online auction application. The main business activities of our auction application, which we'll call **WebAuction**, will be selling, searching and bidding. Each of these areas involve providing Web Services to support client transactions with fundamentally synchronous or asynchronous server responses.

Firstly, we'll focus on how to build a transaction analysis from the use cases. We'll then move on to building the XML Schema to describe the messages involved, and then combine them into a WSDL specification of the service. Once we have our WSDL we'll use .NET Beta 2 tools and the C# language to develop the client and server Web Service layers incrementally (see Chapter 11 for more on .NET and C#). We'll build and test on a transaction-by-transaction basis though we won't do each and every one. Neither will we build or test the actual auction server or auction client applications that would be required for deployment of our Service in the real world.

Lastly we'll look at the possibilities for integrating the Web Services with client and server applications, and take a very high level view of the issues of state management and security.

Requirements

At the start of most projects, the developer has a user to consult about requirements and to agree the scope. For this one the author simply paid a visit to some well-known online auction sites and decided how many features to include or exclude for phase one of a project to add Web Services. This will be the input to our requirement analysis, starting with workflow diagrams that are similar to UML activity diagrams.

The project will implement the following features in phase 1:

❑   Allow all users to register and logon.

❑   Allow sellers to offer items for sale, and receive bids and status reports.

❑   Allow buyers to find items, view item details, bid for them, and receive status reports.

❑   Give both buyers and sellers final status reports on items they have offered or bid for.

The following Use Case diagram gives us a useful requirements summary as an introduction to the project:

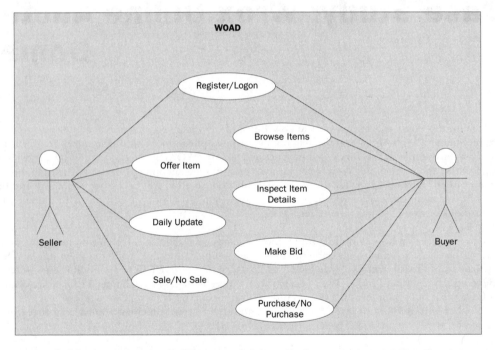

Having decided on our processes, we'll now model the seller's process in more detail, using some different, more precise techniques.

Selling an Item

Let's look at the requirement. Each seller has to be registered so that there is a single person responsible for every item being offered for sale, and so the Web Service can eventually (in phase 2) add value across multiple sales by letting sellers and buyers rate each other and establish higher levels of trust than would otherwise be possible.

We then need to allow the seller to enter details of the item or items that are being offered for sale. Obviously we have to let the seller know if the item has a winning bid by the deadline, but we can make our site more attractive to them by offering an update service to let them know the state of all items they have offered for sale. This will mean additions to our code, but it doesn't involve any extra data on the database, which is a good indication that it should be simple to offer. At this stage we might be thinking of mailing it out to the sellers daily.

Activity Diagrams are useful for modeling workflow logic, so we'll include one for our seller's process here. They're similar to flow-charts and you can think of them as modeling the state(s) of a process. In this case we'll concentrate on the actions in the process, specifically the communications between auction users and the auction system.

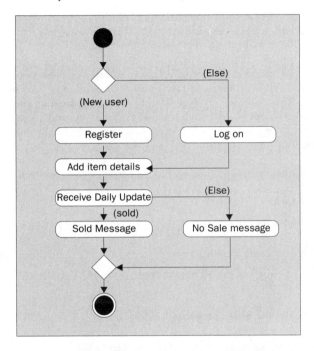

Activity Diagrams go from a start state to an end state via a series of actions, decisions and merges. For more complex systems, with multiple host components, I would usually break out the individual branches and describe the communications in more detail using UML Sequence Diagrams.

We can then document our activities and the paths between them as a use case:

Sell Item

This describes a number of scenarios based around the core activity of selling something on the site

Main Scenario

1. Seller registers new user ID and password. We send an appropriate error if either is invalid, this includes looking up the user ID to ensure that it is not a duplicate.

2. Seller enters item details, timescale and minimum price. Minimum price is public – phase 2 will include the ability to set a reserve price which won't be known to bidders. They can perform this transaction as many times as they wish.

3. System sends daily summary of offers to seller. For each item currently on offer, what bids have been made today if any, by whom, and how long until the deadline. This depends on .Net Web Services supporting asynchronous transactions via protocols such as SMTP, if not we may have to provide this functionality in another way. The system performs this transaction as long as the seller has items on offer.

4. System sends details of winning bid and bidder to seller (and bidder).

"Repeat Seller" Scenario

As above, but different for [1]

1. Seller logs on using existing id and password. We send an appropriate error message for invalid logons.

"No Sale" scenario

As for the Main or Repeat Seller Scenario, but for [4]:

4. System reports absence of any adequate bid to seller.

Obviously a production system would require more complexity, with options to cover seller fees, fee-refunds for non-paying high bidders and so on but this is sufficient for our example. We'll now move on to look at the model for our bidding process.

Buying an Item

The bidding process is similar to the selling process, particularly at the start. We want bidders to register for the same reasons that we want sellers to register. Clearly we want them to be able to find items to bid for, so we'll provide a two-level query mechanism that allows them to do general queries to retrieve item summaries and then drill down to see item details.

If a user decides to bid for an item then we have to accept the bid message. We also want to add value by giving the bidder a summary report on the status of any items for which he or she has outstanding bids. Finally we should let them know if their bid has been successful or not.

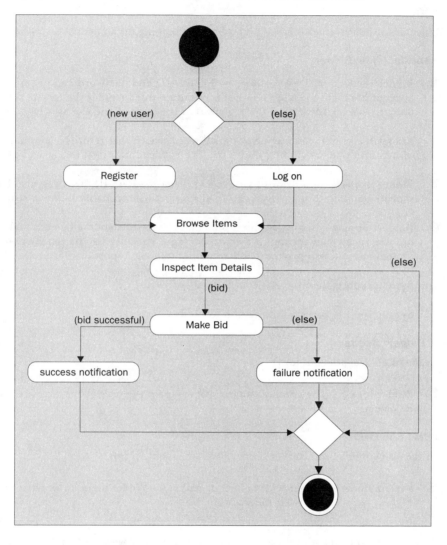

Let's look at the use case for this:

Buy Item

This includes various scenarios based on finding and bidding for an item:

Main Scenario – New Bidder

1. Bidder registers as a user – they send a user ID and password and get an appropriate error message if either is invalid – this includes the case of a non-unique user ID. Otherwise the registration is accepted and the user logged on.

2. Bidder searches for items. This is a keyword search that returns a summary list of items on offer, including their IDs. The bidder can repeat this at will.

3. Bidder inspects item details by querying using the item ID. This can also be repeated at will, though any item details report will probably follow a search.

4. Bidder submits a bid for an item. Bids that are lower than the current highest bid will receive an appropriate error message. This can also be repeated at will, though any bid will probably follow an item details report.

5. System reports item bid status to bidder.

6. System reports success notification to bidder.

"Repeat Bidder" Scenario

As for the Main Scenario, but for [1]:

1. Bidder logs on. They receive an error message if the user ID or password is incorrect.

"Failed Bid" Scenario

As for the "New Bidder" or "Repeat Bidder" Scenarios, but for [6]:

6. System updates Bidder with failure notification. We let them know what their highest bid was and what the winning bid was.

In a real project we might expand the use cases further, but for now we've got enough information to design a set of Web Services.

Transaction Analysis

The first step in the design is to list the **transactions** in the use cases above. We're using the word transactions to mean "individual calls between systems", in the context of this project. In the real world, great satisfaction can be gained from having an increasingly grubby printout of use cases where each of the steps is crossed off in turn, but it's all been done for you in this project.

Here's an initial list of the transactions our Web Services will have to implement:

- ❑ Register User – from both use cases.
- ❑ Logon – from both use cases.
- ❑ Enter item details, minimum price and timescale – from Sell Item, step [2].
- ❑ Receive daily summary of offers – from Sell Item, step [3].
- ❑ Receive details of successful offer – from Sell Item, step [4].
- ❑ Receive no sale message – from Sell Item, No Sale scenario, step [4].
- ❑ Search for items – from Buy Item, step [2].
- ❑ Inspect item – from Buy Item, step [3].
- ❑ Bid for an item – from Buy Item, step [4].
- ❑ Receive daily summary of outstanding bids - from Buy Item, step [5].
- ❑ Receive notification of successful bid - from Buy Item, step [6].
- ❑ Receive notification of failed bid – from Buy Item, Failed Bid Scenario, step [6].

This leaves us with a setback to consider – one of those real life situations where the requirement as stated cannot be met as simply as envisioned. Although the SOAP 1.1 specification (see Appendix A) includes a sample of what a SOAP message would look like with SMTP as the transport protocol (and you have seen examples of SOAP bound to SMTP and to FTP in Chapter 5), there is so far only one official binding, and that is to HTTP. Assuming most users are likely to be using dial-up access, we can't use a synchronous protocol like HTTP for the application to send messages to the users. This is because users may not be online to receive them, and they may not even have a fixed DNS address for us to send the message to, resulting in us possibly sending many messages that will be aborted on non-receipt. However, we don't have the option of using an asynchronous protocol like SMTP because this is not yet a supported feature of .NET Web Services. So this is the point where we would normally go to our business user and lay out the problem and the options with as honest and fair an assessment of the costs and risks as possible.

We could:

- ❑ use a development kit from a different vendor who has implemented SOAP over SMTP.
- ❑ implement SOAP over SMTP ourselves.
- ❑ assume that so many of our users are permanently online that we can send them synchronous messages using HTTP.
- ❑ wait for SOAP over SMTP to be included in .NET.
- ❑ give users their status reports whenever they log in.
- ❑ abandon the project.

In this case the author would recommend giving the user their reports whenever they logon. This reduces the six server-initiated asynchronous transactions to one client-initiated synchronous transaction, while coming close enough to the original requirement.

We will add a ping operation, basically as the simplest-possible transaction to test the client-server connection. This author's experience of client-server projects is that configuring and testing the initial connection is normally the single greatest technological risk factor. Hopefully Web Services will change all this, but it is still useful to have some assistance for this key task built in.

At this point, it's time to consider what SOAP transactions will be needed for our auction site to run properly and for it to have full functionality. The following table shows these operations, the type of user who initiates each operation, and the messages to be sent and returned in each case:

Operation	User Type	Message Sent	Message Returned
Ping	Any user	ping	pingResponse
Register user	Any user	register	reportOk
Logon	Any user	logon	reportOk
Enter item details	Seller	makeOffer	reportItemDetails
Get status of own offers and bids	Any user	requestStatus	reportStatus
Search for items	Buyer	requestItemList	reportItemList
Inspect item	Buyer	RequestItemDetails	reportItemDetails
Bid for an item	Buyer	makeBid	reportBids

Specification

First, we define some plausible structures for the messages. We do this by creating a separate XML Schema, WebAuction.xsd. XML Schemas can be written by hand in a text editor, but I now prefer using relatively mature tools like XML Spy (though at the time of writing Version 4 is still in beta – see http://www.xmlspy.com/) that have a good graphical interface for defining structures, and increasingly effective editing support for creating schema-valid messages. Although a recent W3C recommendation, XML Schema is a key component of .NET and is supported by .NET development tools like wsdl.exe and Visual Studio. Here's the XML Schema that was created to define each of the messages proposed in the above table – the whole schema covers about five sides, so for brevity, only the important parts are walked through below.

> Please note: the full WebAuction.xsd file can be found in the code download for this book on http://www.wrox.com/.

First, we specify the namespaces and defaults:

```
<xsd:schema targetNamespace="http://schemaValid.com/services/webAuction"
            xmlns:xsd="http://www.w3.org/2001/XMLSchema"
            xmlns="http://schemaValid.com/services/webAuction"
            elementFormDefault="qualified">
```

Next, let's specify the structure of the ping messages – an empty call (that is, with no parameters) and a string response:

```
<xsd:element name="ping">
   <xsd:complexType/>
</xsd:element>
<xsd:element name="pingResponse">
   <xsd:complexType>
      <xsd:sequence>
         <xsd:element name="pingResult" type="xsd:string"/>
      </xsd:sequence>
   </xsd:complexType>
</xsd:element>
```

Now, we declare the top-level elements for three other transactions:

```
<xsd:element name="register" type="registerDef"/>
<xsd:element name="logon" type="logonDef"/>
<xsd:element name="makeOffer" type="makeOfferDef"/>
```

and a couple of response messages:

```
<xsd:element name="reportException" type="reportExceptionDef"/>
<xsd:element name="reportOk" type="reportOkDef"/>
```

The remaining message definitions have been truncated for brevity.

This leaves us with five message types to define. `registerDef` combines `userDetails` (which will be reused to describe the user to others) with `password` (which will not be part of a user's public definition):

```
<xsd:complexType name="registerDef">
   <xsd:sequence>
      <xsd:element name="userDetails" type="userDetailsDef"/>
      <xsd:element name="password" type="xsd:string"/>
   </xsd:sequence>
</xsd:complexType>
```

`logonDef` simply contains a `userId` and `password` for a registered user:

```
<xsd:complexType name="logonDef">
   <xsd:sequence>
      <xsd:element name="userId" type="xsd:string"/>
      <xsd:element name="password" type="xsd:string"/>
   </xsd:sequence>
</xsd:complexType>
```

`makeOfferDef` uses a `loggedOnToken` attribute to authenticate the user, and contains enough information to effectively describe and sell an offered item:

```
<xsd:complexType name="makeOfferDef">
   <xsd:sequence>
      <xsd:element name="shortDescription" type="xsd:string"/>
      <xsd:element name="fullDescription" type="xsd:string"/>
      <xsd:element name="startPrice" type="xsd:decimal"/>
      <xsd:element name="reservePrice" type="xsd:decimal"/>
```

```
        <xsd:element name="biddingOpens" type="xsd:dateTime"/>
        <xsd:element name="biddingCloses" type="xsd:dateTime"/>
        <xsd:element name="category" type="categoryDef"
                        maxOccurs="unbounded"/>
    </xsd:sequence>
    <xsd:attribute name="loggedOnToken" type="loggedOnTokenDef"
                        use="required"/>
</xsd:complexType>
```

I've truncated the other definitions here. Remember, you can see the full schema in the code download for the book.

```
<xsd:complexType name="userDetailsDef">
    <xsd:sequence>
        <xsd:element name="userName" type="xsd:string"/>
        <xsd:element name="userId" type="xsd:string"/>
        <xsd:element name="email" type="xsd:string"/>
        <xsd:element name="contactNotes" type="xsd:string"/>
    </xsd:sequence>
</xsd:complexType>
```

We finish off with some re-used messages – the reportOkDef passes back the loggedOnToken:

```
<xsd:complexType name="reportOkDef">
    <xsd:attribute name="loggedOnToken" type="loggedOnTokenDef"/>
</xsd:complexType>
```

The reportExceptionDef passes back information and diagnostics:

```
<xsd:complexType name="reportExceptionDef">
    <xsd:sequence>
        <xsd:element name="exceptionCode">
            <xsd:simpleType>
                <xsd:restriction base="xsd:string">
                    <xsd:maxLength value="16"/>
                </xsd:restriction>
            </xsd:simpleType>
        </xsd:element>
        <xsd:element name="exceptionDescription" type="xsd:string"/>
        <xsd:element name="exceptionData" type="xsd:string"/>
    </xsd:sequence>
</xsd:complexType>
```

categoryDef is a placeholder to allow a stricter definition of categories, perhaps based on Regular Expressions:

```
<xsd:simpleType name="categoryDef">
    <xsd:restriction base="xsd:string"/>
</xsd:simpleType>
```

reportItemDetailsDef is needed because we're re-using this as a response message for the makeOffer transaction where we offer items for sale:

```
<xsd:complexType name="reportItemDetailsDef">
   <xsd:annotation>
      <xsd:documentation
      >define the reportItemDetails message</xsd:documentation>
   </xsd:annotation>
   <xsd:sequence>
      <xsd:element name="shortDescription" type="xsd:string"/>
      <xsd:element name="fullDescription" type="xsd:string"/>
      <xsd:element name="startPrice" type="xsd:decimal"/>
      <xsd:element name="latestPrice" type="xsd:decimal"/>
      <xsd:element name="biddingOpens" type="xsd:dateTime"/>
      <xsd:element name="biddingCloses" type="xsd:dateTime"/>
      <xsd:element name="category" type="categoryDef"
                  maxOccurs="unbounded"/>
   </xsd:sequence>
</xsd:complexType>
```

All that's left is to define a simple type – `loggedOnTokenDef` is used in the `reportOk` and `makeOffer` messages:

```
<xsd:simpleType name="loggedOnTokenDef">
   <xsd:restriction base="xsd:string"/>
</xsd:simpleType>
</xsd:schema>
```

Now we have a structure for our messages, let's use WSDL to specify operations that use them, then bind them to the SOAP protocol and specify where they can be found.

WSDL documents can be generated from scratch (the specification is not too complex) but you may find it simpler to take an existing file – which Visual Studio.NET will generate from any of its sample applications – and adapt it to your requirements. Basically we're going to take four of the transactions listed in the table above and map them to the messages that we've specified in the XML Schema. Then we'll specify that these transactions (or "operations" in WSDL) will run on SOAP using HTTP, and finally we'll say where to find the server running them.

The following code excerpts are taken from the complete `webAuction.wsdl` file that you can get from the code download:

```
<definitions xmlns:s="http://www.w3.org/2001/XMLSchema"
            xmlns:http="http://schemas.xmlsoap.org/wsdl/http/"
            xmlns:mime="http://schemas.xmlsoap.org/wsdl/mime/"
            xmlns:tm="http://microsoft.com/wsdl/mime/textMatching/"
            xmlns:soap="http://schemas.xmlsoap.org/wsdl/soap/"
            xmlns:soapenc="http://schemas.xmlsoap.org/soap/encoding/"
            xmlns:s0="http://schemaValid.com/services/webAuction"
            targetNamespace="http://schemaValid.com/services/webAuction"
            xmlns="http://schemas.xmlsoap.org/wsdl/">

   <types>
```

This is where you can embed XML Schema definitions of your messages. The author cut and pasted the entire contents of `webAuction.xsd` into `webAuction.wsdl`, which has been truncated here for obvious reasons.

WSDL also allows the importation of XML Schemas, which is obviously more elegant, but .Net Beta 2 doesn't appear to support this feature.

```
    </types>
    <message name="pingSoapIn">
        <part name="parameters" element="s0:ping"/>
    </message>
    <message name="pingSoapOut">
        <part name="parameters" element="s0:pingResponse"/>
    </message>
    <message name="register">
        <part name="body" element="s0:register"/>
    </message>
    <message name="reportOk">
        <part name="body" element="s0:reportOk"/>
    </message>
    <message name="reportException">
        <part name="body" element="s0:reportException"/>
    </message>
    <message name="logon">
        <part name="body" element="s0:logon"/>
    </message>
    <message name="makeOffer">
        <part name="body" element="s0:makeOffer"/>
    </message>
```

The rest of the message definitions have been truncated too – you should see a pattern by now. Let's move on to grouping our transactions into a port type (we'll implement the port later by binding it to the SOAP protocol, and specifying an address):

```
<portType name="WebAuctionWebService">
    <operation name="ping">
       <input message="s0:pingSoapIn"/>
       <output message="s0:pingSoapOut"/>
    </operation>
    <operation name="register">
       <input message="s0:register"/>
       <output message="s0:reportOk"/>
       <fault message="s0:reportException"/>
    </operation>
    <operation name="login">
       <input message="s0:logon"/>
       <output message="s0:reportOk"/>
       <fault message="s0:reportException"/>
    </operation>
    <operation name="makeOffer">
       <input message="s0:makeOffer"/>
       <output message="s0:reportItemDetails"/>
       <fault message="s0:reportException"/>
    </operation>
```

The remaining abstract operation definitions that appear at this point have also been skipped:

```
    </portType>
```

Here's where we add any extra information needed to implement the above `portType` as a SOAP port.

The `binding` element allows us to select a protocol or protocols (we could specify HTTP POST as an alternative) that we will use to implement the `port` definition. Within a binding the `soap:binding` extensibility element specifies that we are using SOAP over HTTP as our transport. Each `operation` element refers back to one of the operations defined in the `port`, and allows us to add protocol-specific information. In this case we're specifying SOAP-specific data items, that is the `soapAction` to be included in the HTTP header for each request, and the fact that each input and output uses literal XML rather than SOAP-encoded programming parameters.

```
<binding name="WebAuctionWebServiceSoap" type="s0:WebAuctionWebService">
  <soap:binding transport="http://schemas.xmlsoap.org/soap/http"
                style="document"/>
  <operation name="ping">
    <soap:operation
    soapAction="http://www.schemaValid.com/webservices/WebAuction/ping"
                                                  style="document"/>
    <input>
      <soap:body use="literal"/>
    </input>
    <output>
      <soap:body use="literal"/>
    </output>
  </operation>
  <operation name="register">
    <soap:operation
     soapAction="http://www.schemaValid.com/webservices/
                                        WebAuction/register"
     style="document"/>
    <input>
      <soap:body use="literal"/>
    </input>
    <output>
      <soap:body use="literal"/>
    </output>
  </operation>
  <operation name="login">
    <soap:operation
     soapAction="http://www.schemaValid.com/webservices/
                                        WebAuction/logon"
     style="document"/>
    <input>
      <soap:body use="literal"/>
    </input>
    <output>
      <soap:body use="literal"/>
    </output>
  </operation>
  <operation name="makeOffer">
    <soap:operation
     soapAction="http://www.schemaValid.com/webservices/
                                        WebAuction/makeOffer"
     style="document"/>
    <input>
      <soap:body use="literal"/>
```

```
        </input>
        <output>
            <soap:body use="literal"/>
        </output>
    </operation>
```

The bindings for other operations are defined in `webAuction.wsdl` but have been truncated here.

```
    </binding>
```

The service definition allows us to map one or more bindings to a server. In this case we give it the URL of the .NET Web Service that we are about to create:

```
    <service name="Service1">
        <port name="WebAuctionWebServiceSoap" binding="s0:WebAuctionWebServiceSoap">
            <soap:address location="http://localhost/WebAuction/Service1.asmx"/>
        </port>
    </service>
</definitions>
```

Once we have created this WSDL file, we are now ready to start the next phase of the project, which is implementing our Web Services.

Implementing the WOAD Web Services

As was mentioned at the start, implementing the entire WebAuction client or server application is beyond the scope of this exercise. We will implement and test the client and server Web Services layers using as much automation as possible. We'll write just enough client and server skeleton application code to test the connectivity and to demonstrate how the Web Services layer can be integrated into the rest of the client-server applications.

The first step will be to create the client and server projects in Visual Studio.NET. Then we'll implement and call the simple `ping()` method, finishing off with implementation of three of the operations.

Setting up the Projects

Given that the implementation section of this exercise will use only .NET, we'll use a minimalist, command line and text editor style of development for the client combined with the high automation of the Visual Studio.NET IDE for the server.

For a real project the author would expect to use a combination of Visual Studio.NET for coding both applications, with some .NET and custom command line utilities for initial code generation, depending on the size of the project and the number of operations.

Creating the Server Project

In Visual Studio.NET version 7.0, open a new C# project. Choose the ASP.NET WebService template, and call your project `WebAuction`:

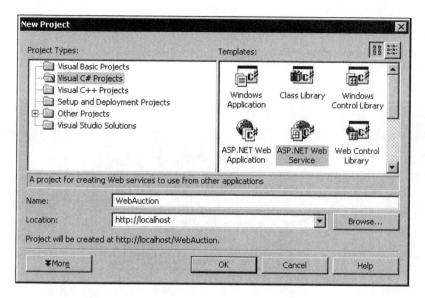

This will create a directory called `C:\Inetpub\wwwroot\WebAuction`, which contains the automatically generated `Service1.asmx` file, as referred to by the service definition and location in `WebAuction.wsdl`. At this stage it is also useful to create a convenient directory somewhere to hold this WSDL file, such as `c:\chap16code`. Download the file (if you haven't already) and save it there.

Creating the Client Project

Create a new directory `C:\webAuctionClient`, then open a Visual Studio.NET command prompt (with public Beta 2 this is available from the Start button, in Visual Studio.Net tools, otherwise just open a command window and set your .NET environment variables), and navigate to this directory.

Implementing the Ping Operation

This is where we can use .NET on our WSDL file to give us a flying start. Using the .NET command prompt, the `wsdl.exe` utility can generate both a complete proxy class for the client project and a useful abstract class for the server project. We'll keep these two classes as intact as possible, in order to minimize the impact of changes to the WSDL. Let's look at the three commands we need to execute to generate the classes.

First we will use the `wsdl.exe` utility to generate a C# class in the server application project directory. Note that we've flagged that we want server code generated, where we want it to be generated, and we have overridden the default filename for the server class. We'll look at how far the utility has been able to help us with the server application a little further down the line.

> **wsdl /server /out:c:\inetpub\wwwroot\webauction\WebAuctionServerBase.cs c:\chap16code\webAuction.wsdl**

Next we use `wsdl.exe` to generate a proxy client class – we can use the default application type, directory and file name here.

> **wsdl c:\chap19code\webAuction.wsdl**

Finally, the client code is compiled as a library for us to link to later:

> csc /debug+ /t:library Service1.cs

The following screen shot shows the full session:

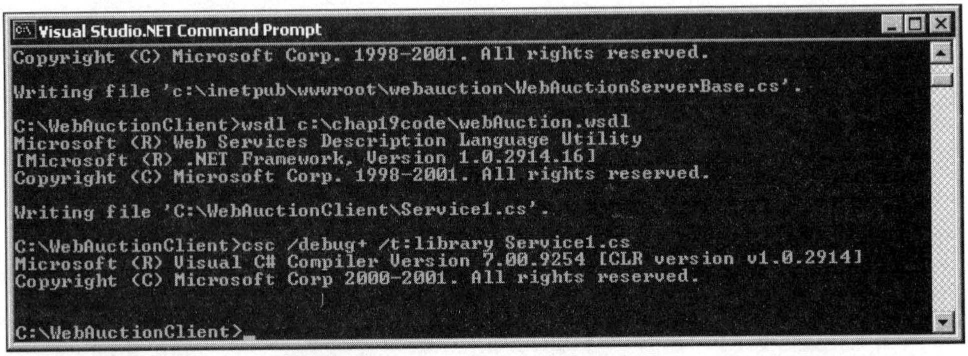

Next switch back to the Visual Studio IDE, and use the menu option File | Add Existing Item to add the newly generated WebAuctionServerBase.cs to the server project. You'll find this file in the C:\inetpub\wwwroot\webAuction folder. Once this file has been added, click on the Solution Explorer button at the top right of the screen to open the Solution Explorer window. Then, double click the WebAuctionServerBase.cs entry that should now be displayed in the Solution Explorer. This will bring up a window headed WebAuctionServerBase design – hit *F7* or select View | Code to reveal the code for this file, as generated by wsdl.exe.

> Please note: the code for each of the following stages, where you are asked to edit a particular file, can be found in the code download for the book. The relevant file name will be given near to where you are asked to alter or amend the code. Each of the files in the download includes all the code necessary to build at the stage where it is introduced.

Implementing Ping on the Server

WebAuctionServerBase.cs contains definitions for an abstract Web Service class called Service1, and for complete classes corresponding to each of the message definitions. It also contains many .NET "attributes" with embedded meta data telling the compiler how these classes and methods are to be mapped to XML serialization and Web Service operations.

We can leave the message classes untouched, but we need to do two things to the service class before we can implement the ping() operation. Firstly, we need to change the class name to WebAuctionBase because its current name of Service1 clashes with the defaults created by Visual Studio's Web Service template. Change the line

```
public abstract class Service1 : System.Web.Services.WebService {
```

to

```
public abstract class WebAuctionBase : System.Web.Services.WebService {
```

Secondly, it's a good idea to simplify the task of implementing a concrete class based on this abstract class. We do this by commenting out any abstract methods that we won't be implementing at this early stage. This avoids the compilation errors we would get unless we implement all abstract methods at once. So we need to comment out any methods we haven't yet implemented in our server class by adding // at the beginning of each of the relevant lines. Begin with `reportOkDef` and end with `reportItemDetailsDef`:

Code with all the above changes already made is available in the file `allcommentedout.txt`.

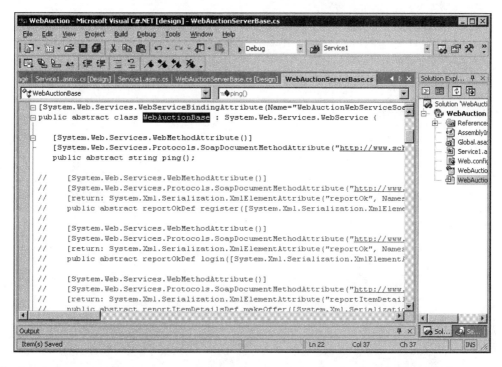

We already have a template server application based on a (currently empty) class called `Service1`, which is defined in `Service1.asmx.cs`. Bring the code for this component up in the Visual Studio IDE, pressing *F7* if necessary, and make the following additions to the component in the places highlighted below. This will implement `WebAuctionBase` in `WebAuction`:

```
namespace WebAuction
{
    /// <summary>
    /// Summary description for Service1.
    /// </summary>
    [WebService(Namespace="http://schemaValid.com/services/webAuction")]
```

Add the `WebService` namespace as above, and change `Service1`'s super class type as below:

```
    public class Service1 : WebAuctionBase
    {
        public Service1()
```

```
        {
        //CODEGEN: This call is required by the ASP.NET Web Services Designer
            InitializeComponent();
        }

        #region Component Designer generated code
        /// <summary>
        /// Required method for Designer support - do not modify
        /// the contents of this method with the code editor.
        /// </summary>
        private void InitializeComponent()
        {
        }
        #endregion

        /// <summary>
        /// Clean up any resources being used.
        /// </summary>
        protected override void Dispose( bool disposing )
        {
        }
```

Lastly, insert the `ping` method implementation by cutting and pasting the method meta data and declaration from the abstract class in `WebAuctionServerBase.cs` into the end of the `Service1.asmx.cs` file, and edit the declaration to override the abstract method. We then provide a nice simple body:

The lines in bold text are the ones you need to edit/add once you've pasted the method in.

```
        [System.Web.Services.WebMethodAttribute()]
        [System.Web.Services.Protocols.SoapDocumentMethodAttribute(
            "http://www.schemaValid.com/webservices/WebAuction/ping",
            RequestNamespace="http://schemaValid.com/services/webAuction",
            ResponseNamespace="http://schemaValid.com/services/webAuction",
            Use=System.Web.Services.Description.SoapBindingUse.Literal,
            ParameterStyle
                =System.Web.Services.Protocols.SoapParameterStyle.Wrapped)]
        public override string ping()
        {
            return "ping: time is " + DateTime.Now;
        }
    }
}
```

Code with all the above changes already made is available from the code download in the file `servicesetup.txt`.

Once we've taken these steps, we should be able to compile everything by hitting *F5* to run. If all has gone to plan, this will bring up a browser instance describing the new service:

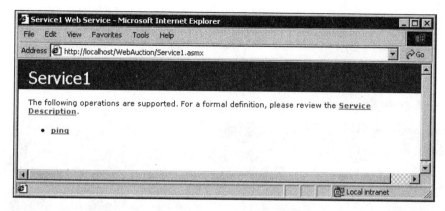

We could now click on the ping link to test this service out interactively, but let's write our own client to demonstrate this simple ping service for illustrative purposes.

Implementing Ping on the Client

Since wsdl.exe generated a complete proxy class we don't need to alter that at all. Instead we just write a small class, WebAuctionClient.cs, to call the proxy. Create this class using your favorite text editor (or get it from the code download in the file webauctionclient1.txt) and save it in the webAuctionClient folder. The code for this class is as follows:

```
using System;

// This class exists to house the application's entry point
class MainApp {

    [System.Diagnostics.DebuggerStepThroughAttribute()]
    static void Main(string[] args)
    {
        // In the client project, Service1 is the proxy class
        Service1 service = new Service1();

        string result = service.ping();
        System.Console.WriteLine(result);

        Console.WriteLine();
        Console.Write("Press Enter to close window.");
        Console.Read();
    }
}
```

We now need to compile and test it from the command window by executing the three commands shown below. To demonstrate the process, we have an unsophisticated little batch file (build.bat) to compile the proxy class (as shown above) to a library, then to compile our new client class, using a /reference option to link in the proxy class library, and finally to run the compiled client. The batch file contains the commands:

```
csc /debug+ /t:library Service1.cs
csc /debug+ /reference:Service1.dll WebAuctionClient.cs
WebAuctionClient
```

To run `build.bat`, download it from http://www.wrox.com/ and save it to the `webAuctionClient` folder and open the Visual Studio.NET command prompt. Navigate to the `webAuctionClient` folder and type:

> **build**

The following screen shot shows the session:

```
Visual Studio.NET Command Prompt                                          _ □ ×
Setting environment for using Microsoft Visual C++.NET 7.0 tools.
(If you also have Visual C++ 6.0 installed and wish to use its tools
from the command line, run vcvars32.bat for Visual C++ 6.0.)

C:\>cd webAuctionClient

C:\webAuctionClient>build

C:\webAuctionClient>csc /debug+ /t:library Service1.cs
Microsoft (R) Visual C# Compiler Version 7.00.9254 [CLR version v1.0.2914]
Copyright (C) Microsoft Corp 2000-2001. All rights reserved.


C:\webAuctionClient>csc /debug+ /reference:Service1.dll WebAuctionClient.cs
Microsoft (R) Visual C# Compiler Version 7.00.9254 [CLR version v1.0.2914]
Copyright (C) Microsoft Corp 2000-2001. All rights reserved.


C:\webAuctionClient>WebAuctionClient
ping: time is 09/07/2001 09:35:50

Press Enter to close window.

C:\webAuctionClient>
```

Now we have a communicating client and server and we've resolved one of the main risk elements for traditional client-server projects, its time to start implementing some of the business services.

Implementing Business Transactions

We are now be able to move to a stage of "normal" application development, where each new transaction is more or less like one we've done already, and the situation is relatively safe and robust. Let's get the rhythm going.

When adding a new transaction, there is a general set of steps that we need to take, which are summarized below:

On the Server Project

❑   Uncomment the method in our abstract class.

❑   Implement the method in our service class.

❑   Recompile and deploy.

On the Client Project

❑   Construct an instance of the message argument (if any) in our client tester program.

❑   Add a call to the method using the message.

❑   Recompile and test.

Let's go through this process with some specific instances:

register()

Let's take the register() operation, server side. Having uncommented the register() abstract method declared in WebAuctionServerBase.cs (available as registeruncommented.txt in the code download), we can then add the code for this method to the Service1 class in Service1.asmx.cs and edit it. Note that this code drops the user details, but it nonetheless provides a hook for saving and validating the details via an existing application:

```
[System.Web.Services.WebMethodAttribute()]
[System.Web.Services.Protocols.SoapDocumentMethodAttribute(
    "http://www.schemaValid.com/webservices/WebAuction/register",
    Use=System.Web.Services.Description.SoapBindingUse.Literal,
    ParameterStyle= System.Web.Services.Protocols.SoapParameterStyle.Bare)]
[return: System.Xml.Serialization.XmlElementAttribute("reportOk",
        Namespace="http://schemaValid.com/services/webAuction",
        IsNullable=false)]
public override reportOkDef register(
[System.Xml.Serialization.XmlElementAttribute("register",
Namespace="http://schemaValid.com/services/webAuction", IsNullable=false)]
registerDef register1)
{
    reportOkDef ok = new reportOkDef();
    ok.loggedOnToken = register1.userDetails.userId + "1000";
    return ok;
}
```

Code with all the above changes already made is available from the code download in the file registerserv.txt.

You'll also notice that the register1 argument to this method has a more complex structure than the one for ping(), mirroring the more complex schema for this message. You can inspect the structure in WebAuctionServerBase.cs where the class is defined.

Now we'll update the client side. This can be achieved by adding a few lines of code to WebAuctionClient.cs and recompiling:

```
userDetailsDef user = new userDetailsDef();
user.userName = "Francis Norton";
user.userId = "fn";
user.email = "francis@redrice.com";
user.contactNotes = "stick to email";

registerDef r = new registerDef();
r.userDetails = user;
r.password = "sesame";

reportOkDef rc = service.register(r);
System.Console.WriteLine(rc.loggedOnToken);
```

Code with all the above changes already made is available from the code download in the file
`webauctionclient2.txt`.

Now we can re-run the batch file, and check the results:

The client prints the requested information to the screen, along with that from the `ping` transaction that
we still have included in our client code.

login()

This is basically very like implementing `register()`, so to make it more interesting we'll call the
service asynchronously. Let's start with the server again. First uncomment the `login()` abstract method
in `WebAuctionServerBase.cs` (the code with this already done is available from the code download
in the file `loginuncommented.txt`). We then add the code for this method to the `Service1` class in
`Service1.asmx.cs`. Again, I'm only suggesting a wire-frame method here, and you'll notice that
there's nothing here in the server code that explicitly supports asynchronous calls – that's all done on
the client side.

```
[System.Web.Services.WebMethodAttribute()]
[System.Web.Services.Protocols.SoapDocumentMethodAttribute(
    "http://www.schemaValid.com/webservices/WebAuction/logon",
    Use=System.Web.Services.Description.SoapBindingUse.Literal,
    ParameterStyle=System.Web.Services.Protocols.SoapParameterStyle.Bare)]
[return: System.Xml.Serialization.XmlElementAttribute("reportOk",
    Namespace="http://schemaValid.com/services/webAuction", IsNullable=false)]
public override reportOkDef login(
    [System.Xml.Serialization.XmlElementAttribute(
        Namespace="http://schemaValid.com/services/webAuction", IsNullable=false)]
    logonDef logon)
{
    reportOkDef ok = new reportOkDef();
    ok.loggedOnToken = logon.userId + "1234";
    return ok;
}
```

Code with all the above changes already made is available from the code download in the file `loginserv.txt`.

Recompile in the usual way, with *F5*.

Now we need to update the client to access this new public method – add the following code to `WebAuctionClient.cs` (available as `webAuctionClient3.txt` from the code download) and recompile:

```
logonDef logon = new logonDef();
logon.userId = "francis";
logon.password = "sesame";

System.Console.WriteLine("about to call login");
IAsyncResult arc = service.Beginlogin(logon, null, null);
while(arc.IsCompleted == false)

    {
        System.Console.Write(".");
    }

rc = service.Endlogin(arc);
System.Console.WriteLine(rc.loggedOnToken);
```

The `Beginlogin()` and `Endlogin()` methods are generated by `wsdl.exe` at the same time as the synchronous version. The two null parameters to `Beginlogin()` allow a more advanced usage, where a delegate method is called back to notify your application that the `async` process has completed. Asynchronous calls allow us to do background processing while our user is waiting at a GUI. They also allow us to write effective multi-threaded applications, though it is complex to write robust, multi-threaded code.

Here is the session that results from building and running our client at this stage:

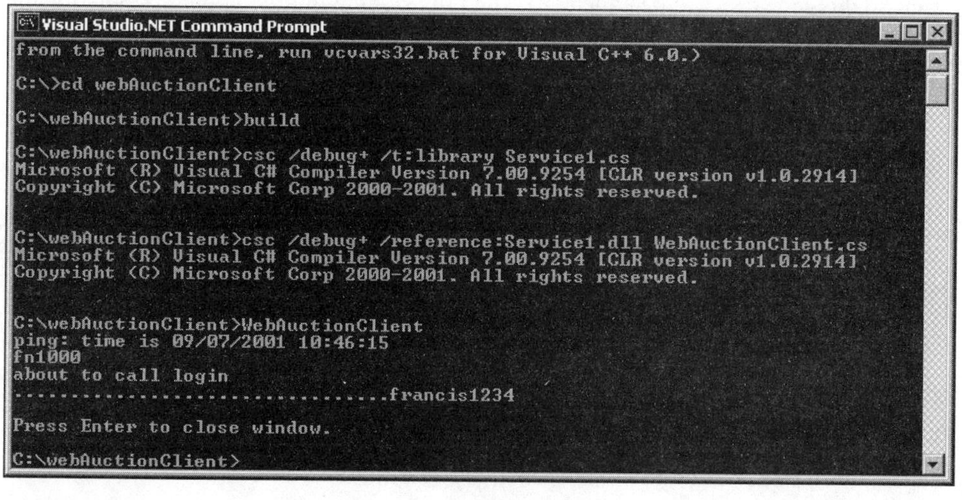

As you can see, we've added two new lines to our screen. about to call login is printed to the screen first after our `ping` and `register` transactions have printed their results, to show us that the `login` transaction has begun. Shortly afterwards, the result is added.

665

makeOffer()

Now let's implement a transaction that involves more complex data structures. Again, uncomment the relevant method in `WebAuctionServerBase.cs` (the full, edited code for this file is available from the code download in the file `offeruncommented.txt`), and paste the following code into `Service1.asmx.cs` (the full, edited code for this file is available from the code download in the file `makeofferserv.txt`):

```
[System.Web.Services.WebMethodAttribute()]
[System.Web.Services.Protocols.SoapDocumentMethodAttribute(
    "http://www.schemaValid.com/webservices/WebAuction/makeOffer",
    Use=System.Web.Services.Description.SoapBindingUse.Literal,
    ParameterStyle=System.Web.Services.Protocols.SoapParameterStyle.Bare)]
[return: System.Xml.Serialization.XmlElementAttribute("reportItemDetails",
    Namespace="http://schemaValid.com/services/webAuction", IsNullable=false)]
public override reportItemDetailsDef makeOffer(
    [System.Xml.Serialization.XmlElementAttribute("makeOffer",
        Namespace="http://schemaValid.com/services/webAuction", IsNullable=false)]
    makeOfferDef makeOffer1)
{
    reportItemDetailsDef result = new reportItemDetailsDef();
    result.shortDescription = makeOffer1.shortDescription;
    result.fullDescription = makeOffer1.fullDescription;
    result.category = makeOffer1.category;
    return result;
}
```

Now use *F5* to recompile the .NET project. You'll notice I've cheated again – I'm borrowing the return structure elements from the client's argument.

So now we need to construct the details of the offered item in the client program by adding the code below and testing it out. This time we've introduced a dependency on the result of the previous `login()`, so this code needs to be added after the call, with the return variable `rc` still in scope:

```
makeOfferDef item = new makeOfferDef();
item.loggedOnToken = rc.loggedOnToken;
item.shortDescription = "Jupiter Ace";
item.fullDescription = "Genuine antique Forth-based personal computer"
    + "with 16k RAM pack and cassette player connector";
item.startPrice = 100.00M;
item.reservePrice = 150.00M;
item.biddingOpens = new System.DateTime(2002, 01, 01);
item.biddingCloses = new System.DateTime(2002, 01, 14);
reportItemDetailsDef rid = service.makeOffer(item);
System.Console.WriteLine(rid.shortDescription);
```

Code with all the above changes already made is available in the file
`webauctionclient4.txt`.

Again, this should compile and run in the usual way, using `build.bat`.

```
C:\>cd webAuctionClient

C:\webAuctionClient>build

C:\webAuctionClient>csc /debug+ /t:library Service1.cs
Microsoft (R) Visual C# Compiler Version 7.00.9254 [CLR version v1.0.2914]
Copyright (C) Microsoft Corp 2000-2001. All rights reserved.


C:\webAuctionClient>csc /debug+ /reference:Service1.dll WebAuctionClient.cs
Microsoft (R) Visual C# Compiler Version 7.00.9254 [CLR version v1.0.2914]
Copyright (C) Microsoft Corp 2000-2001. All rights reserved.


C:\webAuctionClient>WebAuctionClient
ping: time is 09/07/2001 11:02:24
fn1000
about to call login
.............................francis1234
Jupiter Ace

Press Enter to close window.

C:\webAuctionClient>
```

The short description of our added item is printed to the screen after our other transactions have reported their results.

Integrating Web Services With Your Application

The wire-frame client application has been kept as simple as possible in order to enable the author to explain it clearly. The point of a proxy client class like the one we're using is to hide the fact that we're calling a remote system, as our application demonstrates. It doesn't matter which way you write your client application, whether as a command line utility, an onward call from some other Web Service, or as a form-based GUI, you can use the Web Service client proxy as if it was just another local object, if maybe with slower response times.

Similarly the wire-frame server application is very lightweight. In the real world you would design and build your server application with one or more entry points for calling into it. Assuming you had done that, you would implement the abstract server class generated by wsdl.exe, and each method that you went on to implement would then call an appropriate entry point into your server application.

Other aspects of real world implementation would be dealing with state management and security. We will not go into all the key issues these raise in depth here because they could each take up at least a chapter.

State Management and Security

State management can be managed on the server side by using two collections, Application and Session, held in System.Web.Services. They allow the reading and writing of properties for the entire application (such as next available new user ID) or for an individual user's session (such as number of attempts to log on). There are various trade-offs to be made in choosing a state management strategy, where there are choices between performance on the one hand, and robustness and scalability on the other. At one extreme you can have state management scoped to a single application on a single machine, which is fast but vulnerable to crashes and non-scaleable to more machines; at the other you can use SQL Server to store state, which gives you the option to store the state persistently for the use of any machine on a server farm, with robustness against the possibility of all the machines having to be re-booted. These settings are set in the web.config file for .NET projects – check this file for more documentation of these options. Strangely these options are, according to the documentation, only available for the Session object, not for Application. If you have a requirement for heavy-duty, multi-box, application-scoped state management, you may just have to implement it yourself using either SQL Server or an internal Web Service.

Security is inherently troublesome because it's a technology arms race between you and people who may be just as smart as you, are possibly more experienced in the topic, and who don't feel obliged to follow the rules. I recommend reading Bruce Schneier's article about attack trees (http://www.ddj.com/articles/1999/9912/9912a/9912a.htm) just to get into the right frame of mind. Having said that, .NET does include a useful range of security features, correct use of which is a good start to establishing your application's security. The first of these features is the permissions model that is built in to .NET and the CLR (Common Language Runtime). In a real world situation, you need to understand this and use it. The second is the range of authentication features on offer:

❑ Windows logon for intranets

❑ Passport for giving external users a single logon (in the Microsoft-centric universe)

❑ Using session management to store security status - if you are using .NET authentication then the User will be available as a member of your service class. Check the documentation for WebService.User for configuration details.

The third is the correct use of general Internet security features, such as certificates, SSL, firewalls and server security checks.

Some state management and security requirements – like authentication - can also be handled by embedding a session key or user identification in the SOAP header. Search the .NET documentation for 'SOAP header' to find more information on this. The SOAP header is also documented in WSDL. Best practices for this third choice are emerging and are likely to be documented, so keep an eye out.

Publishing the Service

In this section we'll publish the Service to the Microsoft UDDI test registry. The UDDI technology has been described in earlier in the book (in Chapters 6 and 7), so we will focus on the details of publishing our specific Web Service on a typical registry. The process of publishing is mostly a matter of filling in details and making mappings, which I believe makes it a perfect fit for a wizard-style interface, so this section will use the Microsoft registry's web interface.

In order to publish a service to the UDDI registry there are two prerequisites; that the service type definition should be published, and that the service itself should have been deployed. In this case we will emulate the performance of both roles, defining the service and implementing it, although we have not deployed our WOAD application on a production server, so all mappings will be fictitious.

Let's start by defining the service. First, since we're using a Microsoft registry, we have to register ourselves as users using the Microsoft Hotmail and Passport services, so browse to http://test.uddi.microsoft.com/register.aspx and carefully follow the instructions, then click on continue to go to the administration page:

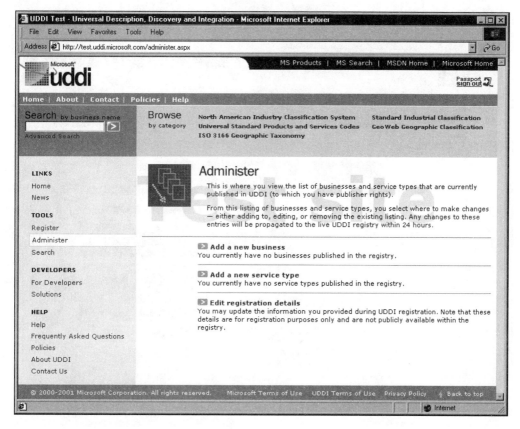

This gives a good overview of what it's all about – publishing service type definitions (which the UDDI spec also refers to as `tModels`), publishing business details, and making mappings between them.

The next step is to add our service type. In a real situation, we would need to have uploaded our `webAuctionInterface.wsdl` (because that is what we have used - UDDI can also use other description languages) to somewhere public before we could do this. For this example situation, you should use a fictitious URL to indicate where you would have hosted the WSDL.

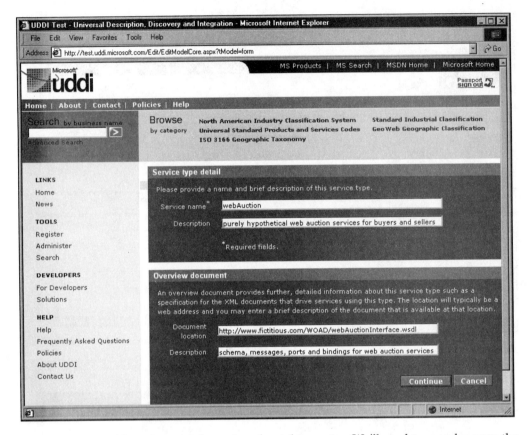

The next step is to add some meta information about this service. We'll need to say who owns the service definition, and then specify technical and business categories for it so that people can find it.

From the service definition page, pick add an identifier and add a business reference. This could be something like a DUNS number – the author selected custom as the identifier type, entered url as the identifier name, and http://www.fictitious.com/WOAD as the identifier value. What you choose will depend on your business requirements, and again for the purposes of this example, it should be fictitious.

Now for more technically interesting steps – we need to add a classification or two. Pick add a classification and move on to the classification screen:

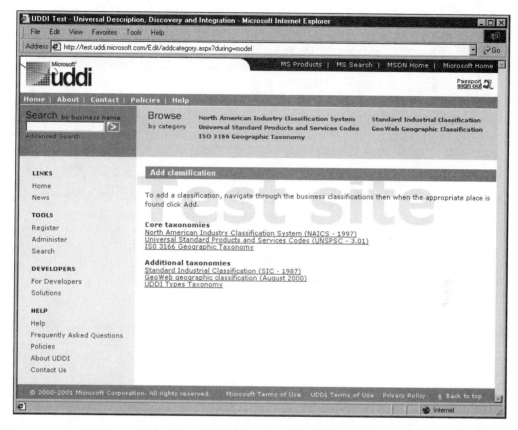

We want to publish the fact that this Web Service definition is defined in a WSDL specification, so we drill down the UDDI Types Taxonomy, through Specification for a web service until we get to a screen where we can add the classification specification for a web service defined in WSDL before clicking on the Add this classification link:

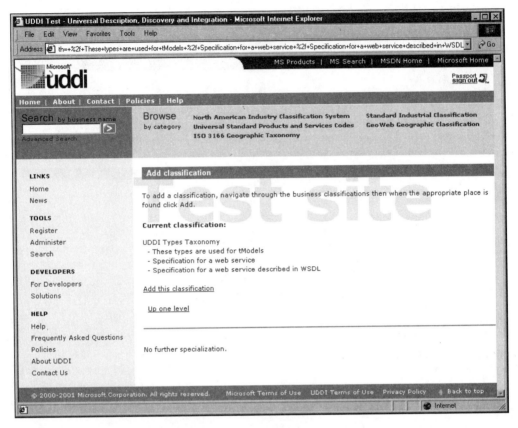

Now we need to select an appropriate service classification. The author browsed the core taxonomies and couldn't find anything plausible there, so moved on and looked up businesses with 'auction' in the name. He found they were commonly classified as SIC business services, within services. As this seemed a bit wide, it made sense to drill down one level and make it Internet business services. This business classification was added by following the same procedure as for the UDDI classification. You could choose to classify your service differently, using the same process.

Having taken these steps we have fulfilled the requirements of our role as a Web Service definition publisher – possible implementers of this definition in a real situation would be able to find the service definition, find the WSDL, and set about implementing server or client applications in the same way we did it ourselves.

In this exercise we are also a Web Service implementer, so the next step is to add our business and tell the world that we have implemented this Web Service. Go back to the Administer screen, and select Add business. This stage is fairly straightforward – the author added the same identifier and business classification, though for a real project these classifications will be determined by business requirements. The interesting bit is linking this business to the Service we have just defined, which we do with Add a service – having added the access point and description, we get to specify which Web Service definition we're implementing here:

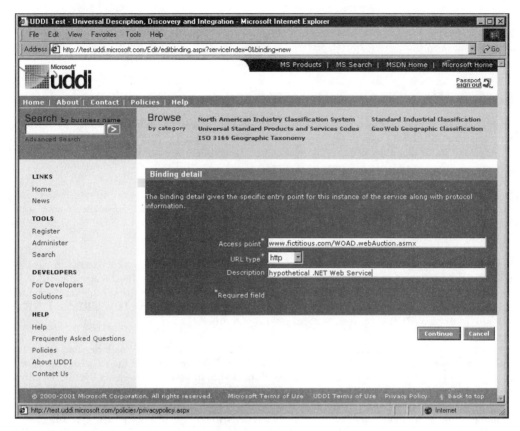

Selecting **Add specification signature** allows you to search for a Web Service definition by name – "webAuction" in our case – then select the correct match from a list. From there we can add additional documentation on service parameters and an overview, and then publish the business and its service.

What Have we Achieved?

Assuming that we had completed these transactions, and implemented them as part of real client and server applications, what if anything would people be able to do with this?

Case 1 – Retail Web Service Clients

Assume you're an end user who wishes to use the service. You may start by searching a UDDI directory for company names which include auction, or – perhaps smarter – for service definition names which include 'auction' and then for companies which support those services.

If you browse to the service definition overview site you will probably be able to find client implementations in Java and .NET that you can download and run with some confidence – apart from technical security features like certificates and sandboxes, you may also have checked that the UDDI registry contains a joint assertion of compatibility from your favorite retailer and the service definition site.

Alternatively this trusted retailer may supply a copy of the client application (just possibly favoring them as a service provider), or, even simpler, you might be able to run the service from the retailer's site as a plug-in or applet, with a rather more sophisticated user interface than would be possible with HTML.

Case 2 – Web Service Developers

A business user would be more likely to use Web Services as a (relatively) plug-and-play extranet, or even as a way of bridging internal system incompatibility problems. Either way is likely to involve development (until or unless some Web Service standards become so dominant that they end up being built in to all the appropriate business packages).

It's an old and occasionally unfashionable truth, but relationships are crucial in commerce. A company is likely to be implementing a Web Service because it wants to do business with someone else who uses it, though once implemented this does create a bias to doing business with others who have compatible services.

To implement the service, a company can be sent a specification by a business partner (for example, "WOAD webAuctions Ltd."). Someone at the company can then look up the service definition's web site on a UDDI registry, or – the lateral approach – if the company finds the service implemented as a .NET Web Service, a developer can simply append a ?wsdl to the .asmx of the URL, and .NET will helpfully return a WSDL specification for the service there.

At this point there will be need to do a gap analysis to see how closely the Web Service operations match the application which will be connected to it as a client or server. If the existing application already has an XML gateway of some kind, developers should consider the use of XSLT to convert messages between your existing formats and the Web Service formats.

If, on the other hand, Web Services are in use internally to bridge otherwise incompatible systems (and the author having spent much of his professional career writing client-server applications involving PCs and mainframes, this makes a very attractive picture) then it may also make sense to implement an internal UDDI Server to act as a services repository. By preventing wheel re-invention and encouraging service re-use this will add to the business case for developing internal Web Services.

Summary

In this exercise we've established, documented and negotiated the requirements for the application. We've designed a set of Web Services to fulfill the requirements, and delivered a WSDL specification from this phase.

Then we used the WSDL specification to get started on writing the client and server Web Service layers using Visual Studio and the .NET environment. We wrote and tested wire-frame `ping()`, `register()`, `login()` and `makeOffer()` operations. The WSDL acted as a well-defined interface between the design and build phases – we could just as well have used a totally different design process that also delivered WSDL, or an alternative development environment – Java being an obvious candidate – which made good use of WSDL as an input.

We established a pattern to adding new operations to the Service, and looked at how the operations would be called from the client application, or would call the server application. We also had a brief, high-level look at state management and security.

Finally we published details of both the web service definition (or tModel) and our business that provides this service via UDDI, using a graphical interface, and we speculated on how our Web Service could be used within retail and business-to-business relationships.

Simple Object Access Protocol (SOAP) 1.1

This appendix is taken from the W3C Note issued on May 8, 2000.

It is available at:

http://www.w3.org/TR/2000/NOTE-SOAP-20000508/

The latest version of the specification can be found at the following URL:

http://www.w3.org/TR/SOAP/

The authors of the original document are as follows:

- ❏ Don Box, DevelopMentor
- ❏ David Ehnebuske, IBM
- ❏ Gopal Kakivaya, Microsoft
- ❏ Andrew Layman, Microsoft
- ❏ Noah Mendelsohn, Lotus Development Corp.
- ❏ Henrik Frystyk Nielsen, Microsoft
- ❏ Satish Thatte, Microsoft
- ❏ Dave Winer, UserLand Software, Inc.

Abstract

SOAP is a lightweight protocol for exchange of information in a decentralized, distributed environment. It is an XML based protocol that consists of three parts: an envelope that defines a framework for describing what is in a message and how to process it, a set of encoding rules for expressing instances of application-defined datatypes, and a convention for representing remote procedure calls and responses. SOAP can potentially be used in combination with a variety of other protocols; however, the only bindings defined in this document describe how to use SOAP in combination with HTTP and HTTP Extension Framework.

Status

This document is a submission to the World Wide Web Consortium (see http://www.w3.org/Submission/2001/07 and http://www.w3.org/Submission/2001/07/Comment) to propose the formation of a working group in the area of XML-based protocols. Comments are welcome to the authors but you are encouraged to share your views on the W3C's public mailing list xml-dist-app@w3.org.

This document is a NOTE made available by the W3C for discussion only. Publication of this Note by W3C indicates no endorsement by W3C or the W3C Team, or any W3C Members. W3C has had no editorial control over the preparation of this Note. This document is a work in progress and may be updated, replaced, or rendered obsolete by other documents at any time.

A list of current W3C technical documents can be found at the Technical Reports page (http://www.w3.org/TR/).

Table of Contents

1.   Introduction
1.1   Design Goals
1.2   Notational Conventions
1.3   Examples of SOAP Messages
2.   The SOAP Message Exchange Model
3.   Relation to XML
4.   SOAP Envelope
4.1.1   SOAP encodingStyle Attribute
4.1.2   Envelope Versioning Model
4.2   SOAP Header
4.2.1   Use of Header Attributes
4.2.2   SOAP actor Attribute
4.2.3   SOAP mustUnderstand Attribute
4.3   SOAP Body
4.3.1   Relationship between SOAP Header and Body

4.4   SOAP Fault
4.4.1   SOAP Fault Codes
5.   SOAP Encoding
5.1   Rules for Encoding Types in XML
5.2   Simple Types
5.2.1   Strings
5.2.2   Enumerations
5.2.3   Array of Bytes
5.3   Polymorphic Accessor
5.4   Compound Types
5.4.1   Compound Values and References to Values
5.4.2   Arrays
5.4.2.1 PartiallyTransmitted Arrays
5.4.2.2 SparseArrays
5.4.3   Generic Compound Types
5.5   Default Values
5.6   SOAP root Attribute
6.   Using SOAP in HTTP
6.1   SOAP HTTP Request
6.1.1   The SOAPAction HTTP Header Field
6.2   SOAP HTTP Response
6.3   The HTTP Extension Framework
6.4   SOAP HTTP Examples
7.   Using SOAP for RPC
7.1   RPC and SOAP Body
7.2   RPC and SOAP Header
8.   Security Considerations
9.   References
A.   SOAP Envelope Examples
A.1   Sample Encoding of Call Requests
A.2   Sample Encoding of Response

1. Introduction

SOAP provides a simple and lightweight mechanism for exchanging structured and typed information between peers in a decentralized, distributed environment using XML. SOAP does not itself define any application semantics such as a programming model or implementation specific semantics; rather it defines a simple mechanism for expressing application semantics by providing a modular packaging model and encoding mechanisms for encoding data within modules. This allows SOAP to be used in a large variety of systems ranging from messaging systems to RPC.

SOAP consists of three parts:

❑   The SOAP envelope (see Section 4) construct defines an overall framework for expressing what is in a message; who should deal with it, and whether it is optional or mandatory.

❑   The SOAP encoding rules (see Section 5) defines a serialization mechanism that can be used to exchange instances of application-defined datatypes.

❑   The SOAP RPC representation (see Section 7) defines a convention that can be used to represent remote procedure calls and responses.

Although these parts are described together as part of SOAP, they are functionally orthogonal. In particular, the envelope and the encoding rules are defined in different namespaces in order to promote simplicity through modularity.

In addition to the SOAP envelope, the SOAP encoding rules and the SOAP RPC conventions, this specification defines two protocol bindings that describe how a SOAP message can be carried in HTTP [5] messages either with or without the HTTP Extension Framework [6].

1.1 Design Goals

A major design goal for SOAP is simplicity and extensibility. This means that there are several features from traditional messaging systems and distributed object systems that are not part of the core SOAP specification. Such features include:

- ❑ Distributed garbage collection
- ❑ Boxcarring (batching) of messages
- ❑ Objects-by-reference (which requires distributed garbage collection)
- ❑ Activation (which requires objects-by-reference)

1.2 Notational Conventions

The keywords "MUST", "MUST NOT", "REQUIRED", "SHALL", "SHALL NOT", "SHOULD", "SHOULD NOT", "RECOMMENDED", "MAY", and "OPTIONAL" in this document are to be interpreted as described in RFC-2119 [2].

The namespace prefixes SOAP-ENV and SOAP-ENC used in this document are associated with the SOAP namespaces http://schemas.xmlsoap.org/soap/envelope/ and http://schemas.xmlsoap.org/soap/encoding/ respectively.

Throughout this document, the namespace prefix xsi is assumed to be associated with the URI http://www.w3.org/1999/XMLSchema-instance defined in the XML Schemas specification [11]. Similarly, the namespace prefix xsd is assumed to be associated with the URI http://www.w3.org/1999/XMLSchema which is defined in [10]. The namespace prefix tns is used to indicate the target namespace of the current document. All other namespace prefixes are samples only.

Namespace URIs of the general form "some-URI" represent some application-dependent or context-dependent URI [4].

This specification uses the augmented Backus-Naur Form (BNF) as described in RFC-2616 [5] for certain constructs.

1.3 Examples of SOAP Messages

In this example, a GetLastTradePrice SOAP request is sent to a StockQuote service. The request takes a string parameter, ticker symbol, and returns a float in the SOAP response. The SOAP Envelope element is the top element of the XML document representing the SOAP message. XML namespaces are used to disambiguate SOAP identifiers from application specific identifiers. The example illustrates the HTTP bindings defined in Section 6. It is worth noting that the rules governing XML payload format in SOAP are entirely independent of the fact that the payload is carried in HTTP.

More examples are available in Appendix A.

Example 1 SOAP Message Embedded in HTTP Request

```
POST /StockQuote HTTP/1.1
Host: www.stockquoteserver.com
Content-Type: text/xml; charset="utf-8"
Content-Length: nnnn
SOAPAction: "Some-URI"

<SOAP-ENV:Envelope
  xmlns:SOAP-ENV="http://schemas.xmlsoap.org/soap/envelope/"
  SOAP-ENV:encodingStyle="http://schemas.xmlsoap.org/soap/encoding/">
  <SOAP-ENV:Body>
      <m:GetLastTradePrice xmlns:m="Some-URI">
          <symbol>DIS</symbol>
      </m:GetLastTradePrice>
  </SOAP-ENV:Body>
</SOAP-ENV:Envelope>
```

Following is the response message containing the HTTP message with the SOAP message as the payload:

Example 2 SOAP Message Embedded in HTTP Response

```
HTTP/1.1 200 OK
Content-Type: text/xml; charset="utf-8"
Content-Length: nnnn

<SOAP-ENV:Envelope
  xmlns:SOAP-ENV="http://schemas.xmlsoap.org/soap/envelope/"
  SOAP-ENV:encodingStyle="http://schemas.xmlsoap.org/soap/encoding/"/>
  <SOAP-ENV:Body>
      <m:GetLastTradePriceResponse xmlns:m="Some-URI">
          <Price>34.5</Price>
      </m:GetLastTradePriceResponse>
  </SOAP-ENV:Body>
</SOAP-ENV:Envelope>
```

2. The SOAP Message Exchange Model

SOAP messages are fundamentally one-way transmissions from a sender to a receiver, but as illustrated above, SOAP messages are often combined to implement patterns such as request/response.

SOAP implementations can be optimized to exploit the unique characteristics of particular network systems. For example, the HTTP binding described in Section 6 provides for SOAP response messages to be delivered as HTTP responses, using the same connection as the inbound request.

Regardless of the protocol to which SOAP is bound, messages are routed along a so-called "message path", which allows for processing at one or more intermediate nodes in addition to the ultimate destination.

A SOAP application receiving a SOAP message MUST process that message by performing the following actions in the order listed below:

1. Identify all parts of the SOAP message intended for that application (see Section 4.2.2)

2. Verify that all mandatory parts identified in step 1 are supported by the application for this message (see Section 4.2.3) and process them accordingly. If this is not the case then discard the message (see Section 4.4). The processor MAY ignore optional parts identified in step 1 without affecting the outcome of the processing.

3. If the SOAP application is not the ultimate destination of the message then remove all parts identified in step 1 before forwarding the message.

Processing a message or a part of a message requires that the SOAP processor understands, among other things, the exchange pattern being used (one way, request/response, multicast, etc.), the role of the recipient in that pattern, the employment (if any) of RPC mechanisms such as the one documented in Section 7, the representation or encoding of data, as well as other semantics necessary for correct processing.

While attributes such as the SOAP `encodingStyle` attribute (see Section 4.1.1) can be used to describe certain aspects of a message, this specification does not mandate a particular means by which the recipient makes such determinations in general. For example, certain applications will understand that a particular `<getStockPrice>` element signals an RPC request using the conventions of Section 7, while another application may infer that all traffic directed to it is encoded as one way messages.

3. Relation to XML

All SOAP messages are encoded using XML (see [7] for more information on XML).

A SOAP application SHOULD include the proper SOAP namespace on all elements and attributes defined by SOAP in messages that it generates. A SOAP application MUST be able to process SOAP namespaces in messages that it receives. It MUST discard messages that have incorrect namespaces (see Section 4.4) and it MAY process SOAP messages without SOAP namespaces as though they had the correct SOAP namespaces.

SOAP defines two namespaces (see [8] for more information on XML namespaces):

❑ The SOAP envelope has the namespace identifier
   http://schemas.xmlsoap.org/soap/envelope/

❑ The SOAP serialization has the namespace identifier
   http://schemas.xmlsoap.org/soap/encoding/

A SOAP message MUST NOT contain a Document Type Declaration. A SOAP message MUST NOT contain Processing Instructions. [7]

SOAP uses the local, unqualified `id` attribute of type `ID` to specify the unique identifier of an encoded element. SOAP uses the local, unqualified attribute `href` of type `uri-reference` to specify a reference to that value, in a manner conforming to the XML Specification [7], XML Schema Specification [11], and XML Linking Language Specification [9].

With the exception of the SOAP `mustUnderstand` attribute (see Section 4.2.3) and the SOAP `actor` attribute (see Section 4.2.2), it is generally permissible to have attributes and their values appear in XML instances or alternatively in schemas, with equal effect. That is, declaration in a DTD or schema with a default or fixed value is semantically equivalent to appearance in an instance.

4. SOAP Envelope

A SOAP message is an XML document that consists of a mandatory SOAP envelope, an optional SOAP header, and a mandatory SOAP body. This XML document is referred to as a SOAP message for the rest of this specification. The namespace identifier for the elements and attributes defined in this section is `http://schemas.xmlsoap.org/soap/envelope/`. A SOAP message contains the following:

❑ The `Envelope` is the top element of the XML document representing the message.

❑ The `Header` is a generic mechanism for adding features to a SOAP message in a decentralized manner without prior agreement between the communicating parties. SOAP defines a few attributes that can be used to indicate who should deal with a feature and whether it is optional or mandatory (see Section 4.2).

❑ The `Body` is a container for mandatory information intended for the ultimate recipient of the message (see Section 4.3). SOAP defines one element for the body, which is the `Fault` element used for reporting errors.

The grammar rules are as follows:

1. `Envelope`

❑ The element name is `Envelope`.

❑ The element MUST be present in a SOAP message.

❑ The element MAY contain namespace declarations as well as additional attributes. If present, such additional attributes MUST be namespace-qualified. Similarly, the element MAY contain additional sub-elements. If present these elements MUST be namespace-qualified and MUST follow the SOAP Body element.

2. `Header` (see Section 4.2)

❑ The element name is `"Header"`.

❑ The element MAY be present in a SOAP message. If present, the element MUST be the first immediate child element of a SOAP Envelope element.

❑ The element MAY contain a set of header entries each being an immediate child element of the SOAP Header element. All immediate child elements of the SOAP Header element MUST be namespace-qualified.

3. `Body` (see Section 4.3)

❑ The element name is `Body`.

❑ The element MUST be present in a SOAP message and MUST be an immediate child element of a SOAP Envelope element. It MUST directly follow the SOAP Header element if present. Otherwise it MUST be the first immediate child element of the SOAP Envelope element.

❑ The element MAY contain a set of body entries each being an immediate child element of the SOAP Body element. Immediate child elements of the SOAP Body element MAY be namespace-qualified. SOAP defines the SOAP Fault element, which is used to indicate error messages (see Section 4.4).

4.1.1 SOAP encodingStyle Attribute

The SOAP encodingStyle global attribute can be used to indicate the serialization rules used in a SOAP message. This attribute MAY appear on any element, and is scoped to that element's contents and all child elements not themselves containing such an attribute, much as an XML namespace declaration is scoped. There is no default encoding defined for a SOAP message.

The attribute value is an ordered space-separated list of one or more URIs identifying the serialization rule or rules that can be used to deserialize the SOAP message indicated in the order of most specific to least specific. Examples of values are:

```
"http://schemas.xmlsoap.org/soap/encoding/"
"http://my.host/encoding/restricted http://my.host/encoding/"
""
```

The serialization rules defined by SOAP in Section 5 are identified by the URI http://schemas.xmlsoap.org/soap/encoding/. Messages using this particular serialization SHOULD indicate this using the SOAP encodingStyle attribute. In addition, all URIs syntactically beginning with http://schemas.xmlsoap.org/soap/encoding/ indicate conformance with the SOAP encoding rules defined in Section 5 (though with potentially tighter rules applied).

A value of the zero-length URI (" ") explicitly indicates that no claims are made for the encoding style of contained elements. This can be used to turn off any claims from containing elements.

4.1.2 Envelope Versioning Model

SOAP does not define a traditional versioning model based on major and minor version numbers. A SOAP message MUST have an Envelope element associated with the http://schemas.xmlsoap.org/soap/envelope/ namespace. If a message is received by a SOAP application in which the SOAP Envelope element is associated with a different namespace, the application MUST treat this as a version error and discard the message. If the message is received through a request/response protocol such as HTTP, the application MUST respond with a SOAP VersionMismatch faultcode message (see Section 4.4) using the SOAP http://schemas.xmlsoap.org/soap/envelope/ namespace.

4.2 SOAP Header

SOAP provides a flexible mechanism for extending a message in a decentralized and modular way without prior knowledge between the communicating parties. Typical examples of extensions that can be implemented as header entries are authentication, transaction management, payment etc.

The Header element is encoded as the first immediate child element of the SOAP Envelope XML element. All immediate child elements of the Header element are called header entries.

The encoding rules for header entries are as follows:

1. A header entry is identified by its fully qualified element name, which consists of the namespace URI and the local name. All immediate child elements of the SOAP Header element MUST be namespace-qualified.

2. The SOAP encodingStyle attribute MAY be used to indicate the encoding style used for the header entries (see Section 4.1.1).

3. The SOAP `mustUnderstand` attribute (see Section 4.2.3) and SOAP `actor` attribute (see Section 4.2.2) MAY be used to indicate how to process the entry and by whom (see Section 4.2.1).

4.2.1 Use of Header Attributes

The SOAP `Header` attributes defined in this section determine how a recipient of a SOAP message should process the message as described in Section 2. A SOAP application generating a SOAP message SHOULD only use the SOAP `Header` attributes on immediate child elements of the SOAP `Header` element. The recipient of a SOAP message MUST ignore all SOAP `Header` attributes that are not applied to an immediate child element of the SOAP `Header` element.

An example is a header with an element identifier of `Transaction`, a `mustUnderstand` attribute of 1, and a value of 5. This would be encoded as follows:

```
<SOAP-ENV:Header>
   <t:Transaction
       xmlns:t="some-URI" SOAP-ENV:mustUnderstand="1">
           5
   </t:Transaction>
</SOAP-ENV:Header>
```

4.2.2 SOAP actor Attribute

A SOAP message travels from the originator to the ultimate destination, potentially by passing through a set of SOAP intermediaries along the message path. A SOAP intermediary is an application that is capable of both receiving and forwarding SOAP messages. Both intermediaries as well as the ultimate destination are identified by a URI.

Not all parts of a SOAP message may be intended for the ultimate destination of the SOAP message but, instead, may be intended for one or more of the intermediaries on the message path. The role of a recipient of a header element is similar to that of accepting a contract in that it cannot be extended beyond the recipient. That is, a recipient receiving a header element MUST NOT forward that header element to the next application in the SOAP message path. The recipient MAY insert a similar header element but in that case, the contract is between that application and the recipient of that header element.

The SOAP `actor` global attribute can be used to indicate the recipient of a header element. The value of the SOAP `actor` attribute is a URI. The special URI `http://schemas.xmlsoap.org/soap/actor/next` indicates that the header element is intended for the very first SOAP application that processes the message. This is similar to the hop-by-hop scope model represented by the `Connection` header field in HTTP.

Omitting the SOAP `actor` attribute indicates that the recipient is the ultimate destination of the SOAP message.

This attribute MUST appear in the SOAP message instance in order to be effective (see Section 3 and 4.2.1).

4.2.3 SOAP mustUnderstand Attribute

The SOAP mustUnderstand global attribute can be used to indicate whether a header entry is mandatory or optional for the recipient to process. The recipient of a header entry is defined by the SOAP actor attribute (see Section 4.2.2). The value of the mustUnderstand attribute is either 1 or 0. The absence of the SOAP mustUnderstand attribute is semantically equivalent to its presence with the value 0.

If a header element is tagged with a SOAP mustUnderstand attribute with a value of 1, the recipient of that header entry either MUST obey the semantics (as conveyed by the fully qualified name of the element) and process correctly to those semantics, or MUST fail processing the message (see Section 4.4).

The SOAP mustUnderstand attribute allows for robust evolution. Elements tagged with the SOAP mustUnderstand attribute with a value of 1 MUST be presumed to somehow modify the semantics of their parent or peer elements. Tagging elements in this manner assures that this change in semantics will not be silently (and, presumably, erroneously) ignored by those who may not fully understand it.

This attribute MUST appear in the instance in order to be effective (see Section 3 and 4.2.1).

4.3 SOAP Body

The SOAP Body element provides a simple mechanism for exchanging mandatory information intended for the ultimate recipient of the message. Typical uses of the Body element include marshalling RPC calls and error reporting.

The Body element is encoded as an immediate child element of the SOAP Envelope XML element. If a Header element is present then the Body element MUST immediately follow the Header element, otherwise it MUST be the first immediate child element of the Envelope element.

All immediate child elements of the Body element are called body entries and each body entry is encoded as an independent element within the SOAP Body element.

The encoding rules for body entries are as follows:

1. A body entry is identified by its fully qualified element name, which consists of the namespace URI and the local name. Immediate child elements of the SOAP Body element MAY be namespace-qualified.

2. The SOAP encodingStyle attribute MAY be used to indicate the encoding style used for the body entries (see Section 4.1.1).

SOAP defines one body entry, which is the Fault entry used for reporting errors (see Section 4.4).

4.3.1 Relationship between SOAP Header and Body

While the Header and Body are defined as independent elements, they are in fact related. The relationship between a body entry and a header entry is as follows: A body entry is semantically equivalent to a header entry intended for the default actor and with a SOAP mustUnderstand attribute with a value of 1. The default actor is indicated by not using the actor attribute (see Section 4.2.2).

4.4 SOAP Fault

The SOAP `Fault` element is used to carry error and/or status information within a SOAP message. If present, the SOAP `Fault` element MUST appear as a body entry and MUST NOT appear more than once within a `Body` element.

The SOAP `Fault` element defines the following four subelements:

❑ `faultcode` - The `faultcode` element is intended for use by software to provide an algorithmic mechanism for identifying the fault. The `faultcode` MUST be present in a SOAP `Fault` element and the `faultcode` value MUST be a qualified name as defined in [8], Section 3. SOAP defines a small set of SOAP fault codes covering basic SOAP faults (see Section 4.4.1)

❑ `faultstring` - The `faultstring` element is intended to provide a human readable explanation of the fault and is not intended for algorithmic processing. The `faultstring` element is similar to the 'Reason-Phrase' defined by HTTP (see [5], Section 6.1). It MUST be present in a SOAP `Fault` element and SHOULD provide at least some information explaining the nature of the fault.

❑ `faultactor` - The `faultactor` element is intended to provide information about who caused the fault to happen within the message path (see Section 2). It is similar to the SOAP `actor` attribute (see Section 4.2.2) but instead of indicating the destination of the header entry, it indicates the source of the fault. The value of the `faultactor` attribute is a URI identifying the source. Applications that do not act as the ultimate destination of the SOAP message MUST include the `faultactor` element in a SOAP `Fault` element. The ultimate destination of a message MAY use the `faultactor` element to indicate explicitly that it generated the fault (see also the `detail` element below).

❑ `detail` - The `detail` element is intended for carrying application specific error information related to the `Body` element. It MUST be present if the contents of the `Body` element could not be successfully processed. It MUST NOT be used to carry information about error information belonging to header entries. Detailed error information belonging to header entries MUST be carried within header entries.

The absence of the `detail` element in the `Fault` element indicates that the fault is not related to processing of the `Body` element. This can be used to distinguish whether the `Body` element was processed or not in case of a fault situation.

All immediate child elements of the `detail` element are called detail entries and each detail entry is encoded as an independent element within the `detail` element.

The encoding rules for detail entries are as follows (see also example 10):

1. A detail entry is identified by its fully qualified element name, which consists of the namespace URI and the local name. Immediate child elements of the `detail` element MAY be namespace-qualified.

2. The SOAP `encodingStyle` attribute MAY be used to indicate the encoding style used for the detail entries (see Section 4.1.1).

Other `Fault` sub-elements MAY be present, provided they are namespace-qualified.

4.4.1 SOAP Fault Codes

The `faultcode` values defined in this section MUST be used in the `faultcode` element when describing faults defined by this specification. The namespace identifier for these `faultcode` values is `http://schemas.xmlsoap.org/soap/envelope/`. Use of this space is recommended (but not required) in the specification of methods defined outside of the present specification.

The default SOAP `faultcode` values are defined in an extensible manner that allows for new SOAP `faultcode` values to be defined while maintaining backwards compatibility with existing `faultcode` values. The mechanism used is very similar to the 1xx, 2xx, 3xx etc basic status classes classes defined in HTTP (see [5] Section 10). However, instead of integers, they are defined as XML qualified names (see [8] Section 3). The character "." (dot) is used as a separator of `faultcode` values indicating that what is to the left of the dot is a more generic fault code value than the value to the right. Example:

```
Client.Authentication
```

The set of `faultcode` values defined in this document is:

Name	Meaning
VersionMismatch	The processing party found an invalid namespace for the SOAP `Envelope` element (see Section 4.1.2)
MustUnderstand	An immediate child element of the SOAP `Header` element that was either not understood or not obeyed by the processing party contained a SOAP `mustUnderstand` attribute with a value of "1" (see Section 4.2.3)
Client	The `Client` class of errors indicate that the message was incorrectly formed or did not contain the appropriate information in order to succeed. For example, the message could lack the proper authentication or payment information. It is generally an indication that the message should not be resent without change. See also Section 4.4 for a description of the SOAP `Fault detail` sub-element.
Server	The `Server` class of errors indicate that the message could not be processed for reasons not directly attributable to the contents of the message itself but rather to the processing of the message. For example, processing could include communicating with an upstream processor, which didn't respond. The message may succeed at a later point in time. See also Section 4.4 for a description of the SOAP `Fault detail` sub-element.

5. SOAP Encoding

The SOAP encoding style is based on a simple type system that is a generalization of the common features found in type systems in programming languages, databases and semi-structured data. A type either is a simple (scalar) type or is a compound type constructed as a composite of several parts, each with a type. This is described in more detail below. This section defines rules for serialization of a graph of typed objects. It operates on two levels. First, given a schema in any notation consistent with the type system described, a schema for an XML grammar may be constructed. Second, given a type-system schema and a particular graph of values conforming to that schema, an XML instance may be constructed. In reverse, given an XML instance produced in accordance with these rules, and given also the original schema, a copy of the original value graph may be constructed.

The namespace identifier for the elements and attributes defined in this section is
`http://schemas.xmlsoap.org/soap/encoding/`. The encoding samples shown assume all
namespace declarations are at a higher element level.

Use of the data model and encoding style described in this section is encouraged but not required; other
data models and encodings can be used in conjunction with SOAP (see Section 4.1.1).

5.1 Rules for Encoding Types in XML

XML allows very flexible encoding of data. SOAP defines a narrower set of rules for encoding. This
section defines the encoding rules at a high level, and the next section describes the encoding rules for
specific types when they require more detail. The encodings described in this section can be used in
conjunction with the mapping of RPC calls and responses specified in Section 7.

To describe encoding, the following terminology is used:

1. A value is a string, the name of a measurement (number, date, enumeration, etc.) or a
    composite of several such primitive values. All values are of specific types.

2. A simple value is one without named parts. Examples of simple values are particular
    strings, integers, enumerated values etc.

3. A compound value is an aggregate of relations to other values. Examples of Compound
    Values are particular purchase orders, stock reports, street addresses, etc.

4. Within a compound value, each related value is potentially distinguished by a role name,
    ordinal or both. This is called its accessor. Examples of compound values include
    particular Purchase Orders, Stock Reports etc. Arrays are also compound values. It is
    possible to have compound values with several accessors each named the same, as RDF
    does for example.

5. An array is a compound value in which ordinal position serves as the only distinction
    among member values.

6. A struct is a compound value in which accessor name is the only distinction among
    member values, and no accessor has the same name as any other.

7. A simple type is a class of simple values. Examples of simple types are the classes
    called string, integer, enumeration classes, etc.

8. A compound type is a class of compound values. An example of a compound type is the
    class of purchase order values sharing the same accessors (shipTo, totalCost, etc.)
    though with potentially different values (and perhaps further constrained by limits on
    certain values).

9. Within a compound type, if an accessor has a name that is distinct within that type but is
    not distinct with respect to other types, that is, the name plus the type together are
    needed to make a unique identification, the name is called "locally scoped." If however
    the name is based in part on a Uniform Resource Identifier, directly or indirectly, such
    that the name alone is sufficient to uniquely identify the accessor irrespective of the type
    within which it appears, the name is called "universally scoped."

689

10. Given the information in the schema relative to which a graph of values is serialized, it is possible to determine that some values can only be related by a single instance of an accessor. For others, it is not possible to make this determination. If only one accessor can reference it, a value is considered "single-reference". If referenced by more than one, actually or potentially, it is "multi-reference." Note that it is possible for a certain value to be considered "single-reference" relative to one schema and "multi-reference" relative to another.

11. Syntactically, an element may be "independent" or "embedded." An independent element is any element appearing at the top level of a serialization. All others are embedded elements.

Although it is possible to use the `xsi:type` attribute such that a graph of values is self-describing both in its structure and the types of its values, the serialization rules permit that the types of values MAY be determinate only by reference to a schema. Such schemas MAY be in the notation described by "XML Schema Part 1: Structures" [10] and "XML Schema Part 2: Datatypes" [11] or MAY be in any other notation. Note also that, while the serialization rules apply to compound types other than `arrays` and `structs`, many schemas will contain only `struct` and `array` types.

The rules for serialization are as follows:

1. All values are represented as element content. A multi-reference value MUST be represented as the content of an independent element. A single-reference value SHOULD not be (but MAY be).

2. For each element containing a value, the type of the value MUST be represented by at least one of the following conditions: (a) the containing element instance contains an `xsi:type` attribute, (b) the containing element instance is itself contained within an element containing a (possibly defaulted) `SOAP-ENC:arrayType` attribute or (c) or the name of the element bears a definite relation to the type, that type then determinable from a schema.

3. A simple value is represented as character data, that is, without any sub-elements. Every simple value must have a type that is either listed in the XML Schemas Specification, part 2 [11] or whose source type is listed therein (see also Section 5.2).

4. A Compound Value is encoded as a sequence of elements, each accessor represented by an embedded element whose name corresponds to the name of the accessor. Accessors whose names are local to their containing types have unqualified element names; all others have qualified names (see also Section 5.4).

5. A multi-reference simple or compound value is encoded as an independent element containing a local, unqualified attribute named `id` and of type `ID` per the XML Specification [7]. Each accessor to this value is an empty element having a local, unqualified attribute named `href` and of type `uri-reference` per the XML Schema Specification [11], with a `href` attribute value of a URI fragment identifier referencing the corresponding independent element.

6. Strings and byte arrays are represented as multi-reference simple types, but special rules allow them to be represented efficiently for common cases (see also Section 5.2.1 and 5.2.3). An accessor to a string or byte-array value MAY have an attribute named `id` and of type `ID` per the XML Specification [7]. If so, all other accessors to the same value are encoded as empty elements having a local, unqualified attribute named `href` and of type `uri-reference` per the XML Schema Specification [11], with a `href` attribute value of a URI fragment identifier referencing the single element containing the value.

7. It is permissible to encode several references to a value as though these were references to several distinct values, but only when it is known from context that the meaning of the XML instance is unaltered.

8. Arrays are compound values (see also Section 5.4.2). SOAP arrays are defined as having a type of SOAP-ENC:Array or a type derived therefrom.

SOAP arrays have one or more dimensions (rank) whose members are distinguished by ordinal position. An array value is represented as a series of elements reflecting the array, with members appearing in ascending ordinal sequence. For multi-dimensional arrays the dimension on the right side varies most rapidly. Each member element is named as an independent element (see rule 2).

SOAP arrays can be single-reference or multi-reference values, and consequently may be represented as the content of either an embedded or independent element.

SOAP arrays MUST contain a SOAP-ENC:arrayType attribute whose value specifies the type of the contained elements as well as the dimension(s) of the array. The value of the SOAP-ENC:arrayType attribute is defined as follows:

```
arrayTypeValue = atype asize
atype          = QName *( rank )
rank           = "[" *( "," ) "]"
asize          = "[" #length "]"
length         = 1*DIGIT
```

The atype construct is the type name of the contained elements expressed as a QName as would appear in the type attribute of an XML Schema element declaration and acts as a type constraint (meaning that all values of contained elements are asserted to conform to the indicated type; that is, the type cited in SOAP-ENC:arrayType must be the type or a supertype of every array member). In the case of arrays of arrays or "jagged arrays", the type component is encoded as the "innermost" type name followed by a rank construct for each level of nested arrays starting from 1. Multi-dimensional arrays are encoded using a comma for each dimension starting from 1.

The asize construct contains a comma separated list of zero, one, or more integers indicating the lengths of each dimension of the array. A value of zero integers indicates that no particular quantity is asserted but that the size may be determined by inspection of the actual members.

For example, an array with 5 members of type array of integers would have an arrayTypeValue value of int[][5] of which the atype value is int[] and the asize value is [5]. Likewise, an array with three members of type two-dimensional arrays of integers would have an arrayTypeValue value of int[,][3] of which the atype value is int[,] and the asize value is [3].

A SOAP array member MAY contain a SOAP-ENC:offset attribute indicating the offset position of that item in the enclosing array. This can be used to indicate the offset position of a partially represented array (see Section 5.4.2.1). Likewise, an array member MAY contain a SOAP-ENC:position attribute indicating the position of that item in the enclosing array. This can be used to describe members of sparse arrays (see Section 5.4.2.2). The value of the SOAP-ENC:offset and the SOAP-ENC:position attribute is defined as follows:

```
arrayPoint = "[" #length "]"
```

with offsets and positions based at 0.

9. A NULL value or a default value MAY be represented by omission of the accessor element. A NULL value MAY also be indicated by an accessor element containing the attribute xsi:null with value '1' or possibly other application-dependent attributes and values.

Note that rule 2 allows independent elements and also elements representing the members of arrays to have names which are not identical to the type of the contained value.

5.2 Simple Types

For simple types, SOAP adopts all the types found in the section "Built-in datatypes" of the "XML Schema Part 2: Datatypes" Specification [11], both the value and lexical spaces. Examples include:

Type	Example
int	58502
float	314159265358979E+1
negativeInteger	-32768
string	Louis "Satchmo" Armstrong

The datatypes declared in the XML Schema specification may be used directly in element schemas. Types derived from these may also be used. An example of a schema fragment and corresponding instance data with elements of these types is:

```
<element name="age" type="int"/>
<element name="height" type="float"/>
<element name="displacement" type="negativeInteger"/>
<element name="color">
  <simpleType base="xsd:string">
    <enumeration value="Green"/>
    <enumeration value="Blue"/>
  </simpleType>
</element>

<age>45</age>
<height>5.9</height>
<displacement>-450</displacement>
<color>Blue</color>
```

All simple values MUST be encoded as the content of elements whose type is either defined in "XML Schema Part 2: Datatypes" Specification [11], or is based on a type found there by using the mechanisms provided in the XML Schema specification.

If a simple value is encoded as an independent element or member of a heterogenous array it is convenient to have an element declaration corresponding to the datatype. Because the "XML Schema Part 2: Datatypes" Specification [11] includes type definitions but does not include corresponding element declarations, the SOAP-ENC schema and namespace declares an element for every simple datatype. These MAY be used.

```
<SOAP-ENC:int id="int1">45</SOAP-ENC:int>
```

5.2.1 Strings

The datatype string is defined in "XML Schema Part 2: Datatypes" Specification [11]. Note that this is not identical to the type called string in many database or programming languages, and in particular may forbid some characters those languages would permit. (Those values must be represented by using some datatype other than xsd:string.)

A string MAY be encoded as a single-reference or a multi-reference value.

The containing element of the string value MAY have an id attribute. Additional accessor elements MAY then have matching href attributes.

For example, two accessors to the same string could appear, as follows:

```
<greeting id="String-0">Hello</greeting>
<salutation href="#String-0"/>
```

However, if the fact that both accessors reference the same instance of the string (or subtype of string) is immaterial, they may be encoded as two single-reference values as follows:

```
<greeting>Hello</greeting>
<salutation>Hello</salutation>
```

Schema fragments for these examples could appear similar to the following:

```
<element name="greeting" type="SOAP-ENC:string"/>
<element name="salutation" type="SOAP-ENC:string"/>
```

(In this example, the type SOAP-ENC:string is used as the element's type as a convenient way to declare an element whose datatype is xsd:string and which also allows an id and href attribute. See the SOAP Encoding schema for the exact definition. Schemas MAY use these declarations from the SOAP Encoding schema but are not required to.)

5.2.2 Enumerations

The "XML Schema Part 2: Datatypes" Specification [11] defines a mechanism called **enumeration**. The SOAP data model adopts this mechanism directly. However, because programming and other languages often define enumeration somewhat differently, we spell-out the concept in more detail here and describe how a value that is a member of an enumerated list of possible values is to be encoded. Specifically, it is encoded as the name of the value.

Enumeration as a concept indicates a set of distinct names. A specific enumeration is a specific list of distinct values appropriate to the base type. For example the set of color names ("Green", "Blue", "Brown") could be defined as an enumeration based on the `string` built-in type. The values 1, 3, 5 are a possible enumeration based on `integer`, and so on. "XML Schema Part 2: Datatypes" [11] supports enumerations for all of the simple types except for `boolean`. The language of "XML Schema Part 1: Structures" Specification [10] can be used to define enumeration types. If a schema is generated from another notation in which no specific base type is applicable, use `string`. In the following schema example `EyeColor` is defined as a string with the possible values of `Green`, `Blue`, or `Brown` enumerated, and instance data is shown accordingly.

```
<element name="EyeColor" type="tns:EyeColor"/>
<simpleType name="EyeColor" base="xsd:string">
    <enumeration value="Green"/>
    <enumeration value="Blue"/>
    <enumeration value="Brown"/>
</simpleType>
<Person>
    <Name>Henry Ford</Name>
    <Age>32</Age>
    <EyeColor>Brown</EyeColor>
</Person>
```

5.2.3 Array of Bytes

An array of bytes MAY be encoded as a single-reference or a multi-reference value. The rules for an array of bytes are similar to those for a string.

In particular, the containing element of the array of bytes value MAY have an `id` attribute. Additional accessor elements MAY then have matching `href` attributes.

The recommended representation of an opaque array of bytes is the 'base64' encoding defined in XML Schemas [10][11], which uses the base64 encoding algorithm defined in 2045 [13]. However, the line length restrictions that normally apply to base64 data in MIME do not apply in SOAP. A `SOAP-ENC:base64` subtype is supplied for use with SOAP.

```
<picture xsi:type="SOAP-ENC:base64">
    aG93IG5vDyBicm73biBjb3cNCg==
</picture>
```

5.3 Polymorphic Accessor

Many languages allow accessors that can polymorphically access values of several types, each type being available at run time. A polymorphic accessor instance MUST contain an `xsi:type` attribute that describes the type of the actual value.

For example, a polymorphic accessor named `cost` with a value of type `xsd:float` would be encoded as follows:

```
<cost xsi:type="xsd:float">29.95</cost>
```

as contrasted with a cost accessor whose value's type is invariant, as follows:

```
<cost>29.95</cost>
```

5.4 Compound types

SOAP defines types corresponding to the following structural patterns often found in programming languages:

- ❏ struct - A struct is a compound value in which accessor name is the only distinction among member values, and no accessor has the same name as any other.

- ❏ array - An array is a compound value in which ordinal position serves as the only distinction among member values.

SOAP also permits serialization of data that is neither a struct nor an array, for example data such as is found in a Directed-Labeled-Graph Data Model in which a single node has many distinct accessors, some of which occur more than once. SOAP serialization does not require that the underlying data model make an ordering distinction among accessors, but if such an order exists, the accessors MUST be encoded in that sequence.

5.4.1 Compound Values, Structs and References to Values

The members of a Compound Value are encoded as accessor elements. When accessors are distinguished by their name (as for example in a struct), the accessor name is used as the element name. Accessors whose names are local to their containing types have unqualified element names; all others have qualified names.

The following is an example of a struct of type Book:

```
<e:Book>
    <author>Henry Ford</author>
    <preface>Prefatory text</preface>
    <intro>This is a book.</intro>
</e:Book>
```

And this is a schema fragment describing the above structure:

```
<element name="Book">
<complexType>
  <element name="author" type="xsd:string"/>
  <element name="preface" type="xsd:string"/>
  <element name="intro" type="xsd:string"/>
</complexType>
</e:Book>
```

Below is an example of a type with both simple and complex members. It shows two levels of referencing. Note that the href attribute of the Author accessor element is a reference to the value whose id attribute matches. A similar construction appears for the Address.

```
<e:Book>
    <title>My Life and Work</title>
    <author href="#Person-1"/>
</e:Book>
<e:Person id="Person-1">
    <name>Henry Ford</name>
    <address href="#Address-2"/>
```

```
   </e:Person>
<e:Address id="Address-2">
   <email>mailto:henryford@hotmail.com</email>
   <web>http://www.henryford.com</web>
</e:Address>
```

The form above is appropriate when the Person value and the Address value are multi-reference. If these were instead both single-reference, they SHOULD be embedded, as follows:

```
<e:Book>
   <title>My Life and Work</title>
   <author>
      <name>Henry Ford</name>
      <address>
         <email>mailto:henryford@hotmail.com</email>
         <web>http://www.henryford.com</web>
      </address>
   </author>
</e:Book>
```

If instead there existed a restriction that no two persons can have the same address in a given instance and that an address can be either a Street-address or an Electronic-address, a Book with two authors would be encoded as follows:

```
<e:Book>
   <title>My Life and Work</title>
   <firstauthor href="#Person-1"/>
   <secondauthor href="#Person-2"/>
</e:Book>
<e:Person id="Person-1">
   <name>Henry Ford</name>
   <address xsi:type="m:Electronic-address">
      <email>mailto:henryford@hotmail.com</email>
      <web>http://www.henryford.com</web>
   </address>
</e:Person>
<e:Person id="Person-2">
   <name>Samuel Crowther</name>
   <address xsi:type="n:Street-address">
      <street>Martin Luther King Rd</street>
      <city>Raleigh</city>
      <state>North Carolina</state>
   </address>
</e:Person>
```

Serializations can contain references to values not in the same resource:

```
<e:Book>
   <title>Paradise Lost</title>
   <firstauthor href="http://www.dartmouth.edu/~milton/"/>
</e:Book>
```

And this is a schema fragment describing the above structures:

```
<element name="Book" type="tns:Book"/>
<complexType name="Book">
    <!-- Either the following group must occur or else the
         href attribute must appear, but not both. -->
    <sequence minOccurs="0" maxOccurs="1">
        <element name="title" type="xsd:string"/>
        <element name="firstauthor" type="tns:Person"/>
        <element name="secondauthor" type="tns:Person"/>
    </sequence>
    <attribute name="href" type="uriReference"/>
    <attribute name="id" type="ID"/>
    <anyAttribute namespace="##other"/>
</complexType>

<element name="Person" base="tns:Person"/>
<complexType name="Person">
    <!-- Either the following group must occur or else the
         href attribute must appear, but not both. -->
    <sequence minOccurs="0" maxOccurs="1">
        <element name="name" type="xsd:string"/>
        <element name="address" type="tns:Address"/>
    </sequence>
    <attribute name="href" type="uriReference"/>
    <attribute name="id" type="ID"/>
    <anyAttribute namespace="##other"/>
</complexType>

<element name="Address" base="tns:Address"/>
<complexType name="Address">
    <!-- Either the following group must occur or else the
         href attribute must appear, but not both. -->
    <sequence minOccurs="0" maxOccurs="1">
        <element name="street" type="xsd:string"/>
        <element name="city" type="xsd:string"/>
        <element name="state" type="xsd:string"/>
    </sequence>
    <attribute name="href" type="uriReference"/>
    <attribute name="id" type="ID"/>
    <anyAttribute namespace="##other"/>
</complexType>
```

5.4.2 Arrays

SOAP arrays are defined as having a type of `SOAP-ENC:Array` or a type derived there from (see also rule 8). Arrays are represented as element values, with no specific constraint on the name of the containing element (just as values generally do not constrain the name of their containing element).

Arrays can contain elements which themselves can be of any type, including nested arrays. New types formed by restrictions of `SOAP-ENC:Array` can also be created to represent, for example, arrays limited to integers or arrays of some user-defined enumeration.

The representation of the value of an array is an ordered sequence of elements constituting the items of the array. Within an array value, element names are not significant for distinguishing accessors. Elements may have any name. In practice, elements will frequently be named so that their declaration in a schema suggests or determines their type. As with compound types generally, if the value of an item in the array is a single-reference value, the item contains its value. Otherwise, the item references its value via an `href` attribute.

The following example is a schema fragment and an array containing integer array members.

```
<element name="myFavoriteNumbers"
        type="SOAP-ENC:Array"/>

<myFavoriteNumbers
  SOAP-ENC:arrayType="xsd:int[2]">
    <number>3</number>
    <number>4</number>
</myFavoriteNumbers>
```

In that example, the array `myFavoriteNumbers` contains several members each of which is a value of type `SOAP-ENC:int`. This can be determined by inspection of the `SOAP-ENC:arrayType` attribute. Note that the `SOAP-ENC:Array` type allows unqualified element names without restriction. These convey no type information, so when used they must either have an `xsi:type` attribute or the containing element must have a `SOAP-ENC:arrayType` attribute. Naturally, types derived from `SOAP-ENC:Array` may declare local elements, with type information.

As previously noted, the `SOAP-ENC` schema contains declarations of elements with names corresponding to each simple type in the "XML Schema Part 2: Datatypes" Specification [11]. It also contains a declaration for `Array`. Using these, we might write

```
<SOAP-ENC:Array SOAP-ENC:arrayType="xsd:int[2]">
    <SOAP-ENC:int>3</SOAP-ENC:int>
    <SOAP-ENC:int>4</SOAP-ENC:int>
</SOAP-ENC:Array>
```

Arrays can contain instances of any subtype of the specified `arrayType`. That is, the members may be of any type that is substitutable for the type specified in the `arrayType` attribute, according to whatever substitutability rules are expressed in the schema. So, for example, an array of integers can contain any type derived from integer (for example `int` or any user-defined derivation of integer). Similarly, an array of `address` might contain a restricted or extended type such as `internationalAddress`. Because the supplied `SOAP-ENC:Array` type admits members of any type, arbitrary mixtures of types can be contained unless specifically limited by use of the `arrayType` attribute.

Types of member elements can be specified using the `xsi:type` attribute in the instance, or by declarations in the schema of the member elements, as the following two arrays demonstrate respectively.

```
<SOAP-ENC:Array SOAP-ENC:arrayType="xsd:ur-type[4]">
    <thing xsi:type="xsd:int">12345</thing>
    <thing xsi:type="xsd:decimal">6.789</thing>
    <thing xsi:type="xsd:string">
        Of Mans First Disobedience, and the Fruit
        Of that Forbidden Tree, whose mortal tast
        Brought Death into the World, and all our woe,
```

```
    </thing>
    <thing xsi:type="xsd:uriReference">
        http://www.dartmouth.edu/~milton/reading_room/
    </thing>
</SOAP-ENC:Array>
<SOAP-ENC:Array SOAP-ENC:arrayType="xsd:ur-type[4]">
    <SOAP-ENC:int>12345</SOAP-ENC:int>
    <SOAP-ENC:decimal>6.789</SOAP-ENC:decimal>
    <xsd:string>
        Of Mans First Disobedience, and the Fruit
        Of that Forbidden Tree, whose mortal tast
        Brought Death into the World, and all our woe,
    </xsd:string>
    <SOAP-ENC:uriReference>
        http://www.dartmouth.edu/~milton/reading_room/
    </SOAP-ENC:uriReference >
</SOAP-ENC:Array>
```

Array values may be `structs` or other compound values. For example an array of `xyz:Order structs`:

```
<SOAP-ENC:Array SOAP-ENC:arrayType="xyz:Order[2]">
    <Order>
        <Product>Apple</Product>
        <Price>1.56</Price>
    </Order>
    <Order>
        <Product>Peach</Product>
        <Price>1.48</Price>
    </Order>
</SOAP-ENC:Array>
```

Arrays may have other arrays as member values. The following is an example of an array of two arrays, each of which is an array of strings.

```
<SOAP-ENC:Array SOAP-ENC:arrayType="xsd:string[][2]">
    <item href="#array-1"/>
    <item href="#array-2"/>
</SOAP-ENC:Array>
<SOAP-ENC:Array id="array-1" SOAP-ENC:arrayType="xsd:string[2]">
    <item>r1c1</item>
    <item>r1c2</item>
    <item>r1c3</item>
</SOAP-ENC:Array>
<SOAP-ENC:Array id="array-2" SOAP-ENC:arrayType="xsd:string[2]">
    <item>r2c1</item>
    <item>r2c2</item>
</SOAP-ENC:Array>
```

The element containing an array value does not need to be named `SOAP-ENC:Array`. It may have any name, provided that the type of the element is either `SOAP-ENC:Array` or is derived from `SOAP-ENC:Array` by restriction. For example, the following is a fragment of a schema and a conforming instance array.

```
<simpleType name="phoneNumber" base="string"/>

<element name="ArrayOfPhoneNumbers">
  <complexType base="SOAP-ENC:Array">
    <element name="phoneNumber" type="tns:phoneNumber" maxOccurs="unbounded"/>
  </complexType>
  <anyAttribute/>
</element>
<xyz:ArrayOfPhoneNumbers SOAP-ENC:arrayType="xyz:phoneNumber[2]">
  <phoneNumber>206-555-1212</phoneNumber>
  <phoneNumber>1-888-123-4567</phoneNumber>
</xyz:ArrayOfPhoneNumbers>
```

Arrays may be multi-dimensional. In this case, more than one size will appear within the `asize` part of the `arrayType` attribute:

```
<SOAP-ENC:Array SOAP-ENC:arrayType="xsd:string[2,3]">
  <item>r1c1</item>
  <item>r1c2</item>
  <item>r1c3</item>
  <item>r2c1</item>
  <item>r2c2</item>
  <item>r2c3</item>
</SOAP-ENC:Array>
```

While the examples above have shown arrays encoded as independent elements, array values MAY also appear embedded and SHOULD do so when they are known to be single references.

The following is an example of a schema fragment and an array of phone numbers embedded in a `struct` of type `Person` and accessed through the accessor `phone-numbers`:

```
<simpleType name="phoneNumber" base="string"/>

<element name="ArrayOfPhoneNumbers">
  <complexType base="SOAP-ENC:Array">
    <element name="phoneNumber" type="tns:phoneNumber" maxOccurs="unbounded"/>
  </complexType>
  <anyAttribute/>
</element>

<element name="Person">
  <complexType>
    <element name="name" type="string"/>
    <element name="phoneNumbers" type="tns:ArrayOfPhoneNumbers"/>
  </complexType>
</element>
<xyz:Person>
  <name>John Hancock</name>
  <phoneNumbers SOAP-ENC:arrayType="xyz:phoneNumber[2]">
      <phoneNumber>206-555-1212</phoneNumber>
      <phoneNumber>1-888-123-4567</phoneNumber>
  </phoneNumbers>
```

Here is another example of a single-reference array value encoded as an embedded element whose containing element name is the accessor name:

```
<xyz:PurchaseOrder>
    <CustomerName>Henry Ford</CustomerName>
    <ShipTo>
        <Street>5th Ave</Street>
        <City>New York</City>
        <State>NY</State>
        <Zip>10010</Zip>
    </ShipTo>
    <PurchaseLineItems SOAP-ENC:arrayType="Order[2]">
        <Order>
            <Product>Apple</Product>
            <Price>1.56</Price>
        </Order>
        <Order>
            <Product>Peach</Product>
            <Price>1.48</Price>
        </Order>
    </PurchaseLineItems>
</xyz:PurchaseOrder>
```

5.4.2.1 Partially Transmitted Arrays

SOAP provides support for partially transmitted arrays, known as **varying** arrays in some contexts [12]. A partially transmitted array indicates in an SOAP-ENC:offset attribute the zero-origin offset of the first element transmitted. If omitted, the offset is taken as zero.

The following is an example of an array of size five that transmits only the third and fourth element counting from zero:

```
<SOAP-ENC:Array SOAP-ENC:arrayType="xsd:string[5]" SOAP-ENC:offset="[2]">
    <item>The third element</item>
    <item>The fourth element</item>
</SOAP-ENC:Array>
```

5.4.2.2 Sparse Arrays

SOAP provides support for sparse arrays. Each element representing a member value contains a SOAP-ENC:position attribute that indicates its position within the array. The following is an example of a sparse array of two-dimensional arrays of strings. The size is 4 but only position 2 is used:

```
<SOAP-ENC:Array SOAP-ENC:arrayType="xsd:string[,][4]">
    <SOAP-ENC:Array href="#array-1" SOAP-ENC:position="[2]"/>
</SOAP-ENC:Array>
<SOAP-ENC:Array id="array-1" SOAP-ENC:arrayType="xsd:string[10,10]">
    <item SOAP-ENC:position="[2,2]">Third row, third col</item>
    <item SOAP-ENC:position="[7,2]">Eighth row, third col</item>
</SOAP-ENC:Array>
```

If the only reference to array-1 occurs in the enclosing array, this example could also have been encoded as follows:

```
<SOAP-ENC:Array SOAP-ENC:arrayType="xsd:string[,][4]">
  <SOAP-ENC:Array SOAP-ENC:position="[2]" SOAP-ENC:arrayType="xsd:string[10,10]>
    <item SOAP-ENC:position="[2,2]">Third row, third col</item>
    <item SOAP-ENC:position="[7,2]">Eighth row, third col</item>
  </SOAP-ENC:Array>
</SOAP-ENC:Array>
```

5.4.3 Generic Compound Types

The encoding rules just cited are not limited to those cases where the accessor names are known in advance. If accessor names are known only by inspection of the immediate values to be encoded, the same rules apply, namely that the accessor is encoded as an element whose name matches the name of the accessor, and the accessor either contains or references its value. Accessors containing values whose types cannot be determined in advance MUST always contain an appropriate xsi:type attribute giving the type of the value.

Similarly, the rules cited are sufficient to allow serialization of compound types having a mixture of accessors distinguished by name and accessors distinguished by both name and ordinal position. (That is, having some accessors repeated.) This does not require that any schema actually contain such types, but rather says that if a type-model schema does have such types, a corresponding XML syntactic schema and instance may be generated.

```
<xyz:PurchaseOrder>
    <CustomerName>Henry Ford</CustomerName>
    <ShipTo>
        <Street>5th Ave</Street>
        <City>New York</City>
        <State>NY</State>
        <Zip>10010</Zip>
    </ShipTo>
    <PurchaseLineItems>
        <Order>
            <Product>Apple</Product>
            <Price>1.56</Price>
        </Order>
        <Order>
            <Product>Peach</Product>
            <Price>1.48</Price>
        </Order>
    </PurchaseLineItems>
</xyz:PurchaseOrder>
```

Similarly, it is valid to serialize a compound value that structurally resembles an array but is not of type (or subtype) SOAP-ENC:Array. For example:

```
<PurchaseLineItems>
    <Order>
        <Product>Apple</Product>
        <Price>1.56</Price>
    </Order>
    <Order>
        <Product>Peach</Product>
        <Price>1.48</Price>
    </Order>
</PurchaseLineItems>
```

5.5 Default Values

An omitted accessor element implies either a default value or that no value is known. The specifics depend on the accessor, method, and its context. For example, an omitted accessor typically implies a `Null` value for polymorphic accessors (with the exact meaning of `Null` accessor-dependent). Likewise, an omitted Boolean accessor typically implies either a `False` value or that no value is known, and an omitted numeric accessor typically implies either that the value is zero or that no value is known.

5.6 SOAP root Attribute

The SOAP root attribute can be used to label serialization roots that are not true roots of an object graph so that the object graph can be deserialized. The attribute can have one of two values, either `1` or `0`. True roots of an object graph have the implied attribute value of `1`. Serialization roots that are not true roots can be labeled as serialization roots with an attribute value of `1` An element can explicitly be labeled as not being a serialization root with a value of `0`.

The SOAP root attribute MAY appear on any sub-element within the SOAP `Header` and SOAP `Body` elements. The attribute does not have a default value.

6. Using SOAP in HTTP

This section describes how to use SOAP within HTTP with or without using the HTTP Extension Framework. Binding SOAP to HTTP provides the advantage of being able to use the formalism and decentralized flexibility of SOAP with the rich feature set of HTTP. Carrying SOAP in HTTP does not mean that SOAP overrides existing semantics of HTTP but rather that the semantics of SOAP over HTTP maps naturally to HTTP semantics.

SOAP naturally follows the HTTP request/response message model providing SOAP request parameters in a HTTP request and SOAP response parameters in a HTTP response. Note, however, that SOAP intermediaries are NOT the same as HTTP intermediaries. That is, an HTTP intermediary addressed with the HTTP Connection header field cannot be expected to inspect or process the SOAP entity body carried in the HTTP request.

HTTP applications MUST use the media type `"text/xml"` according to RFC 2376 [3] when including SOAP entity bodies in HTTP messages.

6.1 SOAP HTTP Request

Although SOAP might be used in combination with a variety of HTTP request methods, this binding only defines SOAP within HTTP POST requests (see Section 7 for how to use SOAP for RPC and Section 6.3 for how to use the HTTP Extension Framework).

6.1.1 The SOAPAction HTTP Header Field

The `SOAPAction` HTTP request header field can be used to indicate the intent of the SOAP HTTP request. The value is a URI identifying the intent. SOAP places no restrictions on the format or specificity of the URI or that it is resolvable. An HTTP client MUST use this header field when issuing a SOAP HTTP Request.

```
soapaction   = "SOAPAction" ":" [ <"> URI-reference <"> ]
URI-reference = <as defined in RFC 2396 [4]>
```

The presence and content of the SOAPAction header field can be used by servers such as firewalls to appropriately filter SOAP request messages in HTTP. The header field value of empty string (" ") means that the intent of the SOAP message is provided by the HTTP Request-URI. No value means that there is no indication of the intent of the message.

Examples:

```
SOAPAction: "http://electrocommerce.org/abc#MyMessage"
SOAPAction: "myapp.sdl"
SOAPAction: ""
SOAPAction:
```

6.2 SOAP HTTP Response

SOAP HTTP follows the semantics of the HTTP Status codes for communicating status information in HTTP. For example, a 2xx status code indicates that the client's request including the SOAP component was successfully received, understood, and accepted etc.

In case of a SOAP error while processing the request, the SOAP HTTP server MUST issue an HTTP 500 "Internal Server Error" response and include a SOAP message in the response containing a SOAP Fault element (see Section 4.4) indicating the SOAP processing error.

6.3 The HTTP Extension Framework

A SOAP message MAY be used together with the HTTP Extension Framework [6] in order to identify the presence and intent of a SOAP HTTP request.

Whether to use the Extension Framework or plain HTTP is a question of policy and capability of the communicating parties. Clients can force the use of the HTTP Extension Framework by using a mandatory extension declaration and the "M-" HTTP method name prefix. Servers can force the use of the HTTP Extension Framework by using the 510 "Not Extended" HTTP status code. That is, using one extra round trip, either party can detect the policy of the other party and act accordingly.

The extension identifier used to identify SOAP using the Extension Framework is

```
http://schemas.xmlsoap.org/soap/envelope/
```

6.4 SOAP HTTP Examples

Example 3 SOAP HTTP Using POST

```
POST /StockQuote HTTP/1.1
Content-Type: text/xml; charset="utf-8"
Content-Length: nnnn
SOAPAction: "http://electrocommerce.org/abc#MyMessage"
```

```
<SOAP-ENV:Envelope...

HTTP/1.1 200 OK
Content-Type: text/xml; charset="utf-8"
Content-Length: nnnn

<SOAP-ENV:Envelope...
```

Example 4 SOAP Using HTTP Extension Framework

```
M-POST /StockQuote HTTP/1.1
Man: "http://schemas.xmlsoap.org/soap/envelope/"; ns=NNNN
Content-Type: text/xml; charset="utf-8"
Content-Length: nnnn
NNNN-SOAPAction: "http://electrocommerce.org/abc#MyMessage"

<SOAP-ENV:Envelope...

HTTP/1.1 200 OK
Ext:
Content-Type: text/xml; charset="utf-8"
Content-Length: nnnn

<SOAP-ENV:Envelope...
```

7. Using SOAP for RPC

One of the design goals of SOAP is to encapsulate and exchange RPC calls using the extensibility and flexibility of XML. This section defines a uniform representation of remote procedure calls and responses.

Although it is anticipated that this representation is likely to be used in combination with the encoding style defined in Section 5 other representations are possible. The SOAP `encodingStyle` attribute (see Section 4.3.2) can be used to indicate the encoding style of the method call and or the response using the representation described in this section.

Using SOAP for RPC is orthogonal to the SOAP protocol binding (see Section 6). In the case of using HTTP as the protocol binding, an RPC call maps naturally to an HTTP request and an RPC response maps to an HTTP response. However, using SOAP for RPC is not limited to the HTTP protocol binding.

To make a method call, the following information is needed:

- The URI of the target object
- A method name
- An optional method signature
- The parameters to the method
- Optional header data

SOAP relies on the protocol binding to provide a mechanism for carrying the URI. For example, for HTTP the request URI indicates the resource that the invocation is being made against. Other than it be a valid URI, SOAP places no restriction on the form of an address (see [4] for more information on URIs).

7.1 RPC and SOAP Body

RPC method calls and responses are both carried in the SOAP `Body` element (see Section 4.3) using the following representation:

❑ A method invocation is modelled as a `struct`.

❑ The method invocation is viewed as a single `struct` containing an accessor for each [in] or [in/out] parameter. The `struct` is both named and typed identically to the method name.

❑ Each [in] or [in/out] parameter is viewed as an accessor, with a name corresponding to the name of the parameter and type corresponding to the type of the parameter. These appear in the same order as in the method signature.

❑ A method response is modelled as a `struct`.

❑ The method response is viewed as a single `struct` containing an accessor for the return value and each [out] or [in/out] parameter. The first accessor is the return value followed by the parameters in the same order as in the method signature.

❑ Each parameter accessor has a name corresponding to the name of the parameter and type corresponding to the type of the parameter. The name of the return value accessor is not significant. Likewise, the name of the `struct` is not significant. However, a convention is to name it after the method name with the string `"Response"` appended.

❑ A method fault is encoded using the SOAP `Fault` element (see Section 4.4). If a protocol binding adds additional rules for fault expression, those also MUST be followed.

As noted above, method and response `structs` can be encoded according to the rules in Section 5, or other encodings can be specified using the `encodingStyle` attribute (see Section 4.1.1).

Applications MAY process requests with missing parameters but also MAY return a fault.

Because a result indicates success and a fault indicates failure, it is an error for the method response to contain both a result and a fault.

7.2 RPC and SOAP Header

Additional information relevant to the encoding of a method request but not part of the formal method signature MAY be expressed in the RPC encoding. If so, it MUST be expressed as a sub-element of the SOAP `Header` element.

An example of the use of the header element is the passing of a transaction ID along with a message. Since the transaction ID is not part of the signature and is typically held in an infrastructure component rather than application code, there is no direct way to pass the necessary information with the call. By adding an entry to the headers and giving it a fixed name, the transaction manager on the receiving side can extract the transaction ID and use it without affecting the coding of remote procedure calls.

8. Security Considerations

Not described in this document are methods for integrity and privacy protection. Such issues will be addressed more fully in a future version(s) of this document.

9. References

[1]   S. Bradner, "The Internet Standards Process -- Revision 3", RFC2026, Harvard University, October 1996

[2]   S. Bradner, "Key words for use in RFCs to Indicate Requirement Levels", RFC 2119, Harvard University, March 1997

[3]   E. Whitehead, M. Murata, "XML Media Types", RFC2376, UC Irvine, Fuji Xerox Info. Systems, July 1998

[4]   T. Berners-Lee, R. Fielding, L. Masinter, "Uniform Resource Identifiers (URI): Generic Syntax", RFC 2396, MIT/LCS, U.C. Irvine, Xerox Corporation, August 1998.

[5]   R. Fielding, J. Gettys, J. C. Mogul, H. Frystyk, T. Berners-Lee, "Hypertext Transfer Protocol -- HTTP/1.1", RFC 2616, U.C. Irvine, DEC W3C/MIT, DEC, W3C/MIT, W3C/MIT, January 1997

[6]   H. Nielsen, P. Leach, S. Lawrence, "An HTTP Extension Framework", RFC 2774, Microsoft, Microsoft, Agranat Systems

[7]   W3C Recommendation "The XML Specification"

[8]   W3C Recommendation "Namespaces in XML"

[9]   W3C Working Draft "XML Linking Language". This is work in progress.

[10]   W3C Working Draft "XML Schema Part 1: Structures". This is work in progress.

[11]   W3C Working Draft "XML Schema Part 2: Datatypes". This is work in progress.

[12]   Transfer Syntax NDR, in "DCE 1.1: Remote Procedure Call"

[13]   N. Freed, N. Borenstein, "Multipurpose Internet Mail Extensions (MIME) Part One: Format of Internet Message Bodies", RFC2045, Innosoft, First Virtual, November 1996

A. SOAP Envelope Examples

A.1 Sample Encoding of Call Requests

Example 5 Similar to Example 1 but with a Mandatory Header

```
POST /StockQuote HTTP/1.1
Host: www.stockquoteserver.com
Content-Type: text/xml; charset="utf-8"
Content-Length: nnnn
SOAPAction: "Some-URI"

<SOAP-ENV:Envelope
  xmlns:SOAP-ENV="http://schemas.xmlsoap.org/soap/envelope/"
  SOAP-ENV:encodingStyle="http://schemas.xmlsoap.org/soap/encoding/"/>
  <SOAP-ENV:Header>
      <t:Transaction
          xmlns:t="some-URI"
          SOAP-ENV:mustUnderstand="1">
              5
      </t:Transaction>
  </SOAP-ENV:Header>
  <SOAP-ENV:Body>
      <m:GetLastTradePrice xmlns:m="Some-URI">
          <symbol>DEF</symbol>
      </m:GetLastTradePrice>
  </SOAP-ENV:Body>
</SOAP-ENV:Envelope>
```

Example 6 Similar to Example 1 but with multiple request parameters

```
POST /StockQuote HTTP/1.1
Host: www.stockquoteserver.com
Content-Type: text/xml; charset="utf-8"
Content-Length: nnnn
SOAPAction: "Some-URI"

<SOAP-ENV:Envelope
  xmlns:SOAP-ENV="http://schemas.xmlsoap.org/soap/envelope/"
  SOAP-ENV:encodingStyle="http://schemas.xmlsoap.org/soap/encoding/"/>
    <SOAP-ENV:Body>
        <m:GetLastTradePriceDetailed
          xmlns:m="Some-URI">
            <Symbol>DEF</Symbol>
            <Company>DEF Corp</Company>
            <Price>34.1</Price>
        </m:GetLastTradePriceDetailed>
    </SOAP-ENV:Body>
</SOAP-ENV:Envelope>
```

A.2 Sample Encoding of Response

Example 7 Similar to Example 2 but with a Mandatory Header

```
HTTP/1.1 200 OK
Content-Type: text/xml; charset="utf-8"
Content-Length: nnnn

<SOAP-ENV:Envelope
  xmlns:SOAP-ENV="http://schemas.xmlsoap.org/soap/envelope/"
  SOAP-ENV:encodingStyle="http://schemas.xmlsoap.org/soap/encoding/"/>
    <SOAP-ENV:Header>
        <t:Transaction
          xmlns:t="some-URI"
          xsi:type="xsd:int" mustUnderstand="1">
            5
        </t:Transaction>
    </SOAP-ENV:Header>
    <SOAP-ENV:Body>
        <m:GetLastTradePriceResponse
          xmlns:m="Some-URI">
            <Price>34.5</Price>
        </m:GetLastTradePriceResponse>
    </SOAP-ENV:Body>
</SOAP-ENV:Envelope>
```

Example 8 Similar to Example 2 but with a Struct

```
HTTP/1.1 200 OK
Content-Type: text/xml; charset="utf-8"
Content-Length: nnnn

<SOAP-ENV:Envelope
  xmlns:SOAP-ENV="http://schemas.xmlsoap.org/soap/envelope/"
  SOAP-ENV:encodingStyle="http://schemas.xmlsoap.org/soap/encoding/"/>
```

```
    <SOAP-ENV:Body>
        <m:GetLastTradePriceResponse
          xmlns:m="Some-URI">
            <PriceAndVolume>
                <LastTradePrice>
                    34.5
                </LastTradePrice>
                <DayVolume>
                    10000
                </DayVolume>
            </PriceAndVolume>
        </m:GetLastTradePriceResponse>
    </SOAP-ENV:Body>
</SOAP-ENV:Envelope>
```

Example 9 Similar to Example 2 but Failing to honor Mandatory Header

```
HTTP/1.1 500 Internal Server Error
Content-Type: text/xml; charset="utf-8"
Content-Length: nnnn

<SOAP-ENV:Envelope
  xmlns:SOAP-ENV="http://schemas.xmlsoap.org/soap/envelope/">
    <SOAP-ENV:Body>
        <SOAP-ENV:Fault>
            <faultcode>SOAP-ENV:MustUnderstand</faultcode>
            <faultstring>SOAP Must Understand Error</faultstring>
        </SOAP-ENV:Fault>
    </SOAP-ENV:Body>
</SOAP-ENV:Envelope>
```

Example 10 Similar to Example 2 but Failing to handle Body

```
HTTP/1.1 500 Internal Server Error
Content-Type: text/xml; charset="utf-8"
Content-Length: nnnn

<SOAP-ENV:Envelope
  xmlns:SOAP-ENV="http://schemas.xmlsoap.org/soap/envelope/">
    <SOAP-ENV:Body>
        <SOAP-ENV:Fault>
            <faultcode>SOAP-ENV:Server</faultcode>
            <faultstring>Server Error</faultstring>
            <detail>
                <e:myfaultdetails xmlns:e="Some-URI">
                    <message>
                        My application didn't work
                    </message>
                    <errorcode>
                        1001
                    </errorcode>
                </e:myfaultdetails>
            </detail>
        </SOAP-ENV:Fault>
    </SOAP-ENV:Body>
</SOAP-ENV:Envelope>
```

THIS DOCUMENT IS PROVIDED "AS IS," AND COPYRIGHT HOLDERS MAKE NO REPRESENTATIONS OR WARRANTIES, EXPRESS OR IMPLIED, INCLUDING, BUT NOT LIMITED TO, WARRANTIES OF MERCHANTABILITY, FITNESS FOR A PARTICULAR PURPOSE, NON-INFRINGEMENT, OR TITLE; THAT THE CONTENTS OF THE DOCUMENT ARE SUITABLE FOR ANY PURPOSE; NOR THAT THE IMPLEMENTATION OF SUCH CONTENTS WILL NOT INFRINGE ANY THIRD PARTY PATENTS, COPYRIGHTS, TRADEMARKS OR OTHER RIGHTS.

THE COPYRIGHT HOLDERS WILL NOT BE LIABLE FOR ANY DIRECT, INDIRECT, SPECIAL OR CONSEQUENTIAL DAMAGES ARISING OUT OF ANY USE OF THE DOCUMENT OR THE PERFORMANCE OR IMPLEMENTATION OF THE CONTENTS THEREOF.

The name and trademarks of copyright holders may NOT be used in advertising or publicity pertaining to this document or its contents without specific, written prior permission. Title to copyright in this document will at all times remain with copyright holders.

Web Services Description Language WSDL) 1.1

This appendix is taken from the W3C Note issued on March 15, 2001, and available at:

http://www.w3.org/TR/2001/NOTE-wsdl-20010315

The latest version of the WSDL specification can be found at the following URL:

http://www.w3.org/TR/wsdl

The authors of the original document are as follows:

- ❑ Erik Christensen, Microsoft
- ❑ Francisco Curbera, IBM Research
- ❑ Greg Meredith, Microsoft
- ❑ Sanjiva Weerawarana, IBM Research

Abstract

WSDL is an XML format for describing network services as a set of endpoints operating on messages containing either document-oriented or procedure-oriented information. The operations and messages are described abstractly, and then bound to a concrete network protocol and message format to define an endpoint. Related concrete endpoints are combined into abstract endpoints (services). WSDL is extensible to allow description of endpoints and their messages regardless of what message formats or network protocols are used to communicate, however, the only bindings described in this document describe how to use WSDL in conjunction with SOAP 1.1, HTTP GET/POST, and MIME.

Status

This document is a submission to the World Wide Web Consortium (see http://www.w3.org/Submission/2001/07/ and http://www.w3.org/Submission/2001/07/Comment/) as a suggestion for describing services for the W3C XML Activity on XML Protocols. For a full list of all acknowledged submissions, please see http://www.w3.org/Submission/.

This draft represents the current thinking with regard to descriptions of services within Ariba, IBM, and Microsoft. It consolidates concepts found in NASSL, SCL, and SDL (earlier proposals in this space). This document is a NOTE made available by the W3C for discussion only. Publication of this Note by W3C indicates no endorsement by W3C or the W3C Team, or any W3C Members. W3C has had no editorial control over the preparation of this Note. This document is a work in progress and may be updated, replaced, or rendered obsolete by other documents at any time.

A list of current W3C technical documents can be found at the Technical Reports page.

Table of Contents

1	Introduction.
1.1	WSDL Document Example
1.2	Notational Conventions
2	Service Definition
2.1	Document Structure
2.1.1	Document Naming and Linking
2.1.2	Authoring Style
2.1.3	Language Extensibility and Binding
2.1.4	Documentation
2.2	Types
2.3	Messages
2.3.1	Message Parts
2.3.2	Abstract vs. Concrete Messages
2.4	Port Types
2.4.1	One-way Operation
2.4.2	Request-response Operation
2.4.3	Solicit-response Operation
2.4.4	Notification Operation
2.4.5	Names of Elements within an Operation
2.4.6	Parameter Order within an Operation
2.5	Bindings
2.6	Ports
2.7	Services

3	SOAP Binding
3.1	SOAP Examples
3.2	How the SOAP Binding Extends WSDL
3.3	`soap:binding`
3.4	`soap:operation`
3.5	`soap:body`
3.6	`soap:fault`
3.7	`soap:header` and `soap:headerfault`
3.8	`soap:address`
4	HTTP GET & POST Binding
4.1	HTTP GET/POST Examples
4.2	How the HTTP GET/POST Binding Extends WSDL
4.3	`http:address`
4.4	`http:binding`
4.5	`http:operation`
4.6	`http:urlEncoded`
4.7	`http:urlReplacement`
5	MIME Binding
5.1	MIME Binding example
5.2	How the MIME Binding extends WSDL
5.3	`mime:content`
5.4	`mime:multipartRelated`
5.5	`soap:body`
5.6	`mime:mimeXml`
6	References
A 1	Notes on URIs
A 1.1	XML namespaces & schema locations
A 1.2	Relative URIs
A 1.3	Generating URIs
A 2	Wire format for WSDL examples
A 2.1	Example 1
A 3	Location of Extensibility Elements
A 4	Schemas
A 4.1	WSDL Schema
A 4.2	SOAP Binding Schema
A 4.3	HTTP Binding Schema
A 4.4	MIME Binding Schema

1. Introduction

As communications protocols and message formats are standardized in the web community, it becomes increasingly possible and important to be able to describe the communications in some structured way. WSDL addresses this need by defining an XML grammar for describing network services as collections of communication endpoints capable of exchanging messages. WSDL service definitions provide documentation for distributed systems and serve as a recipe for automating the details involved in applications communication.

A WSDL document defines **services** as collections of network endpoints, or **ports**. In WSDL, the abstract definition of endpoints and messages is separated from their concrete network deployment or data format bindings. This allows the reuse of abstract definitions: **messages**, which are abstract descriptions of the data being exchanged, and **port types** which are abstract collections of **operations**. The concrete protocol and data format specifications for a particular port type constitutes a reusable **binding**. A port is defined by associating a network address with a reusable binding, and a collection of ports define a service. Hence, a WSDL document uses the following elements in the definition of network services:

- ❑ **Types**– a container for data type definitions using some type system (such as XSD).
- ❑ **Message**– an abstract, typed definition of the data being communicated.
- ❑ **Operation**– an abstract description of an action supported by the service.
- ❑ **Port Type**–an abstract set of operations supported by one or more endpoints.
- ❑ **Binding**– a concrete protocol and data format specification for a particular port type.
- ❑ **Port**– a single endpoint defined as a combination of a binding and a network address.
- ❑ **Service**– a collection of related endpoints.

These elements are described in detail in Section 2. It is important to observe that WSDL does not introduce a new type definition language. WSDL recognizes the need for rich type systems for describing message formats, and supports the XML Schemas specification (XSD) [11] as its canonical type system. However, since it is unreasonable to expect a single type system grammar to be used to describe all message formats present and future, WSDL allows using other type definition languages via extensibility.

In addition, WSDL defines a common **binding** mechanism. This is used to attach a specific protocol or data format or structure to an abstract message, operation, or endpoint. It allows the reuse of abstract definitions.

In addition to the core service definition framework, this specification introduces specific **binding extensions** for the following protocols and message formats:

- ❑ SOAP 1.1 (see Section 3)
- ❑ HTTP GET / POST (see Section 4)
- ❑ MIME (see Section 5)

Although defined within this document, the above language extensions are layered on top of the core service definition framework. Nothing precludes the use of other binding extensions with WSDL.

1.1 WSDL Document Example

The following example shows the WSDL definition of a simple service providing stock quotes. The service supports a single operation called `GetLastTradePrice`, which is deployed using the SOAP 1.1 protocol over HTTP. The request takes a ticker symbol of type `string`, and returns the price as a `float`. A detailed description of the elements used in this definition can be found in Section 2 (Core Language) and Section 3 (SOAP Binding).

This example uses a fixed XML format instead of the SOAP encoding (for an example using the SOAP encoding, see Example 4).

Example 1 SOAP 1.1 Request/Response via HTTP

```xml
<?xml version="1.0"?>
<definitions name="StockQuote"

targetNamespace="http://example.com/stockquote.wsdl"
          xmlns:tns="http://example.com/stockquote.wsdl"
          xmlns:xsd1="http://example.com/stockquote.xsd"
          xmlns:soap="http://schemas.xmlsoap.org/wsdl/soap/"
          xmlns="http://schemas.xmlsoap.org/wsdl/">

    <types>
        <schema targetNamespace="http://example.com/stockquote.xsd"
              xmlns="http://www.w3.org/2000/10/XMLSchema">
            <element name="TradePriceRequest">
                <complexType>
                    <all>
                        <element name="tickerSymbol" type="string"/>
                    </all>
                </complexType>
            </element>
            <element name="TradePrice">
                <complexType>
                    <all>
                        <element name="price" type="float"/>
                    </all>
                </complexType>
            </element>
        </schema>
    </types>

    <message name="GetLastTradePriceInput">
        <part name="body" element="xsd1:TradePriceRequest"/>
    </message>

    <message name="GetLastTradePriceOutput">
        <part name="body" element="xsd1:TradePrice"/>
    </message>

    <portType name="StockQuotePortType">
        <operation name="GetLastTradePrice">
            <input message="tns:GetLastTradePriceInput"/>
            <output message="tns:GetLastTradePriceOutput"/>
        </operation>
    </portType>

    <binding name="StockQuoteSoapBinding" type="tns:StockQuotePortType">
        <soap:binding style="document" transport=
         "http://schemas.xmlsoap.org/soap/http"/>
        <operation name="GetLastTradePrice">
            <soap:operation soapAction="http://example.com/GetLastTradePrice"/>
            <input>
                <soap:body use="literal"/>
            </input>
            <output>
                <soap:body use="literal"/>
```

```
            </output>
        </operation>
    </binding>

    <service name="StockQuoteService">
        <documentation>My first service</documentation>
        <port name="StockQuotePort" binding="tns:StockQuoteBinding">
            <soap:address location="http://example.com/stockquote"/>
        </port>
    </service>

</definitions>
```

1.2 Notational Conventions

1. The keywords "MUST", "MUST NOT", "REQUIRED", "SHALL", "SHALL NOT", "SHOULD", "SHOULD NOT", "RECOMMENDED", "MAY", and "OPTIONAL" in this document are to be interpreted as described in RFC-2119 [2].

2. The following namespace prefixes are used throughout this document:

Prefix	Namespace URI	Definition
wsdl	http://schemas.xmlsoap.org/wsdl/	WSDL namespace for WSDL framework.
soap	http://schemas.xmlsoap.org/wsdl/soap/	WSDL namespace for WSDL SOAP binding.
http	http://schemas.xmlsoap.org/wsdl/http/	WSDL namespace for WSDL HTTP GET & POST binding.
mime	http://schemas.xmlsoap.org/wsdl/mime/	WSDL namespace for WSDL MIME binding.
soapenc	http://schemas.xmlsoap.org/soap/encoding/	Encoding namespace as defined by SOAP 1.1 [8].
soapenv	http://schemas.xmlsoap.org/soap/envelope/	Envelope namespace as defined by SOAP 1.1 [8].
xsi	http://www.w3.org/2000/10/XMLSchema-instance/	Instance namespace as defined by XSD [10].
xsd	http://www.w3.org/2000/10/XMLSchema/	Schema namespace as defined by XSD [10].
tns	*various*	The "this namespace" (tns) prefix is used as a convention to refer to the current document.

Prefix	Namespace URI		Definition
other	*various*		All other namespace prefixes are samples only. In particular, URIs starting `http://example.com` represent some application-dependent or context-dependent URI [4].

3. This specification uses an **informal syntax** to describe the XML grammar of a WSDL document. The syntax appears as an XML instance, but the values indicate the data types instead of values. Characters are appended to elements and attributes as follows: "?" (0 or 1), "*" (0 or more), "+" (1 or more). Elements names ending in "..." (such as `<element.../>` or `<element...>`) indicate that elements/attributes irrelevant to the context are being omitted.

4. Grammar in bold has not been introduced earlier in the document, or is of particular interest in an example. Also note that `<-- extensibility element -->` is a placeholder for elements from some "other" namespace (like ##other in XSD). **The XML** namespace prefixes (defined above) are used to indicate the namespace of the element being defined.

5. Examples starting with `<?xml` contain enough information to conform to this specification; other examples are fragments and require additional information to be specified in order to conform. XSD schemas are provided as a formal definition of **WSDL** grammar (see Section A4).

2. Service Definition

This section describes the core elements of the WSDL language. Binding extensions for SOAP, HTTP and MIME are included in Sections 3, 4 and 5.

2.1 WSDL Document Structure

A WSDL document is simply a **set of definitions**. There is a **definitions** element at the root, **and** definitions inside. The grammar is as follows:

```
<wsdl:definitions name="nmtoken"? targetNamespace="uri"?>

    <import namespace="uri" location="uri"/>*

    <wsdl:documentation .... /> ?

    <wsdl:types> ?
        <wsdl:documentation .... />?
        <xsd:schema .... />*
        <-- extensibility element --> *
    </wsdl:types>
```

```
    <wsdl:message name="nmtoken"> *
        <wsdl:documentation .... />?
        <part name="nmtoken" element="qname"? type="qname"?/> *
    </wsdl:message>

    <wsdl:portType name="nmtoken">*
        <wsdl:documentation .... />?
        <wsdl:operation name="nmtoken">*
            <wsdl:documentation .... /> ?
            <wsdl:input name="nmtoken"? message="qname">?
                <wsdl:documentation .... /> ?
            </wsdl:input>
            <wsdl:output name="nmtoken"? message="qname">?
                <wsdl:documentation .... /> ?
            </wsdl:output>
            <wsdl:fault name="nmtoken" message="qname"> *
                <wsdl:documentation .... /> ?
            </wsdl:fault>
        </wsdl:operation>
    </wsdl:portType>

    <wsdl:binding name="nmtoken" type="qname">*
        <wsdl:documentation .... />?
        <-- extensibility element --> *
        <wsdl:operation name="nmtoken">*
            <wsdl:documentation .... /> ?
            <-- extensibility element --> *
            <wsdl:input> ?
                <wsdl:documentation .... /> ?
                <-- extensibility element -->
            </wsdl:input>
            <wsdl:output> ?
                <wsdl:documentation .... /> ?
                <-- extensibility element --> *
            </wsdl:output>
            <wsdl:fault name="nmtoken"> *
                <wsdl:documentation .... /> ?
                <-- extensibility element --> *
            </wsdl:fault>
        </wsdl:operation>
    </wsdl:binding>

    <wsdl:service name="nmtoken"> *
        <wsdl:documentation .... />?
        <wsdl:port name="nmtoken" binding="qname"> *
            <wsdl:documentation .... /> ?
            <-- extensibility element -->
        </wsdl:port>
        <-- extensibility element -->
    </wsdl:service>

    <-- extensibility element --> *

</wsdl:definitions>
```

Services are defined using six major elements:

❏   **types,** which provides data type definitions used to describe the messages exchanged.

- ❑ **message**, which represents an abstract definition of the data being transmitted. A message consists of logical parts, each of which is associated with a definition within some type system.

- ❑ **portType**, which is a set of abstract operations. Each operation refers to an input message and output messages.

- ❑ **binding**, which specifies concrete protocol and data format specifications for the operations and messages defined by a particular `portType`.

- ❑ **port**, which specifies an address for a binding, thus defining a single communication endpoint.

- ❑ **service**, which is used to aggregate a set of related ports.

These elements will be described in detail in Sections 2.2 to 2.7. In the rest of this section we describe the rules introduced by WSDL for naming documents, referencing document definitions, using language extensions and adding contextual documentation.

2.1.1 Document Naming and Linking

WSDL documents can be assigned an optional `name` attribute of type NCNAME that serves as a lightweight form of documentation. Optionally, a `targetNamespace` attribute of type URI may be specified. The URI MUST NOT be a relative URI. WSDL allows associating a **namespace** with a document **location** using an `import` statement:

```
<definitions .... >
    <import namespace="uri" location="uri"/> *
</definitions>
```

A reference to a WSDL definition is made using a QName. The following types of definitions contained in a WSDL document may be referenced:

- ❑ WSDL definitions: service, port, message, bindings, and `portType`.

- ❑ Other definitions: if additional definitions are added via extensibility, they SHOULD use QName linking.

Each WSDL definition type listed above has its own **name scope** (i.e. port names and message names never conflict). Names within a name scope MUST be unique within the WSDL document.

The resolution of QNames in WSDL is similar to the resolution of QNames described by the XML Schemas specification [11].

2.1.2 Authoring Style

The use of the `import` element allows the separation of the different elements of a service definition into independent documents, which can then be imported as needed. This technique helps writing clearer service definitions, by separating the definitions according to their level of abstraction. It also maximizes the ability to reuse service definitions of all kinds. As a result, WSDL documents structured in this way are easier to use and maintain. Example 2 below shows how to use this authoring style to define the service presented in Example 1. Here we separate the definitions in three documents: data type definitions, abstract definitions, and specific service bindings. The use of this mechanism is of course not limited to the definitions explicitly presented in the example, which uses only language elements defined in this specification. Other types of definitions based on additional language extensions can be encoded and reused in a similar fashion.

Example 2. Alternative authoring style for the service in Example 1.

`http://example.com/stockquote/stockquote.xsd:`

```
<?xml version="1.0"?>
<schema targetNamespace="http://example.com/stockquote/schemas"
        xmlns="http://www.w3.org/2000/10/XMLSchema">

    <element name="TradePriceRequest">
        <complexType>
            <all>
                <element name="tickerSymbol" type="string"/>
            </all>
        </complexType>
    </element>
    <element name="TradePrice">
        <complexType>
            <all>
                <element name="price" type="float"/>
            </all>
        </complexType>
    </element>
</schema>
```

`http://example.com/stockquote/stockquote.wsdl:`

```
<?xml version="1.0"?>
<definitions name="StockQuote"
            targetNamespace="http://example.com/stockquote/definitions"
            xmlns:tns="http://example.com/stockquote/definitions"
            xmlns:xsd1="http://example.com/stockquote/schemas"
            xmlns:soap="http://schemas.xmlsoap.org/wsdl/soap/"
            xmlns="http://schemas.xmlsoap.org/wsdl/">

    <import namespace="http://example.com/stockquote/schemas"
            location="http://example.com/stockquote/stockquote.xsd"/>

    <message name="GetLastTradePriceInput">
        <part name="body" element="xsd1:TradePriceRequest"/>
    </message>

    <message name="GetLastTradePriceOutput">
        <part name="body" element="xsd1:TradePrice"/>
    </message>

    <portType name="StockQuotePortType">
        <operation name="GetLastTradePrice">
            <input message="tns:GetLastTradePriceInput"/>
            <output message="tns:GetLastTradePriceOutput"/>
        </operation>
    </portType>
</definitions>
```

http://example.com/stockquote/stockquoteservice.wsdl:

```xml
<?xml version="1.0"?>
<definitions name="StockQuote"
            targetNamespace="http://example.com/stockquote/service"
            xmlns:tns="http://example.com/stockquote/service"
            xmlns:soap="http://schemas.xmlsoap.org/wsdl/soap/"
            xmlns:defs="http://example.com/stockquote/definitions"
            xmlns="http://schemas.xmlsoap.org/wsdl/">

    <import namespace="http://example.com/stockquote/definitions"
          location="http://example.com/stockquote/stockquote.wsdl"/>

    <binding name="StockQuoteSoapBinding" type="defs:StockQuotePortType">
        <soap:binding style="document"
                      transport="http://schemas.xmlsoap.org/soap/http"/>
        <operation name="GetLastTradePrice">
            <soap:operation soapAction="http://example.com/GetLastTradePrice"/>
            <input>
                <soap:body use="literal"/>
            </input>
            <output>
                <soap:body use="literal"/>
            </output>
        </operation>
    </binding>

    <service name="StockQuoteService">
        <documentation>My first service</documentation>
        <port name="StockQuotePort" binding="tns:StockQuoteBinding">
            <soap:address location="http://example.com/stockquote"/>
        </port>
    </service>
</definitions>
```

2.1.3 Language Extensibility and Binding

In WSDL, the term binding refers to the process associating protocol or data format information with an abstract entity like a message, operation, or portType. WSDL allows elements representing a specific technology (referred to here as **extensibility elements**) under various elements defined by WSDL. These points of extensibility are typically used to specify binding information for a particular protocol or message format, but are not limited to such use. Extensibility elements MUST use an XML namespace different from that of WSDL. The specific locations in the document where extensibility elements can appear are described in detail in Section A3.

Extensibility elements are commonly used to specify some technology specific binding. To distinguish whether the semantic of the technology specific binding is required for communication or optional, extensibility elements MAY place a wsdl:required attribute of type boolean on the element. The default value for required is false. The required attribute is defined in the namespace http://schemas.xmlsoap.org/wsdl/.

Extensibility elements allow innovation in the area of network and message protocols without having to revise the base WSDL specification. WSDL recommends that specifications defining such protocols also define any necessary WSDL extensions used to describe those protocols or formats. See Sections 3, 4, and 5 for examples of extensibility elements defined as part of the base WSDL specification.

2.1.4 Documentation

WSDL uses the optional `wsdl:document` element as a container for human readable documentation. The content of the element is arbitrary text and elements ("mixed" in XSD). The documentation element is allowed inside any WSDL language element.

2.2 Types

The `types` element encloses data type definitions that are relevant for the exchanged messages. For maximum interoperability and platform neutrality, WSDL prefers the use of XSD as the canonical type system, and treats it as the intrinsic type system.

```
<definitions .... >
    <types>
        <xsd:schema .... />*
    </types>
</definitions>
```

The XSD type system can be used to define the types in a message regardless of whether or not the resulting wire format is actually XML, or whether the resulting XSD schema validates the particular wire format. This is especially interesting if there will be multiple bindings for the same message, or if there is only one binding but that binding type does not already have a type system in widespread use. In these cases, the recommended approach for encoding abstract types using XSD is as follows:

- ❑ Use element form (not attribute).

- ❑ Don't include attributes or elements that are peculiar to the wire encoding (e.g. have nothing to do with the abstract content of the message). Some examples are `soap:root`, `xmi:id`, `xmi:name`, `soap:encodingStyle`.

- ❑ Array types should extend the `Array` type defined in the SOAP v1.1 encoding schema (http://schemas.xmlsoap.org/soap/encoding/) (regardless of whether the resulting form actually uses the encoding specified in Section 5 of the SOAP v1.1 document). Use the name `ArrayOfXXX` for array types (where XXX denotes the type of the items in the array). The type of the items in the array and the array dimensions are specified by using a default value for the `soapenc:arrayType` attribute. At the time of this writing, the XSD specification does not have a mechanism for specifying the default value of an attribute which contains a QName value. To overcome this limitation, WSDL introduces the `arrayType` attribute (from the namespace http://schemas.xmlsoap.org/wsdl/) which has the semantic of providing the default value. If XSD is revised to support this functionality, the revised mechanism SHOULD be used in favor of the `arrayType` attribute defined by WSDL.

- ❑ Use the `xsd:anyType` type to represent a field/parameter which can have any type.

However, since it is unreasonable to expect a single type system grammar be used to describe all abstract types present and future, WSDL allows type systems to be added via extensibility elements. An extensibility element may appear under the `types` element to identify the type definition system being used and to provide an XML container element for the type definitions. The role of this element can be compared to that of the `schema` element of the XML Schema language.

```
<definitions .... >
    <types>
        <-- type-system extensibility element --> *
    </types>
</definitions>
```

2.3 Messages

Messages consist of one or more logical **parts**. Each part is associated with a type from some type system using a message-typing attribute. The set of message-typing attributes is extensible. WSDL defines several such message-typing attributes for use with XSD:

- ❏ element: Refers to an XSD element using a QName.

- ❏ type: Refers to an XSD simpleType or complexType using a QName.

Other message-typing attributes may be defined as long as they use a namespace different from that of WSDL. Binding extensibility elements may also use message-typing attributes. The syntax for defining a message is as follows. The message-typing attributes (which may vary depending on the type system used) are shown in **bold**.

```
<definitions .... >
    <message name="nmtoken"> *
        <part name="nmtoken" element="qname"? type="qname"?/> *
    </message>
</definitions>
```

The message name attribute provides a unique name among all messages defined within the enclosing WSDL document. The part name attribute provides a unique name among all the parts of the enclosing message.

2.3.1 Message Parts

Parts are a flexible mechanism for describing the logical abstract content of a message. A binding may reference the name of a part in order to specify binding-specific information about the part. For example, if defining a message for use with RPC, a part MAY represent a parameter in the message. However, the bindings must be inspected in order to determine the actual meaning of the part. Multiple part elements are used if the message has multiple logical units. For example, the following message consists of a Purchase Order and an Invoice.

```
<definitions .... >
    <types>
        <schema .... >
            <element name="PO" type="tns:POType"/>
            <complexType name="POType">
                <all>
                    <element name="id" type="string/>
                    <element name="name" type="string"/>
                    <element name="items">
                        <complexType>
                            <all>
                                <element name="item" type="tns:Item"
                                         minOccurs="0" maxOccurs="unbounded"/>
                            </all>
                        </complexType>
                    </element>
                </all>
            </complexType>

            <complexType name="Item">
                <all>
```

```
                    <element name="quantity" type="int"/>
                    <element name="product" type="string"/>
                </all>
            </complexType>
            <element name="Invoice" type="tns:InvoiceType"/>
            <complexType name="InvoiceType">
                <all>
                    <element name="id" type="string"/>
                </all>
            </complexType>
        </schema>
    </types>

    <message name="PO">
        <part name="po" element="tns:PO"/>
        <part name="invoice" element="tns:Invoice"/>
    </message>
</definitions>
```

However, if the message contents are sufficiently complex, then an alternative syntax may be used to specify the composite structure of the message using the type system directly. In this usage, only one part may be specified. In the following example, the body is either a purchase order, or a set of invoices:

```
<definitions .... >
    <types>
        <schema .... >
            <complexType name="POType">
                <all>
                    <element name="id" type="string/>
                    <element name="name" type="string"/>
                    <element name="items">
                        <complexType>
                            <all>
                                <element name="item" type="tns:Item"
                                        minOccurs="0"
                                    maxOccurs="unbounded"/>
                            </all>
                        </complexType>
                    </element>
                </all>
            </complexType>

            <complexType name="Item">
                <all>
                    <element name="quantity" type="int"/>
                    <element name="product" type="string"/>
                </all>
            </complexType>
            <complexType name="InvoiceType">
                <all>
                    <element name="id" type="string"/>
                </all>
            </complexType>
```

```
                    <complexType name="Composite">
                        <choice>
                            <element name="PO" minOccurs="1" maxOccurs="1"
                            type="tns:POType"/>
                            <element name="Invoice" minOccurs="0" maxOccurs="unbounded"
                            type="tns:InvoiceType"/>
                        </choice>
                    </complexType>
                </schema>
            </types>

            <message name="PO">
                <part name="composite" type="tns:Composite"/>
            </message>
        </definitions>
```

2.3.2 Abstract vs. Concrete Messages

Message definitions are always considered to be an abstract definition of the message content. A message binding describes how the abstract content is mapped into a concrete format. However, in some cases, the abstract definition may match the concrete representation very closely or exactly for one or more bindings, so those binding(s) will supply little or no mapping information. However, another binding of the same message definition may require extensive mapping information. For this reason, it is not until the binding is inspected that one can determine "how abstract" the message really is.

2.4 Port Types

A port type is a named set of abstract operations and the abstract messages involved:

```
<wsdl:definitions .... >
    <wsdl:portType name="nmtoken">
        <wsdl:operation name="nmtoken" .... /> *
    </wsdl:portType>
</wsdl:definitions>
```

The port type name attribute provides a unique name among all port types defined within in the enclosing WSDL document. An operation is named via the name attribute.

WSDL has four transmission primitives that an endpoint can support:

❑ **One-way**. The endpoint receives a message.

❑ **Request-response**. The endpoint receives a message, and sends a correlated message.

❑ **Solicit-response**. The endpoint sends a message, and receives a correlated message.

❑ **Notification**. The endpoint sends a message.

WSDL refers to these primitives as **operations**. Although request/response or solicit/response can be modeled abstractly using two one-way messages, it is useful to model these as primitive operation types because:

❑ They are very common.

❑ The sequence can be correlated without having to introduce more complex flow information.

❑ Some endpoints can only receive messages if they are the result of a synchronous request response.

❑ A simple flow can algorithmically be derived from these primitives at the point when flow definition is desired.

Although request/response or solicit/response are logically correlated in the WSDL document, a given binding describes the concrete correlation information. For example, the request and response messages may be exchanged as part of one or two actual network communications.

Although the base WSDL structure supports bindings for these four transmission primitives, WSDL only defines bindings for the One-way and Request-response primitives. It is expected that specifications that define the protocols for Solicit-response or Notification would also include WSDL binding extensions that allow use of these primitives.

Operations refer to the messages involved using the `message` attribute of type QName. This attribute follows the rules defined by WSDL for linking (see Section 2.1.2).

2.4.1 One-way Operation

The grammar for a one-way operation is:

```
<wsdl:definitions .... > <wsdl:portType .... > *
     <wsdl:operation name="nmtoken">
         <wsdl:input name="nmtoken"? message="qname"/>
     </wsdl:operation>
   </wsdl:portType >
 </wsdl:definitions>
```

The `input` element specifies the abstract message format for the one-way operation.

2.4.2 Request-response Operation

The grammar for a request-response operation is:

```
<wsdl:definitions .... >
   <wsdl:portType .... > *
       <wsdl:operation name="nmtoken" parameterOrder="nmtokens">
           <wsdl:input name="nmtoken"? message="qname"/>
           <wsdl:output name="nmtoken"? message="qname"/>
           <wsdl:fault name="nmtoken" message="qname"/>*
       </wsdl:operation>
     </wsdl:portType >
 </wsdl:definitions>
```

The input and output elements specify the abstract message format for the request and response, respectively. The optional fault elements specify the abstract message format for any error messages that may be output as the result of the operation (beyond those specific to the protocol).

Note that a request-response operation is an abstract notion; a particular binding must be consulted to determine how the messages are actually sent: within a single communication (such as a HTTP request/response), or as two independent communications (such as two HTTP requests).

2.4.3 Solicit-response Operation

The grammar for a solicit-response operation is:

```
<wsdl:definitions .... >
    <wsdl:portType .... > *
        <wsdl:operation name="nmtoken" parameterOrder="nmtokens">
            <wsdl:output name="nmtoken"? message="qname"/>
            <wsdl:input name="nmtoken"? message="qname"/>
            <wsdl:fault name="nmtoken" message="qname"/>*
        </wsdl:operation>
    </wsdl:portType >
</wsdl:definitions>
```

The output and input elements specify the abstract message format for the solicited request and response, respectively. The optional fault elements specify the abstract message format for any error messages that may be output as the result of the operation (beyond those specific to the protocol).

Note that a solicit-response operation is an abstract notion; a particular binding must be consulted to determine how the messages are actually sent: within a single communication (such as a HTTP request/response), or as two independent communications (such as two HTTP requests).

2.4.4 Notification Operation

The grammar for a notification operation is:

```
<wsdl:definitions .... >
    <wsdl:portType .... > *
        <wsdl:operation name="nmtoken">
            <wsdl:output name="nmtoken"? message="qname"/>
        </wsdl:operation>
    </wsdl:portType >
</wsdl:definitions>
```

The output element specifies the abstract message format for the notification operation.

2.4.5 Names of Elements within an Operation

The name attribute of the input and output elements provides a unique name among all input and output elements within the enclosing port type. In order to avoid having to name each input and output element within an operation, WSDL provides some default values based on the operation name. If the name attribute is not specified on a one-way or notification message, it defaults to the name of the operation. If the name attribute is not specified on the input or output messages of a request-response or solicit-response operation, the name defaults to the name of the operation with "Request"/"Solicit" or "Response" appended, respectively.

Each fault element must be named to allow a binding to specify the concrete format of the fault message. The name of the fault element is unique within the set of faults defined for the operation.

2.4.6 Parameter Order within an Operation

Operations do not specify whether they are to be used with RPC-like bindings or not. However, when using an operation with an RPC-binding, it is useful to be able to capture the original RPC function signature. For this reason, a request-response or solicit-response operation MAY specify a list of parameter names via the parameterOrder attribute (of type nmtokens). The value of the attribute is a list of message part names separated by a single space. The value of the parameterOrder attribute MUST follow the following rules:

- ❑ The part name order reflects the order of the parameters in the RPC signature

- ❑ The **return** value part is not present in the list

- ❑ If a part name appears in both the input and output message, it is an **in/out** parameter

- ❑ If a part name appears in only the input message, it is an **in** parameter

- ❑ If a part name appears in only the output message, it is an **out** parameter

Note that this information serves as a "hint" and may safely be ignored by those not concerned with RPC signatures. Also, it is not required to be present, even if the operation is to be used with an RPC-like binding.

2.5 Bindings

A binding defines message format and protocol details for operations and messages defined by a particular portType. There may be any number of bindings for a given portType. The grammar for a binding is as follows:

```
<wsdl:definitions .... >
    <wsdl:binding name="nmtoken" type="qname"> *
        <-- extensibility element (1) --> *
        <wsdl:operation name="nmtoken"> *
            <-- extensibility element (2) --> *
            <wsdl:input name="nmtoken"? > ?
                <-- extensibility element (3) -->
            </wsdl:input>
            <wsdl:output name="nmtoken"? > ?
                <-- extensibility element (4) --> *
            </wsdl:output>
            <wsdl:fault name="nmtoken"> *
                <-- extensibility element (5) --> *
            </wsdl:fault>
        </wsdl:operation>
    </wsdl:binding>
</wsdl:definitions>
```

The name attribute provides a unique name among all bindings defined within the enclosing WSDL document. A binding references the portType that it binds using the type attribute. This QName value follows the linking rules defined by WSDL (see Section 2.1.2). Binding extensibility elements are used to specify the concrete grammar for the input (3), output (4), and fault messages (5). Per-operation binding information (2) as well as per-binding information (1) may also be specified.

An operation element within a binding specifies binding information for the operation with the same name within the binding's portType. Since operation names are not required to be unique (for example, in the case of overloading of method names), the name attribute in the operation binding element might not be enough to uniquely identify an operation. In that case, the correct operation should be identified by providing the name attributes of the corresponding wsdl:input and wsdl:output elements.

A binding MUST specify exactly one protocol.

A binding MUST NOT specify address information.

2.6 Ports

A port defines an individual endpoint by specifying a single address for a binding.

```
<wsdl:definitions .... >
    <wsdl:service .... > *
        <wsdl:port name="nmtoken" binding="qname"> *
            <-- extensibility element (1) -->
        </wsdl:port>
    </wsdl:service>
</wsdl:definitions>
```

The name attribute provides a unique name among all ports defined within in the enclosing WSDL document.

The binding attribute (of type QName) refers to the binding using the linking rules defined by WSDL (see Section 2.1.2).

Binding extensibility elements (1) are used to specify the address information for the port.

A port MUST NOT specify more than one address.

A port MUST NOT specify any binding information other than address information.

2.7 Services

A service groups a set of related ports together:

```
<wsdl:definitions .... >
    <wsdl:service name="nmtoken"> *
        <wsdl:port .... />*
    </wsdl:service>
</wsdl:definitions>
```

The name attribute provides a unique name among all services defined within in the enclosing WSDL document.

Ports within a service have the following relationship:

- ❑ None of the ports communicate with each other (e.g. the output of one port is not the input of another).

- ❑ If a service has several ports that share a port type, but employ different bindings or addresses, the ports are alternatives. Each port provides semantically equivalent behavior (within the transport and message format limitations imposed by each binding). This allows a consumer of a WSDL document to choose particular port(s) to communicate with based on some criteria (protocol, distance, etc.).

- ❑ By examining it's ports, we can determine a service's port types. This allows a consumer of a WSDL document to determine if it wishes to communicate to a particular service based whether or not it supports several port types. This is useful if there is some implied relationship between the operations of the port types, and that the entire set of port types must be present in order to accomplish a particular task.

3. SOAP Binding

WSDL includes a binding for SOAP 1.1 endpoints, which supports the specification of the following protocol specific information:

❑ An indication that a binding is bound to the SOAP 1.1 protocol.

❑ A way of specifying an address for a SOAP endpoint.

❑ The URI for the SOAPAction HTTP header for the HTTP binding of SOAP.

❑ A list of definitions for Headers that are transmitted as part of the SOAP Envelope.

This binding grammar it is not an exhaustive specification since the set of SOAP bindings is evolving. Nothing precludes additional SOAP bindings to be derived from portions of this grammar. For example:

❑ SOAP bindings that do not employ a URI addressing scheme may substitute another addressing scheme by replacing the soap:address element defined in Section 3.8.

❑ SOAP bindings that do not require a SOAPAction omit the soapAction attribute defined in Section 3.4.

3.1 SOAP Examples

In the following example, a SubscribeToQuotes SOAP 1.1 one-way message is sent to a StockQuote service via a SMTP binding. The request takes a ticker symbol of type string, and includes a header defining the subscription URI.

Example 3. SOAP binding of one-way operation over SMTP using a SOAP Header

```
<?xml version="1.0"?>
<definitions name="StockQuote"
            targetNamespace="http://example.com/stockquote.wsdl"
            xmlns:tns="http://example.com/stockquote.wsdl"
            xmlns:xsd1="http://example.com/stockquote.xsd"
            xmlns:soap="http://schemas.xmlsoap.org/wsdl/soap/"
            xmlns="http://schemas.xmlsoap.org/wsdl/">

    <message name="SubscribeToQuotes">
        <part name="body" element="xsd1:SubscribeToQuotes"/>
        <part name="subscribeheader" element="xsd1:SubscriptionHeader"/>
    </message>

    <portType name="StockQuotePortType">
        <operation name="SubscribeToQuotes">
            <input message="tns:SubscribeToQuotes"/>
        </operation>
    </portType>

    <binding name="StockQuoteSoap" type="tns:StockQuotePortType">
        <soap:binding style="document" transport="http://example.com/smtp"/>
        <operation name="SubscribeToQuotes">
            <input message="tns:SubscribeToQuotes">
                <soap:body parts="body" use="literal"/>
                <soap:header message="tns:SubscribeToQuotes"
                        part="subscribeheader"
```

```
                        use="literal"/>
                </input>
            </operation>
    </binding>

    <service name="StockQuoteService">
        <port name="StockQuotePort" binding="tns:StockQuoteSoap">
            <soap:address location="mailto:subscribe@example.com"/>
        </port>
    </service>

    <types>
        <schema targetNamespace="http://example.com/stockquote.xsd"
                xmlns="http://www.w3.org/2000/10/XMLSchema">
            <element name="SubscribeToQuotes">
                <complexType>
                    <all>
                        <element name="tickerSymbol" type="string"/>
                    </all>
                </complexType>
            </element>
            <element name="SubscriptionHeader" type="uriReference"/>
        </schema>
    </types>
</definitions>
```

This example describes that a `GetTradePrice` SOAP 1.1 request may be sent to a `StockQuote` service via the SOAP 1.1 HTTP binding. The request takes a ticker symbol of type `string`, a time of type `timeInstant`, and returns the price as a float in the SOAP response.

Example 4. SOAP binding of request-response RPC operation over HTTP

```
<?xml version="1.0"?>
<definitions name="StockQuote"
            targetNamespace="http://example.com/stockquote.wsdl"
            xmlns:tns="http://example.com/stockquote.wsdl"
            xmlns:xsd="http://www.w3.org/2000/10/XMLSchema"
            xmlns:xsd1="http://example.com/stockquote.xsd"
            xmlns:soap="http://schemas.xmlsoap.org/wsdl/soap/"
            xmlns="http://schemas.xmlsoap.org/wsdl/">

    <message name="GetTradePriceInput">
        <part name="tickerSymbol" element="xsd:string"/>
        <part name="time" element="xsd:timeInstant"/>
    </message>

    <message name="GetTradePriceOutput">
        <part name="result" type="xsd:float"/>
    </message>

    <portType name="StockQuotePortType">
        <operation name="GetTradePrice">
            <input message="tns:GetTradePriceInput"/>
            <output message="tns:GetTradePriceOutput"/>
        </operation>
    </portType>
```

733

```
            <binding name="StockQuoteSoapBinding" type="tns:StockQuotePortType">
                <soap:binding style="rpc"
                 transport="http://schemas.xmlsoap.org/soap/http"/>
                <operation name="GetTradePrice">
                    <soap:operation soapAction="http://example.com/GetTradePrice"/>
                    <input>
                        <soap:body use="encoded"
                                        namespace="http://example.com/stockquote"
                            encodingStyle="http://schemas.xmlsoap.org/soap/encoding/"/>
                    </input>
                    <output>
                        <soap:body use="encoded"
                                namespace="http://example.com/stockquote"
                                encodingStyle="http://schemas.xmlsoap.org
                                                /soap/encoding/"/>
                    </output>
                </operation>>
            </binding>

            <service name="StockQuoteService">
                <documentation>My first service</documentation>
                <port name="StockQuotePort" binding="tns:StockQuoteBinding">
                    <soap:address location="http://example.com/stockquote"/>
                </port>
            </service>
        </definitions>
```

This example describes that a `GetTradePrices` SOAP 1.1 request may be sent to a `StockQuote` service via the SOAP 1.1 HTTP binding. The request takes a stock quote symbol string, an application defined `TimePeriod` structure containing a start and end time and returns an array of stock prices recorded by the service within that period of time, as well as the frequency at which they were recorded as the SOAP response. The RPC signature that corresponds to this service has in parameters `tickerSymbol` and `timePeriod` followed by the output parameter frequency, and returns an array of `floats`.

Example 5. SOAP binding of request-response RPC operation over HTTP

```
<?xml version="1.0"?>
<definitions name="StockQuote"
            targetNamespace="http://example.com/stockquote.wsdl"
            xmlns:tns="http://example.com/stockquote.wsdl"
            xmlns:xsd="http://www.w3.org/2000/10/XMLSchema"
            xmlns:xsd1="http://example.com/stockquote/schema"
            xmlns:soap="http://schemas.xmlsoap.org/wsdl/soap/"
            xmlns:soapenc="http://schemas.xmlsoap.org/soap/encoding/"
            xmlns="http://schemas.xmlsoap.org/wsdl/">

    <types>
        <schema targetNamespace="http://example.com/stockquote/schema"
                xmlns="http://www.w3.org/2000/10/XMLSchema">
            <complexType name="TimePeriod">
                <all>
                    <element name="startTime" type="xsd:timeInstant"/>
                    <element name="endTime" type="xsd:timeInstant"/>
                </all>
```

```
                    </complexType>
                    <complexType name="ArrayOfFloat">
                       <complexContent>
                          <restriction base="soapenc:Array">
                             <attribute ref="soapenc:arrayType"
                                wsdl:arrayType="xsd:float[]"/>
                          </restriction>
                       </complexContent>
                    </complexType>
            </schema>
         </types>

         <message name="GetTradePricesInput">
            <part name="tickerSymbol" element="xsd:string"/>
            <part name="timePeriod" element="xsd1:TimePeriod"/>
         </message>

         <message name="GetTradePricesOutput">
            <part name="result" type="xsd1:ArrayOfFloat"/>
            <part name="frequency" type="xsd:float"/>
         </message>

         <portType name="StockQuotePortType">
            <operation name="GetLastTradePrice" parameterOrder="tickerSymbol
                    timePeriod frequency">
               <input message="tns:GetTradePricesInput"/>
               <output message="tns:GetTradePricesOutput"/>
            </operation>
         </portType>

         <binding name="StockQuoteSoapBinding" type="tns:StockQuotePortType">
            <soap:binding style="rpc"
                          transport="http://schemas.xmlsoap.org/soap/http"/>
            <operation name="GetTradePrices">
               <soap:operation soapAction="http://example.com/GetTradePrices"/>
               <input>
                  <soap:body use="encoded"
                             namespace="http://example.com/stockquote"
                             encodingStyle="http://schemas.xmlsoap.org
                                            /soap/encoding/"/>
               </input>
               <output>
                  <soap:body use="encoded"
                             namespace="http://example.com/stockquote"
                             encodingStyle="http://schemas.xmlsoap.org
                                            /soap/encoding/"/>
               </output>
            </operation>>
         </binding>

         <service name="StockQuoteService">
            <documentation>My first service</documentation>
            <port name="StockQuotePort" binding="tns:StockQuoteBinding">
               <soap:address location="http://example.com/stockquote"/>
            </port>
         </service>
      </definitions>
```

3.2 How the SOAP Binding Extends WSDL

The SOAP Binding extends WSDL with the following extension elements:

```
<definitions .... >
    <binding .... >
        <soap:binding style="rpc|document" transport="uri">
        <operation .... >
            <soap:operation soapAction="uri"? style="rpc|document"?>?
            <input>
                <soap:body parts="nmtokens"? use="literal|encoded"
                           encodingStyle="uri-list"? namespace="uri"?>
                <soap:header message="qname" part="nmtoken" use="literal|encoded"
                             encodingStyle="uri-list"? namespace="uri"?>*
                    <soap:headerfault message="qname" part="nmtoken"
                                      use="literal|encoded"
                                      encodingStyle="uri-list"?
                                      namespace="uri"?/>*
                <soap:header>
            </input>
            <output>
                <soap:body parts="nmtokens"? use="literal|encoded"
                           encodingStyle="uri-list"? namespace="uri"?>
                <soap:header message="qname" part="nmtoken" use="literal|encoded"
                             encodingStyle="uri-list"? namespace="uri"?>*
                    <soap:headerfault message="qname" part="nmtoken"
                                      use="literal|encoded"
                                      encodingStyle="uri-list"? namespace="uri"?/>*
                <soap:header>
            </output>
            <fault>*
                <soap:fault name="nmtoken" use="literal|encoded"
                            encodingStyle="uri-list"? namespace="uri"?>
            </fault>
        </operation>
    </binding>

    <port .... >
        <soap:address location="uri"/>
    </port>
</definitions>
```

Each extension element of the SOAP binding is covered in subsequent sections.

3.3 soap:binding

The purpose of the SOAP binding element is to signify that the binding is bound to the SOAP protocol format: Envelope, Header and Body. This element makes no claims as to the encoding or format of the message (e.g. that it necessarily follows section 5 of the SOAP 1.1 specification).

The soap:binding element MUST be present when using the SOAP binding.

```
<definitions .... >
    <binding .... >
        <soap:binding transport="uri"? style="rpc|document"?>
    </binding>
</definitions>
```

The value of the `style` attribute is the default for the `style` attribute for each contained operation. If the `style` attribute is omitted, it is assumed to be `document`. See Section 3.4 for more information on the semantics of style.

The value of the required `transport` attribute indicates which transport of SOAP this binding corresponds to. The URI value `http://schemas.xmlsoap.org/soap/http` corresponds to the HTTP binding in the SOAP specification. Other URIs may be used here to indicate other transports (such as SMTP, FTP, etc.).

3.4 soap:operation

The `soap:operation` element provides information for the operation as a whole.

```
<definitions .... >
    <binding .... >
        <operation .... >
            <soap:operation soapAction="uri"? style="rpc|document"?>?
        </operation>
    </binding>
</definitions>
```

The `style` attribute indicates whether the operation is RPC-oriented (messages containing parameters and return values) or document-oriented (message containing document(s)). This information may be used to select an appropriate programming model. The value of this attribute also affects the way in which the Body of the SOAP message is constructed, as explained in Section 3.5 below. If the attribute is not specified, it defaults to the value specified in the `soap:binding` element. If the `soap:binding` element does not specify a style, it is assumed to be `document`.

The `soapAction` attribute specifies the value of the `SOAPAction` header for this operation. This URI value should be used directly as the value for the `SOAPAction` header; no attempt should be made to make a relative URI value absolute when making the request. For the HTTP protocol binding of SOAP, this value isrequired (it has no default value). For other SOAP protocol bindings, it MUST NOT be specified, and the `soap:operation` element MAY be omitted.

3.5 soap:body

The `soap:body` element specifies how the message parts appear inside the SOAP Body element. The parts of a message may either be abstract type definitions, or concrete schema definitions. If abstract definitions, the types are serialized according to some set of rules defined by an encoding style. Each encoding style is identified using a list of URIs, as in the SOAP specification. Since some encoding styles such as the SOAP Encoding (http://schemas.xmlsoap.org/soap/encoding/) allow variation in the message format for a given set of abstract types, it is up to the reader of the message to understand all the format variations: "reader makes right". To avoid having to support all variations, a message may be defined concretely and then indicate it's original encoding style (if any) as a hint. In this case, the writer of the message must conform exactly to the specified schema: "writer makes right".

The `soap:body` binding element provides information on how to assemble the different message parts inside the Body element of the SOAP message. The `soap:body` element is used in both RPC-oriented and document-oriented messages, but the style of the enclosing operation has important effects on how the Body section is structured:

❏ If the operation style is RPC each part is a parameter or a return value and appears inside a wrapper element within the body (following Section 7.1 of the SOAP specification). The wrapper element is named identically to the operation name and its namespace is the value of the namespace attribute. Each message part (parameter) appears under the wrapper, represented by an accessor named identically to the corresponding parameter of the call. Parts are arranged in the same order as the parameters of the call.

❏ If the operation style is document there are no additional wrappers, and the message parts appear directly under the SOAP Body element.

The same mechanisms are used to define the content of the Body and parameter accessor elements.

```
<definitions .... >
    <binding .... >
        <operation .... >
            <input>
                <soap:body parts="nmtokens"? use="literal|encoded"?
                            encodingStyle="uri-list"? namespace="uri"?>
            </input>
            <output>
                <soap:body parts="nmtokens"? use="literal|encoded"?
                            encodingStyle="uri-list"? namespace="uri"?>
            </output>
        </operation>
    </binding>
</definitions>
```

The optional parts attribute of type nmtokens indicates which parts appear somewhere within the SOAP Body portion of the message (other parts of a message may appear in other portions of the message such as when SOAP is used in conjunction with the multipart/related MIME binding). If the parts attribute is omitted, then all parts defined by the message are assumed to be included in the SOAP Body portion.

The required use attribute indicates whether the message parts are encoded using some encoding rules, or whether the parts define the concrete schema of the message.

If use is encoded, then each message part references an abstract type using the type attribute. These abstract types are used to produce a concrete message by applying an encoding specified by the encodingStyle attribute. The part names, types and value of the namespace attribute are all inputs to the encoding, although the namespace attribute only applies to content not explicitly defined by the abstract types. If the referenced encoding style allows variations in it's format (such as the SOAP encoding does), then all variations MUST be supported ("reader makes right").

If use is literal, then each part references a concrete schema definition using either the element or type attribute. In the first case, the element referenced by the part will appear directly under the Body element (for document style bindings) or under an accessor element named after the message part (in RPC style). In the second, the type referenced by the part becomes the schema type of the enclosing element (Body for document style or part accessor element for RPC style). For an example that illustrates defining the contents of a composite Body using a type, see Section 2.3.1. The value of the encodingStyle attribute MAY be used when the use is literal to indicate that the concrete format was derived using a particular encoding (such as the SOAP encoding), but that only the specified variation is supported ("writer makes right").

The value of the `encodingStyle` attribute is a list of URIs, each separated by a single space. The URIs represent encodings used within the message, in order from most restrictive to least restrictive (exactly like the `encodingStyle` attribute defined in the SOAP specification).

3.6 soap:fault

The `soap:fault` element specifies the contents of the contents of the SOAP Fault Details element. It is patterned after the `soap:body` element (see Section 3.5).

```
<definitions .... >
    <binding .... >
        <operation .... >
            <fault>*
                <soap:fault name="nmtoken" use="literal|encoded"
                            encodingStyle="uri-list"? namespace="uri"?>
            </fault>
        </operation>
    </binding>
</definitions>
```

The `name` attribute relates the `soap:fault` to the `wsdl:fault` defined for the operation.

The fault message MUST have a single part. The use, `encodingStyle`, and `namespace` attributes are all used in the same way as with `soap:body` (see Section 3.5), only `style="document"` is assumed since faults do not contain parameters.

3.7 soap:header and soap:headerfault

The `soap:header` and `soap:headerfault` elements allow headers to be defined that are transmitted inside the Header element of the SOAP Envelope. It is patterned after the `soap:body` element (see Section 3.5).

It is not necessary to exhaustively list all headers that appear in the SOAP Envelope using `soap:header`. For example, extensions (see Section 2.1.3) to WSDL may imply specific headers should be added to the actual payload and it is not required to list those headers here.

```
<definitions .... >
    <binding .... >
        <operation .... >
            <input>
                <soap:header message="qname" part="nmtoken" use="literal|encoded"
                             encodingStyle="uri-list"? namespace="uri"?>*
                <soap:headerfault message="qname" part="nmtoken"
                                  use="literal|encoded" encodingStyle="uri-list"?
                                  namespace="uri"?/>*
                <soap:header>
            </input>
            <output>
                <soap:header message="qname" part="nmtoken" use="literal|encoded"
                             encodingStyle="uri-list"? namespace="uri"?>*
                <soap:headerfault message="qname" part="nmtoken"
                                  use="literal|encoded"
                                  encodingStyle="uri-list"? namespace="uri"?/>*
                <soap:header>
```

```
            </output>
          </operation>
      </binding>
  </definitions>
```

The use, encodingStyle, and namespace attributes are all used in the same way as with soap:body (see Section 3.5), only style="document" is assumed since headers do not contain parameters.

Together, the message attribute (of type QName) and the part attribute (of type nmtoken) reference the message part that defines the header type. The schema referenced by the part MAY include definitions for the soap:actor and soap:mustUnderstand attributes if use="literal", but MUST NOT if use="encoded". The referenced message need not be the same as the message that defines the SOAP Body.

The optional headerfault elements (which appear inside soap:header and have the same syntax as soap:header) allow specification of the header type(s) that are used to transmit error information pertaining to the header defined by the soap:header. The SOAP specification states that errors pertaining to headers must be returned in headers, and this mechanism allows specification of the format of such headers.

3.8 soap:address

The SOAP address binding is used to give a port an address (a URI). A port using the SOAP binding MUST specify exactly one address. The URI scheme specified for the address must correspond to the transport specified by the soap:binding.

```
<definitions .... >
    <port .... >
        <binding .... >
            <soap:address location="uri"/>
        </binding>
    </port>
</definitions>
```

4. HTTP GET & POST Binding

WSDL includes a binding for HTTP 1.1's GET and POST verbs in order to describe the interaction between a web browser and a web site. This allows applications other than web browsers to interact with the site. The following protocol specific information may be specified:

- ❏ An indication that a binding uses HTTP GET or POST
- ❏ An address for the port
- ❏ A relative address for each operation (relative to the base address defined by the port)

4.1 HTTP GET/POST Examples

The following example shows three ports that are bound differently for a given port type. If the values being passed are part1=1, part2=2, part3=3, the request format would be as follows for each port:

```
port1: GET, URL="http://example.com/o1/A1B2/3"
port2: GET, URL="http://example.com/o1?p1=1&p2=2&p3=3
port3: POST, URL="http://example.com/o1", PAYLOAD="p1=1&p2=2&p3=3"
```

For each port, the response is either a GIF or a JPEG image.

Example 6. GET and FORM POST returning GIF or JPG

```
<definitions .... >
    <message name="m1">
        <part name="part1" type="xsd:string"/>
        <part name="part2" type="xsd:int"/>
        <part name="part3" type="xsd:string"/>
    </message>

    <message name="m2">
        <part name="image" type="xsd:binary"/>
    </message>

    <portType name="pt1">
        <operation name="o1">
            <input message="tns:m1"/>
            <output message="tns:m2"/>
        </operation>
    </portType>

    <service name="service1">
        <port name="port1" binding="tns:b1">
            <http:address location="http://example.com/"/>
        </port>
        <port name="port2" binding="tns:b2">
            <http:address location="http://example.com/"/>
        </port>
        <port name="port3" binding="tns:b3">
            <http:address location="http://example.com/"/>
        </port>
    </service>

    <binding name="b1" type="pt1">
        <http:binding verb="GET"/>
        <operation name="o1">
            <http:operation location="o1/A(part1)B(part2)/(part3)"/>
            <input>
                <http:urlReplacement/>
            </input>
            <output>
                <mime:content type="image/gif"/>
                <mime:content type="image/jpeg"/>
            </output>
        </operation>
    </binding>

    <binding name="b2" type="pt1">
        <http:binding verb="GET"/>
        <operation name="o1">
```

```
                <http:operation location="o1"/>
                <input>
                    <http:urlEncoded/>
                </input>
                <output>
                    <mime:content type="image/gif"/>
                    <mime:content type="image/jpeg"/>
                </output>
            </operation>
        </binding>

        <binding name="b3" type="pt1">
            <http:binding verb="POST"/>
            <operation name="o1">
                <http:operation location="o1"/>
                <input>
                    <mime:content type="application/x-www-form-urlencoded"/>
                </input>
                <output>
                    <mime:content type="image/gif"/>
                    <mime:content type="image/jpeg"/>
                </output>
            </operation>
        </binding>
    </definitions>
```

4.2 How the HTTP GET/POST Binding Extends WSDL

The HTTP GET/POST Binding extends WSDL with the following extension elements:

```
<definitions .... >
    <binding .... >
        <http:binding verb="nmtoken"/>
        <operation .... >
            <http:operation location="uri"/>
            <input .... >
                <-- mime elements -->
            </input>
            <output .... >
                <-- mime elements -->
            </output>
        </operation>
    </binding>

    <port .... >
        <http:address location="uri"/>
    </port>
</definitions>
```

These elements are covered in the subsequent sections.

4.3 http:address

The location attribute specifies the base URI for the port. The value of the attribute is combined with the values of the location attribute of the http:operation binding element. See Section 4.5 for more details.

4.4 http:binding

The `http:binding` element indicates that this binding uses the HTTP protocol.

```
<definitions .... >
    <binding .... >
        <http:binding verb="nmtoken"/>
    </binding>
</definitions>
```

The value of the required `verb` attribute indicates the HTTP verb. Common values are GET or POST, but others may be used. Note that HTTP verbs are case sensitive.

4.5 http:operation

The `location` attribute specifies a relative URI for the operation. This URI is combined with the URI specified in the `http:address` element to form the full URI for the HTTP request. The URI value MUST be a relative URI.

```
<definitions .... >
    <binding .... >
        <operation .... >
            <http:operation location="uri"/>
        </operation>
    </binding>
</definitions>
```

4.6 http:urlEncoded

The `urlEncoded` element indicates that all the message parts are encoded into the HTTP request URI using the standard URI-encoding rules (name1=value&name2=value...). The names of the parameters correspond to the names of the message parts. Each value contributed by the part is encoded using a name=value pair. This may be used with GET to specify URL encoding, or with POST to specify a FORM-POST. For GET, the ? character is automatically appended as necessary.

```
<http:urlEncoded/>
```

For more information on the rules for URI-encoding parameters, see [5], [6], and [7].

4.7 http:urlReplacement

The `http:urlReplacement` element indicates that all the message parts are encoded into the HTTP request URI using a replacement algorithm:

❑ The relative URI value of `http:operation` is searched for a set of search patterns.

❑ The search occurs before the value of the `http:operation` is combined with the value of the location attribute from `http:address`.

❑ There is one search pattern for each message part. The search pattern string is the name of the message part surrounded with parentheses, (and).

❑ For each match, the value of the corresponding message part is substituted for the match at the location of the match.

❑ Matches are performed before any values are replaced (replaced values do not trigger additional matches).

Message parts MUST NOT have repeating values.

```
<http:urlReplacement/>
```

5. MIME Binding

WSDL includes a way to bind abstract types to concrete messages in some MIME format. Bindings for the following MIME types are defined:

❑ multipart/related

❑ text/xml

❑ application/x-www-form-urlencoded (the format used to submit a form in HTML)

❑ Others (by specifying the MIME type string)

The set of defined MIME types is both large and evolving, so it is not a goal for WSDL to exhaustively define XML grammar for each MIME type. Nothing precludes additional grammar to be added to define additional MIME types as necessary. If a MIME type string is sufficient to describe the content, the mime element defined below can be used.

5.11 MIME Binding example

This example describes a GetCompanyInfo SOAP 1.1 request that may be sent to a StockQuote service via the SOAP 1.1 HTTP binding. The request takes a ticker symbol of type string. The response contains multiple parts encoded in the MIME format multipart/related: a SOAP Envelope containing the current stock price as a float, zero or more marketing literature documents in HTML format, and an optional company logo in either GIF or JPEG format.

Example 7. Using multipart/related with SOAP

```
<definitions .... >

    <types>
        <schema .... >
            <element name="GetCompanyInfo">
                <complexType>
                    <all>
                        <element name="tickerSymbol " type="string"/>
                    </all>
                </complexType>
            </element>
            <element name="GetCompanyInfoResult">
                <complexType>
                    <all>
                        <element name="result" type="float"/>
                    </all>
                </complexType>
            </element>
            <complexType name="ArrayOfBinary">
```

```
                    <complexContent>
                        <restriction base="soapenc:Array">
                            <attribute ref="soapenc:arrayType" wsdl:arrayType=
                            "xsd:binary[]"/>
                        </restriction>
                    <complexContent>
                </complexType>
            </schema>
        </types>

        <message name="m1">
            <part name="body" element="tns:GetCompanyInfo"/>
        </message>

        <message name="m2">
            <part name="body" element="tns:GetCompanyInfoResult"/>
            <part name="docs" type="xsd:string"/>
            <part name="logo" type="tns:ArrayOfBinary"/>
        </message>

        <portType name="pt1">
            <operation name="GetCompanyInfo">
                <input message="m1"/>
                <output message="m2"/>
            </operation>
        </portType>

        <binding name="b1" type="tns:pt1">
            <operation name="GetCompanyInfo">
                <soap:operation soapAction="http://example.com/GetCompanyInfo"/>
                <input>
                    <soap:body use="literal"/>
                </input>
                <output>
                    <mime:multipartRelated>
                        <mime:part>
                            <soap:body parts="body" use="literal"/>
                        </mime:part>
                        <mime:part>
                            <mime:content part="docs" type="text/html"/>
                        </mime:part>
                        <mime:part>
                            <mime:content part="logo" type="image/gif"/>
                            <mime:content part="logo" type="image/jpeg"/>
                        </mime:part>
                    </mime:multipartRelated>
                </output>
            </operation>
        </binding>

        <service name="CompanyInfoService">
            <port name="CompanyInfoPort"binding="tns:b1">
                <soap:address location="http://example.com/companyinfo"/>
            </port>
        </service>
</definitions>
```

5.2 How the MIME Binding extends WSDL

The MIME Binding extends WSDL with the following extension elements:

```
<mime:content part="nmtoken"? type="string"?/>

<mime:multipartRelated>
    <mime:part> *
        <-- mime element -->
    </mime:part>
</mime:multipartRelated>

<mime:mimeXml part="nmtoken"?/>
```

They are used at the following locations in WSDL:

```
<definitions .... >
    <binding .... >
        <operation .... >
            <input .... >
                <-- mime elements -->
            </input>
            <output .... >
                <-- mime elements -->
            </output>
        </operation>
    </binding>
</definitions>
```

MIME elements appear under input and output to specify the MIME format. If multiple appear, they are considered to be alternatives.

5.3 mime:content

To avoid having to define a new element for every MIME format, the `mime:content` element may be used if there is no additional information to convey about the format other than its MIME type string.

```
<mime:content part="nmtoken"? type="string"?/>
```

The `part` attribute is used to specify the name of the message part. If the message has a single part, then the `part` attribute is optional. The `type` attribute contains the MIME type string. A type value has two portions, separated by a slash (/), either of which may be a wildcard (*). Not specifying a `type` attribute indicates that all MIME types are acceptable.

If the return format is XML, but the schema is not known ahead of time, the generic `mime` element can be used indicating `text/xml`:

```
<mime:content type="text/xml"/>
```

A wildcard (*) can be used to specify a family of MIME types, for example all text types.

```
<mime:content type="text/*"/>
```

The following two examples both specify all MIME types:

```
<mime:content type="*/*"/>
<mime:content/>
```

5.4 mime:multipartRelated

The `multipart/related` MIME type aggregates an arbitrary set of MIME formatted parts into one message using the MIME type "multipart/related". The `mime:multipartRelated` element describes the concrete format of such a message:

```
<mime:multipartRelated>
    <mime:part> *
        <-- mime element -->
    </mime:part>
</mime:multipartRelated>
```

The `mime:part` element describes each part of a `multipart/related` message. MIME elements appear within `mime:part` to specify the concrete MIME type for the part. If more than one MIME element appears inside a `mime:part`, they are alternatives.

5.5 soap:body

When using the MIME binding with SOAP requests, it is legal to use the `soap:body` element as a MIME element. It indicates the content type is "`text/xml`", and there is an enclosing SOAP Envelope.

5.6 mime:mimeXml

To specify XML payloads that are not SOAP compliant (do not have a SOAP Envelope), but do have a particular schema, the `mime:mimeXml` element may be used to specify that concrete schema. The `part` attribute refers to a message part defining the concrete schema of the root XML element. The `part` attribute MAY be omitted if the message has only a single part. The part references a concrete schema using the `element` attribute for simple parts or `type` attribute for composite parts (see Section 2.3.1).

```
<mime:mimeXml part="nmtoken"?/>
```

6. References

[2]   S. Bradner, "Key words for use in RFCs to Indicate Requirement Levels", RFC 2119, Harvard University, March 1997.

[4]   T. Berners-Lee, R. Fielding, L. Masinter, "Uniform Resource Identifiers (URI): Generic Syntax", RFC 2396, MIT/LCS, U.C. Irvine, Xerox Corporation, August 1998.

[5]   /http://www.w3.org/TR/html401/interact/forms./html - submit-format

[6]   /http://www.w3.org/TR/html401/appendix/notes./html - ampersands-in-uris

[7]   /http://www.w3.org/TR/html401/interact/forms./html - h-17.13.4

[8]   Simple Object Access Protocol (SOAP) 1.1 "/http://www.w3.org/TR/2000/NOTE-SOAP-20000508/"/

[10]   W3C Working Draft "XML Schema Part 1: Structures". This is a work in progress.

[11]   W3C Working Draft "XML Schema Part 2: Datatypes". This is a work in progress.

A 1. Notes on URIs

This section does not directly contribute to the specification, but provides background that may be useful when implementing the specification.

A 1.1 XML namespaces & schema locations

It is a common misperception to equate the `targetNamespace` of an XML schema or the value of the `xmlns` attribute in XML instances with the location of the corresponding schema. Since namespaces are in fact URIs, and URIs may be locations, and you may be able to retrieve a schema from that location, it does not mean that is the only schema that is associated with that namespace. There can be multiple schemas associated with a particular namespace, and it is up to the XML processor to determine which one to use in a particular processing context. The WSDL specification provides the processing context here via the `<import>` mechanism, which is based on the XML schemas grammar for the similar concept.

A 1.2 Relative URIs

Throughout this document you see fully qualified URIs used in WSDL and XSD documents. The use of a fully qualified URI is simply to illustrate the referencing concepts. The use of relative URIs is completely allowed and is warranted in many cases. For information on processing relative URIs, see:

> http://www.normos.org/ietf/rfc/rfc2396.txt

A 1.3 Generating URIs

When working with WSDL, it is sometimes desirable to make up a URI for an entity, but not make the URI globally unique for all time and have it "mean" that version of the entity (schema, WSDL document, etc.). There is a particular URI base reserved for use for this type of behavior: http://tempuri.org/ that can be used to construct a URI without any unique association to an entity. For example, two people or programs could choose to simultaneously use the URI http://tempuri.org/myschema/ for two completely different schemas, and as long as the scope of the use of the URIs does not intersect, then they are considered unique enough. This has the further benefit that the entity referred to by the URI can be versioned without having to generate a new URI, as long as it makes sense within the processing context. It is not recommended that http://tempuri.org/ be used as a base for stable, fixed entities.

A 2. Wire format for WSDL examples

A 2.1. Example 1

SOAP Message Embedded in HTTP Request

```
POST /StockQuote HTTP/1.1
Host: www.stockquoteserver.com
Content-Type: text/xml; charset="utf-8"
Content-Length: nnnn
SOAPAction: "Some-URI"

<soapenv:Envelope xmlns:soapenv="http://schemas.xmlsoap.org/soap/envelope/">
    <soapenv:Body>
        <m:GetLastTradePrice xmlns:m="Some-URI">
```

```
            <m:tickerSymbol>DIS</m:tickerSymbol>
        </m:GetLastTradePrice>
    </soapenv:Body>
</soapenv:Envelope>
```

SOAP Message Embedded in HTTP Response

```
HTTP/1.1 200 OK
Content-Type: text/xml; charset="utf-8"
Content-Length: nnnn

<soapenv:Envelope xmlns:soapenv="http://schemas.xmlsoap.org/soap/envelope/">
    <soapenv:Body>
        <m:GetLastTradePriceResponse xmlns:m="Some-URI">
            <m:price>34.5</m:price>
        </m:GetLastTradePriceResponse>
    </soapenv:Body>
</soapenv:Envelope>
```

A 3. Location of Extensibility Elements

Extensibility elements can appear at the following locations in a WSDL document:

Location	Meaning	Possible usage
definitions	The extensibility element applies to the WSDL document as a whole.	To introduce additional information or definitions to a WSDL document as a whole.
definitions/types	The extensibility element is a type system.	To specify the format of the message in a type system other than XSD.
definitions/service	The extensibility element applies to the service.	To introduce additional information or definitions for the service.
definitions/service/port	The extensibility element applies to the port.	To specify an address for the port.
definitions/binding	The extensibility element applies to the binding as a whole.	To provide protocol specific information that applies to all the operations in the port type being bound.
definitions/binding/operation	The extensibility element applies to the operation as a whole.	To provide protocol specific information that applies to both the input message and the output message.

Table continued on following page

749

Location	Meaning	Possible usage
definitions/binding/operation/ input	The extensibility element applies to the input message for the operation.	To provide details on how abstract message parts map into the concrete protocol and data formats of the binding. To provide additional protocol specific information for the input message.
definitions/binding/operation/ output	The extensibility element applies to the output message of the operation.	To provide details on how abstract message parts map into the concrete protocol and data formats of the binding. To provide additional protocol specific information for the output message.
definitions/binding/operation/ fault	The extensibility element applies to a fault message of the operation.	To provide details on how abstract message parts map into the concrete protocol and data formats of the binding. To provide additional protocol specific information for the fault message.

A 4. Schemas

A 4.1 WSDL Schema

```
<schema xmlns="http://www.w3.org/2000/10/XMLSchema"
        xmlns:wsdl="http://schemas.xmlsoap.org/wsdl/"
        targetNamespace="http://schemas.xmlsoap.org/wsdl/"
        elementFormDefault="qualified">
    <element name="documentation">
        <complexType mixed="true">
            <choice minOccurs="0" maxOccurs="unbounded">
                <any minOccurs="0" maxOccurs="unbounded"/>
            </choice>
            <anyAttribute/>
        </complexType>
    </element>
    <complexType name="documented" abstract="true">
        <sequence>
            <element ref="wsdl:documentation" minOccurs="0"/>
        </sequence>
    </complexType>
    <complexType name="openAtts" abstract="true">
        <annotation>
            <documentation>
```

```
                This type is extended by  component types
                to allow attributes from other namespaces to be added.
                </documentation>
        </annotation>
        <sequence>
            <element ref="wsdl:documentation" minOccurs="0"/>
        </sequence>
        <anyAttribute namespace="##other"/>
    </complexType>
    <element name="definitions" type="wsdl:definitionsType">
        <key name="message">
            <selector xpath="message"/>
            <field xpath="@name"/>
        </key>
        <key name="portType">
            <selector xpath="portType"/>
            <field xpath="@name"/>
        </key>
        <key name="binding">
            <selector xpath="binding"/>
            <field xpath="@name"/>
        </key>
        <key name="service">
            <selector xpath="service"/>
            <field xpath="@name"/>
        </key>
        <key name="import">
                <selector xpath="import"/>
                <field xpath="@namespace"/>
            </key>
        <key name="port">
            <selector xpath="service/port"/>
            <field xpath="@name"/>
        </key>
    </element>
    <complexType name="definitionsType">
        <complexContent>
            <extension base="wsdl:documented">
                <sequence>
                    <element ref="wsdl:import" minOccurs="0" maxOccurs="unbounded"/>
                    <element ref="wsdl:types" minOccurs="0"/>
                    <element ref="wsdl:message" minOccurs="0" maxOccurs="unbounded"/>
                    <element ref="wsdl:portType" minOccurs="0"
                            maxOccurs="unbounded"/>
                    <element ref="wsdl:binding" minOccurs="0" maxOccurs="unbounded"/>
                    <element ref="wsdl:service" minOccurs="0" maxOccurs="unbounded"/>
                    <any namespace="##other" minOccurs="0" maxOccurs="unbounded">
                        <annotation>
                            <documentation>to support extensibility elements
                            </documentation>
                        </annotation>
                    </any>
                </sequence>
                <attribute name="targetNamespace" type="uriReference"
                        use="optional"/>
                <attribute name="name" type="NMTOKEN" use="optional"/>
```

```
            </extension>
        </complexContent>
    </complexType>
    <element name="import" type="wsdl:importType"/>
    <complexType name="importType">
        <complexContent>
    <extension base="wsdl:documented">
    <attribute name="namespace" type="uriReference" use="required"/>
        <attribute name="location" type="uriReference" use="required"/>
    </extension>
    </complexContent>
    </complexType>
    <element name="types" type="wsdl:typesType"/>
    <complexType name="typesType">
        <complexContent>
    <extension base="wsdl:documented">
    <sequence>
    <any namespace="##other" minOccurs="0" maxOccurs="unbounded"/>
    </sequence>
    </extension>
    </complexContent>
    </complexType>
    <element name="message" type="wsdl:messageType">
        <unique name="part">
            <selector xpath="part"/>
            <field xpath="@name"/>
        </unique>
    </element>
    <complexType name="messageType">
        <complexContent>
    <extension base="wsdl:documented">
    <sequence>
    <element ref="wsdl:part" minOccurs="0" maxOccurs="unbounded"/>
    </sequence>
        <attribute name="name" type="NCName" use="required"/>
    </extension>
    </complexContent>
    </complexType>
    <element name="part" type="wsdl:partType"/>
    <complexType name="partType">
        <complexContent>
    <extension base="wsdl:openAtts">
    <attribute name="name" type="NMTOKEN" use="optional"/>
        <attribute name="type" type="QName" use="optional"/>
        <attribute name="element" type="QName" use="optional"/>
    </extension>
    </complexContent>
    </complexType>
    <element name="portType" type="wsdl:portTypeType"/>
    <complexType name="portTypeType">
        <complexContent>
    <extension base="wsdl:documented">
    <sequence>
    <element ref="wsdl:operation" minOccurs="0" maxOccurs="unbounded"/>
    </sequence>
```

```xml
      <attribute name="name" type="NCName" use="required"/>
    </extension>
  </complexContent>
</complexType>
 <element name="operation" type="wsdl:operationType"/>
 <complexType name="operationType">
    <complexContent>
  <extension base="wsdl:documented">
      <choice>
          <group ref="wsdl:one-way-operation"/>
          <group ref="wsdl:request-response-operation"/>
          <group ref="wsdl:solicit-response-operation"/>
          <group ref="wsdl:notification-operation"/>
      </choice>
      <attribute name="name" type="NCName" use="required"/>
  </extension>
</complexContent>
</complexType>
 <group name="one-way-operation">
    <sequence>
        <element ref="wsdl:input"/>
    </sequence>
 </group>
 <group name="request-response-operation">
    <sequence>
        <element ref="wsdl:input"/>
        <element ref="wsdl:output"/>
        <element ref="wsdl:fault" minOccurs="0" maxOccurs="unbounded"/>
    </sequence>
 </group>
 <group name="solicit-response-operation">
    <sequence>
        <element ref="wsdl:output"/>
        <element ref="wsdl:input"/>
        <element ref="wsdl:fault" minOccurs="0" maxOccurs="unbounded"/>
    </sequence>
 </group>
 <group name="notification-operation">
    <sequence>
        <element ref="wsdl:output"/>
    </sequence>
 </group>
 <element name="input" type="wsdl:paramType"/>
 <element name="output" type="wsdl:paramType"/>
 <element name="fault" type="wsdl:faultType"/>
 <complexType name="paramType">
    <complexContent>
  <extension base="wsdl:documented">
  <attribute name="name" type="NMTOKEN" use="optional"/>
      <attribute name="message" type="QName" use="required"/>
  </extension>
</complexContent>
</complexType>
 <complexType name="faultType">
    <complexContent>
```

```
    <extension base="wsdl:documented">
    <attribute name="name" type="NMTOKEN" use="required"/>
      <attribute name="message" type="QName" use="required"/>
    </extension>
</complexContent>
</complexType>
    <complexType name="startWithExtensionsType" abstract="true">
      <complexContent>
    <extension base="wsdl:documented">
    <sequence>
    <any namespace="##other" minOccurs="0" maxOccurs="unbounded"/>
</sequence>
    </extension>
</complexContent>
</complexType>
    <element name="binding" type="wsdl:bindingType"/>
    <complexType name="bindingType">
      <complexContent>
    <extension base="wsdl:startWithExtensionsType">
    <sequence>
    <element name="operation" type="wsdl:binding_operationType" minOccurs="0"
 maxOccurs="unbounded"/>
</sequence>
      <attribute name="name" type="NCName" use="required"/>
      <attribute name="type" type="QName" use="required"/>
    </extension>
</complexContent>
</complexType>
    <complexType name="binding_operationType">
      <complexContent>
    <extension base="wsdl:startWithExtensionsType">
    <sequence>
    <element name="input" type="wsdl:startWithExtensionsType" minOccurs="0"/>
      <element name="output" type="wsdl:startWithExtensionsType" minOccurs="0"/>
      <element name="fault" minOccurs="0" maxOccurs="unbounded">
        <complexType>
          <complexContent>
    <extension base="wsdl:startWithExtensionsType">
    <attribute name="name" type="NMTOKEN" use="required"/>
        </extension>
</complexContent>
</complexType>
    </element>
</sequence>
      <attribute name="name" type="NCName" use="required"/>
    </extension>
</complexContent>
</complexType>
    <element name="service" type="wsdl:serviceType"/>
    <complexType name="serviceType">
      <complexContent>
    <extension base="wsdl:documented">
    <sequence>
    <element ref="wsdl:port" minOccurs="0" maxOccurs="unbounded"/>
      <any namespace="##other" minOccurs="0"/>
```

```
    </sequence>
        <attribute name="name" type="NCName" use="required"/>
    </extension>
    </complexContent>
    </complexType>
    <element name="port" type="wsdl:portType"/>
    <complexType name="portType">
        <complexContent>
    <extension base="wsdl:documented">
    <sequence>
    <any namespace="##other" minOccurs="0"/>
    </sequence>
        <attribute name="name" type="NCName" use="required"/>
        <attribute name="binding" type="QName" use="required"/>
    </extension>
    </complexContent>
    </complexType>
    <attribute name="arrayType" type="string"/>
</schema>
```

A 4.2 SOAP Binding Schema

```
<schema xmlns="http://www.w3.org/2000/10/XMLSchema"
        xmlns:soap="http://schemas.xmlsoap.org/wsdl/soap/"
        targetNamespace="http://schemas.xmlsoap.org/wsdl/soap/">
    <element name="binding" type="soap:bindingType"/>
    <complexType name="bindingType">
        <attribute name="transport" type="uriReference" use="optional"/>
        <attribute name="style" type="soap:styleChoice" use="optional"/>
    </complexType>
    <simpleType name="styleChoice">
        <restriction base="string">
    <enumeration value="rpc"/>
        <enumeration value="document"/>
    </restriction>
    </simpleType>
    <element name="operation" type="soap:operationType"/>
    <complexType name="operationType">
        <attribute name="soapAction" type="uriReference" use="optional"/>
        <attribute name="style" type="soap:styleChoice" use="optional"/>
    </complexType>
    <element name="body" type="soap:bodyType"/>
    <complexType name="bodyType">
        <attribute name="encodingStyle" type="uriReference" use="optional"/>
        <attribute name="parts" type="NMTOKENS" use="optional"/>
        <attribute name="use" type="soap:useChoice" use="optional"/>
        <attribute name="namespace" type="uriReference" use="optional"/>
    </complexType>
    <simpleType name="useChoice">
        <restriction base="string">
    <enumeration value="literal"/>
        <enumeration value="encoded"/>
    </restriction>
    </simpleType>
    <element name="fault" type="soap:faultType"/>
```

```
   <complexType name="faultType">
      <complexContent>
   <restriction base="soap:bodyType">
   <attribute name="parts" type="NMTOKENS" use="prohibited"/>
   </restriction>
   </complexContent>
   </complexType>
   <element name="header" type="soap:headerType"/>
   <complexType name="headerType">
      <all>
         <element ref="soap:headerfault">
      </all>
      <attribute name="message" type="QName" use="required"/>
      <attribute name="parts" type="NMTOKENS" use="required"/>
      <attribute name="use" type="soap:useChoice" use="required"/>
      <attribute name="encodingStyle" type="uriReference" use="optional"/>
      <attribute name="namespace" type="uriReference" use="optional"/>
   </complexType>
   <element name="headerfault" type="soap:headerfaultType"/>
   <complexType name="headerfaultType">
      <attribute name="message" type="QName" use="required"/>
      <attribute name="parts" type="NMTOKENS" use="required"/>
      <attribute name="use" type="soap:useChoice" use="required"/>
      <attribute name="encodingStyle" type="uriReference" use="optional"/>
      <attribute name="namespace" type="uriReference" use="optional"/>
   </complexType>
   <element name="address" type="soap:addressType"/>
   <complexType name="addressType">
      <attribute name="location" type="uriReference" use="required"/>
   </complexType>
</schema>
```

A 4.3 HTTP Binding Schema

```
<schema xmlns="http://www.w3.org/2000/10/XMLSchema"
        xmlns:http="http://schemas.xmlsoap.org/wsdl/http/"
        targetNamespace="http://schemas.xmlsoap.org/wsdl/http/">
   <element name="address" type="http:addressType"/>
   <complexType name="addressType">
      <attribute name="location" type="uriReference" use="required"/>
   </complexType>
   <element name="binding" type="http:bindingType"/>
   <complexType name="bindingType">
      <attribute name="verb" type="NMTOKEN" use="required"/>
   </complexType>
   <element name="operation" type="http:operationType"/>
   <complexType name="operationType">
      <attribute name="location" type="uriReference" use="required"/>
   </complexType>
   <element name="urlEncoded">
      <complexType>
   </complexType>
   </element>
   <element name="urlReplacement">
      <complexType>
   </complexType>
   </element>
</schema>
```

A 4.4 MIME Binding Schema

```
<schema  targetNamespace="http://schemas.xmlsoap.org/wsdl/mime/"
         xmlns:mime="http://schemas.xmlsoap.org/wsdl/mime/"
         xmlns="http://www.w3.org/2000/10/XMLSchema">
  <element name="content" type="mime:contentType"/>
  <complexType name="contentType" content="empty">
     <attribute name="type" type="string" use="optional"/>
     <attribute name="part" type="NMTOKEN" use="optional"/>
  </complexType>
  <element name="multipartRelated" type="mime:multipartRelatedType"/>
  <complexType name="multipartRelatedType" content="elementOnly">
     <element ref="mime:part" minOccurs="0" maxOccurs="unbounded"/>
  </complexType>
  <element name="part" type="mime:partType"/>
  <complexType name="partType" content="elementOnly">
     <any namespace="targetNamespace" minOccurs="0" maxOccurs="unbounded"/>
     <attribute name="name" type="NMTOKEN" use="required"/>
  </complexType>
  <element name="mimeXml" type="mime:mimeXmlType"/>
  <complexType name="mimeXmlType" content="empty">
     <attribute name="part" type="NMTOKEN" use="optional"/>
  </complexType>
</schema>
```

C

UDDI 2.0 Data Types

This appendix consists of material from the *UDDI version 2.0 Data Structure Reference UDDI Open Draft Specification* from UDDI.org, dated 8 June 2001. It gives a detailed list of all UDDI Structures and Substructures, a description of their Fields, and the lengths and data types of these fields.

The original version can be found at:

http://www.uddi.org/pubs/DataStructure-V2.00-Open-20010608.pdf

The editors of the original document are as follows:

❏ David Ehnebuske, IBM

❏ Dan Rogers, Microsoft

❏ Claus von Riegen, SAP

The contributors are as follows:

❏ Tom Bellwood, IBM

❏ Andy Harris, i2 Technologies

❏ Denise Ho, Ariba

❏ Yin-Leng Husband, Compaq

❏ Alan Karp, HP

❏ Keisuke Kibakura, Fujitsu

❏ Jeff Lancelle, Verisign

- ❏ Sam Lee, Oracle

- ❏ Sean MacRoibeaird, Sun

- ❏ Barbara McKee, IBM

- ❏ Tammy Nordan, Compaq

- ❏ Dan Rogers, Microsoft

- ❏ Christine Tomlinson, Sun

- ❏ Cafer Tosun, SAP

Data Structure Notation

Data structures are described by substructure breakdowns in tables of the following form:

Field Name	Description	Data Type	Length

Optional fields are written in `Normal code` font	Description of the field's meaning and whether it's
	
	❏ An attribute or an element
		Possible Data Types include:
		
		`structure`
		
		`string`
		
		`UUID`
			If the field's data type is string, the field's length is given here in Unicode characters

Required fields are written in **`Bold code`** font	❏ Repeatable or not		

Most of the data structures are also given in their XML Schema representation (W3C XML Schema Candidate Recommendation, October 2000). Please use the UDDI XML Schema as the definitive technical reference, if needed.

The businessEntity Structure

The businessEntity structure represents all known information about a business or entity that publishes descriptive information about the entity as well as the services that it offers. From an XML standpoint, the businessEntity is the top-level data structure that accommodates holding descriptive information about a business or entity. Service descriptions and technical information are expressed within a businessEntity by a containment relationship.

Structure Specification

```
<element name = "businessEntity">
   <complexType>
      <sequence>
         <element ref = "discoveryURLs" minOccurs = "0"/>
         <element ref = "name" maxOccurs = "unbounded"/>
         <element ref = "description" minOccurs = "0"
                  maxOccurs = "unbounded"/>
         <element ref = "contacts" minOccurs = "0"/>
         <element ref = "businessServices" minOccurs = "0"/>
         <element ref = "identifierBag" minOccurs = "0"/>
         <element ref = "categoryBag" minOccurs = "0"/>
      </sequence>
      <attribute ref = "businessKey" use = "required"/>
      <attribute ref = "operator"/>
      <attribute ref = "authorizedName">
   </complexType>
</element>
```

Substructure Breakdown

Field Name	Description	Data Type	Length
businessKey	Attribute. This is the unique identifier for a given instance of a businessEntity structure.	UUID	41
authorizedName	Attribute. This is the recorded name of the individual that published the businessEntity data. This data is generated by the controlling operator and should not be supplied within save_business operations.	string	255
operator	Attribute. This is the certified name of the UDDI registry site operator that manages the master copy of the businessEntity data. The controlling operator records this data at the time data is saved. This data is generated and should not be supplied within save_business operations.	string	255

Table continued on following page

Field Name	Description	Data Type	Length
discoveryURLs	Optional element. This is a list of Uniform Resource Locators (URL) that point to alternate, file based service discovery mechanisms. Each recorded businessEntity structure is automatically assigned a URL that returns the individual businessEntity structure. URL search is provided via find_business call.	structure	
name	Required repeating element. These are the human readable names recorded for the businessEntity, adorned with a unique xml:lang value to signify the language that they are expressed in. Name search is provided via find_business call. Names may not be blank.	string	255
description	Optional repeating element. One or more short business descriptions. One description is allowed per national language code supplied.	string	255
contacts	Optional element. This is an optional list of contact information.	structure	
businessServices	Optional element. This is a list of one or more logical business service descriptions.	structure	
identifierBag	Optional element. This is an optional list of name-value pairs that can be used to record identifiers for a businessEntity. These can be used during search via find_business.	structure	
categoryBag	Optional element. This is an optional list of name-value pairs that are used to tag a businessEntity with specific taxonomy information (for example industry, product or geographic codes). These can be used during search via find_business.	structure	

discoveryURLs

The discoveryURLs structure is used to hold pointers to URL addressable discovery documents. The expected retrieval mechanism for URLs referenced in the data within this structure is HTTP-GET. The expected return document is not defined. Rather, a framework for establishing convention is provided, and two such conventions are defined within UDDI behaviors. It is hoped that other conventions come about and use this structure to accommodate alternate means of discovery (An example of an alternate form of service discovery is seen in the ECO Framework as defined by the commerce.net initiative. A convention to provide pointers to ECO discovery entry points could take advantage of the structures provided in discovery URLs by adopting the useType value "ECO").

Field Name	Description	Data Type	Length
`discoveryURL`	Attribute qualified repeating element holding strings that represent web addressable (via `HTTP-GET`) discovery documents.	`string w/attributes`	255

discoveryURL

Each individual discovery URL consists of an attribute whose value designates the URL use type convention, and a string, found within the body of the element. Each time a `businessEntity` structure is saved via a call to `save_business`, the UDDI Operator Site will generate one URL. The generated URL will point to an instance of either a `businessEntity` or `businessEntityExt` structure, and the `useType` attribute of the `discoveryURL` will be set to either "businessEntity" or "businessEntityExt" according to the data type found while processing the `save_business` message. The `discoveryURLs` collection will be augmented so that it includes this generated URL. This URL can then be used to retrieve a specific instance of a `businessEntity`, since the XML returned will be formatted as a normal `businessDetail` message.

Field Name	Description	Data Type	Length
`useType`	Required attribute that designates the name of the convention that the referenced document follows. Two reserved convention values are "businessEntity" and "businessEntityExt". URLs qualified with these values should point to XML documents of the same type as the `useType` value.	`string`	255

An example of the generated data for a given `businessEntity` might look similar to the following:

```
<discoveryURLs>
<discoveryURL useType="businessEntity">
http://www.someOperator?businessKey=BE3D2F08-CEB3-11D3-849F-0050DA1803C0
</discoveryURL>
<discoveryURLs>
```

name

The publishing of several names, for example for romanization purposes, is supported. In order to signify the language that the names are expressed in, they carry unique `xml:lang` values. Not more than one name element may omit specifying its language. Names passed in this way will be assigned the default language code of the registering party. This default language code is established at the time that publishing credentials are established with an individual Operator Site. If no default language is provisioned at the time a publisher signs up, the operator can adopt an appropriate default language code.

The same mechanism applies to the `name` element within the `businessService` structure.

contacts

The `contacts` structure provides a way for information to be registered with a `businessEntity` record so that someone that finds the information can make human contact for any purpose. Since the information held within the UDDI Operator Sites is freely available, some care should be taken when considering the amount of contact information to register. E-mail addresses in particular may be the greatest concern if you are sensitive to receiving unsolicited mail.

The `contacts` structure itself is a simple collection of contact structures. You'll find that there are many collections in the UDDI Version 2.0 API schema. Like the `discoveryURLs` structure – which is a container for one or more `discoveryURL` structures, the `contacts` structure is a simple container where one or more `contact` structures reside.

contact

The `contact` structure lets you record contact information for a person. This information can consist of one or more optional elements, along with a person's name. Contact information exists by containment relationship alone, and no mechanisms for tracking individual contact instances is provided by UDDI specifications.

For transliteration purposes (such as romanization) the suggested approach is to file multiple contacts.

Field Name	Description	Data Type	Length
useType	Optional attribute that is used to describe the type of contact in freeform text. Suggested examples include "technical questions", "technical contact", "establish account", "sales contact", etc.	string	255
description	Optional element. Zero or more language-qualified descriptions* of the reason the contact should be used.	string	255
personName	Required element. Contacts should list the name of the person or name of the job role that will be available behind the contact. Examples of roles include "administrator" or "webmaster".	string	255
phone	Optional repeating element. Used to hold telephone numbers for the contact. This element can be adorned with an optional useType attribute for descriptive purposes. If more than one phone element is saved, useType attributes are required on each.	string w/attributes	50
email	Optional repeating element. Used to hold email addresses for the contact. This element can be adorned with an optional useType attribute for descriptive purposes. If more than one email element is saved, useType attributes are required on each.	string w/attributes	255
address	Optional repeating element. This structure represents the printable lines suitable for addressing an envelope.	structure	

*All fields named `description` behave the same way and are subject to the same language identifier rules as described in the XML usage appendix found in the UDDI programmers API specification. Embedded HTML is prohibited in description fields.

address

The `address` structure is a simple list of `addressLine` elements within the address container. Each `addressLine` element is a simple string. UDDI compliant registries are responsible for preserving the order of any `addressLine` data provided. `address` structures also have three optional attributes. The `useType` describes the address' type in freeform text. The `sortCode` values are not significant within a UDDI registry, but may be used by user interfaces that present contact information in some ordered fashion using the values provided in the `sortCode` attribute. The `tModelKey` references a `tModel` that specifies the meaning of `keyName` `keyValue` pairs given in subordinate `addressLine` elements.

Field Name	Description	Data Type	Length
useType	Optional attribute that is used to describe the type of address in freeform text. Suggested examples include "headquarters", "sales office", "billing department", etc.	string	255
sortCode	Optional attribute that can be used to drive the behavior of external display mechanisms that sort addresses. The suggested values for sortCode include numeric ordering values (like 1, 2, 3), alphabetic character ordering values (like a, b, c) or the first n positions of relevant data within the address.	string	10
tModelKey	Optional attribute. This is the unique key reference that implies that the keyName keyValue pairs given by subsequent addressLine elements are to be interpreted by the taxonomy associated with the tModel that is referenced.	string	255 41*
addressLine	Optional repeating element containing the actual address in freeform text. If the address element contains a tModelKey, these addressLine elements are to be adorned each with an optional keyName/keyValue attribute pair. Together with the tModelKey, keyName and keyValue qualify the addressLine in order to describe its meaning.	string w/attributes	80

The data type for `tModelKey` allows for using URN values in a later revision. In the current release, the key is a generated UUID. Design work around managing duplicate urn claims will allow user supplied URN keys on tModels in the future.

addressLine

addressLine elements contain string data with a line length limit of 80 character positions. Each addressLine element can be adorned with two optional descriptive attributes, keyName and keyValue. Both attributes must be present in each address line if a tModelKey is assigned to the address structure. By doing this, the otherwise arbitrary use of address lines becomes structured. Together with the address' tModelKey, keyName and keyValue virtually build a keyedReference that represents an address line qualifier, given by the referenced tModel. When no tModelKey is provided for the address structure, the keyName and keyValue attributes can be used without restrictions, for example, to provide descriptive information for each addressLine by using the keyName attribute. Since both the keyName and the keyValue attributes are optional, address line order is significant and will always be returned by the UDDI compliant registry in the order originally provided during a call to save_business.

businessServices

The businessServices structure provides a way for describing information about families of services. This simple collection accessor contains zero or more businessService structures and has no other associated structures.

identifierBag

The identifierBag element allows businessEntity or tModel structures to include information about common forms of identification such as D-U-N-S® numbers (see http://www.dnb.com/ for more on these), tax identifiers, etc. This data can be used to signify the identity of the businessEntity, or can be used to signify the identity of the publishing party. Including data of this sort is optional, but when used greatly enhances the search behaviors exposed via the find_xx messages defined in the UDDI Version 2.0 API Specification.

categoryBag

The categoryBag element allows businessEntity, businessService and tModel structures to be categorized according to any of several available taxonomy based classification schemes. Operator Sites automatically provide validated categorization support for three taxonomies that cover industry codes (via NAICS), product and service classifications (via UNSPC) and geography (via ISO 3166). Including data of this sort is optional, but when used greatly enhances the search behaviors exposed by the find_xx messages defined in the UDDI Version 2.0 API Specification.

The businessService Structure

The businessService structures each represent a logical service classification. The name of the element includes the term "business" in an attempt to describe the purpose of this level in the service description hierarchy. Each businessService structure is the logical child of a single businessEntity structure. The identity of the containing (parent) businessEntity is determined by examining the embedded businessKey value. If no businessKey value is present, the businessKey must be obtainable by searching for a businessKey value in any parent structure containing the businessService. Each businessService element contains descriptive information in business terms outlining the type of technical services found within each businessService element.

In some cases, businesses would like to share or reuse services, for example when a large enterprise publishes separate businessEntity structures. This can be established by using the businessService structure as a **projection** to an already published businessService.

Any businessService projected in this way is not managed as a part of the referencing businessEntity, but centrally as a part of the referenced businessEntity. This means that changes of the businessService by the referenced businessEntity are automatically valid for the service projections done by referencing businessEntity structures.

In order to specify both referenced and referencing businessEntity structures correctly, service projections can only be published by a save_business message with the referencing businessKey present in the businessEntity structure and both the referenced businessKey and the referenced businessService present in the businessService structure.

Structure Specification

```
<element name = "businessService">
   <complexType>
      <sequence>
         <element ref = "name" maxOccurs = "unbounded"/>
         <element ref = "description" minOccurs = "0"
                  maxOccurs = "unbounded"/>
         <element ref = "bindingTemplates"/>
         <element ref = "categoryBag" minOccurs = "0"/>
      </sequence>
      <attribute ref = "serviceKey" use = "required"/>
      <attribute ref = "businessKey"/>
   </complexType>
</element>
```

Substructure Breakdown

Field Name	Description	Datatype	Length
businessKey	This attribute is optional when the businessService data is contained within a fully expressed parent that already contains a businessKey value. If the businessService data is rendered into XML and has no containing parent that has within its data a businessKey, the value of the businessKey that is the parent of the businessService is required to be provided. This behavior supports the ability to browse through the parent-child relationships given any of the core elements as a starting point. The businessKey may differ from the publishing businessEntity's businessKey to allow service projections.	UUID	41

Table continued on following page

Field Name	Description	Datatype	Length
serviceKey	This is the unique key for a given businessService. When saving a new businessService structure, pass an empty serviceKey value. This signifies that a UUID value is to be generated. To update an existing businessService structure, pass the UUID value that corresponds to the existing service. If this data is received via an inquiry operation, the serviceKey values may not be blank. When saving a new or updated service projection, pass the serviceKey of the referenced businessService structure.	UUID	41
name	Required repeating element. These are the human readable names recorded for the businessService, adorned with a unique xml:lang value to signify the language that they are expressed in. Name search is provided via find_service call. Names may not be blank. When saving a new or updated service projection, pass the exact name of the referenced businessService, here.	string	255
description	Optional element. Zero or more language-qualified text descriptions of the logical service family.	string	255
bindingTemplates	This structure holds the technical service description information related to a given business service family.	structure	
categoryBag	Optional element. This is an optional list of name-value pairs that are used to tag a businessService with specific taxonomy information (for example, industry, product or geographic codes). These can be used during search via find_service. See categoryBag under businessEntity for a full description.	structure	

bindingTemplates

The bindingTemplates structure is a container for zero or more bindingTemplate structures. This simple collection accessor has no other associated structure.

The bindingTemplate Structure

Technical descriptions of Web Services are accommodated via individual contained instances of bindingTemplate structures. These structures provide support for determining a technical entry point or optionally support remotely hosted services, as well as a lightweight facility for describing unique technical characteristics of a given implementation. Support for technology and application specific parameters and settings files are also supported.

Since UDDI's main purpose is to enable description and discovery of Web Service information, it is the bindingTemplate that provides the most interesting technical data.

Each bindingTemplate structure has a single logical businessService parent, which in turn has a single logical businessEntity parent.

Structure Specification

```
<element name = "bindingTemplate">
    <complexType>
        <sequence>
            <element ref = "description" minOccurs = "0"
                    maxOccurs = "unbounded"/>
                <choice>
                    <element ref = "accessPoint" minOccurs = "0"/>
                    <element ref = "hostingRedirector" minOccurs = "0"/>
                </choice>
            <element ref = "tModelInstanceDetails"/>
        </sequence>
        <attribute ref = "bindingKey" use = "required"/>
        <attribute ref = "serviceKey"/>
    </complexType>
</element>
```

Substructure Breakdown

Field Name	Description	Data Type	Length
bindingKey	This is the unique key for a given bindingTemplate. When saving a new bindingTemplate structure, pass an empty bindingKey value. This signifies that a UUID value is to be generated. To update an existing bindingTemplate structure, pass the UUID value that corresponds to the existing bindingTemplate instance. If this data is received via an inquiry operation, the bindingKey values may not be blank.	UUID	41

Table continued on following page

Field Name	Description	Data Type	Length
serviceKey	This attribute is optional when the bindingTemplate data is contained within a fully expressed parent that already contains a serviceKey value. If the bindingTemplate data is rendered into XML and has no containing parent that has within its data a serviceKey, the value of the serviceKey that is the ultimate containing parent of the bindingTemplate is required to be provided. This behavior supports the ability to browse through the parent-child relationships given any of the core elements as a starting point.	UUID	41
description	Optional repeating element. Zero or more language-qualified text descriptions of the technical service entry point.	string	255
accessPoint	Required attribute qualified element*. This element is a text field that is used to convey the entry point address suitable for calling a particular Web service. This may be a URL, an e-mail address, or even a telephone number. No assumptions about the type of data in this field can be made without first understanding the technical requirements associated with the Web service.	string w/attributes	255
hostingRedirector	Required element if accessPoint not provided. This element is adorned with a bindingKey attribute, giving the redirected reference to a different bindingTemplate. If you query a bindingTemplate and find a hostingRedirector value, you should retrieve that bindingTemplate and use it in place of the one containing the hostingRedirector data.	empty w/attributes	
tModelInstance Details	This structure is a list of zero or more tModelInstanceInfo elements. This data, taken in total, should form a distinct fingerprint that can be used to identify compatible services.	structure	

One of accessPoint or hostingRedirector is required.

The content of the structure named tModelInstanceDetails that is found within a bindingTemplate structure serves as a technical fingerprint. This fingerprint is a series of references to uniquely keyed specifications and/or concepts. To build a new service that is compatible with a tModel, the specifications must be understood. To register a service compatible with a specification, reference a tModelKey within the tModelInstanceDetails data for a bindingTemplate instance.

accessPoint

The `accessPoint` element is an attribute-qualified pointer to a service entry point. The notion of service at the meta data level seen here is fairly abstract and many types of entry points are accommodated.

A single attribute is provided (named `URLType`). The purpose of the `URLType` attribute is to facilitate searching for entry points associated with a particular type of entry point. An example might be a purchase order service that provides three entry points, one for HTTP, one for SMTP, and one for FAX ordering. In this example, we'd find a `businessService` element that contains three `bindingTemplate` entries, each with identical data with the exception of the `accessPoint` value and `URLType` value.

The valid values for `URLType` are:

❑ **mailto**: designates that the `accessPoint` string is formatted as an e-mail address reference, for example, `mailto:purch@fabrikam.com`.

❑ **http**: designates that the `accessPoint` string is formatted as an HTTP compatible Uniform Resource Locator (URL), for example, `http://www.fabrikam.com/purchasing`.

❑ **https**: designates that the `accessPoint` string is formatted as a secure HTTP compatible URL, for example `https://www.fabrikam.com/purchasing`.

❑ **ftp**: designates that the `accessPoint` string is formatted as a FTP directory address, for example `ftp://ftp.fabrikam.com/public`.

❑ **fax**: designates that the `accessPoint` string is formatted as a telephone number that will connect to a facsimile machine, for example 1 425 555 5555.

❑ **phone**: designates that the `accessPoint` string is formatted as a telephone number that will connect to human or suitable voice or tone response based system, for example 1 425 555 5555.

❑ **other**: designates that the `accessPoint` string is formatted as some other address format. When this value is used, one or more of the `tModel` signatures found in the `tModelInstanceInfo` collection must imply that a particular format or transport type is required.

hostingRedirector

The `hostingRedirector` element is used to designate that a `bindingTemplate` entry is a pointer to a different `bindingTemplate` entry. The value in providing this facility is seen when a business or entity wants to expose a service description (for example, advertise that they have a service available that suits a specific purpose) that is actually a service that is described in a separate `bindingTemplate` record. This might occur when a service is remotely hosted (hence the name of this element), or when many service descriptions could benefit from a single service description.

The `hostingRedirector` element has a single attribute and no element content. The attribute is a `bindingKey` value that is suitable within the same UDDI registry instance for querying and obtaining the `bindingDetail` data that is to be used.

More on the `hostingRedirector` can be found in the appendices for the original UDDI Version 2.0 API Specification (see http://www.uddi.org/pubs/ProgrammersAPI-V2.00-Open-20010608.pdf).

tModelInstanceDetails

This structure is a simple accessor container for one or more `tModelInstanceInfo` structures. When taken as a group, the data that is presented in a `tModelInstanceDetails` structure forms a technically descriptive fingerprint by virtue of the unordered list of `tModelKey` references contained within this structure. What this means in English is that when someone registers a `bindingTemplate` (within a `businessEntity` structure), it will contain one or more references to specific and identifiable specifications that are implied by the `tModelKey` values provided with the registration. During an inquiry for a service, an interested party could use this information to look for a specific `bindingTemplate` that contains a specific `tModel` reference, or even a set of `tModel` references. By registering a specific fingerprint in this manner, a software developer can readily signify that they are compatible with the specifications implied in the `tModelKey` elements exposed in this manner.

tModelInstanceInfo

A `tModelInstanceInfo` structure represents the `bindingTemplate` instance specific details for a single `tModel` by reference.

Field Name	Description	Datatype	Length
tModelKey	Required Attribute. This is the unique key reference that implies that the service being described has implementation details that are specified by the specifications associated with the tModel that is referenced	string	255
description	Optional repeating element. This is one or more language qualified text descriptions that designate what role a tModel reference plays in the overall service description.	string	255
instanceDetails	Optional element. This element can be used when tModel reference specific settings or other descriptive information are required to either describe a tModel specific component of a service description or support services that require additional technical data support (for example, via settings or other handshake operations)	structure	

instanceDetails

This structure holds service instance specific information that is required to either understand the service implementation details relative to a specific `tModelKey` reference, or to provide further parameter and settings support. If present, this element should not be empty. Because no single contained element is required in the schema description, this rule is called out here for clarity.

Field Name	Description	Data Type	Length
description	Optional repeating element. This language-qualified text element is intended for holding a description of the purpose and/or use of the particular instanceDetails entry.	string	255
overviewDoc	Optional element. Used to house references to remote descriptive information or instructions related to proper use of a bindingTemplate technical sub-element.	structure	
instanceParms	Optional element. Used to contain settings parameters or a URL reference to a file that contains settings or parameters required to use a specific facet of a bindingTemplate description. If used to house the parameters themselves, the suggested content is a namespace qualified XML string – using a namespace outside of the UDDI schema. If used to house a URL pointer to a file, the suggested format is URL that is suitable for retrieving the settings or parameters via HTTP-GET.	string	255

overviewDoc

This optional structure is provided as a placeholder for metadata that describes overview information about a particular tModel use within a bindingTemplate.

Field Name	Description	Data Type	Length
description	Optional repeating element. This language-qualified string is intended to hold a short descriptive overview of how a particular tModel is to be used.	string	255
overviewURL	Optional element. This string data element is to be used to hold a URL reference to a long form of an overview document that covers the way a particular tModel specific reference is used as a component of an overall web service description. The suggested format is a URL that is suitable for retrieving an HTML based description via a web browser or HTTP-GET operation.	string	255

The tModel structure

Being able to describe a Web Service and then make the description meaningful enough to be useful during searches is an important UDDI goal. Another goal is to provide a facility to make these descriptions useful enough to learn about how to interact with a service that you don't know much about. In order to do this, there needs to be a way to mark a description with information that designates how it behaves, what conventions it follows, or what specifications or standards the service is compliant with. Providing the ability to describe compliance with a specification, concept, or even a shared design is one of the roles that the tModel structure fills.

The tModel structure takes the form of keyed meta data (data about data). In a general sense, the purpose of a tModel within the UDDI registry is to provide a reference system based on abstraction. Thus, the kind of data that a tModel represents is pretty nebulous. In other words, a tModel registration can define just about anything, but in the current revision, two conventions have been applied for using tModels: as sources for determining compatibility and as keyed namespace references.

The information that makes up a tModel is quite simple. There's a key, a name, an optional description, and then a URL that points somewhere – presumably somewhere where the curious can go to find out more about the actual concept represented by the meta data in the tModel itself.

Two Main Uses

There are two places within a businessEntity registration that you'll find references to tModels. In this regard, tModels are special. Whereas the other data within the businessEntity (for example, businessService and bindingTemplate data) exists uniquely with one uniquely keyed instance as a member of one unique parent businessEntity, tModels are used as references. This means that you'll find references to specific tModel instances in many businessEntity structures.

Defining the Technical Fingerprint

The primary role that a tModel plays is to represent a technical specification. An example might be a specification that outlines wire protocols, interchange formats and interchange sequencing rules. Examples can be seen in the RosettaNet Partner Interface Processes Specification (see See http://www.rosettanet.org/), the Open Applications Group Integration Specification (see http://www.openapplications.org/) and various Electronic Document Interchange (EDI) efforts.

Software that communicates with other software across some communication medium invariably adheres to some pre-agreed specifications. In situations where this is true, the designers of the specifications can establish a unique technical identity within a UDDI registry by registering information about the specification in a tModel.

Once registered in this way, other parties can express the availability of Web services that are compliant with a specification by simply including a reference to the tModel identifier (called a tModelKey) in their technical service descriptions bindingTemplate data.

This approach facilitates searching for registered Web Services that are compatible with a particular specification. Once you know the proper tModelKey value, you can find out whether a particular business or entity has registered a Web Service that references that tModel key. In this way, the tModelKey becomes a technical fingerprint that is unique to a given specification.

Defining an Abstract Namespace Reference

The other place where `tModel` references are used is within the `identifierBag`, `categoryBag`, `address` and `publisherAssertion` structures that are used to define organizational identity and various classifications. Used in this context, the `tModel` reference represents a relationship between the keyed name-value pairs to the super-name, or namespace within which the name-value pairs are meaningful.

An example of this can be seen in the way a business or entity can express the fact that their US tax code identifier (which they are sure they are known by to their partners and customers) is a particular value. To do this, let's assume that we find a `tModel` named "US Tax Codes", with a description "United States business tax code numbers as defined by the United States Internal Revenue Service". In this regard, the `tModel` still represents a specific concept – but instead of being a technical specification, it represents a unique area within which tax code ID's have a particular meaning.

Once this meaning is established, a business can use the `tModelKey` for the tax code `tModel` as a unique reference that qualifies the remainder of the data that makes up an entry in the `identifierBag` data.

To get things started, the UDDI Operator Sites have registered a number of useful `tModels`, including NAICS (an industry code taxonomy), UNSPC (a product and service category code taxonomy), and ISO 3166 (a geographical region code taxonomy).

Structure Specification

```
<element name = "tModel">
    <complexType>
        <sequence>
            <element ref = "name"/>
            <element ref = "description" minOccurs = "0"
                    maxOccurs = "unbounded"/>
            <element ref = "overviewDoc" minOccurs = "0"/>
            <element ref = "identifierBag" minOccurs = "0"/>
            <element ref = "categoryBag" minOccurs = "0"/>
        </sequence>
        <attribute ref = "tModelKey" use = "required"/>
        <attribute ref = "operator"/>
        <attribute ref = "authorizedName"/>
    </complexType>
</element>
```

Substructure Breakdown

Field Name	Description	Data Type	Length
tModelKey	Required Attribute. This is the unique key for a given `tModel` structure. When saving a new tModel structure, pass an empty `tModelKey` value. This signifies that a UUID value is to be generated. To update an existing `tModel` structure, pass the `tModelKey` value that corresponds to an existing `tModel` instance.	string	255

Table continued on following page

Field Name	Description	Data Type	Length
authorizedName	Attribute. This is the recorded name of the individual that published the tModel data. This data is calculated by the controlling operator and should not be supplied within save_tModel operations.	string	255
operator	Attribute. This is the certified name of the UDDI registry site operator that manages the master copy of the tModel data. The controlling operator records this data at the time data is saved. This data is calculated and should not be supplied within save_tModel operations.	string	255
name	Required element. This is the name recorded for the tModel. Name search is provided via find_tModel call. Names may not be blank, and should be meaningful to someone who looks at the tModel.	string	255
description	Optional repeating element. One or more short language-qualified descriptions. One description is allowed per national language code supplied.	string	255
overviewDoc	Optional element. Used to house references to remote descriptive information or instructions related to the tModel. See the substructure breakdown for overviewDoc in the *bindingTemplate Structure* section above.	structure	
identifierBag	Optional element. This is an optional list of name-value pairs that can be used to record identification numbers for a tModel. These can be used during search via find_tModel. See the full description of this element in the *identifierBag* section of this document above.	structure	
categoryBag	Optional element. This is an optional list of name-value pairs that are used to tag a tModel with specific taxonomy information (for exmaple, industry, product or geographic codes). These can be used during search via find_tModel. See the full description of this element in the *categoryBag* section of this document above.	structure	

The publisherAssertion Structure

Many businesses, like large enterprises or marketplaces, are not effectively represented by a single businessEntity, since their description and discovery are likely to be diverse. As a consequence, several businessEntity structures can be published, representing individual subsidiaries of a large enterprise or individual participants of a marketplace. Nevertheless, they still represent a more or less coupled community and would like to make some of their relationships visible in their UDDI registrations. Therefore, two related businesses use the xx_publisherAssertion messages, publishing assertions of business relationships.

In order to eliminate the possibility that one publisher claims a relationship between both businesses that is in fact not reciprocally recognized, both publishers have to agree that the relationship is valid by publishing their own `publisherAssertion`. Therefore, both publishers have to publish exactly the same information. When this happens, the relationship becomes visible. More detailed information is given in the appendices for the UDDI Version 2.0 API Specification. (see http://www.uddi.org/pubs/ProgrammersAPI-V2.00-Open-20010608.pdf).

In the case that a publisher is responsible for both businesses, the relationship automatically becomes visible after publishing just one of both assertions that make up the relationship.

The `publisherAssertion` structure consists of the three elements `fromKey` (the first `businessKey`), `toKey` (the second `businessKey`) and `keyedReference`. The `keyedReference` designates the asserted relationship type in terms of a `keyName keyValue` pair within a `tModel`, uniquely referenced by a `tModelKey`.

Structure Specification

```
<element name = "publisherAssertion">
    <complexType>
        <sequence>
            <element ref = "fromKey"/>
            <element ref = "toKey"/>
            <element ref = "keyedReference"/>
        </sequence>
    </complexType>
</element>
```

Substructure Breakdown

Field Name	Description	Data Type	Length
fromKey	Required element. This is the unique key reference to the first businessEntity the assertion is made for.	UUID	41
toKey	Required element. This is the unique key reference to the second businessEntity the assertion is made for.	UUID	41
keyedReference	Required element. This designates the relationship type the assertion is made for, represented by the included tModelKey and described by the included keyName keyValue pair.	empty w/attributes	

Index

A Guide to the Index

The index is arranged hierarchically, in alphabetical order, with symbols preceding the letter A. Most second-level entries and many third-level entries also occur as first-level entries. This is to ensure that users will find the information they require however they choose to search for it.

Symbols

.asmx files, 479
.jar files
  Filesystem Web Service case study, 640
.NET, 42
  .NET Building Block Services, 43
  .NET Enterprise Servers, 43
  background, 470
  classes and namespaces, 472
  operating systems, 43
  VS.NET, 43
  Web Services and .NET
    creating a web service from a WSDL
      Description, 486
    introduction, 467
    prerequisites, 469
    WOAD case study, 643
.NET Building Block Services, 43
.NET compilers, 470
  C#, 470
  C++ with Managed Extension, 470
  JScript.NET, 470
  VB.NET, 470
.NET Enterprise Servers, 43
.NET Framework, 42, 43
  .NET Remoting to build Web Services, 468
    introduction, 517
  ASP.NET, 474
  assemblies, 471
  base classes, 44
  C#, 472
  CIL, 44
  class library, 472
  CLR, 44, 470
  Common Language Specification, 471
  CTS, 471
  data classes, 44
  introduction, 467
  VS.NET, 468
  Web Forms, 44
  web service proxies, 468, 502
  Web Services, 44
  Windows Forms, 44
  XML classes, 44

.NET Framework Redistributable
  downloading, 470
.NET Framework SDK Beta 2
  acquiring, 469
.NET Remoting, 468
  building Web Services
    benefits and limitations, 518
    introduction, 517
  channels
    HTTP, 518
    SMTP, 518
    TCP, 518
  formatters
    binary, 518
    XML using SOAP, 518
.vsdisco files, 502
4NF (Fourth Normal Form), 618
4Suite, 527
  installing, 529
4Suite Server, 527
  Web Service implementations in 4Suite
  Server, 548
    SOAP handler code, 550
    SOAP handlers, setting up, 551
    testing with basic Python library, 554
    testing with SOAP.py, 553
    WSDL description of the Service, 548
4XSLT
  XSLT processor, 546

A

abstract classes, 486
Accept header, 75
Accept request header, 72
Accept-Charset header, 75
accessPoint element (UDDI), 192
Active Server Pages see ASP.
add_publisherAssertions method (UDDI), 208
addType method, SoapTypeMapperFactory
class, 339

Airline Web Service case study, 250
  binding templates, constructing, 267
  creating an account with the UDDI test
  registry, 251
  deploying the Web Service, 253
    Default Mapping Registry Class, 254
    ID, 254
    Java Provider, 254
    Methods, 254
    Provider Type, 254
    Scope, 254
    Script Provider, 254
    Type Mappings, 254
    User-Defined Provider Type, 254
  FareClient class, 274
  FareService class, 252
    getFare method, 252, 274, 279
  tModels
    constructing, 260
    publishing, 257
    tModel keys, 261
algorithms
  assymetric (public key) algorithms, 563
  Diffie-Hellman algorithms, 564
  elliptic curve algorithms, 564
  hash algorithms
    DSA, 565
    RSA-MD2, 565
    RSA-MD5, 565
    SHA, 565
  RSA algorithms, 564
  symmetric (conventional) algorithms, 563
    DES, 564
    IDEA, 564
    Triple-DES, 564
  technology
    CryptoAPI, 565
    JCE, 565
    PGP, 565
Alphaworks
  IBM Web Services, 42
Apache
  Tomcat
    configuring, 414
  Xerces, 414
Apache SOAP, 167, 168
  case studies
    Filesystem Web Service case study, 613
  classes, 169
  deploying Web Services with pluggable
  providers, 634
  installation, 229, 413
  prerequisites, 165, 413
  providers
    diagram, 615
    pluggable providers, 615, 622, 632
  proxy classes, 636
  tunneler, 428
Apache web server
  installing, 166
APIs
  HP UDDI client SDK, 289
  JavaMail API, 628
  JAXB, 46
  JAXM, 46

  JAXP, 46
  JAXR, 48
  JAX-RPC, 46
  Microsoft UDDI SDK, 285
  SOAP APIs
    high level API, 296
    low level API, 296
    SMO Framework, 296
  UDDI4J, 232
Application Layer
  OSI Reference model, 61
application MIME type, 153
applications
  modular
    XML Web Services, 18
  Web Auction application, 643
Area Code Update Service case study
  AreaCodeService class, 475
    CheckForSplit method, 475, 478
    InitializeData method, 476
    ParsePhoneNumber method, 476
  AreaCodeSplitInfo class, 476
  data members
    DateTime, 476
    listExchanges, 476
  dtStartSwitch system 476
  implementation, 476
  introduction, 475
  testing the web service, 481
    client application, 504
    creating a proxy class with VS.NET, 504
  web service
    .asmx extension, 479
    modifications to implementation, 479
  WSDL contract for the web service, 484
AreaCodeClient
  adding a proxy class, 505
  using proxy classes in the application, 511
AreaCodeClient.localhost namespace, 510
AreaCodeService class, 475, 488
  data members, 476
  InitializeData method, 476
  ParsePhoneNumber method, 476
AreaCodeService WSDL description, 487
**AreaCodeService.asmx web service
implementation, 481**
AreaCodeService.cs, 478
AreaCodeService.dll, 478
AreaCodeService.wsdl, 487
AreaCodeService2 class, 490
AreaCodeSplitInfo class, 476
ARPANET, 60
arrays
  SOAP Toolkit, 336
  SOAP encoding, 94
  sparse arrays, 96
AS (Authentication Server), 600
ASP (Active Server Pages), 474
  compared to ASP.NET, 474
ASP listener, 141

ASP.NET
  compared to ASP, 474
  files created by VS.NET template
    .vsdisco files, 494
    Assembly.Info.cs, 494
    Global.asax, 494
    Global.asax.cs, 494
    Web.config, 495
  functionality, 474
  help page, 485
    changing the default namespace, 498
    viewing WebMethod and WebService
      documentation, 496
  intrinsics, 495
  introduction, 474
  protocol support, 484
  stateless protocols, implications, 474
ASP.NET protocol support
  HTTP GET, 485
  HTTP POST, 485
  introduction, 484
  SOAP, 486
ASP.NET Web Services
  see also XML Web Servicesbenefits, 518
  directives, 480
  example, 475
  inline implementations, 493
  methods, renaming, 499
  renaming a service, 500
  System.Web.Services namespace, 479
  testing the web service, 481
  VS.NET, 488
  web service discovery (DISCO), introduction, 502
  WSDL contract for the web service, 484
assemblies, 471
  deployment, 471
  meta data, 471
  MSIL code, 472
  PE Headers, 471
  reflection, 472
  resources, 472
  security, 471
  type scoping, 471
  versioning, 471
  unmanaged stub, 472
asynchronous communication
  compared to synchronous communication, 14
asynchronous proxy classes, creating, 513
ATL Server, 518
attach method, FilesystemProxy class, 636
attachments
  SOAP extensions, 26
    MIME, 27
audio MIME type, 153
auditing, 562
authentication, 562, 614
  .NET example, 668
  basic authentication, 570
  digest authentication, 596
  easy delegation, 600
  mutual authentication, 600
  NT Challenge Reponse, 596
  SOAP messages, 599
  SQL database, 618
  ticket-based authentication, 600
  Windows integrated authentication, 596

Authentication Server see AS.
authenticators, 601
authorization, 562, 614
  HTTP Basic Authorization, 631
  SQL database, 618
Authorization header, 75
Authorization request header, 72

B

BabelFish
  using with SOAPy, 537
Base64 encoding
  MIME objects, 69
base64 module, 525
BaseHTTPServer module, 523, 530
  implementing SOAP Servers, 529
basejoin function, 523
basic authentication, 570
  compared to forms-based authentication, 575
  Java client code modifications, 574
  PERL client code modifications, 575
  Visual Basic client code modifications, 574
  XML Web Service Configuration, 570
BCNF (Boyce-Codd Normal Form) see 4NF.
BeanSerializer, 422
**BeginMessage method, SoapConnector
interface, 325**
Beginxxx method (VS.NET), parameters
  object parameter, 513
  System.AsyncCallback parameter, 513
bid messages, 647
binary data
  SOAP encoding, 93
binding element (WSDL), 113, 120
binding information
  UDDI information model, 191
bindings
  multiple bindings
    WSDL documents example, 136
  SOAP, 24
    SOAP 1.2, 24
  WSDL bindings, 125, 126
bindingTemplates element (UDDI), 190, 233
  bindingKey attribute, 190
  serviceKey attribute, 190
BizTalk Framework, 50
black box reuse, 18
Body element, SOAP messages, 84
BorregoCampground class, 418
Boyce-Codd Normal Form see 4NF.
browse patterns
  UDDI API queries, 211, 236
build.bat file, 662
business entities
  publishing, 236
    limits, 269
business information
  UDDI information model, 188
business service information
  UDDI information model, 190
BusinessEntity class, 233

businessEntity element (UDDI), 188
  authorizedName attribute, 188
  businessKey attribute, 188
  operator attribute, 188
BusinessService class, 233
businessService element (UDDI), 189
  businessKey attribute, 189
  serviceKey attribute, 189
businessServices element (UDDI), 189

C

C#
  compared to C++, 472
C++
  compared to C#, 472
Cache-Control header, 75
call method (SOAP::Lite), 366
Campground Browser client, 412
Campground interface, 418
CampgroundProxy class, 430
Campsite class, 422
CAs (Certification Authorities)
  certificate domains
    root authorities, 580
  digital certificates, 579
case studies
  Airline Web Service case study, 250
  Area Code Update Service case study, 475
  Filesystem Web Service case study, 613
  Organized Campgrounds case study, 411
  WOAD case study, 643
categoryBag element (UDDI), 189
CC/PP (Composite Capabilities/Preference Profiles) specification, 606
CDONTS (Collaboration Data Objects for NT Services), 598
Certificate Signing Request see CSR.
Certification Authorities see CAs.
CGI (Common Gateway Interface) programs, 523
CGIHTTPServer module, 523
character encoding
  WSDL documents, 305
  EasySoap++, 392
  SOAP::Lite, 367
CIL (common intermediate language), 44
classes
  abstract classes, 486
  File class, java.io, 626
  helper classes, 475
  Message class, mimetools module, 524
  proxy classes
  creating class with VS.NET, 504
  creating using wsdl.exe, 657
  WebService class, System.Web.Services namespace, 495
client certificates, 594
  difficulties, 596
  obtaining client certificates
    Tthawte, 595
  X.509, 594
Client class
  get_basic_credentials method, 575

client configuration
  WSDL bindings
    SOAP::Lite, 366
Client element value
  SOAP messages, 87
client requests, 72
  request data, 72
  request headers, 72
  request methods, 72
clients
  client as a servlet, 463
  errors, 421
  examples, 412, 657
  functionality, 393
  passing objects between client and server, 422
  writing clients, 420
CLR (common language runtime), 44, 470
  code access security, 471
code access security, 471
Collaboration Data Objects for NT Services see CDONTS.
COM (Component Object Model), 12
COM objects
  examples, 139
com.organizedCampgrounds package, 418
Commerce XML (cXML), 50
Common Business Library (xCBL), 49
Common Gateway Interface programs see CGI programs.
Common Intermediate Language see CIL.
Common Language Runtime see CLR.
Common Language Specification, 471
Common Object Request Broker Architecture see CORBA.
Common Type System see CTS.
communication types
  asynchronous, 14
  synchronous, 14
Component Object Model see COM.
components
  loosely bound, 18
    limitations, 18
  reusing in WSDL documents, 113
Composite Capabilities/Preference Profiles specification see CC/PP specification.
computing
  services oriented computing, 11
config.bat, 414
CONNECT method (HTTP), 155
connectors
  SOAP Toolkit, 331
    custom connectors, 332
    SOAPClient and connectors, 331
contacts element (UDDI), 189
Content-Length header, 75
Content-Type header, 75
context
  SOAP extensions, 30
context element (UDDI)
  debug attribute, 617
  docBase attribute, 617
  path attribute, 617
  reloadable attribute, 617
  trusted attribute, 617
contractRef elements (XML), 503

copyTo method, Message class, 628
CORBA (Common Object Request Broker
    Architecture), 12
CORBA/IIOP see IIOP.
createNewFile method, 627, 628
CryptoAPI, 565
CSR (Certificate Signing Request), 580, 585
    VeriSign, 585
CTS (Common Type System), 471
cXML see Commerce XML.

D

daemon processes, 353
data
    extensibility of SOAP, 81
DATA command, 64, 164
data definition language see DDL.
data encoding
    SOAP messages, 89
Data Encryption Standard see DES.
Data Link Layer
    OSI Reference model, 61
data members
    DateTime, 476
    ListExchanges, 476
data structures, UDDI see UDDI information model.
data types
    abstract types, using XSD schemas, 116
    catch all (polymorphic accessor), 93
    compound data types
        arrays, 94
        structs, 94
    simple data types
        binary data types, 93
        enumerated data types, 92
        SOAP encoding, 90
DataHandler class, 628
DateTime data member, 476
DCOM (Distributed COM), 12, 13
DDL (data definition language), 618
debugging
    SOAP, 316, 332
definitions element (WSDL), 112
DELETE command, 71
Delete method, File class, 629
delete_binding method (UDDI), 205, 235
delete_business method (UDDI), 205, 235, 281, 283
delete_publisherAssertions method (UDDI), 209
delete_service method (UDDI), 205, 235
delete_tModel method (UDDI), 206, 235
DeleteBusiness class (UDDI), 280
deploy forms
    Encoding style, 426
    ID, 425
    Java to XML serializer, 426
    Java type, 426
    Local part, 426
    Methods, 425
    Namespace URI, 426
    Number of Mappings, 425
    Provider Class, 425
    Provider Type, 425
    Scope, 425
    XML to Java deserializer, 426

DES (Data Encryption Standard), 564
description element (UDDI), 189
deserialization
    example, 462
detach method, FilesystemProxy class, 637
detail element, SOAP messages, 88
Diffie-Hellman algorithms, 564
digest authentication, 596
digest functions see hash functions.
digital certificates, 564
    CA, 579
digital dashboard
    web applications, connecting, 16
Digital Rights Management see DRM.
Digital Signature Standard see DSS.
digital signatures, 566
    digital signature extensions to SOAP, 604
directives
    ASP.NET Web Services
        WebService directive, 480
    Class attribute, 480
    Language attribute, 480
directories
    creating, 415
Directory Services Markup Language see DSML.
discard_authToken method (UDDI), 206, 234
DISCO (web service discovery), 468, 494
    contractRef elements, 503
    discoveryRef elements, 503
    introduction, 502
discoveryRef elements (XML), 503
discoveryURLs element (UDDI), 189
dispatch_to method (SOAP::Lite), 353
dispatching incoming requests
    SOAP::Lite, 367
Disposition Reports
    UDDI see errors, UDDI.
    UDDI4J, 235
Distributed COM see DCOM. .
distributed computing
    COM, 12
    CORBA, 12
    DCOM, 13
    GIOP, 13
    history of, 12
    IIOP, 13
    OMG, 12
    programming models, stateless, 13
    RMI, 14
DNS (Domain Name System), 150
    namespace
        diagram, 151
        zone transfer, 152
do_POST method, BaseHTTPRequestHandler
class, 530
Document Object Module see DOM.
documentation element (WSDL), 112, 115, 497
DOM (Document Object Module), 524
Domain Name System see DNS.
DotNetServices namespace, 475
    AreaCodeService class, 480
drill-down patterns
    UDDI API queries, 211, 236
DRM (Digital Rights Management), 609
DSML (Directory Services Markup Language), 221

DSS (Digital Signature Standard), 565
dynamic discovery see DISCO.
dynamic e-business, 39

E

E_authTokenRequired error code, 235
E_categorizationNotAllowed error code, 235
E_invalidCategory error code, 235
E_invalidKeyPassed erro code, 235
E_keyRetired error code, 235
E_nameTooLong error code, 241
E_operatorMismatch error code, 235
E_unsupported error code, 241
E_userMismatch error code, 236
EAI (Enterprise Application Integration)
  compared to XML Web Services, 17
EasySoap++, 368
  character set encoding, 392
  commands
    make, 371
    make install, 371
  Expat
    installing, 368
  implementing Echo services, 372
    echoIntegerArray server and client, 379
    echoString server and client, 372
    echoStruct server and client, 383
  installing, 368, 370
    prerequisites for installing, 368
  parameter serialization, 389
  XML Schemas, 392
e-business see dynamic e-business.
ebXML (Electronic Business XML), 48, 220
Echo class, 533
Echo servers
  Python SOAP server, 529
Echo services
  explanation of examples, 344
    echoIntegerArray(), 344
    echoString(), 344
    echoStruct(), 344
  implementing with EasySoap++, 372
    echoIntegerArray server and, 379
    echoString server and client, 372
    echoStruct serverand client, 383
  implementing with SOAP::Lite, 352
    echoIntegerArray server and client, 357
    echoString server and client, 352
    echoStruct server and client, 361
  implementing with SOAPx4, 394
    echoIntegerArray server and client, 398
    echoString server and client, 394
    echoStruct server and client, 402
  WSDL description of, 344
EchoHandler method (EasySOAP++), 373
echoIntegerArray server and client, 344
  implementing with EasySoap++, 379
  implementing with SOAP::Lite, 357
  implementing with SOAPx4, 398
  implementing with SOAP::Lite, 357, 358
echoResponse element, 534
echoString server and client
  implementing with EasySoap++, 372
  implementing with SOAP::Lite, 352
  implementing with SOAPx4, 394

echoStruct server and client
  implementing with EasySoap++, 383
  implementing with SOAPx4, 402
  implementing with SOAP::Lite, 361
Electronic Business XML see ebXML.
elements
  MIME elements
    mime:content element, 135
    mime:mimeXml element, 135
    mime:multipartRelated element, 134
  SOAP elements
    Body element, 84
    detail element, 88
    Envelope element, 83
    Fault element, 86
    faultactor element, 88
    faultcode element, 87
    faultstring element, 88
    Header element, 85
    soap:binding element, 126
    soap:body element, 127
    soap:fault element, 130
    soap:header element, 130
    soap:headerfault element, 130
    soap:operation element, 126
  UDDI elements
    accessPoint element, 192
    bindingTemplates element, 190
    businessEntity element, 188
    businessService element, 189
    businessServices element, 189
    categoryBag element, 189
    contacts element, 189
    description element, 189
    discoveryURLs element, 189
    fromKey element, 195
    hostingRedirector element, 192
    identifierBag element, 189
    keyedReference element, 195
    name element, 189
    overviewDoc element, 191
    publisherAssertion element, 191
    tModel element, 191
    tModelInstanceDetails element, 192
    toKey element, 195
  WSDL elements
    binding element, 113, 120
    definitions element, 112
    documentation element, 112, 115, 497
    getCurrentVersion element, 548
    getCurrentVersionFault element, 548
    getCurrentVersionResponse element, 548
    import element, 113
    message element, 113
    operation element, 117
    packageName element, 549
    port element, 121
    portType element, 113, 119, 497
    rdf:Description element, 543
    service element, 117
    types element, 112, 115
    xsd:schema element, 543
  XML elements
    contractRef elements, 503
    discoveryRef elements, 503
elliptic curve algorithms, 564
encoding
  Base64 encoding, 69
  custom encoding in SOAP, 96
  SMTP, 68

encryption, 563
  assymmetric (public key) algorithms, 563
  DES, 564
  Diffie-Hellman algorithms, 564
  digital certificates, 564
  elliptic curve algorithms, 564
  hash (digest) functions, 563
  IDEA, 564
  privacy, 565
  RSA algorithms, 564
  symmetric (conventional) algorithms, 563
  Triple-DES, 564
endpoints, 89
  SOAP messages, 79, 80, 86
end-to-end security, 569
Endxxx method (VS.NET), 514
Enterprise Application Integration see EAI.
enumerations
  SOAP encoding, 92
Envelope element
  SOAP messages, 83
errors
  HTTP errors, 156
  UDDI method call errors, 199-210
  UDDI4J errors, 235-236
e-Services Village (ESV XE), 37
ESMTP (Extended Simple Mail Transfer Protocol), 63
  RFCs, 63
e-Speak, 35
  communities, 36
  contracts, 35
  e-Speak engine, 35
  ESV, 35, 37
  security, 35
  SFS, 35, 37
  vocabulary, 35
Exists method, File class, 629
Expat
  commands
    make, 370
    make install, 370
  installing, 368
Expires header, 75
EXPN command, 64
extensibility, WSDL, 111
extensibility, SOAP, 21, 25, 330
  diagrams, 25
  messages, 80
  SOAP (Simple Object Access Protocol), 341
  SOAP 1.2, 24
Extensible Markup Language see XML.

F

factory functions, 539
FareClient class, 274
FareService class
  getFare method, 252
Fault element, SOAP messages, 86
fault handling
  SOAP::Lite, 353, 355, 356, 365
    global definition of fault handler, 365
    local definition of fault handler, 365
  SOAPx4, 395

Fault class, 355
faultactor element
  SOAP messages, 88
faultcode element
  SOAP messages, 87
    standard element values, 87
faultstring element
  SOAP messages, 88
FaultyConnector class, 332
File class, java.io, 626
  copyTo method, 628
  delete method, 629
  exists method, 629
  getBodyPart method, 627
  getFile method, 627
  getHeader method, 631
  getHomedir method, 628, 632
  getParent method, 630
  getProperty method, 626
  getUsername method, 628, 631
  isDirectory method, 630
  isFile method, 630
  lastModified method, 630
  length method, 630
  list method, 631
  mkdir method, 631
  mkdirs method, 631
  renameTo method, 631
  setLastModified method, 631
File Transfer Protocol see FTP.
filesystem database, 618
  Apache SOAP Web Services, 620
  authentication, 624
  File class, 627
    isAuthenticated method, 624
    isAuthorized method, 624
    marshall method, 626
  FilesystemProvider class, 626
  FilesystemProviderDAO class, 624
  FilesystemProxy class, 626
  homedir field, 620
  IOWriter class, 626
  JDBC datasource, 621
  map tables (join tables), creating, 620
  methods
  MyISAM database, 620
  password field, 620
  primary keys
    composite primary keys, 620
    id, 620
  principal table, 618
  principal webservice map table, 620
  schema, 619
  StringWriter class, 626
  structure, 619
  URI,inserting, 620
  users, granting access to Web Services, 621
  users, creating, 620
  webservice table
    id, 620
    uri, 620

Filesystem Web Service case study
.jar files, 640
benefits, 613
client
testing the client, 641
writing the client, 639
coding the Web Service, 626
database
setting up the database, 618
users, creating, 620
DataHandler class, 628
deploying Web Services, 632
elements
context element, 616
filesystem database, 618
File class, 626, 627
copyTo method, 628
delete method, 629
exists method, 629
getBodyPart method, 627
getFile method, 627
getHeader method, 631
getHomedir method, 628, 632
getParent method, 630
getProperty method, 626
getUsername method, 628, 631
isDirectory method, 630
isFile method, 630
lastModified method, 630
length method, 630
list method, 631
mkdir method, 631
mkdirs method, 631
renameTo method, 631
setLastModified method, 631
FilesystemClient class, 639
FilesystemProvider class, 623
invoke method, 636
FilesystemProviderDAO class, 624
FilesystemProxy class, 636
createNewFile method, 627, 628
HttpServlet class, 626
HttpServletRequest class, 626
HttpServletResponse class, 626
HttpSession class, 626
introduction, 613
JavaMail API, 628
MimeBodyPart class, 628
MsgJavaProvider class, 615
params class, 636
prerequisites, 616
RPCJavaProvider class, 615
security, 614
server, setting up, 616
SOAP Attachments, 627
SOAP Faults, 625
SOAPHTTPConnection class, 636
summary, 641
FilesystemClient class
Filesystem Web Service case study, 639
FilesystemProvider class, 626
implementation, 623
invoke method, 623
locate method, 623
marshall method, 626
target objects, 625
FilesystemProviderDAO class, 624
isAuthenticated method, 624
isAuthorized method, 624

FilesystemProxy class, 636
attach method, 636
createNewFile method, 636
detach method, 637
getBodyPart method, 639
implementation, 636
invoke method, 636
find_binding method (UDDI), 199, 236
find_business method (UDDI), 200, 236, 240
qualifiers, 277
find_relatedBusinesses method (UDDI), 203
find_service method (UDDI), 201, 236, 277
find_tModel method (UDDI), 201, 236
qualifiers, 277
FindBusinessRequest class (UDDI), 290
findQualifiers parameter (UDDI), 237
firewalls
firewall-unfriendly, 15
forms-based authentication
compared to basic authentication, 575
support, 578
Web Services, 578
Fourth Normal Form see 4NF.
frames
web applications, connecting, 15
frameworks
BizTalk, 50
e-Speak, 35
HP Web Services Platform, 35
fromKey element (UDDI), 195
FTP (File Transfer Protocol)
commands, 176
FTP as a transport for SOAP
compared to HTTP and SMTP, 177
example, 176
explanation, 177
prerequisites, 178
introduction, 175
functionality
client, 393
server, 393

G

General Inter-ORB Protocol see GIOP.
GET command, 71
GET method (HTTP), 155
get_assertionStatus method (UDDI), 209
get_authToken method (UDDI), 206, 234, 259, 264
get_bindingDetail method (UDDI), 201, 236
get_businessDetail method (UDDI), 202, 236, 241
get_businessDetailExt method (UDDI), 202
get_publisherAssertions method (UDDI), 210
get_registeredInfo method (UDDI), 206, 236, 282
get_serviceDetail method (UDDI), 202, 236
get_tModelDetail methods (UDDI), 203, 236, 276
getAccessPoint method (UDDI), 243
getBodyPart method, File class, 627
getBodyPart method, Filesystem Proxy class, 639
getBusinessInfos method (UDDI), 241
getBusinessInfoVector method (UDDI), 241
getBusinessKey method (UDDI), 241
getCurrentVersion element (WSDL), 548
getCurrentVersionFault element (WSDL), 548

getCurrentVersionResponse element (WSDL), 548
getFile method, File class, 627
getHeader method, File class, 631
getHomedir method, File class, 628, 632
GetMax method, SoapClient class, 337
getNameString method (UDDI), 242
getParent method, File class, 630
getProperty method, File class, 626
getText method, AccessPoint class, 243
getUsername method, File class, 628, 631
GIOP (General Inter-ORB Protocol), 13
green pages
    UDDI, 187, 191
GUI tools
    browsing the UDDI registry, 245

H

HailStorm
    XML Web Services, 51, 52
        availabilty, 52
        subscription business model, 52
Handle method (EasySOAP++), 374
hash (digest) functions, 563
HEAD method (HTTP), 71, 155
Header elements
    SOAP extensions, 25
    SOAP messages, 85
headers
    HTTP headers, listed, 74
Hello World example service, 490
HELO command (SMTP), 64, 164
HELP command (SMTP), 64
helper classes, 475
high level API, 296
    benefits and limitations, 314
    building the SysInfo class, 300
    compared to low level API, 318
    debugging, 316
        Fault element, 316
        tracing messages, 317
    generating WSDL and WSML, 303
        listeners, 309
    introduction, 299
    proxy classes, 312
    Response class, 312
    services
        systemInfoService, 306
    SoapClient class, 299, 312
    SoapServer class, 299, 310
    SystemInfo class, 300
Host header, 75
hostingRedirector element
    UDDI, 192
HP UDDI client SDK, 289
    FindBusinessRequest class, 290
    UDDISOAPClient class, 290
HP Web Services Platform see HP WSP.
HP WSP (Web Services Platform), 35, 38, 286
    components
        interacting components, 38
        messaging components, 38
        processing components, 39
        security components, 39
        transaction components, 39

HP UDDI browser, 287
HP UDDI client SDK, 289
HP UDDI private registry, 291
HTTP (Hypertext Transfer Protocol), 62
    .NET Remoting, 518
    capabilities and enhancements, 70
    case studies
    Filesystem Web Service case study, 613
    commands, listed, 71
    connection types, 74
    connector properties
        AuthPassword, 574
        AuthUser, 574
    examples, 156
    headers
        extension headers, 74
        listed, 74
    Internet Protocol Stack, 62
    introduction to, 70
    methods
        GET, 155
        list, 155
        POST, 99, 155
    requests, 155
        examples, 154, 162
    required parameters, 71
    responses, 156
        examples, 162
    RPC and HTTP in SOAP messages, 104
    secure HTTP see HTTPS
    security, 569, 614
        basic authentication, 570
        SSL, 570
        SSL, adding to basic authentication, 579
    SOAP messages, 99, 158
        advantages, 158
        creating a client, 161
        creating a server, 159
        examples, 156
    transactions
        client connection and request, 72
        example, 71
        server response to client, 72
HTTP class, 524
HTTP connection types, 74
    persistent connections, 74
    transient connections, 74
HTTP GET/POST bindings, 131
HTTP headers, listed, 74
HttpConnector class, 325
httplib module, 524
httplib.HTTP class, 533
HTTP-Next Generation see HTTP-NG.
HTTP-NG (HTTP-Next Generation), 70
HTTPS (secure HTTP)
    Python Web Services, 523
    SSL, 579
HttpServlet class, 626
HttpServletRequest class, 623, 626
HttpServletResponse class, 626
HttpSession class, 626
Hypertext Transfer Protocol see HTTP.

I

IANA (Internet Assignment Name Authority), 152
IBM SOAP for Java, 110
IBM Web Services
  Alphaworks, 42
  dynamic e-business, 39
  model, 40
  WebSphere, 41
IBM Web Services Toolkit
  compared to SOAP Toolkit, 175
  limitations, 443
  parameters, 443
  proxy generator, 436
  proxygen, 272
  UDDI browser, 248
  UDDI4J API, 232
  WSDL documents
    compared to SOAP Toolkit, 146
    examples, 144
IDEA (International Data Encryption Algorithm), 564
identifierBag element (UDDI), 189
Idoox WASP UDDI, 292
IETF (Internet Engineering Task Force)
  RFCs, 63
If-Modified-Since header, 75
IIOP (Internet Inter-ORB Protocol), 12, 13
image MIME type, 153
implementations
  inline implementations, 493
import element (WSDL), 113
information models, UDDI, 188
  diagram, 196
information, posting
  web applications, connecting, 16
Init method, SOAPServer class, 311
InitializeData method, AreaCodeService class, 476
inline implementations, 493
integration
  user interface (UI)
    web applications, connecting, 16
integrity, 563
interfaces
  ISoapMessagePart interface, 330
  ISoapTypeMapper interface, 338
  org.apache.soap.util.Provider interface, 622
  SoapConnector interface, 318, 324, 331
intermediaries
  SOAP extensions, 27
  SOAP messages, 80
International Data Encryption Algorithm see IDEA.
Internet
  development of ARPANET, 60
  protocols, difficulties with using, 14
    firewall-unfriendly, 15
    single vendor solutions, 15
    symmetrical requirements, 15
  services oriented, 53
  Web Services
    WSDL, 109
    WSDL, examples, 135
  XML Web Services, 53
Internet Assignment Name Authority see IANA.
Internet Engineering Task Force see IETF.
Internet Inter-ORB Protocol see IIOP.

Internet Protocol Security see IPSec.
Internet Protocol Stack, 60
  SMPT and HTTP, 62
  TCP/IP and OSI architecture, 60
Internet transport protocols
  development of, 59
  HTTP, 59, 70
  Internet Protocol Stack, 60
    TCP/IP and OSI architecture, 60
  introduction to, 59
  SMTP, 59, 63
  summary, 75
interoperability
  digital dashboards, 16
  frames, 15
  links, 15
  posting information, 16
  protocols, 13
  screen scraping, 16
  SOAP, 529
intrinsics
  ASP.NET intrinsics, 495
invocation patterns
  UDDI API queries, 211
invoke method, FilesystemProvider class, 623
IOWriter class, 626
IPSec (Internet Protocol Security), 569
ISAPI listener, 141
isAuthenticated method, FilesystemProviderDAO
  class, 624
isAuthorized method, FilesystemProviderDAO
class, 624
isDirectory method, File class, 630
isFile method, File class, 630
ISoapMessagePart interface, 330
ISoapTypeMapper interface, 338

J

Java API for XML Binding see JAXB.
Java API for XML Messaging see JAXM.
Java API for XML Parsing see JAXP.
Java API for XML Registries see JAXR.
Java API for XML-based RPC see JAX-RPC.
Java Class WSDL Generation form, 453
Java Cryptography Extensions see JCE.
Java development kits, 414
Java Filesystem Web Service case study
  see Filesystem Web Service case study.
Java Message Service see JMS.
Javabeans Activation Framework, 414
Javamail, 414
JavaMail API, 628
JAXB (Java API for XML Binding), 46
JAXM
  compared to JAX-RPC, 46
JAXM (Java API for XML Messaging), 46
JAXP (Java API for XML Parsing), 46
JAXR (Java API for XML Registries), 48
JAX-RPC (Java API for XML-based RPC), 46
JCE (Java Cryptography Extensions), 565
JDBC datasource, 621
JDBC-ODBC bridge driver, 621
JIT (just-in-time) compilers, 470

JMS (Java Message Service), 14
JRun
  compared to Tomcat, 462
just-in-time compilers see JIT compilers.
jUUDI, 292

K

KDC (Key Distribution Center), 600
Kerberos
  AS, 601
  authenticators, 601
  benefits, 602
  diagram, 601
  easy delegation, 600
  mutual authentication, 600
  TGS, 601
  TGT, 601
Key Distribution Center see KDC.
keyedReference element (UDDI), 195
keyword arguments
  Python functions, 538

L

lastModified method, File class, 630
legacy Windows applications, 296
length method, File class, 630
links
  web applications, connecting, 15
list method, File class, 631
listeners, 304, 309
  ASP, 141
  ISAPI, 141
listExchanges data member, 476
locate method, FilesystemProvider class, 623
logging, 562
loosely bound components, 18
  limitations, 18
low level API, 296
  clients, 323
  compared to high level API, 318
  components diagram, 318
  errors, 326
  HttpConnector class, 325
  introduction, 318
  SoapConnector interface, 324
    BeginMessage method, 325
  SoapReader class, 321
    load method, 321
  SoapSerializer class, 322
Lye, 526

M

MAIL command, 64, 164
mail delivery agents see MDAs.
mail transfer agents see MTAs.
mail user agents see MUAs.
make command, 352
  EasySoap++, 371
  Expat, 370

make install command, 352
  EasySoap++, 371
  Expat, 370
make test command, 352
MapPath method, Server class, 311
maptype method (SOAP::Lite), 361
marshall method, FilesystemProvider class, 626
md5 module, 525
MDAs (mail delivery agents), 163
members
  iNewAreaCode, 476
  iOldAreaCode, 476
message chains, 79
  diagram, 80
Message class, mimetools module, 524
message element (WSDL), 113
message MIME type, 153
message syntax
  extensibility of SOAP, 81
messages
  SOAP message exchange model, 78
  SOAP messages
    elements and attributes, 83
    endpoints, 79, 80, 86, 89
    example, 82
    intermediaries, 80
    introduction, 149
    senders and receivers, 79
    structure, 81
    XML Namespaces, 82
  XML documents as messages, 79
messaging, reliable
  SOAP extensions, 28
meta data
  assemblies, 471
method namespace, 347
method namespace URI see URI.
Microsoft Intermediate Language see MSIL.
Microsoft Message Queuing see MSMQ.
Microsoft SOAP Toolkit
  .NET, 296
  compared to IBM Web Services Toolkit, 175
  complex types, 336
    arrays, 336
    custom types, 338
  connectors, 331, 335
    custom connectors, 332
    SoapClient and connectors, 331
  creating a client, 161
  creating a server, 159
  debugging, 316
  downloading, 296
  errors, 312
  explanation of examples, 299
  extensibility, 330, 341
  HTTP
    example, 159
  introduction, 295
  SOAP APIs, 296
    high level API, 299
    low level API, 318
    SMO Framework, 326
  summary, 341
  tools and utilities, 297
  WSDL, 298

Microsoft SOAP Toolkit (cont'd)
WSDL documents
compared to IBM Web Services Toolkit, 146
example, 139
WSML, 298
Microsoft UDDI SDK, 285
MIME (Multipurpose Internet Mail Extensions), 27, 63, 152
RFCs, 63
types
composite types, 153
media types, 152
use of MIME in HTTP and SMTP, 152
MIME bindings
WSDL, 133
MIME header fields
Content-Transfer-Encoding headers, 69
Content-Type headers
listed, 68
described, 68
MIME types
composite types
message, 153
multipart, 153
media types
application, 152
audio, 152
image, 152
text, 152
video, 152
mime:content element (WSDL), 135
mime:mimeXml element (WSDL), 135
mime:multipartRelated element (WSDL), 134
mimetools module, 524
MimeWriter module, 524
mkdir method, File class, 631
mkdirs method, File class, 631
models
information models, UDDI, 188
MsgJavaProvider class, 615
MSIL (Microsoft Intermediate Language), 470
MSMQ (Microsoft Message Queuing), 14
mssoapinit method, SoapClient class 314
MSSOAPT, 297
MSTK2 see Microsoft SOAP Toolkit.
MTAs (mail transfer agents), 163
SMTP transactions, 65
MUAs (mail user agents), 163
multipart MIME type, 153
Multipurpose Internet Mail Extensions see MIME.
MustUnderstand element value
SOAP messages, 87
MyISAM database, 620
MySQL
authentication, 624
commands, 618
MyISAM database, 620
setting up
FileSystem Web Services case study, 618

N

NAICS (North American Industrial Classification System), 184, 237
name element (UDDI), 189
Namespace Identifier see NI.

Namespace Specific String see NSS.
namespaces
.NET classes, 472
ASP.NET
changing the default namespace, 498
WSDL documents, list, 114
NASSL (Network Accessibility Service Specification Language), 110
Network Accessibility Service Specification Language see NASSL.
Network Layer
OSI Reference model, 61
NI (Namespace Identifier), 154
non-repudiation, 566
NOOP command, 64, 164
North American Industrial Classification System see NAICS. .
notification operations, 125
NSS (Namespace Specific String), 154
NT challenge response (NTLM), 596

O

Object Linking and Embedding see OLE2.
Object Management Group see OMG.
OLE2 (Object Linking and Embedding), 470
OMG (Object Management Group), 12
on_action method (SOAP::Lite), 353, 354
on_fault method (SOAP::Lite), 365
one-way operations, 122
Open Systems Interconnect see OSI.
OpenSSL, 368
Python installation, 523
operations
WSDL operations see transmission primitives.
operator nodes (UDDI), 183
OPTIONS method (HTTP), 71, 155
Orchard module, 526
Orchard.SOAP, 526
org.apache.soap.util.Provider Interface, 622
Organized Campgrounds case study
Apache SOAP, installing, 413
BorregoCampground class, 418
Campground interface, 418
computePrice method, 417
getCampsite, 425
getNumberOfCampsites, 425
reserveCampsite, 425
CampgroundProxy class, 430
Campsite class, 423
clients
client as a servlet, 463
creating a client, 420
com.organizedCampgrounds package, 418
compiling files, 418
errors, 421
HTTP POST, 430
implementing objects, 423
introduction, 411
passing objects between client and server, 422
proxy classes, 430
creating proxy classes, 436
serialization
writing a serializer, 458
servers, creating, 417

Organized Campgrounds case study (Cont'd)
ServiceRegistryProxy class, 447
services
deploying, 419
redeploying, 425
undeploying, 425
servlet containers
JRun, 462
Tomcat, 414
SOAP message, 430
summary, 464
tunneler, 428
UDDI, 445
UDDI servers, 445
registering services with the server, 449
UDDI structures, 448
Web Services
creating on the same server, 453
OSI (Open Systems Interconnect)
architecture, 60
OSI reference model, 61
SOAP 1.2, 24
layers, 61
functions, 62
overloaded methods, 499
overviewDoc element (UDDI), 191

P

P3P (Platform for Privacy Preferences), 606
benefits and limitations, 608
policy reference files, 607
packageName element (WSDL), 549
parameters
fault handling
SOAP::Lite, 353
findQualifiers parameter, 237
serialization, 390
EasySoap++, 389
SOAPx4, 406
TModelBag parameter, 236
pattern description and process flow see process flow and pattern description.
Perl
ActivePerl, 350
SOAP::Lite, 349
perl Makefile.PL command, 350
persistent connections
HTTP, 74
PEs (portable executables), 471
PGP (Pretty Good Privacy), 565
Physical Layer
OSI Reference model, 62
ping operations, implementing, 657
Platform for Privacy Preferences see P3P.
pluggable providers
Apache SOAP, 615
deploying Web Services using pluggable
providers, 632
writing a pluggable provider, 622
point-to-point security, 568
polymorphic accessor
SOAP encoding, 93
port element (WSDL), 121
portable executables see PEs.

portType element (WSDL), 113, 119
POST method (HTTP), 71, 155
posting information
web applications, connecting, 16
prepared statements, 624
Presentation Layer
OSI Reference model, 61
Pretty Good Privacy see PGP.
PrettyPrint
using with wsdl4py, 541
privacy
P3P, 606
SOAP extensions, 30
XML Web Services
examples, 52
process flow and pattern description
RosettaNet, 54
XML Web Services, 54
processes
daemon processes, 353
processors
4XSLT, 546
programming models
stateless programming models, 13
UDDI, 198
protocols
.NET
difficulties, 649
DCOM, 12, 13
difficulties with existing, 14
distributed protocols
compared to SOAP, 21
firewall-unfriendly, 15
FTP, SOAP transport, 175
GIOP, 13
HTTP, 70
security, 569
IIOP, 12, 13
Internet transport protocols
development of, 59
Internet Protocol Stack, 60
introduction to, 59
interoperability, 13
RMI, 12, 14
single vendor solutions, 15
SMTP
introduction, 63
SOAP transport, 163
SOAP, 17
compared to other distributed protocols, 21
defined, 20
SOAP 1.2, 23
SOAP transports
HTTP, 154
stateless protocols
ASP.NET, 474
HTTP, 569
symmetrical requirements, 15
using with the Internet, 15
XML Protocol see SOAP 1.2.
XML-RPC, 17
limitations, 17
providers
pluggable providers, 615
proxy class constructor, 510

proxy classes, 312
  creating, 502
  creating an asynchronous proxy, 513
  creating proxy classes with IBM Web Services Toolkit,
    430, 436
  creating using wsdl.exe, 516
    WOAD case study, 657
  creating with VS.NET, 504
  example, 430
  SOAP.py, 535
  using in client applications, 511
proxy method (SOAP::Lite), 354
proxygen
  generating service stubs, 272
publisherAssertion element (UDDI), 195
pUDDIng, 293
PUT method (HTTP), 71, 155
Python
  data structures
    tuples, 532
  installing software, 528, 529
  internet data format modules
    base64, 525
    md5, 525
    mimetools, 524
    MimeWriter, 524
    sha, 525
    uu, 525
    xml.dom, 524
    xml.parsers.expat, 524
    xml.sax, 524
  proxy objects, 535
  SOAP and Python
    introduction, 529
    setting up SOAP handlers, 551
    SOAP client, 533
    SOAP handler code XE, 550
    SOAP server, 529
    SOAP.py as SOAP client, 535
    SOAPy as SOAP client, using WSDL, 537
    testing the SOAP implementation with basic Python
      library, 554
    testing the SOAP implementation with SOAP.py, 553
  third-party Python modules and tools
    4Suite, 527
    4Suite Server, 527
    Lye, 526
    Orchard, 526
    PyXML, 527
    SOAP.py, 525
    soaplib.py, 526
    SOAPy, 526
  web architecture modules
    BaseHTTPServer, 523
    CGIHTTPServer, 523
    httplib, 524
    SimpleHTTPServer, 523
    urllib, 523
    urllib2, 523
  Web Services and Python
    implementation in 4Suite Server, 548
    installing software, 528
    internet data format modules, 524
    introduction, 521
    summary, 555
    third-party Python modules and tools, 525
    web architecture modules, 523
  WSDL and Python
    introduction, 539
    using wsdl4py, 539

PyXML, 527
  installing, 528

Q

Quality of Service (QoS)
  Web Services, 566
  SOAP extensions, 29
    Service Level Agreements (SLAs), 29
QUIT command (SMTP), 64, 164

R

RCPT command (SMTP), 64, 164
RDF (Resource Description Framework)
  CC/PP specification, 606
  parsing RDF, 547
  processing WSDL, 542
rdf:Description element (WSDL), 543
read method, ISoapTypeMapper
interface, 338, 530
ReadFromStream method (wsdl4py), 539
ReadFromString method (wsdl4py), 539
ReadFromUri method (wsdl4py), 539
receivers see senders and receivers.
Referer header, 75
Referer request header, 72
registeredInfo class (UDDI), 282
registries
  UDDI, 186
relay agents
  SMTP, 67
Remote Method Invocation protocol see RMI.
Remote Procedure Call see RPC.
renameTo method, File class, 631
request wiredumps
  EasySOAP++, 378, 382, 388, 391
  SOAP::Lite, 356, 359, 363
  SOAPx4, 397, 401, 405
request/response operations, 123
Requests For Comments see RFCs.
Resource Description Framework (RDF), 56
Resource Description Framework see RDF.
response wiredumps
  EasySOAP++, 378, 383, 389
  SOAP::Lite, 357, 360, 364
  SOAPx4, 397, 401, 405
result method (SOAP::Lite), 366
RFCs (Requests For Comments), 63, 70
rfile class, 530
Rivest, Shamir, and Adleman algorithms see RSA
  algorithms.
RMI (Remote Method Invocation) protocol, 12, 14
root authorities, 580
RosettaNet, 49
  process flow, 54
routing
  SOAP extensions, 27
    scalability, 27
RPC (Remote Procedure Call), 13
  convention for SOAP messages, 102
  HTTP and RPC in SOAP messages, 104
  SOAP, 102

RPCJavaProvider class, **615**
rpcrouter, **414**
RSA (Rivest, Shamir, and Adleman) algorithms, **564**
RSA-MD2 (Message Digest 2), **565**
RSA-MD5 (Message Digest 5), **565**
RSET command, **64, 164**

S

S/MIME (Secure/Multipurpose Internet Mail
  Extensions), **63, 585, 597**
  CDONTS, 598
  difficulties, 597
  RFCs, 63
save_binding method (UDDI), **207, 234**
save_business method (UDDI), **207, 234, 267**
save_service method (UDDI), **208, 234**
save_tModel method (UDDI), **208, 234, 260**
SaveBusiness class, **262**
SaveTModel class, **257**
scalability
  XML Web Services
    extensions, impact of, 27
SCL (Service Contract Language), **110**
screen scraping
  web applications, connecting, 16
SDL (Services Description Language), **110**
Secure Hash Algorithm see SHA.
Secure Sockets Layer see SSL.
Secure/Multipurpose Internet Mail Extensions see
  S/MIME.
security
  .NET
    WOAD case study, 668
  approaches to security
    security as a process, 561
    security as an afterthought, 560
  auditing, 562
  authentication, 562
  authorization, 562
  availability, 565
    backup, 566
    failover, 566
    load balancing, 566
    packet filtering, 566
    virus checking, 566
  code access security, 471
  digital signature extensions to SOAP, 604
  digital signatures, 566
  DRM, 609
  encryption, 563
  end-to-end security, 569
  HTTP, 159
  integrity, 563
  introduction, 559
  logging, 562
  non-repudiation, 566
  point-to-point security, 568
  privacy, 565
  privacy and P3P, 606
  Python modules, 525
  resources, 561
  SMTP, 69
  SOAP extensions, 28
    XML Encryption, 29
    XML Signatures, 29

SOAP messages, 599
SQL databases, 618
summary, 610
transport level security, 568
UDDI API, 214
UDDI node operators, 215
Web Services and security
  need for security, 614
Web Services security
  diagram, 567
XML Encryption, 603
XML Signatures, 603
XML Web Services, 560
Semantic Web, **32, 56**
  Resource Description Framework (RDF), 56
senders and receivers
  SOAP messages, 79
SendFault function, **311**
serialization, **422**
  deserialization, 462
  SOAP data see data encoding.
  writing a serializer, 458
Server element value
  SOAP messages, 88
Server class
  MapPath method, 311
server response
  response data, 72
  response header, 72
  status code, 72
servers
  examples
    WOAD case study, 656
  functionality, 393
  passing objects between client and server, 422
  prototype servers
    example, 418
  setting up servers
    Filesystem Web Service case study, 616
Service Contract Language see SCL.
service dispatching
  SOAP::Lite, 367
service elements (WSDL)
  adding to WSDL descriptions, 407
  documentation element, 497
Service Level Agreements (SLAs), **29**
service classes, **366**
Service Specification Framework see SFS.
service type definitions
  publishing service type definitions, 668
service type registrations see tModels. .
service method (SOAP::Lite), **366**
Service1.asmx.cs, **659**
ServiceDetail classes, **278**
ServiceInfo classes, **278**
ServiceRegistryProxy class, **447**
services
  deploying, 419
  redeploying, 425
  systemInfoService, 306
  undeploying, 425
Services Description Language see SDL.
services oriented computing, **11**
servlet containers
  JRun
    compared to Tomcat, 462
  Tomcat, 414

servlets
client as a servlet, 463
rpcrouter, 414
Session Layer
OSI Reference model, 61
set_publisherAssertions method (UDDI), 210
setLastModified method, File class, 631
setName method, FindBusinessRequest class, 290
setPassword method, SOAPHTTPConnection class, 575
setPublishURL method (UDDI), 233
setTransport method (UDDI), 233
setUserName method, SOAPHTTPConnection class, 575
SFS (Service Specification Framework)
e-Speak, 37
SHA (Secure Hash Algorithm), 565
sha module, 525
SIC (Standard Industrial Classification), 184
Simple Mail Transfer Protocol see SMTP.
Simple Messaging Object Framework see SMO Framework, 296
Simple Object Access Protocol see SOAP.
Simple Public Key Infrastructure see SPKI.
SimpleHTTPServer module, 523
single vendor solutions, 15
SLAs see Service Level Agreements.
SMO (Simple Messaging Object) Framework, 296
benefits, 330
code generator see SMO Generator.
diagram, 326
introduction, 326
ISoapMessagePart interface, 330
SoapMessage class, 330
SoapMessageClient class, 330
SMO Generator, 326
XDR schemas, 327
SMTP (Simple Mail Transfer Protocol), 62
.NET Remoting, 518
capabilities and enhancements, 63
commands, 64, 164
encoding methods, 68
ESMTP, 63
extensions, 69
Internet Protocol Stack, 62
introduction, 63, 163
limitations, 67, 175
MDAs, 163
MIME, 63
MTAs, 65, 163
objects, listed, 69
relay agents, 67
restrictions, 69
RFCs, 63
S/MIME, 63
security, 69, 597
S/MIME, 597
SOAP bindings example, 130
SOAP transport
creating a client, 172
limitations, 164
possibilities, 163
status codes
listed, 66
transactions
example, 65

SOAP (Simple Object Access Protocol), 17
attachments
methods, 627
case study, 412
compared to other distributed protocols, 21
configuring for Tomcat, 416
connectors, 331
custom connectors, 332
SOAPClient and connectors, 331
debugging, 316
fault reports, 316
tracing messages, 317
defined, 20
extensibility, 21, 80, 330, 341
further development of, 19
interoperability, 529
introduction of, 19
messages
example code, 169
HTTP, 158, 161
HTTP and SMTP compared, 175
introduction, 149
SMTP, 165
summary, 180
passing objects, 422
proxy objects, 535
Python and SOAP
introduction, 529
setting up SOAP handlers, 551
SOAP client, 533
SOAP server, 529
SOAP.py as SOAP client, 535
SOAPy as SOAP client, using WSDL, 537
testing the SOAP implementation with basic Python library, 554
testing the SOAP implementation with SOAP.py, 553
security, 614
servlets
rpcrouter, 414
specification, 78
transport protocols
FTP, 175
HTTP, 149, 154, 158
SMTP, 149, 163, 165
vendor acceptability, 21
Web Services and SOAP, 78, 109, 110
example, 417
introduction to, 77
possibilities, 106
summary, 107
WOAD case study, 643
webapp, 414
SOAP 1.1 see SOAP (Simple Object Access Protocol).
SOAP 1.2, 77
bindings, 24
development of, 23
diagram, 23
extensibility, 24
extension modules, 24
OSI model, 24
SOAP APIs
high level API, 296
low level API, 296
SMO Framework, 296
SOAP attachments
methods, 627

SOAP bindings, 24
SMTP
example, 130
WSDL, 126
SOAP body, 22
SOAP conventions, 102
SOAP data, 89
encoding, 89
XML Schemas, 90
SOAP encoding, 89, 90
custom encoding, 96
data types
compound data types, 93
simple data types, 90, 91, 92
multi-reference values, 96
XML, 93
SOAP envelope, 22
URI, 367
SOAP extensions, 25
attachments, 26
MIME), 27
context/privacy, 30
diagrams, 25
Header elements, 25
list, 26
MIME, 27
quality of service (QoS), 29
Service Level Agreements (SLAs), 29
reliable messaging, 28
routing/intermediaries, 27
security, 28
XML Encryption, 29
XML Signatures, 29
transactions support, 31
SOAP Faults
Filesystem Web Service case study, 625
SOAP header, 22
SOAP implementations see SOAP toolkits.
SOAP message exchange model, 78
data, 81
design, 80
endpoints, 80
extensibility, 81
message chains, 79
message syntax, 81
purpose, 81
senders and receivers, 79
transports, 81
XML documents as messages, 79
SOAP messages, 22
case studies
Filesystem Web Service case study, 613
data encoding, 89
elements and attributes, 83
actor attribute, 85
arrayType attribute, 95
Body element, 84
detail element, 88
encodingStyleattribute, 84, 90
Envelope element, 83
Envelope namespace, 84
Fault element, 86
faultactor element, 88
faultcode element, 87
faultstring element, 88
Header element, 85
mustUnderstand attribute, 86

SOAP-ENC:offset attribute, 95
SOAP-ENC:postion attribute, 96
xsi:type attribute, 91, 95
endpoints, 79, 80, 86, 89
examples, 22, 79, 82, 169
intermediaries, 80
introduction, 149
message chains
diagram, 80
security, 599
digital signature extensions to SOAP, 604
SOAP body, 22
SOAP envelope, 22
SOAP header, 22
SOAP serializaton, 22
structure
diagram, 81
summary, 180
transports, 98
HTTP, 99, 156
RPC, 102
RPC and HTTP combined, 104
separation of message and transport, 98
UDDI API, 214
XML documents, 106
XML Namespaces, 82
SOAP serializaton, 22
SOAP structure, 347
SOAP Toolkit for Visual Studio, 110
SOAP toolkits
EasySoap++, 368
character set encoding, 392
implementing Echo services, 372, 379, 383
installing, 368, 370
parameter serialization, 389
XML Schemas, 392
Echo service examples, 344
Microsoft SOAP Toolkit, 295
.NET, 296
compared to IBM Web Services Toolkit, 175
complex types, 336
connectors, 331, 335
creating a client, 161
creating a server, 159
debugging, 316
downloading, 296
error handling, 312
extensibility, 330, 341
HTTP, 159
introduction, 295
SOAP APIs, 296
summary, 341
tools and utilities, 297
WSDL, 298
WSML, 298
SOAP::Lite, 349
character set encoding, 367
commands, 352
dispatching incoming requests, 367
error handling, 351
fault handling, 365
implementing Echo services, 352
installing, 349, 350, 352
prerequisites, 350
WDSL bindings, 366

SOAP toolkits (cont'd)
SOAPx4, 392
character set encoding, 406
implementing Echo services, 394, 398, 402
installing, 393
parameter serialization, 406
WSDL binding, 406
XML Schemas, 406
summary, 408
wiredumps with tcpTrace, 347
diagram, 347
example, 348
SOAP transports, 98
HTTP, 99
HTTP POST method, 99
RPC, 102
making a remote procedure call, 102
returning a remote procedure call, 103
RPC and HTTP combined, 104
separation of message and transport, 98
soap.get_proxy function, 538
SOAP.py, 525
compared to SOAPy, 537
confusion with SOAPy, 538
installing, 535
proxy objects, 535
SOAP::Data classes, 353, 358, 362, 366
SOAP::Lite, 349
character set encoding, 367
dispatching incoming requests, 367
error handling, 351
fault handling, 355, 356, 365
global definition of fault handler, 365
local definition of fault handler, 365
parameters, 353
implementing Echo services, 352
echoIntegerArray server and client, 357
echoString server and client, 352
echoStruct server and client, 361
installing, 349
building, testing and installing, 351
error messages, 352
preparing the Makefile, 350
prerequisites for installing, 350
SOAP::Data clasess, 353, 366
UDDI::Lite, 291
WDSL bindings, 366
soap:binding element, 126
soap:body element, 127
soap:fault element, 130
soap:header element, 130
soap:headerfault element, 130
soap:operation element, 126
SoapAction header, 100, 533
SOAPActions, 347
values, 354
SOAPBuilders, 344
SoapClient class
ClientProperty property, 315
connectors, 331
HeaderHandler property, 315
SoapConnector interface, 318, 324, 331
SoapHandler class, 530
SOAPHTTPConnection class, 636
setPassword method, 575
setUserName method, 575
SoapInvoke method, SoapServer class, 312
soaplib.py, 526

SoapMessage class, 330
SoapMessageClient class, 330
SOAPMethod class, 376
request, 374
SOAPParameter class, 376
SOAPProxy initializer, 536
SOAPProxy class, 376
SoapReader class, 318, 321, 326
load method, 321
SOAPResponse class, 365, 376
SoapSerializer class, 318, 322
SoapServer class, 310
Init method, 311
SoapInvoke method, 312
SoapTypeMapperFactory class, 338
SOAPx4, 392
character set encoding, 406
fault handling, 395
implementing Echo services, 394
echoIntegerArray server and client, 398
echoString server and client, 394
echoStruct server and client, 402
installing, 393
prerequisites for installing, 393
parameter serialization, 406
WSDL binding, 406
XML Schemas, 406
SOAPy, 526
compared to SOAP.py, 537
confusion with SOAP.py, 538
using BabelFish, 537
solicit/response operations, 124
sparse arrays
SOAP messages, 96
specifications
Common Language Specification, 471
UDDI, 187
node operators, 214
SPKI (Simple Public Key Infrastructure), 35
SQL databases
4NF, 618
authentication, 624
DDL, 618
MySQL, 618
commands, 618
setting up
FileSystem Web Services case study, 618
SSL (Secure Sockets Layer), 570, 614
adding to basic authentication, 579
HTTPS, 579
client certificates, 590, 594
enabling SSL on a web server, 587
Java client code modifications, 589
PERL client code modifications, 593
SSL certificates, obtaining and installing, 580
Visual Basic client code modifications, 589
Standard Industrial Classification see SIC.
state management, .NET
WOAD case study, 667
stateful autonomous agents
Web agents, 55
stateful objects
Web agents, 55
stateless programming models, 13

stateless protocols
  ASP.NET
    implications, 474
stateless services
  Web agents, 55
statements
  prepared statements, 624
status codes
  HTTP, 156, 159
  SMTP
    listed, 66
  SOAP messages, 100
StringWriter class, 626
structs
  SOAP encoding, 94
subscription business models, 52
Sun ONE (Open Network Environment), 45
  applications and web services layer, 45
  identity and policy layer, 45
  platform layer, 45
  service container layer, 45
  service creation and assembly layer, 45
  service delivery layer, 45
  service integration layer, 45
synchronous communication
  compared to asynchronous communication, 14
SysInfo class, 300
System namespace
  .NET Framework class library, 472
System.Web.Services namespace
  WebMethod attribute, 479
  WebService class, 495
SystemInfo class, 300
SystemInfoService service, 306

T

Target Namespace, 437
target objects, 625
taxonomies
  geographic taxonomies, 185
  NAICS, 184
  SIC, 184
  UNSPSC, 185
TCP (Transport Control Protocol)
  .NET Remoting, 518
TCP/IP (Transport Control Protocol/Internet Protocol)
  architecture, 60
  model, 62
  tools
    DNS, 150
tcpTrace
  examining wiredumps with tcpTrace, 347
    diagram, 347
    example, 348
test bed deployment
  UDDI, 187
text MIME type, 153
TGS (Ticket Granting Service), 600
TGT (Ticket Granting Ticket), 601
Thawte, 595
ticket-based authentication, 600
  Kerberos, 600
tModel class, 233

tModel element (UDDI), 191
  authorizedName attribute, 191
  operator attribute, 191
  tModelKey attribute, 191
tModel keys, 261
TModelBag parameter, 236
TModelDetail class, 234
tModelInstanceDetails element (UDDI), 192
tModels (service type registrations), 187, 193
  canonical tModels, 195
  constructing, 260
  example, 195
  publishing, 236
  publishing service type definitions, 668
toDom method (WSDL), 541
toKey element (UDDI), 195
Tomcat, 167, 414
  configuring, 414
  configuring for SOAP, 416
  elements
    context element, 617
  Filesystem Web Service case study, 616
toolkits
  ApacheSOAP Toolkit, 34
  IBM Web ServicesToolkit, 34
    examples, 144
  Microsoft SOAP Toolkit
    examples, 139, 159
TRACE method (HTTP), 71, 155
transactions
  WOAD case study, 648
transactions support
  SOAP extensions, 31
transient connections
  HTTP, 74
Transmission Control Protocol/Internet Protocol see TCP/IP.
transmission primitives (WSDL operations), 122
  notification operations, 125
  one-way operations, 122
  request/response operations, 123
  solicit/response operations, 124
Transport Layer
  OSI Reference model, 61
transport protocols
  comparing FTP, HTTP, and SMTP, 179
  FTP, 175
  HTTP, 154
  SMTP, 163
transports
  extensibility of SOAP, 81
  Internet transport protocols
    development of, 59
    introduction to, 59
  SOAP messages, 98
    HTTP, 99
    RPC, 102
    separation of message and transport, 98
Triple-DES (Data Encryption Standard), 564
tunnelers
  Apache SOAP tunneler, 428
tuples
  Python data structure, 532
type mapping, 338
types element (WSDL), 112, 115

U

UA see user agent.
UDDI (Universal Description, Discovery, and Integration)
  API
    design principles, 214
    inquiry API, 199
    publishing API, 203
    query patterns, 211
  Business Registry
    browsing the registry programmatically, 238
    browsing the registry using GUI tools, 245
    data stored in the registry, 187
    example of a registration, 197
    introduction, 184
    taxonomies, 184
  case study, 412
    registering services with the server, 449
  data structures
    binding templates, 233
    business entities, 233
    business services, 233
    tModels, 233
  data structures see information model.
  deployment, 186
    test bed deployment, 187
  development, 182
  discovery
    example, 445
  DSML and UDDI, 221
  ebXML and UDDI, 220
  elements
    accessPoint element, 192
    bindingTemplates element, 190
    businessEntity element, 188
    businessService element, 189
    businessServices element, 189
    categoryBag element, 189
    contacts element, 189
    description element, 189
    discoveryURLs element, 189
    fromKey element, 195
    hostingRedirector element, 192
    identifierBag element, 189
    keyedReference element, 195
    name element, 189
    tModelInstanceDetails element, 192
    toKey element, 195
  errors, 210, 214
  implementations
    introduction, 227
    summary, 293
  information model, 188
    binding information, 191
    binding templates, 196
    business entities, 188, 196
    business information, 188
    business service information, 190
    business services, 196
    diagram, 196
    publisher assertions, 195, 196
    specification pointers, 193
    technical information, 193
    tModels, 193
  introduction, 181
  JAXR and UDDI, 221
  operators, 183
    specifications, 214

  programming model, 198
  query patterns, 211
    examples, 212
  service cloud, 183
  specifications, 187
    UDDI node operators, 214
  summary, 223
  Web Services and UDDI, 181
    diagram, 182
    tModels, 193
    WOAD case study, 643
  WSDL and UDDI, 216
    stucture of WSDL, 216
    WSDL for describing Web Services, 218
  XML Web Services, 32
UDDI Business Registry, 249
  browsing the registry
    programmatically, 238
    using GUI tools, 245
  business entities
    deleting programmatically, 280
    deleting using GUI tools, 284
  creating an account with the test registry, 251
  description of services, 250
  developing and deploying Web Services, 252
  discovering Web Services, 250
  methods
    finding and invoking on the Web Service, 271
  private registries, 232, 291
  publishing the business, 250
    publishing using GUI tools, 271
  tModels
    publishing the tModel programmatically, 255
    publishing the tModel using GUI tools, 262
UDDI implementations
  Airline Web Service, 250
    business entities, deleting programmatically, 280
    business entities, deleting using GUI tools, 284
    business entities, publishing programmatically, 262
    business entities, publishing using GUI tools, 271
    creating an account with the UDDI test registry, 251
    developing and deploying the Web Service, 252
    finding and invoking methods on the Web Service, 271
    tModels, publishing programmatically, 255
    tModels, publishing using GUI tools, 262
  Apache SOAP and Tomcat setup, 229
  CLASSPATH settings, 231
  environment settings, 231
  HP WSP, 286
  Idoox WASP UDDI, 292
  introduction, 227
  jUUDI, 292
  prerequisites, 228
    Apache SOAP 2.1 Toolkit, 228
    JAF, 228
    Javamail, 228
    JDK, 228
    JSSE, 228
    Tomcat, 228
    Web Services Toolkit, 228
    Xerces XML parser, 228
  pUDDIng, 293
  summary, 293
  UDDI::Lite, 291
  UDDI4J
    introduction, 232
UDDI queries, 211

UDDI test registry
  publishing a Web Service
    WOAD case study, 668
UDDI::Lite, 291
UDDI4J
  authentication tokens, 234
  BindingTemplate class, 233
    delete_binding method, 235
    find_binding method, 236
    get_bindingDetail method, 236, 238
    save_binding method, 234
  browsing other registries, 247
  browsing the registry using GUI tools, 245
  browsing the UDDI registry programmatically, 238
  business entities
    deleting programmatically, 280
    deleting using GUI tools, 284
    publishing programmatically, 262
    publishing using GUI tools, 271
  business entities and tModels, publishing, 236
  BusinessEntity class, 233
    delete_business method, 235, 281, 283
    discard_authToken method, 234
    find_business method, 236, 237, 240
    get_authToken method, 234, 259, 264
    get_businessDetail method, 236, 238, 241
    getBusinessKey method, 241
    getBusinessInfoVector method, 241
    getBusinessKey method, 241
    save_business method, 234, 267
  BusinessService class, 233
    delete_service method, 235
    find_service method, 236, 237
    get_serviceDetail method, 236, 238
    save_service method, 234
  creating an account with the UDDI test
  registry, 251
  deleting from the UDDI registry, 235
  developing and deploying the Web Service, 252
  Disposition Reports, 235
  errors
    E_authTokenRequired, 235
    E_categorizationNotAllowed, 235
    E_invalidCategory, 235
    E_invalidKeyPassed, 235
    E_keyRetired, 235
    E_nameTooLong, 241
    E_operatorMismatch, 235
    E_unsupported, 241
    E_userMismatch, 236
  inquiries, 236
  introduction, 232
  library, WebSphere, 41
  publishing to the UDDI registry, 234
  registeredInfo class, 282
  ServiceDetail class, 278
  ServiceInfo class, 278
    get_registeredInfo method, 236, 282
    getBusinessInfos method, 241
    getBusinessInfoVector method, 241
  tModel class, 233
    delete_tModel method, 235
    find_tModel method, 236, 237
    get_tModelDetail method, 236, 238
    save_tModel method, 234, 260
  tModels, publishing programmatically, 255
  tModels, publishing using GUI tools, 262
  UDDIClient class, 243

UDDIOperatorURLs class, 243, 244
UDDIProxy class, 233, 239
  setInquiryURL method, 233
  setPublishURL method, 233
  setTransport method, 233
UDDIOperatorURLs class, 244
UDDIProxy class, 233
  constructing, 259, 264, 275
UDDISOAPClient class, 290
Uniform Resource Identifiers see URIs.
Uniform Resource Locators see URLs.
Uniform Resource Names see URNs.
Unique Universal Identifier algorithm see UUID.
Universal Standard Products and Services
  Classification see UNSPSC. .
UNSPSC (Universal Standard Products and Services
  Classification), 185, 237
uri method (SOAP::Lite), 354
URIs (Uniform Resource Identifiers), 153, 367
urlencode function, urllib library module, 523
urllib module, 523
urllib.FancyURLOpener class, urllib library
  module, 523
urllib.URLOpener class, urllib library module, 523
urllib2 module, 523
urlopen function, urllib library module, 523
URLs (Uniform Resource Locators), 153
  accessability, 258
  example, 153
URNs (Uniform Resource Names), 153
use cases
  WOAD case study
    buying an item, 648
    selling an item, 645
user agent (UA), 60
user interface (UI)
  integration
    web applications, connecting, 16
User-Agent header, 75
User-Agent request header, 72
uu module, 525
UUID (Unique Universal Identifier)
algorithm, 188, 216

V

values
  multi-reference values in SOAP, 96
  SOAPAction values, 354
varType method, ISoapTypeMapper interface, 338
vendor acceptability, 21
VeriSign
  CSR, 585
VersionMismatch element value
  SOAP messages, 87
versionString, 549
video MIME type, 153
Virtual Private Network connections see VPN
  connections.
Visual Studio.NET see VS.NET.
VPN (Virtual Private Network) connections, 579
VRFY command, 64

VS.NET, 43
ASP.NET Web Service Template see VS.NET
Template.
ASP.NET Web Services with VS.NET, 488
creating a proxy class, 504
creating an asynchronous proxy, 513
tools, 506
using proxy classes in client applications, 511
ATL Server, 518
VS.NET Beta 2
acquiring, 469
VS.NET Template
classes
System.Web.Services.WebService class, 495
WebService class, 495
compiling, 492
Codebehind attribute, 493
creating a client project, 657
creating a server project, 656
creating a virtual directory, 489
editing the service, 489
files created by the template
.vsdisco files, 494
AssemblyInfo.cs, 494
Global.asax, 494
Global.asax.cs, 494
Web.config, 495
namespaces
changing the default namespace, 498
renaming the service, 500

W

WC3
Specifications
WSDL and XSD, 115
Web agents, 55
stateful autonomous agents, 55
stateless services, 55
web applications, connecting
early attempts, 15
digital dashboards, 16
frames, 15
links, 15
posting informtion, 16
screen scraping, 16
user interface (UI) integration, 16
XML messages over HTTP, 17
Web Auction application see WOAD.
web references, adding see proxy classes,creating.
web service discovery see DISCO.
web service proxies
introduction, 502
Web Services
.NET and Web Services
creating a web service from a WSDL Description, 486
introduction, 467
prerequisites, 469
WOAD case study, 643
.NET Remoting
introduction, 517
case studies
Filesystem Web Service case study, 613
Organized Campgrounds, 411, 453
WOAD, 643
client transactions
WOAD case study, 643

creating on the same server, 453
deploying Web Services using pluggable
providers, 632
implementing Web Services to an existing application
case study, 643
Python and SOAP
introduction, 529
Python and Web Services
implementation in 4Suite Server, 548
installing software, 528
internet data format modules, 524
introduction, 521
network location, 549
standard library modules, 522
summary, 555
third-party Python modules and tools, 525
web architecture modules, 523
Python and WSDL
introduction, 539
Quality of Service (QoS), 566
servers
Filesystem Web Service case study, 616
SOAP and Web Services, 109, 110
example, 279, 417
introduction to, 77, 78
possibilities, 106
summary, 107
Sun ONE, 45
test area web site, 445
UDDI and Web Services, 181
diagram, 182
tModels, 193
WSDL
examples, 112, 135
introduction, 109, 110
WSDL descriptions, 257
Web Services Description Language see WSDL.
**Web Services Description Language Utility see
wsdl.exe.**
Web Services Meta Language see WSML.
Web Services security
application level security, 598
authentication credentials in SOAP messages, 599
point-to-point security, 569
ticket-based authentication, 600
XML security, 602
approaches to Web Services security, 567
auditing, 562
authentication, 562
authorization, 562
availability, 565
diagram, 567
digital signatures, 566
encryption, 563
integrity, 563
introduction, 559
logging, 562
non-repudiation, 566
privacy, 565
summary, 610
transport level security, 568
HTTP, 569
IPSec, 569
point-to-point security, 568
SMTP, 597
Web Services Toolkit
see IBM Web Services Toolkit.
webAuction.wsdl, 653

webAuction.xsd, 653
WebAuctionClient class, 665
WebAuctionServerBase.cs, 658
WebService class, System.Web.Services namespace, 495, 659
WebMethodAttribute class, System.Web.Services namespace, 479, 488
  BufferResponse property, 502
  CacheDuration property, 502
  Description property, 480, 496
  EnableSession property, 502
  MessageName property, 500
  TransactionOption property, 502
WebServiceAttribute class, System.Web.Services namespace, 496
  Description property, 496
  Name property, 500
  Namespace property, 499
WebService directive, 480
WebSphere
  IBM Web Services, 41
  uddi4j Java library, 41
  wsdlgen, 41
white pages
  UDDI, 187, 188
Windows integrated authentication, 596
wiredumps
  request wiredumps
    EasySOAP++, 378, 382, 388, 391
    SOAP::Lite, 356, 359, 363
    SOAPx4, 397, 401, 405
  response wiredumps, 389
    EasySOAP++, 378, 383
    SOAP::Lite, 357, 360, 364
    SOAPx4, 397, 401, 405
  tcpTrace
    examining wiredumps with tcpTrace, 347
      diagram, 347
      example, 348
WOAD (Wrox Online Auction Domain) case study
  bid messages, 647
  bindings, 655
  buying an item
    failed bid scenario, 648
    main scenario (new bidder), 648
    repeat bidder scenario, 648
    use case, 648
  difficulties, 649
  introduction, 643
  possibilities, 673
  requirements, 644
    buying an item, 646
    selling an item, 644
    specification, 650
    transaction analysis, 648
  retail Web Service clients, 673
  selling an item
    main scenario, 646
    no sale scenario, 646
    repeat seller scenario, 646
    use case, 645
  SOAP transactions, 650
    HTTP, 655
  specification
    defaults, 650
    elements, 651
    message types, 651

    namespaces, 650
    ping messages, 650
    response messages, 651
    WSDL documents, 653
    XML Schemas, 650
  summary, 675
  transaction
    list, 648
  transactions
    port type, 654
  use case diagram, 644
  Web Service developers, 674
  webAuction.wsdl, 653
  WOAD Web Services
    implementing, 656
WOAD Web Services
  abstract methods, 659
  classes
    Service1 class, 658
    WebAuctionBase class, 658
    WebAuctionClient class, 661
    WebAuctionServerBase class, 663
  errors, 659
  implementing business transactions, 662
  implementing the ping operation, 657
    client, 661
    server, 658
    testing, 661
  implementing Web Services, 656
  integrating Web Services, 667
    publishing the service, 668
    security and state management, 667
  namespaces
    WebService namespace, 659
  projects, setting up
    creating the server project, 656
  publishing the service
    adding the implemented service, 672
    publishing the service type definition, 668
  UDDI test registry
    prerequisites, 668
  WebAuctionServerBase.cs, 658
wrapping see proxy classes.
write method, ISoapTypeMapper interface, 338
Wrox Online Auction Domain see WOAD.
WSDL (Web Services Description Language), 31
  .NET and WSDL
    WOAD case study, 643
  advantages, 136
  bindings, 125
  creating a web service from a WSDL
  Description, 486
  development of, 110
  documents
    definitions, 111
    elements, 111
    examples, 135, 139, 144
  extensibility, 111
  introduction, 109, 110
  messages, 117, 161
  Python and WSDL
    introduction, 539
    using wsdl4py, 539
  summary, 147
  syntax
    introduction, 111

WSDL (Cont'd)
transmission primitives, 122
 naming of messages, 125
 notification operations, 125
 one-way operations, 122
 request/response operations, 123
 solicit/response operations, 124
type systems
 other type systems, 117
 XSD, 117
UDDI and WSDL, 216
 structure of WSDL, 216
 WSDL for describing Web Services, 218
WSML and WSDL, 299
 similarities and differences, 298
XML Schemas, 115
WSDL and WSML API, 297
WSDL bindings, 125
binding elements, 120
HTTP GET/POST bindings, 131
MIME bindings, 133
multiple bindings, 136
SOAP bindings, 126
 example, SMTP, 130
SOAPx4, 406
SOAP::Lite, 366
WSDL descriptions
creating and manipulating, 541
Echo services, 344
service elements, adding to, 407
URLs, 258
Web Services, 257
WSDL documents
character encoding, 305
components, reusing, 113
definitions, 111
 elements, 115
 example, 112
elements, 111, 115
 binding element, 113, 120
 definitions element, 112
 documentation element, 112, 115
 import element, 113
 message element, 113
 port element, 121
 portType element, 113, 119
 types element, 112, 115
examples, 135
 IBM Web Services Toolkit, 144
 Microsoft SOAP Toolkit, 139
 multiple bindings, 136
generating using WSDL generator, 303
messages, 117
namespaces
 list, 114
operations (transmission primitives), 113, 119, 122
 naming of messages, 125
 notification operations, 125
 one-way operations, 122
 request/response operations, 123
 solicit/response operations, 124
reading in and querying, 539
services, 113, 121
WSDL Generator, 297, 303
benefits of using, 309
complex types, 339
listeners, 309
WSDL messages, 117
naming in an operation, 125

WSDL syntax
introduction, 111
wsdl.exe (Web Services Description Language Utility), 486
creating proxy classes, 516
 WOAD case study, 657
generating code, 487
wsdl4py
installing, 540
processing WSDL, 539
 creating WSDL descriptions, 541
 reading in and querying WSDL documents, 539
 using RDF, 542
 using XSLT, 542
wsdlgen
WebSphere, 41
WSFL (Web Services Flow Language), 42, 55
WSML (Web Services Meta Language), 161, 298
WSDL and WSML, 299
 similarities and differences, 298
WSML documents
example, 298
generating using WSDL generator, 303
WSTK see IBM Web Services Toolkit.

X

xCBL see Common Business Library.
XDR (XML Data Reduced) schemas, 327
Xerces, 167
XLANG, 54
XML (Extensible Markup Language), 11
security, 602
XML Data Reduced schemas see XDR schemas.
XML documents
security, 602
 digital signatures extentions, 604
 DRM, 609
 privacy and P3P, 606
 XML Encryption, 603
 XML Signatures, 603
using as messages in SOAP, 79
XML Encryption, 29, 603
XML Initiatives
see also XML Web Services
ebXML (Electronic Business XML), 48
XML messages over HTTP
web applications, connecting, 17
XML Protocol see SOAP 1.2.
XML Remote Procedure Call see XML-RPC.
XML Repositories, 51
BizTalk.org, 51
XML.org, 51
XML Schemas, 31, 347
EasySoap++, 392
embedding definitions
 example, 653
SOAP data encoding, 90
SOAPx4, 406
UDDI, 188
using abstract types, 116
WSDL, 115
XML Signatures, 29, 603
XML SOAP Admin
deploying services, 419

XML Web Services, 17
  see also ASP.NET Web Services
  see also XML Initiatives.
  agents see Web agents.
  applications
    components, loosely bound, 18
    components, tightly bound, 18
  architecture, 19
    description, 19, 31
    diagram, 33
    discovery, 19, 32
    invocation, 19, 20
    XML Schemas, 31
  BizTalk Framework, 50
  Commerce XML (cXML), 50
  Common Business Library (xCBL), 49
  compared to EAI, 17
  defined, 18
  description, 31
  discovery, 32
    UDDI, 32
  distributed computing, 12
  emerging
    introduction, 11
  example, HailStorm, 51, 52
    availabilty, 52
    subscription business model, 52
  introduction of SOAP, 19
  possibilities, 12, 53
  process flow and pattern description, 54
    RosettaNet, 54
    WSFL, 55
    XLANG, 54
  RosettaNet, 49
  scalability
    extensions, impact of, 27
  security, 560

  Semantic Web, 32
  summary, 57
  WSFL, 55
  XLANG, 54
  XML Repositories, 51
    BizTalk.org, 51
    XML.org, 51
XML Web Services Framework, 33
XML Web Services Tools, 34
  Apache SOAP, 34
  IBM XML Web Services Toolkit, 34
  SOAP Toolkit 2.0, 34
xml.dom module
  minidom, 524
  pulldom, 524
xml.parsers.expat module, 524
xml.sax module, 524
XML-RPC (XML Remote Procedure Call), 17
  limitations, 17
xsd:schema element (WSDL), 543
XSLT
  WSDL descriptions using RDF, 542
  XSLT processors
    4XSLT, 546

Y

yellow pages
  UDDI, 187, 191

Z

zone transfer, 152

p2p.wrox.com
The programmer's resource centre

A unique free service from Wrox Press
with the aim of helping programmers to help each other

Wrox Press aims to provide timely and practical information to today's programmer. P2P
is a list server offering a host of targeted mailing lists where you can share knowledge w
your fellow programmers and find solutions to your problems. Whatever the level of you
programming knowledge, and whatever technology you use, P2P can provide you with t
information you need.

ASP
Support for beginners and professionals, including a resource page wit
hundreds of links, and a popular ASP+ mailing list.

DATABASES
For database programmers, offering support on SQL Server, mySQL,
and Oracle.

MOBILE
Software development for the mobile market is growing rapidly.
We provide lists for the several current standards, including WAP,
WindowsCE, and Symbian.

JAVA
A complete set of Java lists, covering beginners, professionals,and
server-side programmers (including JSP, servlets and EJBs)

.NET
Microsoft's new OS platform, covering topics such as ASP+, C#, and
general .Net discussion.

VISUAL BASIC
Covers all aspects of VB programming, from programming Office macr
to creating components for the .Net platform.

WEB DESIGN
As web page requirements become more complex, programmer sare
taking a more important role in creating web sites. For these
programmers, we offer lists covering technologies such as Flash,
Coldfusion, and JavaScript.

XML
Covering all aspects of XML, including XSLT and schemas.

OPEN SOURCE
Many Open Source topics covered including PHP, Apache, Perl, Linux
Python and more.

FOREIGN LANGUAGE
Several lists dedicated to Spanish and German speaking programmers
categories include .Net, Java, XML, PHP and XML.

How To Subscribe

Simply visit the P2P site, at **http://p2p.wrox.com/**

Select the 'FAQ' option on the side menu bar for more information about the subscripti
process and our service.